THE
BRITISH CATALOGUE
OF MUSIC
1971

The Council of the British National Bibliography, Ltd., by whom this work is published, is a non-profit making organisation set up at the wish of those bodies whose representatives form the Council for the purpose of "compiling, editing and publishing in appropriate bibliographical form lists of books, pamphlets and other recorded material of whatever nature published in Great Britain, the Dominions and Colonies and/or foreign countries, together with such annotations or further information as may be desirable for the use of librarians, bibliographers and others."

During 1971 the Council consisted of the following representatives:

THE
BRITISH CATALOGUE
OF MUSIC
1971

A record of music and books about music recently published in Great Britain, based upon the material deposited at the Copyright Receipt Office of the British Museum, arranged according to a system of classification with an alphabetical index under composers, titles, arrangers, instruments, etc., and a list of music publishers

General Editor: A. J. WELLS, O.B.E., F.L.A.

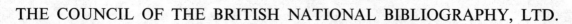

THE COUNCIL OF THE BRITISH NATIONAL BIBLIOGRAPHY, LTD.

7 & 9 RATHBONE STREET, LONDON, W1P 2AL

in association with The Music Department of the British Museum, The U.K. Branch of the International Association of Music Libraries, The Music Publishers Association and The Central Music Library

© 1972   The Council of the British National Bibliography, Ltd.

International Standard Book Number 0 900220 34 1

CONTENTS

1972

Printed in Great Britain by William Clowes & Sons, Limited, London, Beccles and Colchester
and published by the Council of the British National Bibliography, Ltd., 7 & 9 Rathbone Street, London, W1P 2AL
(Registered Office: British Museum, London, W.C.1)

PREFACE

The British Catalogue of Music is a record of new music —with the exception of certain types of popular music— published in Great Britain. In addition, it records foreign music available in this country through a sole agent and books about music. It is based on the works deposited at the British Museum where copies of all new publications must be sent by law and is the most complete list of current British music available.

Hints for tracing information

The Catalogue is presented in three sections:
Classified Section
Composer and Title Index
Subject Index

The purpose of the Classified Section is to arrange works according to the various voices, instruments, and combinations for which they are written. It is not essential to understand the system of classification. To find information, first consult the Composer and Title Index, which makes it possible to find details of which the composer, title, arranger, or any similar fact, is known. The Subject Index provides an alphabetical index of instruments, musical forms, etc., appearing in the Classified Section.

Composer

When the composer or author of a work is known, look under his name in the Composer and Title Index. The information given here, including the publisher and price, will be adequate for most purposes. If, on the other hand, the fullest information about a work is required, turn to the entry in the Classified Section. This may be found by means of the class symbol (group of letters) at the end of the composer or author entry. In tracing class symbols which include ( ) "brackets" or / "stroke", it should be borne in mind that these signs precede letters in the arrangement.

Thus:

	A
is followed by	A(. . . .)
which is followed by	A/ . . . .
which is followed by	AA
which is followed by	AB
which is followed by	B, etc.

Titles, series, editors and arrangers

Entries are made in the Composer and Title Index under the titles of all works, so that, if you do not know the composer or author, a work can be found by looking up its title in the Composer and Title Index.

If you do not know either the composer or the title, it may still be possible to trace the work if the name of the editor or arranger is known and, in the case of vocal works, the author of the words.

Instrument, musical form and character

While the Classified Section displays the works systematically according to the instrument or combination for which a work is written, the Subject Index lists the principal musical forms and musical character and it shows by means of the class symbol where works having such forms or musical character are to be found in the Classified Section. For example, in the Subject Index under the word Sonatas the following entries may be found:

Sonatas: Harp & piano:	
Arrangements for 2 pianos	QNUK/AE
Sonatas: Organ	RE
Sonatas: Piano duets, 4 hands	QNVE
Sonatas: Piano solos	QPE
Sonatas: Violin solos,	
Unaccompanied	SPME

It will be seen that this group of entries enables you to assemble all the works in sonata form no matter for what instrument the music is, or was originally, written.

Under the word Violin the following may be found:	
Violin	S
Violin: Accompanying female	
voices: Choral works	FE/S
Violin: Books	AS
Violin & orchestra	MPS
Violin & string orchestra	RXMPS

This group directs you first to the place S in the Classified Section, where music for the violin is found, including works composed originally for other instruments and arranged for violin. It also directs you to works in which the violin figures in combination with other instruments.

It thus provides at one and the same time the link between an instrument and its place in the Classified Section and an exhaustive guide to all the works in which that particular instrument figures.

Musical literature

Books about music which normally appear in the *British National Bibliography* are also included in this catalogue. They occur in the sequences lettered A and B. They are indexed in exactly the same way as musical works in the Composer and Title Index and are designated by the qualification "Books" in the Subject Index. Thus, in the second group above, the entry Violin: Books, directing you to AS, indicates that books about the violin will be found at that place.

Prices

Prices given are those current at the time of the first recording of an entry in this catalogue. In a few cases prices of parts are not given but can be obtained on application to the publisher.

Abbreviations

Most of the abbreviations used in describing musical works are self-explanatory. The size of a musical work is indicated by one of the following conventional symbols: *8vo* for works up to 10½ in. in height, *4to* for works between 10½ and 12 in. in height, and *fol.* for works over 12 in. in height. The abbreviation *obl.* (oblong) is added to show when a work is of unusual proportions, and a single sheet is designated by the abbreviations *s.sh.* The abbreviations used for the description of books in the sections A and B are those in use in the *British National Bibliography*.

OUTLINE OF THE CLASSIFICATION

The following outline is given for general information only. Users are advised to consult the Subject Index to discover the exact location of required material in the Classified Section.

MUSICAL LITERATURE

A	General works
	Common sub-divisions
A(B)	Periodicals
A(C)	Encyclopaedias
A(D)	Composite works, symposia, essays by several writers
A(E)	Anecdotes, personal reminiscences
A(K)	Economics
A(M)	Persons in music
A(MM)	Musical profession
A(MN)	Music as a career
A(P)	Individuals
A(Q)	Organisations
A(QT)	Terminology
A(QU)	Notation
A(R)	Printing
A(S)	Publishing
A(T)	Bibliographies
A(U)	Libraries
A(V)	Musical education
A(X)	History of music
A(Y)	Music of particular localities
A/AM	Theory of music
A/CC	Aesthetics
A/CY	Technique of music
A/D	Composition
A/E	Performance
A/F	Recording
A/FY	Musical character
A/G	Folk music
A/GM	Music associated with particular occupations
A/H	Dance music
A/HM	Ballet music
A/J	Music accompanying drama
A/JR	Film music
A/KD	Music to accompany social customs
A/L	Religious music
A/LZ	Elements of music
A/R	Harmony
A/S	Forms of music
A/Y	Fugue
AB	Works on vocal music
AC	Works on opera
ACM	Works on musical plays
AD-AX	Works on music for particular vocal or instrumental performers, enumerated like D–X below
B	Works on individual composers (including libretti and other verbal texts of particular musical works)
BZ	Works on non-European music

MUSIC (SCORES AND PARTS)

C/AY	Collections not limited to work of particular composer, executant, form or character
C/AZ	Collections of a particular composer not otherwise limited
C/G-C/Y	Collections illustrating music of particular form, character, etc., enumerated like A/G-A/Y above
CB	Vocal music
CC	Opera. Vocal scores with keyboard
CM	Musical plays. Vocal scores with keyboard
D	Choral music
DC	Religious choral music
DF	Liturgical music
DH	Motets, Anthems, Hymns
DTZ	Secular choral music
DX	Cantatas
DW	Songs, etc.
E	Choral music with instruments other than keyboard
EZ	Choral music unaccompanied
F	Choral music. Female voices
G	Choral music. Male voices
J	Unison vocal works
K	Vocal solos
L	Instrumental music
M	Orchestral music
N	Chamber music
PVV	Music for individual instruments and instrumental groups
PW	Keyboard instruments
Q	Piano
R	Organ
RW	String instruments
S	Violin
SQ	Viola
SR	Cello
SS	Double bass
TQ	Harp
TS	Guitar
U	Wind instruments
V	Woodwind
VR	Flute
VS	Recorder
VT	Oboe
VU	Saxophone
VV	Clarinet
VW	Bassoon
W	Brass
WS	Trumpet
WT	Horn
WU	Trombone
WX	Bass tuba
X	Percussion instruments
Z	Non-European music

CLASSIFIED SECTION

This section contains entries under subjects, executants and instruments according to a system of classification, a synopsis of which appears in the preliminary pages. The key to the classification and to this section is found in the Subject Index at the end of this volume, which is followed by a list of music publishers and their addresses.

The following are used in giving the sizes of musical works:—

8vo for works up to 10½″ in height.
4to for works between 10½″ and 12″ in height.
fol. for works over 12″ in height.
obl. indicates a work of unusual proportions.
s.sh. means a single sheet.

A – MUSICAL LITERATURE
A – Musical literature

Bernstein, Leonard
Leonard Bernstein's young people's concerts/ drawings by Isadore Seltzer. — [Revised and expanded ed.]. — London: Cassell, 1971. — 233p: illus(chiefly col), music(some col), port; 26cm.
This ed. originally published, New York: Simon and Schuster, 1970.
ISBN 0 304 93819 x : £2.10

(B71-25914)

Boulez, Pierre
Boulez on music today/ [by] Pierre Boulez; translated [from the French] by Susan Bradshaw and Richard Rodney Bennett. — London: Faber, 1971. — 144p: illus, music; 23cm.
Originally published as 'Penser la musique aujourd'hui'. Paris: Gothier, 1964.
ISBN 0 571 09420 1 : £2.50

(B71-07322)

Boyden, David Dodge
An introduction to music/ by David D. Boyden; with a preface by Sir Thomas Armstrong and a foreword by Percy A. Scholes. — 2nd ed. — London (3 Queen Sq., Wc1N 3AU): Faber and Faber Ltd, 1971. — xxx,554,xxxvii p,40plates: illus, facsims, music, ports; 20cm.
Pbk. £0.90. sbn 571-09149-0. — Previous ed. 1959.
ISBN 0 571 04745 9 : £2.25

(B71-16009)

Cleary, Vincent
Music course for the Intermediate Certificate/ by Vincent Cleary. — Dublin (John F. Kennedy Drive, Naas Rd, Dublin 12): Folens and Co. Ltd, 1971. — 95p: music; 25cm.
ISBN 0 902592 07 6 Pbk: £0.35

(B71-06906)

Glennon, James
Making friends with music/ [by] James Glennon; decorations by Val Biro. — Slough: Foulsham, 1971. — 64p: illus, music; 22cm.
ISBN 0 572 00774 4 Pbk: £0.60

(B71-27970)

Hendrie, Gerald
Introduction to music/ prepared by Gerald Hendrie and Dinah Barsham for the Humanities Foundation Course Team. — Bletchley (Walton Hall, Bletchley, Bucks.): Open University Press, 1971. — 50p: illus, music; 30cm. — (Humanities: a foundation course, units 13-14) (A100 13 and 14)
ISBN 0 335 00509 8 Pbk: £0.80

(B71-08374)

Mendl, Robert William Sigismund
Reflections of a music lover/ [by] R.W.S. Mendl. — London: Spearman, [1971]. — xii,306p,8plates: illus, ports; 23cm.
bibl p297-302.
ISBN 0 85435 011 x : £2.50

(B71-05263)

Music/ [editors Peter Usborne, Su Swallow, Jennifer Vaughan; illustrated by Michael Ricketts]. — London: Macdonald and Co., 1971. — [2],25p(chiefly col illus); 21cm. — (Macdonald starters)
ISBN 0 356 03759 2 : £0.25

(B71-19965)

Previn, André
Music face to face/ by Andre Previn and Antony Hopkins. — London: Hamilton, 1971. — iii-ix,132p; 23cm.
ISBN 0 241 02036 0 : £1.75

(B71-26599)

Seeley, Charles
To a young music lover/ by Charles Seeley. — Ilfracombe: Stockwell, 1971. — 154p: music; 22cm.
ISBN 0 7223 0050 6 : £1.25

(B71-14239)

A(C) — Encyclopaedias
Blom, Eric
Everyman's dictionary of music/ compiled by Eric Blom. — 5th ed.; revised by Sir Jack Westrup, with the collaboration of [others]. — London: Dent, 1971. — xiii,793p: music; 20cm. — (Everyman's reference library)
Previous ed. 1964.
ISBN 0 460 03022 1 : £4.00

(B71-21647)

Cooper, Martin
The concise encyclopedia of music and musicians/ edited by Martin Cooper. — 2nd ed., revised. — London (3 Fitzroy Sq., W.1): Hutchinson, 1971. — xix,481p: illus, music; 23cm.
Previous ed. 1958. — bibl p.xii-xiii.
ISBN 0 09 107530 0 : £3.25

(B71-30145)

Larousse encyclopaedia of music/ editor Geoffrey Hindley; introduction by Antony Hopkins. — Feltham: Hamlyn, 1971. — 576p,48plates: illus(some col), facsims, music, ports; 30cm.
Illus. on lining papers. — Based on 'La Musique', edited by Norman Dufourcq. Paris: Librarie Larousse, 1965.
ISBN 0 600 02396 6 : £6.30

(B71-25341)

A(D) — Essays
Hughes, Gervase
The music lover's companion/ edited by Gervase Hughes and Herbert Van Thal. — London: Eyre and Spottiswoode, 1971. — 3-533p: illus; 23cm.
Illus. on lining papers.
ISBN 0 413 27920 0 : £3.00

(B71-18712)

The music forum. — New York; London: Columbia University Press. —
Vol.2/ edited by William J. Mitchell and Felix Salzer; Hedi Siegel, editorial assistant. — 1970. — xiii,377p,fold plate: facsims, music; 26cm.
ISBN 0 231 03153 x : £6.05

(B71-06290)

A(D/XKR96) — Essays, 1876-1970
Davies, Laurence, *b.1926*
Paths to modern music: aspects of music from Wagner to the present day/ by Laurence Davies. — London: Barrie and Jenkins, 1971. — xvii,330p; 23cm.
bibl p318-322.
ISBN 0 214 65249 1 : £4.00

(B71-14731)

A(MN) — Careers
Incorporated Society of Musicians
Careers with music. — London (48 Gloucester Place, W1H 3HJ): Incorporated Society of Musicians, 1970. — 79p; 20cm.
ISBN 0 902900 02 1 Pbk: £0.60

(B71-09060)

A(MN/YD) — Careers. Great Britain
Schools Council
Music and the young school leaver: problems and opportunities. — London: Evans Bros: Methuen Educational, 1971. — 36p; 21cm. — (Working paper 31)
ISBN 0 423 46500 7 Sd: £0.23

(B71-18711)

A(Q/YDBCJ/XD471) — Worshipful Company of Musicians. City of London, 1500-1970
Crewdson, Henry Alastair Ferguson
The Worshipful Company of Musicians: a short history/ compiled by H.A.F. Crewdson. — New ed. — London: C. Knight, 1971. — 185p,7plates: illus(some col), coat of arms, ports(incl 1 col), music; 23cm.
Previous ed., London: Constable, 1950.
ISBN 0 85314 086 3 : £4.00

(B71-30640)

A(QU) — Notation
Berry, Marion
Music makers/ [by] Marion Berry; illustrated by Phelps: [in 5 stages]. — Harlow: Longman. —
Stage 4. — 1971. — 48p(chiefly illus(some col), music(some col)); 21x28cm.
ISBN 0 582 18544 0 Sd: £0.40

(B71-06129)

Stage 5. — 1971. — 48p(chiefly illus(some col), music); 21x28cm.
ISBN 0 582 18545 9 Sd: £0.40

(B71-06130)

A(U/YC/BC) — Libraries. *Great Britain. Directories*
Long, Maureen W
Music in British libraries: a directory of resources/ compiled by Maureen W. Long. — London: Library Association, 1971. — 183p; 21cm.
ISBN 0 85365 005 5 Pbk: £1.50(£1.20 to members of the Library Association)

(B71-26836)

A(UJ) — Librarianship. Classification
Universal Decimal Classification. — English full ed. (4th international ed.). — London: British Standards Institution. — (Fédération Internationale de Documentation. Publications; no.179)
78: Music. — 1971. — 14p; 30cm. — (BS1000[78]: 1971)
ISBN 0 580 06563 4 Sd: £0.80

(B71-19565)

A(VC) — Teaching
Kowal, Ada May
Music in school/ by A.M. Kowal. — London (124 New Bond St., W1A 4LJ): Bond Street Publishers, 1970. — [4],123p; 19cm.
ISBN 0 901373 08 7 : £1.00

(B71-10424)

A(VF/VCM) — Schools. Attainment tests
Colwell, Richard
The evaluation of music teaching and learning/ by Richard Colwell. — Englewood Cliffs; Hemel Hempstead: Prentice-Hall, 1970. — x,182p: illus,forms; 24cm. — (Prentice-Hall contemporary perspectives in music education series)
Pbk. £1.50. sbn 13-292144-8. — bibl.
ISBN 0 13 292151 0 : Unpriced

(B71-11816)

A(VG) — Primary schools
Hood, Marguerite Vivian
Teaching rhythm and using classroom instruments/ [by] Marguerite V. Hood. — Englewood Cliffs; Hemel Hempstead: Prentice-Hall, 1970. — xiii,142p: music; 24cm. — (Foundations of music education series)
Pbk. £1.20. sbn 13-894063-0. — bibl.
ISBN 0 13 894089 4 : £3.10

(B71-08201)

Lawrence, Ian
Words and music, by Ian Lawrence, Pamela Montgomery/ Stage 4, illustrations by David Featherstone. — Harlow: Longman, 1971. — 64p: illus(some col),music; 21cm.
ISBN 0 582 18694 3 Pbk: £0.40

(B71-08785)

Lawrence, Ian
Words and music/ [by] Ian Lawrence, Pamela Montgomery. — Harlow: Longman. —
Introduction. — 1971. — 272p: illus, music, maps; 22x28cm.
bibl.
ISBN 0 582 18695 1 Pbk: £2.50

(B71-22574)

Stage 1. — 1971. — 64p(chiefly illus(some col), music); 21cm.
ISBN 0 582 18691 9 Pbk: £0.40

(B71-06126)

Stage 2. — 1971. — 64p(chiefly illus(some col), col map, music); 21cm.
ISBN 0 582 18692 7 Pbk: £0.40

(B71-06127)

Stage 3. — 1971. — 64p(chiefly illus(some col), col chart, col map, music); 21cm.
ISBN 0 582 18693 5 Pbk: £0.40

(B71-06128)

A(VJ) — Junior schools
Garnett, Hugh
Practical music making with juniors/ [by Hugh Garnett]. — London: Schoolmaster Publishing, 1971. — 82p: illus,music; 22cm.
bibl p79.
ISBN 0 900642 10 6 Sd: £0.55

(B71-12945)

A(VK) — Secondary schools
Addison, Richard
Making more music: a book of musical experiments for young people/ [author Richard Addison]. — Edinburgh: Holmes-McDougall, 1970. — 48p: illus(some col), music; 22cm.
ISBN 0 7157 0749 3 Pbk: £0.35(non-net

(B71-17372)

A(VK/YC) — Secondary schools. Great Britain
Brocklehurst, Brian
Response to music: principles of music education/ by Brian Brocklehurst. — London: Routledge and K. Paul, 1971. — vii,141p; 20cm.
ISBN 0 7100 6949 9 : £1.40

(B71-03584)

A(VP/YDJE/X) — Graduate and professional education. Manchester School of Music. History
Kennedy, Michael, *b.1926*
The history of the Royal Manchester College of Music, 1893-1972/ [by] Michael Kennedy. — Manchester: Manchester University Press, 1971. — viii,227p,9plates: illus,ports; 23cm.
ISBN 0 7190 0435 7 : £2.40

(B71-16699)

A(VX/P) — Musicologists. Mendelssohn, Felix
Hendrie, Gerald
Mendelssohn's rediscovery of Bach/ prepared by Gerald Hendrie for the Humanities Foundation Course Team. — Bletchley (Walton Hall, Bletchley, Bucks.): Open University Press, 1971. — 115p: illus, facsim, music, ports; 30cm. — (Humanities: a foundation course, units 27-28) (A100 27 and 28)
ISBN 0 335 00516 0 Pbk: £1.20

(B71-24686)

A(X) — History
Borroff, Edith
Music in Europe and the United States: a history/ [by] Edith Borroff. — Englewood Cliffs; Hemel Hempstead: Prentice-Hall, 1971. — xvi,752p,8plates: illus(some col), facsims, music, plan, ports; 24cm.
ISBN 0 13 608083 9 : £6.00

(B71-21648)

Kirby, F E
An introduction to western music: Bach, Beethoven, Wagner, Stravinsky/ by F.E. Kirby. — New York: Free Press; London: Collier-Macmillan, 1970. — viii,456p: illus,music,ports; 24cm.
bibl p429-439.
ISBN 0 02 917360 4 : £4.00

(B71-10428)

Rosen, Charles
The classical style: Haydn, Mozart, Beethoven/ by Charles Rosen. — London (3 Queen Sq., WC1 3AU): Faber and Faber Ltd, 1971. — 3-467p: music; 26cm.
bibl p13.
ISBN 0 571 09118 0 : £7.00

(B71-09738)

Young, Percy Marshall
Music and its story/ [by] Percy M. Young; drawings by Reginald Haggar. — Revised ed. — London: Dobson, 1970. — 238p: illus, ports; 21cm.
Previous ed. London: Lutterworth Press, 1960.
ISBN 0 234 77346 4 : £1.25

(B71-05265)

A(XKC107) — History, 1863-1969
Ewen, David
David Ewen introduces modern music: a history and appreciation - from Wagner to the avant-garde/ by David Ewen. — Revised, enlarged ed. — Philadelphia; London (67 Jermyn St., S.W.1): Chilton Book Company, 1969. — [13],325p,8plates: ports; 21cm.
Previous ed., Philadelphia: Chilton, 1962.
ISBN 0 8019 5487 8 : £2.75

(B71-24687)

A(XM) — From 1900
Twentieth century composers. — London: Weidenfeld and Nicolson. — In 5 vols.
Vol.1: American music since 1910/ by Virgil Thomson; with an introduction by Nicolas Nabokov. — 1971. — xvii,204p,24plates: music,ports; 23cm.
bibl p187-189.
ISBN 0 297 00264 3 : £3.50

(B71-14732)

A(Y) — MUSIC OF PARTICULAR LOCALITIES
A(YC/WE/Q) — Great Britain. Festival organisation
British Federation of Music Festivals
Year book. — London (106 Gloucester Place, W1H 3DB): British Federation of Music Festivals. —
1971: 50th anniversary. — 1971. — [2],84p,2plates: ports; 25cm.
ISBN 0 901532 02 9 Sd: £0.50

(B71-13106)

A(YH/XM71) — France, 1900-1970
Myers, Rollo Hugh
Modern French music: its evolution and cultural background from 1900 to the present day/ [by] Rollo Myers. — Oxford: Blackwell, 1971. — [9],210p,13plates: illus, music, ports; 23cm. — (Blackwell's music series)
bibl p203-204.
ISBN 0 631 13020 9 : £3.25

(B71-26601)

A/B — PHYSICS OF MUSIC
Backus, John
The acoustical foundations of music/ [by] John Backus. — London: J. Murray, 1970. — xiv,312p: illus; 23cm.
Originally published, New York: Norton, 1969.
ISBN 0 7195 2216 1 : £3.50

(B71-06908)

A/CS — PSYCHOLOGY
A/CS(VC) — Psychology. Teaching
Gordon, Edwin
The psychology of music teaching/ [by] Edwin Gordon. — Englewood Cliffs; [Hemel Hempstead]: Prentice-Hall, 1971. — xvii,138p: form, music; 24cm. — (Prentice-Hall contemporary perspectives in music education series)
Pbk: £2.00. sbn 13-736207-2. — bibl.
ISBN 0 13 736215 3 : £3.50

(B71-30146)

A/D — COMPOSITION
A/D(YB/M) — Europe. Composers
Schonberg, Harold C
The lives of the great composers/ [by] Harold C. Schonberg. — London (Broadwick House, Broadwick St., W1V 2AH): Davis-Poynter Ltd, 1971. — 600p: illus, ports; 26cm.
Originally published, New York: Norton, 1970. — bibl p581-592.
ISBN 0 7067 0001 5 : £5.00

(B71-26600)

A/D(ZF) — Musical composition influenced by spiritualism
Brown, Rosemary
Unfinished symphonies: voices from the beyond/ [by] Rosemary Brown; foreword by the Bishop of Southwark. — London: Souvenir Press, 1971. — 190p,8plates: illus, facsims, music, ports; 23cm.
ISBN 0 285 62009 6 : £1.75

(B71-15624)

A/E — PERFORMANCE
Westrup, *Sir* Jack Allan
Musical interpretation/ by Jack Westrup. — London: British Broadcasting Corporation, 1971. — 72p: illus, facsims, music, ports; 23cm.
'This book accompanies a series of B.B.C. radio programmes first broadcast on Radio 3 (Study), weekly on Thursdays at 7 p.m. from April 1 to June 3, 1971.' - title page verso. — bibl p71.
ISBN 0 563 10352 3 Pbk: £0.90

(B71-06909)

A/EC(P) — Conductors. Barbirolli, Sir John. Biographies
Kennedy, Michael, *b.1926*
Barbirolli: conductor laureate: the authorised biography/ [by] Michael Kennedy; with a full discography compiled by Malcolm Walker. — London: MacGibbon and Kee, 1971. — 416p,17plates: facsim, ports; 23cm.
List of records p338-402.
ISBN 0 261 63336 8 : £2.95

(B71-27973)

Reid, Charles, *b.1900*
John Barbirolli: a biography/ by Charles Reid. — London: Hamilton, 1971. — xvii,446p,17plates: illus,ports; 23cm.
ISBN 0 241 01819 6 : £2.75

(B71-18089)

A/FD — RECORDED MUSIC
A/FD(WM) — Recorded music. Decca Group. Trade catalogues
Decca Group records, including musicassettes and stereo cartridges: main catalogue. — London: Decca. —
1971: [issued] up to and including September 1970. — [1971]. — [637]p; 26cm.
ISBN 0 901364 02 9 : £3.75

(B71-08568)

A/FD(WM) — Recorded music. Philips Records Ltd. Trade catalogues
Philips Group
Catalogue. — London (Stanhope House, Stanhope Place, W.2): Philips Records Ltd, 1971-. — 1v; 33cm.
[438]p. on publication.
ISBN 0 902225 01 4 Ls: Unpriced

(B71-28930)

A/FD(WT/XLT12) — Recorded music. Lists, 1898-1909
Bauer, Roberto
The new catalogue of historical records, 1898-1908/09/ compiled by Roberto Bauer. — London: Sidgwick and Jackson, 1970. — 495p; 21cm.
Originally published 1947.
ISBN 0 283 48420 9 : £6.50

(B71-18315)

A/FH — MECHANICAL MUSIC
A/FM(B) — Fair organs. Periodicals
The **Key** Frame: the journal of the Fair Organ Preservation Society. — Manchester (c/o K. Redfern. 3 Bentley Rd., Dewton, Manchester M34 3AZ): The Fair Organ Preservation Society. — No.1- ; Dec. 1964-. — 1964. — illus; 25cm.
Three or 4 issues a year. 16p. in issue of Winter 1970.
Sd: £0.125(£1.00 yearly)

(B71-18715)

A/FN — Musical boxes
Tallis, David
Musical boxes/ by David Tallis. — London: Muller, 1971. — 143p,20plates: illus(some col); 22cm.
bibl p137-138.
ISBN 0 584 10187 2 : £3.00

(B71-17375)

A/FND — Musical boxes. Disc musical boxes
Webb, Graham
The disc musical box handbook/ by Graham Webb; illustrated by Philip Weston. — London (3 Queen Sq., WC1N 3AU): Faber and Faber Ltd, 1971. — 3-323p,20plates: illus; 23cm.
ISBN 0 571 09378 7 : £3.50

(B71-18092)

A/FP — Pianolas
Ord-Hume, Arthur Wolfgang Julius Gerald
Player piano: the history of the mechanical piano and how to repair it/ [by] Arthur W.J.S. Ord-Hume; illustrated by the author. — London: Allen and Unwin, 1970. — 3-296p,64plates: illus, facsims, music; 25cm.
bibl p285-286.
ISBN 0 04 789003 7 : £4.50

(B71-00206)

A/FP(WM) — Pianolas. Catalogues
The **Hupfeld** player-piano: Solophonola, Duophonola, Triphonola [catalogue, c.1910]. — Bournemouth (19 Glendale Rd, Bournemouth, Hants., BH6 4JA): 'Talking Machine Review', 1971. — [20]p: illus; 25cm.
Facsimile reprint of 1st ed., London: Hupfeld, [1910?].
ISBN 0 902338 11 0 Sd: £0.50

(B71-27974)

A/FS — Aeolian harp
Bonner, Stephen
Aeolian harp/ editor Stephen Bonner. — Cambridge (59 Moorfield Rd, Duxford, Cambridge CB2 4PP): Bois de Boulogne. — In 4 vols.
Vol.3: The Aeolian harp in European literature, 1591-1892/ by Andrew Brown, with additional material by Nicholas Boyle. — 1970. — 8-93,[1]p: 1 illus, facsim; 18cm.
Limited ed. of 180 numbered copies. — bibl p92-93.
ISBN 0 900998 12 1 : £5.30

(B71-24693)

A/FY — MUSICAL CHARACTER
A/G(BC) — Folk music. Great Britain. Yearbooks
Folk directory. — London: English Folk Dance and Song Society. — 1971. — 1971. — 152p: illus, ports; 22cm.
Pbk. £0.50(£0.25 to members). sbn 85418-028-1.
ISBN 0 85418 029 x : £1.00(£0.75 to members)

(B71-07864)

A/GB — Popular music
Jasper, Tony
Pop/ [text by Tony Jasper]. — London: S.C.M. Press, 1970. — 32p: illus; 23cm. — (Probe; 6)
ISBN 0 334 01270 8 Sd: £0.20

(B71-05264)

A/GB(XPQ16) — Popular music, 1955-1970
Cash, Tony
Anatomy of pop/ contributors Peter Cole [and others], editor Tony Cash. — London: British Broadcasting Corporation, 1970. — 132p: illus, music, ports; 21cm.
'...accompanies a series of five programmes under the same title, first broadcast on BBC-1 on Sunday at 11.35 a.m.-12 noon starting 10 January 1971.' - note. — bibl p129.
ISBN 0 563 10261 6 Pbk: £0.70

(B71-03033)

A/GB(YC/BC) — Popular music. Great Britain. Yearbooks
Kemp's music and recording industry year book (international): a comprehensive reference source and marketing guide to the music and recording industry in Great Britain and overseas. — London: Kemp's Printing and Publishing. — 1969/70. — [1971]. — [3],211p: illus; 21cm.
Pbk. £2.25. sbn 901268-29-1.
ISBN 0 901268 28 3 : £3.25

(B71-08164)

1970/71. — [1971]. — [2],212p: illus; 22cm.
Pbk. £3.00. sbn 901268-25-9.
ISBN 0 901268 24 0 : £3.50

(B71-03857)

A/GB(YT/WE) — Popular music. United States. Festivals
Hopkins, Jerry
Festival!: the book of American music celebrations.../ [text Jerry Hopkins, photographs Jim Marshall, Baron Wolman]. — New York: Macmillan (N.Y.); London: Collier-Macmillan, 1970. — 191p: illus,ports; 29cm.
Pbk. £1.25. sbn 02-061950-2.
ISBN 0 02 580170 8 : £4.00

(B71-11123)

A/GB(YT/XEW350/TC) — Popular music. United States, 1620-1969. Bibliographies of scores
Mattfeld, Julius
'Variety' music cavalcade, 1620-1969: a chronology of vocal and instrumental music popular in the United States/ by Julius Mattfeld. — 2nd ed.; [edited by Alfred Cain], with an introduction by Abel Green. — Englewood Cliffs; Hemel Hempstead: Prentice-Hall, 1971. — xxii,766p; 24cm.
Previous ed., Englewood Cliffs: Prentice-Hall, 1962.
ISBN 0 13 940718 9 : £7.50

(B71-23694)

A/H/G(YDL/XQP) — Dance music. Folk dances. Scotland, to 1966
Emmerson, George Sinclair
Rantin' pipe and tremblin' string: a history of Scottish dance music/ George S. Emmerson. — London: Dent, 1971. — xvi,278p,8plates: illus,facsim,music,ports; 26cm.
bibl p233-251.
ISBN 0 460 03891 5 : £5.00

(B71-16700)

A/JR — Film music
Manvell, Roger
The technique of film music/ written and compiled by Roger Manvell and John Huntley. — [1st ed.] reprinted. — London: Focal Press, 1971. — 299p: illus, facsims, music; 22cm. — (The library of communication techniques)
Originally published 1957. — bibl p285-291.
ISBN 0 240 44943 6 : £3.00

(B71-05268)

A/LZ — ELEMENTS OF MUSIC
A/RGD — Figured bass
Schneider, Max
Die Anfänge des Basso continuo und seiner Bezifferung/ von Max Schneider. — Farnborough: Gregg, 1971. — x,205p: facsims, music; 22cm.
Facsimile reprint of 1st ed., Leipzig: Breitkopf and Härtel, 1918.
ISBN 0 576 28963 9 : £7.20

(B71-17374)

Williams, Peter, b.1937
Figured bass accompaniments/ [by] Peter Williams. — Edinburgh: Edinburgh University Press, 1970. — 2v.([8],117p; [6],131p): illus, music; 30cm.
Music on lining papers. — bibl p107-115.
ISBN 0 85224 054 6 Pbk: £5.00

(B71-05794)

A/S — MUSICAL FORM
A/S — Form
Warburton, Annie Osborne
Analyses of musical classics/ [by] Annie O. Warburton. — [Harlow]: Longman. —
Book 3. — 1971. — [10],306p; 19cm.
ISBN 0 582 32487 4 Pbk:£1.40

(B71-27230)

Wishart, Peter
Key to music/ [by] Peter Wishart. — London: British Broadcasting Corporation, 1971. — 56p: facsims, music; 30cm.
'Written to accompany the BBC radio... series "Key to Music" ' - cover. — bibl p54.
ISBN 0 563 10589 5 Sd: £0.90

(B71-24688)

A/Y — Fugues
Bullivant, Roger
Fugue/ [by] Roger Bullivant. — London: Hutchinson, 1971. — 198p: music; 23cm. — (Hutchinson university library, music)
Pbk. £1.00. sbn 09-108441-5. List of music p194. — bibl p193.
ISBN 0 09 108440 7 : £2.25

(B71-25915)

AB – MUSICAL LITERATURE. VOCAL MUSIC
AB/E – Singing. Performance
Hewlett, Arthur Donald
Think afresh about the voice: a reappraisal of the teaching of Ernest George White/ by Arthur D. Hewlett. – Deal (Hillcrest, Ringwood, Deal, Kent): The Ernest George White Society, 1970. – v,60p,8plates: form, music; 21cm.
ISBN 0 9501610 0 4 Pbk: £0.45

(B71-19971)

Lehmann, Lotte
Eighteen song cycles: studies in their interpretations/ [by] Lotte Lehmann; with a foreword by Neville Cardus. – London: Cassell, 1971. – xiii,185p; 21cm.
ISBN 0 304 93842 4 : £2.40

(B71-25345)

Rose, Arnold
The singer and the voice: vocal physiology and technique for singers/ by Arnold Rose; foreword by Harold Rosenthal. – 2nd ed. – London (3 Queen Sq., WC1N 3AU): Faber and Faber Ltd, 1971. – 267p: illus; 23cm.
Previous ed. 1962. – bibl p262-263.
ISBN 0 571 04725 4 : £3.00

(B71-10432)

Rushmore, Robert
The singing voice/ by Robert Rushmore. – London: Hamilton, 1971. – xx,332p,16plates: illus,music,ports; 24cm.
bibl p307-316.
ISBN 0 241 01947 8 : £3.00

(B71-12557)

Schiotz, Aksel
The singer and his art/ [by] Aksel Schiotz; with a preface by Gerald Moore. – London: Hamilton, 1971. – 222p: music; 23cm.
bibl p215-216.
ISBN 0 241 01949 4 : £3.00

(B71-06912)

AB/E(M/C) – Singers. Encyclopaedias
Kutsch, K J
A concise biographical dictionary of singers: from the beginning of recorded sound to the present/ by K.J. Kutsch and Leo Riemens; translated from the German, expanded and annotated by Harry Earl Jones. – Philadelphia; London (67 Jermyn St., S.W.1): Chilton Book Company, 1969. – xxiv,487p; 21cm.
Originally published as 'Unvergängliche Stimmen: kleines Sängerlexicon'. 2.Aufl. Bern: Francke, 1966.
ISBN 0 8019 5516 5 : £7.50

(B71-24692)

AB/E(P) – Singers. Drifters. Biographies
Millar, Bill
The Drifters: the rise and fall of the black vocal group/ [by] Bill Millar. – London: Studio Vista, 1971. – 112p: illus, facsims, ports; 21cm. – (Rockbooks)
List of recordings, p105-110. Pbk. £0.60. sbn 289-70132-5. – bibl p102.
ISBN 0 289 70133 3 : £1.40

(B71-16703)

AB/E(P) – Singers. The Who. Biographies
Herman, Gary
The Who/ [by] Gary Herman. – London: Studio Vista, 1971. – 112p: illus, facsims, ports; 21cm. – (Rockbooks)
List of recordings, p108-112. Pbk. £0.60. sbn 289-70134-1.
ISBN 0 289 70135 x : £1.40

(B71-16698)

AB/E(VG) – Singing. Primary schools
Evans, Ken
Creative singing: the story of an experiment in music and creativity in the Primary classroom/ [by] Ken Evans. – London: Oxford University Press, 1971. – [7],95p: illus, music; 19cm.
ISBN 0 19 317411 1 : £1.25

(B71-20921)

AC – MUSICAL LITERATURE. OPERA
Jacobs, Arthur
Opera: a modern guide/ [by] Arthur Jacobs and Stanley Sadie. – Newton Abbot: David and Charles, 1971. – 492p: music; 23cm.
Originally published as 'The Pan book of opera'. London: Pan, 1964. – bibl p489-492.
ISBN 0 7153 5013 7 : £3.00

(B71-08377)

Morley, *Sir* **Alexander Francis**
The Harrap opera guide/ by Sir Alexander F. Morley. – London: Harrap, 1970. – 320p; 23cm.
ISBN 0 245 50509 1 : £2.10

(B71-00713)

AC(X) – History
Brody, Elaine
Music in opera: a historical anthology/ by Elaine Brody. – Englewood Cliffs; Hemel Hempstead: Prentice-Hall, 1970. – xix,604p(chiefly music); 29cm.
bibl p593-598.
ISBN 0 13 608109 6 : £7.50

(B71-12556)

AC(X) – Opera. History
Matthews, Thomas
The splendid art: a history of the opera/ [by] Thomas Matthews. – [New York]: Crowell-Collier; London: Collier-Macmillan, 1970. – ix,217p,26plates: illus, ports; 22cm.
bibl p206-208.
ISBN 0 02 765290 4 : £1.75

(B71-19967)

AC(XE311) – Opera, 1600-1911
Hoover, Kathleen O'Donnell
Makers of opera/ [by] Kathleen O'Donnell Hoover; introduction by Carleton Sprague Smith. – Port Washington; London (11 Southampton Row, WC1B 5HA): Kennikat Press, 1971. – xiii,209p,50plates: illus, facsims, music, ports; 24cm. – ('Essay and General Literature Index' reprint series)
Originally published, New York: H. Bittner, 1948.
ISBN 0 8046 1412 1 : £5.50

(B71-21649)

AC/E – Opera. Performance
Mitchell, Ronald Elwy
Opera dead or alive: production performance, and enjoyment of musical theatre/ [by] Ronald E. Mitchell. – Madison; London: University of Wisconsin Press, 1970. – xii,322p,16plates: illus, music, plans; 25cm.
bibl p311-312.
ISBN 0 299 05811 5 : £6.00

(B71-19966)

AC/E(YC/Q) – Opera. Performance. Great Britain. Organisations
National Operatic and Dramatic Association
Year book. – London (1 Crestfield St., WC1H 8AV): National Operatic and Dramatic Association. –
1971. – [1971]. – 340p: illus, form, map; 18cm.
ISBN 0 901318 02 7 Pbk: £0.75

(B71-05795)

AC/E(YJ/X) – Performance. Italy. History
Galatopoulos, Stelios
Italian opera/ by Stelios Galatopoulos. – London: Dent, 1971. – vii,179p,16plates: illus, music; 25cm.
List of records p165-166.
ISBN 0 460 05798 7 : £2.00

(B71-07324)

AC/EP(P) – Producers. Wagner, Wieland. Biographies
Skelton, Geoffrey
Wieland Wagner: the positive sceptic/ by Geoffrey Skelton. – London: Gollancz, 1971. – 222p,23plates: illus,facsim,geneal table,ports; 23cm.
bibl p215-216.
ISBN 0 575 00709 5 : £2.80

(B71-16012)

ACBM(X) – Opera. Librettos
Smith, Patrick John
The tenth muse: a historical study of the opera libretto/ by Patrick J. Smith. – London: Gollancz, 1971. – xxii,419,xvi p,16plates: illus, facsims, ports; 24cm.
Originally published, New York: Knopf, 1970. – bibl p411-417.
ISBN 0 575 00669 2 : £4.00

(B71-13107)

ACM – MUSICAL LITERATURE. MUSICAL PLAYS
ACN(VF) – Children's musical plays. Schools
John, Malcolm
Music drama in schools/ edited by Malcolm John. – London: Cambridge University Press, 1971. – xii,176p: music; 24cm. – (The resources of music series; 4)
bibl p173.
ISBN 0 521 08003 7 : £3.80

(B71-20590)

AD – MUSICAL LITERATURE. CHORAL MUSIC
AD/E(QB/DB) – London Emmanuel Choir
Capon, John
Sing Emmanuel: the story of Edwin Shepherd and the London Emmanuel Choir/ by John Capon. – Hemel Hempstead (Park La., Hemel Hempstead, Herts.): Word Books, 1971. – 124p,8plates: illus, ports; 18cm.
List of records p119-124.
ISBN 0 85009 031 8 Pbk: £0.50

(B71-27971)

AD/E(QB/YDLSH) — Choral societies. Aberdeen. Haddo House Choral Society
Linklater, Eric
The music of the north/ [by] Eric Linklater. — Aberdeen (Haddo House, Aberdeen): Haddo House Choral Society, 1970. — 20p,4plates: illus,ports; 22cm.
ISBN 0 9501767 0 2 Sd: £0.30

(B71-09739)

AD/E(VK) — Choral singing. Secondary schools
Roe, Paul F
Choral music education/ [by] Paul F. Roe. — Englewood Cliffs; Hemel Hempstead: Prentice-Hall, 1970. — xi,400p: illus, forms, music; 24cm.
bibl.
ISBN 0 13 133348 8 : £4.50

(B71-02480)

AD/LD(D) — Church music. Essays
English church music: a collection of essays. — Croydon (Addington Palace, Croydon, CR9 5AD): Royal School of Church Music. — 1971. — [1971]. — 3-68p: music; 22cm.
ISBN 0 85402 021 7 Pbk: £0.76

(B71-16701)

AD/LSB/E — Choral music. Roman Catholic Church. Singing
Tamblyn, Bill
Sing up: a guide and encouragement to sing in church/ [by] Bill Tamblyn; with cartoons by Peter Johnson. — London: G. Chapman, 1971. — 87p: illus, form; 22cm.
bibl p74.
ISBN 0 225 65904 2 Pbk: £0.80

(B71-16702)

ADD/LH — Oratorios. Holy Week
Smallman, Basil
The background of Passion music: J.S. Bach and his predecessors/ by Basil Smallman. — 2nd revised and enlarged ed. — New York: Dover; London: Constable, 1970. — 3,180p: facsims,music; 22cm.
Previous ed., London: S.C.M. Press, 1957. — bibl p169-175.
ISBN 0 486 22250 0 Pbk: £0.75

(B71-13108)

ADE/KM(YD/XEY161) — Cantatas. Court odes. England, 1660-1820
McGuinness, Rosamond
English court odes, 1660-1820/ [by] Rosamond McGuinness. — Oxford: Clarendon Press, 1971. — [9],249p: music; 28cm. — (Oxford monographs on music)
bibl p231-239.
ISBN 0 19 816119 0 : £7.00

(B71-27232)

ADH(YT/X) — Motets, Anthems, Hymns, etc. United States. History
Wienandt, Elwyn Arthur
The anthem in England and America/ [by] Elwyn A. Wienandt and Robert H. Young. — New York: Free Press; London: Collier-Macmillan, 1970. — xiii,495p: illus, facsims, music; 24cm.
bibl p460-470.
ISBN 0 02 093523 4 : £6.00
Also classified at ADK(YT/X)

(B71-20591)

ADK(YT/X) — Anthems. United States. History
Wienandt, Elwyn Arthur
The anthem in England and America/ [by] Elwyn A. Wienandt and Robert H. Young. — New York: Free Press; London: Collier-Macmillan, 1970 — xiii,495p: illus, facsims, music; 24cm.
bibl p460-470.
ISBN 0 02 093523 4 : £6.00
Primary classification ADH(YT/X)

(B71-20591)

ADTDS — Byzantine chant
Wellesz, Egon
Studies in Eastern Chant/ general editors Egon Wellesz and Milos Velimirović. — London: Oxford University Press. — Vol.2/ edited by Milos Velimirović. — 1971. — x,198p,8plates: illus,facsims,music,ports; 22cm.
bibl p41-50.
ISBN 0 19 316318 7 : £3.50

(B71-16013)

ADW — Songs, etc
Ivey, Donald
Song: anatomy, imagery, and styles/ by Donald Ivey. — New York: Free Press; London: Collier-Macmillan, 1970. — xiii,273p: 1 illus, music; 25cm.
bibl p257-259.
ISBN 0 02 091580 2 : £3.00

(B71-19968)

ADW(X) — Songs, etc. History
Stevens, Denis
A history of song/ edited by Denis Stevens. — London: Hutchinson, 1971. — 3-491p: music; 24cm.
Pbk. £1.50. sbn 09-104681-5. — Originally published 1960.
ISBN 0 09 104680 7 : £3.75

(B71-06292)

ADW(YD) — Songs, etc. England
Coprario, John
Funeral teares, 1606; [and], Songs of mourning, 1613, [by] John Coprario; [and], Ayres to sing and play to the lute, 1610; [and], The second book of ayres, 1612, [by] William Corkine; [and], Songs for the lute, 1606, [by] John Danyel/ edited by David Greer. — Menston: Scolar Press, 1970. — [168]p(chiefly music); 37cm. — (English lute songs, 1597-1632; vol.3)
Facsimile reprint of 1st eds, London, 1606-1613.
ISBN 0 85417 413 3 : £10.00

(B71-04595)

ADW(YH/XHK51) — Songs, etc. France, 1830-1880
Noske, Frits
French song from Berlioz to Duparc: the origin and development of the mélodie/ [by] Frits Noske. — 2nd ed.; revised by Rita Benton & Frits Noske [and] translated [from the French] by Rita Benton. — New York: Dover; London: Constable, 1970. — xiv,454p,35plates: illus, facsims, music, ports; 22cm. — (American Musicological Society. Reprint series) (Music Library Association. Reprint series)
Previous ed. published as 'La Mélodie francaise de Berlioz à Duparc'. Amsterdam: North-Holland Publishing Company; Paris: Presses Universitaires de France, 1954. — bibl p432-446.
ISBN 0 486 22104 0 Pbk: £3.00

(B71-05796)

ADW/G(YDCR) — Folksongs. Sussex
Copper, Bob
A song for every season: a hundred years of a Sussex farming family/ [by] Bob Copper. — London: Heinemann, 1971. — xiii,288p,8plates: illus, music, ports; 23cm.
ISBN 0 434 14455 x : £2.75

(B71-28161)

ADW/G(YDEVU) — Folk songs. Upper Thames
Williams, Alfred
Folk-songs of the Upper Thames: with an essay on folk-song activity in the Upper Thames neighbourhood/ collected and edited by Alfred Williams. — [1st ed. reprinted]; with a new preface by Stewart F. Sanderson. — Wakefield: S.R. Publishers, [1971]. — x,306p; 23cm. — ([Dialect reprints])
Facsimile reprint of 1st ed., London: Duckworth, 1923.
ISBN 0 85409 610 8 : £3.15

(B71-10430)

ADW/G(YDJH) — Folksongs. Durham County
Graham, Frank, *b.1913*
The Geordie song book/ edited by Frank Graham. — Newcastle upon Tyne: Graham, 1971. — 47p: ill, music; 22cm.
ISBN 0 902833 81 2 Sd: £0.31
Primary classification ADW/G(YDJJ)

(B71-18090)

ADW/G(YDJJ) — Folksongs. Northumberland
Graham, Frank, *b.1913*
The Geordie song book/ edited by Frank Graham. — Newcastle upon Tyne: Graham, 1971. — 47p: ill, music; 22cm.
ISBN 0 902833 81 2 Sd: £0.31
Also classified at ADW/G(YDJH)

(B71-18090)

ADW/G(YDL) — Folksongs. Scotland
Angus-Butterworth, Lionel Milner
Scottish folk-song/ by L.M. Angus-Butterworth. — [Ashton on Mersey (Ashton New Hall, The Old Village, Ashton on Mersey, Cheshire)]: L.M. Angus-Butterworth, 1971. — 18p; 22cm.
ISBN 0 9501956 0 x Sd: Unpriced

(B71-19970)

ADW/G(YDT) — Folksongs. Northern Ireland
Morton, Robin
Folksongs sung in Ulster/ compiled by Robin Morton. — Cork (4 Bridge St., Cork): The Mercier Press, 1970. — [10],95p: music; 18cm.
ISBN 0 85342 221 4 Pbk: £0.50

(B71-06293)

ADW/G(YSXD) — Folksongs. Newfoundland
Karpeles, Maud
Folk songs from Newfoundland/ collected and edited by Maud Karpeles. — London (3 Queen Sq., WC1N 3AU): Faber and Faber Ltd, 1971. — 3-340p: map, music; 26cm.
ISBN 0 571 09297 7 : £7.00

(B71-07869)

ADW/G/E(P) — Folk singers. Baez, Joan. Biographies
Baez, Joan
    Daybreak/ [by] Joan Baez. — London: Panther, 1971. — 141p;
18cm.
    Originally published, New York: Dial Press, 1968; London: MacGibbon and
Kee, 1970.
    ISBN 0 586 03502 8 Pbk: £0.30
        :
                              (B71-19969)

AF/E — Female voices. Performance
National Federation of Women's Institutes
    Accent on music. — London: N.F.W.I., 1971. — vi,89p: illus, music;
21cm.
    ISBN 0 900556 12 9 Pbk: £0.30
                              (B71-07868)

AK — MUSICAL LITERATURE. VOCAL SOLOS
AKDW/HHW — Blues
Groom, Bob
    The blues revival/ [by] Bob Groom. — London: Studio Vista, 1971.
— 112p: illus,facsims,ports; 21cm.
    Pbk(Blues paperbacks). £0.70. sbn 289-70148-1. — bibl p112.
    ISBN 0 289 70149 x : £1.40
                              (B71-16011)

AKDW/HHW(YTQ) — Blues. Mississippi
Ferris, William
    Blues from the Delta/ [by] William Ferris, Jr. — London: Studio
Vista, 1970. — 111p: illus, facsims, map, ports; 21cm.
    Pbk. (Blues paperbacks). £0.65. sbn 289-70071-x. — bibl p108-109.
    ISBN 0 289 70072 8 : £1.35
                              (B71-06291)

AKDW/HHW/(P) — Blues. Singing. Wheatstraw, Peetie. Biographies
Garon, Paul
    The Devil's son-in-law: the story of Peetie Wheatstraw and his songs/
[by] Paul Garon. — London: Studio Vista, 1971. — 111p: illus,
facsims, music, ports; 20cm.
    List of records p.107-111. Pbk. (Blues paperbacks). £0.70. sbn 289-70211-9.
— bibl p106.
    ISBN 0 289 70212 7 : £1.40
                              (B71-25346)

AKDW/HHW/E(YTNW) — Blues. Singing. United States. North
Carolina
Bastin, Bruce
    Crying for the Carolines/ [by] Bruce Bastin. — London: Studio Vista,
1971. — 112p: illus, facsims, maps, ports; 20cm.
    List of records p.109-112. Pbk. (Blues paperbacks). £0.70. sbn 289-70209-7.
— bibl p108-109.
    ISBN 0 289 70210 0 : £1.40
    Primary classification AKDW/HHW/E(YTNX)
                              (B71-25347)

AKDW/HHW/E(YTNX) — Blues. Singing. United States. South
Carolina
Bastin, Bruce
    Crying for the Carolines/ [by] Bruce Bastin. — London: Studio Vista,
1971. — 112p: illus, facsims, maps, ports; 20cm.
    List of records p.109-112. Pbk. (Blues paperbacks). £0.70. sbn 289-70209-7.
— bibl p108-109.
    ISBN 0 289 70210 0 : £1.40
    Also classified at AKDW/HHW/E(YTNW)
                              (B71-25347)

AKDW/HK(C) — Songs, etc. Rock 'n' roll. Encyclopaedias
Wood, Graham
    An A-Z of rock and roll/ by Graham Wood. — London: Studio
Vista, 1971. — 128p: illus,facsims,ports; 21cm.
    List of films p121. List of records p122-128. Pbk. £1.25. sbn 289-70005-1.
    ISBN 0 289 70006 x : £2.50
                              (B71-12553)

AKDW/HK/E(Y)M — Rock 'n' roll singers. Biographies
Hallowell, John
    Inside Creedence/ by John Hallowell. — New York: Bantam, 1971. —
viii,88p,64plates: illus,ports; 18cm.
    List of recordings, p88.
    ISBN 0 552 66901 6 Pbk: £0.40
                              (B71-14240)

AKDW/K/G(YC) — Ballads. Great Britain
Kidson, Frank
    Traditional tunes: a collection of ballad airs/ collected and edited with
illustrated notes by Frank Kidson. — [1st ed. reprinted]; with a new
foreword by A.E. Green. — Wakefield: S.R. Publishers, 1970. —
xviii,iii-174p: music; 24cm.
    Facsimile reprint of 1st ed., Oxford: Taphouse, 1891.
    ISBN 0 85409 637 x : £2.10
                              (B71-03034)

AKDW/K/G/KDX — Ballads. Bawdy
Cray, Ed
    Bawdy ballads/ [compiled and edited by Ed Cray]. — London:
Blond, 1970. — iii-xxxvi,272p: illus; 27cm.
    bibl p266-267.
    ISBN 0 218 51471 9 : £3.00
                              (B71-04596)

AKFQ/E(P) — Ferrier, Kathleen. Biographies
Kathleen Ferrier: comprising: The life of Kathleen Ferrier by her sister
Winifred Ferrier, and; Kathleen Ferrier: a memoir; edited by Neville
Cardus. — London: Pan Books, 1971. — [6],280p,16plates: facsim,
ports; 18cm.
    'The life of Kathleen Ferrier' originally published, London: Hamilton, 1955. —
'Kathleen Ferrier: a memoir' originally published, London: Hamilton, 1954.
    ISBN 0 330 02627 5 Pbk: £0.50
                              (B71-27231)

AKG/E(P) — Chevalier, Maurice. Biographies
Chevalier, Maurice
    I remember it well/ [by] Maurice Chevalier; preface by Marcel
Pagnol; translated from the French by Cornelia Higginson. —
London: W.H. Allen, 1971. — 221p,16plates: 1 illus, facsim, ports;
23cm.
    This translation originally published, New York: Macmillan (N.Y.), 1970.
    Originally published as 'Môme à cheveux blancs'. Paris: Presses de la Cité,
1969.
    ISBN 0 491 00436 2 : £2.00
                              (B71-06910)

AKGH/E(P) — Lanza, Mario. Biographies
Burrows, Michael
    Mario Lanza; and, Max Steiner/ by Michael Burrows. — St Austell
(21 Highfield Ave, St Austell, Cornwall): Primestyle Ltd, 1971. —
44p: illus, port; 22cm. — (Formative films series)
    Sd. £0.30. sbn 902421-04-2. — List of films p41 & p44. — bibl p41.
    ISBN 0 902421 14 x Sd: £0.75
    Also classified at BSNN(N)
                              (B71-27972)

AKGH/E(P) — Tenor voice. Tauber, Richard. Biographies
Castle, Charles, *b.1939*
    This was Richard Tauber/ [by] Charles Castle; in collaboration with
Diana Napier Tauber. — London: W.H. Allen, 1971. —
209p,33plates: illus, facsims(on lining papers), ports; 23cm.
    ISBN 0 491 00117 7 : £3.50
                              (B71-11818)

AL — MUSICAL LITERATURE. INSTRUMENTAL MUSIC
AL/B(XDWC378) — Instruments, 1523-1900
Paganelli, Sergio
    Musical instruments from the Renaissance to the 19th century/ [by]
Sergio Paganelli; [translated from the Italian by Anthony Rhodes]. —
Feltham: Hamlyn, 1970. — 157p: col illus; 20cm. — (Cameo)
    Originally published as 'Gli strumenti musicali nell'arte'. Milano: Fabbri,
1967.
    ISBN 0 600 35920 4 : £0.90
                              (B71-07323)

AL/BC — Instruments. Instrument making
Mandell, Muriel
    Make your own musical instruments/ by Muriel Mandell and Robert
E. Wood; illustrations by Margaret Krivak. — New ed. — Folkestone:
Bailey Bros and Swinfen, 1970. — 128p: illus; 20cm.
    Previous ed., London: Oak Tree, 1962.
    ISBN 0 561 00083 2 : £1.40
                              (B71-01700)

AL/Y — Fugues
Nalden, Charles
    Fugal answer/ [by] Charles Nalden. — Auckland: Auckland
University Press; London: Oxford University Press, 1970. —
xiii,192p: music; 26cm.
    bibl p189-190.
    ISBN 0 19 647552 x : £5.75
                              (B71-04593)

AM — MUSICAL LITERATURE. ORCHESTRAL MUSIC
AM/DF — Orchestration
Kennan, Kent Wheeler
    The technique of orchestration/ [by] Kent Wheeler Kennan. — 2nd
ed. — Englewood Cliffs; Hemel Hempstead: Prentice-Hall, 1970. —
xv,364p: illus, music; 24cm.
    Previous ed., New York: Prentice-Hall, 1952. — bibl p344-346.
    ISBN 0 13 903316 9 : £4.00
                              (B71-01701)

AMM/E(DCVB/X/QB) – Symphony orchestra. Performance. England. Hampshire. Bournemouth. History. Bournemouth Symphony Orchestra
Miller, Geoffrey
The Bournemouth Symphony Orchestra/ [by] Geoffrey Miller; introduction by Sir Adrian Boult. – Sherborne (3 Railway Cottages, Milborne Port, Sherborne, Dorset): Dorset Publishing Company, 1970. – ix,197p,32plates: illus, ports; 23cm.
ISBN 0 902129 06 6 : £4.00

(B71-05269)

AMT – MUSICAL LITERATURE. JAZZ
AMT(T) – Bibliographies
Kennington, Donald
The literature of jazz: a critical guide/ by Donald Kennington. – London: Library Association, 1970. – xv,142p; 22cm.
bibl.
ISBN 0 85365 074 8 Pbk: £1.75(£1.40 to members)

(B71-03232)

AMT/E(M) – Jazz musicians. Biographies
Blesh, Rudi
Combo: U.S.A.: eight lives in jazz/ by Rudi Blesh. – Philadelphia; London (67 Jermyn St., S.W.1): Chilton Book Company, 1971. – [11],240p,8plates: illus,ports; 25cm.
List of records p227-230. – bibl p225-226.
ISBN 0 8019 5250 6 : £3.50

(B71-14733)

AMT/E(M/XMK41) – Jazz musicians, 1910-1950
McCarthy, Albert John
The dance band era: the dancing decades from ragtime to swing, 1910-1950/ [by] Albert McCarthy. – London: Studio Vista, 1971. – 176p: illus, facsims, map, music, ports; 31cm.
List of records p171-173. – bibl p173.
ISBN 0 289 70218 6 : £4.20

(B71-30152)

AMT/E(P) – Armstrong, Louis. Biographies
Jones, Max
Louis: the Louis Armstrong story, 1900-1971/ [by] Max Jones & John Chilton. – London: Studio Vista, 1971. – 256p: illus, facsims, ports; 26cm.
ISBN 0 289 70215 1 : £3.20

(B71-25343)

AMT/E(P) – Ellington, Duke
Dance, Stanley
The world of Duke Ellington/ [by] Stanley Dance. – London: Macmillan, 1971. – xvi,301p,12plates: illus, ports; 23cm.
Originally published, New York: Scribner's Sons, 1970.
ISBN 0 333 13019 7 : £3.50

(B71-30153)

AMT/E(P) – Jazz. Wells, Dicky. *Biographies*
Wells, Dicky
The night people: reminiscences of a jazzman/ by Dicky Wells, as told to Stanley Dance; foreword by Count Basie. – London: Hale, 1971. – vi,122p: illus, ports; 23cm.
Originally published, Boston: Crescendo Publishing, 1971.
ISBN 0 7091 2397 3 : £2.00

(B71-25916)

AMT/E(P) – Mingus. Charles. Biographies
Mingus, Charles
Beneath the underdog: his world as composed by Mingus/ edited by Nel King. – London: Weidenfeld and Nicolson, 1971. – [7],366p; 23cm.
Originally published, New York: Knopf, 1971.
ISBN 0 297 00446 8 : £2.10

(B71-19348)

AP – MUSICAL LITERATURE. INDIVIDUAL INSTRUMENTS & INSTRUMENTAL GROUPS
APS – Musical literature. Musique concrète
Dwyer, Terence
Composing with tape recorders: musique concrète for beginners/ by Terence Dwyer. – London: Oxford University Press, 1971. – v,74p,4plates: illus; 20cm.
ISBN 0 19 311912 9 Pbk: £0.90

(B71-14737)

APW – MUSICAL LITERATURE. KEYBOARD INSTRUMENTS
AQ(X) – Piano. History
Sumner, William Leslie
The pianoforte/ by W.L. Sumner. – 3rd ed., with corrections and additions. – London: Macdonald and Co., 1971. – 223p,32plates: illus,ports,music; 23cm.
Previous ed. 1967. – bibl p206-217.
ISBN 0 356 03516 6 : £2.50

(B71-11124)

AQ/D/ED – Piano. Accompaniment. Composition
Lovelock, William
Elementary accompaniment writing/ by William Lovelock. – London: Bell, 1971. – 152p(chiefly music); 21cm.
ISBN 0 7135 1961 4 : £1.40

(B71-24689)

AQ/E(M) – Pianists
Kaiser, Joachim
Great pianists of our time/ by Joachim Kaiser; translated from the German by David Wooldridge and George Unwin; discography adapted and expanded by F.F. Clough. – London: Allen and Unwin, 1971. – 230p,12plates: music,ports; 25cm.
List of records p199-224. – Originally published as 'Grosse Pianisten in unserer Zeit'. Munich: Rutten und Loening, 1965.
ISBN 0 04 780019 4 : £3.25

(B71-16015)

AQ/E(VC) – Piano. Performance. Teaching
Booth, Victor
We piano teachers/ [by] Victor Booth. – [1st ed.] 8th impression (revised); revised by Adele Franklin; preface by Margaret Hubicki. – Richmond (Victoria); London: Hutchinson, 1971. – 135p,9plates: illus,facsim,music,port; 23cm.
Previous ed., London: Skeffington, 1964. – bibl p129-131.
ISBN 0 09 106190 3 : £1.25

(B71-05270)

Sharp, Mary, *b.1907*
Humour in music/ by Mary Sharp. – Ilfracombe: Stockwell, 1970. – 20p; 19cm.
ISBN 0 7223 0133 2 Sd: £0.175

(B71-04182)

AQ/E(VCL) – Piano. Performance. Examinations
The **piano** teachers' yearbook for the Associated Board Syllabus. – London: H. Freeman. –
1970/ compiled by Betty Reeves. – 1969. – 90p; 22cm.
ISBN 0 900385 00 6 Sd: £0.50

(B71-02482)

1971/ compiled by Betty Reeves. – 1970. – 84p; 22cm.
ISBN 0 900385 01 4 Sd: £0.50

(B71-02481)

AQPE – Piano solos. Sonatas
Hopkins, Antony
Talking about sonatas: a book of analytical studies, based on a personal view/ [by] Antony Hopkins. – London: Heinemann Educational, 1971. – 184p: music; 23cm.
ISBN 0 435 81425 7 : £2.50

(B71-26602)

AQR/E – Harpsichord. Performance
Schott, Howard
Playing the harpsichord/ [by] Howard Schott. – London (3 Queen Sq., WC1N 3AU): Faber and Faber Ltd, 1971. – 3-223p,8plates: illus, music; 23cm.
List of music p215-216.
ISBN 0 571 09203 9 : £2.75

(B71-29388)

AR(YC/VP/Q) – Organ. Great Britain. Graduate and professional education. Organisations
Royal College of Organists
Year book. – London (Kensington Gore, S.W.7): Royal College of Organists. –
1970/1971. – 1970. – [1],132p,plate: port; 19cm.
ISBN 0 902462 01 6 Pbk: £0.525

(B71-04184)

AR/B(X) – Organ. History
Perrot, Jean
The organ, from its invention in the Hellenistic period to the end of the thirteenth century/ by Jean Perrot; translated from the French by Norma Deane. – London: Oxford University Press, 1971. – xxviii,317p,28plates: illus,facsims,music; 26cm.
Originally published as 'L'orgue de ses origines hellénistiques à la fin du XIIIe siècle'. Paris: Picard, 1965.
ISBN 0 19 318418 4 : £8.50

(B71-14734)

AR/BL – Organ. Blowers
Elvin, Laurence
Organ blowing: its history and development/ by Laurence Elvin; foreword by Herbert Norman. – Lincoln (10 Almond Ave., Swanpool, Lincoln): L. Elvin, 1971. – [2],198p,25plates: illus,facsims,ports; 26cm.
bibl p177-185.
ISBN 0 9500049 1 x : £3.75

(B71-16704)

AR/E — Organ. Performance
Reynolds, Gordon
Organo pleno/ [by] Gordon Reynolds; with drawings by Bernard
Hollowood. — London: Novello, 1970. — 48p: illus, music; 19cm.
ISBN 0 85360 004 x Pbk: £0.35(non-net)

(B71-04183)

ARPV/BT — Electronic organs. Servicing
Middleton, Robert Gordon
Electronic organ servicing guide/ by Robert G. Middleton; with a
specially written chapter for the guidance of the English reader by W.
Oliver. — Slough: Foulsham, 1971. — [7],3-128p: illus; 29cm. —
(Foulsham-Sams technical books)
Originally published, Indianapolis: Sams, 1971.
ISBN 0 572 00785 x : £2.25

(B71-25917)

ARW — MUSICAL LITERATURE. STRING INSTRUMENTS
AS/EB — Violinists. Physiology
Szende, Ottó
The physiology of violin playing/ by Ottó Szende and Mihály
Nemessuri; with a foreword by Yehudi Menuhin; preface by Paul
Rolland; [translated from the Hungarian by I. Szmodis]. — London:
Collet's, 1971. — 202p: illus(some col); 25cm.
Originally published as 'A hegedüjáték élettani alapjai'. Budapest:
Zeneműkiadó Vállalat, 1971. — bibl p193-202.
ISBN 0 569 06196 2 : £3.50

(B71-16546)

ASTU(B) — Viola da gamba. Periodicals
Chelys: the journal of the Viola da Gamba Society. — Hedley (26
Churchill Cres., Hedley, Hants.): Viola da Gamba Society. —
Vol.1-. — 1970-. — music; 22cm.
55p. in first issue.
Sd: £2.10(free to members)

(B71-01190)

**AT — MUSICAL LITERATURE. PLUCKED STRING
INSTRUMENTS**
ATQ/B — Harp
Armstrong, Robert Bruce
[Musical instruments]. The Irish and Highland harps/ [by] Robert
Bruce Armstrong; introduction by Seóirse Bodley. — Shannon: Irish
University Press, 1969. — ix,xviii,199p,40plates(3fold): illus(some
col), 2facsims, music, ports; 32cm.
Quarter leather. — Facsimile reprint of Part 1 of the author's 'Musical
instruments'. Edinburgh: Douglas, 1904.
ISBN 0 7165 0073 6 : £10.00

(B71-30155)

ATQ/E(P) — Ventura, Angelo Benedetto
Bonner, Stephen
Angelo Benedetto Ventura: teacher, inventor, & composer: a study in
English Regency music/ by Stephen Bonner. — Harlow (128
Bishopsfield, Harlow, Essex): Bois de Boulogne, 1971. —
7-68p,15plates: illus(incl 1col),facsims,music,ports; 26cm.
Limited ed. of 180 numbered copies. Record (2 sides. 7in. 33 1/3 rpm) in
pocket. — bibl p66.
ISBN 0 900998 08 3 : £10.00

(B71-18714)

ATS/B(X) — Guitar. Instruments. History
Grunfeld, Frederic V
The art and times of the guitar: an illustrated history of guitars and
guitarists/ [by] Frederic V. Grunfeld. — New York: Macmillan
(N.Y.); London: Collier-Macmillan, 1969. — viii,340p: illus, facsims,
music, ports; 25cm.
bibl p323-334.
ISBN 0 02 546290 3 : £2.50

(B71-19972)

ATS/BC — Guitar. Instrument making
McLeod, Donald, b.1921
The classical guitar: design and construction/ [by] Donald McLeod,
Robert Welford. — Leicester: Dryad Press, 1971. — [1],107p: illus;
26cm.
ISBN 0 85219 077 8 : £2.50

(B71-14735)

ATWTJ — Appalachian dulcimer
Pearse, John
The dulcimer book/ by John Pearse. — London: A.T.V. Kirshner
Music; London (138 Old St., E.C.1): Distributed by Rosetti and Co.
Ltd, 1970. — [2],74p: illus, music, ports; 28cm.
ISBN 0 903052 00 8 Sd: £0.75

(B71-18091)

AU — MUSICAL LITERATURE. WIND INSTRUMENTS
AVV/B(X) — Clarinet. History
Rendall, Francis Geoffrey
The clarinet: some notes upon its history and construction/ by F.
Geoffrey Rendall. — 3rd ed.; revised and with some additional
material by Philip Bate. — London: Benn, 1971. — xx,206p,15plates:
illus, music; 23cm. — (Instruments of the orchestra)
Previous ed. 1957. — bibl p184-189.
ISBN 0 510 36701 1 : £2.75

(B71-20593)

AVV/E(M/XA1950) — Clarinettists, to 1950
Weston, Pamela
Clarinet virtuosi of the past/ [by] Pamela Weston. — London: Hale,
1971. — 292p,32plates: illus, facsims, music, ports; 23cm.
bibl.
ISBN 0 7091 2442 2 : £5.00

(B71-30156)

AWU/E — Trombone. Performance
Wick, Denis
Trombone technique/ by Denis Wick. — London: Oxford University
Press, 1971. — vii,152p,4plates: illus,music; 19cm.
List of music, p115-152.
ISBN 0 19 318704 3 Pbk: £1.15

(B71-14736)

AX — MUSICAL LITERATURE. PERCUSSION INSTRUMENTS
AX(X) — History
Blades, James
Percussion instruments and their history/ [by] James Blades. —
London (3 Queen Sq., WC1N 3AU): Faber and Faber Ltd, 1970. —
3-509p,72plates: illus, music, ports; 26cm.
bibl.
ISBN 0 571 08858 9 : £10.00

(B71-05797)

AXSR(YDCR) — Church bells. Sussex
Elphick, George Philip
Sussex bells and belfries/ by George P. Elphick. — Chichester:
Phillimore, 1970. — xx,427p,2fold plates: illus, ports; 23cm.
ISBN 0 900592 08 7 : £5.50

(B71-11121)

AXSR/B(YDFS) — Bells. Church bells. England. Scilly Isles
Sharpe, Frederick
The bells of the Isles of Scilly/ by Frederick Sharpe. — [Bicester
('Derwen', Launton, Bicester, Oxon.)]: [Sharpe], [1965]. — 7p;
22cm.
ISBN 0 9500835 2 6 Sd: £0.10

(B71-07870)

AXSR/B(YDHR) — Bells. Church bells. England. Herefordshire
Sharpe, Frederick
The church bells of Herefordshire: their inscriptions and founders/ by
Frederick Sharpe. — Launton ('Derwen', Launton, Bicester, Oxon.):
F. Sharpe. —
Vol.3: Kington-Pudlestone. — 1970. — xii,257-416p: illus, facsim, ports;
22cm.
ISBN 0 9500835 1 8 Pbk: £1.75

(B71-04597)

AXSR/E — Church bells. Change ringing
Duckworth, Richard
Tintinnalogia; or, The art of ringing/ [by Richard Duckworth and
Fabian Stedman]. — [1st ed. reprinted]; with an introduction by
Frederick Sharpe. — Bath: Kingsmead Reprints, 1970. — [16],136p;
19cm.
'... evidence that Duckworth was the writer and that Stedman supplied much
of the subject matter.' - Introduction. — Facsimile reprint of 1st ed., London:
Printed by W.G. for Fabian Stedman, 1668.
ISBN 0 901571 41 5 : £2.10

(B71-04185)

B — INDIVIDUAL COMPOSERS
BBG — Bartok, Bela
Lendvai, Ernő
Béla Bartók: an analysis of his music/ by Ernő Lendvai; with an
introduction by Alan Bush. — London (25 Thurloe St., S.W.7): Kahn
and Averill, 1971. — xi,115p: ill, music; 23cm.
ISBN 0 900707 04 6 : £2.00

(B71-30147)

BBG(N) — Bartok, Béla. Biographies
Bartók, Béla
Béla Bartók - letters/ collected, selected, edited and annotated by
János Demény; prefaced by Sir Michael Tippett; translated [from the
Hungarian] into English by Péter Balabán and István Farkas;
translation revised by Elisabeth West and Colin Mason. — London (3
Queen Sq., WC1N 3AU): Faber and Faber Ltd, 1971. —
466p,13plates: illus, facsims, music, ports; 25cm.
bibl p453-454.
ISBN 0 571 09638 7 : £5.50

(B71-18713)

Helm, Everett
Bartok/ by Everett Helm. — London (3 Queen Sq., WC1N 3AU):
Faber and Faber Ltd, 1971. — 80p,8plates: illus,facsim,music,ports;
26cm. — (The great composers)
bibl p77.
ISBN 0 571 09105 9 : £1.25

(B71-17373)

BBGAQ — Bartók, Béla. Piano. Manuals
Suchoff, Benjamin
Guide to Bartók's 'Mikrokosmos'/ [by] Benjamin Suchoff. — Revised
ed. — London: Boosey and Hawkes, 1971. — vii,152p: music; 23cm.
Previous ed. published on microfilm as 'Béla Bartók and a guide to the
"Mikrokosmos"'. Ann Arbor: University Microfilms, 1957. — bibl p143-147.
ISBN 0 85162 002 7 : £2.50

(B71-09061)

BBJ(N) — Beethoven, Ludwig van. Biographies
Arnold, Denis
The Beethoven companion/ edited by Denis Arnold and Nigel
Fortune. — London (3 Queen Sq., WC1N 3AU): Faber and Faber
Ltd, 1971. — 3-542p,8plates: illus, facsims, port; 23cm.
ISBN 0 571 09003 6 : £7.00

(B71-05266)

Gimpel, Herbert J.
Beethoven: master composer/ [by] Herbert J. Gimpel. — London (18
Grosvenor St., W.1): Franklin Watts Ltd, 1970. — iii-viii,250p:
illus,facsims,music,ports; 23cm. — (Immortals of mankind)
ISBN 0 85166 321 4 : £1.25

(B71-12554)

BBJASRPE — Beethoven, Ludwig van. Cello & piano. Sonatas
Beethoven, Ludwig van
[Sonata for cello & piano, no.3 in A major. Op.69]. Sonata for
violoncello and pianoforte. Opus 69, first movement [by] Ludwig van
Beethoven: facsimile of the autograph/ introductory note by Lewis
Lockwood; presented by 'The music forum'. — New York; London:
Columbia University Press, 1970. — [24]p of music; 28x36cm.
Facsimile reproduction of the autograph MSS, ca 1809.
ISBN 0 231 03417 2 Pbk:£1.75

(B71-06294)

BBKR(N) — Berg, Alban. Biographies
Berg, Alban
Alban Berg: letters to his wife/ edited, translated [from the German]
and annotated by Bernard Grun. — London (3 Queen Sq., WC1N
3AU): Faber and Faber Ltd, 1971. — 3-456p,17plates: illus, facsims,
maps, music, ports; 23cm.
ISBN 0 571 08395 1 : £4.50

(B71-05267)

BBTP — Bridge, Frank
Pirie, Peter John
Frank Bridge/ [by] Peter J. Pirie. — London (5 Mayfield Rd, W.3):
Triad Press, 1971. — 2-30p; 23cm.
Limited ed. of 180 numbered copies.
ISBN 0 902070 02 9 Sd:£0.80

(B71-24084)

BBV(N) — Bull, John. Biographies
Chappell, Paul
A portrait of John Bull, c.1563-1628/ by Paul Chappell. — Hereford:
Hereford Cathedral, 1970. — 25p: port; 22cm.
bibl p22.
ISBN 0 9501011 2 5 Sd:£0.10

(B71-03035)

BCBG — Cage, John
Kostelanetz, Richard
John Cage/ edited by Richard Kostelanetz. — London: Allen Lane,
1971. — iv-xvii,237p,32plates: illus,facsims,music,ports; 23cm. —
(Documentary monographs in modern art)
'...told mostly in his Cage's own words and writings...' - Preface. — Originally
published, New York: Praeger, 1970. — biblp211-230.
ISBN 0 7139 0210 8 : £3.15

(B71-14242)

BDL(N) — Delius, Frederick. Biographies
Fenby, Eric
Delius/ by Eric Fenby. — London (3 Queen Sq., WC1N 3AU): Faber
and Faber Ltd, 1971. — 100p,12plates: illus, facsims, ports, music;
26cm. — (The great composers)
bibl p94.
ISBN 0 571 09296 9 : £1.50

(B71-19346)

BDTWADW — Dowland, John. Songs
Dowland, John
The first booke of songes or ayres, 1597; [and], The first booke of
songs, 1613; [and], The second booke of songs or ayres, 1600; [and],
The third and last booke of songs or ayres, 1603; [and], A pilgrimes
solace, 1612, [by] John Dowland; [and], A musicall banquet, 1610,
[by] Robert Dowland/ edited by Diana Poulton. — Menston: Scolar
Press, 1970. — [313]p(chiefly music); 37cm. — (English lute songs,
1597-1632; Vol.4)
Facsimile reprints of 1st eds, London, 1597-1613.
ISBN 0 85417 414 1 : £10.00

(B71-04594)

BDX(N) — Dvořák, Antonin. Biographies
Young, Percy Marshall
Dvořák/ [by] Percy M. Young; [illustrated by Paul Newland]. —
London: Benn, 1970. — 80p: illus, music, ports; 23cm. — (Masters of
music)
ISBN 0 510 13717 2 : £0.90

(B71-01698)

BENAC — Einem, Gottfried von. Opera
Dürrenmatt, Friedrich
Der Besuch der alten Dame/ [by] Friedrich Durrenmatt; Oper in drei
Akten von Gottfried von Einem; Opernfassung des Textes von
Friedrich Dürrenmatt. — London: Boosey & Hawkes, 1970. — 87p;
19cm.
ISBN 0 85162 000 0 Pbk: Unpriced

(B71-04180)

BEP(N) — Elgar, Sir Edward, bart. Biographies
Parrott, Ian
Elgar/ by Ian Parrott. — London: Dent, 1971. — xi,143p,8plates:
illus,facsims,music,ports; 20cm. — (The master musicians series)
bibl p125-129.
ISBN 0 460 03109 0 : £1.75

(B71-14243)

BFURAKDW — French, Percy. Songs, etc.
French, Percy
Best Irish songs of Percy French/ edited with an introduction by
Tony Butler. — London: Wolfe, 1971. — 64p; 17cm.
ISBN 0 7234 0428 3 Sd:£0.25

(B71-11819)

BHE(N) — Haydn, Joseph. Biographies
Hughes, Rosemary
Haydn/ by Rosemary Hughes. — Revised ed. — London: Dent, 1970.
— xiii,271p,6plates: illus, facsim, music, ports; 20cm. — (The master
musicians series)
Previous ed. 1962. — bibl p252-258.
ISBN 0 460 03111 2 : £1.50

(B71-07862)

BJFAC — Janáček, Leos. Opera
Chisholm, Erik
The operas of Leos Janáček/ by Erik Chisholm. — Oxford:
Pergamon, 1971. — xxiv,390p,17plates: illus, music, port; 21cm. —
(The Commonwealth and international library, music division)
Pbk. £1.75. sbn 08-012853-x.
ISBN 0 08 012854 8 : £2.50

(B71-07865)

BLJ(N) — Liszt, Franz. Biographies
Walker, Alan, *b.1930*
Liszt/ by Alan Walker. — London (3 Queen Sq., WC1N 3AU);
Faber and Faber Ltd, 1971. — 3-108p,8plates:
illus,facsims,music,ports; 26cm. — (The great composers)
List of records p102-104. — bibl p99.
ISBN 0 571 09120 2 : £1.50

(B71-10425)

BMBH — Machaut, Guillaume de
Reaney, Gilbert
Guillaume de Machaut/ [by] Gilbert Reaney. — London: Oxford
University Press, 1971. — 76p: music; 22cm. — (Oxford studies of
composers; 9)
bibl p75-76.
ISBN 0 19 315218 5 Pbk:£0.90

(B71-30148)

BMS(N) — Mozart, Wolfgang Amadeus. Biographies
Einstein, Alfred
Mozart: his character - his work/ [by] Alfred Einstein; translated
[from the German] by Arthur Mendel and Nathan Broder. —
London: Panther, 1971. — 510p: music; 18cm.
This translation originally published, New York: Oxford University Press,
1945; London: Cassell, 1946.
ISBN 0 586 03277 0 Pbk:£0.75

(B71-06907)

BMS(N) — Mozart, Wolfgang Amadeus. Biographies
Levey, Michael
The life & death of Mozart/ [by] Michael Levey. — London:
Weidenfeld and Nicolson, 1971. — [1],ii-ix,278p,16plates: illus,
facsims, music, ports; 24cm.
bibl p271-272.
ISBN 0 297 00477 8 : £3.00

(B71-28693)

Valentin, Erich
Mozart and his world/ by Erich Valentin; [translated from the
German by Margaret Shenfield]. — London: Thames and Hudson,
1970. — 144p: illus, facsims, map, music, ports; 24cm.
This translation originally published as 'Mozart: a pictorial biography'. 1959.
Originally published as 'Mozart, eine Bildbiographie'. Munich: Kindler, 1959.
ISBN 0 500 13029 9 : £1.75

(B71-08375)

BMSAC — Mozart, Wolfgang Amadeus. Così fan tutte. Librettos
Da Ponte, Lorenzo
Le Nozze di Figaro; [and], Così fan tutte; [librettos by Lorenzo da
Ponte to the operas by] W.A. Mozart/ introduction by Dennis
Arundell. — London: Cassell, 1971. — 237p; 23cm. — (Cassell opera
guides)
List of records p235-237. Parallel Italian libretti and English translations by
Lionel Salter.
ISBN 0 304 93826 2 : £1.75
Primary classification BMSAC

(B71-25344)

**BMSAC — Mozart, Wolfgang Amadeus. Die Entführung aus dem
Serail. Librettos**
Schikaneder, Emanuel
Die Zauberflöte; [libretto by Emanuel Schikaneder to the opera by]
W.A. Mozart; [and], Die Entführung aus dem Serail; [libretto by
Gottlieb Stephanie to the opera by] W.A. Mozart/ introduction by
Brigid Brophy. — London: Cassell, 1971. — [2],163p; 23cm. —
(Cassell opera guides)
List of records p161-163. Parallel German libretti and English translations by
Lionel Salter.
ISBN 0 304 93825 4 : £1.75
Primary classification BMSAC

(B71-24690)

BMSAC — Mozart, Wolfgang Amadeus. Die Zauberflöte. Librettos
Schikaneder, Emanuel
Die Zauberflöte; [libretto by Emanuel Schikaneder to the opera by]
W.A. Mozart; [and], Die Entführung aus dem Serail; [libretto by
Gottlieb Stephanie to the opera by] W.A. Mozart/ introduction by
Brigid Brophy. — London: Cassell, 1971. — [2],163p; 23cm. —
(Cassell opera guides)
List of records p161-163. Parallel German libretti and English translations by
Lionel Salter.
ISBN 0 304 93825 4 : £1.75
Also classified at BMSAC

(B71-24690)

BMSAC — Mozart, Wolfgang Amadeus. Don Giovanni. Librettos
Da Ponte, Lorenzo
Don Giovanni; [libretto by Lorenzo da Ponte to the opera by] W.A.
Mozart; [and], Idomeneo; [libretto by Giambattista Varesco to the
opera by] W.A. Mozart/ introduction by Anthony Burgess. —
London: Cassell, 1971. — 150p; 23cm. — (Cassell opera guides)
List of records p147-150. Parallel Italian libretti and English translations by
Lionel Salter.
ISBN 0 304 93824 6 : £1.75
Also classified at BMSAC

(B71-24691)

BMSAC — Mozart, Wolfgang Amadeus. Idomeneo. Librettos
Da Ponte, Lorenzo
Don Giovanni; [libretto by Lorenzo da Ponte to the opera by] W.A.
Mozart; [and], Idomeneo; [libretto by Giambattista Varesco to the
opera by] W.A. Mozart/ introduction by Anthony Burgess. —
London: Cassell, 1971. — 150p; 23cm. — (Cassell opera guides)
List of records p147-150. Parallel Italian libretti and English translations by
Lionel Salter.
ISBN 0 304 93824 6 : £1.75
Primary classification BMSAC

(B71-24691)

BMSAC — Mozart, Wolfgang Amadeus. Le Nozze di Figaro. Librettos
Da Ponte, Lorenzo
Le Nozze di Figaro; [and], Così fan tutte; [librettos by Lorenzo da
Ponte to the operas by] W.A. Mozart/ introduction by Dennis
Arundell. — London: Cassell, 1971. — 237p; 23cm. — (Cassell opera
guides)
List of records p235-237. Parallel Italian libretti and English translations by
Lionel Salter.
ISBN 0 304 93826 2 : £1.75
Also classified at BMSAC

(B71-25344)

**BMSAMPQ/U — Mozart, Wolfgang Amadeus. Piano & orchestra. First
movement or Sonata form**
Forman, Denis
Mozart's concerto form: the first movements of the piano concertos/
[by] Denis Forman. — London: Hart-Davis, 1971. — 303p: music;
23cm.
Text on lining papers.
ISBN 0 246 64008 1 : £6.95

(B71-30154)

BPC(N) — Palestrina, Giovanni Pierluigi da. Biographies
Roche, Jerome
Palestrina/ [by] Jerome Roche. — London: Oxford University Press,
1971. — 60p: music; 22cm. — (Oxford studies of composers; 7)
List of music p.54-60.
ISBN 0 19 314117 5 Pbk: £0.90

(B71-29385)

BPP(N) — Prokofiev, Sergei. Biographies
Samuel, Claude
Prokofiev/ [by] Claude Samuel; translated [from the French] by
Miriam John. — London: Calder and Boyars, 1971. — 191p: illus,
facsims, music, ports; 22cm. — (Illustrated calderbooks; CB74)
Pbk. £0.90. sbn 7145-0490-4. — Originally published as 'Prokofiev'. Bourges:
Editions du Seuil, 1960.
ISBN 0 7145 0489 0 : £2.25

(B71-24085)

BRE — Ravel, Maurice
Myers, Rollo Hugh
Ravel: life and works/ by Rollo H. Myers. — London: Duckworth,
1971. — 239p,7plates: illus,facsim,music,ports; 23cm. — (Paperduck)
Originally published 1960. — bibl p228-230.
ISBN 0 7156 0566 6 Pbk: £1.00

(B71-10426)

BSET — Schoenberg, Arnold
Reich, Willi
Schoenberg: a critical biography/ [by] Willi Reich; translated [from
the German] by Leo Black. — Harlow: Longman, 1971. —
xi,268p,12plates: facsims, music, ports; 23cm.
Originally published as 'Arnold Schönberg, oder der konservative
Revolutionär'. Wien: Molden, 1968. — bibl p253-255.
ISBN 0 582 12753 x : £3.50

(B71-16010)

BSF — Schubert, Franz
Einstein, Alfred
Schubert/ by Alfred Einstein; translated [from the German MS] by
David Ascoli. — London: Panther, 1971. — 384p: music; 18cm.
Originally published, New York: Oxford University Press; London: Cassell,
1951.
ISBN 0 586 03480 3 Pbk: £0.75

(B71-14241)

BSF(N) — Schubert, Franz. Biographies
Kobald, Karl
Franz Schubert and his times/ by Karl Kobald; translated from the
German by Beatrice Marshall. — Port Washington; London (11
Southampton Row, WC1 B5HA): Kennikat Press, 1970. —
ix,277p,16plates: illus, ports; 23cm.
This translation originally published, New York: Knopf, 1928. Originally
published as 'Franz Schubert und seine Zeit'. Zürich: Amalthea-Verlag, 1928.
ISBN 0 8046 0756 7 : £6.25

(B71-02479)

Young, Percy Marshall
Schubert/ [by] Percy M. Young; [illustrated by Paul Newland]. —
London: Benn, 1970. — 80p: illus, music, ports; 23cm. — (Masters of
music)
ISBN 0 510 13732 6 : £0.90

(B71-01699)

BSGR(N) — Shostakovich, Dmitri. Biographies
Kay, Norman
Shostakovich/ [by] Norman Kay. — London: Oxford University
Press, 1971. — 80p: music; 22cm. — (Oxford studies of composers; 8)
List of music p.79-80.
ISBN 0 19 315422 6 Pbk: £0.90

(B71-29386)

BSHM — Simpson, Robert. Essays
Johnson, Edward
Robert Simpson: [fiftieth birthday] essays/ edited by Edward
Johnson. — London (5 Mayfield Rd., W.3): Triad Press, 1971. —
28p: facsim,music,ports; 23cm.
Limited ed. of 300 numbered copies, of which 275 are for sale.
ISBN 0 902070 01 0 Sd: £0.75

(B71-10427)

BSNN(N) — Steiner, Max. Biographies
Burrows, Michael
Mario Lanza; and, Max Steiner/ by Michael Burrows. — St Austell
(21 Highfield Ave. St Austell, Cornwall): Primestyle Ltd, 1971. —
44p: illus, port; 22cm. — (Formative films series)
Sd. £0.30. sbn 902421-04-2. — List of films p41 & p44. — bibl p41.
ISBN 0 902421 14 x Sd: £0.75
Primary classification AKGH/E(P)

(B71-27972)

BSQB(N) — Strauss family. Biographies
Fantel, Hans
Johann Strauss: father and son, and their era/ [by] Hans Fantel. —
Newton Abbot: David and Charles, 1971. — 246p,8plates: illus,
facsim, ports; 23cm.
bibl p222-227.
ISBN 0 7153 5421 3 : £2.75

(B71-30149)

BSW(N) — Sullivan, Sir Arthur. Biographies
Young, Percy Marshall
Sir Arthur Sullivan/ [by] Percy M. Young. — London: Dent, 1971. —
xiii,304p,16plates: illus, facsims, music, ports; 24cm.
List of musical works p271-285. — bibl p289-294.
ISBN 0 460 03934 2 : £4.00

(B71-28694)

BTD(N) — Tchaikovsky, Peter. Biographies
Bowen, Catherine Drinker
The music lovers: the story of Tchaikowsky and Nadejda von Meck/
[by] Catherine Drinker Bowen and Barbara von Meck. — 2nd ed.
abridged. — London: Hodder Paperbacks, 1971. — 317p: music,
plan; 18cm.
Full ed. originally published as 'Beloved friend'. New York: Random House,
1937.
ISBN 0 340 15154 4 Pbk: £0.35

(B71-04592)

BVD(N) — Vaughan Williams, Ralph. Biographies
Kennedy, Michael, *b.1926*
The works of Ralph Vaughan Williams/ [by] Michael Kennedy. —
London: Oxford University Press, 1971. — iii-xi,405p: music; 21cm.
Originally published 1964.
ISBN 0 19 315423 4 Pbk: £0.90

(B71-30151)

Lunn, John E
Ralph Vaughan Williams: a pictorial biography/ [by] John E. Lunn
and Ursula Vaughan Williams. — London: Oxford University Press,
1971. — [6],121p(chiefly illus, facsims, ports, music); 26cm.
ISBN 0 19 315420 x : £3.30

(B71-30150)

BVE(N) — Verdi, Giuseppe. Biographies
Verdi, Giuseppe
Letters of Giuseppe Verdi/ selected, translated and edited by Charles
Osborne. — London: Gollancz, 1971. — 280p,9plates: illus, facsim,
music, ports; 24cm.
ISBN 0 575 00759 1 : £3.00

(B71-21046)

BVJ — Vivaldi, Antonio
Kolneder, Walter
Antonio Vivaldi: his life and works/ [by] Walter Kolneder; translated
[from the German] by Bill Hopkins. — London (3 Queen Sq., WC1N
3AU): Faber and Faber Ltd, 1970. — x,288p,17plates: illus, facsims,
music, col port; 25cm.
Illus. on lining papers. — Originally published as 'Antonio Vivaldi, 1678-1741'.
Wiesbaden: Breitkopf und Härtel, 1965. — bibl p213-219.
ISBN 0 571 09386 8 : £6.00

(B71-07863)

BWC(N) — Wagner, Richard. Biographies
Gutman, Robert William
Richard Wagner: the man, his mind and his music/ [by] Robert W.
Gutman. — Harmondsworth: Penguin, 1971. — 693p; 18cm. —
(Pelican biographies)
Originally published, London: Secker and Warburg, 1968. — bibl p637-651.
ISBN 0 14 021168 3 Pbk: £0.75

(B71-05793)

Padmore, Elaine
Wagner/ by Elaine Padmore. — London (3 Queen Sq., WC1N 3AU):
Faber and Faber Ltd, 1971. — 3-100p,8plates: illus, facsims, ports,
music; 26cm. — (The great composers)
bibl p95.
ISBN 0 571 08785 x : £1.50

(B71-29387)

BZ — LITERATURE ON NON-EUROPEAN MUSIC
BZFL — North India
Jairazbhoy, Nazir Ali
The rags of North Indian music: their structure and evolution/ by
N.A. Jairazbhoy. — London (3 Queen Sq., WC1N 3AU): Faber and
Faber Ltd, 1971. — 3-222p,plate: illus,music; 26cm.
Record (2 sides. 7 in 45 rpm) in pocket. — bibl p211-212.
ISBN 0 571 08315 3 : £10.00

(B71-11817)

BZFMNT — Madras (State). Nilgiri Hills. Toda peoples
Emeneau, Murray Barnson
Toda songs/ [edited by] M.B. Emeneau. — Oxford: Clarendon Press,
1971. — xlviii,1004p,5plates(1 fold): 1 illus, geneal table, 3ports;
24cm.
Parallel Toda text and English translation. — bibl p xiii-xiv.
ISBN 0 19 815129 2 : £11.00

(B71-06911)

BZGVJAL/B(WJ) — Indonesia. Java. Instruments. Exhibitions
Fagg, William
The Raffles 'gamelan': a historical note/ edited by William Fagg with
a biographical note by Douglas Barrett. — London: British Museum,
1970. — [1],32p: illus(some col), facsims, music, ports; 21cm.
ISBN 0 7141 1514 2 Pbk: £0.40

(B71-04179)

C/AY — GENERAL COLLECTIONS
C/AYD — England
Musica Britanica: a national collection of music/ Vol.19; John Bull:
Keyboard music II, transcribed and edited by Thurston Dart. — 2nd
revised ed. — London: Stainer and Bell, 1970. — xxiii,238p; fol.
Unpriced
Also classified at PWP/AZ

(B71-50002)

Musica Britannica: a national collection of music. — London: Stainer
and Bell. —
Vol.33: English songs, 1625-1660/ transcribed and edited by Ian Spink. —
1971. — xxiii,210p; fol.
Unpriced
Also classified at KDW/AYD

(B71-50001)

C/AZ — Collected works of individual composers
Byrd, William
The collected works of William Byrd, edited by Edmund H. Fellowes
and revised under the direction of Thurston Dart/ Vol. 17; Consort
music, newly edited from manuscript and printed sources by Kenneth
Elliott. — London: Stainer and Bell, 1971. — ix,167p; 8vo.
£4.75
Also classified at STN

(B71-50723)

Byrd, William
The collected works of William Byrd/ edited by Edmund H. Fellowes
and revised under the direction of Thurston Dart. — London: Stainer
and Bell. —
Vol.15: Consort songs for voice & viols/ newly edited from manuscript
sources by Philip Brett. — 1970. — xii,180p; 8vo.
Pbk: Unpriced
Also classified at KE/STDW

(B71-50003)

Purcell, Henry
The works of Henry Purcell. — London: Novello. —
Vol.26: King Arthur; edited by Dennis Arundell, revised by Margaret Laurie.
— 1971. — xxxviii,205p; 8vo.
£4.50
Also classified at CB/JM

(B71-50156)

**C/CY — COLLECTIONS, EXERCISES, ETC., ILLUSTRATING
TECHNIQUES OF PERFORMANCE**
C/EF — Aural training
Warburton, Annie O
Graded aural tests for all purposes: with suggested methods of
working/ by Annie O. Warburton. — [Harlow]: Longman, 1971. —
285p; 8vo.
ISBN 0 582 32585 4 : Unpriced

(B71-50724)

CB — VOCAL MUSIC
CB/EG — Sight singing
London College of Music
Examinations in pianoforte playing and singing: sight reading tests,
sight singing tests as set throughout 1970. Grades I-VIII & diplomas.
— London: Ashdown, 1971. — 15p; 4to.
£0.25
Primary classification Q/EG

(B71-50084)

CB/JM — Incidental music
Purcell, Henry
The works of Henry Purcell. — London: Novello. —
Vol.26: King Arthur; edited by Dennis Arundell, revised by Margaret Laurie.
— 1971. — xxxviii,205p; 8vo.
£4.50
Primary classification C/AZ

(B71-50156)

CB/LD — Church music
Tallis, Thomas
English sacred music/ by Thomas Tallis; transcribed and edited by
Leonard Ellinwood. — London: Stainer and Bell. — (Early English
church music)
1: Anthems. — 1971. — xvii,124p; 8vo.
Unpriced

(B71-50726)

2: Service music. — 1971. — xvii,214p; 8vo.
Unpriced

(B71-50727)

CB/NM — Rhythm
Jones, E Olwen
Gweithdy cerddorol y plant/ [by] E. Olwen Jones. — Llandybie:
Christopher Davies, 1971. — 30p; obl. 4to.
Unpriced

(B71-50728)

CC — OPERA. VOCAL SCORES
Einem, Gottfried von
Der Besuch der alten Dame. Op. 35: Oper in drei Akten nach
Friedrich Dürrenmatts tragischer Komödie/ [by] Gottfried von
Einem; Opernfassung von Friedrich Dürrenmatt. — London: Boosey
and Hawkes, 1971. — 463p; fol.
Vocal score.
Unpriced

(B71-50729)

Humperdinck, Engelbert
Hansel and Gretel: a fairy opera in three acts/ the music by E.
Humperdinck; complete vocal score by R. Kleinmichel, translated
and adapted into English by Tom Hammond. — London: Schott,
1971. — 179p; 4to.
Vocal score.
Unpriced

(B71-50157)

McCabe, John
The lion, the witch and the wardrobe: an opera/ by John McCabe;
libretto by Gerald Larner (based on the book by C.S. Lewis). —
Borough Green: Novello, 1971. — 159p; 8vo.
Vocal score.
£1.25

(B71-50158)

Maw, Nicholas
The rising of the moon: an opera in three acts/ by Nicholas Maw;
libretto by Beverley Cross, piano reduction by David Matthews. —
London: Boosey and Hawkes, 1971. — 418p; 4to.
Vocal score.
Unpriced

(B71-50159)

Searle, Humphrey
Hamlet. Op. 48: opera in three acts/ by Humphrey Searle; libretto by
the composer after William Shakespeare, German translation by
Hans Keller and Paul Hamburger after August Wilhelm von
Schlegel. — London: Faber, 1971. — 316p; 4to.
Vocal score.
Unpriced

(B71-50160)

Stoker, Richard
Johnson preserved: opera in 3 acts/ by Richard Stoker; libretto by Jill
Watt. — London: Peters. [Hinrichsen], 1971. — 129p; 4to.
Vocal score.
£5.00

(B71-50161)

Verdi, Giuseppe
La Forza del destino: opera in three acts/ by Giuseppe Verdi; libretto
by Francesco Maria Piave, English translation by Ruth and Thomas
Martin. — New York: Schirmer; London: Chappell, 1970. — iv,367p;
8vo.
Vocal score.
Unpriced

(B71-50162)

Tchaikovsky, Peter
Eugene Onegin: lyric scenes in three acts and seven scenes/ by Pyotr
Tchaikovsky; libretto by Konstantin Shilovsky and Pyotr
Tchaikovsky, English version by David Lloyd-Jones. — London:
Schauer and May, 1971. — 243p; 4to.
Vocal score.
Unpriced

(B71-50730)

CF — OPERETTAS, VOCAL SCORES
Offenbach, Jacques
Ba-ta-clan: a masquerade in one act/ by Jacques Offenbach; libretto
by Ludovic Halévy, English adaptation and translation by Ian
Strasfogel. — New York: Schirmer; [London]: [Chappell], 1971. —
vi,114p; 8vo.
Vocal score.
Unpriced

(B71-50163)

Offenbach, Jacques
La Belle Hélène/ by Jacques Offenbach; music adapted and arranged
by Graham Ripley; new libretto and lyrics by Brian Anderson. —
London: United Music, 1971. — 145p; 4to.
Unpriced

(B71-50004)

CM — MUSICAL PLAYS. VOCAL SCORES
Hanmer, Ronald
Viva Mexico!: a comedy musical in three acts/ by Ronald Hanmer;
book and lyrics by Phil Park with the music of Latin-America
adapted and arranged by Ronald Hanmer. [Vocal score]. — London:
Weinberger, 1971. — 221p; 4to.
Vocal score.
Unpriced

(B71-50164)

Loewe, Frederick
Paint your wagon: a musical play/ by Frederick Loewe and Alan Jay
Lerner; book and lyrics by Alan Jay Lerner. — London: Chappell,
1971. — 260p; 4to.
Unpriced

(B71-50731)

CN — Children's musical plays with keyboard accompaniment
Hopkins, Antony
Doctor Musicus: an opera designed especially for the young/ words
and music by Antony Hopkins. — London: Chester, 1971. — 101p;
8vo.
Vocal score.
Unpriced

(B71-50732)

Sansom, Clive A
Oh! Noah/ words and music by Clive A. Sansom. — London: Studio
Music, 1971. — 28p; 8vo.
Vocal score. Duration 15 mins.
Unpriced

(B71-50165)

CN/L — Children's religious musical plays with piano accompaniment
Chappell, Herbert
The Goliath jazz: for unison voices with piano accompaniment and
guitar chords/ by Herbert Chappell; words by Tracey Lloyd and
Herbert Chappell. — London (145 Castlenau, S.W.13): Clarabella
Music, 1971. — 32p; 8vo.
Vocal score.
Unpriced

(B71-50166)

Chappell, Herbert
The Jericho jazz: for unison voices with piano accompaniment and
guitar chords/ by Herbert Chappell; words by Tracey Lloyd. —
London (145 Castlenau, S.W.13): Clarabella Music, 1971. — 34p;
8vo.
Vocal score.
Unpriced

(B71-50167)

Chappell, Herbert
The Noah jazz: for unison voices with piano accompaniment and
guitar chords/ by Herbert Chappell; words by Tracey Lloyd and
Herbert Chappell. — London (145 Castlenau, S.W.13): Clarabella
Music, 1971. — 30p; 8vo.
Vocal score.
Unpriced

(B71-50168)

Chappell, Herbert
The prodigal son jazz: for unison voices with piano accompaniment
and guitar chords/ by Herbert Chappell; words by Tracey Lloyd. —
London (145 Castlenau, S.W.13): Clarabella Music, 1971. — 27p;
8vo.
Vocal score.
Unpriced

(B71-50169)

Chappell, Herbert
The Red Sea jazz: for unison voices with piano accompaniment and guitar chords/ by Herbert Chappell; words by Tracey Lloyd. — London (145 Castlenau, S.W.13): Clarabella Music, 1971. — 31p; 8vo.
Vocal score.
Unpriced

(B71-50170)

Chappell, Herbert
The Christmas jazz: for unison voices with piano accompaniment and guitar chords/ by Herbert Chappell; words by Tracey Lloyd and Herbert Chappell. — London (145 Castlenau, S.W.13): Clarabella Music, 1971. — 30p; 8vo.
Vocal score.
Unpriced

(B71-50171)

CQC — OPERA. FULL SCORES
Holst, Gustav
[The tale of the wandering scholar. Op.50]. The wandering scholar. Op.50: a chamber opera in one act/ by Gustav Holst; edited by Benjamin Britten and Imogen Holst, libretto by Clifford Bax. — London: Faber, 1971. — 104p; 8vo.
Unpriced

(B71-50172)

CQF — OPERETTAS. FULL SCORES
Tate, Phyllis
Twice in a blue moon: a fantasy operetta, the accompaniment for two pianos, percussion and double bass/ by Phyllis Tate; libretto by Christopher Hassall. — London: Oxford University Press, 1971. — 50p; 4to.
ISBN 0 19 338377 2 : £1.25

(B71-50733)

CQM — MUSICAL PLAYS. FULL SCORES
Berger, Jean
The pied piper: a play with music/ by Jean Berger; text based on the poem by Robert Browning. — New York: Schirmer; [London]: [Chappell], 1971. — 120p; 8vo.
Unpriced

(B71-50173)

Birtwistle, Harrison
Down by the greenwood side: a dramatic pastoral/ by Harrison Birtwistle, text by Michael Nyman. — London: Universal, 1971. — 70p; 4to.
Unpriced

(B71-50734)

CQN — Children's musical plays. Full scores
Tate, Phyllis
A pride of lions: a story for singing and staging/ by Phyllis Tate, book by Ian Serraillier. — London: Oxford University Press, 1971. — 4to.
Score (v,40p.), choral score (8p.) & 3 parts.
Unpriced

(B71-50735)

DADW — SONGS, ETC. CHORAL SCORES
Tchaikovsky, Peter
1812 overture. Op.49: a festive overture/ by Peter Tchaikovsky; transcribed for chorus and orchestra by Igor Buketoff. — London: Sunbury Music, 1968. — 11p; 8vo.
Choral score. The editor suggests that various folk-melodies occurring in this orchestral work be transcribed for chorus.
£0.40

(B71-50736)

DD — ORATORIOS. VOCAL SCORES
Steel, Christopher
Paradise lost. Op. 34: a dramatic cantata in two parts, for soprano, tenor and baritone soli, SATB and orchestra/ by Christopher Steel; words by John Milton. — Borough Green: Novello, 1971. — 83p; 8vo.
Vocal score.
£0.90

(B71-50737)

DE — RELIGIOUS CANTATAS WITH KEYBOARD ACCOMPANIMENT
Crosse, Gordon
The covenant of the rainbow: festival anthem for mixed chorus, organ and piano duet; text from the Chester miracle play and the liturgy. Opus 24/ by Gordon Crosse. — London: Oxford University Press, 1970. — 63p; 4to.
Duration 20 mins.
ISBN 0 19 335610 4 : £1.50

(B71-50005)

Cruft, Adrian
A Bemerton cantata. Op.59: for mezzo-soprano solo, chorus, organ, string orchestra, harp, percussion/ by Adrian Cruft; words by John Norris. — London: Leeds Music, 1971. — 20p; 8vo.
Unpriced

(B71-50006)

Smith, Gregg
Babel: for four-part chorus of mixed voices (or solo quartet), five speaking groups and piano (2 players)/ by Gregg Smith; [words from] Genesis 2. — New York: Schirmer; London: Chappell, 1970. — 27p; 8vo.
£0.25

(B71-50007)

Tavener, John
Coplas: chorus (SATB-16 voices), soloists-SATB/ by John Tavener; verses of St John of the Cross. — London: Chester, 1971. — 18p; 4to.
Duration 11 mins. In this work a tape recording of extract from Crucifixus section from Bach's B minor Mass is employed.
Unpriced

(B71-50174)

Williamson, Malcolm
Genesis: a cassation for audience and instruments/ by Malcolm Williamson. — London: Weinberger, 1971. — 4to & 8vo.
Vocal score (16p.) and voices part.
Unpriced

(B71-50738)

DE/LEZ — Religious cantatas. Advent
Fischer, Theo
Die goldene Zeit: vorweihnachtliche Musik in neun Sätzen, für gleiche Stimmen, Männerchor und Kammerorchester (klavier oder Orgel) [by] Theo Fischer. — Cologne; London: Bosworth, 1971. — 23p; 4to.
Vocal score.
£0.50

(B71-50739)

DE/LF — Christmas
Rorem, Ned
Miracles of Christmas: for four-part mixed chorus and organ (or piano)/ by Ned Rorem; text by Ruth Apprich Jacob. — New York; [London]: Boosey and Hawkes, 1971. — 44p; 8vo.
£1.05

(B71-50175)

DFF — ROMAN LITURGY
DG — Ordinary of the Mass
Haydn, Joseph
[Mass no.16, 'Theresa mass']. Mass in B flat (Theresienmesse): for four-part chorus of mixed voices and solo quartet/ by Joseph Haydn; edited with keyboard reduction by William Herrmann. — New York: Schirmer; [London]: [Chappell], 1971. — vi,133p; 8vo.
Vocal score.
Unpriced

(B71-50176)

DGKJ/LF — Divine Office. Vespers. Christmas
Gabrieli, Giovanni
Hodie Christus natus est: for double chorus of mixed voices with organ accompaniment/ by Giovanni Gabrieli; edited by Dale Jergensen and Daniel Wolfe. — New York: Schirmer; [London]: [Chappell], 1971. — ii,22p; 8vo.
From 'Reliquiae sacrorum concentum' comprising works by Gabrieli and Hassler.
Unpriced

(B71-50740)

DGLBT — Other services. Benediction. Tantum ergo
Schubert, Franz
Tantum ergo in E flat (1828). [D.962]: for four-part chorus of mixed voices and solo quartet (ad lib.) with organ or piano accompaniment/ by Franz Schubert; edited with keyboard reduction by William Herrmann, text: St Thomas Aquinas. — New York: Schirmer; [London]: [Chappell], 1971. — 10p; 8vo.
Unpriced

(B71-50177)

DGM — ANGLICAN LITURGY
Royal School of Church Music
Festival service book. — Croydon: Royal School of Church Music. — 5. — 1971. — 62p; 8vo.
ISBN 0 85402 018 7 : Unpriced

(B71-50178)

DGM/KDD — Weddings
Royal School of Church Music
Choral wedding service. — Revised [ed.]. — Croydon: Royal School of Church Music, 1971. — 40p; 8vo.
ISBN 0 85402 019 5 : Unpriced

(B71-50179)

DGNQ — Morning Prayer. Te Deum
Williamson, Malcolm
Te Deum: for S.A.T.B. choir, organ and optional brass ensemble/ by Malcolm Williamson. — London: Weinberger, 1971. — 19p; 8vo.
Vocal score.
£0.25

(B71-50180)

DGNR — Morning Prayer. Benedicite
Sumsion, Herbert
Festival Benedicite in D: in shortened form/ by Herbert Sumsion. — South Croydon: Lengnick, 1971. — 16p; 8vo.
Unpriced

(B71-50741)

DGNT — Morning prayer. Jubilate
Kelly, Bryan
O be joyful in the Lord: a Caribbean Jubilate, for SATB and organ/ by Bryan Kelly. — London: Novello, 1970. — 15p; 8vo.
£0.15

(B71-50008)

DGPP — Anglican liturgy. Evening Prayer. Canticles
Byrd, William
[Short service. Excerpts]. Magnificat and Nunc dimittis: SAATTB and organ/ by William Byrd; edited by E.H. Fellowes, revised by Anthony Greening. — Revised ed. — London: Oxford University Press, 1971. — 14p; 8vo.
ISBN 0 19 352024 9 : £0.25

(B71-50181)

DGPP — Evening Prayer. Canticles
Humphrey, Pelham
Evening Service: SATB and organ with verses for SSAATB/ by Pelham Humphrey; edited by Christopher Dearnley. — London: Oxford University Press, 1971. — 16p; 8vo.
ISBN 0 19 351634 9 : £0.20

(B71-50182)

Purcell, Daniel
Magnificat and Nunc dimittis in E minor: for SATB and organ/ by Daniel Purcell; [reconstructed by Sir John Stainer], edited by Christopher Dearnley. — London: Novello, 1971. — 13p; 8vo.
£0.15

(B71-50742)

Tomkins, Thomas
[Musica Deo Sacra. Service no.1. Excerpts]. Magnificat and Nunc dimittis: for SATB/ by Thomas Tomkins; edited by Bernard Rose. — Borough Green: Novello, 1971. — 14p; 8vo.
Unpriced

(B71-50743)

DGPQ — Evening Prayer. Magnificat
Glarum, Leonard Stanley
Canticle of Mary (Magnificat) for four-part chorus of mixed voices with organ accompaniment/ by L. Stanley Glarum. — New York: Schirmer; London: Chappell, 1971. — 11p; 8vo.
Unpriced

(B71-50183)

DGS — Communion service
Wills, Arthur
Communion service in C: for congregation, SATB and organ/ by Arthur Wills; Series II text. — Croydon: Royal School of Church Music, 1970. — 2v.(16p; 4p); 8vo.
Unpriced

(B71-50009)

DGT — LITURGIES OF DENOMINATIONS OTHER THAN ROMAN & ANGLICAN
DGUB — Jewish liturgy. Sabbath
Bloch, Ernest
Avodath Hakodesh. Sacred service: a Sabbath morning service according to the Union Prayer Book, for baritone (cantor), mixed chorus and organ or full orchestra/ by Ernest Bloch; English text by David Stephens. — London: Boosey and Hawkes, 1970. — 97p; 8vo.
Vocal score.
Unpriced

(B71-50010)

DH — MOTETS, ANTHEMS, HYMNS, ETC.
Aldridge, Richard
Fill thou my life: anthem for SATB organ/ by Richard Aldridge; words by Horatius Bonar. — Croydon: Lengnick, 1971. — 12p; 8vo.
£0.13

(B71-50184)

Ball, Eric
Hail to the Lord's annointed: anthem for SATB and organ (or brass band)/ by Eric Ball; words by James Montgomery. — Borough Green: Novello, 1971. — 15p; 8vo.
£0.15

(B71-50185)

Chapman, Edward
Christ is the flower within my heart: a Christmas anthem, SATB/ words and music by Edward Chapman. — London: Oxford University Press, 1971. — 6p; 8vo.
Duration 3-1/4 mins.
ISBN 0 19 351110 x : Unpriced

(B71-50744)

Forrester, Leon
St Christopher. Stupendous thought/ by Leon Forrester; words by Milton P. Allen. — York: Banks, 1970. — 4p; 8vo.
Unpriced

(B71-50011)

Friend, Jerry R
On my way to the hill I saw my Lord: S.A.B. with piano and optional string bass/ words and music by Jerry R. Friend. — New York: Warner; [London]: [Blossom Music], 1971. — 15p; 8vo.
Unpriced

(B71-50745)

Gordon, Philip
Within thy light: SATB with organ or piano/ by Philip Gordon; words by Ilo Orleans. — New York; Warner; [London: Blossom Music], 1971. — 11p; 8vo.
Unpriced

(B71-50186)

Haydn, Joseph
[Mass, no.6 'Harmoniemesse'. - Dona nobis pacem]. Dona nobis pacem/ by Joseph Haydn: for four-part chorus of mixed voices with organ or piano accompaniment; edited and with keyboard reduction by William Herrmann. — New York: Schirmer; [London]: [Chappell], 1971. — 20p; 8vo.
Unpriced

(B71-50746)

Hovhaness, Alan
[I will lift up mine eyes. Op.93. Excerpts]. My help cometh from the Lord: for mixed voices and organ/ by Alan Hovhaness; from Psalm 121. — New York: Peters; [London]: [Hinrichsen], 1970. — 14p; 8vo.
£0.30

(B71-50187)

Howells, Herbert
Thee will I love: motet for SATB and organ/ by Herbert Howells; words by R.S. Bridges. — Borough Green: Novello, 1970. — 14p; 8vo.
£0.15

(B71-50012)

Pedrette, Edward
Almighty God: for four-part chorus of mixed voices with organ or piano accompaniment/ by Edward Pedrette; [words from] the Book of Common Prayer. — New York: Schirmer; London: Chappell, 1971. — 4p; 8vo.
Unpriced

(B71-50188)

Peter, Johann Friedrich
[Der Herr segne euch]. The Lord shall increase you: for SSAB chorus (or SATB)/ by Johann Friedrich Peter; edited and arranged by Roy E. Stilwell and Ewald V. Nolte, [text from] Psalm 115, English adaptation by R.E.S.. — New York; [London]: [Boosey and Hawkes], 1971. — 7p; 8vo.
£0.09

(B71-50189)

Peter, Johann Friedrich
[Ich will dir ein Frendenopfer]. I will freely sacrifice to thee: for SSTB chorus (or SATB)/ by Johann Friedrich Peter; edited and arranged by Roy E. Stillwell and Ewald V. Nolte, [text from] Psalm 54, English adaptation by R.E.S. and E.V.N. — New York; [London]: Boosey and Hawkes, 1971. — 9p; 8vo.
£0.15

(B71-50190)

Smith, Noel
Great mover of all hearts: anthem/ by Noel Smith; words by C. Coffin, translated by I. Williams. — South Croydon: Lengnick, 1971. — 8p; 8vo.
Unpriced

(B71-50747)

Webber, Lloyd
Four introits: for SATB and organ/ by Lloyd Webber. — Borough Green: Novello, 1971. — 7p; 8vo.
Contents: 1.Bee still, my soul; words by K. von Schlegel, translated by J. Borthwick. — 2.Let your light so shine; text from St. Matthew. — 3.Lo, God is here; words by G. Tersteegen, translated by J. Wesley. — 4.Jesus, where'er thy people meet; words by William Cowper.
£0.09

(B71-50013)

DH/LF — Christmas
Hammerschmidt, Andreas
[Alleluja. Freuet euch ihr Christen alle]. Alleluia! O rejoice ye Christians loudly: for mixed voices, organ (piano) and strings (ad lib)/ by Andreas Hammerschmidt; edited by Diethard Hellmann; [words by] Christian Reimann, [translated from the German] by Catherine Winkworth. — New York: Peters; [London]: [Hinrichsen], 1970. — 22p; 8vo.
Vocal score.
£0.45

(B71-50191)

DH/LFL — Epiphany
Marcello, Benedetto
[Psalm 45. Excerpts]. Heart's adoration: two-part/ by Benedetto Marcello, adapted by Lionel Lethbridge; words from the hymn by Bishop Heber. — London: Oxford University Press, 1971. — 3p; 8vo.
Duration 2 mins.
Unpriced

(B71-50014)

DH/LG — Lent
Matthews, Walter E
Oh, come and mourn with us: SATB/ by Walter E. Matthews; text by Frederick W. Faber. — New York: Warner; [London]: [Blossom], 1971. — 11p; 8vo.
Unpriced

(B71-50748)

DH/LL — Easter
Thiman, Eric Harding
Come, ye faithful, raise the strain: Easter anthem, for SATB and organ/ by Eric H. Thiman; words by St John Damascene; translated by J.M. Neale. — Borough Green: Novello, 1971. — 8p; 8vo.
Staff & tonic sol-fa notation.
Unpriced

(B71-50015)

DH/LM — Ascension
Rorem, Ned
Lift up your heads. (The ascension)/ by Ned Rorem; [words by] John Beaumont. — New York; [London]: Boosey and Hawkes, 1969. — 19p; 8vo.
Vocal score.
y4.50

(B71-50749)

DJ — MOTETS
Gabrieli, Giovanni
Jubilemus singuli: for eight-part chorus of mixed voices with organ accompaniment/ by Giovanni Gabrieli; edited by Dale Jergenson and Daniel Wolfe. — New York: Schirmer; London: Chappell, 1970. — 22p; 8vo.
Unpriced

(B71-50016)

Tamblyn, William
You are Peter: anthem for SATB, organ and/or brass/ by William Tamblyn; text from the Jerusalem Bible. — London: Boosey and Hawkes, 1971. — 8p; 8vo.
Unpriced

(B71-50192)

DK — ANTHEMS
Aston, Peter
For I went with the multitude: anthem for SATB and organ/ by Peter Aston; [from] Psalm 42. — Borough Green: Novello, 1971. — 7p; 8vo.
Unpriced

(B71-50750)

Beck, John Ness
Anthem of unity: for four-part chorus of mixed voices with piano or organ accompaniment/ by John Ness Beck; text adapted from Ephesians 4. — New York: Schirmer; [London]: [Chappell], 1971. — 11p; 8vo.
Unpriced

(B71-50751)

Handel, George Frideric
Coronation anthem no.2 (The King shall rejoice): for six-part chorus of mixed voices, by George Frideric Handel; edited with keyboard reduction by William Herrmann; text from Psalm 21. — New York: Schirmer; [London]: [Chappell], 1971. — vii,38p; 8vo.
Vocal score.
Unpriced

(B71-50194)

Handel, George Frideric
Coronation anthem no.3 (My heart is inditing): for five-part chorus of mixed voices and solo quartet (ad lib.) with organ or piano accompaniment/ by George Frideric Handel; edited and with keyboard reduction by William Herrmann, text [from] Psalm 45. — New York: Schirmer; London: Chappell, 1971. — vii,41p; 8vo.
Unpriced

(B71-50193)

Locke, Matthew
Turn thy face from my sins: verse anthem for A.T.B. and chorus, SSATB/ by Matthew Locke; edited by Anthony Greening; [text from] Psalm 51 with Gloria. — London: Oxford University Press, 1971. — 11p; 8vo.
Unpriced

(B71-50195)

Newbury, Kent A
Great is the Lord: for full chorus of mixed voices with organ or piano accompaniment/ by Kent A. Newbury; [words] adapted from Psalms 48 and 148. — New York: Schirmer; [London]: [Chappell], 1971. — 8p; 8vo.
Unpriced

(B71-50196)

Pasfield, W R
Grieve not the holy Spirit of God: anthem for SATB and organ/ by W.R. Pasfield; words from Ephesians 4. — London: Ashdown, 1971. — 4p; 8vo.
Unpriced

(B71-50752)

Rhodes, Joseph W
They shall see the glory of the Lord: SATB/ by Joseph W. Rhodes; text from Isaiah 35. — New York: Warner, Seven Arts; London: Blossom Music, 1971. — 11p; 8vo.
Unpriced

(B71-50197)

Silk, Richard
Sing and rejoice: SATB/ by Richard Silk; text from Zechariah 2. — London: Oxford University Press, 1971. — 12p; 8vo.
ISBN 0 19 350315 8 : Unpriced

(B71-50198)

Standford, Patric
How amiable are thy dwellings: anthem for SATB and organ/ by Patric Standford; words adapted from Psalm 84. — Borough Green: Novello, 1971. — 17p; 8vo.
Unpriced

(B71-50199)

Steel, Christopher
O clap your hands together. Op.50: anthem for SATB and organ (or brass)/ by Christopher Steel; [words from] Psalms 46, 47, 145, 149. — Borough Green: Novello, 1971. — 15p; 8vo.
£0.15

(B71-50200)

DK/KDD — Weddings
Handel, George Frideric
Sing unto God. (Wedding anthem for Frederick, Prince of Wales, 1736): for soloists, chorus and orchestra/ by G.F. Handel; edited by Paul Steinitz. — London: Oxford University Press, 1971. — 38p; 8vo.
Vocal score.
ISBN 0 19 336660 6 : £0.80

(B71-50201)

DK/LF — Christmas
Gibbons, Orlando
Almighty God, which hast given: verse anthem for Christmas Day/ by Orlando Gibbons; reconstructed by Paul Vining. — Borough Green; London: Novello, 1970. — 12p; 8vo.
£0.15

(B71-50017)

DM — HYMNS
Bach, Johann Sebastian
[Wachet auf. S.140. Excerpts]. Zion hears the watchmen's voices: for unison & SATB chorale/ by J.S. Bach; edited by John Rutter, [words by] P. Nicolai, English words by John Rutter. — London: Oxford University Press, 1971. — 7p; 8vo.
ISBN 0 19 343013 4 : Unpriced

(B71-50202)

Williams, W Matthews
Tannau moliant/ [by] W. Matthews Williams. — Caernarfon: Llyfrfa'r Methodistiaid Calfinaidd, 1971. — 63p; 8vo.
Unpriced

(B71-50753)

DM/AY — Collections
Gathered together: a service book for senior schools. — London: Oxford University Press, 1971. — 4to.
Music ed. (505p.) & melody ed.
Unpriced

(B71-50203)

Green, Frederick Pratt
26 hymns/ [by] F. Pratt Green. — London: Epworth Press, 1971. — 64p: music; 8vo.
ISBN 0 7162 0181 x Sd: £0.40

(B71-50754)

Old, Margaret V
Sing to God: Christian songs for juniors/ compiled by Margaret V. Old and Elspeth M. Stephenson. — London: Scripture Union, 1971. — [158]p; obl. 8vo.
ISBN 0 85421 302 3 : £1.25

(B71-50755)

Shepherd, Edwin T
Emmanuel songs, compiled by Edwin T. Shepherd/ Vol.2. — London: Marshall, Morgan and Scott, 1971. — 73p; 8vo.
ISBN 0 551 05416 6 : £0.45

(B71-50757)

Shepherd, Edwin T
Emmanuel songs/ compiled by Edwin T. Shepherd. — London: Marshall, Morgan and Scott. —
Vol.3. — 1971. — 65p; 8vo.
ISBN 0 551 05049 7 : £0.45

(B71-50756)

DM/AYDK — Collections. Wales
Battye, Ken
Welsh flavour: a selection of Welsh hymn tunes set to English words/ compiled by Ken Battye. — Carnforth (3 Wood View, Burton in Lonsdale, Via Carnforth, Lancs.): K. Battye. —
Vol.1. — 1971. — 31p; 8vo.
Unpriced

(B71-50204)

Vol.2. — 1971. — 27p; 8vo.
Unpriced

(B71-50205)

Vol.3. — 1971. — 27p; 8vo.
Unpriced

(B71-50206)

Vol.4. — 1971. — 27p; 8vo.
Unpriced

(B71-50207)

Vol.5. — 1971. — 27p; 8vo.
Unpriced

(B71-50208)

DM/LL — Easter
Rutter, John
Christ the Lord is risen again: SATB/ by John Rutter; words by Michael Weisse; [translated from the German by] Catherine Winkworth. — London: Oxford University Press, 1971. — 8p; 8vo.
ISBN 0 19 351109 6 : £0.09

(B71-50209)

DM/LL/AY — Easter. Collections
Brooks, Nigel
Songs for Easter/ arranged by Nigel Brooks. — London: Boosey and Hawkes, 1971. — 28p; 4to.
Unpriced

(B71-50210)

DM/LSB/AY — Roman Catholic Church. Collections
Petti, Anthony
New Catholic hymnal/ compiled and edited by Anthony Petti and Geoffrey Laycock. — London: Faber Music, 1971. — xix,374p; 8vo.
ISBN 0 571 10001 5 : Unpriced

(B71-50758)

DP — CAROLS
DP/LF — Christmas
Curtis, Frederick Vernon
O the morn, the merry merry morn/ by Frederick Vernon Curzon; [words by] G.R. Woodward. — York: Banks, 1970. — 1p; 8vo.
Unpriced

(B71-50018)

Ehret, Walter
Where sleeps the infant Jesus: Mexican carol, SATB/ arranged by Walter Ehret, English text by W.E. — New York: Warner; London: Blossom Music, 1971. — 7p; 8vo.
Unpriced

(B71-50211)

Gardner, John
Four carols. Op.109: for mixed or S.A. voices/ by John Gardner. — London: Oxford University Press. —
1: Chanticleer's carol/ [text by] William Austin. — 1971. — 3p; 8vo.
ISBN 0 19 343017 7 : Unpriced
Also classified at FDP/LF

(B71-50759)

2: Balulalow/ [text by] Wedderburn. — 1971. — 4p; 8vo.
ISBN 0 19 343018 5 : Unpriced
Also classified at FDP/LF

(B71-50760)

3: Remember/ [text by] T. Ravenscroft. — 1971. — 6p; 8vo.
ISBN 0 19 343019 3 : Unpriced
Also classified at FDP/LF

(B71-50761)

4: A gallery carol. — 1971. — 6p; 8vo.
ISBN 0 19 343020 7 : Unpriced

(B71-50762)

Gruber, Franz
[Stille Nacht, heilige Nacht]. Silent night/ by Franz Gruber; arranged by Edward Chapman, SATB; words by Joseph Mohr, trans. David Willcocks. — London: Oxford University Press, 1971. — 3p; 8vo.
ISBN 0 19 343022 3 : Unpriced

(B71-50763)

Mathias, William
[Ave rex. Excerpts]. Sir Christmas: SATB/ by William Mathias; words anon. — London: Oxford University Press, 1971. — 6p; 8vo.
ISBN 0 19 343008 8 : Unpriced

(B71-50212)

Rutter, John
Flemish carol: tune old Flemish, SATB/ arranged by John Rutter, words translated by R.C. Trevelyan. — London: Oxford University Press, 1971. — 4p; 8vo.
ISBN 0 19 343014 2 : Unpriced

(B71-50213)

Rutter, John
Love came down at Christmas: SATB/ by John Rutter; [words by] Christina Rossetti. — London: Oxford University Press, 1971. — 3p; 8vo.
ISBN 0 19 343025 8 : Unpriced

(B71-50764)

Willcocks, David
Masters in this hall: French traditional carol, SATB/ arranged by David Willcocks; words by William Morris. — London: Oxford University Press, 1971. — 7p; 8vo.
ISBN 0 19 343009 6 : Unpriced

(B71-50214)

Willcocks, David
Quelle est cette odeur agréable? Whence is that goodly fragrance flowing?: French traditional carol, S.A.T.B./ arranged by David Willcocks, tr. A.B. Ramsey. — London: Oxford University Press, 1971. — 7p; 8vo.
ISBN 0 19 343010 x : Unpriced

(B71-50215)

Willcocks, David
Resonemus laudibus: SATB/ arranged by David Willcocks; transcribed and edited by Frank Ll. Harrison. — London: Oxford University Press, 1971. — 5p; 8vo.
ISBN 0 19 343011 8 : Unpriced

(B71-50216)

Wilson, Robert Barclay
All poor men and humble. O deued pob Christio: a Welsh carol/ arranged by R. Barclay Wilson. — London: Cramer, 1971. — 4p; 8vo.
£0.06

(B71-50765)

Wilson-Dickson, Andrew
A little hymn to Mary: carol for SATB and piano or organ/ by Andrew Wilson-Dickson; words anonymous, 16th century. — Borough Green: Novello, 1971. — 4p; 8vo.
Unpriced

(B71-50766)

DP/LF/AY — Christmas. Collections
Willcocks, David
[Carols for choirs. Excerpts]. Six Christmas hymns: for mixed voices and organ (or orchestra)/ arranged by David Willcocks. — London: Oxford University Press, 1971. — 15p; 8vo.
Vocal score.
ISBN 0 19 353568 8 : £0.20

(B71-50217)

DP/LF/AYDFRP – Christmas. Collections. Cornwall. Padstow
Worden, John
Strike sound: a collection of Padstow carols/ by John Worden. –
Padstow: Lodenek Press, 1971. – 22p; 4to.
Unpriced

(B71-50767)

DP/LFP – Epiphany
Hurford, Peter
Bethlehem, of noblest cities: Australian folk melody and a melody
from Psalmodia sacra, Gotha, 1715, for SATB/ arranged by Peter
Hurford, words by Prudentius [translated from the Latin by] E.
Caswall. – London: Oxford University Press, 1971. – 4p; 8vo.
Unpriced

(B71-50218)

DR – PSALMS
Aston, Peter
Praise ye the Lord: anthem for SATB with divisions, and organ (or
brass)/ by Peter Aston; text Psalm 150. – Borough Green: Novello,
1971. – 11p; 8vo.
£0.13

(B71-50219)

Bruckner, Anton
Psalm 112: for double chorus of mixed voices/ by Anton Bruckner;
English adaptation by Maynard Klein. – New York: Schirmer;
[London]: [Chappell], 1971. – 80p; 8vo.
Vocal score.
Unpriced

(B71-50220)

Hoag, Charles K
May God have mercy upon us: for four-part chorus of mixed voices
with organ accompaniment/ by Charles K. Hoag; [text] Psalm 6. –
New York: Schirmer; [London]: [Chappell], 1971. – 6p; 8vo.
Unpriced

(B71-50768)

Hovhaness, Alan
I will lift up mine eyes. Opus 93: mixed voices (boys choir and bass
solo ad lib.) and organ/ by Alan Hovhaness; [text] Psalm 121. –
New York: Peters; [London]: [Hinrichsen], 1970. – 31p; 8vo.
Duration 15 mins.
£0.75

(B71-50221)

Joubert, John
I will lift up mine eyes unto the hills. Op. 63: anthem for SSAA and
piano/ by John Joubert; text: Psalm 121. – Borough Green: Novello,
1971. – 12p; 8vo.
£0.15

(B71-50222)

Kelly, Bryan
Out of the deep. De profundis: anthem for SATB and organ (or brass
band)/ by Bryan Kelly; text Psalm 130. – London: Novello, 1971. –
14p; 8vo.
£0.15

(B71-50223)

Tamblyn, William
Antiphons and Psalm 150: for cantor, congregation, SATB choir and
organ/ by William Tamblyn; text from the Jerusalem Bible.
London: Boosey and Hawkes, 1971. – 7p; 8vo.
Unpriced

(B71-50224)

DT – PLAINSONG
DTD – Gregorian chant
Briggs, H B
A manual of plainsong for Divine Service/ as edited by H.B. Briggs
and W.H. Frere based on the edition by J.H. Arnold, adapted for
'The Revised Psalter' by John Dykes Bower and Gerald H. Knight. –
London: Novello, 1969. – xxviii,268p; 8vo.
£1.25

(B71-50019)

DW – SONGS, ETC.
Artman, Ruth
Well, what do you know!: SATB, with piano accompaniment and
optional violins, strings bass and guitar/ words and music by Ruth
Artman. – New York: Warner; [London]: [Blossom Music], 1971.
– 8vo.
Score (16p.) & part.
Unpriced

(B71-50770)

Brahms, Johannes
Abendlied. Evening song. Op.91, no.3: for four-part chorus of mixed
voices with piano accompaniment/ by Johannes Brahms, edited by
Maynard Klein; [words by] Friedrich Hebbel, English text by M.K..
– New York: Schirmer; London: Chappell, 1971. – 8p; 8vo.
Text in German and English.
Unpriced

(B71-50225)

Brahms, Johannes
Nachtens. Nightly visions. Op.112, no.2: for four-part chorus of
mixed voices with piano accompaniment/ by Johannes Brahms,
edited by Maynard Klein; English text by M.K. – New York:
Schirmer; London: Chappell, 1971. – 10p; 8vo.
Text in German and English.
Unpriced

(B71-50226)

Brahms, Johannes
O schöne Nacht. O lovely night. Op.92, no.1: for four-part chorus of
mixed voices with piano accompaniment/ by Johannes Brahms,
edited by Maynard Klein; [words by] Daumer, English text by M.K.
– New York: Schirmer; London: Chappell, 1971. – 11p; 8vo.
Text in German and English.
Unpriced

(B71-50227)

Brahms, Johannes
Sehnsucht. Longing. Op.112, no.1: for four-part chorus of mixed
voices with piano accompaniment/ by Johannes Brahms, edited by
Maynard Klein; [words by] Frans Kugler, English text by M.K.. –
New York: Schirmer; London: Chappell, 1971. – 8p; 8vo.
Text in German and English.
Unpriced

(B71-50228)

Brahms, Johannes
Spätherbst. Late autumn. Op.92, no.2: for four-part chorus of mixed
voices with piano accompaniment/ by Johannes Brahms, edited by
Maynard Klein; English text by M.K.. – New York: Schirmer;
London: Chappell, 1971. – 4p; 8vo.
Text in German and English.
Unpriced

(B71-50229)

Brahms, Johannes
Warum. Wherefore should our singing soar. Op.91, no.4: for
four-part chorus of mixed voices with piano accompaniment/ by
Johannes Brahms; edited by Maynard Klein, [words by] Goethe,
English text by M.K.. – New York: Schirmer; London: Chappell,
1971. – 8p; 8vo.
Text in German and English.
Unpriced

(B71-50230)

Dougherty, Celius
Buffalo boy: for four-part chorus of mixed voices with piano
accompaniment/ by Celius Dougherty; [words] traditional. – New
York: Schirmer; [London]: [Chappell], 1971. – 16p; 8vo.
Unpriced

(B71-50231)

Engelhart, Franz Xaver
[Wenn ich ein Glöcklein wär]. The Vesper bell/ by F.X. Engelhart;
arrangement for SATB by F. Naylor, English lyrics by Peter Carroll.
– London: Bosworth, 1971. – 4p; 8vo.
Staff and tonic sol-fa notation.
Unpriced

(B71-50771)

Faith, Richard
Music I heard with you: for four-part chorus of mixed voices with
piano accompaniment/ by Richard Faith; words by Conrad Aiken. –
New York: Schirmer; London: Chappell, 1971. – 8p; 8vo.
Unpriced

(B71-50232)

Friend, Jerry R
Hear my dream: S.A.B. and piano/ words and music by J.R. Friend.
– New York: Warner; [London]: [Blossom Music], 1971. – 12p;
8vo.
Unpriced

(B71-50772)

House, L Marguerite
We three: two-part chorus with piano, optional guitars and claves/ by
L.M. House; words by L.M. House. – New York: Warner; London:
Blossom Music, 1970. – 4p; 8vo.
Unpriced

(B71-50233)

Muradeli, Vano
Lenin in Siberia/ by Vano Muradeli, arranged for mixed choir and pianoforte by Alan Bush; poem by U. Kamenetz, English version [from the Russian] by Nancy Bush. — London: Workers' Music Association, 1971. — 11p; 4to.
£0.13

(B71-50773)

Pooler, Marie
Simple gifts: American Shaker song/ arranged for four-part chorus of mixed voices with piano accompaniment by Marie Pooler. — New York: Schirmer; [London]: [Chappell], 1971. — 11p; 8vo.
Unpriced

(B71-50769)

Ridout, Alan
A farewell/ by Alan Ridout; words by Alfred, Lord Tennyson. — London: Stainer and Bell, 1971. — 7p; 8vo.
Unpriced

(B71-50020)

Rocherolle, Eugénie R
A joyful song: SATB/ by Eugénie R. Rocherolle. — New York: Warner: Seven Arts; London: Blossom Music, 1971. — 8p; 8vo.
Unpriced

(B71-50021)

Rocherolle, Eugénie R
Lookin' ahead (six feet under): S.A.B./ words and music by Eugénie R. Rocherolle. — New York: Warner; [London]: [Blossom Music], 1971. — 7p; 8vo.
Unpriced

(B71-50774)

Schuman, William
Orpheus with his lute: arranged by the composer for four-part chorus of mixed voices with piano accompaniment/ by William Schuman; [words by] William Shakespeare. — New York: Schirmer; London: Chappell, 1970. — 4p; 8vo.
£0.10

(B71-50022)

Simpson, John
The piper o'Dundee: for S.A.B./ arranged by John Simpson. — London: Feldman, 1970. — 11p; 8vo.
Unpriced

(B71-50234)

DW/G/AY — Folk songs. Collections
Cooper, Irvin
Singers all: ten songs arranged for four-part singing (unchanged and changing voices)/ by Irvin Cooper. — London: Oxford University Press, 1971. — 37p; 8vo.
ISBN 0 19 330240 3 : £0.45

(B71-50775)

DW/JR — Film songs
Gold, Ernest
[Exodus. Excerpts]. The Exodus song, by Ernest Gold; arranged SATB by Charles N. Smith, lyrics by Pat Boone. — London: Chappell, 1971. — 7p; 8vo.
£0.09

(B71-50235)

DW/JR — Films
Gold, Ernest
[Exodus. Excerpts]. The Exodus song: S.A.B./ by Ernest Gold; arranged by Charles N. Smith, lyric by Pat Boone. — London: Chappell, 1971. — 7p; 8vo.
Unpriced

(B71-50236)

DW/LC — Spirituals
Hudson, Hazel
Go tell it on the mountain. He's got the whole world in His hands: a quodlibet based on two negro spirituals/ arr. by Hazel Hudson. — London: Ashdown, 1971. — 10p; 8vo.
£0.10

(B71-50776)

Hudson, Hazel
Oh Mary, and all that jazz!: a quodlibet/ arr. by Hazel Hudson. — London: Ashdown, 1971. — 11p; 8vo.
£0.10

(B71-50777)

Hudson, Hazel
The old ark's a-moverin' (amongst other things): a quodlibet for two female, two male, or one female and one male voice parts/ arr. from negro spirituals by Hazel Hudson. — London: Ashdown, 1971. — 8p; 8vo.
Unpriced

(B71-50778)

DX — SECULAR CANTATAS
Burgon, Geoffrey
Think on dredful domesday: for s.S.A.T.B and chamber orchestra/ by Geoffrey Burgon; words [from] parts of the Requiem Mass, two anonymous 15th century poems, 'Nuits de l'enfer' by Rimbaud and 'After long storms' from Spenser's 'Amoretti'. — London: Stainer and Bell, 1970. — 32p; 8vo.
Vocal score. Duration 22 min.
Unpriced

(B71-50779)

Williamson, Malcolm
The stone wall: a cassation for audience and orchestra/ by Malcolm Williamson. — London: Weinberger, 1971. — 12p; 4to.
Vocal score.
Unpriced

(B71-50780)

E — CHORAL WORKS WITH ACCOMPANIMENT OTHER THAN KEYBOARD
EL — With instrumental accompaniment
Heider, Werner
Edition: multiple Musik für Instrumental - oder Vokalgruppen/ [by] Werner Heider. — Frankfurt: Litolff, Peters; London: [Hinrichsen], 1970. — 7p; 4to.
£0.90
Primary classification LN

(B71-50374)

EMDD — With orchestra. Oratorios
Berlioz, Hector
L'Enfance du Christ. Op.25: [chorus and orchestra]/ by Hector Berlioz; edited by Roger Fiske, [German translation by] Peter Cornelius, English translation by H.F. Chorley. — London: Eulenburg, 1971. — xi,258p; 8vo.
£4.75

(B71-50237)

EMDE — With orchestra. Religious cantatas
Vaughan Williams, Ralph
Dona nobis pacem: a cantata for soprano and baritone soli, chorus and orchestra/ by Ralph Vaughan Williams. — London: Oxford University Press, 1971. — 129p; 8vo.
Study score.
ISBN 0 19 338860 x : £3.50

(B71-50781)

EMDG — With orchestra. Ordinary of the Mass
Charpentier, Marc Antoine
[Mass for eight voices & eight violins & flutes]. Mass: for soloists, double chorus & orchestra/ by Marc-Antoine Charpentier; transcribed by Carl de Nys. — London: Oxford University Press, 1971. — xiv,128p; 4to.
Duration 45 mins.
ISBN 0 19 335500 0 : £3.50

(B71-50238)

EMDH — With orchestra. Motets. Anthems, Hymns, etc
Leonard, Harry
The power and the glory/ by Harry Leonard; arranged for SATB by Desmond Ratcliffe, orchestration by Ted Brennan; words by Paul Hollingdale and Bob Halfin. — Borough Green: Novello, 1970. — 12p; 4to.
Score & 13 parts.
£1.75

(B71-50023)

EMDP/LF — With orchestra. Carols. Christmas
Jacques, Reginald
[Carols for choirs. Bk.1, nos. 33, 27, 13]. Three carol orchestrations/ arranged for voices and orchestra by Reginald Jacques and David Willcocks. — London: Oxford University Press, 1971. — 16p; 4to.
Unpriced

(B71-50782)

EMDX — With orchestra. Secular cantatas
Bedford, David
A dream of the seven lost stars/ by David Bedford. — London: Universal, 1971. — 2v.(6p;9p); 8vo.
Choral score and instrumental score.
Unpriced

(B71-50239)

ENUXPNQDH/LL — With brass, strings & keyboard. Motets, Anthems, Hymns, etc. Easter
Hammerschmidt, Andreas
[Wer walset uns den Stein]. An Easter dialogue: for mixed voices, organ (piano), 2 trumpets, 4 trombones and double bass/ by Andreas Hammerschmidt; edited by Diethard Hellmann, [text] adapted from the Gospels by Walter E. Buszin. — New York: Peters; London: Hinrichsen, 1970. — 21p; 8vo.
£0.45

(B71-50240)

ENYEXPNSDP/LF — With brass, string & percussion quartet. Carols. Christmas
Roe, Betty
Out of your sleep arise and wake: carol for SATB and trumpet, horn, cello and percussion/ by Betty Roe. — London: Thames, 1971. — [7]p; 8vo.
Unpriced

(B71-50783)

ENYHXPNRDH/LM — With brass and percussion quintet. Motets, Anthems, Hymns, etc. Ascension
Rorem, Ned
Lift up your heads. (The ascension)/ by Ned Rorem: brass accompaniment, [words by] John Beaumont. — New York; [London]: Boosey and Hawkes, 1971. — 5pt; 8vo.
£1.10

(B71-50784)

ENYLNSDX — With keyboard & percussion quartet. Secular cantatas
Mathias, William
Culhwch and Olwen. Op. 32: an entertainment/ by William Mathias; words by Gwyn Thomas. — Cardiff: University of Wales Press, 1971. — 80p; 4to.
Duration 28 min.
Unpriced

(B71-50785)

EPWNUDJ — With keyboard duet. Motets
Smith, Gregg
Ave Maria: for chorus of treble voices and four-part chorus of mixed voices with celeste (or bells) and organ (or piano) accompaniment/ by Gregg Smith. — New York: Schirmer; [London]: [Chappell], 1971. — 15p; 8vo.
Unpriced

(B71-50786)

ERXMDE — With string orchestra. Religious cantatas
Effinger, Cecil
Paul of Tarsus: three episodes in the life of Paul the apostle, for four-part chorus of mixed voices with baritone solo, strings and organ/ by Cecil Effinger; text freely adapted from the Scriptures. — New York: Schirmer; London: Chappell, 1971. — 91p; 4to.
Unpriced

(B71-50241)

EUMDH — With wind band. Motets, Anthems, Hymns, etc
Beethoven, Ludwig van
[Christus am Olberger. Excerpts]. Hallelujah/ by Ludwig van Beethoven; transcribed for band and mixed chorus by Harold Pottenger. — New York: Schirmer; London: Chappell, 1971. — 4to.
Full score (28p.) & 57 parts.
Unpriced

(B71-50242)

EVRDW — With flute. Songs, etc
Roe, Betty
Shadwell Stair: part-song for SATB and flute/ by Betty Roe; words by Wilfred Owen. — London: Thames, 1970. — [3]p; 8vo.
Unpriced

(B71-50787)

EWNNDH — With brass octet. Motets, Anthems, Hymns, etc
Schütz, Heinrich
[Psalmen Davids sampt etlichen Moteten und Concerten, no.19]. Ist nicht Ephraim mein teurer Sohn? Is not Ephraim my precious Son?: Motete a 8 e 16 con due cappelle in fine, for mixed voices and instruments/ by Heinrich Schütz; edited by Paul Steinitz. — London: Oxford University Press, 1971. — 4to.
Score (14p.) & choral score.
ISBN 0 19 338084 6 : £0.95

(B71-50788)

EZ — UNACCOMPANIED CHORAL WORKS
EZ/X — Canons
Binkerd, Gordon
Institutional canons: for mixed chorus/ by Gordon Binkerd. — New York; [London]: Boosey and Hawkes. —
1: The wealth of Illinois: S.A.T.B.. — 1971. — 13p; 8vo.
£0.15

(B71-50243)

2: There is in souls: SATB/ text by William Cowper. — 1971. — 6p; 8vo.
£0.09

(B71-50244)

3: To thy happy children: SSATBB/ text by Loredo Taft [and from] Proverbs 31. — 1971. — 8p; 8vo.
£0.09

(B71-50245)

EZ/X/AY — Canons. Collections
Buszin, Walter E
60 canons on secular texts: four centuries, 2 to 8 voices/ edited by Walter E. Buszin. — New York: Peters; [London]: [Hinrichsen]. —
Vol.1: Nos 1-30. — 1970. — 15p; 8vo.
£0.45

(B71-50246)

Vol.2: 31-60. — 1970. — 18p; 8vo.
£0.45

(B71-50247)

EZDG — Roman liturgy. Ordinary of the Mass
Putterill, Jack
Thaxted Mass: three part unaccompanied/ by Jack Putterill. — Hoddesdon: St Gregory Publishing Co., 1971. — 7p; 8vo.
£0.20

(B71-50789)

Taverner, John
'Gloria tibi trinitas': mass for six-part unaccompanied choir, S.A.T.T.B.B./ by John Taverner; transcribed and edited by Hugh Benham. — London: Stainer and Bell, 1971. — 72p; 8vo.
As in most masses of the period, there are four movements, the Kyrie not being set. Text omissions from the Credo were normal. — Editor's note.
£1.15

(B71-50302)

EZDGKAH — Roman liturgy. Proper of the Mass. Communion
Byrd, William
Beata viscera, Hail Mary, full of grace: motet for five voices, S.A.A.T.B. for feasts of the Blessed Virgin/ by William Byrd; edited with an alternative English text by Anthony G. Petti. — London: Chester, 1971. — 5p; 8vo.
Duration 2 min.
Unpriced

(B71-50248)

EZDGKJ — Roman liturgy. Divine Office. Vespers
Gabrieli, Giovanni
Beata es virgo: part chorus of mixed voices with organ accompaniment (optional), by Giovanni Gabrieli; edited by Dale Jorgensen and Daniel Wolfe. — New York: Schirmer; London: Chappell, 1970. — 18p; 8vo.
Unpriced

(B71-50024)

Palestrina, Giovanni Pierluigi da
Assumpta est Maria: motet for six voices/ by Giovanni Pierluigi da Palestrina; edited by Nigel Davison. — London: Chester, 1971. — iii,21p; 8vo.
Unpriced

(B71-50249)

EZDGPS — Anglican liturgy. Evening Prayer. Deus misereatur
Tye, Christopher
O God be merciful unto us. (Deus misereatur): SATB (full)/ by [Christopher] Tye; edited by John Langdon. — Revised ed. — London: Oxford University Press, 1971. — 7p; 8vo.
ISBN 0 19 352146 6 : Unpriced

(B71-50250)

Tye, Christopher
O God be merciful unto us. (Deus misereatur): SATB (full) with verse for SATB/ by [Christopher] Tye; edited by John Langdon. — Revised ed. — London: Oxford University Press, 1971. — 9p; 8vo.
ISBN 0 19 352147 4 : Unpriced

(B71-50251)

EZDH — Motets, Anthems, Hymns, etc
Chorbajian, John
The lamb: for full chorus of mixed voices a cappella/ by John Chorbajian; [words by] William Blake. — New York: Schirmer; London: Chappell, 1971. — 8p; 8vo.
Unpriced

(B71-50252)

Ford, Virgil T
Come, O thou God of grace: for three-part chorus of mixed voices a cappella/ by Virgil T. Ford; [text by] William B. Evans. — New York: Schirmer; [London]: [Chappell], 1971. — 4p; 8vo.
Unpriced

(B71-50790)

Glarum, Leonard Stanley
When one knows thee: for four-part chorus of mixed voices a cappella/ by L. Stanley Glarum, [words by] Rabindranath Tagore. — New York: Schirmer; [London]: [Chappell], 1971. — 8p; 8vo.
Unpriced

(B71-50253)

Kodály, Zoltan
Jesus and the traders: for S.A.T.B./ by Zoltan Kodály; [text from] St John II, St Mark XII and St Luke XIX, English translation by Geoffry Russell-Smith. — Revised ed. — London: Universal Music, 1971. — 16p; 8vo.
Unpriced

(B71-50254)

Le Jeune, Claude
[Meslanges. Liv. 2 - Excerpts]. Hélas! mon Dieu: SAATB unacc./ by Claude Le Jeune; edited, with English text, by John Eliot Gardiner, [words] 'Souspir d'un malade' (1573). — Borough Green: Oxford University Press, 1971. — 15p; 8vo.
Unpriced

(B71-50791)

Lord, David
A prayer for peace: SATB unacc./ by David Lord, words anon. — London: Oxford University Press, 1971. — 3p; 8vo.
Duration 2 min. 40 sec.
ISBN 0 19 350320 4 : Unpriced

(B71-50025)

Nevens, David
3 canticles of Thomas à Kempis: for unaccompanied mixed voices/ by David Nevens. — Borough Green: Novello, 1971. — 23p; 8vo.
Contains the words and music of over 20 folk and other songs.
Unpriced

(B71-50792)

EZDH/AYD — Motets, Anthems, Hymns, etc. Collections. England
Wulstan, David
An anthology of English church music/ compiled by David Wulstan; edited by Peter James and others. — London: Chester, 1971. — 160p; 8vo.
Unpriced

(B71-50793)

EZDJ — Motets
Anerio, Felice
Christus factus est. Jesus who for our salvation: four-part chorus of mixed voices a cappella/ by Felice Anerio; edited by Robert S. Hines, translation [from the Latin] by R.S.H. — New York: Schirmer; [London]: [Chappell], 1971. — 4p; 8vo.
Unpriced

(B71-50794)

EZDJ/AYK — Motet collections. Spain
Lewkovitch, Bernhard
Twelve motets of the Spanish golden age/ edited by Bernhard Lewkovitch. — London: Chester, 1971. — 22p; 8vo.
Unpriced

(B71-50795)

EZDJ/LF — Motets. Christmas
Monteverdi, Claudio
Hodie Christus natus est. On this day Christ appears: motet for three-part chorus of women's voices a cappella/ by Claudio Monteverdi; edited by Maynard Klein. — New York: Schirmer; London: Chappell, 1971. — 8p; 8vo.
Unpriced

(B71-50256)

EZDK — Anthems
Billings, William
I heard a great voice: SAATBB a cappella/ by William Billings; [text from] Revelations 14; edited by Oliver Daniel. — New York: Peters; [London]: [Hinrichsen], 1971. — 5p; 8vo.
£0.35

(B71-50257)

Morgan, Haydn
They who considereth the poor shall be blest: SATB, ad. lib/ by Haydn Morgan; adapted from Psalms 41-42. — New York: Warner; London: Blossom Music], 1971. — 7p; 8vo.
Unpriced

(B71-50258)

Nares, James
Try me, O God: short full anthem/ by James Nares; edited by Watkins Shaw, [text from] Psalm 139. — London: Novello, 1970. — 4p; 8vo.
£0.06

(B71-50026)

Newbury, Kent A
Behold, I stand at the door: for four-part chorus of mixed voices a cappella/ by Kent A. Newbury; [text from] Rev.3. — New York: Schirmer; London: Chappell, 1971. — 7p; 8vo.
Unpriced

(B71-50259)

Tye, Christopher
I will exalt thee: full anthem for four voices/ by Christopher Tye; edited by John Langdon; [text from] Psalm 30. — London: Novello, 1970. — 13p; 8vo.
£0.15

(B71-50027)

EZDP — Carols
Diplock, Cyril
Peace to every neighbour: a carol/ words and music by Cyril Diplock. — Croydon: Royal School of Church Music, 1971. — 4p; 8vo.
Unpriced

(B71-50796)

EZDP/LF — Carols. Christmas
Blyton, Carey
A lullaby: Christmas carol, SATB unaccompanied/ by Carey Blyton; [words] anon. — Croydon: Royal School of Church Music, 1971. — 4p; 8vo.
Unpriced

(B71-50797)

Costeley, Guillaume
Noel: Sus, debout gentilz pasteurs. Now arise ye shepherds mild: for four-part chorus of mixed voices a capella/ by Guillaume Costeley; edited by Maynard Klein, English text by M.K. — New York: Schirmer; [London]: [Chappell], 1971. — 15p; 8vo.
Unpriced

(B71-50798)

Higdon, George
He is born. Il est né: traditional French carol/ arranged by George Higdon, English text by George Higdon. — Cincinnati: Willis Music, 1971. — 8p; 8vo.
Unpriced

(B71-50799)

Lawson, Gordon
How far is it to Bethlehem?: West country carol/ arranged by Gordon Lawson; [words by Frances Chesterton]. — Croydon: Royal School of Church Music, 1971. — 4p; 8vo.
£0.05

(B71-50800)

Paynter, John
There is no rose: a Christmas carol, mixed, or female or male voices unacc./ by John Paynter; anonymous words. — London: Oxford University Press, 1971. — 3p; 8vo.
ISBN 0 19 353340 5 : Unpriced
Also classified at FEZDP/LF; GEZDP/LF

(B71-50801)

Rutter, John
Quem pastores laudavere. Shepherds left their flocks a-straying: German [carol] SATB unacc./ arranged by John Rutter; tr. Imogen Holst. — London: Oxford University Press, 1971. — 3p; 8vo.
ISBN 0 19 343012 6 : Unpriced

(B71-50260)

Simpson, Lionel
Song of the refugee children; and, Chorus of the Holy Innocents/ by Lionel Simpson; verse by Eiluned Lewis. — London: Feldman, 1971. — 11p; 8vo.
Unpriced

(B71-50802)

EZDP/LF — Unaccompanied choral works. Carols. Christmas
Robinson, Douglas
God rest you merry/ arranged by Douglas Robinson. — London: Ashdown, 1971. — 8p; 8vo.
£0.09

(B71-50803)

Robinson, Douglas
Good King Wenceslas/ arranged by Douglas Robinson. — London: Ashdown, 1971. — 7p; 8vo.
£0.09

(B71-50804)

Tomblings, Philip
Behold the great Creator: carol for SATB unaccompanied/ by Philip Tomblings; words by Thomas Pestel. — London: Ashdown, 1971. — 3p; 8vo.
£0.05

(B71-50805)

EZDP/LF/AY — Carols. Christmas. Collections
Brooks, Nigel
More carols for Christmas/ arranged by Nigel Brooks. — London: Boosey and Hawkes, 1971. — 4to.
Full music ed. (8p.) & voice part.
Unpriced

(B71-50261)

EZDP/LL — Carols. Easter
Hurford, Peter
Magdalen, cease from sobs and sighs: SATB unacc./ arranged by Peter Hurford from melody of Nicht rahen Magdalena Kundt. — London: Oxford University Press, 1971. — 3p; 8vo.
Unpriced

(B71-50028)

EZDR — Psalms
Deiss, Lucien
More Biblical hymns and psalms/ by Lucien Deiss. — London: G. Chapman, 1971. — 126p; 8vo.
£1.00

(B71-50806)

Goudimel, Claude
[Psalm 42]. Ainsi qu'on oit le cerf bruire. So my heart seeks ever after: for four-part chorus of mixed voices a cappella/ by Claude Goudimel; edited by George Lynn, text translated by Lucile Lynn. — New York: Schirmer; London: Chappell, 1971. — 4p; 8vo.
Unpriced

(B71-50262)

Hopson, Hal H
God is our refuge, God is our strength: SATB chorus of choral and speaking voices with optional congregational declamation/ by Hal H. Hopson; words Psalm 46. — New York: Warner; [London]: [Blossom Music], 1971. — 11p; 8vo.
Unpriced

(B71-50807)

Vann, Stanley
Behold, how good and joyful: S.A.T.B. unacc./ by Stanley Vann; Psalm 133. — London: Oxford University Press, 1971. — 4p; 8vo.
Duration 2-1/4 min.
ISBN 0 19 350327 1 : Unpriced

(B71-50808)

EZDR/KDN — Psalms. Funerals
Dowland, John
[Mr Henry Noell, his funerall psalmes]. Seven hymn tunes. Lamentio Henrici Noel: S.A.T.B./ by John Dowland; edited by Edmund H. Fellowes. — Revised ed.; by Peter le Huray and David Willcocks. — London: Oxford University Press. —
Nos. 1-4. — 1971. — 11p; 8vo.
ISBN 0 19 352157 1 : Unpriced

(B71-50809)

EZDR/KDN — Unaccompanied choral works. Psalms. Funerals
Dowland, John
[Mr Henry Noell, his funerall psalmes]. Seven hymn tunes. Lamentio Henrici Noel: S.A.T.B./ by John Dowland; edited by Edmund H. Fellowes. — Revised ed.; by Peter le Huray and David Willcocks. — London: Oxford University Press. —
Nos. 5-7. — 1971. — 11p; 8vo.
ISBN 0 19 352160 1 : Unpriced

(B71-50810)

EZDTM — Amens
Blyton, Carey
Seven polyphonic amens: for unaccompanied voices/ by Carey Blyton. — London: Leeds Music, 1971. — 5p; 8vo.
Unpriced

(B71-50811)

EZDU — Madrigals
Gastoldi, Giovanni
[Balletti for five voices (1591)]. Fifteen balletti: SSATB a cappella (recorders and strings ad libitum)/ by Giovanni Gastoldi. — New ed.; by Harold C. Schmidt, English translation [from the Italian] by Gail Meadows. — New York: Peters; [London]: [Hinrichsen]. —
Introduttioni a i Balletti: O compagni allegrezza. (Companions, be happy). — 1970. — 10p; 8vo.
£0.40

(B71-50263)

Set 3. — 1970. — 19p; 8vo.
Contents:- 7.Il Piacere (On happiness). — 8.L'Ardito. (The bold warrior). — 9.Il Contento. (The contented one). — 10.Lo Schernito. (The rebuffed). — 11. Il Premiato. (The prize-winner).
£0.40

(B71-50264)

Set 4. — 1970. — 15p; 8vo.
Contents:- 12.L'Innamorata. (In praise of love). — 13.Il Martellato. (Torture). — 14.L'Acceso. (Enamored). — 15.Amor Vittorioso (Victorious love).
£0.40

(B71-50265)

Gastoldi, Giovanni Giacomo
[A lieta vita]. Such happy living: SSATB/ by Giovanni Gastoldi; edited by Walter Ehret, English text by Melinda Edwards. — New York: Warner; [London]: [Blossom Music], 1971. — 7p; 8vo.
Unpriced

(B71-50266)

Scandello, Antonio
[Canzoni napoletane. Lib 1, no.14. Voria che ta cantass']. Neapolitan song/ by Antonio Scandello; arr. and ed. for SATB chorus by Walter Ehret, English text by Melinda Edwards. — New York: Warner; [London]: [Blossom Music], 1971. — 5p; 8vo.
Unpriced

(B71-50812)

Verdelot, Philippe
[Madonna, per voi ardo]. Ah love, my heart is burning: for SATB chorus/ by Philippe Verdelot; edited by Walter Ehret, English text by Melinda Edwards. — New York: Warner; London: Blossom Music, 1971. — 6p; 8vo.
Unpriced

(B71-50267)

EZDU/AY — Madrigals. Collections
Dart, Thurston
Invitation to madrigals/ compiled by Thurston Dart. — London: Stainerand Bell. —
5: for SATB. — 1971. — 60p: facsim; 8vo.
£0.40

(B71-50813)

EZDU/AYD — Madrigals. Collections. England
Stevens, Denis
The second Penguin book of English madrigals: for five voices/ [compiled by] Denis Stevens. — Harmondsworth: Penguin, 1970. — 158p; 8vo.
ISBN 0 14 070837 5 : £0.50

(B71-50029)

EZDW — Songs, etc
Bartholomew, Marshall
Gaudeamus igitur: traditional German melody arranged for chorus of mixed voices a cappella/ by Marshall Bartholomew. — New York: Schirmer; [London]: [Chappell], 1971. — 4p; 8vo.
Unpriced

(B71-50268)

Byrt, John
Dashing away with the smoothing iron: traditional song SATB unacc./ arranged by John Byrt. — London: Oxford University Press, 1971. — 8p; 8vo.
ISBN 0 19 343007 x : Unpriced

(B71-50269)

Chagrin, Francis
Mother, I cannot mind my wheel/ [by] Francis Chagrin, poem by Walter Savage Landor. — Chesham (Bucks.): Ricordi, 1970. — 4p; 8vo.
Unpriced

(B71-50030)

Chorbajian, John
Come away, come away, Death: for full chorus of mixed voices a cappella/ by John Chorbajian; words by William Shakespeare. — New York: Schirmer; [London]: [Chappell], 1971. — 10p; 8vo.
Unpriced

(B71-50814)

Chorbajian, John
Two doves: for full chorus of mixed voices a cappella by John Chorbajian; [words by] Christina Rossetti. — New York: Schirmer; [London]: [Chappell], 1971. — 8p; 8vo.
Unpriced

(B71-50270)

Crosse, Gordon
[The demon Adachigahara. Op. 21. Excerpts]. Night wind: S.A.T.B./ adapted by Gordon Crosse; [words by] Ted Hughes. — London: Oxford University Press, 1971. — 8p; 8vo.
Duration 5 mins.
ISBN 0 19 342986 1 : Unpriced

(B71-50815)

Dalby, Martin
Four miniature songs from Ezra Pound: S.A.T.B. unaccompanied/ by Martin Dalby. — Croydon: Lengnick, 1971. — 4p; 8vo.
Contents: 1.Ts'ai chi'h - 2.Alba. — 3.The faces. — 4.Fan-piece.
Unpriced

(B71-50031)

Effinger, Cecil
Three contemporary madrigals: for four-part chorus of mixed voices a cappella/ by Cecil Effinger. — New York: Schirmer; [London]: [Chappell]. —
If you your lips would keep from slips/ [words anonymous. — 1971. — 10p; 8vo.
Unpriced

(B71-50271)

My love and I for kisses played/ [words by] Poor Richard. — 1971. — 6p; 8vo.
Unpriced

(B71-50272)

Why was Cupid a boy?/ [words by] William Blake. — 1971. — 12p; 8vo.
Unpriced

(B71-50273)

Hovdesven, E A
Fold to thy heart thy brother: for four-part chorus of mixed voices a cappella/ by E.A. Hovdesven; [words by] John Greenleaf Whittier. — New York: Schirmer; [London]: [Chappell], 1971. — 7p; 8vo.
Unpriced

(B71-50816)

Kent, Richard
Here's Jupiter: SATB a cappella (or improvised rock accompaniment ad lib)/ by Richard Kent; lyric by Burt Shepherd. — New York: Warner: Seven Arts; [London]: [Blossom Music], 1971. — 12p; 8vo.
Unpriced

(B71-50032)

Kodály, Zoltán
Invocation of peace: Bekesser ohajtas: S.A.T.B. unaccompanied/ by Zoltán Kodály; [words] Benedek Virág, English translation [from the Hungarian] by Geoffry Russell-Smith. — London: Boosey and Hawkes, 1970. — 7p; 8vo.
Unpriced

(B71-50274)

Kodály, Zoltán
Prayer for honour: Szep Kőnyőrgés: S.A.T.B. unaccompanied/ by Zoltán Kodály; [words] Bálint Balissi, English translation [from the Hungarian] by Geoffry Russell-Smith. — London: Boosey and Hawkes, 1970. — 7p; 8vo.
Unpriced

(B71-50275)

Leaf, Robert
I hear a song: for full chorus of mixed voices a cappella/ by Robert Leaf; [words by] R.L. — New York: Schirmer; [London]: [Chappell], 1971. — 7p; 8vo.
Unpriced

(B71-50276)

Lekberg, Sven
Come o'er the eastern hills: for four-part chorus of mixed voices a cappella/ by Sven Lekberg; [words by] William Blake. — New York: Schirmer; London: Chappell, 1971. — 8p; 8vo.
Unpriced

(B71-50278)

Lekberg, Sven
Little sorrows sit and weep: for four-part chorus of mixed voices a cappella/ by Sven Lekberg; words by William Blake. — New York: Schirmer; London: Chappell, 1971. — 4p; 8vo.
Unpriced

(B71-50279)

Lekberg, Sven
Three peavinations: for mixed chorus/ by Sven Lekberg; words by Leigh McBradd. — New York: Schirmer; London: Chappell. —
1: Pavane. — 1970. — 6p; 8vo.
Unpriced

(B71-50280)

2: Moment musical. — 1970. — 6p; 8vo.
Unpriced

(B71-50281)

3: Counterpoint. — 1971. — 7p; 8vo.
Unpriced

(B71-50282)

Newbury, Kent A
Ring out, wild bells: for four-part chorus of mixed voices a cappella/ by Kent A. Newbury; words by Alfred, Lord Tennyson. — New York: Schirmer; London: Chappell, 1971. — 19p; 8vo.
Unpriced

(B71-50283)

Roe, Betty
Sweet Thames flow softly: part-song, SATB/ by Betty Roe; words by Ewan MacColl. — London: Thames, 1970. — [8]p; 8vo.
Unpriced

(B71-50817)

Wilson, Richard
Soaking: for four-part chorus of mixed voices a cappella/ by Richard Wilson; words by Stephen Sandy. — New York: Schirmer; London: Chappell, 1971. — 11p; 8vo.
Unpriced

(B71-50284)

EZDW/AY — Songs, etc. Collections
Parkinson, John Alfred
Renaissance song book: seven songs for mixed voices/ edited by John A. Parkinson. — London: Oxford University Press, 1971. — 16p; 8vo.
ISBN 0 19 330610 7 : £0.23

(B71-50033)

EZDW/G/AYG — Folk song collections. Hungary
Kodály, Zoltán
Mátra pictures: a set of Hungarian folksongs for S.A.T.B./ by Zoltán Kodály; English translation by Geoffry Russell-Smith. — Revised ed. — London: Universal, 1971. — 24p; 8vo.
Unpriced

(B71-50285)

EZDW/G/AYPK — Folk song collections. Yugoslavia
Srebotnjak, Alojz
Six folksongs from Yugoslavia: [arranged] for four-part chorus of mixed voices a cappella/ by Alojz Srebotnjak; English version by Maria Pelikan. — New York: Schirmer; [London]: [Chappell]. —
1: The things my mother buys. — 1971. — 8p; 8vo.
Unpriced

(B71-50818)

2: Katya and the Czar. — 1971. — 5p; 8vo.
Unpriced

(B71-50819)

3: The farmer's daughter. — 1971. — 9p; 8vo.
Unpriced

(B71-50820)

4: Love song from Ohrid. — 1971. — 5p; 8vo.
Unpriced

(B71-50821)

5: Wake up, Melinda. — 1971. — 7p; 8vo.
Unpriced

(B71-50822)

6: Oro (Yugoslav dance). — 1971. — 9p; 8vo.
Unpriced

(B71-50823)

EZDW/G/AYULD — Folk song collections. Jamaica
Murray, Tom
Three Jamaican folk-songs/ arranged for unaccompanied voices by Tom Murray. — London: Oxford University Press, 1971. — 15p; 8vo.
Contents: Heaby Load. — Hog eena me coco. — 'Oman Tung.
£0.25

(B71-50034)

EZDW/LC — Songs. Spirituals
Billings, William
[The dying Christian's last farewell]. Fare you well, my friends: SATB a cappella/ by William Billings; edited by Oliver Daniel. — New York: Peters; [London]: [Hinrichsen], 1970. — 10p; 8vo.
£0.75

(B71-50286)

F — FEMALE VOICES, CHILDREN'S VOICES
FDD — Oratorios
Swann, Donald
The song of Caedmon/ by Donald Swann; words by Arthur Scholey. — London: Bodley Head, 1971. — 76p; 8vo.
£1.50

(B71-50824)

FDE — Religious cantatas
Flanders, Michael
Captain Noah and his floating zoo: cantata in popular style for unison or two-part voices & piano, with optional bass & drums/ by Michael Flanders and Joseph Horovitz. — Borough Green: Novello, 1970. — 57p; 8vo.
Vocal score.
£0.40

(B71-50035)

FDG — Roman liturgy. Ordinary of the Mass
Henriksen, Josef
English mass: two-part with organ accompaniment by Josef Henriksen. — Hoddesdon: St Gregory Publishing Co., 1970. — 16p; 4to.
£0.40

(B71-50825)

FDGKJ — Roman liturgy. Divine Office. Vespers
Mozart, Wolfgang Amadeus
[Vesperae solennes de confessore. K.339 - Excerpts]. Laudate Dominum. K.339, no.5/ by W.A. Mozart; arranged for S.S.A. by Lionel Lethbridge. — London: Oxford University Press, 1971. — 8p; 8vo.
Vocal score.
ISBN 0 19 342590 4 : Unpriced

(B71-50826)

FDM/AYDK — Hymn collections. Wales
Battye, Ken
Children's Welsh flavour: a selection of Welsh children's hymn tunes set to English words/ by Ken Battye. — Carnforth (3 Wood View, Burton in Lonsdale, Carnforth, Lancs.): Ken Battye. —
Vol.1. — 1971. — 27p; 8vo.
Unpriced

(B71-50827)

FDP/LF — Carols. Christmas

Bennett, F Roy
Three Christmas carols/ words and music by F. Roy Bennett. —
London: Ashdown, 1971. — 8p; 8vo.
Contents:- The Holy Child. — Carol of the Holy Thorn. — African crib carol.
Unpriced

(B71-50830)

Britten, Benjamin
The oxen: a carol for women's voices and piano/ by Benjamin
Britten; words by Thomas Hardy. — London: Faber Music, 1968. —
7p; 8vo.
Unpriced

(B71-50036)

Broad, D F
Born to be King/ by D.F. Broad, arr. for two voices by A.G.
Warren-Smith; words by Hazel Oliver. — York: Banks, 1970. — 3p;
8vo.
Staff and tonic solfa notation.
Unpriced

(B71-50287)

Gardner, John
Four carols. Op.109: for mixed or S.A. voices/ by John Gardner. —
London: Oxford University Press. —
1: Chanticleer's carol/ [text by] William Austin. — 1971. — 3p; 8vo.
ISBN 0 19 343017 7 : Unpriced
Primary classification DP/LF

(B71-50759)

2: Balulalow/ [text by] Wedderburn. — 1971. — 4p; 8vo.
ISBN 0 19 343018 5 : Unpriced
Primary classification DP/LF

(B71-50760)

3: Remember/ [text by] T. Ravenscroft. — 1971. — 6p; 8vo.
ISBN 0 19 343019 3 : Unpriced
Primary classification DP/LF

(B71-50761)

Gibbs, Alan
Spell out the news: carol for unison voices with divisions, and organ
or piano (or brass)/ words and music by Alan Gibbs. — Borough
Green: Novello, 1971. — 4p; 8vo.
£0.06

(B71-50288)

Hunter, Ian T
Ding dong! merrily on high: carol arranged for women's or boys'
voices & organ/piano/ by Ian T. Hunter; words by G.R. Woodward.
— London: Thames, 1971. — 5p; 8vo.
Unpriced

(B71-50828)

Nelson, Havelock
La lo and lullaby: berceuse de Noé: two part song/ by Havelock
Nelson; words by Dorothy Dumbrille. — Croydon: Lengnick, 1970.
— 4p; 8vo.
£0.05

(B71-50037)

Parry, William Howard
Riding into Bethlehem: for unison or two-part voices with piano,
optional recorders, and optional percussion by W.H. Parry; words by
L. Bell. — London: Oxford University Press, 1971. — 7p; 8vo.
ISBN 0 19 342048 1 : Unpriced
Also classified at JFDP/LF

(B71-50829)

Rutter, John
Nativity carol: S.S.A./ words and music by John Rutter. — London:
Oxford University Press, 1971. — 4p; 8vo.
ISBN 0 19 342591 2 : Unpriced

(B71-50289)

Verrall, Pamela Motley
Sing a lullabye for Jesus/ words and music by P.M. Verrall. —
London: Freeman, 1971. — 2p; 8vo.
Unpriced

(B71-50290)

Verrall, Pamela Motley
A stable bare/ words and music by P.M. Verrall. — London:
Freeman, 1971. — 2p; 8vo.
Unpriced

(B71-50291)

FDP/LF/AYB — Carols. Christmas. Collections. Europe

Phillips, John Charles
World rejoice!: a suite of traditional carols from five nations arranged
for female and/or boys' voices, piano, strings and percussion, with
alternative accompaniment for piano and optional percussion only/
by John Charles Phillips. — Borough Green: Novello, 1970. — 18p;
8vo.
Vocal score.
£0.25

(B71-50292)

FDW — Songs, etc

Arch, Gwyn
Over the stone: Welsh folk-song/ arranged for S.S.A. by Gwyn Arch.
— London: Feldman, 1971. — 5p; 8vo.
Unpriced

(B71-50038)

Bliss, *Sir* Arthur
Two ballads: for S.A. and piano/ by Arthur Bliss. — Borough Green:
Novello. —
1: The mountain-plover. Ushagreaisht. — 1971. — 8p; 8vo.
£0.125

(B71-50039)

2: Flowers in the valley. — 1971. — 16p; 8vo.
£0.19

(B71-50040)

Brown, Oscar
[Joy. Excerpts]. Brown baby: for chorus of treble voices (SSA) and
piano/ by Oscar Brown; arranged by Ollie McFarland. — Borough
Green: Novello, 1970. — 7p; 8vo.
Duration 3 mins.
£0.09

(B71-50041)

Dale, Mervyn
I arise from dreams of thee: two-part song, optional unison/ by
Mervyn Dale; words by Percy Bysshe Shelley. — London: Ashdown,
1971. — 5p; 8vo.
Unpriced

(B71-50831)

Dale, Mervyn
So we'll go no more a-roving: two-part song, optional unison/ by
Mervyn Dale; words by Lord Byron. — London: Ashdown, 1971. —
3p; 8vo.
Unpriced

(B71-50832)

Debussy, Claude
Beau soir. Beautiful evening/ by Claude Debussy; transcribed for
SSC and piano by Joseph Penna; [words by Paul Bourget], English
translation by Joseph Penna. — London: Boosey and Hawkes, 1971.
— 8p; 8vo.
Unpriced

(B71-50833)

Dexter, Harry
Are there any here?: based on the French folksong 'Dites-nous
messieurs'/ arranged for two-part singing with piano, violins and
descant recorders and cellos and/or basses ad lib by Harry Dexter;
English words by Harry Dexter. — London: Ashdown, 1971. — 8p;
8vo.
Unpriced

(B71-50834)

Dexter, Harry
Mary Ann. (Down by the sea-shore siftin' sand): a popular Jamaican
[sic] song in calypso style/ arranged for two-part singing by Harry
Dexter. — London: Ashdown, 1971. — 10p; 8vo.
Unpriced

(B71-50835)

Dougherty, Celius
Declaration of independence: arranged for three-part chorus of
women's voices with piano accompaniment/ by Celius Dougherty:
[words by] Wolcott Gibbs. — New York: Schirmer; [London]:
[Chappell], 1971. — 8p; 8vo.
Unpriced

(B71-50836)

Enfield, Patrick
Last voyage: part-song for S.A. and piano/ by Patrick Enfield; words
by Michael Goymour. — Borough Green: Elkin, 1971. — 4p; 8vo.
£0.07

(B71-50042)

Gardner, John
Three amorous airs. Op.104: for female voices and piano/ by John
Gardner. — London: Oxford University Press. —
1: Waly waly: three-part/ [text] anon. — 1971. — 8p; 8vo.
Duration 4 1/2 mins.
ISBN 0 19 342587 4 : Unpriced

(B71-50293)

2: The German flute: three-part/ [text] anon. — 1971. — 8p; 8vo.
Duration 2 1/2 mins.
ISBN 0 19 342588 2 : Unpriced

(B71-50294)

3: The ballad of Nancy Dee: four-part/ words by John Gardner. — 1971. — 8p; 8vo.
Duration 4 mins.
ISBN 0 19 342589 0 : Unpriced

(B71-50295)

Parke, Dorothy
Has sorrow thy young days shaded?: for soprano and alto/ by Dorothy Parke. — London: Cramer, 1971. — 7p; 8vo.
Air 'Sly Patrick' from Moore's Irish melodies.
£0.09

(B71-50837)

[Pax], [C E]
You! you!: a German folk tune/ [by] C.E. Pax]; arranged as two-part song (optional unison) by Laurence H. Davies, English words by Laurence H. Davies. — London: Ashdown, 1971. — 4p; 8vo.
£0.05

(B71-50838)

Schumann, Robert
[Lied. Op. 29, no.2]. In meinen Garten. In my garden/ by Robert Schumann; edited for three-part chorus of women's voices with piano accompaniment by Maynard Klein, [text by Emanuel Geibel], English text by M.K. — New York: Schirmer; [London]: [Chappell], 1971. — 7p; 8vo.
Unpriced

(B71-50839)

Thiman, Eric Harding
Honeybrook: part-song for SSA and piano/ by Eric H. Thiman; words by K.M. Warburton. — Borough Green: Novello, 1971. — 6p; 8vo.
Unpriced

(B71-50043)

Williams, Patrick
How sweet I roamed from field to field: two part song/ by Patrick Williams; words by William Blake. — London: Bosworth, 1971. — 4p; 8vo.
Staff and tonic sol-fa notation.
£0.07

(B71-50840)

FDW/LC — Songs, etc. Spirituals
Arch, Gwyn
Standing in the need of prayer: spiritual/ arranged by Gwyn Arch. — London: Feldman, 1971. — 8p; 8vo.
Unpriced

(B71-50296)

FDW/XC — Songs, etc. Rounds
Mozart, Wolfgang Amadeus
[O du eselhafter Peierl. K.559a]. Peter, Peter: a round for four groups of singers/ by Mozart; arr., by W. Michael Dennison, words anon. — London: Ashdown, 1971. — 11p; 8vo.
£0.10

(B71-50841)

FDX — Secular cantatas
Hurd, Michael
Charms and ceremonies: for unison voices, S(S)A and piano/ by Michael Hurd; words by Robert Herrick. — Borough Green: Novello, 1971. — 18p; 8vo.
Duration 10 min.
£0.30

(B71-50842)

Schoenfield, Paul
A children's game: for women's voices with piano four-hand accompaniment/ by Paul Schoenfield; text by Christina Rossetti and Paul Schoenfield. — New York: Schirmer; [London]: [Chappell], 1971. — 46p; 8vo.
Unpriced

(B71-50297)

FE/MDX — With orchestra. Secular cantatas
Bush, Geoffrey
Seven limericks: for two-part choir & small orchestra/ by Geoffrey Bush; words chiefly from Edward Lear. — London: Novello, 1970. — 29p; 4to.
Duration 5 mins.
£0.50

(B71-50044)

Liszt, Franz
[Dante symphony]. Symphonie zu Dantes Divina commedia: für Frauenchor und Orchester/ [by] Franz Liszt; herausgegeben von Imre Sulyok. — London: Eulenburg, 1970. — vii,109p; 8vo.
Duration 45 mins.
£2.10

(B71-50298)

FE/NYFSDE — With recorders, keyboard and percussion. Religious cantatas
Verrall, Pamela
Johnny Appleseed: a cantata for all ages, for narrator, speaking chorus, singing chorus, dancers, mimers/ by Pamela Verrall; the accompaniment arranged for recorders, percussion (tuned and untuned) and piano. — London: Feldman, 1971. — 17p; 4to.
£0.30

(B71-50843)

FE/NYHSDX — With recorders and percussion. Secular contatas
Verrall, Pamela Motley
Summer water: a cantata for recorders and percussion, two-part singing chorus, soprano solo and speaking chorus/ by Pamela M. Verrall. — London: Bosworth, 1971. — 8vo.
Piano score (16p.) & 6 parts.
£0.75

(B71-50844)

FE/NYLDW — With keyboard & percussion. Songs, etc
Self, George
The evening draws in: for solo vocalist, chorus, piano and percussion/ by George Self; text by J. Beckett. — London: Universal, 1971. — s.sh; obl.fol.
Unpriced

(B71-50299)

FE/VRDP/LF — With flute. Carols. Christmas
Cumming, Richard
The cherry-tree carol: for women's voices, S.A. and flute/ by Richard Cumming; words traditional. — New York; [London]: Boosey and Hawkes, 1971. — 8p; 8vo.
£0.09

(B71-50300)

FE/VSDW/XC — With recorders. Songs. Rounds
Lawrence, Ian
Fifty simple rounds: for singers, recorders and other instruments/ by Ian Lawrence. — Borough Green: Novello, 1971. — 20p; 8vo.
£0.30

(B71-50301)

FEZDH/LF — Motets, Anthems, Hymns, etc. Christmas
Hoag, Charles K
Sing softly: for two-part chorus of young voices with organ accompaniment (ad lib.)/ by Charles K. Hoag. — New York: Schirmer; [London]: [Chappell], 1971. — 3p; 8vo.
Unpriced

(B71-50845)

FEZDJ — Motets
Monteverdi, Claudio
Angelus ad pastores ait. The angel hosts declare: motet for three-part chorus of women's voices a cappella/ by Claudio Monteverdi; edited by Maynard Klein, English text by M.K. — New York: Schirmer; London: Chappell, 1971. — 6p; 8vo.
Unpriced

(B71-50303)

FEZDJ/LF — Motets. Christmas
Lasso, Orlando di
[Resonet in laudibus. Excerpts]. Hodie apparuit. On this day the Christ appears: SSA or TTB/ by Orlando di Lasso; edited by Maynard Klein, English text by M.K. — New York: Schirmer; London: Chappell, 1971. — 6p; 8vo.
Unpriced
Also classified at GEZDJ/LF

(B71-50304)

FEZDP/LF — Carols. Christmas
Hunter, Ian T
Hodie Christus natus est: Christmas introit for women's or boys' voices/ by Ian T. Hunter. — London: Thames, 1971. — 6p; 8vo.
Unpriced

(B71-50846)

Hunter, Ian T
The shadows are falling: Tyrolean cradle song; words by T.A. Armstrong; [with], Christmas day: Lancashire carol: carols for women's or boys' voices/ arranged by Ian T. Hunter. — London: Thames, 1971. — [3]p; 8vo.
Unpriced

(B71-50847)

FEZDP/LF — Carols, Christmas
Paynter, John
There is no rose: a Christmas carol, mixed, or female or male voices
unacc./ by John Paynter: anonymous words. — London: Oxford
University Press, 1971. — 3p; 8vo.
ISBN 0 19 353340 5 : Unpriced
Primary classification EZDP/LF

(B71-50801)

FEZDP/LF — Carols. Christmas
Roe, Betty
Children's songs of the nativity: carol for woodwind (recorder, flute
& clarinet or oboe), two-part women's or boy's voices, piano/organ
and optional percussion/ by Betty Roe; words by Frances
Chesterton. — London: Thames, 1971. — [7]p; 8vo.
Unpriced

(B71-50848)

Willcocks, David
How far is it to Bethlehem?: English traditional melody, S.A.A.
unacc./ arranged by David Willcocks; words by Frances Chesterton.
— London: Oxford University Press, 1971. — [2]p; 8vo.
ISBN 0 19 342592 0 : Unpriced

(B71-50305)

FEZDW — Songs, etc
Barber, Samuel
To be sung on the water. Op. 42, no.2: transcribed for four-part
chorus of women's voices a cappella/ by Samuel Barber; [words by]
Louise Bogan. — New York: Schirmer; London: Chappell, 1971. —
10p; 8vo.
£0.35

(B71-50306)

FEZDW — Songs etc
Kodaly, Zoltán
Bicinia hungarica/ by Zoltan Kodaly; English words and annotations
by Percy M. Young. — Revised English ed.; Geoffry Russell-Smith. —
London: Boosey and Hawkes. — (Kodaly choral method)
Vol.4: 60 progressive two-part songs. — 1970. — 32p; 8vo.
Unpriced

(B71-50045)

FEZDW/G/AYVB — Folk song collections. Turkey
Erkin, Ulvi Cemal
Six Turkish songs/ arranged in two parts by U.C. Erkin; English
translations by Donald Hoffmann. — London: Schott, 1971. — 6p;
4to.
£0.60

(B71-50849)

FEZDW/LC/AY — Spirituals. Collections
Phillips, John Charles
Eight negro spirituals: arranged for SSA unaccompanied/ by John C.
Phillips. — Borough Green: Novello, 1971. — 38p; 8vo.
£0.35

(B71-50850)

FEZDX — Secular cantatas
Self, George
Take a shape: for voices/ by George Self; text taken from the
'Illustrated dictionary' published by the Oxford University Press. —
London: Universal, 1971. — 5p; obl.fol.
Duration 4 min.
£0.20

(B71-50307)

FHYE/NYLDX — Speakers. With keyboard & percussion. Secular
cantatas
Pehkonen, Elis
My cats: for speaker, chorus and percussion/ by Elis Pehkonen,
words by Stevie Smith. — London: Universal, 1971. — 2s.sh.; obl.fol.
Printed on one side of the leaf only.
£0.20

(B71-50308)

FLDEDP/LF — Treble voices. Carol cantatas
Britten, Benjamin
A ceremony of carols. Ein Kranz von Lobechörens. Op.28: for treble
voices and harp/ by Benjamin Britten; übersetzung aus dem
Englischen von Herbert E. Herlitschka. — New English-German ed.
— London: Boosey and Hawkes, 1970. — 8vo.
Score (64p.) & 3 vocal parts. In this edition bars have been numbered and two
changes made in instructions to performers.
Unpriced

(B71-50309)

FLDH — Soprano voices. Motets, Anthems, Hymns, etc
Macpherson, Charles
Thou, O God art praised in Sion: short anthem/ by Charles
Macpherson; arranged for SS and organ by C.H. Trevor, [text from]
Psalm 65. — Borough Green: Novello, 1971. — 4p; 8vo.
£0.06

(B71-50310)

FLDP/LF — Soprano voices. Carols. Christmas
Hamilton, Alasdair
Good cheer: a Christmas carol/ by Alasdair Hamilton; words:
medieval English. — London: Oxford University Press, 1971. — 6p;
8vo.
ISBN 0 19 341505 4 : Unpriced

(B71-50851)

Roe, Betty
As I sat on a sunny bank: carol for treble voices and piano/ by Betty
Roe. — London: Thames, 1970. — [3]p; 4to.
Unpriced

(B71-50852)

Roe, Betty
Unto us is born a son: carol for treble voices and piano/ by Betty
Roe; words adapted from the translation by G.R. Woodward. —
London: Thames, 1970. — [3]p; 4to.
Unpriced

(B71-50853)

FLDW — Soprano voices. Songs, etc
Dvorák, Antonin
[Moravian duets. Op.32]. Songs from Moravia/ by Antonin Dvorák;
translated and arranged for soprano voices and piano by Neil
Butterworth. — London: Chappell. —
Book 1. — 1971. — 30p; 8vo.
Unpriced

(B71-50855)

Dvorak, Antonin
[Moravian duets. Op.32]. Songs from Moravia/ by Antonin Dvorák;
translated and arranged for soprano voices and piano by Neil
Butterworth. — London: Chappell. —
Book 1. — 1971. — 30p; 8vo.
Unpriced

(B71-50856)

Dvorák, Antonin
[Moravian duets. Op.32]. Songs from Moravia/ by Antonin Dvorák;
translated and arranged for soprano voices and piano by Neil
Butterworth. — London: Chappell. —
Book 2. — 1971. — [32]p; 8vo.
Unpriced

(B71-50854)

FLE/NYLDW — Soprano voices. With keyboard & percussion. Songs,
etc
Pitfield, Thomas Baron
Rhymes and rhythms: pieces for youth choir, piano, perc. and
various optional instruments/ words & music by Thomas B. Pitfield.
— London: Hinrichsen, 1970. — 23p; 4to.
£1.60
Also classified at GE/NYLDW

(B71-50311)

FLEZDGM — Unaccompanied treble voices. Anglican liturgy
Holman, Derek
Versicles, Responses and the Lord's Prayer: for treble voices/ by
Derek Holman. — Croydon: Lengnick, 1971. — 7p; 8vo.
Unpriced

(B71-50312)

G — MALE VOICES
GDH/LF — Motets, Anthems, Hymns, etc. Christmas
Hammerschmidt, Andreas
[Ehre sey Gott in der Höhe]. Glory to God in the highest: for mixed
voices, organ (piano) and strings (ad lib)/ by Andreas
Hammerschmidt; edited by Diethard Hellmann, [words] adapted
from Luke 2 by Walter E. Buszin. — New York: Peters; [London]:
[Hinrichsen], 1970. — 19p; 8vo.
Vocal score.
£0.45

(B71-50313)

GDW — Songs, etc
Adler, Richard
[The pajama game - Excerpts]. Hernando's hideaway: T.T.B.B./ by
Richard Adler; arranged by William Stickles. — London: Frank
Music, 1971. — 8p; 8vo.
£0.90

(B71-50314)

Williams, Arnold
Going to see my long-haired babe/ arranged for tenor solo and
accompanied men's chorus by Arnold Williams. — York: Banks,
1970. — 8p; 8vo.
Unpriced

(B71-50046)

GE/NYLDW — With keyboard & percussion. Songs, etc
Pitfield, Thomas Baron
Rhymes and rhythms: pieces for youth choir, piano, perc. and
various optional instruments/ words & music by Thomas B. Pitfield.
— London: Hinrichsen, 1970. — 23p; 4to.
£1.60
Primary classification FLE/NYLDW

(B71-50311)

GE/SNTPWDJ — Male voices with two violins and keyboard. Motets
Monteverdi, Claudio
[Selve morale e spirituale. Excerpts]. Deus tuorum militum: himnus
unius martyris for T.T.B. with two violins and continuo/ by Claudio
Monteverdi; edited by Roger Norrington. — London: Oxford
University Press, 1971. — 8vo & 4to.
Score (3p.) & 3 parts.
ISBN 0 19 353272 7 : Unpriced

(B71-50900)

GEZDJ/LF — Motets. Christmas
Lasso, Orlando di
[Resonet in laudibus. Excerpts]. Hodie apparuit. On this day the
Christ appears: SSA or TTB/ by Orlando di Lasso; edited by
Maynard Klein, English text by M.K. — New York: Schirmer;
London: Chappell, 1971. — 6p; 8vo.
Unpriced
Primary classification FEZDJ/LF

(B71-50304)

GEZDP/LF — Carols, Christmas
Paynter, John
There is no rose: a Christmas carol, mixed, or female or male voices
unacc./ by John Paynter; anonymous words. — London: Oxford
University Press, 1971. — 3p; 8vo.
ISBN 0 19 353340 5 : Unpriced
Primary classification EZDP/LF

(B71-50801)

GEZDW — Unaccompanied male voices. Songs, etc
Dinham, Kenneth J
Kwmbayah: African tune/ arranged T.T.B.B. unacc. by K.J.
Dinham. — London: Oxford University Press, 1971. — [2]p; 8vo.
ISBN 0 19 341019 2 : £0.04

(B71-50857)

J — VOICES IN UNISON
JDGPQ — Magnificat
Glarum, Leonard Stanley
Canticle of Mary (Magnificat) for unison voices with organ
accompaniment/ by L. Stanley Glarum. — New York: Schirmer;
London: Chappell, 1971. — 6p; 8vo.
Unpriced

(B71-50315)

JDH — Motets, Anthems, Hymns, etc
Steer, Michael
Easter song: for unison voices and organ/ by Michael Steer; words
by W.R. Champion. — Borough Green: Novello, 1971. — 4p; 8vo.
Unpriced

(B71-50316)

JDM — Hymns
Kearney, Peter
Songs of brotherhood/ by Peter Kearney; words and music by Peter
Kearney. — London: Feldman, 1971. — 18p; 4to.
Unpriced

(B71-50317)

JDM/AY — Hymns. Collections
20th Century Church Light Music Group
Hymns for all seasons/ [compiled by] the 20th Century Church Light
Music Group. — London: Weinberger, 1971. — 13p; 8vo.
Unpriced

(B71-50047)

JDP/LF — Carols. Christmas
Verrall, Pamela Motley
Star bright, starlight/ words and music by P.M. Verrall. — London:
Freeman, 1971. — 1p; 8vo.
Unpriced

(B71-50318)

JDP/LF/AY — Carols. Christmas. Collections
The **Christmas** tree: a garland of 20th century carols and songs for the
young. — London: Weinberger, 1971. — 16p; 8vo.
Includes three carols by Malcolm Williamson.
£0.35

(B71-50858)

JDW — Songs, etc
Bush, Alan
Songs of struggle/ by Alan Bush. — London (236 Westbourne Park
Rd, W.11): Workers' Music Association, 1971. — 2p; 8vo.
With tonic sol-fa notation.
Unpriced

(B71-50048)

Bush, Alan
Songs of struggle/ by Alan Bush. — London: Workers' Music
Association, 1971. — 27p; 4to.
£0.35

(B71-50859)

Carter, Sydney
Songs of Sydney Carter. — Great Yarmouth: Galliard. —
4: Riding a tune. — 1971. — 33p; 8vo.
Vols 1-3 published under the title of 'In the present tense'.
Unpriced

(B71-50860)

JDW/G/AY — Folk songs. Collections
Stuart, Forbes
A medley of folk songs/ compiled by Forbes Stuart, musical
arrangements by Geoffrey Winters. — London: Longman Young
Books, 1971. — 159p; 4to.
ISBN 0 582 15331 x : £2.50

(B71-50861)

JE/TSDW — With guitar. Songs, etc
Rowe, Christopher
Man on the move: songs on the past, present and future of transport/
by Christopher Rowe and Ian Clark. — Great Yarmouth: Galliard,
1971. — 24p; 8vo.
Unpriced

(B71-50319)

**JE/TSDW/G/AYT — With guitar. Folk songs. Collections. United
States**
Travis, Dave
103 folk songs/ compiled and arranged by Dave Travis. — London:
Campbell, Connelly, 1971. — 113p; 4to.
£0.95

(B71-50320)

JEZDW — Unaccompanied voices. Songs, etc
Campbell, David
Search: songs of the sun/ by David Campbell; [words by] David
Campbell. — Great Yarmouth: Galliard, 1971. — 24p; 8vo.
ISBN 0 85249 160 3 : Unpriced

(B71-50862)

JFDE — Female voices, Children's voices. Religious cantatas
Fairbanks, Terry
Noah and all that jazz: cantata for unison voices with piano
accompaniment/ doggerel and music by Terry Fairbanks. — London:
Leeds Music, 1970. — 27p; 8vo.
Unpriced

(B71-50049)

JFDH — Female voices, children's voices. Motets, Anthems, Hymns
Graves, Richard
Calypso praise/ words and music by Richard Graves. — London:
Bosworth, 1970. — 4p; 8vo.
£0.06

(B71-50050)

JFDM — Female voices, Children's voices. Hymns
Williamson, Malcolm
6 Wesley songs for the young/ by Malcolm Williamson; words by
Charles Wesley. — London: Weinberger, 1971. — 9p; 4to.
£0.30

(B71-50864)

JFDM/AY — Female voices, Children's voices. Hymns. Collections
Brace, Geoffrey
Something to sing at assembly/ compiled by Geoffrey Brace. —
Cambridge: Cambridge University Press, 1971. — 59p; 8vo.
ISBN 0 521 07570 x : Unpriced

(B71-50322)

A **Hymn** for children: a selection of hymns from the television series.
— London (10 Denmark St., WC2H 8LU): High-Fye Music, 1971. —
20p: illus; 4to.
£0.50

(B71-50321)

**JFDM/GJ/AY — Female voices, Children's voices. Children's hymns.
Collections**
Dowman, Pamela
Come and sing: a selection of Christian songs for under-eights/
compiled by Pamela Dowman and Elspeth M. Stephenson. —
London: Scripture Union, 1971. — 45p; 4to.
ISBN 0 85421 301 5 : Unpriced

(B71-50863)

JFDP/LF — Female voices, Children's voices. Carols. Christmas
Ager, Lawrence
Rhythm of the beating wings: a carol/ by Lawrence Ager; words by Kenneth A. Allen. — London: Feldman, 1971. — 4p; 8vo.
Unpriced

(B71-50865)

Bennett, F Roy
Three carols for Christ's nativity: unison/ words and music by R. Roy Bennett. — London: Ashdown, 1971. — 7p; 8vo.
Contents:- The carol of the kings. — Mary's lullaby. — The carol of the bells.
Unpriced

(B71-50866)

Coates, Douglas
The cherub carol: unison/ by Douglas Coates: words by J.L. St C. Garrington. — London: Bosworth, 1971. — 3p; 8vo.
Staff and tonic sol-fa notation.
£0.05

(B71-50867)

Parry, William Howard
Riding into Bethlehem: for unison or two-part voices with piano, optional recorders, and optional percussion by W.H. Parry; words by L. Bell. — London: Oxford University Press, 1971. — 7p; 8vo.
ISBN 0 19 342048 1 : Unpriced
Primary classification FDP/LF

(B71-50829)

JFDP/LF — Female voices, children's voices. Christmas
Thorpe, Frank
The light of Christmas: unison with piano or 2-stave organ, the winner of the 1970 'Carol for a future' competition/ by Frank Thorpe. — London: Weinberger, 1970. — 5p; 8vo.
£0.05

(B71-50051)

JFDW — Female voices, Children's voices. Songs, etc
Doherty, Christopher
Follow me: eight songs for young people/ by Christopher Doherty; arranged for piano by David Storey. — London: Weinberger, 1971. — 17p; 8vo.
Unpriced

(B71-50868)

JFDW — Female voices, children's voices. Songs, etc
Harris, Will
The cold encounter: unison song/ words and music by Will Harris. — London: Bosworth, 1970. — 4p; 8vo.
£0.06

(B71-50052)

JFDW — Female voices, Children's voices. Songs, etc
Hunt, Reginald
I had a hippopotamus/ by Reginald Hunt; words by Patrick Barrington. — London: Ashdown, 1971. — 8p; 8vo.
Unpriced

(B71-50869)

JFDW — Female voices, children's voices. Songs, etc
Veal, Arthur
The Irish fiddler: unison/ by Arthur Veal; words by Clive Sansom. — London: Oxford University Press, 1970. — 5p; 8vo.
Unpriced

(B71-50053)

JFDW/G/AYD — Female voices, Children's voices. Folk song collections. England
Palmer, Roy
Room for company: folk songs and ballads selected and edited by/ Roy Palmer. — Cambridge: Cambridge University Press, 1971. — 4to & obl.8vo.
Piano score (75p.) & melody edition (76p.).
ISBN 0 521 08173 4 : y1.38

(B71-50870)

JFDW/GJ — Female voices, Children's voices. Children's songs
Beaumont, Adrian
Songs for little children/ by Adrian Beaumont. — London: Boosey and Hawkes. —
Set 1. — 1971. — 14p; 8vo.
£0.50

(B71-50054)

JFDW/GJ — Female voices, children's voices. Children's songs
Horscroft, Elizabeth
Space songs for infants/ melodies and words by Elizabeth Horscroft; pianoforte, guitar and 'additional' accompaniment by Denise Narcisse-Muir. — London: Ashdown, 1971. — 20p; 8vo.
£0.25

(B71-50323)

JFDW/GJ/AYB — Female voices, Children's voices. Children's songs. Collections. Europe
Offer, Charles Karel
European songs for children: 15 traditional songs/ selected with words by Charles K. Offer, pianoforte arrangements by A.W. Benoy. — London: Paxton, 1971. — 16p; 8vo.
Unpriced

(B71-50324)

JFDW/GK/AY — Female voices, Children's voices. Nursery rhymes. Collections
Poston, Elizabeth
Bye, Baby Bunting/ [compiled by] Elizabeth Poston. — London: Bodley Head, 1971. — 48p; col illus, music; 4to. — (Poston, Elizabeth. The baby's song book; part 1)
ISBN 0 370 01526 6 : £1.10

(B71-50871)

Poston, Elizabeth
Girls and boys come out to play/ [compiled by] Elizabeth Poston. — London: Bodley Head, 1971. — 48p; col illus, music; 4to. — (Poston, Elizabeth. The baby's song book; part 2)
ISBN 0 370 01527 4 : £1.10

(B71-50872)

Poston, Elizabeth
I had a little nut tree/ [compiled by] Elizabeth Poston. — London: Bodley Head, 1971. — 48p; col illus; 4to. — (Poston, Elizabeth. The baby's song book; part 3)
ISBN 0 370 01528 2 : £1.10

(B71-50873)

Poston, Elizabeth
Where are you going to, my pretty maid?/ [compiled by] Elizabeth Poston. — London: Bodley Head, 1971. — 48p; col illus, music; 4to. — (Poston, Elizabeth. The baby's song book; part 4)
ISBN 0 370 01529 0 : £1.10

(B71-50874)

JFE/NYESDW/G/AYT — Female voices, Children's voices. With recorder, keyboard and percussion. Folk song collections. United States
Jamson, Bruce
Songs of America/ text and song arrangements by Bruce Jamson. — Yarmouth: Stainer and Bell, 1971. — 28p; obl. 8vo.
ISBN 0 903000 01 6 : Unpriced

(B71-50875)

JFE/NYHSDE/LF — Female voices, Children's voices. With recorders & percussion. Religious cantatas. Christmas
Mendoza, Anne
A children's Christmas festival: for voices, recorders and percussion/ by Anne Mendoza and Joan Rimmer. — London: Oxford University Press, 1971. — 17p; 4to.
ISBN 0 19 330566 6 : £0.50

(B71-50876)

JFE/NYJDW/GK/AY — Female voices, Children's voices. With strings & percussion. Nursery rhymes. Collections
Room, Peter
Nursery rhymes/ [compiled by] Peter Room; with guitar & percussion accompaniment. — London: Leeds Music, 1971. — 28p; obl.4to.
Unpriced

(B71-50877)

JFE/NYLDW — Female voices, Children's voices with keyboard & percussion. Songs, etc
McNeill, Mary
Songs of the seaside: three songs for unison voices, piano, tuned and rhythm percussion/ words and music by Mary McNeill. — London: Keith Prowse Music, 1971. — 4to.
Score (15p.) & 10 parts.
£0.90

(B71-50325)

JFE/NYLDW — Female voices, children's voices. With keyboard & percussion. Songs, etc
Senator, Ronald
A basket of eggs and other rhymes: for infants and juniors/ by Ronald Senator; words from the Puffin Book of Nursery Rhymes. — London: Boosey and Hawkes, 1970. — 20p; 4to.
Piano score with instrumental score (8p.) and voice part (8p.) as insert.
£0.75

(B71-50055)

JFE/TQTDW/GS/AY — Female voices, Children's voices. With autoharp. Songs. Games. Collections
Jeremiah, Dorothy Adams
Yes! I can play: songs and singing games/ by Dorothy Adams Jeremiah. — London: Leeds Music, 1971. — 15p; 4to.
Unpriced

(B71-50878)

JFE/TSDW/G/AY — Female voices, Children's voices. With guitar. Folk songs. Collections

Rose, Margaret E
Folk and vision: book of words and melody/ |compiled by] Margaret E. Rose and Mabel Rose Cook. — London: Hart-Davis, 1971. — 122p; obl. 8vo.
ISBN 0 247 54443 4 : Unpriced

(B71-50879)

JFE/XMDW — Female voices, Childrens voices. With percussion band. Songs, etc

Eckert, Alex
Galgenlieder nach Gedichten von Christian Morgenstern: Aleatorische Komposition für Kinder, Solosprecher, Sprech-und Sing-Chor, Bläser Streicher, Stabspiel, Geräuschinstrumente und Schlagwerk/ [by] Alex Eckert. — Mainz; London: Schott, 1971. — 31p; obl.8vo.
£1.70

(B71-50326)

JFE/XMDX — Female voices, Children's voices. With percussion band. Secular cantatas

Hutchinson, Godfrey
The Lambton worm: a folk tale from the North, for speakers, singers and tuned percussion/ by Godfrey Hutchinson; words Michael Langley. — London: Leeds Music, 1971. — 15p; 8vo.
Unpriced

(B71-50327)

JFEZDW/G/AY — Unaccompanied unison female voices, children's voices. Folk songs. Collections

Silverman, Jerry
Folk songs for schools and camps: 81 favourite songs/ [compiled by] Jerry Silverman. — New York: Robbins Music; London: Francis, Day and Hunter, 1971. — 96p; 4to.
£0.75

(B71-50328)

JN — SINGLE VOICES IN COMBINATION

Heider, Werner
Edition: multiple Musik für Instrumental - oder Vokalgruppen/ [by] Werner Heider. — Frankfurt: Litolff, Peters; London: [Hinrichsen], 1970. — 7p; 4to.
£0.90
Primary classification LN

(B71-50374)

JNAYE/MDX — Octets. Accompanied by orchestra. Secular cantatas

Berio, Luciano
Sinfonia (1968): for eight voices and orchestra/ by Luciano Berio. — London: Universal, 1971. — 129p; fol.
Unpriced

(B71-50329)

JNCDW/JR — Quartets. Film songs

Lennon, John
Let it be: souvenir song album [of] 8 songs from the film/ [composed] by John Lennon and Paul McCartney. — London: Northern Songs, 1970. — 24p; 4to.
£0.75

(B71-50330)

JNFDE/MDW — Female voices. Trios. With orchestra. Songs, etc

Maw, Nicholas
Scenes and arias/ by Nicholas Maw; words anon. — London: Boosey and Hawkes, 1971. — 140p; 8vo.
Miniature score.
£2.50

(B71-50880)

KDH — MOTETS, ANTHEMS, HYMNS, ETC. SOLOS
George Beverley Shea solos: songs/ by John W. Peterson [and others]. — London: Marshall, Morgan and Scott, 1971. — 32p; 8vo.
ISBN 0 551 05069 1 : £0.40

(B71-50881)

KDP — CAROLS. SOLOS
KDP/LF — Christmas
Head, Michael
The carol of the field mice/ by Michael Head; words by Kenneth Grahame. — London: Boosey and Hawkes, 1971. — 7p; 4to.
Unpriced

(B71-50331)

KDP/LF/AY — Christmas. Collections
Westmore, Peter
Come to Bethlehem: twelve original carols/ words by Peter Westmore. — London: Vanguard Music, 1969. — 32p; 4to.
Unpriced

(B71-50882)

KDW — SONGS, ETC. SOLOS
Binkerd, Gordon
The fair morning/ by Gordon Binkerd; text by Jones Very. — New York; London: Boosey and Hawkes, 1971. — 20p; 4to.
£0.65

(B71-50332)

Binkerd, Gordon
If thou wilt ease thine heart/ by Gordon Binkerd; poem by Thomas L. Beddoes. — New York; London: Boosey and Hawkes, 1971. — 8p; 4to.
£0.40

(B71-50333)

Binkerd, Gordon
Nursery ode/ by Gordon Binkerd; poem by Ambrose Philips. — New York; London: Boosey and Hawkes, 1971. — 10p; 4to.
£0.40

(B71-50334)

Binkerd, Gordon
The wishing caps/ by Gordon Binkerd; poem by Rudyard Kipling. — New York; London: Boosey and Hawkes, 1971. — 10p; 8vo.
£0.65

(B71-50335)

Bliss, *Sir* Arthur
Simples: a setting of James Joyce's poem/ by Arthur Bliss. — London: Oxford University Press, 1971. — 5p; fol.
Limited edition of 500 copies.
ISBN 0 19 345165 4 : £0.80

(B71-50336)

Bononcini, Giovanni Battista
[Selections]. Arias from the Vienna operas/ by Giovanni Bononcini; edited by Anthony Ford. — London: Oxford University Press for the University of Hull, 1971. — vii,80p; 4to. — (Baroque operatic arias; 1)
ISBN 0 19 713412 2 : £2.50

(B71-50337)

Cage, John
Aria: voice (any range)/ by John Cage. — New York: Peters; London: [Hinrichsen], 1967. — 20p; 4to.
Words in Armenian, Russian, Italian, French and English.
£4.25

(B71-50338)

Dylan, Bob
New morning: complete vocal/piano folio with guitar diagrams & chord symbols/ arrangements and words by Bob Dylan. — London: Feldman, 1970. — 68p; 4to.
Unpriced

(B71-50056)

Goehr, Alexander
Four songs from the Japanese. Op.9:: voice and piano/ by Alexander Goehr; the words adapted from Lafcadio Hearn's 'Gleanings in Buddha fields', translation of Japanese texts. — London: Schott, 1971. — 14p; 4to.
Unpriced

(B71-50339)

Jeffreys, John, *b.*1927
A book of songs/ by John Jeffreys. — Private facsimile ed. — Hertford (13 Queens Rd, Hertford): B. Hill, 1971. — 32p; 8vo.
Unpriced

(B71-50340)

Lawes, William
Six songs/ by William Lawes, edited by Edward Huws Jones; words by Robert Herrick. — London: Schott, 1971. — 14p; 4to.
£0.65

(B71-50883)

Lennon, John
Songs of John Lennon. — London: Wise Publications, Music Sales, 1971. — 80p; 4to.
£1.50

(B71-50884)

Lorenzo Fernández, Oscar
Cancao do mar: canto e piano/ [by] Oscar Lorenzo Fernandez; poesias de Manoel Bandeira em português e francês, letra italiana V. Spinelli. — Rio de Janeiro: Arthur Napoleao; [London]: [Essex Music], 1971. — [3]p; 4to.
Unpriced

(B71-50341)

Lorenzo Fernández, Oscar
Noturno: canto e piano/ [by] Oscar Lorenzo Fernández; poesia em português e francês de Eduardo Tourinho. — Rio de Janeiro: Arthur Napoleao; [London]: [Essex Music], 1971. — 4p; 4to.
Unpriced

(B71-50342)

Mahler, Gustav
[Symphony no.5 in C minor. Excerpts. Adagietto]. The timeless moment: [song]/ based on a theme by Gustav Mahler; music by Roger Webb, words by Norman Newell. — London: Chappell, 1971. — 3p; 4to.
£0.20

(B71-50885)

Rubbra, Edmund
Rune of hospitality. Op. 15: song with piano accompaniment/ by Edmund Rubbra; [words] old Gaelic rune recovered by Kenneth Macleod. — Revised [ed.]. — South Croydon: Lengnick, 1971. — 3p; 4to.
Unpriced

(B71-50886)

Villa-Lobos, Heitor
[Serestas. Excerpts]. Cancao do Carreiro ou Cancao um crepúsculo caricioso: canto e piano/ de Heitor Villa-Lobos; poesia de Ribeiro Couto. — Rio de Janeiro: Arthur Napoleao; London: Essex Music, 1970. — 7p; 4to.
Unpriced

(B71-50057)

Warren, Raymond
Songs of old age: a song cycle for voice and piano/ by Raymond Warren; poems by W.B. Yeats. — Borough Green: Novello, 1971. — 37p; 4to.
£0.75

(B71-50887)

Webern, Anton von
Four Stefan George songs: voice and piano/ by Anton von Webern; edited by Peter Westergaard. — London: Boosey and Hawkes, 1971. — 16p; 4to.
Unpriced

(B71-50343)

Wishart, Peter
Six miniatures/ by Peter Wishart, poems by James McAuley. — [London]: Stainer and Bell, 1971. — 26p; 4to.
£1.50

(B71-50344)

KDW/AYD — Collections. England
Musica Britannica: a national collection of music. — London: Stainer and Bell. —
Vol.33: English songs, 1625-1660/ transcribed and edited by Ian Spink. — 1971. — xxiii,210p; fol.
Unpriced
Primary classification C/AYD

(B71-50001)

KDW/AYEE — Collections. East Germany
Lenin Lieder: für Gesang und Klavier von Komponisten der Deutschen Demokratischen Republik. — Leipzig: Peters; [London]: [Hinrichsen], 1970. — 30p; 4to.
£1.05

(B71-50345)

KDW/G/AYG — Folk songs. Collections. Hungary
Bartók, Béla
[Hungarian folksongs (1906). Excerpts]. Five Hungarian folksongs: for voice and piano/ [arranged] by Béla Bartók; edited by Denijs Dille, English words by Nancy Bush. — London: Boosey and Hawkes, 1970. — 11p; 4to.
Unpriced

(B71-50346)

KDW/G/AYT — Folk songs. Collections. United States
Okun, Milton
Something to sing about!: the personal choices of America's folk singers/ collected and arranged by Milton Okun. — New York: Collier Books; London: Collier-Macmillan, 1970. — 241p; 4to.
£1.25

(B71-50347)

KDW/JR — Film songs
Greig, Edvard
Song of Norway/ by Edvard Greig; song album [from the film] musical adaptation and lyrics by Robert Wright and George Forrest. — London: Chappell: Frank Music, 1971. — 47p; 4to.
£0.60

(B71-50058)

KDW/KC/AYDJJ — Sea songs. Collections. Northumberland
Tate, Phyllis
Coastal ballads: Northumbrian sea songs/ arranged by Phyllis Tate. — London: Oxford University Press. —
No.1: The water of Tyne. — 1971. — 4p; 4to.
ISBN 0 19 345820 9 : £0.25

(B71-50348)

No.2: O the bonny fisher lad. — 1971. — 4p; 4to.
ISBN 0 19 345819 5 : £0.25

(B71-50349)

No.3: Billy boy. — 1971. — 5p; 4to.
ISBN 0 19 345821 7 : £0.25

(B71-50350)

KE — VOCAL SOLOS WITH ACCOMPANIMENT OTHER THAN KEYBOARD
KE/MDX — With orchestra. Secular cantatas
Henze, Hans Werner
Versuch über Schweine: für Stimme und Orchester/ [by] Hans Werner Henze; Gedicht Gaston Salvatore. — Mainz; London: Schott, 1970. — 83p; 4to.
Duration 20 mins.
£3.20

(B71-50059)

KE/NYDPNQDW — With woodwind, strings, keyboard & percussion. Songs, etc
Davies, Peter Maxwell
Eight songs for a mad king: [for voice], flute (doubling piccolo), clarinet, piano (doubling harpsichord and dulcimer), violin, violoncello and percussion/ by Peter Maxwell Davies; words by Randolph Stow. — London: Boosey and Hawkes, 1971. — 33p; fol.
Duration 33 min.
Unpriced

(B71-50351)

KE/SPLRDH — With violin & organ. Motets, Anthems, Hymns, etc
Høgner, Friedrich
Zwei Trauungsgesänge und Tanflied: für Singstimme, Violine und Orgel/ [by] Friedrich Høgner. — Frankfurt: Litolff, Peters; London: [Hinrichsen], 1970. — 4to.
Score (11p.) & part.
£1.75

(B71-50352)

KE/STDW — With viol accompaniment. Songs, etc
Byrd, William
The collected works of William Byrd/ edited by Edmund H. Fellowes and revised under the direction of Thurston Dart. — London: Stainer and Bell. —
Vol.15: Consort songs for voice & viols/ newly edited from manuscript sources by Philip Brett. — 1970. — xii,180p; 8vo.
Pbk: Unpriced
Primary classification C/AZ

(B71-50003)

KE/TSDW — With guitar. Songs, etc
Guthrie, Arlo
This is the Arlo Guthrie book/ editor: Herbert Wise. — New York: Amsco Music Publishing; London: Distributed by Collier-Macmillan, 1969. — 96p: illus, ports; 4to.
ISBN 0 02 060680 x Pbk: £0.90

(B71-50888)

KE/TSDW/AY — With guitar. Song collections
Campell, Alex
Alex Campbell songs/ [collected or composed by Alex Campbell]. — Great Yarmouth: Galliard, 1971. — 24p; obl. 8vo.
Unpriced

(B71-50889)

KE/TSDW/G/AY — With guitar. Folk songs. Collections
Norriss, Eileen
Folk songs for guitar/ arranged by Eileen Norriss. — London: Keith Prowse, 1970. — 12p; 4to.
£0.30

(B71-50060)

KE/TSDW/G/AYD — With guitar. Folk songs. Collections. England
Wales, Tony
The Yetties song book/ edited by Tony Wales; transcriptions by Dave Kettlewell. — London: English Folk Dance and Song Society, 1971. — 34p; 4to.
Unpriced

(B71-50353)

KE/TSDW/G/AYDGH — With guitar. Folk songs. Collections. Lincolnshire
O'Shaughnessy, Patrick
More folk songs from Lincolnshire: guitar chords added/ edited by Patrick O'Shaughnessy. — London: Oxford University Press in conjunction with the Lincolnshire Association, 1971. — vii,64p; 8vo.
ISBN 0 19 343687 6 : £0.75

(B71-50354)

KE/TVDW — With vihuela. Songs, etc
Milan, Luis
El Maestro/ by Luis de Milan; edited, translated, and transcribed by Charles Jacobs. — University Park (Pa.); London: Pennsylvania University Press, 1971. — 319p; 8vo.
ISBN 0 271 00091 0 : Unpriced
Primary classification TVPMJ

(B71-50616)

KF — FEMALE VOICE, CHILD'S VOICE
KFDW — Songs, etc
Webber, Andrew Lloyd
[Jesus Christ Superstar- Excerpts]. I don't know how to love him/ by Lloyd Webber; lyrics by Tim Rice. — London: Leeds Music, 1971. — 5p; 4to.
£0.20

(B71-50890)

KFE/TSDW/G/AYC — With guitar. Folk songs. Collections. Great Britain
McDonald, Jacqueline
Songs for singing folk: Jackie and Bridies second song book/ [compiled by] Jacqueline McDonald & Bridie O'Donnell; edited by Tony Wales. — London: Galliard, 1971. — 25p; 8vo.
Unpriced

(B71-50355)

KFLDW — Soprano voice. Songs, etc
Furnivall, Anthony
Si tu veux, nous nous aimerons: for soprano and piano/ by Anthony Furnivall; words by Stephen Mallarmé. — Oxford (4 Benson Place, Oxford): Sycamore Press, 1970. — 2p; 8vo.
Unpriced

(B71-50356)

KFLE/MDX — Soprano voice. With orchestra. Secular cantatas
Birtwistle, Harrison
Cantata: by Harrison Birtwistle. — London: Universal, 1971. — 22p; obl.4to.
Duration 11 min.
Unpriced

(B71-50891)

KFLE/MPPSDW — Soprano voice. With electronic instrument & orchestra. Songs, etc
Bussotti, Sylvano
Due voci: per soprano, martenot solo ed orchestra su un frammento di Jean de la Fontaine/ [by] Sylvano Bussotti. — London: Universal, 1970. — 32p; fol.
The 'martenot solo' is an electronic generator of sound.
Unpriced

(B71-50357)

KFLE/MRDX — Soprano voice. With chamber orchestra
Denisov, Edisson
Die Sonne der Inkas: für Sopran, 3 Sprecher und 11 Instrumentalisten/ [by] Edisson Denisov; Gedichte von Gabriela Mistral, russisch von Owady Sawitsch, Rückübertragung von Natalie Leufgen. — London: Universal, 1971. — 48p; 4to.
Duration 18 min.
Unpriced

(B71-50358)

KFLE/MRDX — Soprano voice. With chamber orchestra. Secular cantatas
Davies, Peter Maxwell
Revelation and fall. Offenbarung und Untergang: [for soprano and sixteen instrumentalists]/ [by] Peter Maxwell Davies; text by Georg Trakl. — London: Boosey and Hawkes, 1971. — 66p; fol.
Three full-size colour reproductions of the original sketches are included.
Unpriced

(B71-50359)

KFLE/RXNDX — Soprano voice. With string ensemble. Secular cantatas
Pergolesi, Giovanni Battista
Orfeo: Kantate für Sopran, Streicher und Basso continuo/ [by] Giovanni Battista Pergolesi; herausgegeben von Raimund Rüegge. — Frankfurt: Litolff: London: Hinrichsen, 1970. — 29p; 4to.
£1.80

(B71-50360)

KFLE/VVPDW — Soprano voice. With clarinet & piano. Songs, etc
Greaves, Terence
A garden of weeds: 5 songs for soprano, clarinet and piano/ by Terence Greaves; words by Jacqueline Froom. — London: Thames, 1971. — 14p; 8vo.
Unpriced

(B71-50892)

KFNDW — Mezzo-soprano voice. Songs, etc
Binkerd, Gordon
Three songs: for mezzo-soprano/ by Gordon Binkerd. — New York; [London]: Boosey and Hawkes, 1971. — 24p; 4to.
Contents: Never the nightingale: text by Adelaide Crapsey. How lillies came white; text by Robert Herrick. Upon parting; text by Robert Herrick.
£1.25

(B71-50361)

KFNE/NYDDW — Mezzo-soprano voice. With wind, strings, keyboard & percussion. Songs, etc
Rands, Bernard
Ballad 1: mezzo-soprano, flute/altoflute, tenor, trombone, contra-bass, piano, percussion/ by Bernard Rands; [words by] Gilbert Sorrentino. — London: Universal, 1971. — 18p; obl. fol.
Duration 14 mins.
Unpriced

(B71-50362)

KFNE/NYLNUDW — Mezzo-soprano voice. With keyboard and percussion duet. Songs, etc
Tavener, John
Three surrealist songs: for mezzo-soprano, tape and piano doubling bongos by John Tavener; poems by Edward Lucie-Smith. — London: Chester, 1971. — 10p; 4to.
Unpriced

(B71-50893)

KFT — HIGH VOICE
KFTDH — Motets, Anthems, Hymns, etc
Bach, Johann Sebastian
Five spiritual songs (Geistliche Lieder)/ by Johann Sebastian Bach; realized for high voice and piano by Benjamin Britten [from Anna Magdalena's Notebook, 1725 and Schmelli's Gesangbuch, 1736], with English translations by Peter Pears. — London: Faber Music, 1970. — 12p; 4to.
German & English text.
£1.00

(B71-50062)

KFTDW — Songs, etc
Binkerd, Gordon
What sweeter musick: high voice/ music by Gordon Binkerd; poem by Robert Herrick. — New York; [London]: Boosey and Hawkes, 1971. — 6p; 4to.
This song has appeared with a different text entitled 'A bygone occasion'.
£0.40

(B71-50363)

Dowland, John
Fifty songs for high voice/ by John Dowland; selected and edited by Edmund H. Fellowes, revised by David Scott. — Revised ed. — London: Stainer and Bell. —
Book 1. — 1970. — 50p; 8vo.
Unpriced

(B71-50063)

Book 2. — 1970. — 52p; 8vo.
Unpriced

(B71-50064)

Griffes, Charles Tomlinson
Four German songs: medium (high) voice and piano/ by Charles T. Griffes; translated and edited by Donna K. Anderson. — New York: Peters; London: [Hinrichsen], 1970. — 13p; 4to.
Contents:- Am Kreuzweg wird begraben. They buried him at the crossroads; text by H. Heine. — An den Wind. To the wind; text by N. Lenau. — Meeres Stille. Calm sea; text by J.W. von Goethe. — So halt' ich endlich dich umfangen. At last I hold you; text by E. Geibel.
£1.10
Primary classification KFVDW

(B71-50365)

Griffes, Charles Tomlinson
Four impressions: medium (high) voice and piano/ by Charles T. Griffes; editor Donna K. Anderson, [words by] Oscar Wilde. — New York: Peters; London: [Hinrichsen], 1970. — 19p; 4to.
'As in the original Wilde poems, Griffes' texts are in English although the titles are French'. — Publisher's note. — Contents:- Le Jardin. The garden. — 2.Impression du matin. Early morning in London. — 3.La Mer. The sea. — 4.Le Réveillon. Dawn.
£1.10
Primary classification KFVDW

(B71-50366)

Joubert, John
Six poems of Emily Brontë. Op.63: for high voice and piano/ by John Joubert. — Borough Green: Novello, 1971. — 34p; 4to.
£1.75

(B71-50895)

Roe, Betty
Ponder' songs of the seasons: for high voice and piano/ by Betty Roe; words by Barbara Softley. — London: Thames, 1971. — 16p; 4to.
Unpriced

(B71-50894)

KFV — MIDDLE VOICE
Beethoven, Ludwig van
La Tivanna, Kinsky 125: canzonetta for medium voice and piano/ by Ludwig van Beethoven; edited by Alan Tyson, words by William Wennington. — Borough Green: Novello, 1970. — 4p; 4to.
£0.20

(B71-50364)

Griffes, Charles Tomlinson
Four German songs: medium (high) voice and piano/ by Charles T.
Griffes; translated and edited by Donna K. Anderson. — New York:
Peters; London: [Hinrichsen], 1970. — 13p; 4to.
Contents:- Am Kreuzweg wird begraben. They buried him at the crossroads;
text by H. Heine. — An den Wind. To the wind; text by N. Lenau. — Meeres
Stille. Calm sea; text by J.W. von Goethe. — So halt' ich endlich dich
umfangen. At last I hold you; text by E. Geibel.
£1.10
Also classified at KFTDW

(B71-50365)

Griffes, Charles Tomlinson
Four impressions: medium (high) voice and piano/ by Charles T.
Griffes; editor Donna K. Anderson, [words by] Oscar Wilde. — New
York: Peters; London: [Hinrichsen], 1970. — 19p; 4to.
'As in the original Wilde poems, Griffes' texts are in English although the titles
are French'. — Publisher's note. — Contents:- Le Jardin. The garden. —
2.Impression du matin. Early morning in London. — 3.La Mer. The sea. —
4.Le Réveillon. Dawn.
£1.10
Also classified at KFTDW

(B71-50366)

KFX — LOW VOICE
Binkerd, Gordon
What sweeter musick: low voice/ music by Gordon Binkerd; poem
by Robert Herrick. — New York; [London]: Boosey and Hawkes,
1971. — 6p; 4to.
This song has appeared with a different text entitled 'A bygone occasion'.
£0.40

(B71-50367)

Dowland, John
Fifty songs for low voice/ by John Dowland; selected and edited by
Edmund H. Fellowes, revised by David Scott. — Revised ed. —
London: Stainer and Bell. —
Book 1. — 1970. — 50p; 8vo.
Unpriced

(B71-50065)

Book 2. — 1970. — 52p; 8vo.
Unpriced

(B71-50066)

KG — MALE VOICE
KGHE/VRPDW — Tenor voice. With flute & piano. Songs, etc
Rameau, Jean Philippe
Arias: for tenor, flute, continuo/ by J. Ph. Rameau; [edited by] Renée
Viollier. — London: Musica rara. —
Each volume consists of two scores, one with and the other without a
realisation of the keyboard continuo.
Vol.1. — 1971. — 39p; 4to.
£3.15

(B71-50368)

KGNDW — Baritone voice. Songs, etc
Bliss, *Sir* **Arthur**
[Serenade. Excerpts]. Two love songs: for baritone and orchestra/ by
Arthur Bliss. — London: Oxford University Press, 1971. — 15p; 4to.
Piano score. — Contents:- Fair is my love; words by Edmund Spenser. — In
praise of his Daphnis; words by Sir J. Wotton.
ISBN 0 19 345166 2 : £0.75

(B71-50369)

Reutter, Hermann
[Der Tod des Empedokles. Excerpts]. Drei Monologue des
Empedokles von Friedrich Hölderlin: für Bariton und Klavier oder
Orchester/ [by] Hermann Reutter. — Mainz, London: Schott, 1971.
— 20p; 4to.
£1.30

(B71-50370)

KGNE/NUPNRDW — Baritone voice. With woodwind, string &
keyboard quartet. Songs, etc
Sutermeister, Heinrich
Vier Lieder Bariton: Fassung mit Violine, Flöte, Oboe, Faggott und
Cembalo/ [by] Heinrich Sutermeister; nach Texten schweizerischer
Minnesänger. — Mainz; London: Schott, 1971. — 4to.
Score (40p.) & 4 parts.
£2.40

(B71-50371)

LH — DANCES
LH/G/AYD — Folk dances. Collections England
Fleming-Williams, Nan
A popular selection of English dance airs/ edited by Nan
Fleming-Williams and Pat Shaw. — London: English Folk Dance and
Song Society. —
Book 4: Sword and ceremony. — 1971. — 20p; obl.8vo.
£0.25

(B71-50896)

LJ — Miscellaneous works
Cardew, Cornelius
Treatise handbook including Bun no.2, Volo solo/ by Cornelius
Cardew. — London: Peters, [Hinrichsen], 1971. — 72p; 4to.
Duration 10 mins.
£3.50

(B71-50372)

Cardew, Cornelius
Volo solo: for a virtuoso performer on any instrument/ by Cornelius
Cardew. — London: Peters, [Hinrichsen], 1971. — 16p; 4to.
£0.90

(B71-50373)

LN — ENSEMBLES
Brace, Geoffrey
Something to play: an instrumental workbook for the classroom/
compiled by Geoffrey Brace. — London: Cambridge University
Press, 1971. — 40p; 4to.
Unpriced

(B71-50897)

Heider, Werner
Edition: multiple Musik für Instrumental - oder Vokalgruppen/ [by]
Werner Heider. — Frankfurt: Litolff, Peters; London: [Hinrichsen],
1970. — 7p; 4to.
£0.90
Also classified at EL; JN

(B71-50374)

LNS — Quartets
Orton, Richard
Cycle: for two or four players/ by Richard Orton. — London: Ars
Viva: Schott, 1971. — 1v; fol.
The 'score' comprises three rotating concentric dials.
£2.25
Primary classification LNU

(B71-50067)

LNU — Duets
Arnell, Richard
Five inventions: for two or more treble-clef instruments of equal
pitch/ by Richard Arnell. — London: Hinrichsen, 1970. — 9p; 4to.
Unpriced

(B71-50375)

Orton, Richard
Cycle: for two or four players/ by Richard Orton. — London: Ars
Viva: Schott, 1971. — 1v; fol.
The 'score' comprises three rotating concentric dials.
£2.25
Also classified at LNS

(B71-50067)

LXNUE/X — Bass instruments. Duets. Sonatas. Canons
Telemann, Georg Philipp
Sonatas in canon for two bass instruments. Opus 5/ by Georg Philipp
Telemann; edited by Rodney Slatford. — London: Yorke. —
Vol.2: Sonata in C minor, no.3; [and], Sonata in C major, no.4. — 1971. — 7p;
4to.
Unpriced

(B71-50898)

M/T — VARIATIONS
Hand, Colin
Variations and fugue on a Cheshire souling song: for orchestra/ by
Colin Hand. — Borough Green: Novello, 1971. — 8vo.
Score (66p.) & 21 parts.
Unpriced

(B71-50899)

MH — DANCES
Debussy, Claude
[Petite suite. Excerpts]. Ballet/ by Claude Debussy; arranged by
David Stone. — London: Boosey and Hawkes, 1971. — 4to.
Score (26p.) & 26 parts.
£1.05

(B71-50901)

MJ — MISCELLANEOUS WORKS
Chagrin, Francis
Lullaby: for four solo instruments, optional solo bassoon or solo
cello, and string orchestra or piano/ by Francis Chagrin. — Borough
Green: Novello, 1971. — 4to.
Score (12p.) & 11 parts.
£1.55

(B71-50902)

Gluck, Christoph Willibald von
[Alceste. Excerpts]. Overture: arranged for school, amateur or
professional orchestras [or] for strings with optional full orchestra/
by C.P. Arnell & K.W. Rokos. — London: Bosworth. 1970. — 28p;
4to.
Score & 14 parts. Duration 5 mins.
£0.375

(B71-50068)

Szőnyi, Erzsebét
Allegro: per orchestra/ [by] Erzsebét Szőnyi. — London: Boosey and
Hawkes, 1971. — 4to.
Score (31p.) & 17 parts.
y1.10

(B71-50903)

MK — ARRANGEMENTS
MK/AH — Dances
Kodály, Zoltán
[Children's dances. Excerpts]. Four dances [nos 9, 5, 4 & 12]/
arranged for orchestra by Denis Bloodworth and Alan Fluck. —
London: Boosey and Hawkes, 1970. — 30p; 4to.
Score (£1.70) & 21 parts (£2.30).
£4.00

(B71-50069)

MM — WORKS FOR SYMPHONY ORCHESTRA
MM/JR — Film music
Ireland, John
The overlanders: suite for orchestra/ / [from the film]/ by John
Ireland; arranged by Charles Mackerras. — London: Boosey and
Hawkes, 1971. — 116p; 8vo.
Miniature score. Duration 18 mins.
£2.50
Primary classification MMG

(B71-50070)

Ireland, John
[The overlanders]. Two symphonic studies [on themes from 'The
overlanders']/ by John Ireland; arranged by Geoffrey Bush. —
London: Boosey and Hawkes, 1971. — 59p; 8vo.
Miniature score. Duration 11 mins.
£0.65
Primary classification MMJ

(B71-50072)

Thomson, Virgil
[Journey to America. Excerpts]. Pilgrims and pioneers: for
orchestra/ by Virgil Thomson. — New York: Schirmer; [London]:
[Chappell], 1971. — 4to.
Score (54p.) & 19 parts.
Unpriced

(B71-50376)

MME — Symphonies
Baird, Tadeusz
Symphony no.3/ by Tadeusz Baird. — London: Chester, 1971. —
32p; fol.
Unpriced

(B71-50377)

Berkeley, Lennox
Symphony no.3 in one movement/ by Lennox Berkeley. — London:
Chester, 1971. — 83p; 8vo.
Miniature score. Duration 14 mins.
Unpriced

(B71-50378)

Gerhard, Roberto
Symphony 4 'New York'/ by Roberto Gerhard. — London: Oxford
University Press, 1971. — 197p; 8vo.
Miniature score. Duration 26 mins.
ISBN 0 19 363614 x : £4.50

(B71-50379)

Haydn, Joseph
Symphony no.50 in C major/ by Joseph Haydn; edited by Gwilym
Beechey. — London: Eulenburg, 1970. — ix,49p; 8vo.
Miniature score.
Unpriced

(B71-50380)

Hoddinott, Alun
Symphony no.3. Opus 61/ by-Alun Hoddinott. — London: Oxford
University Press, 1971. — 119p; 8vo.
Duration 21 mins.
ISBN 0 19 364551 3 : £3.00

(B71-50381)

Hoddinott, Alun
Symphony no.4. Op.70/ by Alun Hoddinott. — London: Oxford
University Press, 1971. — 119p; 8vo.
Study score.
ISBN 0 19 364553 x : y3.50

(B71-50904)

Kadosa, Pál
Symphony no.8. Op.66/ by Pál Kadosa. — London: Boosey and
Hawkes, 1971. — 143p; 8vo.
Unpriced

(B71-50382)

Klemperer, Otto
Symphony no.2/ by Otto Klemperer. — London: Hinrichsen. 1970. —
67p; fol.
£5.00

(B71-50383)

Mozart, Wolfgang Amadeus
[Symphony no.35 in D major. K.385, 'Haffner']. Symphony in D.
K.385, 'Haffner' symphony/ by Wolfgang Amadeus Mozart: edited
from the autograph manuscript and the authentic first edition of
Artaria by doctoral students of the City University of New York
under the supervision of H.C. Robbins Landon. — London: Faber
Music, 1971. — xv,48p; 8vo.
£2.75

(B71-50905)

MMG — Suites
Bliss, *Sir* Arthur
Conquest of the air: suite/ by Arthur Bliss. — London: Boosey and
Hawkes, 1971. — 70p; 4to.
Duration 12 min.
Unpriced

(B71-50384)

Ireland, John
The overlanders: suite for orchestra/ / [from the film]/ by John
Ireland; arranged by Charles Mackerras. — London: Boosey and
Hawkes, 1971. — 116p; 8vo.
Miniature score. Duration 18 mins.
£2.50
Also classified at MM/JR

(B71-50070)

MMH — Dances
Barber, Samuel
[Vanessa. Excerpts]. Under the willow tree: country dance, for
orchestra/ by Samuel Barber. — New York: Schirmer; London:
Chappell, 1971. — 22p; 4to.
Unpriced

(B71-50385)

Hoddinott, Alun
Investiture dances: for orchestra. Opus 66/ by Alun Hoddinott. —
London: Oxford University Press, 1971. — 64p; 8vo.
Miniature score. Duration 8-9 mins.
ISBN 0 19 364505 x : £2.00

(B71-50386)

MMJ — Miscellaneous works
Bacon, Ernst
The muffin man: for orchestra/ by Ernst Bacon. — New York:
Schirmer; [London]: [Chappell], 1971. — 4to.
Score (38p.) & 29 parts.
Unpriced

(B71-50387)

Birtwistle, Harrison
Nomos: [for orchestra]/ [by] Harrison Birtwistle. — London:
Universal, 1971. — 66p; 8vo.
Unpriced

(B71-50388)

Cardew, Cornelius
Bun no.2: for orchestra/ by Cornelius Cardew. — London: Peters,
[Hinrichsen], 1971. — 32p; 4to.
Unpriced

(B71-50389)

Chavez, Carlos
Clio: symphonic ode/ by Carlos Chavez. — New York: Schirmer;
London: Chappell, 1970. — 38p; 8vo.
Miniature score.
Unpriced

(B71-50071)

Christou, Jani
Enantiodromia: [for orchestra]/ [by Jani Christou]. — London:
Chester, 1971. — 19p; fol.
Unpriced

(B71-50906)

Copland, Aaron
Happy anniversary: a well-known tune/ arranged for symphony
orchestra by Aaron Copland. — London: Boosey and Hawkes, 1971.
— 5p; 4to.
Unpriced

(B71-50911)

Durkó, Zsolt
Fioriture: for orchestra/ by Zsolt Durkó. — London: Boosey and Hawkes, 1971. — 35p; 8vo.
Miniature score. Duration 11 min.
£0.75

(B71-50907)

Feldman, Morton
On time and the instrumental factor/ by Morton Feldman. — London: Universal, 1971. — 14p; 8vo.
Miniature score.
Unpriced

(B71-50390)

Halffter, Cristobal
Anillos: [for orchestra]/ [by] Cristobal Halffter. — Revised version. — London: Universal, 1971. — 39p; fol.
Unpriced

(B71-50391)

Hamilton, Iain
Cantus: for orchestra (1964)/ by Iain Hamilton. — London: Schott, 1971. — 35p; 8vo.
Miniature score.
£0.60

(B71-50908)

Hirsch, Hans Ludwig
Omaggi a Rossini: für Orchester/ [by] Hans Ludwig Hirsch. — Frankfurt: Litolff, Peters: London: [Hinrichsen], 1970. — 88p; 8vo.
Study score.
£2.50

(B71-50392)

Huber, Klaus
Tenebrae: für grosses Orchester/ [by] Klaus Huber. — Mainz: Ars Viva; London: Schott, 1969. — 65p; fol.
Study score.
£5.60

(B71-50393)

Ireland, John
[The overlanders]. Two symphonic studies [on themes from 'The overlanders']/ by John Ireland; arranged by Geoffrey Bush. — London: Boosey and Hawkes, 1971. — 59p; 8vo.
Miniature score. Duration 11 mins.
£0.65
Also classified at MM/JR

(B71-50072)

Kupkovic, Ladislav
Dio: Orchesterspiele mit Dirigieren/ [by] Ladislav Kupkovic. — London: Universal, 1971. — 88p; fol.
Unpriced

(B71-50394)

McCabe, John
Concertante music/ by John McCabe. — London: Novello, 1971. — 125p; 4to.
Duration 24 mins.
£2.50

(B71-50395)

Panufnik, Andrzej
Nocturne: for orchestra/ by Andrzej Panufnik. — London: Boosey and Hawkes, 1971. — 15p; 8vo.
Miniature score. Duration 6 mins.
Unpriced

(B71-50396)

Panufnik, Andrzej
Nocturne: for orchestra/ by Andrzej Panufnik. — London: Boosey and Hawkes, 1971. — 15p; fol.8vo.
Duration 16 mins.
Unpriced

(B71-50397)

Schnittke, Alfred
Pianissimo.../ [by] Alfred Schnittke. — London: Universal, 1971. — 25p; fol.
Unpriced

(B71-50398)

Schubert, Franz
Overture in C major (in the Italian style) D. 591/ by Franz Schubert. — London: Eulenburg, 1971. — 47p; 8vo.
Miniature score.
£0.75

(B71-50909)

Schubert, Franz
Overture in D major (in the Italian style) D. 590/ by Franz Schubert. — London: Eulenberg, 1971. — 47p; 8vo.
Miniature score.
£0.75

(B71-50910)

Stravinsky, Igor
[Four études for orchestra]. Quatre études: pour orchestre., [by] Igor Stravinsky. — Revision 1952. — London: Boosey and Hawkes, 1971. — 51p; 8vo.
Miniature score. Duration 12 mins.
£0.65

(B71-50073)

Stravinsky, Igor
[Four études for orchestra]. Quatre études: pour orchestre/ [by] Igor Stravinsky. — Revision 1952. — London: Boosey and Hawkes, 1970. — 51p; 4to.
Unpriced

(B71-50399)

Vaughan Williams, Ralph
Norfolk rhapsody: founded on folk-tunes collected orally in Norfolk and set as an orchestral piece/ by Ralph Vaughan Williams. — London: Oxford University Press, 1971. — 40p; 8vo.
ISBN 0 19 369227 9 : £1.75

(B71-50400)

Zimmerman, Bernd Alois
Photoptosis: Prelude für grosser Orchester/ [by] Bernd Alois Zimmerman. — Mainz; London: Schott, 1971. — 87p; 4to.
£3.20

(B71-50074)

Zimmerman, Bernd Alois
Stille und Umkehr: Orchesterskizzen/ [by] Bernd Alois Zimmerman. — Mainz; London: Schott, 1971. — 30p; 8vo.
Miniature score.
£1.90

(B71-50401)

MMK/JM — Arrangements. Incidental music
Ireland, John
Scherzo & cortege, on themes from Julius Caesar/ by John Ireland arranged by Geoffrey Bush. — London: Boosey and Hawkes, 1971. — 34p; 8vo.
Incidental music for a radio production. Duration 6 mins. Miniature score.
£1.10

(B71-50075)

MP — WORKS FOR SOLO INSTRUMENT (S) & ORCHESTRA
MPQ/T — Piano & orchestra. Variations
Hindemith, Paul
Thema mit vier Variationen: die Vier Temperamente, für Klavier und Streichorchester/ by Paul Hindemith. — Mainz; London: Schott, 1971. — 91p; 8vo.
Miniature score.
£2.80

(B71-50402)

MPQNVFL — One piano, 4 hands & orchestra. Concertinos
McCabe, John
Concertino for piano duet & orchestra (1968)/ by John McCabe. — Borough Green: Novello, 1970. — 52p; 8vo.
Miniature score.
Unpriced

(B71-50076)

MPR — Organ & orchestra
Hindemith, Paul
Kammermusik no.7: Konzert für Orgel und Kammerorchester. Opus 46, no.2/ by Paul Hindemith. — Mainz; London: Schott, 1971. — 39p; 4to.
Miniature score. Duration 17 mins.
£1.70

(B71-50912)

MPSF — Violin & orchestra. Concertos
Einem, Gottfried von
[Concerto for violin. Op.33]. Violin concerto. Op.33/ by Gottfried von Einem. — London: Boosey and Hawkes, 1970. — 152p; 8vo.
Miniature score. Duration 33 mins.
Unpriced

(B71-50077)

MPSQ — Viola and orchestra
Bozay, Attila
Pezzo concertato. Op.11: per viola solo e orchestra/ by Attila Bozay. — London: Boosey and Hawkes, 1970. — 60p; 8vo.
Miniature score.
£1.15

(B71-50078)

MPSQ — Viola & orchestra
Henze, Hans Werner
  Compases para preguntas ensimismadas: music for viola and 22 players/ by Hans Werner Henze. — Mainz; London: Schott, 1971. — 84p; 4to.
  £3.20

(B71-50913)

MPSQQF — Viola d'amore & orchestra. Concertos
Hindemith, Paul
  Kammermusik no.6. Op.46, no.1: Konzert für Viola d'amore und Kammerorchester/ [by] Paul Hindemith. — London: Schott, 1971. — 35p; 8vo.
  Study score.
  £1.60

(B71-50403)

MPSRF — Cello & orchestra. Concertos
Bliss, *Sir* **Arthur**
  Concerto for cello & orchestra/ by Arthur Bliss; cello part edited by Mstislav Rostropovich. — Borough Green: Novello, 1971. — 120p; 4to.
  Duration 26 min.
  £2.50

(B71-50404)

MPTQ — Harp & orchestra
Berio, Luciano
  Chemins I (sur Sequenza II): per arpa principale ed orchestra/ [by] Luciano Berio. — London: Universal, 1971. — 33p; fol.
  Unpriced

(B71-50405)

MPTQF — Harp & orchestra. Concertos
Hoddinott, Alun
  Concerto for harp. Opus 11/ by Alun Hoddinott. — London: Oxford University Press, 1971. — 149p; 8vo.
  Duration 17 mins.
  ISBN 0 19 364487 8 : £3.00

(B71-50406)

MR — WORKS FOR CHAMBER ORCHESTRA
MRE — Symphonies
Bach, Wilhelm Friedemann
  [Symphony in D major. Falck 64]. Sinfonie D-Dur. Falck 64/ by Wilhelm Friedemann Bach; Erstmals herausgegeben von Walter Lebermann. — Mainz; London: Schott, 1971. — 24p; 4to.
  £1.20

(B71-50407)

Dittersdorf, Carl Ditters von
  [Sinfonia in D major]. Sinfonia, D-Dur/ [by] Carl Ditters von Dittersdorf. Krebs vakat; Erstmals herausgegeben von Walter Lebermann. — Mainz; London: Schott, 1971. — 26p; 4to.
  £1.50

(B71-50408)

Richter, Franz Xaver
  [Symphony with fugue in G minor]. Sinfonia con fuga, g-Moll/ [by] Franz Xaver Richter; herausgegeben von Günter Kehr. — Mainz; London: Schott, 1971. — 28p; 4to.
  £1.50

(B71-50409)

MRG — Suites
Blomdahl, Karl-Birger
  Game for eight: choreographic suite for chamber orchestra/ by Karl-Birger Blomdahl. — London: Schott, 1971. — 90p; 8vo.
  Miniature score.
  £1.75

(B71-50914)

MRHP — Gigues
Rathaus, Karol
  Praeludium and gigue: [for orchestra]/ by Karol Rathaus. — New York; [London]: Boosey and Hawkes, 1971. — 32p; 4to.
  Duration 7 mins.
  £2.10

(B71-50410)

MRJ — Miscellaneous works
Boyce, William
  Twelve overtures, by William Boyce; edited, with realization of the basso continuo by Richard Platt/ No.2: [in G major]; for oboes, flutes, horns, strings, and continuo. — London: Oxford University Press, 1971. — 4to.
  Score (14p.) & 7 parts.
  ISBN 0 19 361812 5 : £1.25

(B71-50916)

Boyce, William
  Twelve overtures, by William Boyce; edited, with realization of the basso continuo by Richard Platt/ No.4: [in D major]; for oboes, trumpets, horns, timpani, strings, and continuo. — London: Oxford University Press, 1971. — 4to.
  Score (14p.) & 7 parts.
  ISBN 0 19 361834 6 : £1.25

(B71-50918)

Boyce, William
  Twelve overtures/ by William Boyce; edited, with realization of the basso continuo by Richard Platt. — London: Oxford University Press. —
  Score (14p.) & 7 parts.
  No.1: [in D major]; for oboes, strings and continuo. — 1971. — 4to.
  ISBN 0 19 361802 8 : £1.25

(B71-50915)

  No.3: [in Bflat major]; for oboes, strings and continuo. — 1971. — 4to.
  ISBN 0 19 361824 9 : Unpriced

(B71-50917)

  No.5: [in F major]; for oboes, strings and continuo. — 1971. — 4to.
  ISBN 0 19 361849 4 : £1.25

(B71-50919)

  No.6: [in D minor]; for oboes, flutes, horns, strings, and continuo. — 1971. — 4to.
  ISBN 0 19 361859 1 : £1.25

(B71-50920)

Feldman, Morton
  Madame Press died last week at ninety: [for small orchestra]/ [by] Morton Feldman. — London: Universal, 1971. — 5p; obl.4to.
  Duration 4 min.
  Unpriced

(B71-50411)

Fortner, Wolfgang
  Zyklus (1964): Fassung für Violoncello, Bläser, Harfen und Schlagzeug (1969)/ by Wolfgang Fortner. — Mainz; London: Schott, 1971. — 46p; 8vo.
  Miniature score. Duration 18 mins.
  £2.00

(B71-50412)

Hovhaness, Alan
  Mountains and rivers without end. Op.225: chamber symphony for 10 players/ by Alan Hovhaness. — New York: Peters; London: Hinrichsen, 1969. — 48p; 8vo.
  £1.50

(B71-50413)

Lipkin, Malcolm
  Mosaics: for chamber orchestra/ by Malcolm Lipkin. — London: Chester, 1971. — 28p; 8vo.
  Duration 10 mins.
  Unpriced

(B71-50921)

Panufnik, Andrzej
  Autumn music/ by Andrzej Panufnik. — London: Boosey and Hawkes, 1971. — 20p; 4to.
  £1.50

(B71-50922)

Panufnik, Andrzej
  Autumn music/ by Andrzej Panufnik. — London: Boosey and Hawkes, 1971. — 20p; 8vo.
  Miniature score.
  £0.50

(B71-50923)

MRK — Arrangements
Schubert, Franz
  [Overture for strings in C minor. D.8]. Ouverture, C-moll: für Kammerorchester, nach der Ouverture C-moll für Streicher/ [by] Franz Schubert; instrumentiert von Wolfgang Hofman. — Frankfurt: Litolff, Peters; London: [Hinrichsen], 1970. — 32p; 4to.
  Unpriced

(B71-50414)

MS — WORKS FOR LIGHT ORCHESTRA
MSHJMR — Dances. Cha-chas
Cartwright, Kenneth
  Clarinet cha-cha: for orchestra/ [by] Kenneth Cartwright. — London: Feldman, 1971. — 24p; 4to.
  Unpriced

(B71-50415)

MV — WORKS FOR ORCHESTRAS INCLUDING TOY INSTRUMENTS
MVF — Toy instruments. Concertos
Elenor, John
  Concerto for toy orchestra: in one movement/ by John Elenor. — Borough Green: Novello, 1971. — Score (14p) and 8 parts; 4to.
  £0.95

(B71-50416)

NU – WIND, STRINGS & KEYBOARD
NUPNSE – Woodwind, strings & keyboard. Quartets. Sonatas
Janitsch, Johann Gottlieb
[Sonata for flute, violin, oboe & basso continuo in C major. Op.4].
Sonata da camera in C major. Op.4: for flute, violin, oboe & basso
continuo/ by Johann Gottlieb Janitsch, [edited by] David Lasocki,
realisation of basso continuo by Robert Paul Block. – London:
Musica rara, 1971. – 4to.
Score (23p.) & 4 parts.
£1.50

(B71-50079)

NUTNTK/LF – Clarinet, string & keyboard trios. Arrangements.
Concertos
Bach, Johann Sebastian
[Concerto for violin & oboe. S1060]. Concerto in C minor: for violin,
oboe and piano or two violins & piano/ by Johann Sebastian Bach. –
New York: Schirmer; London: Chappell, 1970. – 4to.
Score (23p.) & 3 parts.
Unpriced

(B71-50417)

NUVNT – Clarinet, string & keyboard. Trios
Gál, Hans
Trio for violin, clarinet and pianoforte. Op.97/ by Hans Gál. –
London: Simrock, 1971. – 460.
Score (32p.) & part.
Unpriced

(B71-50924)

NUXPNP – Brass, strings & keyboard. Septets
Macero, Ted
One-three quarters: piccolo (flute), violin, violoncello, trombone, tuba
and two pianos/ by Ted Macero. – New York: Peters; London:
[Hinrichsen], 1970. – 4to.
Score & 6 parts.
£1.75

(B71-50418)

NUXUNSE – Trombone, strings & keyboard. Quartets. Sonatas
Bertali, Antonio
[Sonata for two violins, trombone & basso continuo, no.1, in D
minor]. Sonata à 3, no.1 in D minor: for 2 violins, trombone & organ
continuo/ by Antonio Bertali; [edited by] John D. Hill, Robert Paul
Block. – London: Musica rara, 1971. – 4to.
Score (12p.) & 4 parts.
Unpriced

(B71-50419)

Bertali, Antonio
[Sonata for two violins, trombone & basso continuo, no.2, in D
minor]. Sonata à 3, no.2 in D minor: for 2 violins, trombone & organ
continuo/ by Antonio Bertali; [edited by] John D. Hill, Robert Paul
Block. – London: Musica rara, 1971. – 4to.
Score (12p.) & 4 parts.
Unpriced

(B71-50420)

NV – WIND & STRINGS
NVNR – Quintets
Reicha, Anton Joseph
[Quintet for horn and strings in E major. Op.106]. Quintet in E
major. Op.106: for horn and string quartet (double bass ad lib)/ by
Anton Reicha; [edited by] David Lasocki, William Blackwell. –
London: Musica rara, 1971. – 4to.
Score (35p.) & 6 parts.
Unpriced

(B71-50926)

Spinner, Leopold
Quintet for clarinet, horn, bassoon, guitar and double bass. Op.14/
by Leopold Spinner. – London: Boosey and Hawkes, 1971. – 16p;
4to.
Unpriced

(B71-50421)

NVNS – Wind & strings. Quartets
Krommer, Franz
[Quartet for bassoon, 2 violas & cello in B flat major. Op.46, no.1].
Quartet in B flat. Op.46, no.1: for bassoon, 2 violas & cello or
bassoon, violin, viola and cello/ by Franz Krommer; [edited] by
Roger Hellyer. – London: Musica rara, 1970. – 4to.
Score (27p.) & 5 parts.
Unpriced

(B71-50422)

NVRNR – Flute & strings. Quintets
Dushkin, Dorothy
Quintet for flute and strings/ by Dorothy Dushkin. – London:
Musica rara, 1971. – 4to.
Score (28p.) & 5 parts.
Unpriced

(B71-50927)

NVSK – Recorders & strings
Parkinson, Patricia
Two little pieces: for recorders & strings/ by Patricia Parkinson;
arranged by Patricia Parkinson. – London: Feldman, 1971. – 7p;
4to.
Contents:- Schubert, Franz. Cradle song. – Schumann, Robert. Soldier's
march.
Unpriced

(B71-50928)

NVSRNK/DW/AY – Descant recorder and strings. Arrangements.
Songs. Collections
Medley of melodies for descant recorder: arranged for classroom
ensemble with chord symbol guide for piano, guitar, uke and chime
bars, [with] chord diagrams for guitar and ukelele. – London:
Feldman, 1971. – 16p; 4to.
Unpriced

(B71-50929)

NVTNS – Oboe & strings. Quartets
Berkeley, Lennox
[Quartet for oboe & strings]. Oboe quartet/ by Lennox Berkeley. –
London: Chester, 1971. – 5v; 4to.
Unpriced

(B71-50423)

Holliger, Heinz
[Trio for oboe, viola and harp]. Trio für Oboe, Viola und Harfe/ [by]
Heinz Holliger. – Mainz; London: Schott, 1971. – 3pt; 4to.
Unpriced

(B71-50930)

Le Fanu, Nicola
Variations for oboe quartet/ by Nicola Le Fanu. – Borough Green:
Novello, 1971. – 4to.
Score (27p.) & 4 parts.
£1.75

(B71-50931)

NWPNSE – Woodwind & keyboard quartet. Sonatas
Janitsch, Johann Gottlieb
[Sonata for flute, violin, oboe and basso continuo in C major. Op.4].
Sonata da camera in C major. Op.4: for flute, violin, oboe and basso
continuo/ by Johann Gottlieb Janitsch; [edited by] David Lasocki,
realisation of the basso continuo by Robert Paul Block. – London:
Musica rara, 1970. – 4to.
Score (23p.) & 5 parts.
£1.50

(B71-50424)

NWXP – BRASS & KEYBOARD
NWXPNM – Nonets
Weeks, John
Jubilate: for organ and brass/ by John Weeks. – London:
Hinrichsen, 1970. – 12p; 4to.
£1.50

(B71-50425)

NWXPNP – Brass & keyboard. Septets
Dickinson, Peter
Fanfares and elegies: for brass and organ/ by Peter Dickinson. –
Borough Green: Novello, 1971. – 4to.
Score (22p.) & 6 parts.
£1.25

(B71-50426)

NWXPNS – Brass and keyboard. Quartets
Hingeston, John
Fantasia for 2 trumpets (cornetti), bass trombone (sackbutt) and
organ continuo/ by John Hingeston; [edited by] Robert Paul Block.
– London: Musica rara, 1971. – 4to.
Score (5p.) & 3 parts.
Unpriced

(B71-50936)

NWXPNT – Trios
Hingeston, John
Fantasia for cornetto (trumpet), sackbutt (bass trombone) and organ
continuo/ by John Hingeston; [edited by] Robert Paul Block. –
London: Musica rara, 1971. – 4to.
Score (5p.) & 2 parts.
Unpriced

(B71-50934)

NX – STRINGS & KEYBOARD
NXNR – Quintets
Elgar, Sir Edward, bart
[Quintet for piano and strings in A minor. Op. 84]. Piano quintet in
A minor. Op. 84/ by Edward Elgar. – London: Eulenburg, 1971. –
67p; 8vo.
Miniature score.
£0.35

(B71-50935)

NXNT — Trios
Jungk, Klaus
Alterationen. Op.54: für Violine, Violoncello und Klavier/ [by] Klaus Jungk. — Frankfurt: Litolff, Peters; London: [Hinrichsen], 1970. — 4to.
Score (12p.) & part.
£3.00

(B71-50427)

Kurzbach, Paul
[Trio for violin, cello & piano]. Trio für Violine, Violoncello und Klavier/ [by] Paul Kurzbach. — Leipzig: Litolff; [London]: [Hinrichsen], 1971. — 31p; 4to.
£1.40

(B71-50428)

NXNTE — Trios. Sonatas
Francoeur, Francois
[Sonata for violin, cello and basso continuo in E major. Liv.2, no.12]. Triosonate, E-Dur: für Violine, Violoncello oder Viola da gamba und Basso continuo/ [by] Francois Francoeur le Cadet; herausgegeben von Hugo Ruf. — Mainz; London: Schott, 1971. — 4to.
Score (16p.) & 3 parts.
£1.20

(B71-50430)

Telemann, Georg Philipp
[Sonata for violin, viola da gamba & harpsichord in G minor]. Sonate g-moll für Violine, Viola da gamba (Viola) und Cembalo [by] Georg Philipp Telemann; herausgegeben von Karlheinz Schultz-Hauser. — Leipzig: Peters; London: Hinrichsen, 1969. — 4to.
Score (17p) & 3 parts.
£1.05

(B71-50429)

NYD — WIND, STRINGS, KEYBOARD & PERCUSSION
NYDPNQ — Woodwind, strings, keyboard & percussion. Sextets
Rands, Bernard
Tableau: flute/alto flute, B flat clarinet/bass clarinet, viola, cello, piano/celesta, percussion/ by Bernard Rands. — London: Universal, 1971. — 16p; obl. fol.
Unpriced

(B71-50431)

NYDRK/DW/AYB — Flute, string, keyboard & percussion.
Arrangements. Songs, etc. Collections. Europe
Buhé, Klaus
Europäische Volks-und Tanzweisen: für Flöte, Akkordeon I/II, Gitarre (banjo), Bass und Schlagzeug/ [arranged by] Klaus Buhé. — Mainz; London: Schott, 1971. — 46p; 4to.
£1.20

(B71-50432)

NYDRK/DW/AYT — Flute, string, keyboard & percussion.
Arrangements. Songs, etc. Collections. United States
Buhé, Klaus
Volks- und Tanzweisen aus Amerika: für Flöte, Akkordeon I/II (E-Gitarre), Gitarre (Banjo), Bass und Schlagzeug/ [arranged by] Klaus Buhé. — Mainz; London: Schott, 1971. — 38p; 4to.
£1.20

(B71-50433)

NYE — WIND, STRINGS & PERCUSSION
NYESK/AAY — Recorder, strings and percussion. Collections
Sadleir, Richard
Four easy scores: arranged for recorder, guitar and percussion/ by Dick Sadleir. — London: Feldman, 1971. — 8p; 4to.
£0.25

(B71-50937)

NYESK/DW/G/AYB — Recorder, strings & percussion.
Arrangements. Folksongs. Collections. Europe
Draths, Willi
Rund um die Welt: folkloristische Tanzmelodien für Blockflötenquartett (Streicher) und Schlagwerke, Gitarre ad lib/ bearbeitet von Willi Draths. — Mainz; London: Schott, 1971. — 31p; 4to.
£1.00

(B71-50434)

NYEVNR — Clarinet, strings and percussion. Quintets
Fink, Siegfried
Serenade in percussione: for clarinet, double-bass and percussion (3 players)/ [by] Siegfried Fink. — Hamburg; London: Simrock, 1971. — 4to.
Score & 5 parts.
£0.85

(B71-50435)

NYH — WIND & PERCUSSION
NYHNR — Quintets
Chihara, Paul
Willow, willow: for flute, tuba, and three percussionists/ by Paul Chihara. — Hollywood: Protone Music: Henmer Music; London: Hinrichsen, 1970. — 12p; 4to.
£1.75

(B71-50436)

NYHWNT — Bassoons & percussion. Trios
Chihara, Paul
Branches: for 2 bassoons and percussion/ by Paul Chihara. — New York: Peters; London: Hinrichsen, 1968. — 7p; 4to.
£1.25

(B71-50437)

NYHXPNNGN — Brass & percussion octets. Fanfares
Bliss, *Sir* Arthur
Fanfare for heroes: for 3 trumpets, 3 trombones, timpani & cymbals/ by Arthur Bliss. — Borough Green: Novello, 1971. — 8vo.
Score (4p.) & 8 parts.
Unpriced

(B71-50438)

NYL — KEYBOARD & PERCUSSION
NYLNS — Quartets
Mellnäs, Arne
Capricorn flakes: [for keyboard & percussion]/ by Arne Mellnäs. — New York: Peters; [London]: [Hinrichsen], 1970. — 2p; fol.
£2.00

(B71-50439)

Rudzinski, Zbigniew
[Quartet for two pianos and percussion]. Quartett für zwei Klaviere und Schlagzeug/ [by] Zbigniew Rudzinski. — Mainz; London: Schott, 1971. — 28p; obl.4to.
£1.80

(B71-50440)

PS — MUSIQUE CONCRETE
Kagel, Mauricio
Ludwig van: hommage von Beethoven/ by Mauricio Kagel. — London: Universal, 1971. — xii,[90]p; obl.fol.
The score consists of photographs of objects completely pasted over with compositions by Beethoven.
Unpriced

(B71-50441)

Ligeti, György
Artikulation: electronic music: an aural score/ [devised] by Rainer Wehinger. — Mainz; London: Schott, 1971. — 55p; obl.fol.
Unpriced

(B71-50080)

Reynolds, Roger
Traces: piano, cello, signal generator, ring modulator; 6 channels of taped sound/ by Roger Reynolds. — New York: Peters; London: Hinrichsen, 1969. — 18p; 4to.
£2.50

(B71-50442)

PW — KEYBOARD INSTRUMENTS
PW/EG — Sight reading
Keilmann, Wilhelm
Ich spiele vom Blatt: Schule des Prima-Vista-Spiels für Klavier und andere Tasteninstrumente/ [by] Wilhelm Keilmann. — Frankfurt: Litolff, Peters; London: Hinrichsen, 1970. — 58p; 4to.
£3.00

(B71-50443)

PWNU — KEYBOARD DUETS
PWNUK/LF — Arrangements. Concertos
Francaix, Jean
[Concerto for harpsichord]. Concerto pour clavecin et ensemble instrumental/ [by] Jean Francaix. — Mainz; London: Schott, 1971. — 53p; 4to.
£2.40

(B71-50444)

PWNV/AY — Keyboard duets, one keyboard instrument, 4 hands. Collections
Ferguson, Howard
Style and interpretation: an anthology of keyboard music, edited and annotated by Howard Ferguson/ Vol.5: Keyboard duets (1): 17th and 18th centuries. — London: Oxford University Press, 1971. — 78p; 4to.
ISBN 0 19 372628 9 : £1.25
Also classified at PWP/AY

(B71-50938)

Ferguson, Howard
Style and interpretation: an anthology of keyboard music, edited and annotated by Howard Ferguson/ Vol.6; Keyboard duets (2): 19th and 20th centuries. — London: Oxford University Press, 1971. — 77p; 4to.
ISBN 0 19 372629 7 : £1.25
Also classified at PWP/AY

(B71-50939)

PWP — KEYBOARD SOLOS
PWP/AY — Collections
Ferguson, Howard
Style and interpretation: an anthology of keyboard music, edited and annotated by Howard Ferguson/ Vol.5; Keyboard duets (1): 17th and 18th centuries. — London: Oxford University Press, 1971. — 78p; 4to.
ISBN 0 19 372628 9 : £1.25
Primary classification PWNV/AY

(B71-50938)

Ferguson, Howard
Style and interpretation: an anthology of keyboard music, edited and annotated by Howard Ferguson/ Vol.6; Keyboard duets (2): 19th and 20th centuries. — London: Oxford University Press, 1971. — 77p; 4to.
ISBN 0 19 372629 7 : £1.25
Primary classification PWNV/AY

(B71-50939)

PWP/AYD — Collections. England
Ferguson, Howard
Early English keyboard music: an anthology/ edited by Howard Ferguson. — London: Oxford University Press. —
Vol.1. — 1971. — 64p; 4to.
ISBN 0 19 372622 x : £0.95

(B71-50081)

Vol.2. — 1971. — 64p; 4to.
ISBN 0 19 372623 8 : £0.95

(B71-50082)

PWP/AZ — Collected works of individual composers
Musica Britanica: a national collection of music/ Vol.19; John Bull: Keyboard music II, transcribed and edited by Thurston Dart. — 2nd revised ed. — London: Stainer and Bell, 1970. — xxiii,238p; fol.
Unpriced
Primary classification C/AYD

(B71-50002)

PWP/T — Variations
Hassler, Hans Leo
Variationen 'Ich geing einmal Spatieren': für Cembalo (Orgel, Klavier)/ [by] Hans Leo Hassler; herausgegeben von Georges Kiss. — Mainz; London: Schott, 1971. — 39p; obl.fol.
£1.50

(B71-50445)

Q — PIANO
Q/AC — Tutors
Duckworth, Guy
Keyboard musicianship/ by Guy Duckworth. — New York: Free Press; London: Collier-Macmillan, 1971. — 261p; 4to.
Unpriced

(B71-50446)

Miller, Allan
Beginning piano for adults/ by Allan Miller. — New York: Collier Books; London: Collier-Macmillan, 1970. — 127p: illus, music; 26cm.
bibl p124-127.
ISBN 0 02 080890 9 Pbk: £1.00

(B71-50083)

Runze, Klaus
Zwei Hände-zwölf Tasten/ by Klaus Runze. — Mainz; London: Schott. —
Band 1: Ein Buch mit Bildern für kleine Klavierspieler. — 1971. — 64p; obl.4to.
£2.40

(B71-50940)

Squire, Russel Nelson
Class piano for adult beginners/ [by] Russel N. Squire, Virginia R. Mountney. — 2nd ed. — Englewood Cliffs; Hemel Hempstead: Prentice-Hall, 1971. — xvii,173p: illus; 4to.
Previous ed., Englewood Cliffs: Prentice-Hall, 1964. — bibl p160.
ISBN 0 13 135160 5 Sp: £3.00

(B71-50447)

Q/AF — Exercises
Last, Joan
Freedom technique: exercises and studies for piano/ by Joan Last. — London: Oxford University Press. —
Book 1: Beginners to grade 3 (USA2). — 1971. — 12p; 4to.
ISBN 0 19 373117 7 : £0.40

(B71-50941)

Book 2: Grades 3-4 (USA 2-2 1/2). — 1971. — 16p; 4to.
ISBN 0 19 373118 5 : £0.40

(B71-50942)

Book 3: Grade 5 (USA3) upwards. — 1971. — 24p; 4to.
ISBN 0 19 373119 3 : £0.50

(B71-50943)

Lerchner, Juliane
New compendium of piano technique/ by Juliane Lerchner. — Leipzig: Peters; London: Hinrichsen. —
Book 2: Reiteration with and without changing fingers. — 1969. — 41p; 4to.
£1.25

(B71-50448)

Q/AL — Examinations
Associated Board of the Royal Schools of Music
Pianoforte examinations, 1972. — London: Associated Board of the Royal Schools of Music. —
Grade 1: Lists A and B (primary). — 1971. — 10p; 4to.
£0.35

(B71-50944)

Grade 2: Lists A and B (elementary). — 1971. — 10p; 4to.
£0.35

(B71-50945)

Grade 3: Lists A and B (transitional). — 1971. — 15p; 4to.
£0.35

(B71-50946)

Grade 4: Lists A and B (Lower). — 1971. — 15p; 4to.
£0.35

(B71-50947)

Grade 5: List A (Higher). — 1971. — 13p; 4to.
£0.35

(B71-50949)

Grade 5: List B (Higher). — 1971. — 12p; 4to.
£0.35

(B71-50948)

Grade 6. List A (Intermediate). — 1971. — 22p; 4to.
£0.35

(B71-50951)

Grade 6: List B (Intermediate). — 1971. — 22p; 4to.
£0.35

(B71-50950)

Grade 7. List A (Advanced). — 1971. — 21p; 4to.
£0.35

(B71-50952)

Grade 7. List B (Advanced). — 1971. — 21p; 4to.
£0.35

(B71-50953)

Guildhall School of Music and Drama
Pianoforte examinations. — London: Lengnick. —
Grade 1. — 1971. — 15p; 4to.
£0.35

(B71-50956)

Grade 2. — 1971. — 19p; 4to.
£0.35

(B71-50957)

Grade 3. — 1971. — 16p; 4to.
£0.35

(B71-50958)

Grade 4. — 1971. — 18p; 4to.
£0.35

(B71-50959)

Junior. — 1971. — 15p; 4to.
£0.35

(B71-50955)

Preliminary. — 1971. — 12p; 4to.
£0.35

(B71-50954)

Guildhall School of Music and Drama
Pianoforte examinations, series 9. — London: Lengnick. —
Introductory. — 1971. — 11p; 4to. —
£0.35

(B71-50960)

Q/EG — Sight reading
London College of Music
Examinations in pianoforte playing and singing: sight reading tests, sight singing tests as set throughout 1970. Grades I-VIII & diplomas. — London: Ashdown, 1971. — 15p; 4to.
£0.25
Also classified at CB/EG

(B71-50084)

Q/R — Harmony
Chatterley, Albert
101 tunes to explore/ compiled by Albert Chatterley and Gordon Reynolds. — Borough Green: Novello, 1971. — xv,40p; 8vo.
£0.75

(B71-50961)

QNU — TWO PIANOS, 4 HANDS
Bach, Carl Philipp Emanuel
Four little duets for two pianos. Wq.155/ by Carl Philipp Emanuel
Bach; edited by Arthur Gold and Robert Fizdale. — New York:
Schirmer; London: Chappell, 1971. — 11p; 4to.
Unpriced

(B71-50962)

Sary, Laszlo
Catacoustics: for two pianos/ by Laszlo Sary. — London: Boosey
and Hawkes, 1970. — 24p; 4to.
£0.86

(B71-50449)

QNUK/LF — Arrangements. Concertos
Corigliano, John
Concerto for piano and orchestra/ by John Corigliano; reduction by
the composer. — New York: Schirmer; [London]: [Chappell], 1971.
— 106p; 4to.
Two-piano score.
Unpriced

(B71-50963)

Kasschau, Howard
Country concerto for young pianists: for piano and orchestra/ by
Howard Kasschau. — New York: Schirmer; [London]: [Chappell],
1971. — 18p; 4to.
Two-piano score.
Unpriced

(B71-50964)

QNV — ONE PIANO, 4 HANDS
Fly, Leslie
Forest themes: piano duets/ by Leslie Fly. — London: Forsyth, 1971.
— 15p; 4to.
Unpriced

(B71-50450)

Helps, Robert
Saccade: piano, four hands/ by Robert Helps. — New York: Peters;
London: [Hinrichsen], 1969. — 15p; 4to.
Duration 7 1/2 min.
£0.90

(B71-50451)

Reger, Max
[Selections]. Walzer-Capricen, deutsche Tänze und andere Stücke:
für Klavier zu vier Händen/ [by] Max Reger; ausgewählt und
herausgegeben von Walter Frickert. — Leipzig: Peters; [London]:
[Hinrichsen], 1969. — 39p: obl.4to.
£1.40

(B71-50452)

QNV/AL — Examinations
Associated Board of the Royal Schools of Music
Pianoforte duet examinations. — London: Associated Board of the
Royal Schools of Music. —
Junior division. List A. — 1970. — 15p; 4to.
£0.175

(B71-50966)

Middle division. List A. — 1971. — 21p; 4to.
£0.20

(B71-50967)

Senior division. List A. — 1969. — 49p; 4to.
£0.35

(B71-50965)

QNVE — Sonatas
Bach, Johann Christian
[Sonata for piano duet in F major. Op. 18, no.6]. Sonata in F: for
pianoforte duet/ by Johann Christian Bach. — London: Associated
Board of the Royal Schools of Music, 1969. — 19p; 4to.
£0.175

(B71-50968)

Schubert, Franz
[Sonata for piano duet in B flat major]. Grand sonata. Op.30: for
pianoforte duet/ by Franz Schubert. — London: Associated Board of
the Royal Schools of Music, 1969. — 39p; 4to.
Unpriced

(B71-50969)

QNVEM — Sonatinas
Kubelik, Rafael
[Sonatina for piano, 2 hands]. Sonatina: für Klavier zu zwei Händen/
[by] Rafael Kubelik. — Frankfurt: Litolff, Peters; London:
[Hinrichsen], 1970. — 20p; 4to.
£1.50

(B71-50453)

QNVK — Arrangements
Gomes, Antonio Carlos
[Il Guarany - Excerpts]. O Guarani: sinfonia/ [by] Antonio Carlos
Gomes; [reducaa] piano 4 maos por Nicolo Celega, revisada por
Arthur Napoleao. — Rio de Janeiro: Arthur Napoleao; London:
Essex Music, 1971. — 22p; 4to.
Unpriced

(B71-50454)

QP — PIANO SOLOS
QP/AY — Collections
Waterman, Fanny
The young pianist's repertoire/ selected by Fanny Waterman &
Marion Harewood. — London: Faber. —
Book 1. — 1971. — 46p; 4to.
Unpriced

(B71-50455)

Book 2. — 1971. — 48p; 4to.
Unpriced

(B71-50456)

QP/LF — Christmas
Beck, John Ness
Five carol fantasies: for piano/ by John Ness Beck. — New York:
Schirmer; [London]: [Chappell], 1971. — 11p; 4to.
Contents:- 1.What Child is this? - 2.Bring a torch, Jeanette, Isabella. —
3.Appalachian Christmas carol. — 4.God rest ye merry, gentlemen. — 5.Joy to
the world.
Unpriced

(B71-50457)

QP/RM/AY — Counterpoint. Collections
Messenger, Thomas
Two-part counterpoint from the great Masters/ collected by Thomas
Messenger. — Borough Green: Faber, 1970. — 55p; 4to.
£0.55

(B71-50458)

QP/T — Variations
Stravinsky, Soulima
[Variations for piano]. Piano variations/ by Soulima Stravinsky. —
New York: Peters; London: [Hinrichsen]. —
1st series. — 1970. — 18p; 4to.
Duration 12 min.
£0.90

(B71-50459)

2nd series. — 1970. — 16p; 4to.
Duration 13 min.
£0.90

(B71-50460)

Viera Rios, Graziela
Evocacao: tema con variacoes [for] piano/ [by] Graziela Viera Rios.
— Rio de Janeiro: Arthur Napoleao, 1971. — 7p; 4to.
Unpriced

(B71-50970)

QP/W — Rondos
Webern, Anton von
Sonatensatz (Rondo) für Klavier/ by Anton von Webern. — London:
Boosey and Hawkes, 1970. — 8p; 4to.
Unpriced

(B71-50461)

QP/Y — Fugues
Hartmann, Karl Amadeus
Jazz-Toccata und - Fuge: für Klavier/ [by] Karl Amadeus
Hartmann. — Mainz; London: Schott, 1970. — 19p; 4to.
£1.20

(B71-50085)

Mendelssohn, Felix
[Preludes and fugues for piano. Op.35]. Six preludes and fugues.
Op.35: piano solo/ by F. Mendelssohn-Bartholdy; edited by A.
Ruthardt. — London: Peters, [Hinrichsen], 1970. — 39p; 4to.
£0.60

(B71-50462)

QPE — Sonatas
Keats, Donald
[Sonata for piano]. Piano sonata/ by Donald Keats. — New York;
London: Boosey and Hawkes, 1971. — 28p; 4to.
£1.10

(B71-50463)

Kelly, Brian
Sonata for piano/ by Brian Kelly. — London: Novello, 1971. — 20p;
4to.
Unpriced

(B71-50971)

Mozart, Wolfgang Amadeus
[Sonata for piano in B flat major. K281]. Sonata in B flat: pianoforte.
K.281/ by W.A. Mozart; edited by Stanley Sadie, fingering by Denis
Matthews. — London: Associated Board of the Royal Schools of
Music, 1970. — 21p; 4to.
£0.35

(B71-50086)

Mozart, Wolfgang Amadeus
[Sonata for piano in D major. K.311]. Sonata in D. K.311/ by
Mozart; edited by Stanley Sadie, fingering and notes on performance
by Denis Matthews. — London: Associated Board of the Royal
Schools of Music, 1971. — 23p; 4to.
£0.35

(B71-50464)

Mozart, Wolfgang Amadeus
[Sonata for piano in E flat major. K.282]. Sonata in E flat. K.282/ by
Mozart; edited by Stanley Sadie, fingering and notes on performance
by Denis Matthews. — London: Associated Board of the Royal
Schools of Music, 1971. — 13p; 4to.
£0.35

(B71-50465)

Shostakovich, Dmitri
[Sonata for piano, no.1. Opus 12]. Sonate für Klavier, no.1. Opus
12/ [by] D. Schostakowitsch. — Leipzig: Peters; [London]:
[Hinrichsen], 1969. — 20p; 4to.
£0.90

(B71-50466)

Wilson, Thomas
[Sonata for piano (1959, rev. 1964)]. Piano sonata (1959: revised
1964)/ by Thomas Wilson. — London: Stainer & Bell, 1971. — 14p;
4to.
Unpriced

(B71-50972)

QPEM — Sonatinas
Hartmann, Karl Amadeus
[Sonatina for piano]. Sonatine für Klavier/ [by] Karl Amadeus
Hartmann. — Mainz; London: Schott, 1971. — 12p; 4to.
£0.90

(B71-50087)

Pitfield, Thomas
[Sonatina for piano in C major]. Sonatina in C: for piano/ by
Thomas Pitfield. — London: Freeman, 1971. — 5p; 4to.
Unpriced

(B71-50467)

QPG — Suites
Camilleri, Charles
Little African suite: for piano. Opus 44/ by Charles Camilleri. —
London: Novello, 1971. — 14p; 4to.
Unpriced

(B71-50469)

Hall, Richard
[Suite for piano]. Suite/ by Richard Hall. — Borough Green: Novello,
1971. — 13p; 4to.
£0.50

(B71-50973)

Johnson, Thomas Arnold
A day in the country: suite/ by Thomas A. Johnson. — London:
Freeman, 1971. — 7p; 4to.
£0.20

(B71-50088)

Johnson, Thomas Arnold
In the forest: suite/ by Thomas A. Johnson. — London: Freeman,
1971. — 7p; 4to.
£0.20

(B71-50089)

Johnson, Thomas Arnold
Puppets on parade: suite/ by Thomas A. Johnson. — London:
Freeman, 1971. — 7p; 4to.
£0.20

(B71-50090)

Villa-Lobos, Heitor
Carnaval das criancas: colecao de 8 pecas [for] piano/ [by] H.
Villa-Lobos; revisao do Barrozo Netto. — Rio de Janeiro: Arthur
Napoleao; London: Essex Music. —
No.7: A Gaita de um precoce fantasiado. — 1971. — 3p; 4to.
Unpriced

(B71-50470)

Villa-Lobos, Heitor
La suite infantil: colecao de 5 pecas [for piano]/ by H. Villa-Lobos. —
Rio de Janeiro: Arthur Napoleao; London: Essex Music. —
No.2: Nene vai dormir. — 1971. — 2p; 4to.
Unpriced

(B71-50468)

Villa-Lobos, Heitor
Suite floral: colecao de 3 pecas [for] piano. Op.97/ [by] H.
Villa-Lobos. — Rio de Janeiro: Arthur Napoleao; London: Essex
Music. —
No.3: Alegria na Horta. — 1971. — 5p; 4to.
Unpriced

(B71-50471)

QPHMH — Dances. Habaneras
Napoleao, Arthur
Romance and habanera: piano. Op.71/ by Arthur Napoleao. — Rio
de Janeiro: Arthur Napoleao; London: Essex Music, 1971. — 11p;
4to.
Unpriced
Primary classification QPJ

(B71-50493)

QPHQ — Dances. Mazurkas
Messina, Alfredo
Confidencia: mazurca no.3, piano/ by Alfredo Messina. — Rio de
Janeiro: Arthur Napoleao; [London]: [Essex Music], 1971. — [2]p;
4to.
Unpriced

(B71-50974)

QPJ — Miscellaneous works
Allanbrook, Douglas
40 changes: for piano/ by Douglas Allanbrook. — New York;
London: Boosey and Hawkes, 1971. — 36p; 4to.
£1.50

(B71-50472)

Berio, Luciano
Erdenklavier: pastorale [for piano]/ [by] Luciano Berio. — London:
Universal, 1971. — [2]p; obl.4to.
Unpriced

(B71-50473)

Berio, Luciano
Wasserklavier: [for piano]/ [by] Luciano Berio. — London:
Universal, 1971. — [2]p; obl.4to.
Unpriced

(B71-50474)

Blackburn, Maria
A score of nursery rhymes/ by Maria Blackburn. — London:
Feldman, 1971. — 10p; 4to.
y0.25

(B71-50975)

Boguslawski, Edward
Per pianoforte/ [by] Edward Boguslawski. — Mainz: Ars viva;
London: Schott, 1971. — 5p; fol.
£1.80

(B71-50475)

Bozay, Attila
Medailles: for piano/ by Attila Bozay. — London: Boosey and
Hawkes, 1970. — 13p; 4to.
£0.57

(B71-50476)

Castaldi, Paolo
Moll: für das Pianoforte/ [by] Paulo Castaldi. — London: Universal,
1971. — 2p; fol.
Unpriced

(B71-50477)

Dawe, Margery
Diversions on the new road to pianoforte playing/ by Margery Dawe.
— London: Cramer, 1971. — 12p; 4to.
Unpriced

(B71-50091)

Debussy, Claude
Selected piano works [of] Claude Debussy/ edited by Eberhardt
Klemm. — Leipzig: Peters; [London]: [Hinrichsen]. —
Vol.3: Préludes, 2e livre. — 1971. — 76p; 4to.
£1.75

(B71-50478)

Debussy, Claude
Selected piano works [of]Claude Debussy/ edited by Eberhardt
Klemm. — Leipzig: Peters; [London]: [Hinrichsen]. —
Vol.4: Images. — 1971. — 67p; 4to.
£1.50

(B71-50479)

Debussy, Claude
The music of Claude Debussy/ edited by Josephine Rayner. —
Manchester: Forsyth. —
Book 1: La Fille aux cheveux de lin; [and], The little shepherd; [and], Jimbo's
lullaby. — 1970. — 8p; 4to.
Unpriced

(B71-50480)

Book 2: Clair de lune; [and], Des Pas sur la neige; [and], Snow is dancing. —
1970. — 15p; 4to.
Unpriced

(B71-50481)

Book 3: Serenade of the doll; [and], La Puerta del vino; [and] Sarabande. —
1970. — 8p; 4to.
Unpriced

(B71-50482)

Diemer, Emma Lou
Sound pictures: for piano/ by Emma Lou Diemer. — New York;
London: Boosey and Hawkes, 1971. — 11p; 4to.
£0.65

(B71-50483)

Duke, Henry
Album for the youngsters: for piano/ by Henry Duke. — London:
Feldman, 1971. — 11p; 4to.
y0.30

(B71-50976)

Farinello, Orestes
Intermezzo, Impressoes do teatro: piano/ [by] Orestes Farinello. —
Rio de Janeiro: Arthur Napoleao; [London]: [Essex Music], 1971. —
[3]p; 4to.
Unpriced

(B71-50484)

Ferneyhough, Brian
Three pieces: for piano/ by Brian Ferneyhough. — London: Peters,
Hinrichsen, 1971. — 19p; 4to.
£1.10

(B71-50485)

Griffes, Charles Tomlinson
Roman sketches. Op.7: for piano/ by Charles T. Griffes. — New
York: Schirmer; London: Chappell, 1971. — 32p; 4to.
Contents: The white peacock. — Nightfall. — The fountain of the Acqua
Paola. — Clouds.
Unpriced

(B71-50092)

Heider, Werner
Landschaftspartitur: für Klavier/ [by] Werner Heider. — Frankfurt:
Litolff; London: [Hinrichsen], 1970. — 10 leaves; 4to.
Ls: £3.25

(B71-50486)

Hopkins, Bill
Etudes: piano solo/ by Bill Hopkins. — London: Schott. —
Book 1. — 1969. — 32p; 4to.
Unpriced

(B71-50093)

Lambert, Cecily
Greek scenes/ by Cecily Lambert. — London: Forsyth, 1970. — 11p;
4to.
Unpriced

(B71-50094)

Lawson, Peter
Momenta 94: for solo piano/ by Peter Lawson. — London: Peters,
Hinrichsen, 1971. — 14p; 4to.
£1.25

(B71-50487)

Lehmann, Hans Ulrich
Instants: pour piano/ [by] Hans Ulrich Lehmann. — Mainz; London:
Schott, 1971. — 5p; fol.
£1.50

(B71-50488)

Leighton, Kenneth
Conflicts. Op. 51: fantasy on two themes for piano/ by Kenneth
Leighton. — London: Novello, 1971. — 34p; 4to.
Unpriced

(B71-50977)

Liszt, Franz
[Ballades for piano]. Two ballades/ [by] Franz Liszt; [edited by]
Emil von Sauer. — London: Peters, [Hinrichsen], 1971. — 33p; 4to.
Contents: No.1 in D flat major. — No.2 in B minor.
£0.50

(B71-50489)

Liszt, Franz
[Légendes]. Two legends/ by Franz Liszt; [edited by] Emil von
Sauer. — New York: Peters; London: [Hinrichsen], 1970. — 30p; 4to.
Contents:- St Francois d'Assise 'La Prédication aux oiseaux'. — St Francois
de Paule marchant sur les flots.
£0.40

(B71-50490)

Longmire, John
Fancy free: for piano/ by John Longmire. — London: Freeman,
1971. — 13p; 4to.
£0.30

(B71-50978)

Longmire, John
Playing for pleasure: for piano/ by John Longmire. — London:
Bosworth. —
Book 3: Grade 1. — 1971. — 16p; 4to.
£0.225

(B71-50095)

Longmire, John
Twelve floral sketches: for piano/ by John Longmire. — London:
Bosworth, 1971. — 15p; 4to.
£0.20

(B71-50096)

McCabe, John
Capriccio (1969): for piano/ by John McCabe. — Borough Green:
Novello, 1971. — 12p; 4to.
£0.50

(B71-50491)

Muczynski, Robert
Toccata: for piano/ by Robert Muczynski. — New York: Schirmer;
[London]: [Chappell], 1971. — 14p; 4to.
Unpriced

(B71-50492)

Napoleao, Arthur
Romance and habanera: piano. Op.71/ by Arthur Napoleao. — Rio
de Janeiro: Arthur Napoleao; London: Essex Music, 1971. — 11p;
4to.
Unpriced
Also classified at QPHMH

(B71-50493)

Nepomuceno, Alberto
Noturno: piano/ [by] Alberto Nepomuceno. — Rio de Janeiro:
Arthur Napoleao; London: Essex Music, 1971. — 5p; 4to.
Unpriced

(B71-50494)

Netto, Barrozo
Na rede: piano/ de Barrozo Neto [i.e. Netto]. — Rio de Janeiro:
Arthur Napoleao; London: Essex Music, 1971. — 2p; 4to.
Unpriced

(B71-50495)

Netto, Barrozo
Romance sem palavras: piano/ de Barrozo Neto [i.e. Netto]. — Rio
de Janeiro: Arthur Napoleao; London: Essex Music, 1971. — 4p;
4to.
Unpriced

(B71-50496)

Papp, Lajos
Improvvisazione: per pianoforte/ [by] Lajos Papp. — London:
Boosey and Hawkes, 1971. — 9p; 4to.
Unpriced

(B71-50497)

Phillips, Sally
Two pictures: for piano/ by Sally Phillips. — London: Oxford
University Press, 1970. — 4p; 4to.
Contents: March of the toy soldiers. — Waltz of the dolls.
Unpriced

(B71-50097)

Pope, Roger Hugh
Five short solos: for piano/ by Roger Hugh Pope. — London:
Bosworth, 1971. — 7p; 4to.
£0.18

(B71-50979)

Reger, Max
[Selections]. Ausgewählte Klavierwerke/ [by] Max Reger. — Leipzig:
Peters; London: Hinrichsen. —
Band 3: Aus meinem Tagebuch. Op.82/ herausgegeben von Heinz Volger. —
1968. — 40p; 4to.
£1.25

(B71-50498)

Robinson, L Woodroffe
Holiday tunes: 18 easy pieces for pianoforte/ by L. Woodroffe
Robinson. — London: Freeman, 1970. — 12p; 4to.
Unpriced

(B71-50098)

Sári, József
Episodi: per pianoforte/ [by] József Sári. — London: Boosey and
Hawkes, 1971. — 10p; 8vo.
Unpriced

(B71-50499)

Shostakovich, Dmitri
[Selections]. Piano compositions/ by D. Schostakowitsch. — Leipzig:
Peters; London: Hinrichsen, 1971. — 31p; 4to.
Contents: - Three fantastic dances. Op.1. — Aphorisms. Op.13. — Five
preludes.
£1.00

(B71-50500)

Szalonek, Witold
Mutanza: per pianoforte/ [by] Witold Szalonek. — London: Chester,
1971. — 9p; obl.4to.
Unpriced

(B71-50980)

Villa-Lobos, Heitor
[Fabulas caracteristicas. Op.65. Excerpts]. O Gato e o rato: piano/
[by] Heitor Villa-Lobos. — Rio de Janeiro: Arthur Napoleao;
London: Essex Music, 1971. — 7p; 4to.
Unpriced

(B71-50501)

Villa-Lobos, Heitor
Ondulando: estudo [for] piano. Op.31/ [by] H. Villa-Lobos. — Rio
de Janeiro: Arthur Napoleao; London: Essex Music, 1971. — 5p;
4to.
Unpriced

(B71-50502)

Villa-Lobos, Heitor
Simples coletanea: colecao de 3 pecas [for] piano/ [by] H.
Villa-Lobos. — Rio de Janeiro: Arthur Napoleao; London: Essex
Music. —
No.1: Valsa mistica. — 1971. — 4p; 4to.
Unpriced

(B71-50503)

No.3: Rodante. — 1971. — 6p; 4to.
Unpriced

(B71-50504)

Villa-Lobos, Heitor
[Suite infantil no.2. Excerpts]. Allegro/ by Heitor Villa-Lobos. — Rio
de Janeiro: Arthur Napoleao; London: Essex Music, 1970. — [3]p;
4to.
Unpriced

(B71-50099)

Webern, Anton von
Satz für Klavier/ by Anton von Webern. — London: Boosey and
Hawkes, 1970. — 11p; 4to.
Unpriced

(B71-50505)

Wilson, Robert Barclay
Two short pieces: piano/ by R. Barclay Wilson. — London: Cramer,
1971. — 3p; 4to.
Contents:- Lullaby for Titania. Puck dances.
Unpriced

(B71-50506)

Wolpe, Stefan
Form IV: broken sequences: for piano/ by Stefan Wolpe. — New
York: Peters; London: Hinrichsen, 1970. — 9p; 4to.
Duration 4 min.
Unpriced

(B71-50507)

Wyttenbach, Jürg
Drei Klavierstücke (1969)/ [by] Jürg Wyttenbach. — Mainz;
London: Schott, 1970. — 7p; 4to.
£1.20

(B71-50508)

QPK — Arrangements
Bach, Johann Sebastian
[Selections]. Get to know Mister Bach: an informal introduction with
simple piano arrangements of his music/ by Felton Rapley. —
London: Chappell, 1971. — 26p; 4to.
Unpriced

(B71-50981)

Mozart, Wolfgang Amadeus
[Eine kleine Nachtmusik. K.525. Allegro]. Mozart 13: serenade
no.13 in G major/ adapted by Waldo de los Rios. — London: Rondor
Music: Hansen, 1971. — 7p; 4to.
£0.20

(B71-50982)

Mozart, Wolfgang Amadeus
[Symphony no.40 in G minor. K.550. Molto allegro]. Mozart 40/
arranged for piano by B. Kelsey and Ellis Rich. — London: Feldman,
1971. — 4p; 4to.
Unpriced

(B71-50509)

Mozart, Wolfgang Amadeus
[Symphony no.40 in G minor. K.550. Molto allegro]. Mozart
(Symphony no.40)/ adapted by Waldo de los Rios. — London (1 St
George St., W.1): Rondor Music, 1971. — 8p; 4to.
£0.20

(B71-50510)

Musical excerpts of the masters. — London: Campbell Connelly, 1970.
— 57p; 4to.
£0.60

(B71-50100)

Rios, Waldo de los
Symphonies for the seventies/ adapted by Waldo de los Rios. —
London: Rondor Music, 1971. — 47p; 4to.
£1.25

(B71-50983)

Tchaikovsky, Peter
Piano arrangements for all to play/ arranged by Cecil Bolton. —
London: Francis, Day and Hunter, 1970. — 100p; 4to.
£0.90

(B71-50511)

QPK/AHM/JR — Arrangements. Ballet music. Films
Lanchbery, John
Tales of Beatrix Potter: music from the film/ arranged for the piano
by John Lanchbery. — London: E.M.I. Film Music: Keith Prowse
Music, 1971. — 17p; 4to.
£0.40

(B71-50512)

QPK/CC — Arrangements. From opera
Bizet, Georges
Carmen: the story and music/ by Georges Bizet; arranged for piano
solo by Harry Dexter. — London: Keith Prowse, 1970. — 31p; 4to.
£0.20

(B71-50101)

QPK/CM — Arrangements. Musical plays
Coward, Noel
Bitter sweet: easy-to-play piano selection/ by Noel Coward; arranged
by Howard Evans. — London: Chappell, 1971. — 16p; obl. 4to.
£0.25

(B71-50102)

Lane, Burton
On a clear day you can see forever/ by Burton Lane; piano selection
arranged by Walter Paul. — London: Chappell, 1971. — 16p; 4to.
£0.25

(B71-50984)

Novello, Ivor
The dancing years/ by Ivor Novello; easy-to-play piano or organ
selection arranged by Howard Evans. — London: Chappell, 1970. —
15p; obl. 4to.
£0.25
Also classified at RK/CM

(B71-50103)

QPK/CM/JR — Arrangements. Musical plays. Film music
Greig, Edvard
[Selections]. The song of Norway: piano selection [from the film]/
[music] by Edvard Greig; musical adaptation by Robert Wright and
George Forrest, arranged by Bert Brewis. — London: Chappell:
Frank Music, 1971. — 14p; 4to.
£0.25

(B71-50104)

QPK/DW — Arrangements. Songs, etc
Mussorgsky, Modeste
[Boris Goudonov - Excerpts]. Varlaam's song/ by Mussorgsky;
freely transcribed by John Ogdon. — London: Ascherberg, Hopwood
and Crew, 1971. — 8p; 4to.
£0.25

(B71-50985)

QPK/DW — Piano solo. Arrangements. Songs, etc
The **Beatles** complete: piano vocal/easy organ. — London: Northern Songs (Music Sales), 1971. — 217p: illus, port; 4to.
£2.50
Also classified at RK/DW

(B71-50986)

QPK/DW/GJ/AY — Arrangements. Children's songs. Collections
Gabschuss, Klaus Ulbrich
Kinderlieder und Volkslieder: für den systematischen Unterricht am Klavier/ herausgegeben von K.U. Gabschuss. — Mainz; London: Schott, 1971. — 30p; 8vo.
£1.30

(B71-50513)

QPK/JR — Arrangements. Film music
Liszt, Franz
[Two episodes from Lenau's Faust. No.2. First Mephisto waltz]. The Mephisto waltz/ by Franz Liszt; love theme from the film adapted for piano by Jerry Goldsmith. — London: Twentieth Century Music, 1971. — 3p; 4to.
£0.20

(B71-50514)

QPK/JS — Arrangements. Television music *record*
Khachaturian, Aram
[Spartak - Excerpts]. Spartacus: love theme/ by Khachaturian; arranged by E. Charles and N. Newell. — London: Plantagenet Music, 1971. — 4p; 4to.
£0.20

(B71-50987)

QRP — HARPSICHORD SOLOS
QRPE — Sonatas
Paradisi, Pietro Domenico
[Sonatas for harpsichord]. Sonate di gravicembalo/ by Pietro Domenico Paradisi; herausgegeben von Hugo Ruf und Hans Bemmann. — Mainz; London: Schott. —
Band 1: Sonate 1-6. — 1971. — 47p; 4to.
£1.40

(B71-50989)

Band 2: Sonate 7-12. — 1971. — 56p; 4to.
£1.40

(B71-50988)

QRPJ — Miscellaneous works
Couperin, Francois
[Pièces de clavecin. Excerpts]. Selected harpischord music/ by Francois Couperin; edited and annotated by Sylvia Marlowe. — New York: Schirmer; London: Chappell, 1971. — xvi,117p; 4to.
Unpriced

(B71-50105)

Ligeti, György
Continuum: für Cembalo/ [by] György Ligeti. — Mainz; [London]: Schott, 1970. — 11p; 4to.
£1.20

(B71-50106)

QSQ — VIRGINALS
QSQ/AZ — Collected works of individual composers
Tisdall, William
Complete keyboard works [of] William Tisdall/ newly transcribed and edited from the Fitzwilliam Virginal Book and the John Bull Virginal Book by Howard Ferguson. — 2nd, revised ed. — London: Stainer and Bell, 1971. — 12p; fol.
Unpriced

(B71-50515)

R — ORGAN
R/AC — Tutors
Trevor, Caleb Henry
The Oxford organ method/ by C.H. Trevor. — London: Oxford University Press, 1971. — 142p; 8vo.
Unpriced

(B71-50107)

R/AY — Collections
Funk, Heinrich
Contemporary organ music for liturgical use/ [compiled by] Heinrich Funk. — London: Eulenburg, Hinrichsen, 1970. — 148p; obl.4to.
The numeration IV on the cover is to be ignored, on the advice of the publishers.
£2.50

(B71-50516)

Trevor, Caleb H
Organ books/ edited by C.H. Trevor. — London: Oxford University Press. —
No.3. — 1971. — 32p; 4to.
£0.65

(B71-50990)

R/AYJ — Collections. Italy
Szigeti, Kilian
Liber organi. Altitalienische Orgelmeister/ ausgewählt und für den praktischen Gebrauch bezeichnet von Kilian Szigeti. — Mainz; London: Schott. —
2. — 1971. — 32p; 4to.
£0.30

(B71-50991)

R/AZ — Collected works of individual composers
Liszt, Franz
Complete organ works [of] Franz Liszt/ edited by Sandor Margittay. — London: Boosey and Hawkes. —
Vol.1. — 1971. — 87p; obl.fol.
Unpriced

(B71-50517)

R/LH — Holy Week
Förtig, Peter
Stationes für Orgel/ [by] Peter Förtig. — Mainz; London: Schott, 1971. — 36p; 4to.
£3.00

(B71-50992)

R/T — Variations
Amner, John
Variations on 'O Lord in Thee is all my trust': for organ/ by John Amner; edited by Anthony Greening. — London: Schott, 1970. — 16p; 4to.
Unpriced

(B71-50108)

Henriksen, Josef
Variations for organ on the Lourdes Hymn/ by Josef Henriksen. — Hoddesdon: St Gregory Publishing Co., 1970. — 19p; obl. 8vo.
£0.53

(B71-50993)

RE — Symphonies
Williamson, Malcolm
Symphony: for organ/ by Malcolm Williamson. — Borough Green: Novello, 1971. — 62p; obl.4to.
Duration 35 min.
£1.50

(B71-50994)

RF — Concertos
Bach, *Monsieur*
[Concerto for organ solo in E flat major]. Concerto in E flat: for two manuals and pedals/ anon., once attributed to J.S. Bach; edited by Martin Neary. — London: Oxford University Press, 1971. — 8p; 4to.
The manuscript was ascribed to 'Monsieur Bach'; the work is not regarded as being by J.S. Bach. No attribution is possible.
Unpriced

(B71-50109)

RG — Suites
Hovhaness, Alan
Sanahin: partita for organ/ by Alan Hovhaness. — New York: Peters; London: [Hinrichsen], 1970. — 19p; 4to.
Duration 12 mins.
£0.90

(B71-50518)

RJ — Miscellaneous works
Bach, Johann Sebastian
[Selections]. A Bach organ book for students/ edited by C.H. Trevor. — London: Elkin, 1971. — xiv,68p; obl.fol.
£1.50

(B71-50519)

Barrett, Gavin
Introduction, allegro and finale: organ/ by Gavin Barrett. — London: Boosey and Hawkes, 1970. — 12p; 4to.
£0.55

(B71-50110)

Berkeley, Lennox
Three pieces: for organ/ by Lennox Berkeley. — London: Chester, 1971. — 17p; 4to.
Contents:- 1.Aubade. — 2.Aria. — 3.Toccata.
Unpriced

(B71-50520)

Blow, John
Two voluntaries: [for organ]/ by John Blow; edited, from the Nanki manuscript, by Hugh McLean. — Borough Green: Novello, 1971. — 9p; 4to.
These works are published for the first time; they are attributed to John Blow.
£0.35

(B71-50521)

Fricker, Peter Racine
Praeludium. Opus. 60: [for organ]/ by Peter Racine Fricker. — London: Oxford University Press, 1971. — 16p; 4to.
ISBN 0 19 375390 1 : £0.80

(B71-50522)

Garlick, George T
A little tune for St Mark's Day. Op.71, no.1: organ solo/ by George T. Garlick. — Bristol (18 Wathen Rd, St Andrews, Bristol): George T. Garlick, 1971. — 3p; obl.4to.
Unpriced

(B71-50995)

Genzmer, Harald
Die Tageszeiten: für Orgel/ [by] Harald Genzmer. — New York: Litolff, Peters; London: [Hinrichsen], 1968. — 20p; obl. 4to.
£0.75

(B71-50523)

Harvey, Jonathan
Laus Deo: [for organ]/ by Jonathan Harvey. — Borough Green: Novello, 1971. — 8p; obl.4to.
Duration 3 mins.
£0.30

(B71-50524)

Hopkins, Douglas
Postlude on 'Love divine' [by] John Stainer: for organ/ by Douglas Hopkins. — London: Paxton, 1971. — 5p; 4to.
Unpriced

(B71-50525)

Klerk, Albert de
Twelve images. — Borough Green: Novello. —
Score (27p.) & 4 parts.
b for organ/ by Albert de Klerk. — 1971. — 25p; 4to.
£0.50

(B71-50996)

Kraft, Walter
Toccata, 'Ite, missa est': für Orgel/ [by] Walter Kraft. — Mainz: London: Schott, 1971. — 16p; obl.4to.
£1.00

(B71-50526)

Leigh, Eric
Two hymn preludes: for organ/ by Eric Leigh. — London: Feldman, 1971. — 5p; 4to.
Contents:- Dundee. — Song 67.
£0.20

(B71-50997)

Maine, Basil
Three plainsong preludes: for organ/ by Basil Maine. — London: Boosey and Hawkes, 1971. — 7p; 4to.
Unpriced

(B71-50527)

Waters, Charles Frederick
Cornet fantasy: for the organ/ by Charles F. Waters. — London: Leonard, Gould and Bolttler, 1971. — 3p; 4to.
£0.18

(B71-50998)

Wehrle, Heinz
Vier Orgelstücke/ [by] Heinz Wehrle. — London: Eulenburg, Hinrichsen, 1970. — 27p; 4to.
Contents:- Sons d'orgue. — Aria variata. — Chant de paix. — Final.
£1.10

(B71-50528)

RK — Arrangements
Ceremonial music for organ: fanfares and trumpet tunes. — London: Oxford University Press, 1970. — 16p; 4to.
ISBN 0 19 375120 8 : £0.40

(B71-50111)

RK/AAY — Arrangements. Collections
Williams, Patrick
First easy album for the organ/ arranged by Patrick Williams. — London: Bosworth, 1969. — 35p; 8vo.
£0.30

(B71-50529)

Williams, Patrick
Second easy album for the organ/ arranged by Patrick Williams. — London: Bosworth, 1969. — 30p; 8vo.
Unpriced

(B71-50530)

RK/CM — Arrangements. Musical plays
Novello, Ivor
The dancing years/ by Ivor Novello; easy-to-play piano or organ selection arranged by Howard Evans. — London: Chappell, 1970. — 15p; obl. 4to.
£0.25
Primary classification QPK/CM

(B71-50103)

RK/CM/JR — Arrangements. Musical plays. Films
Grieg, Edvard
[Selections]. Song of Norway: selection for all organs/ [from music by] Edvard Grieg; musical adaptation and lyrics by Robert Wright and George Forrest. — London: Chappell, 1971. — 24p; 4to.
£0.40

(B71-50999)

RK/DM/ED/AY — Collections
Knight, Gerald Hocken
Accompaniments for unison hymn-singing/ compiled and edited by Gerald H. Knight. — Croydon: Royal School of Church Music, 1971. — 64p; 4to.
Unpriced

(B71-50531)

RK/DW — Arrangements. Songs, etc
The **Beatles** complete: piano vocal/easy organ. — London: Northern Songs (Music Sales), 1971. — 217p: illus, port; 4to.
£2.50
Primary classification QPK/DW

(B71-50986)

Handel, George Frideric
[Rodelinda. - Dove sei]. Art thou troubled?: organ/ by Handel; arranged by Douglas Hopkins. — London: Paxton, 1971. — 4p; 4to.
Unpriced

(B71-50532)

Lennon, John
50 great songs/ by John Lennon and Paul McCartney; arranged for all organs. — London: Northern Songs (Music Sales), 1971. — 128p; 4to.
£1.50

(B71-51000)

RPV — ELECTRIC ORGANS
RPVCK/DP/LF/AYB — Chord organ. Arrangements. Carols. Christmas. Collections. Europe
Duke, Henry
Christmas carols/ arranged for chord organ by Henry Duke. — London: Feldman, 1971. — 16p; 4to.
y0.40

(B71-51001)

RPVK — Arrangements. Collections
Rothenberg, Peter
Elektronische Orgel klassisch/ bearbeitet von Peter Rothenberg. — Mainz; London: Schott, 1971. — 31p; 4to.
£1.20

(B71-51002)

RPVK/B/FL — Arrangements. Automata. Cassette organs
Philips philicorda cassette album. — London: Chappell, 1971. — 32p; 4to.
Unpriced

(B71-50533)

RPVK/CM — Electronic organ. Arrangements. Musical plays
Kern, Jerome
Show boat/ by Jerome Kern; selection; arranged for all G and C electric chord organs by Bert Brewis. — London: Chappell, 1971. — 12p; obl.4to.
£0.30

(B71-51003)

RPVK/CM/AY — Arrangements. Musical plays. Collections
Sullivan, *Sir* Arthur
Gilbert and Sullivan songs/ by Sir Arthur Sullivan; arranged for 12 18 button chord organs by Cecil Bolton. — London: Francis, Day and Hunter, 1971. — 44p; 4to.
£0.50

(B71-51004)

RPVK/DW — Arrangements. Songs, etc
Lennon, John
50 great songs, by John Lennon and Paul McCartney; arranged for C and G chord organs. — London: Northern Songs (Music Sales), 1971. — 65p; 4to.
£1.25

(B71-51005)

RSPM — UNACCOMPANIED ACCORDION SOLOS
RSPMJ — Miscellaneous works
Leslie, John
Tyrolean carnival: accordion solo/ by John Leslie. — London:
Bosworth, 1971. — 4p; 4to.
£0.15

(B71-50112)

Surdin, Morris
Serious I-VIII: piano accordion/ by Morris Surdin. — London:
Boosey and Hawkes, 1970. — 21p; 4to.
Unpriced

(B71-50113)

RSPMK/DW — Arrangements. Songs, etc
Crossman, Gerald
Two accordion pieces/ arranged by Gerald Crossman. — London:
Feldman, 1971. — 5p; 4to.
Contents:- The bailiff's daughter of Islington. — Annie Laurie.
£0.20

(B71-51006)

RXM — STRING ORCHESTRA
RXME — Sonatas
Albinoni, Tommaso
[Trattenimenti armonici per camera divisi in dodici sonate. Op.6, no.
2]. Sonata for string orchestra. Op. 6, no. 2/ by Tommaso Albinoni;
arranged and edited by Frederick F. Polnauer. — London: Chester,
1971. — 4to.
Score (16p.) & 6 parts.
Unpriced

(B71-51008)

Kendell, Iain
Sonata for strings/ by Iain Kendell. — London: Chester, 1971. — 8vo.
Score (18p.) & 6 parts.
Unpriced

(B71-51007)

RXMG — Suites
O Riada, Sean
Hercules dux Ferrariae: Nomos no.1 for strings/ [by] Sean O' Riada.
— Dublin (29 Westland Row, Dublin): Woodtown Music, 1970. —
viii,29p; fol.
Unpriced

(B71-50114)

Walker, George
The Anthony Gell suite (in olden style): for strings and woodwind
(optional)/ by George Walker. — London: Bosworth, 1970. — 4to.
Score (18p.) & 9 parts. Duration 26 mins.
Unpriced

(B71-50115)

RXMJ — Miscellaneous works
Berger, Jean
Divertissement: for string orchestra/ by Jean Berger. — New York:
Schirmer; London: Chappell, 1971. — 4to.
Score (25p.) & 5 parts.
Unpriced

(B71-50534)

Tomlinson, Geoffrey
Divertimento: for string orchestra/ by Geoffrey Tomlinson. —
London: Boosey and Hawkes, 1970. — 4to.
Score (35p.) & 6 parts. Duration 15 mins.
£4.10

(B71-50116)

Trimble, Lester
Notturno: for strings/ by Lester Trimble. — New York: Peters;
[London]: [Hinrichsen], 1970. — 8vo.
Score (12p,) & 5 parts.
£1.60

(B71-50535)

RXMP — SOLO INSTRUMENT (S) & STRING ORCHESTRA
RXMPSF — Violin & string orchestra. Concertos
Vivaldi, Antonio
[Concerto for violin in B flat major, (The Posthorn), P.350]. Konzert,
B-dur (das Posthorn): für Violino und Streichorchester/ [by] Antonio
Vivaldi; herausgegeben von Manfred Fechner. — Leipzig: Peters;
London: Hinrichsen, 1969. — 19p; 4to.
£1.25

(B71-50536)

RXMPSNTSRF — Two violins, cello & string orchestra. Concertos
Boyce, William
Concerto grosso in B minor: for two solo violins, solo violoncello and
string orchestra/ by William Boyce; edited by Gwilym Beechey. —
London: Eulenburg, 1971. — vi,19p; 8vo.
Miniature score.
£0.60

(B71-51009)

RXMPSSF — Double bass & string orchestra. Concertos
Hofmann, Wolfgang
[Concerto for double bass & string orchestra]. Konzert: für
Kontrabass und Streicher/ [by] Wolfgang Hofmann. — Frankfurt:
Litolff, Peters; London: [Hinrichsen], 1970. — 32p; 8vo.
Study score.
£1.00

(B71-50537)

RXMPUNS — Wind quartet & string orchestra
Sutermeister, Heinrich
Sérénade pour Montreux: pour 2 hautbois, 2 cors et orchestre à
cordes/ [by] Heinrich Sutermeister. — London: Schott, 1971. — 32p;
8vo.
Study score.
£1.60

(B71-50538)

RXMPVRF — Flute & string orchestra. Concertos
Quantz, Johann Joachim
[Concerto for flute & string orchestra in G major]. Concerto in sol
maggiore: per flauto, archi e continuo/ by Johann Joachim Quantz;
edited with cadenzas by Oliver Nagy. — London: Boosey and
Hawkes, 1969. — 4to.
Score (36p.) & 6 parts.
Unpriced

(B71-50117)

RXMPVRG — Flute & string orchestra. Suites
Telemann, Georg Philip
[Suite for flute & string orchestra in A minor]. Suite in A minor: for
flute and strings/ by Georg Phillip Telemann; edited by Louis Moyse.
— New York: Schirmer; London: Chappell, 1971. — 4to.
Score (28p.) & 5 parts.
Unpriced

(B71-50539)

RXMPVRNU/Y — Two flutes & string orchestra. Fugues
Bach, Wilhelm Friedemann
[Adagio and fugue for two flutes & string orchestra]. Adagio und
Fuge: für 2 Querflöten und Streichorchester. Falck 65/ [by] Wilhelm
Friedemann Bach; herausgegeben von Walter Lebermann. — Mainz;
London: Schott, 1971. — 15p; 4to.
£1.00

(B71-50540)

RXMPVWF — Bassoon & string orchestra. Concertos
Vivaldi, Antonio
[Concerto for bassoon in F major. P.318]. Konzert, F-dur: für
Fagott und Streichorchester/ [by] Antonio Vivaldi; herausgegeben
von Walter Kolneder. — Leipzig: Peters; London: Hinrichsen, 1970.
— 23p; 4to.
£1.75

(B71-50541)

RXMPWSF — Trumpet & string orchestra. Concertos
Genzmer, Harald
[Concerto for trumpet & string orchestra]. Konzert: für Trompete
und Streicher/ [by] Harald Genzmer. — Frankfurt: Litolff, Peters;
London: [Hinrichsen], 1970. — 39p; 8vo.
Study score.
£1.50

(B71-50542)

RXN — Ensembles
Schubert, Franz
[Overture for strings in C minor. D.8]. Ouverture, C-moll: für
Streicher (Zweite Fassung)/ [by] Franz Schubert; zum ersten Mal
herausgegeben von Ernst Hess. — Frankfurt: Litolff, Peters;
[London]: [Hinrichsen], 1971. — 21p; 4to.
Five-part version.
£1.60

(B71-50543)

Schubert, Franz
[Overture for strings in C minor. D.8]. Overture, C-moll: für
Streicher/ [by] Franz Schubert; zum ersten Mal herausgegeben von
Ernst Hess. — Frankfurt: Litolff, Peters; London: [Hinrichsen],
1970. — 16p; 4to.
Four-part version.
£1.60

(B71-50544)

RXN/AY — Collections
Fletcher, Stanley
New tunes for strings/ by Stanley Fletcher. — New York; [London]:
Boosey and Hawkes, 1971. — 4to.
Teacher's book (68p.) & 4 parts.
£4.90

(B71-51010)

RXNS — Quartets
Dessau, Paul
[Quartet for strings, no.1]. Streichquartett no.1/ [by] Paul Dessau. —
Leipzig: Litolff; [London]: [Hinrichsen], 1969. — 4v; 4to.
£2.10

(B71-50545)

Durko, Zsolt
[Quartet for strings, no.2]. Quatuor à cordes no.2/ by Zsolt Durko.
— London: Boosey and Hawkes, 1971. — 16p; obl. fol.
Unpriced

(B71-50546)

Forbes, Sebastian
[Quartet for strings, no.1]. String quartet no.1/ by Sebastian Forbes.
— London: Chester, 1971. — 39p; 8vo.
Unpriced

(B71-50547)

Hedges, Anthony
[Quartet for strings (1970). Op. 41]. String quartet (1970). Op. 41/
by Anthony Hedges. — London: British & Continental Music, 1971.
— 32p; 8vo.
Miniature score.
Unpriced

(B71-50548)

Kelemen, Milko
Motion: für Streichquartett/ [by] Milko Kelemen. — Frankfurt:
Litolff, Peters; London: [Hinrichsen], 1970. — 23p; 8vo.
Study score.
£0.90

(B71-50549)

Porter, Quincy
[Quartet for strings, no.3]. String quartet no.3/ by Quincy Porter. —
New York: Peters; [London]: [Hinrichsen], 1970. — 32p; 8vo.
£1.10

(B71-50550)

Stevens, Bernard
[Quartet for strings, no.2]. String quartet no.2/ by Bernard Stevens.
— [Great Yarmouth]: Galliard, 1966. — 4to.
Score (45p.) & 4 parts. Title page imprint: London.
Unpriced

(B71-51011)

RXNT — Trios
Haydn, Michael
Divertimento for viola, cello and double bass [in E flat major]/ by
Michael Haydn; edited by Ian White & Rodney Slatford. — London:
Yorke Edition, 1971. — 4to.
Score (6p.) & 3 parts.
Unpriced

(B71-50551)

Haydn, Michael
Divertimento for viola, cello & double bass [in E flat major]/ by
Michael Haydn; edited by Ian White & Rodney Slatford. — London:
Yorke, 1971. — 4to.
Score (6p.) & 3 parts.
Unpriced

(B71-50552)

S — VIOLIN
S/AC — Tutors
Suzuki, Shinichi
Suzuki violin school: Suzuki method. — Revised ed. — London:
Boosey and Hawkes. —
Vol.1. — 1970. — 2v; 4to.
Piano part (24p.), violin part (23p.).
Unpriced

(B71-50553)

Vol.2. — 1970. — 2v; 4to.
Piano part (24p.), violin (23p.).
Unpriced

(B71-50554)

Vol.3. — 1970. — 2v; 4to.
Piano part (26p.), violin part (20p.).
Unpriced

(B71-50555)

Vol.4. — 1970. — 2v; 4to.
Piano part (32p.), violin part (22p.).
Unpriced

(B71-50556)

SM — VIOLIN BAND
SMK/DM/AY — Arrangements. Hymns. Collections
Henriksen, Josef
Fifty hymn melodies for school assembly/ arranged for violin class
beginners with piano accompaniment by Josef Henriksen. —
Hoddesdon: St Gregory Publishing Co., 1969. — 53p; obl. 8vo.
£0.825

(B71-51012)

SNTPW — TWO VIOLINS & KEYBOARD
SNTQE — Two violins & piano. Sonatas
Gal, Hans
Sonata for two violins & pianoforte. Op. 96/ by Hans Gal. —
Hamburg; London: Simrock, 1971. — 4to.
Score (52p.) & 2 parts.
£1.75

(B71-51013)

SNU — VIOLIN DUETS
SNUEM — Sonatinas
Fletcher, Stanley
[Sonatina for violin duet]. Sonatina for two violins/ by Stanley
Fletcher. — New York; [London]: Boosey and Hawkes, 1971. — 2v;
4to.
£1.10

(B71-50557)

SNUK/DW — Arrangements. From songs, etc
Villa-Lobos, Heitor
Modinha [Serestas no.5]: 1 violao [with] Adeus, Bela Morena; [and,
Cirandinhas no.2]: 2 violaoes/ [by] H. Villa-Lobos; arranjos para
violao de Isaias Savio. — Rio de Janeiro: Arthur Napoleao;
[London]: [Essex Music], 1971. — 4p; 4to.
Unpriced
Primary classification SPMK

(B71-50581)

SP — VIOLIN & PIANO
SP/AY — Collections
Doflein, Elma
Music for violin and piano: a collection in 4 books in progressive
order/ [compiled by] Elma and Erich Doflein. — Mainz; London:
Schott. —
3: From Vivaldi to Viotti: 25 pieces and 1 sonata (changes of position). —
1971. — 48p; 4to.
£1.50

(B71-50558)

SP/T — Variations
Chávez, Carlos
Variations for violin with piano/ by Carlos Chávez. — New York:
Schirmer; London: Chappell, 1971. — 4to.
Score (15p.) & part.
Unpriced

(B71-50559)

SPE — Sonatas
Croft, William
[Sonata for violin and basso continuo in G minor]. Sonata in G
minor: for violin and continuo (cello ad lib.)/ by William Croft; edited
by Michael Tilmouth. — 4to.
Score (7p.) & part.
£0.60

(B71-51014)

Veracini, Francesco Maria
[Sonatas for violin & harpsichord. Op.2]. Sonate accademiche. Op.2:
für Violine und bezifferten Bass, Violine und Klavier (Cembalo,
Orgel) mit Violoncello ad libitum/ [by] Francesco Maria Veracini;
herausgegeben von Walter Kolneder. — Leipzig: Peters; [London]:
[Hinrichsen]. —
Sonata 1, D-dur. — 1961. — 4to.
Score (23p) & 2 parts.
£0.525

(B71-50560)

Sonata 2, B-dur. — 1963. — 19p; 4to.
Score (19p) & 2 parts.
£0.525

(B71-50561)

Sonata 3, C-dur. — 1964. — 4to.
Score (22p) & 2 parts.
£0.525

(B71-50562)

Sonata 4, F-dur. — 1966. — 4to.
Score (20p) & 2 parts.
£0.725

(B71-50563)

Sonata 7, d-moll. — 1968. — 4to.
Score (15p) & 2 parts.
Unpriced

(B71-50564)

Sonata 8, e-moll. — 1970. — 4to.
Score (12p) & 2 parts.
£0.80

(B71-50565)

Sonata 9, A-dur. — 1970. — 12p; 4to.
Score (12p) & 2 parts.
£0.80

(B71-50566)

Sonata 12, d-moll. — 1961. — 24p; 4to.
Score (24p) & 2 parts.
£0.80

(B71-50567)

SPG — Suites
Philidor, Anne Danican
[Suite for oboe and basso continuo no.1 in G minor (1er livre)]. Suite 1, g-Moll: für Oboe (Querflöte, Violine) und Basso continuo./ [by] Anne Danican-Philidor; herausgegeben von Hugo Ruf. — Mainz; London: Schott, 1971. — 4to.
Score (10p.) & 2 parts.
£0.90
Primary classification VTPG

(B71-50664)

SPJ — Miscellaneous works
Russell, Leslie
[Suite for flute & piano, no.1]. Suite one: for flute (or violin) and piano/ by Leslie Russell. — London: Boosey and Hawkes, 1971. — 4to.
Score (7p.) & part.
y0.50
Primary classification VRPJ

(B71-51072)

Sáry, László
Fluttuazioni: per violino e pianoforte/ [by] László Sáry. — London: Boosey and Hawkes, 1971. — 14p; fol.
Unpriced

(B71-50568)

Villa-Lobos, Heitor
[Os martírios dos insetos - Excerpts]. A Mariposa na luz: violino e piano/ [by] H. Villa-Lobos. — Rio de Janeiro: Arthur Napoleão; London: Essex Music, 1971. — 4to.
Score (4p.) & part.
Unpriced

(B71-50569)

SPK — Arrangements
Beethoven, Ludwig van
[Romances for violin & orchestra. Op.40 & 50]. Romanzen. Op.40 (G-dur), Op.50 (F-dur): für Violine und Orchester/ [by] L. van Beethoven; Bezeichnung der Violinstimme von Igor Oistrach; Klavierauszug von Manfred Fechner. — Leipzig: Peters; [London]: [Hinrichsen], 1970. — 4to.
Score (16p.) & part.
£0.90

(B71-50571)

Manicke, Dietrich
Aria: for violin and orchestra (1949/69)/ [by] Dietrich Manicke. — Piano score. — Hamburg; London: Simrock, 1971. — 4to.
Score (7p.) & part.
£0.55

(B71-50570)

SPK/AAY — Arrangements. Collections
Lenkei, Gabriella
Violin music for beginners/ edited by Gabriella Lenkei. — London: Boosey and Hawkes, 1971. — 4to.
Score & part.
£0.80

(B71-50572)

SPK/LF — Arrangements. Concertos
Beethoven, Ludwig van
[Concerto for violin in D major. Op.61]. Violin-Konzert, D-Dur: für Violine und Orchester. Op.61/ [by] Ludwig van Beethoven; herausgegeben von Max Rostal. — Klavierauszug. — Mainz; London: Schott, 1971. — 4to.
Score (58p.) & part.
£1.50

(B71-50573)

Paganini, Nicolo
[Concerto for violin, no.3, in E major]. Concerto no.3: per violino ed orchestra/ by Nicolò Paganini. — [Eindhoven]: N.V. Philips' Photographische Industrie; [London]: [Chappell], 1971. — 40p; fol.
A newly discovered work. Reduction for violin and piano.
Unpriced

(B71-51015)

Shostakovich, Dmitri
[Concerto for violin, no.2. Op.129]. Konzert No.2 für Violine und Orchester. Op.129/ by Dmitri Schostakowitsch; bezeichnung der Violinstimme von David Oistrach. — Leipzig: Peters; London: Hinrichsen. —
Ausgabe für Violine und Klavier vom Komponisten. — 1970. — 4to.
Score (43p.) & part.
£2.00

(B71-50574)

Tchaikovsky, Peter
[Concerto for violin in D major. Op.35]. Konzert, D-dur. Op.35: für Violine und Orchester/ [by] P. Tchaikovski. — Leipzig: Peters; London: Hinrichsen. —
Ausgabe für Violine und Klavier von Komponisten/ herausgegeben von Konstantin Mostras und David Oistrach. — 1969. — 4to.
Score (70p.) & part.
£1.40

(B71-50575)

Vivaldi, Antonio
[Concerto for violin in B flat major, (The Posthorn). P.350]. Konzert, B-dur (das Posthorn): für Violine und Streichorchester/ [by] Antonio Vivaldi; herausgegeben von Manfred Fechner. — Leipzig: Peters; London: Hinrichsen. —
Score (12p) & part.
Klavierauszug/ von Erhard Franke. — 1969. — 12p; 4to.
£0.90

(B71-50576)

SPLTQ — VIOLIN & HARP
SPLTQE — Sonatas
Donizetti, Gaetano
[Sonata for violin & harp in G major]. Sonate: Violine (Flöte) und Harfe/ [by] Gaetano Donizetti; zum ersten Mal herausgegeben von Raymond Meylan. — Frankfurt: Litolff, Peters; [London]: [Hinrichsen], 1970. — 4to.
Score (7p.) & part. The original manuscript bears no title; reasons of analogy justify naming the work a sonata'. — Publisher's note.
£0.80
Also classified at VRPLTQK/AE

(B71-50577)

SPLX — VIOLIN & PERCUSSION
Dubrovay, László
Sei duo: per violino e percussioni/ [by] László Dubrovay. — London: Boosey and Hawkes, 1971. — 7p; fol.
Unpriced

(B71-50578)

SPM — UNACCOMPANIED VIOLIN SOLOS
Prokofiev, Sergei
[Sonata for violin solo. Op.115]. Sonate für Violine solo. Opus 115/ [by] Sergej Prokofjew; herausgegeben von Ruggiero Ricci. — Leipzig: Peters; [London]: [Hinrichsen], 1969. — 8p; 4to.
£0.90

(B71-50579)

SPMK — Arrangements
Lorenzo Fernández, Oscar
[Suites for piano. Excerpts]. Caminho da serra; [and], Cacando Borboletas; [and], Madrugada; [and], Na Beira do Rio/ [by] Oscar Lorenzo Fernandez; arranjos por violao de Isaias Savio. — Rio de Janeiro: Arthur Napoleao; [London]: [Essex Music], 1971. — 5p; 4to.
Unpriced

(B71-50580)

Villa-Lobos, Heitor
Modinha [Serestas no.5]: 1 violao [with] Adeus, Bela Morena; [and, Cirandinhas no.2]: 2 violaoes/ [by] H. Villa-Lobos; arranjos para violao de Isaias Savio. — Rio de Janeiro: Arthur Napoleao; [London]: [Essex Music], 1971. — 4p; 4to.
Unpriced
Also classified at SNUK/DW

(B71-50581)

SQ — VIOLA
SQNTPWK/LF — Two violas & keyboard. Arrangements. Concertos
Telemann, Georg Philip
[Concerto for two violas, strings & basso continuo in G major]. Konzert, G-Dur: für 2 Violen, Streicher und Basso continuo/ [by] Georg Philip Telemann; herausgegeben von Walter Lebermann. Klavierauszug. — Mainz; London: Schott, 1971. — 4to.
Score (18p.) & 2 parts.
Unpriced

(B71-50119)

SQP — VIOLA & PIANO
SQPK/DW/G/AYB — Arrangements. Folk songs. Collections. Europe
Widdicombe, Trevor
Forty tunes: for the viola/ graded and arranged with piano accompaniments by Trevor Widdicombe. — London: Curwen, 1971. — 4to.
Score (24p.) & part.
Unpriced

(B71-50582)

SQPK/LF — Arrangements. Concertos
Brixi, Franz Xaver
[Concerto fur viola in C major]. Konzert, C-Dur: für Viola und Orchestra/ [by] Franz Xaver Brixi; Erstmals herausgegeben und mit Kadenzen versehen von Walter Lebermann. Klavierauszug vom Herausgeber. — Mainz; London: Schott, 1970. — 4to.
Score (34p.) & part.
£1.30

(B71-50120)

Hoffstetter, Roman
[Concerto for viola in C major]. Konzert, C-Dur: für Viola, Streicher, 2 Oboen und 2 Hörner/ [by] Roman Hoffstetter; Erstmals herausgegeben und mit Kadenzen versehen von Walter Lebermann. — Mainz; London: Schott. —
Klavierauszug von Helmut May. — 1971. — 4to.
Score (36p) & part.
£1.80

(B71-50583)

SQPLSR — VIOLA & CELLO
SQPLSSVE — Sonatas
Dittersdorf, Carl Ditters von
Duetto for viola & violone (or double bass) [in E flat major]/ by K. Ditters von Dittersdorf; edited by Wolfgang Stert. — London: Yorke, 1971. — 15p; 4to.
'... well known as a sonata for viola and pianoforte, Dittersdorf's 'Duetto' is published here for the first time in the so-called 'Schwerin' version ...' - Publisher's note.
Unpriced

(B71-50584)

SQPM — UNACCOMPANIED VIOLA SOLOS
SQPMJ — Miscellaneous works
Berio, Luciano
Sequenza VI: per viola solo/ [by] Luciano Berio. — London: Universal, 1971. — 6 leaves; fol.
Unpriced

(B71-50585)

SR — CELLO
SR/AC — Tutors
Cole, Hugo
Playing the cello: an approach through live music making/ by Hugo Cole and Anna Shuttleworth. — London: Novello, 1971. — 2v.(87p; 48p); 4to.
1.50

(B71-50586)

Friss, Antal
Violoncello tutor/ by Antal Friss. — London: Boosey and Hawkes. —
Vol.3. — 1971. — 88p; 4to.
Piano accompaniments (16p.) as insert.
Unpriced

(B71-50587)

SR/AF — Exercises
Bunting, Christopher
Six string-crossing studies: for cello solo/ by Christopher Bunting. — London: Oxford University Press, 1971. — 7p; 4to.
ISBN 0 19 355751 7 : Unpriced

(B71-50588)

Bunting, Christopher
Six velocity studies: for cello solo/ by Christopher Bunting. — London: Oxford University Press, 1971. — 4p; 4to.
ISBN 0 19 355752 5 : £0.40

(B71-50589)

Popper, David
[10 mittelschwere grosse Etüden. Op.76,II]. Studies (preparatory to the high school of cello playing). Op. 76/ by David Popper. — New York: Schirmer; [London]: [Chappell], 1971. — 21p; 4to.
Unpriced

(B71-51016)

SRNU — CELLO DUETS
Alcock, John, b.1740
A favorite duet: for two bassoons or violoncellos/ by John Alcock; edited by Stanley Sadie. — Banbury (Overthorpe Hall, Banbury, Oxon.): Piers Press, 1970. — 7p; 4to.
Unpriced
Primary classification VWNU

(B71-50148)

Dotzauer, Justus Johann Friedrich
[Duets for cellos. Opus 15]. Duos: für zwei Violoncelli. Opus 15/ herausgegeben von Bernhard Weigart. Spielpartitur. — Mainz; London: Schott, 1970. — 24p; 4to.
£0.90

(B71-50121)

Offenbach, Jacques
[Duets for cellos, nos.1-3. Op.51]. Drei Duette: für Violoncelli. Op.51/ [by] Jacques Offenbach; herausgegeben von Walter Lebermann. — Mainz; London: Schott, 1971. — 2v; 4to.
£1.20

(B71-50590)

SRP — CELLO & PIANO
SRP/T — Variations
Dinn, Freda
Variations on 'Good morrow, gossip Joan'/ by Freda Dinn. — London: Schott, 1971. — 4to.
Score (3p.) & part.
Unpriced

(B71-51017)

SRP/W — Rondos
Hellendaal, Pieter, b.1721
[Sonata for cello and keyboard in B flat major. Op.5, no.3 - Excerpts]. Rondo: for cello and piano/ by Peter Hellendaal; edited by Freda Dinn. — London: Schott, 1971. — 4to.
Score (3p.) & part.
Unpriced

(B71-51018)

SRPE — Sonatas
Binkerd, Gordon
Sonata: for cello and piano/ by Gordon Binkerd. — New York; [London]: Boosey and Hawkes, 1971. — 56p; 4to.
£3.15

(B71-50591)

Boccherini, Luigi
[Sonatas for cello & piano]. Six sonatas: for violoncello and piano/ by Luigi Boccherini; solo part edited and bass part realised by Analee Bacon. — New York: Schirmer; London: Chappell, 1970. — 4to.
Score (86p.) & part.
Unpriced

(B71-50122)

Brahms, Johannes
[Sonata for cello & piano in F major. Op.99]. Sonata in F major. Op.99: for cello and piano/ by Johannes Brahms. — New York: Schirmer; [London]: [Chappell], 1971. — 4to.
Score (31p.) & part.
Unpriced

(B71-51019)

Defesch, Willem
[Sonata for cello & basso continuo in G minor. Op.8, no.5]. Sonata, g moll: für Violoncello und Basso continuo/ [by] Willem de Fesch; herausgegeben von Edwin Koch und Bernhard Weigart. — Mainz; London: Schott, 1971. — 4to.
Score (8p.) & part.
£0.80

(B71-50592)

Galliard, Johann Ernst
[Sonata for bassoon and basso continuo in G major]. Sonata, G-Dur: für Fagott oder Violoncello und Basso continuo/ [by] Johann Ernst Galliard; herausgegeben von Hugo Ruf. — Mainz; London: Schott, 1971. — 4to.
Score (7p.) & 2 parts.
£0.90
Primary classification VWPE

(B71-50684)

Muczynski, Robert
[Sonata for cello & piano. Op.25]. Sonata for cello and piano. Op.25/ by Robert Muczynski; cello part edited by Gordon Epperson. — New York: Schirmer; London: Chappell, 1971. — 4to.
Score (32p.) & part.
Unpriced

(B71-50123)

Paxton, Stephen
[Sonata for cello and keyboard in D major. Op.3, No.2]. Sonata. Op.3, No.2/ by Stephen Paxton; edited by Freda Dinn. — London: Schott, 1971. — 4to.
Score (7p.) &part.
Unpriced

(B71-51020)

Webern, Anton von
[Sonata for cello & piano]. Cello sonata: for cello and piano/ by Anton von Webern; edited by Friedrich Gulda. — London: Boosey and Hawkes, 1970. — 2v; 4to.
Two copies, the second 'provided for the convenience of the soloist' with the cello part printed on p.8.
Unpriced

(B71-50593)

SRPH — Dances
Maxwell, Michael
A little dance; and, Waltz: for cello and piano/ by Michael Maxwell.
— London: Schott, 1971. — 4to.
Score (6p.) & part.
Unpriced

(B71-51021)

SRPHR/T — Minuets. Variations
Flackton, William
[Sonata for cello and keyboard in F major. Op.2, No.3 - Excerpts].
Minuet and variation/ by William Flackton; edited by Freda Dinn. —
London: Schott, 1971. — 4to.
Score (3p.) & part.
Unpriced

(B71-51022)

SRPJ — Miscellaneous works
Alexander, Arthur
Southward bound/ by Arthur Alexander; cello part edited by Herbart
Withers. — London: Schott, 1971. — 4to.
Score (3p.) & part. — Contents:- Song of the voyager. — Ocean calm.
Unpriced

(B71-51024)

Alwyn, William
Mountain scenes: for cello and piano/ by William Alwyn. — London:
Schott, 1971. — 4to.
Score (7p.) & part. — Contents: - In the canoe. — Emerald lake. — On the trail.
Unpriced

(B71-51025)

Corker, Marjorie
In Ireland/ [by] Marjorie Corker. — London: Schott, 1971. — 4to.
Score (3p.) & part. — Contents:- On the hills. — On the lake.
Unpriced

(B71-51026)

Davidov, Charles
Romance sans paroles. [Op.23]/ by Carl Davidoff. — London:
Schott, 1971. — 4to.
Score (5p.) & part.
Unpriced

(B71-51027)

Graves, John
Cathedral city/ by John Graves. — London: Schott, 1971. — 4to.
Score (8p.) & part. — Contents:- The swans glide on the Bishop's Palace moat.
— In the cathedral. — It is market day in the square.
Unpriced

(B71-51028)

Paxton, Stephen
Allegro moderato. [Op.3, no. 5]/ by Stephen Paxton; arranged for
cello and piano by Freda Dinn. — London: Schott, 1971. — 4to.
Score (3p.) & part.
Unpriced

(B71-51029)

Ridout, Alan
Bagatelles/ by Alan Ridout. — London: Schott, 1971. — 4to.
Score (7p.) & part.
Unpriced

(B71-51030)

Swain, Freda
Walking; and, Dream tide/ by Freda Swain. — London: Schott, 1971.
— 4to.
Score (4p.) & part.
Unpriced

(B71-51031)

SRPK — Arrangements
Bach, Johann Sebastian
[Concerto for clavier in F minor. S1056 - Excerpts]. Largo and
allegretto/ by J.S. Bach; arranged by Herbert Withers. — London:
Schott, 1971. — 4to.
Score (4p.) & part.
Unpriced

(B71-51032)

Elgar, *Sir* Edward, *bart*
Dream children. [Op.43,no.2]/ by Edward Elgar; arranged for cello
and piano by Herbert Withers. — London: Schott, 1971. — 4to.
Score (4p.) &part.
Unpriced

(B71-51033)

Haydn, Joseph
[Concerto for cello in D major. Hob. VII b/2. - Excerpts]. Adagio/
by Joseph Haydn; simplified version by Herbert Withers. — London:
Schott, 1971. — 4to.
Score (4p.) & part.
Unpriced

(B71-51023)

Lalo, Edouard
[Concerto for violin in G minor, 'Concerto russe'. Op. 29 - Excerpts].
Chants russes/ by Eduard Lalo; violoncello part revised by Herbert
Withers. — London: Schott, 1971. — 4to.
Score (3p.) & part.
Unpriced

(B71-51034)

Purcell, Henry
Air [in D minor]/ by Henry Purcell; arranged for cello and piano by
A. Moffat [and] P. Such. — London: Schott, 1971. — 4to.
Not in Zimmermann; an attribution to Henry Purcell is suppositious. — Score
(3p.) & part.
Unpriced

(B71-51035)

Schumann, Robert
Abendlied. [Op.85, no.12]/ by Robert Schumann; arranged for cello
and piano by S. Lee. — London: Schott, 1971. — 4to.
Score (3p.) & part.
Unpriced

(B71-51036)

SRPK/AAY — Arrangements. Collections
Forbes, Watson
Easy classics for cello/ arranged by Watson Forbes, Irene Demuth
and Shena Fraser. — London: Oxford University Press. —
Book 2/ arranged for cello and piano by Irene Demuth and Shena Fraser. —
1971. — Score (11p.) and part; 4to.
Score & part. Book 1, arranged by Watson Forbes, is entered under his name.
ISBN 0 19 356578 1 : £0.40

(B71-50594)

Lengyel, Endre
Violoncello music for beginners/ edited by Endre Lengyel and Árpád
Pejtsik. — London: Boosey and Hawkes, 1971. — 4to.
Score (44p.) & part.
£0.80

(B71-50595)

SRPK/AH — Arrangements. Dances
Mozart, Wolfgang Amadeus
[Six German dances for violins, bass and wind instruments. K.600,
no.2]. German dance/ by W.A. Mozart; arranged for cello and piano
by E. Rapp. — London: Schott, 1971. — 4to.
Score (3p.) & part.
Unpriced

(B71-51037)

SRPK/AHPP — Arrangements. Malaguenas
Albéniz, Isaac
[Espana. Op. 165 - Excerpts]. Malaguena. Op. 165, no.3/ by Isaac
Albéniz; arranged for cello and piano by J. Stutschewsky. — London:
Schott, 1971. — 4to.
Score (8p.) & part.
Unpriced

(B71-51038)

SRPK/AHR — Arrangements. Minuets
Marshall, Nicholas
Two minuets/ arranged by Nicholas Marshall. — London: Schott,
1971. — 4to.
Score (3p.) & part. — Contents:- Böhm, Georg. Minuet. — Fesch, Willem de.
Minuet from Sonata no.12, Op.8.
Unpriced

(B71-51039)

SRPK/AHVL — Arrangements. Sarabandes
Handel, George Frideric
[Rinaldo - Sorge nel petto]. Sarabande/ by George Frideric Handel;
arranged for cello and piano by W. Burmester [and] A. Moffat. —
London: Schott, 1971. — 4to.
Score (3p.) and part.
Unpriced

(B71-51040)

SRPK/DW — Arrangements. Songs, etc
Schubert, Franz
Wiegenlied. Op.98, no.2/ by Franz Schubert; arranged for cello and
piano by Hugo Becker. — London: Schott, 1971. — 4to.
Score (3p.) & part.
Unpriced

(B71-51041)

SRPK/DW/G/AYDM — Arrangements. Folk songs. Collections.
Ireland
Price, Beryl
Emerald isle: five Irish airs arranged for cello (1st position) and
piano/ by Beryl Price. — London: Oxford University Press, 1971. —
Score (7p) and part; 4to.
Score (7p.) & part.
ISBN 0 19 358302 x : £0.40

(B71-50596)

SRPK/LF — Arrangements. Concertos
Bliss, *Sir* **Arthur**
Concerto for cello & orchestra/ by Arthur Bliss; cello part edited by Mstislav Rostropovich. — Borough Green: Novello. —
Score (45p.) & part.
Cello & piano score. — 1971. — 45p; 4to.
£1.50

(B71-50597)

SRPM — UNACCOMPANIED CELLO SOLOS
SRPME — Sonatas
Leighton, Kenneth
Sonata for cello solo. Op.52/ by Kenneth Leighton. — Borough Green: Novello, 1971. — 17p; 4to.
£0.50

(B71-50598)

SRPMG — Suites
Muczynski, Robert
Gallery: suite for unaccompanied cello/ by Robert Muczynski; edited by Gordon Epperson. — New York: Schirmer; London: Chappell, 1971. — 6p; 4to.
Unpriced

(B71-50599)

SRPMJ — Miscellaneous works
Bozay, Attila
Formazion. Op.16: per violoncello solo/ by Attila Bozay. — London: Boosey and Hawkes, 1971. — 10p; 4to.
Unpriced

(B71-50600)

SS — DOUBLE BASS
SSN — Viol ensembles
Chihara, Paul
Logs: for 1 or more string basses/ by Paul Chihara. — [Hollywood]: Protone Music: Henmar Music; London: Hinrichsen, 1970. — 3p; 4to.
£1.00

(B71-50601)

SSP — DOUBLE BASS & PIANO
SSPGM — Marches
Cruft, Adrian
Prelude and march. Op.60: for double bass or other bass clef instrument and pianoforte/ by Adrian Cruft. — London: Leeds Music, 1971. — 4to.
Score (3p.) & part.
Unpriced

(B71-51042)

SSPH — Dances
Cruft, Adrian
Prelude and dance. Op.68: two light pieces, for double bass and pianoforte/ by Adrian Cruft. — London: Leeds Music. 1971. — 4to.
Score (7p.) & part.
Unpriced

(B71-51043)

SSPJ — Miscellaneous works
Cruft, Adrian
Prelude and scherzo. Op.65: for double bass or other bass clef instrument and pianoforte/ by Adrian Cruft. — London: Leeds Music. 1971. — 4to.
Score (3p.) & part.
Unpriced

(B71-51044)

Elliott, Vernon
Odd man out: for double bass and piano/ by Vernon Elliott. — London: Yorke, 1971. — 4to.
Score (3p.) & part.
Unpriced

(B71-50124)

Maconchy, Elizabeth
Music for double bass and piano/ by Elizabeth Maconchy. — London: Yorke, 1971. — 4to.
2 parts.
Unpriced

(B71-50125)

SSPK/AAY — Arrangements. Collections
Bukalski, Jur Stanislaw
Short pieces: for double bass with piano accompaniment/ ed. [and compiled by] J.S. Bukalski. — Cracow: PWM; Leipzig; [London]: Peters, 1969. — 4to.
Score (20p.) & part.
£0.75

(B71-50602)

ST — VIOL
STN — Ensembles
Byrd, William
The collected works of William Byrd, edited by Edmund H. Fellowes and revised under the direction of Thurston Dart/ Vol. 17; Consort music, newly edited from manuscript and printed sources by Kenneth Elliott. — London: Stainer and Bell, 1971. — ix,167p; 8vo.
£4.75
Primary classification C/AZ

(B71-50723)

STNQR — FIVE VIOLS & ORGAN
Jenkins, John
Consort music in five parts/ by John Jenkins; edited by Richard Nicholson. — London: Faber Music, 1970. — 4to.
Title-page headed 'The Viola da gamba Society of Great Britain'. Score (93p.) & 6 parts.
Unpriced

(B71-50126)

TS — GUITAR
TS/AC — Tutors
Crimlisk, Anthony
Play guitar!: a comprehensive tutor for the complete beginner, of classical folk and creative techniques for the finger style Spanish guitar, by Anthony Crimlisk/ Supplement on chords, chord-shapes and fingerboard harmony. — London: Boosey and Hawkes, 1971. — 38p; 4to.
Contains the words and music of over 20 folk and other songs.
Unpriced

(B71-51045)

Crimlisk, Anthony
Play guitar!: a comprehensive tutor, for the complete beginner, of classical, folk and creative techniques for the finger style Spanish guitar/ by Anthony Crimlisk. — London: Boosey and Hawkes. — Vol.1. — 1971. — 39p; 4to.
With a separate leaf headed 'Appendix C. Chart of the guitar fingerboard' inserted.
Unpriced

(B71-50603)

Vol.2. — 1971. — 41p; 4to.
With a separate leaf headed 'Appendix C. Chart of the guitar fingerboard' inserted.
Unpriced

(B71-50604)

Economides, George C
Classic guitar method including chords and 20 studies/ by George C. Economides. — London: Keith Prowse Music. —
Vol.1. — 1970. — 40p; 4to.
£0.60

(B71-50127)

Vol.2. — 1970. — 41-80p; 4to.
£0.60

(B71-50128)

Economides, George C
The study of the guitar simplified: a complete guitar course in 30 lessons/ by George Economides. — London: Keith Prowse Music. —
Vol.1. — 1970. — 48p; 4to.
Unpriced

(B71-50129)

Gilbert, Bryan Edward
Playing the guitar for the Lord's work/ [by] Bryan Gilbert. — Revised ed. — London (Blundell House, Goodwood Rd, S.E.14): Marshall, Morgan and Scott Ltd, 1971. — 31p: illus, music; 22cm.
Previous ed. 1965.
ISBN 0 551 05435 2 Sd: £0.30

(B71-50130)

Hall, Alan
The classical guitar: a method for beginners/ by Alan Hall; edited by John Pearse. — London (64 Dean St., W1V 6AU): Scratchwood Music, 1971. — 50p; 4to.
£0.75

(B71-50605)

Herfurth, Clarence Paul
A tune a day: for classical guitar: a third instruction book/ by C. Paul Herfurth and Stanley George Urwin. — London: Chappell, 1971. — 35p; 4to.
£0.40

(B71-50606)

Hunt, Edgar
An introduction to playing the Spanish guitar/ by Edgar Hunt. — London: Schott, 1971. — 15p; obl.8vo.
£0.25

(B71-51047)

Sadleir, Richard
Master method for guitar: based on progressive arrangements of
excerpts from the works of great masters/ by Dick Sadleir. —
London: Feldman, 1971. — 45p; 4to.
£0.50

(B71-51048)

TSNT — GUITAR TRIOS
TSNTK — Arrangements
Haydn, Joseph
[Trios for strings. Hob.IV, 1-3]. London trios/ by Joseph Haydn;
transcribed for three guitars by Theodore Norman. — New York:
Schirmer; [London]: [Chappell], 1971. — viii,31p; 4to.
Unpriced

(B71-51049)

TSNU — GUITAR DUETS
Gastoldi, Giovanni Giacomo
Acht Duette: für Gitarren/ [by] Giovanni Giacomo Gastoldi;
herausgegeben von Alf Zschiesche. — Mainz; London: Schott, 1971.
— 19p; 4to.
£0.80

(B71-50607)

Jeffery, Brian
Elizabethan duets/ transcribed from the original and arranged for
guitars by Brian Jeffery. — London: Schott, 1970. — 8p; 4to.
£0.40

(B71-50131)

TSNUK/AG — Duets. Arrangements. Suites
Kuhnau, Johann
[Clavier Übung. Tl.2. Partie for keyboard, no.3 in E minor]. Suite in
A minor/ by Johann Kuhnau; arranged for guitar duet [and
transcribed from E minor] by Jeremy Allison. — Borough Green:
Novello, 1971. — 11p; 4to.
Unpriced

(B71-51050)

TSNUK/AHM — Duets. Arrangements. Ballet music
Sadleir, Dick
Album for guitar/ arranged by Dick Sadleir. — London: Feldman,
1971. — 8p; 4to.
Contents: Tango. Op.165, no.2 by I. Albeniz. — Cygnet's dance (from 'Swan
Lake') by Tschaikowsky. — Granada by I. Albeniz.
£0.35
Primary classification TSPMK/AAY

(B71-50613)

TSPM — UNACCOMPANIED GUITAR SOLOS
TSPMJ — Miscellaneous works
Bresgen, Cesar
Malinconia: fünf Gitarrenstücke/ [by] Cesar Bresgen; eingerichtet
von Barna Kovats. — Mainz; London: Schott, 1971. — 10p; 4to.
£0.80

(B71-50608)

Economides, George
24 études: for the guitar/ by George Economides. — London: KPM
Music, 1971. — 16p; 4to.
£0.50

(B71-50609)

Kovats, Barna
Minutenstücke: für Gitarre/ [by] Barna Kovats. — Mainz; London:
Schott, 1970. — 7p; 4to.
£0.70

(B71-50132)

Mairants, Ivor
Six easy pieces: for classic guitar/ by Ivor Mairants. — London:
British and Continental, 1970. — 9p; 4to.
Unpriced

(B71-50133)

Paganini, Niccolò
Kleine Stücke: für Gitarre/ [by] Niccolò Paganini; bearbeitet und
herausgegeben von László Vereczkey. — Mainz; London: Schott,
1971. — 39p; 4to.
£1.40

(B71-51051)

Visée, Robert de
Gitarrenbuch/ [by] Robert de Visée; aus der Tabulatur übertragen
bezeichnet und herausgegeben von F.J. Giesbert. — Mainz; London:
Schott, 1971. — 27p; 4to.
£1.20

(B71-50610)

TSPMK — Arrangements
Bartók, Béla
[For children. Excerpts]. For children: 25 selected pieces/ by Béla
Bartók; selected and arranged for guitar by Ferenc Brodszky. —
London: Boosey and Hawkes, 1970. — 16p; 4to.
£0.75

(B71-50611)

Beethoven, Ludwig van
Für Elise/ by Ludwig van Beethoven; arranged for solo guitar by
Ivor Mairants. — London: British and Continental, 1970. — 7p; 4to.
Unpriced

(B71-50135)

Brodszky, Ferenc
Lieder und Tänze der Vorklassik: Stücke aus dem 16. bis 18.
Jahrhundert für Gitarre sehr leicht gesetzt/ von Ferenc Brodszky. —
Mainz; [London]: Schott, 1971. — 16p; 4to.
Unpriced

(B71-50612)

Hodgson, Martyn
Seven easy pieces by Elizabethan composers/ transcribed from the
lute tablature and arranged for guitar by Martyn Hodgson. — Leeds:
Regina Music, 1971. — 7p; 4to.
Unpriced

(B71-50134)

Myers, Stanley
Cavatina/ by Stanley Myers: arranged for guitar by John Williams.
— London: Francis, Day and Hunter, 1971. — 3p; 4to.
£0.40

(B71-51052)

TSPMK/AAY — Arrangements. Collections
Sadleir, Dick
Album for guitar/ arranged by Dick Sadleir. — London: Feldman,
1971. — 8p; 4to.
Contents: Tango. Op.165, no.2 by I. Albeniz. — Cygnet's dance (from 'Swan
Lake') by Tschaikowsky. — Granada by I. Albeniz.
£0.35
Also classified at TSNUK/AHM

(B71-50613)

TSPMK/AE — Arrangements. Sonatas
Seixas, Carlos de
[Sonatas for harpsichord in A minor. S.K.74, 80]. Zwei Sonaten/
[by] Carlos Seixas; für Gitarre übertragen und herausgegeben von
Javier Hinojosa. — Mainz; London: Schott, 1971. — 5p; 4to.
£0.50

(B71-50614)

TSPMK/AH/AYD — Arrangements. Dance collections. England
Duarte, John
A delight of English lute music/ transcribed for guitar by John W.
Duarte. — London: Schott, 1971. — 12p; 4to.
£0.60

(B71-51053)

TSPMK/DP/LF/AY — Arrangements. Carols. Christmas. Collections
Brewis, Bert
Christmas songs for guitar/ by Bert Brewis. — London: Chappell,
1970. — 20p; 4to.
Unpriced

(B71-51054)

TSPMK/DP/LF/AYB — Arrangements. Christmas carol collections. Europe
Smith, Isabel
Six carols for guitar/ arranged by Isabel Smith. — London: Schott,
1971. — 6p; 8vo.
£0.30

(B71-51055)

TSPMK/DW/G/AYB — Arrangements. Folk song collections. Europe
Noble, Robert
Folk tunes to accompany: a guide to simple accompaniment for
beginners of all ages in schools, clubs, colleges or the home/ by
Robert Noble. — London: Novello. —
Book 3: Modes and minors. — 1971. — 22p; obl. 8vo.
£0.90

(B71-51056)

TSPMK/DW/G/AYD — Arrangements. From folk songs. Collections. England
Bayford, Dudley Escott
English folk songs: for guitar or banjo/ arranged by Dudley E.
Bayford. — London: Francis, Day and Hunter, 1971. — 65p; 4to.
£0.75

(B71-50615)

TUNU — ZITHER DUETS
TVPMJ — Miscellaneous works
Milan, Luis
El Maestro/ by Luis de Milan; edited, translated, and transcribed by Charles Jacobs. — University Park (Pa.); London: Pennsylvania University Press, 1971. — 319p; 8vo.
ISBN 0 271 00091 0 : Unpriced
Also classified at KE/TVDW

(B71-50616)

TW — LUTE
TW/AZ — Collected works of individual composers
Francesco, *da Milano*
The lute music of Francesco Canova da Milano (1497-1543)/ edited by Arthur J. Ness. — Cambridge (Mass.): Harvard University Press; London Oxford University Press. —
Vols I and II. — 1971. — xxxii,473p: facsim; fol.
Unpriced

(B71-50617)

TWPMJ — Miscellaneous works
Dowland, John
[Varietie of lute-lessons. Excerpts]. Fantasia no.7: per liuto/ [by] John Dowland; bearbeitet für Gitarre von Javier Hinojosa. — Mainz; London: Schott, 1971. — 4p; 4to.
£0.80

(B71-50618)

TX — MANDOLINE
TX/AC — Tutors
Francis & Day's mandoline tutor. — London: Francis, Day and Hunter, 1971. — 28p; 8vo.
£0.25

(B71-50619)

UM — WIND BAND
UMJ — Miscellaneous works
Creston, Paul
Kalevala. Op.95: fantasy on Finnish folksongs, for concert band/ by Paul Creston. — New York: Schirmer; London: Chappell, 1971. — 4to.
Score (38p.) & 65 parts. Duration 10 min.
Unpriced

(B71-50620)

Finney, Ross Lee
Summer in Valley City: for band/ by Ross Lee Finney. — New York: Peters; London: [Hinrichsen], 1971. — 76p; 4to.
Duration 16 1/2 min.
£3.50

(B71-50621)

UMK/Y/JR — Arrangements. Fugues. Film music
Thomson, Virgil
[Tuesday in November. Excerpts]. Fugue and chorale on Yankee Doodle/ by Virgil Thomson; transcribed for concert band by Frank Erickson. — New York: Schirmer; London: Chappell, 1971. — 4to.
Full score (24p.), condensed score (8p.) & 50 parts.
Unpriced

(B71-50622)

UMM — MILITARY BAND
UMMGM — Marches
Turner, J Godfrey
The highlander march/ by J. Godfrey Turner. — London: Feldman, 1971. — 8vo.
Conductor (4p.) & 24 parts.
Unpriced

(B71-51057)

Turner, J Godfrey
Youth on parade: [for military band]/ by J. Godfrey Turner. — London: Feldman, 1971. — 8vo.
Conductor & 22 parts.
Unpriced

(B71-51058)

UMMHLF — Galops
Barsotti, Roger
Gay gnu galop/ by Roger Barsotti. — London: Bosworth, 1971. — 8vo.
Conductor (8p.) & 32 parts.
£1.25

(B71-51059)

UMMJ — Miscellaneous works
Farnon, Dennis
Clarinet caprice/ by Dennis Farnon. — London: Boosey and Hawkes, 1971. — 4to.
Conductor (5p.) & 42 parts.
£2.05

(B71-51060)

Grundman, Clare
An Irish rhapsody: for military band/ by Clare Grundman. — New York; [London]: Boosey and Hawkes, 1971. — 4to.
Full score (32p.) & Condensed score (11p.) & 72 parts.
£8.75

(B71-50623)

Hattori, Koh-Ichi
From the North Country: overture for band/ by Koh-Ichi Hattori. — New York; [London]: Boosey and Hawkes, 1971. — 4to.
Score (19p.), conductor (8p.) & 48 parts.
£2.00

(B71-51061)

Willan, Healey
Elegie heroique/ by Healey Willan. — London: Boosey and Hawkes, 1971. — 4to.
Score & 29 parts.
Unpriced

(B71-50624)

UMMK/DW — Military band. Arrangements. Songs, etc
Gershwin, George
George Gershwin: a symphonic portrait for concert band; arranged by Bruce Chase. — London: Chappell, 1971. — 4to.
Condensed score (20p.) &34 parts.
Unpriced

(B71-51062)

MacLellan, Gene
Snowbird/ by Gene MacLellan; arranged for military band by Edrich Siebert. — London: Ardmore and Beechwood, 1970. — 8vo.
Conductor & 26 parts.
Unpriced

(B71-51063)

UMMK/JR — Arrangements. Film music
Lai, Francis
Love story: theme from [the film]/ by Francis Lai; arranged for military band by John Edmundson. — London: Chappell, 1971. — 4to.
Conductor (6p.) & 48 parts.
Unpriced

(B71-51064)

UMMK/Y/JR — Arrangements. Fugues. Film music
Walton, *Sir* **William**
[Prelude & fugue, 'The Spitfire'. Excerpts]. Spitfire fugue/ by William Walton, arranged by J.L. Wallace. — London: Boosey and Hawkes, 1970. — lv.p; 4to.
Score, conductor & 28 parts (parts £1.70).
Unpriced

(B71-50136)

UMP — WORKS FOR SOLO INSTRUMENT (S) & WIND BAND
UMPVR — Flute & wind band
Griffes, Charles T
Poem: for flute and band/ by Charles T. Griffes; arranged by James Thornton. — New York: Schirmer; London: Chappell, 1971. — 4to.
Score (53p.) & 34 parts.
Unpriced

(B71-50626)

UMPVRF — Flute & wind band. Concertos
Badings, Henk
Concerto: for flute and wind symphony orchestra/ by Henk Badings. — New York: Peters; London: [Hinrichsen], 1970. — 50p; 4to.
Duration 12 min.
£3.50

(B71-50625)

UN — WIND ENSEMBLE
UNN — Wind octets
Lachner, Franz
[Octet for wind instruments in B flat major. Op.156]. Octet for flute, oboe, 2 clarinets, 2 horns and 2 bassoons. Op.156/ by Franz Lachner. — London: Musica rara, 1971. — 4to.
Score (67p.) & 8 parts.
£5.25

(B71-50137)

UNNG — Suites
Krommer, Franz
Octet-partita. Op.79: for 2 oboes, 2 clarinets, 2 horns, 2 bassoons and contrabassoon ad lib/ by Franz Krommer; edited by Roger Hellyer. — London: Musica rara, 1971. — 4to.
Score (30p.) & 9 parts.
Unpriced

(B71-50627)

Krommer, Franz
[Suite for wind octet, no.4, in F major]. Octet-partita: for 2 oboes, 2 clarinets, 2 horns, 2 bassoons and contrabassoon ad. lib. Op.57/ by Franz Krommer, [edited by] Roger Hellyer. — London: Musica rara, 1971. — 4to.
Score (28p.) & 9 parts.
£5.50

(B71-50138)

Krommer, Franz
[Suite for wind octet, no.5, in B flat major]. Octet-partita: for 2 oboes, 2 clarinets, 2 horns, 2 bassoons and contrabassoon ad. lib. Op.67/ by Franz Krommer [edited by] Roger Hellyer. — London: Musica rara, 1971. — 4to.
Score (28p.) & 9 parts.
£5.25

(B71-50139)

UNQ — Sextets
Castil-Blaze, Francois Henri Joseph
[Sextet for wind instruments, no.1 in E flat major]. Sextet no.1 in E flat for 2 clarinets, 2 horns and 2 bassoons/ by Francois Henri Joseph Castil-Blaze; edited by Roger Hellyer. — London: Musica rara, 1971. — 4to.
Score (32p.) & 6 parts.
Unpriced

(B71-51065)

Genzmer, Harald
[Sextet for wind instruments]. Sextett: für Klarinetten in B, 2 Fagotte, 2 Hörner/ [by] Harald Genzmer. — Frankfurt: Litolff, Peters; London: [Hinrichsen], 1970. — 47p; 8vo.
Study score.
£1.50

(B71-50628)

Genzmer, Harald
[Sextet for wind instruments]. Sextett: 2 Klarinetten, 2 Fagotte, 2 Hörner/ [by] Harald Genzmer. — Frankfurt: Litolff, Peters; London: [Hinrichsen], 1970. — 6v; 4to.
Six parts.
£6.00

(B71-50629)

UNR — Quintets
Balassa, Sándor
[Quintet for woodwind instruments. Op.9]. Quintetto a fiati. Op.9/ [by] Sándor Balassa. — London: Boosey and Hawkes, 1971. — 4to.
Score (24p.) & 5 parts.
Unpriced

(B71-50630)

Durkó, Zsolt
Improvvisazioni: per quintetto a fiati/ [by] Zsolt Durkó. — London: Boosey and Hawkes, 1970. — 12p; 4to.
£0.50

(B71-50631)

Reicha, Anton
Two andantes and adagio 'pour le Cor Anglais': for flute, cor anglais, clarinet, horn and bassoon/ by Anton Reicha; edited by Frans Vester. — London: Universal Edition, 1971. — 4to.
Score (18p.) & 5 parts.
Unpriced

(B71-50632)

Stoker, Richard
[Quintet for wind instruments]. Wind quintet: for flute, oboe, clarinet, bassoon, horn/ by Richard Stoker; edited by Leonard Brain. — [London]: Hinrichsen, 1970. — 4to.
Score (12p.) & 5 parts.
Unpriced

(B71-50633)

UNRK — Quintets. Arrangements
Beethoven, Ludwig van
[Sonatas for piano. Op.49, nos.1,2 - Excerpts]. Divertimento in G major/ by Ludwig van Beethoven; arranged for wind quintet, flute, oboe, clarinet, horn, bassoon by Boris Mersson. — London: Bosworth, 1971. — 4to.
Score (18p.) & 5 parts.
£2.25

(B71-51066)

UNRK/A/FK — Quintets. From works for musical clock
Beethoven, Ludwig van
[Five pieces for the musical clock, nos.1,3]. Adagio and allegro for the musical clock/ by L. van Beethoven; realisation for flute, oboe, clarinet, horn & bassoon by Frans Vester. — London: Universal, 1971. — 4to.
Score (12p.) and 6 parts.
Unpriced

(B71-50634)

V — WOODWIND INSTRUMENTS
V/AC — Tutors
Hilton, Lewis B
Learning to teach through playing: a woodwind method/ by Lewis B. Hilton. — Reading (Mass.); London: Addison-Wesley, 1970. — vii,184p; 4to.
Unpriced

(B71-50140)

Oboussier, Philippe
Workbook for woodwind: an elementary group method/ by Philippe Oboussier. — Borough Green: Novello, 1971. — vii,30p; 8vo.
With two cards bearing fingering charts for flute, bassoon, oboe and clarinet.
£0.90

(B71-51067)

VR — FLUTE
VR/AF/AY — Exercises. Collections
Zöller, Karlheinz
Moderne Orchester-Studien: für Flöte/ [compiled by] Karlheinz Zöller. — Mainz; London: Schott. —
Band 1. — 1971. — 72p; 4to.
£3.00

(B71-50635)

Band 2. — 1971. — 56p; 4to.
£2.75

(B71-50636)

VRNTPW — TWO FLUTES & KEYBOARD
VRNTPWE — Sonatas
Handel, George Frideric
[Sonata for two flutes in E minor]. Triosonate e-Moll: für 2 Querflöten und Basso continuo/ [by] Georg Friedrich Händel; herausgegeben von Frank Nagel, Generalbassaussetzung von Winfried Radeke. — Mainz; London: Schott, 1971. — 4to.
Score (15p.) & 3 parts.
£1.10

(B71-50637)

VRNTQ — TWO FLUTES & PIANO
Fürstenau, Anton Bernhard
L'Union: introduction and rondo brilliant. Op.115, on themes from Norma (Bellini), for two flutes and piano/ by Anton Bernhard Fürstenau; edited by András Adorján. — London: Musica rara, 1971. — 4to.
Score (12p.) & part.
Unpriced

(B71-51068)

VRNTQ/W — Rondos
Doppler, Albrecht Franz
Andante & rondo. Op.25: for two flutes & piano/ by Franz Doppler; edited by András Adorján. — London: Musica rara, 1971. — 4to.
Score (15p.) & part.
Unpriced

(B71-50638)

VRNTQK — Two flutes and piano. Arrangements
Doppler, Franz
[Fantasy on Hungarian themes. Op.35]. Hungarian phantasy: for two flutes and piano/ by Franz and Carl Doppler; edited by András Adorján. — London: Musica rara, 1971. — 4to.
Score (23p.) & part. — Originally for two flutes and orchestra.
Unpriced

(B71-51069)

VRP — FLUTE & PIANO
VRP/AY — Collections
Modern flute music/ Book 2; Capriccio, by William Mathias; [and], Canzonetta, by Phylis Tate; [and], Greek pastoral, by Arthur Veal; [and], Bagatelle, by John Addison. — London: Oxford University Press, 1971. — 4to.
Score (22p.) & part.
ISBN 0 19 357821 2 : £0.90

(B71-51070)

Parry, William Howard
Modern flute music/ Book 1; Marcia capricciosa, by Kenneth Leighton; [and], Pavane, by Arnold Cook; [and], Scherzo, by Colin Hand. — London: Oxford University Press, 1971. — 4to.
Score (16.) & part.
ISBN 0 19 357820 4 : £0.90

(B71-51071)

VRPE — Sonatas
Richardson, Alan
Sonatina for flute and piano/ by Alan Richardson. — London: Weinberger, 1971. — 4to.
Score (21p.) & part.
Unpriced

(B71-50639)

Ries, Ferdinand
Sonate sentimentale: for flute or clarinet. Op.169/ by Ferdinand Ries; edited by Georgina Dobrée. — London: Musica rara, 1971. — 8vo.
Score (34p.) & 2 parts.
£2.25

(B71-50141)

VRPG — Suites
Boismortier, Joseph Bodin de
[Suite for flute & basso continuo in B minor. Op.35, no.5]. Suite h-Moll: für Querflöte und Basso continuo/ [by] Joseph Bodin de Boismortier; herausgegeben von Hugo Ruf. — Mainz; London: Schott, 1971. — 4to.
Score (15p.) & 2 parts.
£1.10

(B71-50640)

Boismortier, Joseph Bodin de
[Suite for flute & basso continuo in G major. Op.35, no.2]. Suite, g-Dur: für Querflöte und Basso continuo/ [by] Joseph Bodin de Boismortier; herausgegeben von Hugo Ruf. — Mainz; London: Schott, 1971. — 4to.
Score (12p.) & 2 parts.
£1.00

(B71-50641)

Philidor, Anne Danican
[Suite for oboe and basso continuo no.1 in G minor (1er livre)]. Suite 1, g-Moll: für Oboe (Querflöte, Violine) und Basso continuo,/ [by] Anne Danican-Philidor; herausgegeben von Hugo Ruf. — Mainz; London: Schott, 1971. — 4to.
Score (10p.) & 2 parts.
£0.90
Primary classification VTPG

(B71-50664)

Telemann, Georg Philipp
[Petite Musique de Chambre. Excerpts]. Partita no.3 in C minor: for descant recorder and piano/ by Georg Philipp Telemann; edited by Walter Bergmann. — London: Faber Music, 1971. — 4to.
Score (13p.) & parts.
Unpriced

(B71-50642)

VRPJ — Miscellaneous works
Doppler, Albrecht Franz
Fantasie pastorale hongroise: for flute and piano/ by Albrecht Franz Doppler; edited by Louis Moyse. — New York: Schirmer; London: Chappell, 1971. — 4to.
Score (13p.) & part.
Unpriced

(B71-50142)

Gilbert, Anthony
The incredible flute music. Op.11: for flute and piano/ by Anthony Gilbert. — London: Schott, 1970. — 2v.(14p; 14p); 4to.
Two copies.
Unpriced

(B71-50643)

Rózmann, Akos
Improvvisazione: per flauto e pianoforte/ [by] Akos Rózmann. — London: Boosey and Hawkes, 1971. — 22p; 4to.
Unpriced

(B71-50644)

Russell, Leslie
[Suite for flute & piano, no.1]. Suite one: for flute (or violin) and piano/ by Leslie Russell. — London: Boosey and Hawkes, 1971. — 4to.
Score (7p.) & part.
y0.50
Also classified at SPJ

(B71-51072)

VRPK/LF — Arrangements. Concertos
Boccherini, Luigi
[Concerto for cello & string orchestra, no.3 in G major. WV480]. Konzert no.3, G-Dur: für Violoncello und Streichorchester/ by Luigi Boccherini; herausgegeben und mit Kadenzen versehen von Walter Lebermann. — Mainz; London: Schott, 1971. — 4to.
Score (30p.) & part.
£1.50

(B71-50143)

Quantz, Johann Joachim
[Concerto for flute & string orchestra in G major]. Concerto in sol maggiore: per flauto, archi e continuo/ by Johann Joachim Quantz; arranged for flute and piano, provided with cadences (sic) and edited according to the original manuscript by Oliver Nagy. — London: Boosey and Hawkes, 1969. — 4to.
Score (40p.) & part.
£1.45

(B71-50144)

VRPLSQ — FLUTE & VIOLA
Borgulya, András
4 duetti: per flauto (o flauto dolce) e viola/ [by] András Borgulya. — London: Boosey and Hawkes, 1971. — 11p; 4to.
Unpriced

(B71-50645)

VRPLTQ — FLUTE & HARP
VRPLTQK/AE — Arrangements. Sonatas
Donizetti, Gaetano
[Sonata for violin & harp in G major]. Sonate: Violine (Flöte) und Harfe/ [by] Gaetano Donizetti; zum ersten Mal herausgegeben von Raymond Meylan. — Frankfurt: Litolff, Peters; [London]: [Hinrichsen], 1970. — 4to.
Score (7p.) & part. 'The original manuscript bears no title; reasons of analogy justify naming the work a sonata'. — Publisher's note.
£0.80
Primary classification SPLTQE

(B71-50577)

VRPLVT — FLUTE & OBOE
Binkerd, Gordon
Duo for flute and oboe/ by Gordon Binkerd. — New York; London: Boosey and Hawkes, 1971. — 4to.
£1.25

(B71-50646)

VRPM — UNACCOMPANIED FLUTE SOLOS
VRPM/AY — Collections
Doflein, Erich
16 Stücke: für Flöte allein/ gesammelt und herausgegeben von Erich Doflein. — Mainz; London: Schott, 1971. — 16p; 4to. — (Flauto traverso)
£0.80

(B71-50145)

VRPMG — Suites
Boismortier, Joseph Bodin de
[Suites for flute. Op.36 nos.1-6]. Sechs Suiten: für Querflöte solo/ [by] Joseph Bodin de Boismortier; herausgegeben von Hugo Ruf. — Mainz; London: Schott, 1971. — 28p; 4to.
£1.20

(B71-50647)

VRPMJ — Miscellaneous works
Jungk, Klaus
Appunti: für Flöte/ [by] Klaus Jungk. — Frankfurt: Litolff, Peters; London: [Hinrichsen], 1970. — 7p; 4to.
Unpriced

(B71-50648)

VS — RECORDER
VSK/DH/LL/AY — Arrangements. Motets, anthems, hymns, etc
Bayford, Dudley Escott
Easter hymns and carols/ [arranged] for recorder by Dudley Bayford. — London: Francis, Day and Hunter, 1971. — 17p; 8vo.
Unpriced

(B71-50649)

VSM — RECORDER BAND
VSMJ — Miscellaneous works
Capriccio fugato a dodice/ by Domenico Scarlatti[?]; arranged for four descant, two treble, two tenor and two bass recorders by Francis Baines. — London: Schott, 1971. — 4to.
Eg2451, from which this piece is taken, does not provide the fore-name of the composer. It could, therefore, by Alessandro Scarlatti or, indeed, by anyone else with that surname. No indication is given as to the original instrumentation.
£1.00

(B71-51073)

VSN — Ensembles
Dale, Gordon
A dozen duets: for recorder groups of mixed ability/ by Gordon Dale. — London: Feldman, 1970. — 7p; obl. 8vo.
£0.20

(B71-51074)

VSNQ — RECORDER SEXTETS
VSNQK/DW — Arrangements. Songs, etc
Josquin des Prés
Three six-part pieces/ by Josquin des Prés; transcribed and edited for six recorders descant, two trebles, two tenors and bass, by Kenneth McLeish. — London: Schott, 1971. — 9p; 4to.
Contents:- Pour souhaitter. — J'ay bien cause de lamenter. — Vous ne l'aurez pas.
£0.30

(B71-51075)

VSNQPW – FIVE RECORDERS & KEYBOARD
VSNQQ – Five recorders & piano
Bonsor, Brian
Three into five: for descant, treble (divisi) and tenor (divisi) recorders and piano/ by Brian Bonsor. – London: Schott, 1971. – 4to.
Score (10p.) & part.
£0.50

(B71-50933)

VSNR – RECORDER QUINTETS
VSNRK/DW – Arrangements. Songs
Josquin des Prés
Two five-part pieces/ by Josquin des Prés; transcribed and edited for five recorders, descant, treble I, tenor I (or treble II), tenor II and bass, by Kenneth McLeish. – Mainz; London: Schott, 1971. – 7p; 4to.
Contents:-.
£0.40

(B71-51076)

VSNS – RECORDER QUARTETS
VSNS/T – Variations
Cook, Douglas
Octave variations: for recorder quartet/ by Douglas Cook. – London: Schott, 1971. – 4to.
Score (10p.) & 4 parts.
£0.50

(B71-50650)

VSNSG – Suites
Clover, David
A mini-blues suite: for descant, treble and tenor recorders/ by David Clover. – London: Feldman, 1971. – 4p; 4to.
Unpriced

(B71-50651)

VSNSK/DH – Arrangements. Motets, Anthems, Hymns, etc
Franco, Fernando
Dios itlazu nantzine/ by Hernando Franco; arranged for descant, treble, tenor and bass with percussion ad lib by Roberto Rivera y Rivera, percussion ad lib. part by Manuel Jorge de Elias. – London: Schott, 1971. – 3p; 4to.
£0.40

(B71-51077)

VSNSK/Y – Arrangements. Fugues
Telemann, Georg Philipp
[Twenty little fugues for organ. Excerpts]. Four fugues [nos.20, 7, 9, 13]/ by George Philipp Telemann; arranged for recorder quartet, D. TR. T. B., by Walter Bergmann. – London: Faber Music, 1971. – 9p; 4to.
Unpriced

(B71-50652)

VSNU – RECORDER DUETS
VSNUE/AYD – Sonata collections. England
Ruf, Hugo
Zwei Duos alter englischer Meister: für Altblockflöten (Querflöten, Oboen)/ herausgegeben von Hugo Ruf. – Mainz; London: Schott, 1971. – 11p; 4to.
Contents:- Sonata in F major, by Daniel Purcell. – Sonata in F major, by William Williams.
£0.70

(B71-50653)

VSNUK/AAY – Arrangements. Collections
Rohr, Heinrich
Vortragsbüchlein für das Zusammenspiel: Sopran-und Altblockflöte, Schlagwerk ad lib/ [compiled by] Heinrich Rohr und Franz Lehn. – Mainz; London: Schott, 1971. – 30p; 8vo.
Unpriced

(B71-50654)

VSP – RECORDER & PIANO
VSPJ – Miscellaneous works
Rudrum, Kenneth
Gay recorders: for descant or treble recorder with piano accompaniment/ by Kenneth Rudrum. – London: Paterson, 1971. – 4to.
Unpriced

(B71-51078)

VSPM – UNACCOMPANIED RECORDER
VSPMK/AAY – Arrangements. Collections
Bayford, Dudley Escott
Songs and dances of many nations: for recorder/ arr. by Dudley E. Bayford. – London: Francis, Day and Hunter, 1971. – 29p; 8vo.
£0.25

(B71-51079)

VSRN – Descant recorder ensemble
Self, George
Shriek: for 4, 8 or more descant recorders/ by George Self. – London: Universal, 1971. – 3p; obl.fol.
£0.15

(B71-50655)

VSRPG – Descant recorder & piano. Suites
Hand, Colin
Petite suite champêtre. Op.67: for descant recorder (or flute or oboe) and piano/ by Colin Hand. – London: Boosey and Hawkes, 1971. – 8vo.
Score (8p.) & part.
Unpriced

(B71-51080)

VSRPK/DW/G/AYB – Descant recorder & piano. Arrangements. Folk song collections. Europe
McMullen, Elli
Twelve folk dances from many lands/ arranged for descant recorder, piano and/or percussion by Elli McMullen. – London: Schott, 1971. – obl.8vo.
Score (21p.) & 2 parts.
£0.70

(B71-51081)

VSRPMK – Unaccompanied descant recorder solos. Arrangements
Mendelssohn, Felix
Melodies/ by Felix Mendelssohn; arranged for descant recorder by M.D. Manson. – London: Schott, 1970. – 15p; obl. 8vo.
£0.25

(B71-50146)

VSRPMK/DW/LF/AY – Unaccompanied descant recorder. Arrangements. Christmas songs. Collections
Evans, Howard
Christmas songs for descant recorder/ arranged by Howard Evans and Bert Brewis. – London: Chappell, 1971. – 4to.
Unpriced

(B71-51082)

VSSNUE – Treble recorder duets. Sonatas
Courtville, Raphael
[Sonatas for two treble recorders, nos. 1-6]. Sechs Sonaten: für zwei Altblockflöten/ [by] Raphael Courtville; herausgegeben von F.J. Giesbert. – Mainz; London: Schott, 1971. – 18p; 4to.
£0.80

(B71-50656)

VSSPE – Treble recorder & piano. Sonatas
Konink, Servaas van
[Sonatas for treble recorder in C minor & F major]. Zwei Sonaten, c-Moll, f-Dur: für Altenblockflöte und Basso continuo/ [by] Servaass van Konink; herausgegeben von Georges Kiss und Henri Murgier. – Mainz; London: Schott, 1971. – 4to.
Score (12p.) & 2 parts.
£0.80

(B71-51083)

Vivaldi, Antonio
[Sonata for treble recorder & basso continuo in F major. Rinaldi op.67]. Sonate F-Dur: für Altblockflöte und Basso continuo/ [by] Antonio Vivaldi; herausgegeben von Frank Nagel, Generalbassaussetzung von Winfried Radeke. – Mainz; London: Schott, 1971. – 4to.
Score (6p.) & 2 parts.
£0.80

(B71-50657)

VSSPK/AAY – Treble recorder & piano. Arrangements. Collections
Camden, John
Solos for the alto (treble) recorder player: with piano accompaniment/ selected and edited by John Camden and Peter Devereux. – New York: Schirmer; London: Chappell, 1971. – 4to.
Score (63p.) & part.
Unpriced

(B71-50658)

VSSPMG/AY – Unaccompanied treble recorder
Ruf, Hugo
Einzelstücke und Suiten: für Altblockflöte solo/ herausgegeben von Hugo Ruf. – Mainz; London: Schott, 1971. – 24p; 4to.
Selected from Daniel Demsivre's 'Aires made on purpose for a flute. 3rd collection' and George Bingham's '50 airs anglais'.
£0.80

(B71-50659)

VSSPMJ – Unaccompanied treble recorder. Miscellaneous works
Berio, Luciano
Gesti: for alto recorder/ by Luciano Berio. – London: Universal, 1971. – 2p; fol.
Unpriced

(B71-50661)

Linde, Hans Martin
Music for a bird: for treble recorder solo/ by Hans Martin Linde. —
Mainz; London: Schott, 1971. — 7p; 4to.
£0.70

(B71-50660)

VTNTVTT — OBOE & COR ANGLAIS
Beethoven, Ludwig van
[Trio for two oboes and cor anglais in C major. Op.87]. Trio, C
major. Opus 87: for 2 oboes and cor anglais/ by L. van Beethoven. —
London: Peters, Hinrichsen, 1970. — 3v; 4to.
£0.80

(B71-50662)

VTP — OBOE & PIANO
VTPE — Sonatas
Chédeville, Nicolas
[Sonata for oboe & basso continuo in E minor]. Sonata e-Moll: für
Oboe (Querflöte, Violine) und Basso continuo/ [by] Nicolas
Chédeville; herausgegeben von Hugo Ruf. — Mainz; London: Schott,
1971. — 4to.
Score (10p.) & part.
£0.90

(B71-50663)

VTPG — Suites
Philidor, Anne Danican
[Suite for oboe and basso continuo no.1 in G minor (1er livre)]. Suite
1, g-Moll: für Oboe (Querflöte, Violine) und Basso continuo,/ [by]
Anne Danican-Philidor; herausgegeben von Hugo Ruf. — Mainz;
London: Schott, 1971. — 4to.
Score (10p.) & 2 parts.
£0.90
Also classified at VRPG; SPG

(B71-50664)

VTPJ — Miscellaneous works
Bozay, Attila
Tétélpár: two movements for oboe and piano/ by Attila Bozay. —
London: Boosey and Hawkes, 1971. — 13p; fol.
Unpriced

(B71-51084)

Darke, Harold
Six miniatures: for oboe and piano/ by Harold Darke. — London:
Schott, 1971. — 4to.
Score (18p.) & part.
£0.60

(B71-51085)

Ferneyhough, Brian
Coloratura: for oboe and piano/ by Brian Ferneyhough. — London:
Hinrichsen, 1970. — 4to.
Score (12p) & part.
£1.10

(B71-50665)

VTPK — Arrangements
Korn, Peter Jona
Rhapsody: for oboe and strings (1951)/ [by] Peter Jona Korn.
Op.14. — Piano score. — Hamburg; London: Simrock, 1971. — 12p;
4to.
£1.00

(B71-50666)

VTPK/AAY — Arrangements. Collections
Craxton, Janet
First book of oboe solos/ edited and arranged for oboe and piano by
Janet Craxton and Alan Richardson. — London: Faber Music, 1971.
— 4to.
Score (26p.) & part.
£0.75

(B71-50147)

VTPK/LF — Arrangements. Concertos
Vivaldi, Antonio
[Il Cimento dell'armonia e dell'inventione. Op.8. Concerto for oboe
& string orchestra in C major]. Konzert, C-Dur: für Oboe,
Streichorchester und General bass/ [by] Antonio Vivaldi;
herausgegeben von Walter Lebermann; Klavierauszug vom
Herausgeber. — Mainz; London: Schott, 1971. — 4to.
Score (11p.) & part.
£0.90

(B71-50667)

Zehm, Friedrich
Concerto da camera: für Oboe und Streichorchester/ [by] Friedrich
Zehm. — Klavierauszug. — Mainz; London: Schott, 1971. — 4to.
Score (28p.) and part.
£2.00

(B71-50668)

VTPLR/T — Variations
Pinkham, Daniel
Variations: for oboe and organ by Daniel Pinkham. — New York:
Peters; London: Hinrichsen, 1970. — 4to.
Score (18p) & part. Duration 11 min.
£1.10

(B71-50669)

VV — CLARINET
VV/AC — Tutors
Dawe, Margery
The new road to clarinet playing/ by Margery Dawe. — London:
Cramer, 1971. — 48p; 4to.
y0.45

(B71-51086)

VVNS — CLARINET QUARTETS
VVNSH — Quartets. Dances
Dillon, Robert
Rhythmic dance: for four B flat clarinets/ by Robert Dillon. — New
York; London: Boosey and Hawkes, 1971. — 4to.
Score (5p) & 4 parts.
£0.65

(B71-50670)

VVNT — CLARINET TRIOS
Simpson, John
Divertimento: for 3 clarinets in B flat/ by John Simpson. — London:
Feldman, 1971. — 4to.
Score (11p.) & 3 parts.
Unpriced

(B71-51087)

VVNT/AY — Trios. Collections
Weston, Pamela
Eight clarinet trios of the 18th century/ edited by Pamela Weston. —
London: Schott, 1971. — 16p: facsim; 4to.
£0.40

(B71-50671)

VVNTK — Trios. Arrangements
Haydn, Joseph
[Symphony, no.99, in E flat major. B and H. 99. Adagio]. Adagio/
by Joseph Haydn; arranged for three clarinets by A.D. Harris. —
London: Feldman, 1971. — 4to.
Score (6p.) & 3 parts.
Unpriced

(B71-51088)

VVNU — CLARINET DUETS
Grundman, Clare
Puppets: for two B flat clarinets/ by Clare Grundman. — New York;
London: Boosey and Hawkes, 1971. — 3p; 4to.
Another copy as insert.
£0.45

(B71-50672)

VVP — CLARINET & PIANO
VVPE — Sonatas
Wanhal, Johann Baptist
[Sonata for clarinet & piano in E flat major]. Sonate, Es-Dur: für
Klarinette in B und Klavier/ [by] Johann Baptist Wanhal;
herausgegeben von Doris Stofer. — Mainz; London: Schott, 1971. —
4to.
Score (40p.) & part.
£2.00

(B71-50673)

VVPG — Suites
Pitfield, Thomas
Conversations: suite for B flat clarinet and piano (or string orchestra
and harp)/ by Thomas Pitfield. — London: Leeds Music, 1970. — 4to.
Score (19p.) & part.
Unpriced

(B71-51089)

VVPHVS — Tarantellas
Dillon, Robert
Tarantella: for B flat clarinet/ by Robert Dillon. — New York;
London: Boosey and Hawkes, 1971. — 4to.
Score (7p.) & part.
£0.65

(B71-50674)

VVPJ — Miscellaneous works
Burgmüller, Norbert
[Duo for clarinet & piano in E flat major. Op.15]. Duo. Op.15: for
clarinet and piano/ by Norbert Burgmüller; [edited by] Jost
Michaels. — Hamburg; London: Simrock, 1971. — 4to.
Score (16p) & part.
Unpriced

(B71-50675)

Hoffmeister, Franz Anton
[Duet for clarinet & piano in A major]. Duo für Klarinette und
Klavier, A-Dur/ [by] Franz Anton Hoffmeister; herausgegeben von
Doris Stofer. — Mainz; London: Schott, 1971. — 4to.
Score (43p.) & part.
£2.00

(B71-50676)

Verrall, Pamela
Six conversations: for clarinet with piano accompaniment/ by
Pamela Verrall. — London: Feldman, 1971. — 4to.
Score (13p.) & part.
Unpriced

(B71-50677)

VVPK/AAY — Clarinet and piano. Arrangements. Collections
Weston, Pamela
Classical album: for 2 clarinets in B flat and piano/ arranged by
Pamela Weston. — London: Boosey and Hawkes, 1971. — 4to.
Unpriced

(B71-51090)

VVPK/LF — Arrangements. Concertos
Stamitz, Carl
[Concerto for clarinet & string orchestra, no.1, in F major]. Konzert
no.1, F-Dur: für Klarinette (B) und Streicher, zwei Oboen und zwei
Hörner ad lib./ [by] Carl Stamitz; herausgegeben und mit Kadenzen
versehen von Walter Lebermann. — Klavierauszug. — Mainz;
London: Schott, 1971. — 4to.
Score (4p.) & part.
£2.00

(B71-50678)

VVPM — UNACCOMPANIED CLARINET SOLOS
VVPMJ — Miscellaneous works
Donizetti, Gaetano
[Study for clarinet, no.1]. Studie: für Klarinette/ [by] Gaetano
Donizetti; zum ersten Mal herausgegeben von Raymond Meylan. —
Frankfurt: Litolff, Peters; London: Hinrichsen, 1970. — 6p; 4to.
£0.50

(B71-50679)

Laporte, André
Reflections. Inner-space music: clarinet solo/ by André Laporte. —
London: Chester, 1971. — 3p; 4to.
Unpriced

(B71-50680)

Waters, Charles Frederick
Little cycle: for solo clarinet/ by Charles F. Waters. — London:
Hinrichsen, 1970. — 7p; 4to.
£0.35

(B71-50681)

VWNTPW — TWO BASSOONS & KEYBOARD
Selma y Salaverde, Bartolomeo de
[Canzon for two bassoons & basso continuo]. XXIII Canzon a 2
Bassi: für 2 Fagotte oder Posaune und Fagott und Basso continuo/
[by] Bartolomeo de Selma y Salaverde; herausgegeben von M.S.
Kastner. — London: Schott, 1971. — 4to.
The numbering in the title refers to its place in the collection of his works
published in 1638. Score (11p.) & part.
£1.00

(B71-50682)

VWNU — BASSOON DUETS
Alcock, John, *b.1740*
A favorite duet: for two bassoons or violoncellos/ by John Alcock;
edited by Stanley Sadie. — Banbury (Overthorpe Hall, Banbury,
Oxon.): Piers Press, 1970. — 7p; 4to.
Unpriced
Also classified at SRNU

(B71-50148)

VWPE — Sonatas
Bertoli, Giovanni Antonio
[Sonata for bassoon and basso continuo, no.1, in D minor]. Sonata
prima: für Fagott und Basso continuo/ [by] Giovanni Antonio
Bertoli; herausgegeben von M.S. Kastner, [figured bass realized with
the co-operation of Willy Burger]. — Mainz; London: Schott, 1971.
— 4to.
Score (16p.) & part.
£1.10

(B71-50683)

Galliard, Johann Ernst
[Sonata for bassoon and basso continuo in G major]. Sonata,
G-Dur: für Fagott oder Violoncello und Basso continuo/ [by] Johann
Ernst Galliard; herausgegeben von Hugo Ruf. — Mainz; London:
Schott, 1971. — 4to.
Score (7p.) & 2 parts.
£0.90
Also classified at SRPE

(B71-50684)

VWPEM — Sonatinas
Feld, Jindrich
[Sonatina for bassoon & piano (1969)]. Sonatine: für Fagott und
Klavier/ [by] Jindrich Feld. — Mainz; London: Schott, 1970. — 4to.
Score (22p.) & part.
£1.30

(B71-50149)

VWPJ — Miscellaneous works
Selma y Salaverde, Bartolomeo de
[Fantasia for bassoon in D minor]. V Fantasia ex D: für Fagott und
Basso continuo/ [by] Bartolomeo de Selma y Salaverde;
herausgegeben von M.S. Kastner. — London: Schott, 1971. — 4to.
The numbering in the title refers to its place in the collection of his works
published in 1638. Score (13p.) & part.
£1.10

(B71-50685)

VWPK/DH — Arrangements. Motets, Anthems, Hymns, etc
Handel, George Frideric
[Selections]. A Handel solo album: for trumpet or trombone & piano
(or bassoon & piano)/ arranged & edited by Lionel Lethbridge. —
London: Oxford University Press, 1971. — 4to.
Score (22p.) & 2 parts.
ISBN 0 19 356971 x : £0.60
Primary classification WSPK/DH

(B71-50717)

VWPK/LF — Arrangements. Concertos
Vivaldi, Antonio
[Concerto for bassoon in F major. P.318]. Konzert, F-dur: für
Fagott und Streichorchester/ [by] Antonio Vivaldi; herausgegeben
von Walter Kolneder. — Leipzig: Peters; London: Hinrichsen. —
Ausgabe für Fagott und Klavier. — 1970. — 19p; 4to.
£1.20

(B71-50686)

VY — BAGPIPES
VY/AC — Tutors
Logan's complete tutor: for the Highland bagpipe, and [with] a
selection of marches, quicksteps, laments, strathspeys, reels &
country dances followed by piobaireachd exercises & the famous
piobaireachd, Cha till McCruimein (MacCrimmon will never return).
— Revised ed. — London: Paterson, 1968. — 44p; obl. 4to.
Unpriced

(B71-50687)

WM — BRASS BAND
WM/AY — Collections
Salvation Army
Salvation Army Brass Band Journal (Festival series)/ Nos. 337-340.
— London: Salvationist Publishing and Supplies, 1971. — 60p; obl.
8vo.
Contents: The joy-bringer: march phantasy, by Kenneth Downie. — Happy,
saved and free: suite, by J.V. Key. — Wondrous truth: double quartet, by Tom
Brevik. — The magic flute: overture, by Mozart, arr. Michael Kenyon.
Unpriced

(B71-51091)

Salvation Army
Salvation Army Brass Band Journal (General series)/
Nos.1617-1620; A prayer: meditation by Erik Leidzen; [and],
Happiness and harmony: suite, by Terry Camsey; [and], Angels
watching over me: negro spiritual, arr. Joy Webb (trs. Ray
Steadman-Allen); [and], The joyful sound: march, by Ray Shotton.
— London: Salvationist Publishing, 1970. — 32p; obl.8vo.
Unpriced

(B71-50688)

Salvation Army
Salvation Army Brass Band Journal (General series)/
Nos.1613-1616; Dalaro; march by Edward Gregson. Someone
cares: cornet solo, from 'Take-over bid' by John Larsson, arr. Ray
Steadman-Allen. The triumph of Calvary; meditation by Phil. B.
Catelinet. Chile; march by Erik Silfverberg. — London: Salvationist
Publishing and Supplies, 1970. — 32p; obl. 4to.
£0.50

(B71-50689)

Salvation Army
Salvation Army Brass Band Journal (General series)/ Nos.
1621-1624. — London: Salvationist Publishing and Supplies, 1971. —
52p; obl. 8vo.
Contents: - St. Columba; prelude by Keith Griffin; and, Whosoever heareth;
song arrangement by Allen Pengilly. — Nobody knows the trouble I've seen;
negro spiritual, [arranged by] Erik Silfverberg; and, In the sanctuary; song
setting by Eiliv Herikstad. — The Saviour comes; selection by Charles Skinner.
— The colour guard; festival march, by Phil. B. Catelinet.
Unpriced

(B71-51092)

Salvation Army
Salvation Army Brass Band Journal (Triumph series)/ 729-732;
Summertime: march, by Paul Martin; [and]; Jesus bids us shine; by
Brian Bowes; [and], Consolation: trombone solo by J. Hatton, arr.
Brian Bowes; [and], Voice of assurance: selection, by E.A. Smith. —
London: Salvationist Publishing, 1970. — 36p; obl.8vo.
Unpriced

(B71-50690)

Salvation Army
Salvation Army Brass Band Journal (Triumph series)/ Nos.733-736;
Cheerful song; march by Keith Griffin; [and], Visions of youth no.2;
suite, by J.S. Bach, arr. Phil. B. Catelinet; [and], Jesus is strong to
deliver; song arrangement by David Wells; [and], Joyous
discipleship; march by Allen Pengilly. — London: Salvationist
Publishing, 1971. — 32p; obl.8vo.
Unpriced

(B71-50691)

Salvation Army
Salvation Army Brass Band Journal (Triumph series)/ Nos.737-740;
Thoughts of Calvary: selection by Ray Steadman-Allen. Sailing
homeward: air varié by Charles Dove. We three kings: carol setting
by Ray Bowes, [and] His love remains the same; cornet trio by John
Larsson, arr. Ray Steadman-Allen. Blessed sunshine: march by
Folke Andersson. — London: Salvationist Publishing and Supplies,
1971. — 40p; obl. 8vo.
Unpriced

(B71-51093)

WMEM — Sinfoniettas
Horovitz, Joseph
Sinfonietta: for brass band/ by Joseph Horovitz, scored by Bram
Gay. — Borough Green: Novello, 1971. — 4to.
Score (58p.) & 19 parts.
£3.00

(B71-51094)

WMG — Suites
Ball, Eric
English country scenes: suite for brass band/ by Eric Ball. — London:
Paxton, 1971. — obl. 8vo & 8vo.
Score (32p.) & 24 parts. Duration 9 min.
Unpriced

(B71-50692)

Hanmer, Ronald
Mexican fiesta: for brass band/ by Ronald Hanmer. — London:
Studio Music, 1970. — 40p; obl.4to.
Unpriced

(B71-50693)

Siebert, Edrich
The rising generation/ by Edrich Siebert. — London: Boosey and
Hawkes, 1971. — obl.8vo & 8vo.
Score (17p.) & 25 parts.
y2.64

(B71-51095)

Street, Allan
Nott'num Town/ by Allan Street. — London: Boosey and Hawkes,
1971. — 8vo.
Score (35p.)& 27 parts.
£2.90

(B71-51096)

WMGM — Marches
Kelly, Bryan
March: Washington D.C./ by Bryan Kelly; scored for brass band by
F. Bryce. — Borough Green: Novello, 1971. — 4to.
Score (26p.) & 16 parts.
Unpriced

(B71-51097)

Siebert, Edrich
The big parade: quick march/ by Edrich Siebert. — London: Studio
Music, 1970. — 25 parts; obl. 8vo.
Unpriced

(B71-50694)

WMGN — Fanfares
Uber, David
Symphonic fanfare for brass choir/ by David Uber. — New York:
Schirmer; [London]: [Chappell], 1971. — 4to.
Score (10p.) & 19 parts.
Unpriced

(B71-50695)

WMH — Dances
Street, Allan
Song and dances: brassband/ by Allan Street. — London: Boosey
and Hawkes, 1970. — 44p; obl.8vo & 8vo.
Score (£1.15) & 18 parts.
Unpriced

(B71-50150)

WMHVR — Tangos
Siebert, Edrich
Tango militaire: cornet solo/ by Edrich Siebert. — London: Studio
Music, 1971. — 4to.
Conductor (3p.) & 26 parts.
Unpriced

(B71-51098)

WMJ — Miscellaneous works
Ball, Eric
Celebration: fantasia for brass band/ by Eric Ball. — London: Boosey
and Hawkes, 1971. — obl. 8vo & 8vo.
Score (30p.) & 23 parts.
Unpriced

(B71-51100)

Barraclough, C
Three lazy gents/ by C. Barraclough. — London: Studio Music, 1971.
— 8vo.
Conductor & 25 parts. Various parts are in duplicate.
Unpriced

(B71-50696)

Butterworth, Arthur
The path across the moor: for brass band/ by Arthur Butterworth. —
London: Hinrichsen, 1970. — 16p; obl.4to.
£0.90

(B71-50697)

Hovhaness, Alan
[Five fantasies for brass choir. Op. 70]/ by Alan Hovhaness. — New
York: Peters; London: Hinrichsen. —
Fantasy no.1: trumpets, horns, trombones. — 1969. — 8vo.
Score (4p.) & 3 parts.
£0.60

(B71-50698)

Fantasy no.2: trumpets, horns, trombones. — 1969. — 8vo.
Score (4p.) & 3 parts.
£0.625

(B71-50699)

Fantasy no.3: trumpets, horns, trombones. — 1969. — 8vo.
Score (6p.) & 3 parts.
£0.625

(B71-50700)

Fantasy no.4: 2 trumpets, horns, trombones (tubas). — 1969. — 8vo.
Score (11p.) & 4 parts.
£0.875

(B71-50701)

Fantasy no.5: 2 trumpets, horns, trombones (tubas). — 1969. — 8vo.
Score (7p.) & 4 parts.
£0.90

(B71-50702)

Jacob, Gordon
Two chorale preludes: for brass band/ by Gordon Jacob. — Borough
Green: Novello, 1971. — 4to & 8vo.
Score (10p.) & 18 parts. — Contents:- Melcombe, by S. Webbe the elder. —
Abridge, by I. Smith.
£1.45

(B71-50703)

Richardson, Norman
Avalon: diversions on an original theme/ by Norman Richardson. —
London: Boosey and Hawkes, 1971. — obl. 8vo & 8vo.
Score (28p.) and 26 parts.
Unpriced

(B71-51101)

Simpson, Robert
Energy: symphonic study for brass band/ by Robert Simpson. —
London: Boosey and Hawkes, 1971. — obl. 8vo and 8vo.
Score (53p.) and 24 parts.
Unpriced

(B71-51102)

Stapleton, Eric
Overture for a festival/ by Eric Stapleton. — London: Feldman, 1971.
— 20p; 8vo.
Unpriced

(B71-51099)

Turok, Paul
Elegy in memory of Karol Rathaus. Op.23: for 3 trumpets, 2 horns, 3
trombones and baritone and tuba/ by Paul Turok. — London: Musica
rara, 1971. — 4to.
Score (23p.) & 10 parts.
Unpriced

(B71-51103)

WMK — Arrangements
Coates, Eric
[Selections]. Eric Coates for brass: musical extracts from At the
dance, The jester at the wedding, London Bridge, The three
Elizabeths, The three bears; arranged for brass and reed band by
Allan Street. — London: Chappell, 1971. — 8vo.
Conductor (12p.) & 27 parts.
Unpriced

(B71-50704)

Farnon, Robert J
[Selections]. Robert Farnon for brass: arranged for brass and reed
band by Allan Street. — London: Chappell, 1971. — 8vo.
Unpriced

(B71-51104)

Mozart, Wolfgang Amadeus
[Symphony no.40 in G minor. K.550 - Molto allegro]. Mozart 40/
[arranged] by B. Kelsey and Ellis Rich; arranged for brass band by
N. Royston. — London: Feldman, 1971. — 8vo.
Conductor (2p.) & 23 parts.
Unpriced

(B71-51105)

Siebert, Edrich
Amazing grace: traditional/ arranged by Edrich Siebert. — London:
Studio Music, 1971. — 8vo.
Solo conductor & 24 parts.
Unpriced

(B71-50705)

WMK/AGM — Arrangements. Marches
Osterling, Eric
Sunburst: concert march/ by Eric Osterling [with] Royal hunt from
'Sarajevo suite', by Morton Gould; adaptation for concert band by
Louis Brunelli. — London: Chappell, 1970. — 1v; 4to.
Conductor & 39 parts.
Unpriced

(B71-50151)

Rosas, Juventino
Mexican march/ [arranged for brass band] by Barsotti. — London:
Bosworth, 1970. — 8vo.
£0.875

(B71-50152)

WMK/AH — Arrangements. Dances
Falla, Manuel de
[El Amor brujo-Danza ritual del fuego]. Ritual fire dance/ by Manuel
de Falla; arranged by Allan Street. — London: Chester, 1971. — 4to.
Conductor (3p.) & 25 parts.
Unpriced

(B71-51106)

WMK/AHG — Arrangements. Dance suites
Warlock, Peter
Capriol suite/ by Peter Warlock; arranged for brass band by
Geoffrey Brand. — London (210 Strand, WC2R 1AP): Curwen, R.
Smith, 1970. — 41p; obl.4to.
Duration 9 1/2 mins.
Unpriced

(B71-50706)

WMK/AHM/JR — Arrangements. Ballet music. Film music
Lanchbery, John
Tales of Beatrix Potter: selection from the ballet/ by John Lanchbery;
arranged for brass band by Edrich Siebert. — London: E.M.I. Film
Music: Keith Prowse Music, 1971. — 8vo.
Conductor & 24 parts.
y1.50

(B71-51107)

WMK/CM — Arrangements. From musical plays
Lane, Burton
On a clear day you can see forever/ by Burton Lane; selection for
brass band arranged by Howard Evans. — London: Chappell, 1970.
— 1v; 8vo.
Conductor & 26 parts. Parts £1.70.
Unpriced

(B71-50153)

WMK/CM/JR — Arrangements. Musical plays. Films
Grieg, Edvard
[Selections]. Song of Norway/ [comprising] music by Edvard Grieg;
arranged for brass and reed band by Allan Street, lyrics and musical
adaptation by Robert Wright and George Forrest. — London:
Chappell, 1971. — 8vo.
Conductor (8p.) & 26 parts.
Unpriced

(B71-51108)

WMK/DW — Arrangements. Songs, etc
Gluck, Christoph Willibald von
[Orfeo. Che faro]. Air from 'Orpheus and Euridice': popularly
known as 'What is life?'/ by Gluck; arr. by Ronald Hanmer. —
London: Studio Music, 1971. — 1v; 8vo.
Conductor & 25 parts.
Unpriced

(B71-50707)

MacLellan, Gene
Snowbird/ by Gene MacLellan: arranged for brass band by Edrich
Siebert. — London: Ardmore and Beechwood, 1970. — 8vo.
Unpriced

(B71-51109)

WMK/DW/AYDK — Arrangements. Songs, etc. Collections. Wales
Siebert, Edrich
A Welsh cameo/ arranged for brass band by Edrich Siebert. —
London: Studio Music, 1970. — obl. 8vo.
Solo conductor & 24 parts.
Unpriced

(B71-50708)

WMK/DW/AYDL — Arrangements. Songs, etc. Collections. Scotland
Siebert, Edrich
A Scottish cameo/ arranged for band by Edrich Siebert. — London:
Studio Music, 1970. — obl. 8vo.
Solo conductor & 24 parts.
Unpriced

(B71-50709)

WMK/JR — Arrangements. Film music
Lai, Francis
Love story: theme from the film/ music by Francis Lai; arranged for
brass and reed band by Allan Street. — London: Chappell, 1971. —
1v; 4to.
Conductor and 26 parts as insert.
Unpriced

(B71-50710)

WN — BRASS ENSEMBLE
WNMK/AF — Nonets. Arrangements. Exercises
Diabelli, Anton
[28 melodious exercises for piano duet. Op.149, nos. 16,11,26,6]. A
Diabelli suite: for small brass ensemble/ [arranged] by Arthur
Butterworth. — London: Feldman, 1971. — 8vo.
Score (21p.) & 9 parts.
Unpriced

(B71-51110)

WNR — Quintets
Connolly, Justin
Cinquepaces. Op. 5: for brass quintet/ by Justin Connolly. —
London: Oxford University Press, 1971. — [56]p; 4to.
£2.00

(B71-51111)

WNR/AZ — Quintets. Complete works of individual composers
Holborne, Antony
[Pavans, galiards, almains and other short airs]. Complete music for
brass: for 2 trumpets and 3 trombones (2 trumpets, horn and 2
trombones)/ by Anthony Holborne; [edited by] Robert Paul Block. —
London: Musica rara. —
Vol.1. — 1971. — 4to.
Score (39p.) & 7 parts.
Unpriced

(B71-51112)

Vol.2. — 1971. — 4to.
Score (39p.) & 7 parts.
Unpriced

(B71-51113)

WNRK/LF — Quintets. Arrangements. Concertos
Ross, Walter
Concerto for brass quintet & orchestra/ by Walter Ross. — Piano
reduction. — New York; [London]: Boosey and Hawkes, 1971. —
48p; 4to.
£2.10

(B71-50711)

WNS — Quartets
Horsch, Hans
[Suite for brass, no.2]. Blechbläser Suite No.2/ [by] Hans Horsch;
herausgegeben von Willy Schneider. — Mainz; London: Schott, 1971.
— 8vo.
Score (18p.) & 7 parts.
£1.60

(B71-50712)

Spurgin, Anthony
Foursome for brass/ by Anthony Spurgin. — London: Feldman,
1971. — 8vo.
Score (8p.) & 4 parts.
Unpriced

(B71-51114)

WNSK — Quartets. Arrangements
Beethoven, Ludwig van
[Quartets for strings, nos.1, 6 and 2 - Excerpts]. Quartet no.1 on themes from Beethoven/ transcribed [for brass quartet] by Edrich Siebert. — London: Studio Music, 1971. — 8vo.
Score (15p.) & 4 parts.
Unpriced

(B71-50713)

WNT — Trios
Pinkham, Daniel
[Trio for trumpet, horn & trombone]. Brass trio: trumpet, horn, trombone/ by Daniel Pinkham. — New York: Peters; London: Hinrichsen, 1970. — 11p; 4to.
Duration 5 min.
£1.25

(B71-50714)

WNUK/AF — Duets. Arrangements. Exercises
Bergmann, Walter
[Ten canonic studies for recorders, nos. 1-7]. Seven canonic studies/ by Walter Bergmann; arranged for brass instruments by Patrick Rivers. — London: Schott, 1971. — 15p; obl.8vo.
Unpriced

(B71-51115)

WRP — CORNET & PIANO
WRP/W — Rondos
Street, Allan
Rondino: solo for B flat trumpet (or cornet) with piano accompaniment/ by Allan Street. — London: Boosey and Hawkes, 1970. — 4to.
Score (6p.) & part.
£0.35
Primary classification WSP/W

(B71-50154)

WSNTPW — TWO TRUMPETS & KEYBOARD
WSNTPWEM — Sonatinas
Pezel, Johann
[Bicinia variorum instrumentum. Excerpts]. Sonatinas nos. 61, 62, 65 and 66: for 2 trumpets in B flat (C) & continuo/ by Johann Pezel; [edited by] Robert Paul Block. — London: Musica rara, 1971. — 4to.
Score (10p.) & 5 parts.
Unpriced

(B71-50715)

WSP — TRUMPET & PIANO
WSP/W — Rondos
Street, Allan
Rondino: solo for B flat trumpet (or cornet) with piano accompaniment/ by Allan Street. — London: Boosey and Hawkes, 1970. — 4to.
Score (6p.) & part.
£0.35
Also classified at WRP/W

(B71-50154)

WSPK — Arrangements
Haydn, Joseph
A Haydn solo album: eleven short pieces/ by Joseph Haydn; arranged and edited for trumpet and piano by Ian Lawrence. — London: Oxford University Press, 1971. — 4to.
Score (14p.) & part.
ISBN 0 19 357066 1 : £0.60

(B71-50716)

WSPK — Trumpet & piano. Arrangements
Barsham, Eve
Shore's trumpet: eight pieces for B flat trumpet and piano/ arranged by Eve Barsham. — London: Boosey and Hawkes, 1971. — 4to.
Score (8p.) & part. — Includes works by Jeremiah Clarke.
£0.55

(B71-51116)

WSPK/AAY — Arrangements. Collections
Richardson, Norman
Six more trumpet tunes/ arranged for trumpet or cornet in B flat and piano by Norman Richardson. — London: Boosey and Hawkes, 1971. — 4to.
Score (20p.) & part.
£0.65

(B71-51117)

WSPK/DH — Arrangements. Motets, Anthems, Hymns, etc
Handel, George Frideric
[Selections]. A Handel solo album: for trumpet or trombone & piano (or bassoon & piano)/ arranged & edited by Lionel Lethbridge. — London: Oxford University Press, 1971. — 4to.
Score (22p.) & 2 parts.
ISBN 0 19 356971 x : £0.60
Also classified at VWPK/DH

(B71-50717)

WT — HORN
WTNRR — Four horns & organ
Watson, Walter
Music for organ and horns/ by Walter Watson. — New York: Schirmer; [London]: [Chappell], 1971. — 4to.
Score (16p.) & 4 parts.
Unpriced

(B71-51118)

WTNU — HORN DUETS
WTNU/GT — Hunting
Sperger, Johann Matthias
Jagdmusik: 12 kleine Stücke, für zwei Hörner/ [by] Johann Matthias Sperger; herausgegeben von Karlheinz Schultz-Hauser. — Mainz; London: Schott, 1971. — 12p; 4to.
£0.70

(B71-50155)

WTP — HORN & PIANO
WTP/T — Variations
Kalabis, Viktor
[Variations for horn & piano. Opus 31]. Variationen für Horn und Klavier. Op.31/ [by] Viktor Kalabis. — Mainz; London: Schott, 1971. — 4to.
Score (20p.) & part.
£1.10

(B71-51119)

WTPE — Sonatas
Beethoven, Ludwig van
[Sonata for horn & piano in F major. Op. 17]. Sonata. Op.17: for horn & piano/ by Ludwig van Beethoven. — New York: Schirmer; [London]: [Chappell], 1971. — 4to.
Score (19p.) & part.
Unpriced

(B71-51120)

WTPK/LF — Arrangements. Concertos
Harutjunian, Alexander
[Concerto for horn]. Konzert: für Horn und Orchester/ [by] Alexander Harutjunjan. — Leipzig: Peters; London: Hinrichsen. — Ausgabe für Horn und Klavier vom Komponisten. — 1970. — 4to.
Score (18p.) & part.
£1.20

(B71-50718)

WTPM — UNACCOMPANIED HORN SOLOS
WTZNUG — Duets. Suites
Catelinet, Philip B
Suite in miniature: three movements in contrasting styles for two trombones or baritones or euphoniums/ by Philip B. Catelinet. — London: Hinrichsen, 1966. — 5p; 4to.
£0.20
Primary classification WUNUG

(B71-50719)

WUNU — TROMBONE DUETS
Catelinet, Philip B
Suite in miniature: three movements in contrasting styles for two trombones or baritones or euphoniums/ by Philip B. Catelinet. — London: Hinrichsen, 1966. — 5p; 4to.
£0.20
Also classified at WTZNUG

(B71-50719)

WUP — TROMBONE & PIANO
WUPJ — Miscellaneous works
Ross, Walter
Cryptical triptych: for trombone and piano/ by Walter Ross. — New York; [London]: Boosey and Hawkes, 1971. — 4to.
Score (10p.) & part.
£1.05

(B71-50720)

XN — PERCUSSION ENSEMBLE
Lisken, Gerd
Vibration: model for a group improvisation with Orff instrumentation or other intstruments [sic]/ by Gerd Lisken. — Mainz; London: Schott, 1971. — 15p; obl.4to.
£1.20

(B71-51121)

O'Reilly, John
Three episodes: for percussion ensemble/ by John O'Reilly. — New York: Schirmer; [London]: [Chappell], 1971. — 17p; 4to.
Score (17p.) & 5 parts. Duration 6 mins.
Unpriced

(B71-50721)

XNGM — Marches
Fink, Siegfried
Percussio antiqua: improvisations based on Sundgauer Marsch 1469 on historic percussion instruments, for percussion solo/ by Siegfried Fink. — Hamburg; London: Simrock, 1971. — 8p; 4to.
£0.65

(B71-51122)

XNN — Octets
Soler, Josep
Sonidas de la noche. Sounds in the night: for six percussionists/ by Josep Soler. — Mainz; London: Schott, 1971. — 15p; 8vo.
Unpriced

(B71-50722)

XNP — Septets
Fink, Siegfried
Ritmo (Latin-American music): for percussion ensemble (7 players)/ by Siegfried Fink. — Hamburg; London: Simrock, 1971. — 4to.
Score (20p.) & 7 parts.
£1.10

(B71-51123)

XNT — Trios
Hiller, Wilfried
Catalogue for percussion III: 3 players/ by Wilfried Hiller. — Mainz; London: Schott, 1971. — 32p; 4to.
£1.60

(B71-51124)

COMPOSER
AND
TITLE INDEX

(B71-51101)
Ave Maria: for chorus of treble voices and four-part chorus of mixed voices with celeste (or bells) and organ (or piano) accompaniment. (Smith, Gregg). *Schirmer; Chappell. Unpriced* EPWNUDJ (B71-50786)
Ave rex. Excerpts. Sir Christemas: SATB. (Mathias, William). *Oxford University Press. Unpriced* DP/LF (B71-50212) ISBN 0 19 343008 8
Avodah Hakodesh. Sacred service: a Sabbath morning service according to the Union Prayer Book, for baritone (cantor), mixed chorus and organ or full orchestra. (Bloch, Ernest). *Boosey and Hawkes. Unpriced* DGUB (B71-50010)
Ba-ta-clan: a masquerade in one act. (Offenbach, Jacques). *Schirmer; Chappell. Unpriced* CF (B71-50163)
Babel: for four-part chorus of mixed voices (or solo quartet), five speaking groups and piano (2 players). (Smith, Gregg). *Schirmer; Chappell. £0.25* DE (B71-50007)
Bach, Carl Philipp Emanuel. Four little duets for two pianos. Wq.155. *Schirmer; Chappell. Unpriced* QNU (B71-50962)
Bach, Johann Christian. Sonata for piano duet in F major. Op. 18, no.6. Sonata in F: for pianoforte duet. *Associated Board of the Royal Schools of Music. £0.175* QNVE (B71-50968)
Bach, Johann Sebastian.
A Bach organ book for students. *Elkin. £1.50* RJ (B71-50519)
Concerto for clavier in F minor. S1056 - Excerpts. Largo and allegretto. *Schott. Unpriced* SRPK (B71-51032)
Concerto for violin & oboe. S1060. Concerto in C minor: for violin, oboe and piano or two violins & piano. *Schirmer; Chappell. Unpriced* NUTNTK/LF (B71-50417)
Five spiritual songs (Geistliche Lieder). *Faber Music. £1.00* KFTDH (B71-50062)
Get to know Mister Bach: an informal introduction with simple piano arrangements of his music. *Chappell. Unpriced* QPK (B71-50981)
Wachet auf. S.140. Excerpts. Zion hears the watchmen's voices: for unison & SATB chorale. *Oxford University Press. Unpriced* DM (B71-50202) ISBN 0 19 343013 4
Bach, *Monsieur*. Concerto for organ solo in E flat major. Concerto in E flat: for two manuals and pedals. *Oxford University Press. Unpriced* RF (B71-50109)
Bach, Wilhelm Friedemann.
Adagio and fugue for two flutes & string orchestra. Adagio und Fuge: fur 2 Querfloten und Streicher. Falck 65. *Schott. £1.00* RXMPVRNU/Y (B71-50540)
Symphony in D major. Falck 64. Sinfonie D-Dur. Falck 64. *Schott. £1.20* MRE (B71-50407)
Background of Passion music: J.S. Bach and his predecessors. (Smallman, Basil). 2nd revised and enlarged ed. *Dover; Constable. £0.75* ADD/LH (B71-13108) ISBN 0 486 22250 0
Backus, John. The acoustical foundations of music. *J. Murray. £3.50* A/B (B71-06908) ISBN 0 7195 2216 1
Bacon, Analee. Sonatas for cello & piano. Six sonatas: for violoncello and piano. (Boccherini, Luigi). *Schirmer; Chappell. Unpriced* SRPE (B71-50122)
Bacon, Ernst. The muffin man: for orchestra. *Schirmer Chappell. Unpriced* MMJ (B71-50387)
Badings, Henk. Concerto: for flute and wind symphony orchestra. *Peters; Hinrichsen. £3.50* UMPVRF (B71-50625)
Baez, Joan. Daybreak. *Panther. £0.30* ADW/G/E(P) (B71-19969) ISBN 0 586 03502 8
Bagatelles. (Ridout, Alan). *Schott. Unpriced* SRPJ (B71-51030)
Baird, Tadeusz. Symphony no.3. *Chester. Unpriced* MME (B71-50377)
Balaban, Peter. Bela Bartok - letters. (Bartok, Bela). *Faber and Faber Ltd. £5.50* BBG(N) (B71-18713) ISBN 0 571 09638 7
Balassa, Sandor. Quintet for woodwind instruments. Op.9. Quintetto a fiati. Op.9. *Boosey and Hawkes. Unpriced* UNR (B71-50630)
Balissi, Balint. Prayer for honour: Szep Konyorges: S.A.T.B. unaccompanied. (Kodaly, Zoltan). *Boosey and Hawkes. Unpriced* EZDW (B71-50275)
Ball, Eric.
Celebration: fantasia for brass band. *Boosey and Hawkes. Unpriced* WMJ (B71-51100)
English country scenes: suite for brass band. *Paxton. Unpriced* WMG (B71-50692)
Hail to the Lord's annointed: anthem for SATB and organ (or brass band). *Novello. £0.15* DH (B71-50185)
Ballad 1: mezzo-soprano, flute/altoflute, tenor, trombone, contra-bass, piano, percussion. (Rands, Bernard). *Universal. Unpriced* KFNE/NYDDW (B71-50362)
Ballet. (Debussy, Claude). *Boosey and Hawkes. £1.05* MH (B71-50901)
Balletti for five voices (1591). Fifteen balletti: SSATB a cappella (recorders and strings ad libitum)
Introduttioni a i Balletti: O compagni allegrezza. (Companions, be happy). (Gastoldi, Giovanni). New ed. *Peters; Hinrichsen. £0.40* EZDU (B71-50263)
Balletti for five voices (1591). Fifteen balletti: SSATB a cappella (recorders and strings ad libitum)
Set 3. (Gastoldi, Giovanni). New ed. *Peters; Hinrichsen. £0.40* EZDU (B71-50264)
Balletti for five voices (1591). Fifteen balletti: SSATB a cappella (recorders and strings ad libitum)
Set 4. (Gastoldi, Giovanni). New ed. *Peters; Hinrichsen. £0.40* EZDU (B71-50265)
Bandeira, Manoel. Cancao do mar: canto e piano. (Lorenzo Fernandez, Oscar). *Arthur Napoleao; Essex Music. Unpriced* KDW (B71-50341)
Barber, Samuel.
To be sung on the water. Op. 42, no.2: transcribed for four-part chorus of women's voices a cappella. *Schirmer; Chappell. £0.35* FEZDW (B71-50306)
Vanessa. Excerpts. Under the willow tree: country dance, for orchestra. *Schirmer; Chappell. Unpriced* MMH (B71-50385)
Barbirolli: conductor laureate: the authorised biography. (Kennedy, Michael, *b.1926*). *MacGibbon and Kee. £2.95* A/EC(P) (B71-27973) ISBN 0 261 63336 8
Baroque operatic arias. *(Oxford University Press for the University of Hull)* Bononcini, Giovanni Battista. Arias from the Vienna operas. *Oxford University Press for the University of Hull. £2.50* KDW (B71-50337) ISBN 0 19 713412 2
Barraclough, C. Three lazy gents. *Studio Music. Unpriced* WMJ (B71-50696)
Barrett, Gavin. Introduction, allegro and finale: organ. *Boosey and Hawkes. £0.55* RJ (B71-50110)
Barrington, Patrick. I had a hippopotamus. (Hunt, Reginald). *Ashdown. Unpriced* JFDW (B71-50869)
Barsham, Dinah. Introduction to music. (Hendrie, Gerald). *Open University Press. £0.80* A (B71-08374) ISBN 0 335 00509 8
Barsham, Eve. Shore's trumpet: eight pieces for B flat trumpet and piano. *Boosey and Hawkes. £0.55* WSPK (B71-51116)
Barsotti, Roger.
Gay gnu galop. *Bosworth. £1.25* UMMHLF (B71-51059)
Mexican march. (Rosas, Juventino). *Bosworth. £0.875* WMK/AGM (B71-50152)
Bartholomew, Marshall. Gaudeamus igitur: traditional German melody arranged for chorus of mixed voices a cappella. *Schirmer; Chappell. Unpriced* EZDW (B71-50268)
Bartok, Bela.
Bela Bartok - letters. *Faber and Faber Ltd. £5.50* BBG(N) (B71-18713) ISBN 0 571 09638 7
For children. Excerpts. For children: 25 selected pieces. *Boosey and Hawkes. £0.75* TSPMK (B71-50611)
Hungarian folksongs (1906). Excerpts. Five Hungarian folksongs: for voice and piano. *Boosey and Hawkes. Unpriced* KDW/G/AYG (B71-50346)
Bartok. (Helm, Everett). *Faber and Faber Ltd. £1.25* BBG(N) (B71-17373) ISBN 0 571 09105 9
Basket of eggs and other rhymes: for infants and juniors. (Senator, Ronald). *Boosey and Hawkes. £0.75* JFE/NYLDW (B71-50055)
Bastin, Bruce. Crying for the Carolines. *Studio Vista. £1.40* AKDW/HHW/E(YTNX) (B71-25347) ISBN 0 289 70210 0
Bate, Philip. The clarinet: some notes upon its history and construction. (Rendall, Francis Geoffrey). 3rd ed. *Benn. £2.75* AVV/B(X) (B71-20593) ISBN 0 510 36701 1
Battye, Ken.
Children's Welsh flavour: a selection of Welsh children's hymn tunes set to English words
Vol.1. *Ken Battye. Unpriced* FDM/AYDK (B71-50827)
Welsh flavour: a selection of Welsh hymn tunes set to English words
Vol.1. *K. Battye. Unpriced* DM/AYDK (B71-50204)
Vol.2. *K. Battye. Unpriced* DM/AYDK (B71-50205)
Vol.3. *K. Battye. Unpriced* DM/AYDK (B71-50206)
Vol.4. *K. Battye. Unpriced* DM/AYDK (B71-50207)
Vol.5. *K. Battye. Unpriced* DM/AYDK (B71-50208)
Bauer, Roberto. The new catalogue of historical records, 1898-1908/09. *Sidgwick and Jackson. £6.50* A/FD(WT/XLT12) (B71-18315) ISBN 0 283 48420 9
Bawdy ballads. (Cray, Ed). *Blond. £3.00* AKDW/K/G/KDX (B71-04596) ISBN 0 218 51471 9
Bax, Clifford. The tale of the wandering scholar. Op.50. The wandering scholar. Op.50: a chamber opera in one act. (Holst, Gustav). *Faber. Unpriced* CQC (B71-50172)
Bayford, Dudley Escott.
Easter hymns and carols. *Francis, Day and Hunter. Unpriced* VSK/DH/LL/AY (B71-50649)
English folk songs: for guitar or banjo. *Francis, Day and Hunter. £0.75* TSPMK/DW/G/AYD (B71-50615)
Songs and dances of many nations: for recorder. *Francis, Day and Hunter. £0.25* VSPMK/AAY (B71-51079)
Beata es virgo: part chorus of mixed voices with organ accompaniment (optional). (Gabrieli, Giovanni). *Schirmer; Chappell. Unpriced* EZDGKJ (B71-50024)
Beata viscera, Hail Mary, full of grace: motet for five voices, S.A.A.T.B. for feasts of the Blessed Virgin. (Byrd, William). *Chester. Unpriced* EZDGKAH (B71-50248)
Beatles complete: piano vocal/easy organ. *Northern Songs (Music Sales). £2.50* QPK/DW (B71-50986)
Beau soir. Beautiful evening. (Debussy, Claude). *Boosey and Hawkes. Unpriced* FDW (B71-50833)
Beaumont, Adrian. Songs for little children
Set 1. *Boosey and Hawkes. £0.50* JFDW/GJ (B71-50054)
Beaumont, John.
Lift up your heads. (The ascension). (Rorem, Ned). *Boosey and Hawkes. y4.50* DH/LM (B71-50749)
Lift up your heads. (The ascension). (Rorem, Ned). *Boosey and Hawkes. £1.10* ENYHXPNRDH/LM (B71-50784)
Beck, John Ness.
Anthem of unity: for four-part chorus of mixed voices with piano or organ accompaniment. *Schirmer; Chappell. Unpriced* DK (B71-50751)
Five carol fantasies: for piano. *Schirmer; Chappell. Unpriced* QP/LF (B71-50457)
Becker, Hugo. Wiegenlied. Op.98, no.2. (Schubert, Franz). *Schott. Unpriced* SRPK/DW (B71-51041)
Beckett, J. The evening draws in: for solo vocalist, chorus, piano and percussion. (Self, George). *Universal. Unpriced* FE/NYLDW (B71-50299)
Beddoes, Thomas Lovell. If thou wilt ease thine heart. (Binkerd, Gordon). *Boosey and Hawkes. £0.40* KDW (B71-50333)
Bedford, David. A dream of the seven lost stars. *Universal. Unpriced* EMDX (B71-50239)
Beechey, Gwilym.
Concerto grosso in B minor: for two solo violins, solo violoncello and string orchestra. (Boyce, William). *Eulenburg. £0.60* RXMPSNTSRF (B71-51009)
Symphony no.50 in C major. (Haydn, Joseph). *Eulenburg. Unpriced* MME (B71-50380)
Beethoven, Ludwig van.
Christus am Olberger. Excerpts. Hallelujah. *Schirmer; Chappell. Unpriced* EUMDH (B71-50242)
Concerto for violin in D major. Op.61. Violin-Konzert, D-Dur: fur Violine und Orchester. Op.61. Klavierauszug. *Schott. £1.50* SPK/LF (B71-50573)
Five pieces for the musical clock, nos.1,3. Adagio and allegro for the musical clock. *Universal. Unpriced* UNRK/A/FK (B71-50634)
Fur Elise. *British and Continental. Unpriced* TSPMK (B71-50135)
Quartets for strings, nos.1, 6 and 2 - Excerpts. Quartet no.1 on themes from Beethoven. *Studio Music. Unpriced* WNSK (B71-50713)
Romances for violin & orchestra. Op.40 & 50. Romanzen. Op.40 (G-dur), Op.50 (F-dur): fur Violine und Orchester. *Peters; Hinrichsen. £0.90* SPK (B71-50571)
Sonata for cello & piano, no.3 in A major. Op.69. Sonata for violoncello and pianoforte. Opus 69, first movement by Ludwig van Beethoven: facsimile of the autograph. *Columbia University Press. £1.75* BBJASRPE (B71-06294) ISBN 0 231 03417 2
Sonata for horn & piano in F major. Op. 17. Sonata. Op.17: for horn & piano. *Schirmer; Chappell. Unpriced* WTPE (B71-51120)
Sonatas for piano. Op.49, nos.1,2 - Excerpts. Divertimento in G major. *Bosworth. £2.25* UNRK (B71-51066)
La Tivanna, Kinsky 125: canzonetta for medium voice and piano. *Novello. £0.20* KFVDW (B71-50364)
Trio for two oboes and cor anglais in C major. Op.87. Trio, C major. Opus 87: for 2 oboes and cor anglais. *Peters, Hinrichsen. £0.80* VTNTVTT (B71-50662)
Beethoven companion. (Arnold, Denis). *Faber and Faber Ltd. £7.00* BBJ(N) (B71-05266) ISBN 0 571 09003 6
Beethoven: master composer. (Gimpel, Herbert J.). *Franklin Watts Ltd. £1.25* BBJ(N) (B71-12554) ISBN 0 85166 321 4
Beginning piano for adults. (Miller, Allan). *Collier Books; Collier-Macmillan. £1.00* Q/AC (B71-50083) ISBN 0 02 080890 9
Behold, how good and joyful: S.A.T.B. unacc.,. (Vann, Stanley). *Oxford University Press. Unpriced* EZDR (B71-50808) ISBN 0 19 350327 1
Behold, I stand at the door: for four-part chorus of mixed voices a cappella. (Newbury, Kent A). *Schirmer; Chappell. Unpriced* EZDK (B71-50259)
Behold the great Creator: carol for SATB unaccompanied. (Tomblings, Philip). *Ashdown. £0.05* EZDP/LF (B71-50805)
Bela Bartok: an analysis of his music. (Lendvai, Erno). *Kahn and Averill. £2.00* BBG (B71-30147) ISBN 0 900707 04 6
Bell, . Modern flute music. (Parry, William Howard). *Oxford University Press. £0.90* VRP/AY (B71-51071) ISBN 0 19 357820 4
Bell, L. Riding into Bethlehem: for unison or two-part voices with piano, optional recorders, and optional percussion by W.H. Parry; words by L. Bell. (Parry, William Howard). *Oxford University Press. Unpriced* FDP/LF (B71-50829) ISBN 0 19 342048 1
Belle Helene. (Offenbach, Jacques). *United Music. Unpriced* CF (B71-50004)
Bells of the Isles of Scilly. (Sharpe, Frederick). *Sharpe. £0.10* AXSR/B(YDFS) (B71-07870) ISBN 0 9500835 2 6
Beloved friend. The music lovers: the story of Tchaikowsky and Nadejda von Meck. (Bowen, Catherine Drinker). 2nd ed. abridged. *Hodder Paperbacks. £0.35* BTD(N) (B71-04592) ISBN 0 340 15154 4
Bemerton cantata. Op.59: for mezzo-soprano solo, chorus, organ, string orchestra, harp, percussion. (Cruft, Adrian). *Leeds Music. Unpriced* DE (B71-50006)
Bemmann, Hans.
Sonatas for harpsichord. Sonate di gravicembalo
Band 1: Sonate 1 -6. (Paradisi, Pietro Domenico). *Schott. £1.40* QRPE (B71-50989)
Sonatas for harpsichord. Sonate di gravicembalo
Band 2: Sonate 7-12. (Paradisi, Pietro Domenico). *Schott. £1.40* QRPE (B71-50988)
Beneath the underdog: his world as composed by Mingus. (Mingus, Charles). *Weidenfeld and Nicolson. £2.10* AMT/E(P) (B71-19348) ISBN 0 297 00446 8
Benham, Hugh. 'Gloria tibi trinitas': mass for six-part unaccompanied choir, S.A.T.T.B.B. (Taverner, John). *Stainer and Bell. £1.15* EZDG (B71-50302)
Bennett, F Roy.
Three carols for Christ's nativity: unison. *Ashdown. Unpriced* JFDP/LF (B71-50866)
Three Christmas carols. *Ashdown. Unpriced* FDP/LF (B71-50830)
Bennett, Richard Rodney. Boulez on music today. (Boulez, Pierre). *Faber. £2.50* A (B71-07322) ISBN 0 571 09420 1
Benoy, Arthur William. European songs for children: 15 traditional songs. (Offer, Charles Karel). *Paxton. Unpriced* JFDW/GJ/AYB (B71-50324)
Benton, Rita. French song from Berlioz to Duparc: the origin and development of the melodie. (Noske, Frits). 2nd ed. *Dover; Constable. £3.00* ADW(YH/XHK51) (B71-05796) ISBN 0 486 22104 0
Berg, Alban. Alban Berg: letters to his wife. *Faber and Faber*

Ltd. *£4.50* BBKR(N) (B71-05267) ISBN 0 571 08395 1
Berger, Jean.
Divertissement: for string orchestra. *Schirmer; Chappell. Unpriced* RXMJ (B71-50534)
The pied piper: a play with music. *Schirmer; Chappell. Unpriced* CQM (B71-50173)
Bergmann, Walter.
Petite Musique de Chambre. Excerpts. Partita no.3 in C minor: for descant recorder and piano. (Telemann, Georg Philipp). *Faber Music. Unpriced* VRPG (B71-50642)
Ten canonic studies for recorders, nos. 1-7. Seven canonic studies. *Schott. Unpriced* WNUK/AF (B71-51115)
Twenty little fugues for organ. Excerpts. Four fugue nos.20, 7, 9, 13. (Telemann, Georg Philipp). *Faber Music. Unpriced* VSNSK/Y (B71-50652)
Berio, Luciano.
Chemins I (sur Sequenza II): per arpa principale ed orchestra. *Universal. Unpriced* MPTQ (B71-50405)
Erdenklavier: pastorale for piano. *Universal. Unpriced* QPJ (B71-50473)
Gesti: for alto recorder. *Universal. Unpriced* VSSPMJ (B71-50661)
Sequenza VI: per viola solo. *Universal. Unpriced* SQPMJ (B71-50585)
Sinfonia (1968): for eight voices and orchestra. *Universal. Unpriced* JNAYE/MDX (B71-50329)
Wasserklavier: for piano. *Universal. Unpriced* QPJ (B71-50474)
Berkeley, Lennox.
Quartet for oboe & strings. Oboe quartet. *Chester. Unpriced* NVTNS (B71-50423)
Symphony no.3 in one movement. *Chester. Unpriced* MME (B71-50378)
Three pieces: for organ. *Chester. Unpriced* RJ (B71-50520)

Berlioz, Hector. L'Enfance du Christ. Op.25: chorus and orchestra. *Eulenburg. £4.75* EMDD (B71-50237)
Bernstein, Leonard. Leonard Bernstein's young people's concerts. Revised and expanded ed.. *Cassell. £2.10* A (B71-25914) ISBN 0 304 93819 x
Berry, Marion.
Music makers: in 5 stages Stage 4. *Longman. £0.40* A(QU) (B71-06129) ISBN 0 582 18544 0
Stage 5. *Longman. £0.40* A(QU) (B71-06130) ISBN 0 582 18545 9
Bertali, Antonio.
Sonata for two violins, trombone & basso continuo, no.1, in D minor. Sonata a 3, no.1 in D minor: for 2 violins, trombone & organ continuo. *Musica rara. Unpriced* NUXUNSE (B71-50419)
Sonata for two violins, trombone & basso continuo, no.2, in D minor. Sonata a 3, no.2 in D minor: for 2 violins, trombone & organ continuo. *Musica rara. Unpriced* NUXUNSE (B71-50420)
Bertoli, Giovanni Antonio. Sonata for bassoon and basso continuo, no.1, in D minor. Sonata prima: fur Fagott und Basso continuo. *Schott. £1.10* VWPE (B71-50683)
Best Irish songs of Percy French. (French, Percy). *Wolfe. £0.25* BFURAKDW (B71-11819) ISBN 0 7234 0428 3
Besuch der alten Dame. (Durrenmatt, Friedrich). *Boosey & Hawkes. Unpriced* BENAC (B71-04180) ISBN 0 85162 000 0
Besuch der alten Dame. Op. 35: Oper in drei Akten nach Friedrich Durrenmatts tragischer Komodie. (Einem, Gottfried von). *Boosey and Hawkes. Unpriced* CC (B71-50729)
Bethlehem, of noblest cities: Australian folk melody and a melody from Psalmodia sacra, Gotha, 1715, for SATB. (Hurford, Peter). *Oxford University Press. Unpriced* DP/LFP (B71-50218)
Bicinia hungarica
Vol.4: 60 progressive two-part songs. (Kodaly, Zoltan). Revised English ed. *Boosey and Hawkes. Unpriced* FEZDW (B71-50045)
Bicinia variorum instrumentum. Excerpts. Sonatinas nos. 61, 62, 65 and 66: for 2 trumpets in B flat (C) & continuo. (Pezel, Johann). *Musica rara. Unpriced* WSNTPWEM (B71-50715)
Big parade: quick march. (Siebert, Edrich). *Studio Music. Unpriced* WMGM (B71-50694)
Billings, William.
The dying Christian's last farewell. Fare you well, my friends: SATB a cappella. *Peters; Hinrichsen. £0.75* EZDW/LC (B71-50286)
I heard a great voice: SAATBB a cappella. *Peters Hinrichsen. £0.35* EZDK (B71-50257)
Bingham, George. 50 airs anglais. Einzelstucke und Suiten fur Altblockflote solo. (Ruf, Hugo). *Schott. £0.80* VSSPMG/AY (B71-50659)
Bingham, George. Cinquante airs anglais. *See* Bingham, George. 50 airs anglais.
Binkerd, Gordon. A bygone occasion. *See* Binkerd, Gordon. What sweeter musick.
Binkerd, Gordon.
Duo for flute and oboe. *Boosey and Hawkes. £1.25* VRPLVT (B71-50646)
The fair morning. *Boosey and Hawkes. £0.65* KDW (B71-50332)
If thou wilt ease thine heart. *Boosey and Hawkes. £0.40* KDW (B71-50333)
Institutional canons: for mixed chorus
1: The wealth of Illinois: S.A.T.B. *Boosey and Hawkes. £0.15* EZ/X (B71-50243)
2: There is in souls: SATB. *Boosey and Hawkes. £0.09* EZ/X (B71-50244)
3: To thy happy children: SSATBB. *Boosey and Hawkes. £0.09* EZ/X (B71-50245)
Nursery ode. *Boosey and Hawkes. £0.40* KDW (B71-50334)
Sonata: for cello and piano. *Boosey and Hawkes. £3.15* SRPE (B71-50591)
Three songs: for mezzo-soprano. *Boosey and Hawkes. £1.25* KFNDW (B71-50361)
What sweeter musick: high voice. *Boosey and Hawkes. £0.40* KFTDW (B71-50363)
What sweeter musick: low voice. *Boosey and Hawkes. £0.40* KFXDW (B71-50367)
The wishing caps. *Boosey and Hawkes. £0.65* KDW (B71-50335)
Biro, Val. Making friends with music. (Glennon, James). *Foulsham. £0.60* A (B71-27970) ISBN 0 572 00774 4
Birtwistle, Harrison.
Cantata: by Harrison Birtwistle. *Universal. Unpriced* KFLE/MDX (B71-50891)
Down by the greenwood side: a dramatic pastoral. *Universal. Unpriced* CQM (B71-50734)
Nomos: for orchestra. *Universal. Unpriced* MMJ (B71-50388)
Bitter sweet: easy-to-play piano selection. (Coward, Noel). *Chappell. £0.25* QPK/CM (B71-50102)
Bizet, Georges. Carmen: the story and music. *Keith Prowse. £0.20* QPK/CC (B71-50101)
Black, Leo. Schoenberg: a critical biography. (Reich, Willi). *Longman. £3.50* BSET (B71-16010) ISBN 0 582 12753 x
Blackburn, Maria. A score of nursery rhymes. *Feldman. y0.25* QPJ (B71-50975)
Blackwell, William. Quintet for horn and strings in E major. Op.106. Quintet in E major. Op.106: for horn and string quartet (double bass ad lib). (Reicha, Anton Joseph). *Musica rara. Unpriced* NVNR (B71-50926)
Blackwell's music series. *(Blackwell)* Myers, Rollo Hugh. Modern French music: its evolution and cultural background from 1900 to the present day. *Blackwell. £3.25* A(YH/XM71) (B71-26601) ISBN 0 631 13020 9
Blades, James. Percussion instruments and their history. *Faber and Faber Ltd. £10.00* AX(X) (B71-05797) ISBN 0 571 08858 9
Blake, William.
Come o'er the eastern hills: for four-part chorus of mixed voices a cappella. (Lekberg, Sven). *Schirmer; Chappell. Unpriced* EZDW (B71-50278)
How sweet I roamed from field to field: two part song. (Williams, Patrick). *Bosworth. £0.07* FDW (B71-50840)
The lamb: for full chorus of mixed voices a cappella. (Chorbajian, John). *Schirmer; Chappell. Unpriced* EZDH (B71-50252)
Little sorrows sit and weep: for four-part chorus of mixed voices a cappella. (Lekberg, Sven). *Schirmer; Chappell. Unpriced* EZDW (B71-50279)
Three contemporary madrigals: for four-part chorus of mixed voices a cappella
Why was Cupid a boy?. (Effinger, Cecil). *Schirmer Chappell. Unpriced* EZDW (B71-50273)
Blaze, Francois Henri Joseph. *See* Castil-Blaze, Francois Henri Joseph.
Blesh, Rudi. Combo: U.S.A.: eight lives in jazz. *Chilton Book Company. £3.50* AMT/E(M) (B71-14733) ISBN 0 8019 5250 6
Bliss, *Sir* Arthur.
Concerto for cello & orchestra. *Novello. £2.50* MPSRF (B71-50404)
Concerto for cello & orchestra
Cello & piano score. *Novello. £1.50* SRPK/LF (B71-50597)
Conquest of the air: suite. *Boosey and Hawkes. Unpriced* MMG (B71-50384)
Fanfare for heroes: for 3 trumpets, 3 trombones, timpani & cymbals. *Novello. Unpriced* NYHXPNNGN (B71-50438)

Serenade. Excerpts. Two love songs: for baritone and orchestra. *Oxford University Press. £0.75* KGNDW (B71-50369) ISBN 0 19 345166 2
Simples: a setting of James Joyce's poem. *Oxford University Press. £0.80* KDW (B71-50336) ISBN 0 19 345165 4
Two ballads: for S.A. and piano
1: The mountain-plover. Ushagreaisht. *Novello. £0.125* FDW (B71-50039)
2: Flowers in the valley. *Novello. £0.19* FDW (B71-50040)
Bloch, Ernest. Avodath Hakodesh. Sacred service: a Sabbath morning service according to the Union Prayer Book, for baritone (cantor), mixed chorus and organ or full orchestra. *Boosey and Hawkes. Unpriced* DGUB (B71-50010)
Block, Robert Paul.
Bicinia variorum instrumentum. Excerpts. Sonatinas nos. 61, 62, 65 and 66: for 2 trumpets in B flat (C) & continuo. (Pezel, Johann). *Musica rara. Unpriced* WSNTPWEM (B71-50715)
Fantasia for 2 trumpets (cornetti), bass trombone (sackbutt) and organ continuo. (Hingeston, John). *Musica rara. Unpriced* NWXPNS (B71-50936)
Fantasia for cornetto (trumpet), sackbutt (bass trombone) and organ continuo. (Hingeston, John). *Musica rara. Unpriced* NWXPNT (B71-50934)
Pavans, galiards, almains and other short airs. Complete music for brass: for 2 trumpets and 3 trombones (2 trumpets, horn and 2 trombones)
Vol.1. (Holborne, Antony). *Musica rara. Unpriced* WNR/AZ (B71-51112)
Pavans, galiards, almains and other short airs. Complete music for brass: for 2 trumpets and 3 trombones (2 trumpets, horn and 2 trombones)
Vol.2. (Holborne, Antony). *Musica rara. Unpriced* WNR/AZ (B71-51113)
Sonata for flute, violin, oboe and basso continuo in C major. Op.4. Sonata da camera in C major: for flute, violin, oboe and basso continuo. (Janitsch, Johann Gottlieb). *Musica rara. £1.50* NWPNSE (B71-50424)
Sonata for flute, violin, oboe & basso continuo in C major. Op.4. Sonata da camera in C major. Op.4: for flute, violin, oboe & basso continuo. (Janitsch, Johann Gottlieb). *Musica rara. £1.50* NUPNSE (B71-50079)
Sonata for two violins, trombone & basso continuo, no.1, in D minor. Sonata a 3, no.1 in D minor: for 2 violins, trombone & organ continuo. (Bertali, Antonio). *Musica rara. Unpriced* NUXUNSE (B71-50419)
Sonata for two violins, trombone & basso continuo, no.2, in D minor. Sonata a 3, no.2 in D minor: for 2 violins, trombone & organ continuo. (Bertali, Antonio). *Musica rara. Unpriced* NUXUNSE (B71-50420)
Blom, Eric. Everyman's dictionary of music. 5th ed. *Dent. £4.00* A(C) (B71-21647) ISBN 0 460 03022 1
Blomdahl, Karl-Birger. Game for eight: choreographic suite for chamber orchestra. *Schott. £1.75* MRG (B71-50914)
Bloodworth, Denis. Children's dances. Excerpts. Four dances nos 9, 5, 4 & 12. (Kodaly, Zoltan). *Boosey and Hawkes. £4.00* MK/AH (B71-50069)
Blow, John. Two voluntaries: for organ. *Novello. £0.35* RJ (B71-50521)
Blue paperbacks. The blues revival. (Groom, Bob). *Studio Vista. £1.40* AKDW/HHW (B71-16011) ISBN 0 289 70149 x
Blues from the Delta. (Ferris, William). *Studio Vista. £1.35* AKDW/HHW(YTQ) (B71-06291) ISBN 0 289 70072 8
Blues paperbacks. Blues from the Delta. (Ferris, William). *Studio Vista. £1.35* AKDW/HHW(YTQ) (B71-06291) ISBN 0 289 70072 8
Blues revival. (Groom, Bob). *Studio Vista. £1.40* AKDW/HHW (B71-16011) ISBN 0 289 70149 x
Blyton, Carey.
A lullaby: Christmas carol, SATB unaccompanied. *Royal School of Church Music. Unpriced* EZDP/LF (B71-50797)
Seven polyphonic amens: for unaccompanied voices. *Leeds Music. Unpriced* EZDTM (B71-50811)
Boccherini, Luigi.
Concerto for cello & string orchestra, no.3 in G major. WV480. Konzert no.3, G-Dur: fur Violoncello und Streichorchester. *Schott. £1.50* VRPK/LF (B71-50143)
Sonatas for cello & piano. Six sonatas: for violoncello and piano. *Schirmer; Chappell. Unpriced* SRPE (B71-50122)
Bogan, Louise. To be sung on the water. Op. 42, no.2: transcribed for four-part chorus of women's voices a cappella. (Barber, Samuel). *Schirmer; Chappell. £0.35* FEZDW (B71-50306)
Boguslawski, Edward. Per pianoforte. *Ars viva; Schott. £1.80* QPJ (B71-50475)
Boismortier, Joseph Bodin de.
Suite for flute & basso continuo in B minor. Op.35, no.5. Suite h-Moll: fur Querflote und Basso continuo. *Schott. £1.10* VRPG (B71-50640)
Suite for flute & basso continuo in G major. Op.35, no.2. Suite, g-Dur: fur Querflote und Basso continuo. *Schott. £1.00* VRPG (B71-50641)
Suites for flute. Op.36 nos.1-6. Sechs Suiten: fur Querflote solo. *Schott. £1.20* VRPMG (B71-50647)
Bolton, Cecil.
Gilbert and Sullivan songs. (Sullivan, *Sir* Arthur). *Francis, Day and Hunter. £0.50* RPVK/CM/AY (B71-51004)
Piano arrangements for all to play. (Tchaikovsky, Peter). *Francis, Day and Hunter. £0.90* QPK (B71-50511)
Bonar, Horatius. Fill thou my life: anthem for SATB organ. (Aldridge, Richard). *Lengnick. £0.13* DH (B71-50184)
Bonner, Stephen.
Aeolian harp
Vol.3: The Aeolian harp in European literature, 1591-1892. *Bois de Boulogne. £5.30* A/FS (B71-24693) ISBN 0 900998 12 1
Angelo Benedetto Ventura: teacher, inventor, & composer: a study in English Regency music. *Bois de Boulogne. £10.00* ATQ/E(P) (B71-18714) ISBN 0 900998 08 3
Bononcini, Giovanni Battista. Arias from the Vienna operas. *Oxford University Press for the University of Hull. £2.50* KDW (B71-50337) ISBN 0 19 713412 2
Bonsor, Brian. Three into five: for descant, treble (divisi) and tenor (divisi) recorders and piano. *Schott. £0.50* VSNQQ (B71-50933)
Boone, Pat.
Exodus. Excerpts. The Exodus song. (Gold, Ernest). *Chappell. £0.09* DW/JR (B71-50235)
Exodus. Excerpts. The Exodus song: S.A.B. (Gold, Ernest). *Chappell. Unpriced* DW/JR (B71-50236)
Booth, Victor. We piano teachers. 1st ed. 8th impression (revised). *Hutchinson. £1.25* AQ/E(VC) (B71-05270) ISBN 0 09 106190 3
Borgulya, Andras. 4 duetti: per flauto (o flauto dolce) e viola. *Boosey and Hawkes. Unpriced* VRPLSQ (B71-50645)
Boris Goudonov - Excerpts. Varlaam's song. (Mussorgsky, Modeste). *Ascherberg, Hopwood and Crew. £0.25* QPK/DW (B71-50985)
Born to be King. (Broad, D F). *Banks. Unpriced* FDP/LF (B71-50287)
Borroff, Edith. Music in Europe and the United States: a history. *Prentice-Hall. £6.00* A(X) (B71-21648) ISBN 0 13 608083 9
Boulez, Pierre. Boulez on music today. *Faber. £2.50* A (B71-07322) ISBN 0 571 09420 1
Boulez on music today. (Boulez, Pierre). *Faber. £2.50* A (B71-07322) ISBN 0 571 09420 1
Bourget, Paul. Beau soir. Beautiful evening. (Debussy, Claude). *Boosey and Hawkes. Unpriced* FDW (B71-50833)
Bournemouth Symphony Orchestra. (Miller, Geoffrey). *Dorset Publishing Company. £4.00*

AMM/E(DCVB/X/QB) (B71-05269) ISBN 0 902129 06 6

Bowen, Catherine Drinker. The music lovers: the story of Tchaikowsky and Nadejda von Meck. 2nd ed. abridged. *Hodder Paperbacks. £0.35* BTD(N) (B71-04592) ISBN 0 340 15154 4

Bower, John Dykes. A manual of plainsong for Divine Service. (Briggs, H B). *Novello. £1.25* DTD (B71-50019)

Boyce, William.
Concerto grosso in B minor: for two solo violins, solo violoncello and string orchestra. *Eulenburg. £0.60* RXMPSNTSRF (B71-51009)
Twelve overtures: in D major; for oboes, trumpets, horns, timpani, strings, and continuo. *Oxford University Press. £1.25* MRJ (B71-50918) ISBN 0 19 361834 6
Twelve overtures: in G major; for oboes, flutes, horns, strings, and continuo. *Oxford University Press. £1.25* MRJ (B71-50916) ISBN 0 19 361812 5
Twelve overtures
No.1: in D major; for oboes, strings and continuo. *Oxford University Press. £1.25* MRJ (B71-50915) ISBN 0 19 361802 8
No.3: in Bflat major; for oboes, strings and continuo. *Oxford University Press. Unpriced* MRJ (B71-50917) ISBN 0 19 361824 9
No.5: in F major; for oboes, strings and continuo. *Oxford University Press. £1.25* MRJ (B71-50919) ISBN 0 19 361849 4
No.6: in D minor; for oboes, flutes, horns, strings, and continuo. *Oxford University Press. £1.25* MRJ (B71-50920) ISBN 0 19 361859 1

Boyden, David Dodge. An introduction to music. 2nd ed. *Faber and Faber Ltd. £2.25* A (B71-16009) ISBN 0 571 04745 9

Boyle, Nicholas. Aeolian harp
Vol.3: The Aeolian harp in European literature, 1591-1892. (Bonner, Stephen). *Bois de Boulogne. £5.30* A/FS (B71-24693) ISBN 0 900998 12 1

Bozay, Attila.
Formazion. Op.16: per violoncello solo. *Boosey and Hawkes. Unpriced* SRPMJ (B71-50600)
Medailles: for piano. *Boosey and Hawkes. £0.57* QPJ (B71-50476)
Pezzo concertato. Op.11: per viola solo e orchestra. *Boosey and Hawkes. £1.15* MPSQ (B71-50078)
Tetelpar: two movements for oboe and piano. *Boosey and Hawkes. Unpriced* VTPJ (B71-51084)

Brace, Geoffrey.
Something to play: an instrumental workbook for the classroom. *Cambridge University Press. Unpriced* LN (B71-50897)
Something to sing at assembly. *Cambridge University Press. Unpriced* JFDM/AY (B71-50322) ISBN 0 521 07570 x

Bradshaw, Susan. Boulez on music today. (Boulez, Pierre). *Faber. £2.50* A (B71-07322) ISBN 0 571 09420 1

Brahms, Johannes.
Abendlied. Evening song. Op.91, no.3: for four-part chorus of mixed voices with piano accompaniment. *Schirmer; Chappell. Unpriced* DW (B71-50225)
Nachtens. Nightly visions. Op.112, no.2: for four-part chorus of mixed voices with piano accompaniment. *Schirmer; Chappell. Unpriced* DW (B71-50226)
O schone Nacht. O lovely night. Op.92, no.1: for four-part chorus of mixed voices with piano accompaniment. *Schirmer; Chappell. Unpriced* DW (B71-50227)
Sehnsucht. Longing. Op.112, no.1: for four-part chorus of mixed voices with piano accompaniment. *Schirmer; Chappell. Unpriced* DW (B71-50228)
Sonata for cello & piano in F major. Op.99. Sonata in F major. Op.99: for cello and piano. *Schirmer; Chappell. Unpriced* SRPE (B71-51019)
Spatherbst. Late autumn. Op.92, no.2: for four-part chorus of mixed voices with piano accompaniment. *Schirmer; Chappell. Unpriced* DW (B71-50229)
Warum. Wherefore should our singing soar. Op.91, no.4: for four-part chorus of mixed voices with piano accompaniment. *Schirmer; Chappell. Unpriced* DW (B71-50230)

Brain, Leonard. Quintet for wind instruments. Wind quintet: for flute, oboe, clarinet, bassoon, horn. (Stoker, Richard). *Hinrichsen. Unpriced* UNR (B71-50633)

Branches: for 2 bassoons and percussion. (Chihara, Paul). *Peters; Hinrichsen. £1.25* NYHWNT (B71-50437)

Brand, Geoffrey. Capriol suite. (Warlock, Peter). *Curwen, R. Smith. Unpriced* WMK/AHG (B71-50706)

Brennan, Ted. The power and the glory. (Leonard, Harry). *Novello. £1.75* EMDH (B71-50023)

Bresgen, Cesar. Malinconia: funf Gitarrenstucke. *Schott. £0.80* TSPMJ (B71-50608)

Brett, Philip. The collected works of William Byrd
Vol.15: Consort songs for voice & viols. (Byrd, William). *Stainer and Bell. Unpriced* C/AZ (B71-50003)

Brewis, Bert.
Christmas songs for descant recorder. (Evans, Howard). *Chappell. Unpriced* VSRPMK/DW/LF/AY (B71-51082)
Christmas songs for guitar. *Chappell. Unpriced* TSPMK/DP/LF/AY (B71-51054)
Show boat. (Kern, Jerome). *Chappell. £0.30* RPVK/CM (B71-51003)
The song of Norway: piano selection from the film. (Greig, Edvard). *Chappell; Frank Music. £0.25* QPK/CM/JR (B71-50104)

Bridges, R S. Thee will I love: motet for SATB and organ. (Howells, Herbert). *Novello. £0.15* DH (B71-50012)

Briggs, H B. A manual of plainsong for Divine Service. *Novello. £1.25* DTD (B71-50019)

British Broadcasting Corporation.
Anatomy of pop. (Cash, Tony). *British Broadcasting Corporation. £0.70* A/GB(XPQ16) (B71-03033) ISBN 0 563 10261 6
Musical interpretation. (Westrup, *Sir* Jack Allan). *British Broadcasting Corporation. £0.90* A/E (B71-06909) ISBN 0 563 10352 3

British Federation of Music Festivals. Year book
1971: 50th anniversary. *British Federation of Music Festivals. £0.50* A(YC/WE/Q) (B71-13106) ISBN 0 901532 02 9

British Museum. The Raffles 'gamelan': a historical note. (Fagg, William). *British Museum. £0.40* BZGVJAL/B(WJ) (B71-04179) ISBN 0 7141 1514 2

British Standards Institution. Universal Decimal Classification
78: Music. English full ed. (4th international ed.). *British Standards Institution. £0.80* A(UJ) (B71-19565) ISBN 0 580 06563 4

Britten, Benjamin.
A ceremony of carols. Ein Kranz von Lobechorens. Op.28: for treble voices and harp. New English-German ed. *Boosey and Hawkes. Unpriced* FLDEDP/LF (B71-50309)
Five spiritual songs (Geistliche Lieder). (Bach, Johann Sebastian). *Faber Music. £1.00* KFTDH (B71-50062)
The oxen: a carol for women's voices and piano. *Faber Music. Unpriced* FDP/LF (B71-50036)
The tale of the wandering scholar. Op.50. The wandering scholar. Op.50: a chamber opera in one act. (Holst, Gustav). *Faber. Unpriced* CQC (B71-50172)

Brixi, Franz Xaver. Concerto fur viola in C major. Konzert, C-Dur: fur Viola und Orchestra. *Schott. £1.30* SQPK/LF (B71-50120)

Broad, D F. Born to be King. *Banks. Unpriced* FDP/LF (B71-50287)

Brocklehurst, Brian. Response to music: principles of music education. *Routledge and K. Paul. £1.40* A(VK/YC) (B71-03584) ISBN 0 7100 6949 9

Broder, Nathan. Mozart: his character - his work. (Einstein, Alfred). *Panther. £0.75* BMS(N) (B71-06907) ISBN 0 586 03277 0

Brodszky, Ferenc.
For children. Excerpts. For children: 25 selected pieces. (Bartok, Bela). *Boosey and Hawkes. £0.75* TSPMK (B71-50611)
Lieder und Tanze der Vorklassik: Stuke aus dem 16. bis 18. Jahrhundert fur Gitarre sehr leicht gesetzt. *Schott. Unpriced* TSPMK (B71-50612)

Brody, Elaine. Music in opera: a historical anthology. *Prentice-Hall. £7.50* AC(X) (B71-12556) ISBN 0 13 608109 6

Bronte, Emily. Six poems of Emily Bronte. Op.63: for high voice and piano. (Joubert, John). *Novello. £1.75* KFTDW (B71-50895)

Brooks, Nigel.
More carols for Christmas. *Boosey and Hawkes. Unpriced* EZDP/LF/AY (B71-50261)
Songs for Easter. *Boosey and Hawkes. Unpriced* DM/LL/AY (B71-50210)

Brown, Andrew. Aeolian harp
Vol.3: The Aeolian harp in European literature, 1591-1892. (Bonner, Stephen). *Bois de Boulogne. £5.30* A/FS (B71-24693) ISBN 0 900998 12 1

Brown, Oscar. Joy. Excerpts. Brown baby: for chorus of treble voices (SSA) and piano. *Novello. £0.09* FDW (B71-50041)

Brown, Rosemary. Unfinished symphonies: voices from the beyond. *Souvenir Press. £1.75* A/D(ZF) (B71-15624) ISBN 0 285 62009 6

Brown baby: for chorus of treble voices (SSA) and piano. (Brown, Oscar). *Novello. £0.09* FDW (B71-50041)

Browning, Robert. The pied piper: a play with music. (Berger, Jean). *Schirmer; Chappell. Unpriced* CQM (B71-50173)

Bruckner, Anton. Psalm 112: for double chorus of mixed voices. *Schirmer; Chappell. Unpriced* DR (B71-50220)

Brunelli, Louis. Sunburst: concert march. (Osterling, Eric). *Chappell. Unpriced* WMK/AGM (B71-50151)

Bryce, F. March: Washington D.C. (Kelly, Bryan). *Novello. Unpriced* WMGM (B71-51097)

Buffalo boy: for four-part chorus of mixed voices with piano accompaniment. (Dougherty, Celius). *Schirmer; Chappell. Unpriced* DW (B71-50231)

Buhe, Klaus.
Europaische Volks-und Tanzweisen: fur Flote, Akkordeon I/II, Gitarre (banjo), Bass und Schlagzeug. *Schott. £1.20* NYDRK/DW/AYB (B71-50432)
Volks- und Tanzweisen aus Amerika: fur Flote, Akkordeon I/II (E-Gitarre), Gitarre (Banjo), Bass und Schlagzeug. *Schott. £1.20* NYDRK/DW/AYT (B71-50433)

Bukalski, Jur Stanislaw. Short pieces: for double bass with piano accompaniment. *PWM; Peters. £0.75* SSPK/AAY (B71-50602)

Buketoff, Igor. 1812 overture. Op.49: a festive overture. (Tchaikovsky, Peter). *Sunbury Music. £0.40* DADW (B71-50736)

Bull, John. Musica Britanica: a national collection of music. 2nd revised ed. *Stainer and Bell. Unpriced* C/AYD (B71-50002)

Bullivant, Roger. Fugue. *Hutchinson. £2.25* A/Y (B71-25915) ISBN 0 09 108440 7

Bun no.2: for orchestra. (Cardew, Cornelius). *Peters Hinrichsen. Unpriced* MMJ (B71-50389)

Bunting, Christopher.
Six string-crossing studies: for cello solo. *Oxford University Press. Unpriced* SR/AF (B71-50588) ISBN 0 19 355751 7
Six velocity studies: for cello solo. *Oxford University Press. £0.40* SR/AF (B71-50589) ISBN 0 19 355752 5

Burger, Willy. Sonata for bassoon and basso continuo, no.1, in D minor. Sonata prima: fur Fagott und Basso continuo. (Bertoli, Giovanni Antonio). *Schott. £1.10* VWPE (B71-50683)

Burgmuller, Norbert. Duo for clarinet & piano in E flat major. Op.15. Duo. Op.15: for clarinet and piano. *Simrock. Unpriced* VVPJ (B71-50675)

Burgon, Geoffrey. Think on dredful domesday: for s.S.A.T.B and chamber orchestra. *Stainer and Bell. Unpriced* DX (B71-50779)

Burmester, W. Rinaldo - Sorge nel petto. Sarabande. (Handel, George Frideric). *Schott. Unpriced* SRPK/AHVL (B71-51040)

Burrows, Michael. Mario Lanza; and, Max Steiner. *Primestyle Ltd. £0.75* AKGH/E(P) (B71-27972) ISBN 0 902421 14 x

Bush, Alan.
Lenin in Siberia. (Muradeli, Vano). *Workers' Music Association. £0.13* DW (B71-50773)
Songs of struggle. *Workers' Music Association. Unpriced* JDW (B71-50048)
Songs of struggle. *Workers' Music Association. £0.35* JDW (B71-50859)

Bush, Geoffrey.
The overlanders. Two symphonic studies on themes from 'The overlanders'. (Ireland, John). *Boosey and Hawkes. £0.65* MMJ (B71-50072)
Scherzo & cortege, on themes from Julius Caesar. (Ireland, John). *Boosey and Hawkes. £1.10* MMK/JM (B71-50075)
Seven limericks: for two-part choir & small orchestra. *Novello. £0.50* FE/MDX (B71-50044)

Bush, Nancy.
Hungarian folksongs (1906). Excerpts. Five Hungarian folksongs: for voice and piano. (Bartok, Bela). *Boosey and Hawkes. Unpriced* KDW/G/AYG (B71-50346)
Lenin in Siberia. (Muradeli, Vano). *Workers' Music Association. £0.13* DW (B71-50773)

Bussotti, Sylvano. Due voci: per soprano, martenot solo ed orchestra su un frammento di Jean de la Fontaine. *Universal. Unpriced* KFLE/MPPSDW (B71-50357)

Buszin, Walter E.
60 canons on secular texts: four centuries, 2 to 8 voices
Vol.1: Nos 1-30. *Peters; Hinrichsen. £0.45* EZ/X/AY (B71-50246)
Vol.2: 31-60. *Peters; Hinrichsen. £0.45* EZ/X/AY (B71-50247)
Ehre sey Gott in der Hohe. Glory to God in the highest: for mixed voices, organ (piano) and strings (ad lib). (Hammerschmidt, Andreas). *Peters; Hinrichsen. £0.45* GDH/LF (B71-50313)
Wer walset uns den Stein. An Easter dialogue: for mixed voices, organ (piano), 2 trumpets, 4 trombones and double bass. (Hammerschmidt, Andreas). *Peters; Hinrichsen. £0.45* ENUXPNQDH/LL (B71-50240)

Butler, Tony. Best Irish songs of Percy French. (French, Percy). *Wolfe. £0.25* BFURAKDW (B71-11819) ISBN 0 7234 0428 3

Butterworth, Arthur.
28 melodious exercises for piano duet. Op.149, nos. 16,11,26,6. A Diabelli suite: for small brass ensemble. (Diabelli, Anton). *Feldman. Unpriced* WNMK/AF (B71-51110)
The path across the moor: for brass band. *Hinrichsen. £0.90* WMJ (B71-50697)

Butterworth, Lionel Milner Angus-. *See* Angus-Butterworth, Lionel Milner.

Butterworth, Neil.
Moravian duets. Op.32. Songs from Moravia
Book 1. (Dvorak, Antonin). *Chappell. Unpriced* FLDW (B71-50855)
Moravian duets. Op.32. Songs from Moravia
Book 1. (Dvorak, Antonin). *Chappell. Unpriced* FLDW (B71-50856)
Moravian duets. Op.32. Songs from Moravia
Book 2. (Dvorak, Antonin). *Chappell. Unpriced* FLDW (B71-50854)

Bye, Baby Bunting. (Poston, Elizabeth). *Bodley Head. £1.10* JFDW/GK/AY (B71-50871) ISBN 0 370 01526 6

Bygone occasion. *See* Binkerd, Gordon.

Byrd, William.
Beata viscera, Hail Mary, full of grace: motet for five voices, S.A.A.T.B. for feasts of the Blessed Virgin. *Chester. Unpriced* EZDGKAH (B71-50248)
The collected works of William Byrd. *Stainer and Bell. £4.75* C/AZ (B71-50723)
The collected works of William Byrd
Vol.15: Consort songs for voice & viols. *Stainer and Bell. Unpriced* C/AZ (B71-50003)
Short service. Excerpts. Magnificat and Nunc dimittis: SAATTB and organ. Revised ed. *Oxford University Press. £0.25* DGPP (B71-50181) ISBN 0 19 352024 9

Byron, George Gordon Noel, *Baron Byron*. So we'll go no more a-roving: two-part song, optional unison. (Dale, Mervyn). *Ashdown. Unpriced* FDW (B71-50832)

Byrt, John. Dashing away with the smoothing iron: traditional song SATB unacc. *Oxford University Press. Unpriced* EZDW (B71-50269) ISBN 0 19 343007 x

Cage, John.
Aria: voice (any range). *Peters; Hinrichsen. £4.25* KDW (B71-50338)
John Cage. (Kostelanetz, Richard). *Allen Lane. £3.15* BCBG (B71-14242) ISBN 0 7139 0210 8

Cain, Alfred. 'Variety' music cavalcade, 1620-1969: a chronology of vocal and instrumental music popular in the United States. (Mattfeld, Julius). 2nd ed. *Prentice-Hall. £7.50* A/GB(YT/XEW350/TC) (B71-23694) ISBN 0 13 940718 9

Calypso praise. (Graves, Richard). *Bosworth. £0.06* JFDH (B71-50050)

Camden, John. Solos for the alto (treble) recorder player: with piano accompaniment. *Schirmer; Chappell. Unpriced* VSSPK/AAY (B71-50658)
Cameo. *(Hamlyn)* Paganelli, Sergio. Musical instruments from the Renaissance to the 19th century. *Hamlyn. £0.90* AL/B(XDWC378) (B71-07323) ISBN 0 600 35920 4
Camilleri, Charles. Little African suite: for piano. Opus 44. *Novello. Unpriced* QPG (B71-50469)
Caminho da serra; and, Cacando Borboletas; and, Madrugada; and, Na Beira do Rio. (Lorenzo Fernandez, Oscar). *Arthur Napoleao; Essex Music. Unpriced* SPMK (B71-50580)
Campbell, David. Search: songs of the sun. *Galliard. Unpriced* JEZDW (B71-50862) ISBN 0 85249 160 3
Campell, Alex. Alex Campbell songs. *Galliard. Unpriced* KE/TSDW/AY (B71-50889)
Cancao do Carreiro ou Cancao um crepusculo caricioso: canto e piano. (Villa-Lobos, Heitor). *Arthur Napoleao; Essex Music. Unpriced* KDW (B71-50057)
Cancao do mar: canto e piano. (Lorenzo Fernandez, Oscar). *Arthur Napoleao; Essex Music. Unpriced* KDW (B71-50341)
Cantata: by Harrison Birtwistle. (Birtwistle, Harrison). *Universal. Unpriced* KFLE/MDX (B71-50891)
Canticle of Mary (Magnificat) for four-part chorus of mixed voices with organ accompaniment. (Glarum, Leonard Stanley). *Schirmer; Chappell. Unpriced* DGPQ (B71-50183)
Canticle of Mary (Magnificat) for unison voices with organ accompaniment. (Glarum, Leonard Stanley). *Schirmer; Chappell. Unpriced* JDGPQ (B71-50315)
Cantus: for orchestra (1964). (Hamilton, Iain). *Schott. £0.60* MMJ (B71-50908)
Canzon for two bassoons & basso continuo. XXIII Canzon a 2 Bassi: fur 2 Fagotte oder Posaune und Fagott und Basso continuo. (Selma y Salaverde, Bartolomeo de). *Schott. £1.00* VWNTPW (B71-50682)
Canzoni napoletane. Lib 1, no.14. Voria che ta cantass'. Neapolitan song. (Scandello, Antonio). *Warner; Blossom Music. Unpriced* EZDU (B71-50812)
Capon, John. Sing Emmanuel: the story of Edwin Shepherd and the London Emmanuel Choir. *Word Books. £0.50* AD/E(QB/DB) (B71-27971) ISBN 0 85009 031 8
Capriccio (1969): for piano. (McCabe, John). *Novello. £0.50* QPJ (B71-50491)
Capriccio fugato a dodice. *Schott. £1.00* VSMJ (B71-51073)
Capricorn flakes: for keyboard & percussion. (Mellnas, Arne). *Peters; Hinrichsen. £2.00* NYLNS (B71-50439)
Capriol suite. (Warlock, Peter). *Curwen, R. Smith. Unpriced* WMK/AHG (B71-50706)
Captain Noah and his floating zoo: cantata in popular style for unison or two-part voices & piano, with optional bass & drums. (Flanders, Michael). *Novello. £0.40* FDE (B71-50035)
Cardew, Cornelius.
Bun no.2: for orchestra. *Peters, Hinrichsen. Unpriced* MMJ (B71-50389)
Treatise handbook including Bun no.2, Volo solo. *Peters Hinrichsen. £3.50* LJ (B71-50372)
Volo solo: for a virtuoso performer on any instrument. *Peters, Hinrichsen. £0.90* LJ (B71-50373)
Careers with music. (Incorporated Society of Musicians). *Incorporated Society of Musicians. £0.60* A(MN) (B71-09060) ISBN 0 902900 02 1
Carmen: the story and music. (Bizet, Georges). *Keith Prowse. £0.20* QPK/CC (B71-50101)
Carnaval das criancas: colecao de 8 pecas for piano
No.7: A Gaita de um precoce fantasiado. (Villa-Lobos, Heitor). *Arthur Napoleao; Essex Music. Unpriced* QPG (B71-50470)
Carol of the field mice. (Head, Michael). *Boosey and Hawkes. Unpriced* KDP/LF (B71-50331)
Carols for choirs. Bk.1, nos. 33, 27, 13. Three carol orchestrations. (Jacques, Reginald). *Oxford University Press. Unpriced* EMDP/LF (B71-50782)
Carols for choirs. Excerpts. Six Christmas hymns: for mixed voices and organ (or orchestra). (Willcocks, David). *Oxford University Press. £0.20* DP/LF/AY (B71-50217) ISBN 0 19 353568 8
Carroll, Peter. Wenn ich ein Glocklein war. The Vesper bell. (Engelhart, Franz Xaver). *Bosworth. Unpriced* DW (B71-50771)
Carter, Sydney. Songs of Sydney Carter
4: Riding a tune. *Galliard. Unpriced* JDW (B71-50860)
Cartwright, Kenneth. Clarinet cha-cha: for orchestra. *Feldman. Unpriced* MSHJMR (B71-50415)
Cash, Tony. Anatomy of pop. *British Broadcasting Corporation. £0.70* A/GB(XPQ16) (B71-03033) ISBN 0 563 10261 6
Cassell opera guides. *(Cassell)*
Da Ponte, Lorenzo. Don Giovanni; libretto by Lorenzo da Ponte to the opera by W.A. Mozart; and, Idomeneo libretto by Giambattista Varesco to the opera by W.A. Mozart. *Cassell. £1.75* BMSAC (B71-24691) ISBN 0 304 93824 6
Da Ponte, Lorenzo. Le Nozze di Figaro; and, Cosi fan tutte; librettos by Lorenzo da Ponte to the operas by W.A. Mozart. *Cassell. £1.75* BMSAC (B71-25344) ISBN 0 304 93826 2
Schikaneder, Emanuel. Die Zauberflote; libretto by Emanuel Schikaneder to the opera by W.A. Mozart; and, Die Entfuhrung aus dem Serail; libretto by Gottlieb Stephanie to the opera by W.A. Mozart. *Cassell. £1.75* BMSAC (B71-24690) ISBN 0 304 93825 4
Castaldi, Paolo. Moll: fur das Pianoforte. *Universal. Unpriced* QPJ (B71-50477)
Castil-Blaze, Francois Henri Joseph. Sextet for wind instruments, no.1 in E flat major. Sextet no.1 in E flat for 2 clarinets, 2 horns and 2 bassoons. *Musica rara. Unpriced* UNQ (B71-51065)
Castle, Charles, *b.1939*. This was Richard Tauber. *W.H. Allen. £3.50* AKGH/E(P) (B71-11818) ISBN 0 491 00117 7
Caswall, Edward. Bethlehem, of noblest cities: Australian folk melody and a melody from Psalmodia sacra, Gotha, 1715, for SATB. (Hurford, Peter). *Oxford University Press. Unpriced* DP/LFP (B71-50218)
Catacoustics: for two pianos. (Sary, Laszlo). *Boosey and Hawkes. £0.86* QNU (B71-50449)
Catalogue for percussion III: 3 players. (Hiller, Wilfried). *Schott. £1.60* XNT (B71-51124)
Catelinet, Philip B. Suite in miniature: three movements in contrasting styles for two trombones or baritones or euphoniums. *Hinrichsen. £0.20* WUNUG (B71-50719)
Cathedral Church of the Blessed Virgin Mary and St Ethelbert, *Hereford*. *See* Hereford Cathedral.
Cathedral city. (Graves, John). *Schott. Unpriced* SRPJ (B71-51028)
Cavatina: arranged for guitar by John Williams. (Myers, Stanley). *Francis, Day and Hunter. £0.40* TSPMK (B71-51052)
Celebration: fantasia for brass band. (Ball, Eric). *Boosey and Hawkes. Unpriced* WMJ (B71-51100)
Celega, Nicolo. Il Guarany - Excerpts. O Guarani: sinfonia. (Gomes, Antonio Carlos). *Arthur Napoleao; Essex Music. Unpriced* QNVK (B71-50454)
Ceremonial music for organ: fanfares and trumpet tunes. *Oxford University Press. £0.40* RK (B71-50111) ISBN 0 19 375120 8
Ceremony of carols. Ein Kranz von Lobechorens. Op.28: for treble voices and harp. (Britten, Benjamin). New English-German ed. *Boosey and Hawkes. Unpriced* FLDEDP/LF (B71-50309)
Chagrin, Francis.
Lullaby: for four solo instruments, optional solo bassoon or solo cello, and string orchestra or piano. *Novello. £1.55* MJ (B71-50902)
Mother, I cannot mind my wheel. *Ricordi. Unpriced* EZDW (B71-50030)
Champion, W R. Easter song: for unison voices and organ. (Steer, Michael). *Novello. Unpriced* JDH (B71-50316)
Chants russes. (Lalo, Edouard). *Schott. Unpriced* SRPK (B71-51034)
Chapman, Edward.
Christ is the flower within my heart: a Christmas anthem, SATB. *Oxford University Press. Unpriced* DH (B71-50744) ISBN 0 19 351110 x
Stille Nacht, heilige Nacht. Silent night. (Gruber, Franz). *Oxford University Press. Unpriced* DP/LF (B71-50763) ISBN 0 19 343022 3
Chappell, Herbert.
The Christmas jazz: for unison voices with piano accompaniment and guitar chords. *Clarabella Music. Unpriced* CN/LF (B71-50171)
The Goliath jazz: for unison voices with piano accompaniment and guitar chords. *Clarabella Music. Unpriced* CN/L (B71-50166)
The Jericho jazz: for unison voices with piano accompaniment and guitar chords. *Clarabella Music. Unpriced* CN/L (B71-50167)
The Noah jazz: for unison voices with piano accompaniment and guitar chords. *Clarabella Music. Unpriced* CN/L (B71-50168)
The prodigal son jazz: for unison voices with piano accompaniment and guitar chords. *Clarabella Music. Unpriced* CN/L (B71-50169)
The Red Sea jazz: for unison voices with piano accompaniment and guitar chords. *Clarabella Music. Unpriced* CN/L (B71-50170)
Chappell, Paul. A portrait of John Bull, c.1563-1628. *Hereford Cathedral. £0.10* BBV(N) (B71-03035) ISBN 0 9501011 2 5
Charles, E. Spartak - Excerpts. Spartacus: love theme. (Khachaturian, Aram). *Plantagenet Music. £0.20* QPK/JS (B71-50987)
Charms and ceremonies: for unison voices, S(S)A and piano. (Hurd, Michael). *Novello. £0.30* FDX (B71-50842)
Charpentier, Marc Antoine. Mass for eight voices & eight violins & flutes. Mass: for soloists, double chorus & orchestra. *Oxford University Press. £3.50* EMDG (B71-50238) ISBN 0 19 335500 0
Chase, Bruce. George Gershwin: a symphonic portrait for concert band; arranged by Bruce Chase. (Gershwin, George). *Chappell. Unpriced* UMMK/DW (B71-51062)
Chatterley, Albert. 101 tunes to explore. *Novello. £0.75* Q/R (B71-50961)
Chavez, Carlos. Clio: symphonic ode. *Schirmer; Chappell. Unpriced* MMJ (B71-50071)
Chavez, Carlos. Variations for violin with piano. *Schirmer; Chappell. Unpriced* SP/T (B71-50559)
Chedeville, Nicolas. Sonata for oboe & basso continuo in E minor. Sonata e-Moll: fur Oboe (Querflote, Violine) und Basso continuo. *Schott. £0.90* VTPE (B71-50663)
Chelys: the journal of the Viola da Gamba Society
Vol.1-. *Viola da Gamba Society. £2.10(free to members)* ASTU(B) (B71-01190)
Chemins I (sur Sequenza II): per arpa principale ed orchestra. (Berio, Luciano). *Universal. Unpriced* MPTQ (B71-50405)
Cherry-tree carol: for women's voices, S.A. and flute. (Cumming, Richard). *Boosey and Hawkes. £0.09* FE/VRDP/LF (B71-50300)
Cherub carol: unison. (Coates, Douglas). *Bosworth. £0.05* JFDP/LF (B71-50867)
Chesterton, Frances.
Children's songs of the nativity: carol for woodwind (recorder, flute & clarinet or oboe), two-part women's or boy's voices, piano/organ and optional percussion. (Roe, Betty). *Thames. Unpriced* FEZDP/LF (B71-50848)
How far is it to Bethlehem?: English traditional melody, S.A.A. unacc. (Willcocks, David). *Oxford University Press. Unpriced* FEZDP/LF (B71-50305) ISBN 0 19 342592 0
How far is it to Bethlehem?: West country carol. (Lawson, Gordon). *Royal School of Church Music. £0.05* EZDP/LF (B71-50800)
Chevalier, Maurice. I remember it well. *W.H. Allen. £2.00* AKG/E(P) (B71-06910) ISBN 0 491 00436 2
Chihara, Paul.
Branches: for 2 bassoons and percussion. *Peters; Hinrichsen. £1.25* NYHWNT (B71-50437)
Logs: for 1 or more string basses. *Protone Music; Henmar Music; Hinrichsen. £1.00* SSN (B71-50601)
Willow, willow: for flute, tuba, and three percussionists. *Protone Music; Henmer Music; Hinrichsen. £1.75* NYHNR (B71-50436)
Children's Christmas festival: for voices, recorders and percussion. (Mendoza, Anne). *Oxford University Press. £0.50* JFE/NYHSDE/LF (B71-50876) ISBN 0 19 330566 6
Children's dances. Excerpts. Four dances nos 9, 5, 4 & 12. (Kodaly, Zoltan). *Boosey and Hawkes. £4.00* MK/AH (B71-50069)
Children's game: for women's voices with piano four-hand accompaniment. (Schoenfield, Paul). *Schirmer; Chappell. Unpriced* FDX (B71-50297)
Children's songs of the nativity: carol for woodwind (recorder, flute & clarinet or oboe), two-part women's or boy's voices, piano/organ and optional percussion. (Roe, Betty). *Thames. Unpriced* FEZDP/LF (B71-50848)
Children's Welsh flavour: a selection of Welsh children's hymn tunes set to English words
Vol.1. (Battye, Ken). *Ken Battye. Unpriced* FDM/AYDK (B71-50827)
Chilton, John. Louis: the Louis Armstrong story, 1900-1971. (Jones, Max). *Studio Vista. £3.20* AMT/E(P) (B71-25343) ISBN 0 289 70215 1
Chisholm, Erik. The operas of Leos Janacek. *Pergamon. £2.50* BJFAC (B71-07865) ISBN 0 08 012854 8
Choral music education. (Roe, Paul F). *Prentice-Hall. £4.50* AD/E(VK) (B71-02480) ISBN 0 13 133348 8
Choral wedding service. (Royal School of Church Music). Revised ed.. *Royal School of Church Music. Unpriced* DGM/KDD (B71-50179) ISBN 0 85402 019 5
Chorbajian, John.
Come away, come away, Death: for full chorus of mixed voices a cappella. *Schirmer; Chappell. Unpriced* EZDW (B71-50814)
The lamb: for full chorus of mixed voices a cappella. *Schirmer; Chappell. Unpriced* EZDH (B71-50252)
Two doves: for full chorus of mixed voices a cappella by John Chorbajian; words by Christina Rossetti. *Schirmer Chappell. Unpriced* EZDW (B71-50270)
Chorley, H F. L'Enfance du Christ. Op.25: chorus and orchestra. (Berlioz, Hector). *Eulenburg. £4.75* EMDD (B71-50237)
Christ is the flower within my heart: a Christmas anthem, SATB. (Chapman, Edward). *Oxford University Press. Unpriced* DH (B71-50744) ISBN 0 19 351110 x
Christ the Lord is risen again: SATB. (Rutter, John). *Oxford University Press. £0.09* DM/LL (B71-50209) ISBN 0 19 351109 6
Christmas jazz: for unison voices with piano accompaniment and guitar chords. (Chappell, Herbert). *Clarabella Music. Unpriced* CN/LF (B71-50171)
Christmas songs for descant recorder. (Evans, Howard). *Chappell. Unpriced* VSRPMK/DW/LF/AY (B71-51082)
Christmas songs for guitar. (Brewis, Bert). *Chappell. Unpriced* TSPMK/DP/LF/AY (B71-51054)
Christmas tree: a garland of 20th century carols and songs for the young. *Weinberger. £0.35* JDP/LF/AY (B71-50858)
Christou, Jani. Enantiodromia: for orchestra. *Chester. Unpriced* MMJ (B71-50906)
Christus am Olberger. Excerpts. Hallelujah. (Beethoven, Ludwig van). *Schirmer; Chappell. Unpriced* EUMDH (B71-50242)
Christus factus est. Jesus who for our salvation: four-part chorus of mixed voices a cappella. (Anerio, Felice). *Schirmer; Chappell. Unpriced* EZDJ (B71-50794)
Church bells of Herefordshire: their inscriptions and founders
Vol.3: Kington-Pudlestone. (Sharpe, Frederick). *F. Sharpe. £1.75* AXSR/B(YDHR) (B71-04597) ISBN 0 9500835 1 8
Cimentia dell'armonia e dell'inventione. Op.8. Concerto for oboe & string orchestra in C major. Konzert, C-Dur: fur Oboe, Streichorchester und General bass. (Vivaldi, Antonio). *Schott. £0.90* VTPK/LF (B71-50667)
Cinquante airs anglais. *See* Bingham, George.
Cinquepaces. Op. 5: for brass quintet. (Connolly, Justin). *Oxford University Press. £2.00* WNR (B71-51111)
Clarinet caprice. (Farnon, Dennis). *Boosey and Hawkes. £2.05* UMMJ (B71-51060)
Clarinet cha-cha: for orchestra. (Cartwright, Kenneth). *Feldman. Unpriced* MSHJMR (B71-50415)
Clarinet: some notes upon its history and construction. (Rendall, Francis Geoffrey). 3rd ed. *Benn. £2.75* AVV/B(X) (B71-20593) ISBN 0 510 36701 1
Clarinet virtuosi of the past. (Weston, Pamela). *Hale. £5.00* AVV/E(M/XA1950) (B71-30156) ISBN 0 7091 2442 2
Clark, Ian. Man on the move: songs on the past, present and future of transport. (Rowe, Christopher). *Galliard. Unpriced* JE/TSDW (B71-50319)
Class piano for adult beginners. (Squire, Russel Nelson). 2nd ed. *Prentice-Hall. £3.00* Q/AC (B71-50447)

ISBN 0 13 135160 5

Classic guitar method including chords and 20 studies
Vol.1. (Economides, George C). *Keith Prowse Music. £0.60* TS/AC (B71-50127)
Vol.2. (Economides, George C). *Keith Prowse Music. £0.60* TS/AC (B71-50128)

Classical album: for 2 clarinets in B flat and piano. (Weston, Pamela). *Boosey and Hawkes. Unpriced* VVPKf AAY (B71-51090)

Classical guitar: design and construction. (McLeod, Donald, *b.1921*). *Dryad Press. £2.50* ATS/BC (B71-14735) ISBN 0 85219 077 8

Classical style: Haydn, Mozart, Beethoven. (Rosen, Charles). *Faber and Faber Ltd. £7.00* A(X) (B71-09738) ISBN 0 571 09118 0

Clavier Ubung. Tl.2. Partie for keyboard, no.3 in E minor. Suite in A minor. (Kuhnau, Johann). *Novello. Unpriced* TSNUK/AG (B71-51050)

Cleary, Vincent. Music course for the Intermediate Certificate. *Folens and Co. Ltd. £0.35* A (B71-06906) ISBN 0 902592 07 6

Clio: symphonic ode. (Chavez, Carlos). *Schirmer; Chappell. Unpriced* MMJ (B71-50071)

Clough, Francis Frederick. Great pianists of our time. (Kaiser, Joachim). *Allen and Unwin. £3.25* AQ/E(M) (B71-16015) ISBN 0 04 780019 4

Clover, David. A mini-blues suite: for descant, treble and tenor recorders. *Feldman. Unpriced* VSNSG (B71-50651)

Coastal ballads: Northumbrian sea songs
No.1: The water of Tyne. (Tate, Phyllis). *Oxford University Press. £0.25* KDW/KC/AYDJJ (B71-50348) ISBN 0 19 345820 9
No.2: O the bonny fisher lad. (Tate, Phyllis). *Oxford University Press. £0.25* KDW/KC/AYDJJ (B71-50349) ISBN 0 19 345819 5
No.3: Billy boy. (Tate, Phyllis). *Oxford University Press. £0.25* KDW/KC/AYDJJ (B71-50350) ISBN 0 19 345821 7

Coates, Douglas. The cherub carol: unison. *Bosworth. £0.05* JFDP/LF (B71-50867)

Coates, Eric. Eric Coates for brass: musical extracts from At the dance, The jester at the wedding, London Bridge, The three Elizabeths, The three bears; arranged for brass and reed band by Allan Street. *Chappell. Unpriced* WMK (B71-50704)

Coffin, C. Great mover of all hearts: anthem. (Smith, Noel). *Lengnick. Unpriced* DH (B71-50747)

Cold encounter: unison song. (Harris, Will). *Bosworth. £0.06* JFDW (B71-50052)

Cole, Hugo. Playing the cello: an approach through live music making. *Novello. 1.50* SR/AC (B71-50586)

Cole, Peter. Anatomy of pop. (Cash, Tony). *British Broadcasting Corporation. £0.70* A/GB(XPQ16) (B71-03033) ISBN 0 563 10261 6

Coloratura: for oboe and piano. (Ferneyhough, Brian). *Hinrichsen. £1.10* VTPJ (B71-50665)

Colwell, Richard. The evaluation of music teaching and learning. *Prentice-Hall. Unpriced* A(VF/VCM) (B71-11816) ISBN 0 13 292151 0

Combo: U.S.A.: eight lives in jazz. (Blesh, Rudi). *Chilton Book Company. £3.50* AMT/E(M) (B71-14733) ISBN 0 8019 5250 6

Come and sing: a selection of Christian songs for under-eights. (Dowman, Pamela). *Scripture Union. Unpriced* JFDM/GJ/AY (B71-50863) ISBN 0 85421 301 5

Come away, come away, Death: for full chorus of mixed voices a cappella. (Chorbajian, John). *Schirmer; Chappell. Unpriced* EZDW (B71-50814)

Come, O thou God of grace: for three-part chorus of mixed voices a cappella. (Ford, Virgil T). *Schirmer; Chappell. Unpriced* EZDH (B71-50790)

Come o'er the eastern hills: for four-part chorus of mixed voices a cappella. (Lekberg, Sven). *Schirmer; Chappell. Unpriced* EZDW (B71-50278)

Come to Bethlehem: twelve original carols. (Westmore, Peter). *Vanguard Music. Unpriced* KDP/LF/AY (B71-50882)

Come, ye faithful, raise the strain: Easter anthem, for SATB and organ. (Thiman, Eric Harding). *Novello. Unpriced* DH/LL (B71-50015)

Commonwealth and international library, music division. *(Pergamon)* Chisholm, Erik. The operas of Leos Janacek. *Pergamon. £2.50* BJFAC (B71-07865) ISBN 0 08 012854 8

Compases para preguntas ensimismadas: music for viola and 22 players. (Henze, Hans Werner). *Schott. £3.20* MPSQ (B71-50913)

Composing with tape recorders: musique concrete for beginners. (Dwyer, Terence). *Oxford University Press. £0.90* APS (B71-14737) ISBN 0 19 311912 9

Concertante music. (McCabe, John). *Novello. £2.50* MMJ (B71-50395)

Concerto for harpsichord. Concerto pour clavecin et ensemble instrumental. (Francaix, Jean). *Schott. £2.40* PWNUK/LF (B71-50444)

Concise biographical dictionary of singers: from the beginning of recorded sound to the present. (Kutsch, K J). *Chilton Book Company. £7.50* AB/E(M/C) (B71-24692) ISBN 0 8019 5516 5

Concise encyclopedia of music and musicians. (Cooper, Martin). 2nd ed., revised. *Hutchinson. £3.25* A(C) (B71-30145) ISBN 0 09 107530 0

Confidencia: mazurca no.3, piano. (Messina, Alfredo). *Arthur Napoleao; Essex Music. Unpriced* QPHQ (B71-50974)

Conflicts. Op. 51: fantasy on two themes for piano. (Leighton, Kenneth). *Novello. Unpriced* QPJ (B71-50977)

Connolly, Justin. Cinquepaces. Op. 5: for brass quintet. *Oxford University Press. £2.00* WNR (B71-51111)

Conquest of the air: suite. (Bliss, *Sir* Arthur). *Boosey and Hawkes. Unpriced* MMG (B71-50384)

Consort music in five parts. (Jenkins, John). *Faber Music. Unpriced* STNQR (B71-50126)

Contemporary organ music for liturgical use. (Funk, Heinrich). *Eulenburg, Hinrichsen. £2.50* R/AY (B71-50516)

Continuum: fur Cembalo. (Ligeti, Gyorgy). *Schott. £1.20* QRPJ (B71-50106)

Conversations: suite for B flat clarinet and piano (or string orchestra and harp). (Pitfield, Thomas). *Leeds Music. Unpriced* VVPG (B71-51089)

Cook, Douglas. Octave variations: for recorder quartet. *Schott. £0.50* VSNS/T (B71-50650)

Cook, Mabel Rose. Folk and vision: book of words and melody. (Rose, Margaret E). *Hart-Davis. Unpriced* JFE/TSDW/G/AY (B71-50879) ISBN 0 247 54443 4

Cooper, Irvin. Singers all: ten songs arranged for four-part singing (unchanged and changing voices). *Oxford University Press. £0.45* DW/G/AY (B71-50775) ISBN 0 19 330240 3

Cooper, Martin. The concise encyclopedia of music and musicians. 2nd ed., revised. *Hutchinson. £3.25* A(C) (B71-30145) ISBN 0 09 107530 0

Coperario, John. *See* Coprario, John.

Copland, Aaron. Happy anniversary: a well-known tune. *Boosey and Hawkes. Unpriced* MMJ (B71-50911)

Coplas: chorus (SATB-16 voices), soloists-SATB. (Tavener, John). *Chester. Unpriced* DE (B71-50174)

Copper, Bob. A song for every season: a hundred years of a Sussex farming family. *Heinemann. £2.75* ADW/G(YDCR) (B71-28161) ISBN 0 434 14455 x

Coprario, John. Funeral teares, 1606; and, Songs of mourning, 1613, by John Coprario; and, Ayres to sing and play to the lute, 1610; and, The second book of ayres, 1612, by William Corkine; and, Songs for the lute, 1606 by John Danyel. *Scolar Press. £10.00* ADW(YD) (B71-04595) ISBN 0 85417 413 3

Corigliano, John. Concerto for piano and orchestra. *Schirmer; Chappell. Unpriced* QNUK/LF (B71-50963)

Corker, Marjorie. In Ireland. *Schott. Unpriced* SRPJ (B71-51026)

Cornelius, Peter. L'Enfance du Christ. Op.25: chorus and orchestra. (Berlioz, Hector). *Eulenburg. £4.75* EMDD (B71-50237)

Cornet fantasy: for the organ. (Waters, Charles Frederick). *Leonard, Gould and Bolttler. £0.18* RJ (B71-50998)

Coronation anthem no.2 (The king shall rejoice): for six-part chorus of mixed voices. (Handel, George Frideric). *Schirmer; Chappell. Unpriced* DK (B71-50194)

Coronation anthem no.3 (My heart is inditing): for five-part chorus of mixed voices and solo quartet (ad lib.) with organ or piano accompaniment. (Handel, George Frideric). *Schirmer; Chappell. Unpriced* DK (B71-50193)

Costeley, Guillaume. Noel: Sus, debout gentilz pasteurs. Now arise ye shepherds mild: for four-part chorus of mixed voices a capella. *Schirmer; Chappell. Unpriced* EZDP/LF (B71-50798)

Country concerto for young pianists: for piano and orchestra. (Kasschau, Howard). *Schirmer; Chappell. Unpriced* QNUK/LF (B71-50964)

Couperin, Francois. Pieces de clavecin. Excerpts. Selected harpsichord music. *Schirmer; Chappell. Unpriced* QRPJ (B71-50105)

Courtiville, Raphael. Sonatas for two treble recorders, nos. 1-6. Sechs Sonaten: fur zwei Altblockfloten. *Schott. £0.80* VSSNUE (B71-50656)

Couto, Ribiero. Serestas. Excerpts. Cancao do Carreiro ou Cancao um crepusculo caricioso: canto e piano. (Villa-Lobos, Heitor). *Arthur Napoleao; Essex Music. Unpriced* KDW (B71-50057)

Covenant of the rainbow: festival anthem for mixed chorus, organ and piano duet; text from the Chester miracle play and the liturgy. Opus 24. (Crosse, Gordon). *Oxford University Press. £1.50* DE (B71-50005) ISBN 0 19 335610 4

Coward, Noel. Bitter sweet: easy-to-play piano selection. *Chappell. £0.25* QPK/CM (B71-50102)

Cowper, William. Institutional canons: for mixed chorus
2: There is in souls: SATB. (Binkerd, Gordon). *Boosey and Hawkes. £0.09* EZ/X (B71-50244)

Craxton, Janet. First book of oboe solos. *Faber Music. £0.75* VTPK/AAY (B71-50147)

Cray, Ed. Bawdy ballads. *Blond. £3.00* AKDW/K/G/KDX (B71-04596) ISBN 0 218 51471 9

Creative singing: the story of an experiment in music and creativity in the Primary classroom. (Evans, Ken). *Oxford University Press. £1.25* AB/E(VG) (B71-20921) ISBN 0 19 317411 1

Creston, Paul. Kalevala. Op.95: fantasy on Finnish folksongs, for concert band. *Schirmer; Chappell. Unpriced* UMJ (B71-50620)

Crewdson, Henry Alastair Ferguson. The Worshipful Company of Musicians: a short history. New ed. *C. Knight. £4.00* A(Q/YDBCJ/XD471) (B71-30640) ISBN 0 85314 086 3

Crimlisk, Anthony.
Play guitar!: a comprehensive tutor for the complete beginner, of classical folk and creative techniques for the finger style Spanish guitar. *Boosey and Hawkes. Unpriced* TS/AC (B71-51045)
Play guitar!: a comprehensive tutor, for the complete beginner, of classical, folk and creative techniques for the finger style Spanish guitar
Vol.1. *Boosey and Hawkes. Unpriced* TS/AC (B71-50603)
Vol.2. *Boosey and Hawkes. Unpriced* TS/AC (B71-50604)

Croft, William. Sonata for violin and basso continuo in G minor. Sonata in G minor: for violin and continuo (cello ad lib.). *£0.60* SPE (B71-51014)

Cross, Beverley. The rising of the moon: an opera in three acts. (Maw, Nicholas). *Boosey and Hawkes. Unpriced* CC (B71-50159)

Crosse, Gordon.
The covenant of the rainbow: festival anthem for mixed chorus, organ and piano duet; text from the Chester miracle play and the liturgy. Opus 24. *Oxford University Press. £1.50* DE (B71-50005) ISBN 0 19 335610 4
The demon Adachigahara. Op. 21. Excerpts. Night wind: S.A.T.B. *Oxford University Press. Unpriced* EZDW (B71-50815) ISBN 0 19 342986 1

Crossman, Gerald. Two accordion pieces. *Feldman. £0.20* RSPMK/DW (B71-51006)

Cruft, Adrian.
A Bemerton cantata. Op.59: for mezzo-soprano solo, chorus, organ, string orchestra, harp, percussion. *Leeds Music. Unpriced* DE (B71-50006)
Prelude and dance. Op.68: two light pieces, for double bass and pianoforte. *Leeds Music. Unpriced* SSPH (B71-51043)
Prelude and march. Op.60: for double bass or other bass clef instrument and pianoforte. *Leeds Music. Unpriced* SSPGM (B71-51042)
Prelude and scherzo. Op.65: for double bass or other bass clef instrument and pianoforte. *Leeds Music. Unpriced* SSPJ (B71-51044)

Crying for the Carolines. (Bastin, Bruce). *Studio Vista. £1.40* AKDW/HHW/E(YTNX) (B71-25347) ISBN 0 289 70210 0

Cryptical triptych: for trombone and piano. (Ross, Walter). *Boosey and Hawkes. £1.05* WUPJ (B71-50720)

Culhwch and Olwen. Op. 32: an entertainment. (Mathias, William). *University of Wales Press. Unpriced* ENYLNSDX (B71-50785)

Cumming, Richard. The cherry-tree carol: for women's voices, S.A. and flute. *Boosey and Hawkes. £0.09* FE/VRDP/LF (B71-50300)

Curtis, Frederick Vernon. O the morn, the merry merry morn. *Banks. Unpriced* DP/LF (B71-50018)

Cycle: for two or four players. (Orton, Richard). *Ars Viva; Schott. £2.25* LNU (B71-50067)

Da Palestrina, Giovanni Pierluigi. *See* Palestrina, Giovanni Pierluigi da.

Da Ponte, Lorenzo.
Don Giovanni; libretto by Lorenzo da Ponte to the opera by W.A. Mozart; and, Idomeneo; libretto by Giambattista Varesco to the opera by W.A. Mozart. *Cassell. £1.75* BMSAC (B71-24691) ISBN 0 304 93824 6
Le Nozze di Figaro; and, Cosi fan tutte; librettos by Lorenzo da Ponte to the operas by W.A. Mozart. *Cassell. £1.75* BMSAC (B71-25344) ISBN 0 304 93826 2

Dalby, Martin. Four miniature songs from Ezra Pound: S.A.T.B. unaccompanied. *Lengnick. Unpriced* EZDW (B71-50031)

Dale, Gordon. A dozen duets: for recorder groups of mixed ability. *Feldman. £0.20* VSN (B71-51074)

Dale, Mervyn.
I arise from dreams of thee: two-part song, optional unison. *Ashdown. Unpriced* FDW (B71-50831)
So we'll go no more a-roving: two-part song, optional unison. *Ashdown. Unpriced* FDW (B71-50832)

Dance, Stanley.
The night people: reminiscences of a jazzman. (Wells, Dicky). *Hale. £2.00* AMT/E(P) (B71-25916) ISBN 0 7091 2397 3
The world of Duke Ellington. *Macmillan. £3.50* AMT/E(P) (B71-30153) ISBN 0 333 13019 7

Dance band era: the dancing decades from ragtime to swing, 1910-1950. (McCarthy, Albert John). *Studio Vista. £4.20* AMT/E(M/XMK41) (B71-30152) ISBN 0 289 70218 6

Dancing years. (Novello, Ivor). *Chappell. £0.25* QPK/CM (B71-50103)

Danican-Philidor, Anne. *See* Philidor, Anne Danican.

Daniel, Oliver.
The dying Christian's last farewell. Fare you well, my friends: SATB a cappella. (Billings, William). *Peters Hinrichsen. £0.75* EZDW/LC (B71-50286)
I heard a great voice: SAATBB a cappella. (Billings, William). *Peters; Hinrichsen. £0.35* EZDK (B71-50257)

Dante Alighieri. Divina commedia. Dante symphony. Symphonie zu Dantes Divina commedia: fur Frauenchor und Orchester. (Liszt, Franz). *Eulenburg. £2.10* FE/MDX (B71-50298)

Dante symphony. Symphonie zu Dantes Divina commedia fur Frauenchor und Orchester. (Liszt, Franz). *Eulenburg. £2.10* FE/MDX (B71-50298)

Darke, Harold. Six miniatures: for oboe and piano. *Schott. £0.60* VTPJ (B71-51085)

Dart, Thurston.
The collected works of William Byrd
Vol.15: Consort songs for voice & viols. (Byrd, William). *Stainer and Bell. Unpriced* C/AZ (B71-50003)
Invitation to madrigals
5: for SATB. *Stainerand Bell. £0.40* EZDU/AY (B71-50813)
Musica Britanica: a national collection of music. 2nd revised ed. *Stainer and Bell. Unpriced* C/AYD (B71-50002)

Dashing away with the smoothing iron: traditional song SATB unacc. (Byrt, John). *Oxford University Press. Unpriced* EZDW (B71-50269) ISBN 0 19 343007 x

Daumer, Georg Friedrich. O schone Nacht. O lovely night. Op.92, no.1: for four-part chorus of mixed voices with piano accompaniment. (Brahms, Johannes). *Schirmer;*

Chappell. Unpriced DW (B71-50227)
Davidoff, Carl. *See* Davidov, Carl.
Davidov, Charles. Romance sans paroles. Op.23. *Schott. Unpriced* SRPJ (B71-51027)
Davies, Laurence, *b.1926*. Paths to modern music: aspects of music from Wagner to the present day. *Barrie and Jenkins. £4.00* A(D/XKR96) (B71-14731) ISBN 0 214 65249 1
Davies, Laurence H. You! you!: a German folk tune. (Pax, C E). *Ashdown. £0.05* FDW (B71-50838)
Davies, Peter Maxwell.
Eight songs for a mad king: for voice, flute (doubling piccolo), clarinet, piano (doubling harpsichord and dulcimer), violin, violoncello and percussion. *Boosey and Hawkes. Unpriced* KE/NYDPNQDW (B71-50351)
Revelation and fall. Offenbarung und Untergang: for soprano and sixteen instrumentalists. *Boosey and Hawkes. Unpriced* KFLE/MRDX (B71-50359)
Davison, Nigel. Assumpta est Maria: motet for six voices. (Palestrina, Giovanni Pierluigi da). *Chester. Unpriced* EZDGKJ (B71-50249)
Dawe, Margery.
Diversions on the new road to pianoforte playing. *Cramer. Unpriced* QPJ (B71-50091)
The new road to clarinet playing. *Cramer. y0.45* VV/AC (B71-51086)
Day in the country: suite. (Johnson, Thomas Arnold). *Freeman. £0.20* QPG (B71-50088)
Daybreak. (Baez, Joan). *Panther. £0.30* ADW/G/E(P) (B71-19969) ISBN 0 586 03502 8
De Boismortier, Joseph. *See* Boismortier, Joseph Bodin de.
De Boismortier, Joseph Bodin. *See* Boismortier, Joseph Bodin de.
De Falla, Manuel. *See* Falla, Manuel de.
De Klerk, Albert. *See* Klerk, Albert de.
De la Fontaine, Jean. *See* La Fontaine, Jean de.
De los Rios, Waldo. *See* Rios, Waldo de los.
De los Rios, Waldo. See Rios, Waldo de los.
De Nys. *Carl. See* Nys, Carl de.
De Seixas, Carlos. *See* Seixas, Carlos de.
De Selma y Salaverde, Bartolomeo. *See* Selma y Salaverde, Bartolomeo de.
Deane, Norma. The organ, from its invention in the Hellenistic period to the end of the thirteenth century. (Perrot, Jean). *Oxford University Press. £8.50* AR/B(X) (B71-14734) ISBN 0 19 318418 4
Dearnley, Christopher.
Evening Service: SATB and organ with verses for SSAATB. (Humphrey, Pelham). *Oxford University Press. £0.20* DGPP (B71-50182) ISBN 0 19 351634 9
Magnificat and Nunc dimittis in E minor: for SATB and organ. (Purcell, Daniel). *Novello. £0.15* DGPP (B71-50742)
Debussy, Claude.
Beau soir. Beautiful evening. *Boosey and Hawkes. Unpriced* FDW (B71-50833)
Petite suite. Excerpts. Ballet. *Boosey and Hawkes. £1.05* MH (B71-50901)
Selected piano works of Claude Debussy
Vol.3: Preludes, 2e livre. *Peters; Hinrichsen. £1.75* QPJ (B71-50478)
Selected piano works ofClaude Debussy
Vol.4: Images. *Peters; Hinrichsen. £1.50* QPJ (B71-50479)

The music of Claude Debussy
Book 1: La Fille aux cheveux de lin; and, The little shepherd; and, Jimbo's lullaby. *Forsyth. Unpriced* QPJ (B71-50480)
Book 2: Clair de lune; and, Des Pas sur la neige; and, Snow is dancing. *Forsyth. Unpriced* QPJ (B71-50481)
Book 3: Serenade of the doll; and, La Puerta del vino; and Sarabande. *Forsyth. Unpriced* QPJ (B71-50482)
Decca Group records, including musicassettes and stereo cartridges: main catalogue
1971: issued up to and including September 1970. *Decca. £3.75* A/FD(WM) (B71-08568) ISBN 0 901364 02 9
Declaration of independence: arranged for three-part chorus of women's voices with piano accompaniment. (Dougherty, Celius). *Schirmer; Chappell. Unpriced* FDW (B71 50836)
Defesch, Willem. Sonata for cello & basso continuo in G minor. Op.8, no.5. Sonata, g moll: fur Violoncello und Basso continuo. *Schott. £0.80* SRPE (B71-50592)
Deiss, Lucien. More Biblical hymns and psalms. *G. Chapman. £1.00* EZDR (B71-50806)
Delight of English lute music. (Duarte, John). *Schott. £0.60* TSPMK/AH/AYD (B71-51053)
Delius. (Fenby, Eric). *Faber and Faber Ltd. £1.50* BDL(N) (B71-19346) ISBN 0 571 09296 9
Demeny, Janos. Bela Bartok - letters. (Bartok, Bela). *Faber and Faber Ltd. £5.50* BBG(N) (B71-18713) ISBN 0 571 09638 7
Demon Adachigahara. Op. 21. Excerpts. Night wind: S.A.T.B. (Crosse, Gordon). *Oxford University Press. Unpriced* EZDW (B71-50815) ISBN 0 19 342986 1
Demsivre, Daniel. Aires made on purpose for a flute. 3rd collection. Einzelstucke und Suiten: fur Altblockflote solo. (Ruf, Hugo). *Schott. £0.80* VSSPMG/AY (B71-50659)
Demuth, Irene. Easy classics for cello
Book 2. (Forbes, Watson). *Oxford University Press. £0.40* SRPK/AAY (B71-50594) ISBN 0 19 356578 1
Denisov, Edisson. Die Sonne der Inkas: fur Sopran, 3 Sprecher und II Instrumentalisten. *Universal. Unpriced* KFLE/MRDX (B71-50358)
Dennison, W Michael. O du eselhafter Peierl. K.559a. Peter, Peter: a round for four groups of singers. (Mozart, Wolfgang Amadeus). *Ashdown. £0.10* FDW/XC (B71-50841)
Des Pres, Josquin. *See* Josquin des Pres.
Dessau, Paul. Quartet for strings, no.1. Streichquartett no.1. *Litolff; Hinrichsen. £2.10* RXNS (B71-50545)
Deus tuorum militum: himnus unius martyris for T.T.B. with two violins and continuo. (Monteverdi, Claudio). *Oxford University Press. Unpriced* GE/SNTPWDJ (B71-50900) ISBN 0 19 353272 7
Devereux, Peter. Solos for the alto (treble) recorder player: with piano accompaniment. (Camden, John). *Schirmer; Chappell. Unpriced* VSSPK/AAY (B71-50658)
Devil's son-in-law: the story of Peetie Wheatstraw and his songs. (Garon, Paul). *Studio Vista. £1.40* AKDW/HHW/(P) (B71-25346) ISBN 0 289 70212 7
Dexter, Harry.
Are there any here?: based on the French folksong 'Dites-mois messieurs'. *Ashdown. Unpriced* FDW (B71-50834)
Carmen: the story and music. (Bizet, Georges). *Keith Prowse. £0.20* QPK/CC (B71-50101)
Mary Ann. (Down by the sea-shore siftin' sand): a popular Jamacian sic song in calypso style. *Ashdown. Unpriced* FDW (B71-50835)
Diabelli, Anton. 28 melodious exercises for piano duet. Op.149, nos. 16,11,26,6. A Diabelli suite: for small brass ensemble. *Feldman. Unpriced* WNMK/AF (B71-51110)
Dialect reprints. *(S.R. Publishers)* Williams, Alfred. Folk-songs of the Upper Thames: with an essay on folk-song activity in the Upper Thames neighbourhood 1st ed. reprinted. *S.R. Publishers. £3.15* ADW/G(YDEVU) (B71-10430) ISBN 0 85409 610 8
Dickinson, Peter. Fanfares and elegies: for brass and organ. *Novello. £1.25* NWXPNP (B71-50426)
Dickson, Andrew Wilson-. *See* Wilson-Dickson, Andrew.
Die goldene Zeit: vorweihnachtliche Musik in neun Satzen fur gleiche Stimmen, Mannerchor und Kammerorchester (klavier oder Orgel) by Theo Fischer. (Fischer, Theo). *Bosworth. £0.50* DE/LEZ (B71-50739)
Diemer, Emma Lou. Sound pictures: for piano. *Boosey and Hawkes. £0.65* QPJ (B71-50483)
Dille, Denijs. Hungarian folksongs (1906). Excerpts. Five Hungarian folksongs: for voice and piano. (Bartok, Bela). *Boosey and Hawkes. Unpriced* KDW/G/AYG (B71-50346)
Dillon, Robert.
Rhythmic dance: for four B flat clarinets. *Boosey and Hawkes. £0.65* VVNSH (B71-50670)
Tarantella: for B flat clarinet. *Boosey and Hawkes. £0.65* VVPHVS (B71-50674)
Ding dong! merrily on high: carol arranged for women's or boys' voices & organ/piano. (Hunter, Ian T). *Thames. Unpriced* FDP/LF (B71-50828)
Dinham, Kenneth J. Kwmbayah: African tune. *Oxford University Press. £0.04* GEZDW (B71-50857) ISBN 0 19 341019 2
Dinn, Freda.
Allegro moderato. Op.3, no. 5. (Paxton, Stephen). *Schott. Unpriced* SRPJ (B71-51029)
Sonata for cello and keyboard in B flat major. Op.5, no.3 - Excerpts. Rondo: for cello and piano. (Hellendaal, Pieter, *b.1721*). *Schott. Unpriced* SRP/W (B71-51018)
Sonata for cello and keyboard in D major. Op.3, No.2. Sonata. Op.3, No.2. (Paxton, Stephen). *Schott. Unpriced* SRPE (B71-51020)
Sonata for cello and keyboard in F major. Op.2, No.3 - Excerpts. Minuet and variation. (Flackton, William). *Schott. Unpriced* SRPHR/T (B71-51022)
Variations on 'Good morrow, gossip Joan'. *Schott. Unpriced* SRP/T (B71-51017)
Dio: Orchesterspiele mit Dirigieren. (Kupkovic, Ladislav). *Universal. Unpriced* MMJ (B71-50394)
Dios itlazu nantzine. (Franco, Fernando). *Schott. £0.40* VSNSK/DH (B71-51077)
Diplock, Cyril. Peace to every neighbour: a carol. *Royal School of Church Music. Unpriced* EZDP (B71-50796)
Disc musical box handbook. (Webb, Graham). *Faber and Faber Ltd. £3.50* A/FND (B71-18092) ISBN 0 571 09378 7
Dittersdorf, Carl Ditters von.
Duetto for viola & violone (or double bass) in E flat major. *Yorke. Unpriced* SQPLSSVE (B71-50584)
Sinfonia in D major. Sinfonia, D-Dur. *Schott. £1.50* MRE (B71-50408)
Diversions on the new road to pianoforte playing. (Dawe, Margery). *Cramer. Unpriced* QPJ (B71-50091)
Divertimento: for 3 clarinets in B flat. (Simpson, John). *Feldman. Unpriced* VVNT (B71-51087)
Divertissement: for string orchestra. (Berger, Jean). *Schirmer; Chappell. Unpriced* RXMJ (B71-50534)
Divina commedia. *See* Dante Alighieri.
Dobree, Georgina. Sonate sentimentale: for flute or clarinet. Op.169. (Ries, Ferdinand). *Musica rara. £2.25* VRPE (B71-50141)
Doctor Musicus: an opera designed especially for the young. (Hopkins, Antony). *Chester. Unpriced* CN (B71-50732)
Documentary monographs in modern art. *(Allen Lane)* Kostelanetz, Richard. John Cage. *Allen Lane. £3.15* BCBG (B71-14242) ISBN 0 7139 0210 8
Doflein, Elma. Music for violin and piano: a collection in 4 books in progressive order
3: From Vivaldi to Viotti: 25 pieces and 1 sonata (changes of position). *Schott. £1.50* SP/AY (B71-50558)
Doflein, Erich.
16 Stucke: fur Flote allein. *Schott. £0.80* VRPM/AY (B71-50145)
Music for violin and piano: a collection in 4 books in progressive order
3: From Vivaldi to Viotti: 25 pieces and 1 sonata (changes of position). (Doflein, Elma). *Schott. £1.50* SP/AY (B71-50558)
Doherty, Christopher. Follow me: eight songs for young people. *Weinberger. Unpriced* JFDW (B71-50868)
Don Giovanni; libretto by Lorenzo da Ponte to the opera by W.A. Mozart; and, Idomeneo; libretto by Giambattista Varesco to the opera by W.A. Mozart. (Da Ponte, Lorenzo). *Cassell. £1.75* BMSAC (B71-24691) ISBN 0 304 93824 6
Dona nobis pacem. (Haydn, Joseph). *Schirmer; Chappell. Unpriced* DH (B71-50746)
Dona nobis pacem: a cantata for soprano and baritone soli, chorus and orchestra. (Vaughan Williams, Ralph). *Oxford University Press. £3.50* EMDE (B71-50781) ISBN 0 19 338860 x
Donizetti, Gaetano.
Sonata for violin & harp in G major. Sonate: Violine (Flote) und Harfe. *Litolff, Peters; Hinrichsen. £0.80* SPLTQE (B71-50577)
Study for clarinet, no.1. Studie: fur Klarinette. *Litolff, Peters; Hinrichsen. £0.50* VVPMJ (B71-50679)
Doppler, Albrecht Franz.
Andante & rondo. Op.25: for two flutes & piano. *Musica rara. Unpriced* VRNTQ/W (B71-50638)
Fantasie pastorale hongroise: for flute and piano. *Schirmer; Chappell. Unpriced* VRPJ (B71-50142)
Doppler, Carl. Fantasy on Hungarian themes. Op.35. Hungarian phantasy: for two flutes and piano. (Doppler, Franz). *Musica rara. Unpriced* VRNTQK (B71-51069)
Doppler, Franz. Fantasy on Hungarian themes. Op.35. Hungarian phantasy: for two flutes and piano. *Musica rara. Unpriced* VRNTQK (B71-51069)
Dotzauer, Justus Johann Friedrich. Duets for cellos. Opus 15. Duos: fur zwei Violoncelli. Opus 15. *Schott. £0.90* SRNU (B71-50121)
Dougherty, Celius.
Buffalo boy: for four-part chorus of mixed voices with piano accompaniment. *Schirmer; Chappell. Unpriced* DW (B71-50231)
Declaration of independence: arranged for three-part chorus of women's voices with piano accompaniment. *Schirmer; Chappell. Unpriced* FDW (B71-50836)
Dowland, John.
Fifty songs for high voice
Book 1. Revised ed. *Stainer and Bell. Unpriced* KFTDW (B71-50063)
Book 2. Revised ed. *Stainer and Bell. Unpriced* KFTDW (B71-50064)
Fifty songs for low voice
Book 1. Revised ed. *Stainer and Bell. Unpriced* KFXDW (B71-50065)
Book 2. Revised ed. *Stainer and Bell. Unpriced* KFXDW (B71-50066)
The first booke of songes or ayres, 1597; and, The first booke of songs, 1613; and, The second booke of songs or ayres, 1600; and, The third and last booke of songs or ayres, 1603; and, A pilgrimes solace, 1612, by John Dowland; and, A musicall banquet, 1610, by Robert Dowland. *Scolar Press. £10.00* BDTWADW (B71-04594) ISBN 0 85417 414 1
Mr Henry Noell, his funerall psalmes. Seven hymn tunes. Lamentio Henrici Noel: S.A.T.B.
Nos. 1-4. Revised ed. *Oxford University Press. Unpriced* EZDR/KDN (B71-50809) ISBN 0 19 352157 1
Mr Henry Noell, his funerall psalmes. Seven hymn tunes. Lamentio Henrici Noel: S.A.T.B.
Nos. 5-7. Revised ed. *Oxford University Press. Unpriced* EZDR/KDN (B71-50810) ISBN 0 19 352160 1
Varietie of lute-lessons. Excerpts. Fantasia no.7: per liuto. *Schott. £0.80* TWPMJ (B71-50618)
Dowman, Pamela. Come and sing: a selection of Christian songs for under-eights. *Scripture Union. Unpriced* JFDM/GJ/AY (B71-50863) ISBN 0 85421 301 5
Down by the greenwood side: a dramatic pastoral. (Birtwistle, Harrison). *Universal. Unpriced* CQM (B71-50734)
Dozen duets: for recorder groups of mixed ability. (Dale, Gordon). *Feldman. £0.20* VSN (B71-51074)
Draths, Willi. Rund um die Welt: folkloristische Tanzmelodien fur Blockflotenquartett (Streicher) und Schlagwerke, Gitarre ad lib;. *Schott. £1.00* NYESK/DW/G/AYB (B71-50434)
Dream children. Op.43,no.2. (Elgar, *Sir* Edward, *bart*). *Schott. Unpriced* SRPK (B71-51033)
Dream of the seven lost stars. (Bedford, David). *Universal. Unpriced* EMDX (B71-50239)
Drei Monologue des Empedokles von Friedrich Holderlin fur Bariton und Klavier oder Orchester. (Reutter, Hermann). *Schott. £1.30* KGNDW (B71-50370)
Drifters: the rise and fall of the black vocal group. (Millar, Bill). *Studio Vista. £1.40* AB/E(P) (B71-16703) ISBN 0 289 70133 3
Duarte, John. A delight of English lute music. *Schott. £0.60* TSPMK/AH/AYD (B71-51053)
Dubrovay, Laszlo. Sei duo: per violino e percussioni. *Boosey and Hawkes. Unpriced* SPLX (B71-50578)
Duckworth, Guy. Keyboard musicianship. *Free Press; Collier-Macmillan. Unpriced* Q/AC (B71-50446)
Duckworth, Richard. Tintinnalogia; or, The art of ringing 1st ed. reprinted. *Kingsmead Reprints. £2.10* AXSR/E (B71-04185) ISBN 0 901571 41 5
Duke, Henry.
Album for the youngsters: for piano. *Feldman. y0.30* QPJ (B71-50976)
Christmas carols. *Feldman. y0.40* RPVCK/DP/LF/AYB (B71-51001)
Dulcimer book. (Pearse, John). *A.T.V. Kirshner Music; Distributed by Rosetti and Co. Ltd. £0.75* ATWTJ (B71-18091) ISBN 0 903052 00 8
Dumbrille, Dorothy. La lo and lullaby: berceuse de Noe: two part song. (Nelson, Havelock). *Lengnick. £0.05* FDP/LF (B71-50037)

Durko, Zsolt.

Fioriture: for orchestra. *Boosey and Hawkes. £0.75* MMJ (B71-50907)

Improvvisazioni: per quintetto a fiati. *Boosey and Hawkes. £0.50* UNR (B71-50631)

Durko, Zsolt. Quartet for strings, no.2. Quatuor a cordes no.2. *Boosey and Hawkes. Unpriced* RXNS (B71-50546)

Durrenmatt, Friedrich.

Der Besuch der alten Dame. *Boosey & Hawkes. Unpriced* BENAC (B71-04180) ISBN 0 85162 000 0

Der Besuch der alten Dame. Op. 35: Oper in drei Akten nach Friedrich Durrenmatts tragischer Komodie. (Einem, Gottfried von). *Boosey and Hawkes. Unpriced* CC (B71-50729)

Dushkin, Dorothy. Quintet for flute and strings. *Musica rara. Unpriced* NVRNR (B71-50927)

Dvorak, Antonin. Moravian duets. Op.32. Songs from Moravia

Book 1. *Chappell. Unpriced* FLDW (B71-50855)

Dvorak, Antonin. Moravian duets. Op.32. Songs from Moravia

Book 1. *Chappell. Unpriced* FLDW (B71-50856)

Dvorak, Antonin. Moravian duets. Op.32. Songs from Moravia

Book 2. *Chappell. Unpriced* FLDW (B71-50854)

Dvorak. (Young, Percy Marshall). *Benn. £0.90* BDX(N) (B71-01698) ISBN 0 510 13717 2

Dwyer, Terence. Composing with tape recorders: musique concrete for beginners. *Oxford University Press. £0.90* APS (B71-14737) ISBN 0 19 311912 9

Dying Christian's last farewell. Fare you well, my friends: SATB a cappella. (Billings, William). *Peters; Hinrichsen. £0.75* EZDW/LC (B71-50286)

Dylan, Bob. New morning: complete vocal/piano folio with guitar diagrams & chord symbols. *Feldman. Unpriced* KDW (B71-50056)

Early English church music. *(Stainer and Bell)*

Tallis, Thomas. English sacred music

1: Anthems. *Stainer and Bell. Unpriced* CB/LD (B71-50726)

Tallis, Thomas. English sacred music

2: Service music. *Stainer and Bell. Unpriced* CB/LD (B71-50727)

Early English keyboard music: an anthology

Vol.1. (Ferguson, Howard). *Oxford University Press. £0.95* PWP/AYD (B71-50081) ISBN 0 19 372622 x

Vol.2. (Ferguson, Howard). *Oxford University Press. £0.95* PWP/AYD (B71-50082) ISBN 0 19 372623 8

Easter dialogue: for mixed voices, organ (piano), 2 trumpets, 4 trombones and double bass. (Hammerschmidt, Andreas). *Peters; Hinrichsen. £0.45* ENUXPNQDH/LL (B71-50240)

Easter song: for unison voices and organ. (Steer, Michael). *Novello. Unpriced* JDH (B71-50316)

Easy classics for cello

Book 2. (Forbes, Watson). *Oxford University Press. £0.40* SRPK/AAY (B71-50594) ISBN 0 19 356578 1

Eckert, Alex. Galgenlieder nach Gedichten von Christian Morgenstern: Alcatorische Komposition fur Kinder, Solosprecher, Sprech-und Sing-Chor, Blaser Streicher, Stabspiel, Gerauschinstrumente und Schlagwerk. *Schott. £1.70* JFE/XMDW (B71-50326)

Economides, George. 24 etudes: for the guitar. *KPM Music. £0.50* TSPMJ (B71-50609)

Economides, George C.

Classic guitar method including chords and 20 studies

Vol.1. *Keith Prowse Music. £0.60* TS/AC (B71-50127)

Vol.2. *Keith Prowse Music. £0.60* TS/AC (B71-50128)

The study of the guitar simplified: a complete guitar course in 30 lessons

Vol.1. *Keith Prowse Music. Unpriced* TS/AC (B71-50129)

Edition: multiple Musik fur Instrumental - oder Vokalgruppen. (Heider, Werner). *Litolff, Peters Hinrichsen. £0.90* LN (B71-50374)

Edmundson, John. Love story: theme from the film. (Lai, Francis). *Chappell. Unpriced* UMMK/JR (B71-51064)

Edwards, Melinda.

A lieta vita. Such happy living: SSATB. (Gastoldi, Giovanni Giacomo). *Warner; Blossom Music. Unpriced* EZDU (B71-50266)

Canzoni napoletane. Lib 1, no.14. Voria che ta cantass'. Neapolitan song. (Scandello, Antonio). *Warner; Blossom Music. Unpriced* EZDU (B71-50812)

Madonna, per voi ardo. Ah love, my heart is burning: for SATB chorus. (Verdelot, Philippe). *Warner; Blossom Music. Unpriced* EZDU (B71-50267)

Effinger, Cecil.

Paul of Tarsus: three episodes in the life of Paul the apostle, for four-part chorus of mixed voices with baritone solo, strings and organ. *Schirmer; Chappell. Unpriced* ERXMDE (B71-50241)

Three contemporary madrigals: for four-part chorus of mixed voices a cappella

If you your lips would keep from slips. *Schirmer; Chappell. Unpriced* EZDW (B71-50271)

My love and I for kisses played. *Schirmer; Chappell. Unpriced* EZDW (B71-50272)

Why was Cupid a boy?. *Schirmer; Chappell. Unpriced* EZDW (B71-50273)

Ehre sey Gott in der Hohe. Glory to God in the highest: for mixed voices, organ (piano) and strings (ad lib). (Hammerschmidt, Andreas). *Peters; Hinrichsen. £0.45* GDH/LF (B71-50313)

Ehret, Walter.

A lieta vita. Such happy living: SSATB. (Gastoldi, Giovanni Giacomo). *Warner; Blossom Music. Unpriced* EZDU (B71-50266)

Canzoni napoletane. Lib 1, no.14. Voria che ta cantass'. Neapolitan song. (Scandello, Antonio). *Warner; Blossom Music. Unpriced* EZDU (B71-50812)

Madonna, per voi ardo. Ah love, my heart is burning: for SATB chorus. (Verdelot, Philippe). *Warner; Blossom Music. Unpriced* EZDU (B71-50267)

Where sleeps the infant Jesus: Mexican carol, SATB. *Warner; Blossom Music. Unpriced* DP/LF (B71-50211)

Eight negro spirituals: arranged for SSA unaccompanied. (Phillips, John Charles). *Novello. £0.35* FEZDW/LC/AY (B71-50850)

Eight songs for a mad king: for voice, flute (doubling piccolo), clarinet, piano (doubling harpsichord and dulcimer), violin, violoncello and percussion. (Davies, Peter Maxwell). *Boosey and Hawkes. Unpriced* KE/NYDPNQDW (B71-50351)

Eighteen song cycles: studies in their interpretations. (Lehmann, Lotte). *Cassell. £2.40* AB/E (B71-25345) ISBN 0 304 93842 4

Einem, Gottfried von.

Der Besuch der alten Dame. (Durrenmatt, Friedrich). *Boosey & Hawkes. Unpriced* BENAC (B71-04180) ISBN 0 85162 000 0

Der Besuch der alten Dame. Op. 35: Oper in drei Akten nach Friedrich Durrenmatts tragischer Komodie. *Boosey and Hawkes. Unpriced* CC (B71-50729)

Concerto for violin. Op.33. Violin concerto. Op.33. *Boosey and Hawkes. Unpriced* MPSF (B71-50077)

Einstein, Alfred.

Mozart: his character - his work. *Panther. £0.75* BMS(N) (B71-06907) ISBN 0 586 03277 0

Schubert. *Panther. £0.75* BSF (B71-14241) ISBN 0 586 03480 3

Einzelstucke und Suiten: fur Altblockflote solo. (Ruf, Hugo). *Schott. £0.80* VSSPMG/AY (B71-50659)

Electronic organ servicing guide. (Middleton, Robert Gordon). *Foulsham. £2.25* ARPV/BT (B71-25917) ISBN 0 572 00785 x

Elegie heroique. (Willan, Healey). *Boosey and Hawkes. Unpriced* UMMJ (B71-50624)

Elegy in memory of Karol Rathaus. Op.23: for 3 trumpets, 2 horns, 3 trombones and baritone and tuba. (Turok, Paul). *Musica rara. Unpriced* WMJ (B71-51103)

Elektronische Orgel klassisch. (Rothenberg, Peter). *Schott. £1.20* RPVK (B71-51002)

Elementary accompaniment writing. (Lovelock, William). *Bell. £1.40* AQ/D/ED (B71-24689) ISBN 0 7135 1961 4

Elenor, John. Concerto for toy orchestra: in one movement. *Novello. £0.95* MVF (B71-50416)

Elgar, *Sir* Edward, *bart.*

Dream children. Op.43,no.2. *Schott. Unpriced* SRPK (B71-51033)

Quintet for piano and strings in A minor. Op. 84. Piano quintet in A minor. Op. 84. *Eulenburg. £0.35* NXNR (B71-50935)

Elgar. (Parrott, Ian). *Dent. £1.75* BEP(N) (B71-14243) ISBN 0 460 03109 0

Elias, Manuel Jorge de. Dios itlazu nantzine. (Franco, Fernando). *Schott. £0.40* VSNSK/DH (B71-51077)

Elizabethan duets. (Jeffery, Brian). *Schott. £0.40* TSNUK (B71-50131)

Ellinwood, Leonard.

English sacred music

1: Anthems. (Tallis, Thomas). *Stainer and Bell. Unpriced* CB/LD (B71-50726)

2: Service music. (Tallis, Thomas). *Stainer and Bell. Unpriced* CB/LD (B71-50727)

Elliott, Kenneth. The collected works of William Byrd. (Byrd, William). *Stainer and Bell. £4.75* C/AZ (B71-50723)

Elliott, Vernon. Odd man out: for double bass and piano. *Yorke. Unpriced* SSPJ (B71-50124)

Elphick, George Philip. Sussex bells and belfries. *Phillimore. £5.50* AXSR(YDCR) (B71-11121) ISBN 0 900592 08 7

Elvin, Laurence. Organ blowing: its history and development. *L. Elvin. £3.75* AR/BL (B71-16704) ISBN 0 9500049 1 x

Emeneau, Murray Barnson. Toda songs. *Clarendon Press. £11.00* BZFMNT (B71-06911) ISBN 0 19 815129 2

Emerald isle: five Irish airs arranged for cello (1st position) and piano. (Price, Beryl). *Oxford University Press. £0.40* SRPK/DW/G/AYDM (B71-50596) ISBN 0 19 358302 x

Emmanuel songs. (Shepherd, Edwin T). *Marshall, Morgan and Scott. £0.45* DM/AY (B71-50757) ISBN 0 551 05416 6

Emmanuel songs

Vol.3. (Shepherd, Edwin T). *Marshall, Morgan and Scott. £0.45* DM/AY (B71-50756) ISBN 0 551 05049 7

Emmerson, George Sinclair. Rantin' pipe and tremblin' string: a history of Scottish dance music. *Dent. £5.00* A/H/G(YDL/XQP) (B71-16700) ISBN 0 460 03891 5

Enantiodromia: for orchestra. (Christou, Jani). *Chester. Unpriced* MMJ (B71-50906)

Energy: symphonic study for brass band. (Simpson, Robert). *Boosey and Hawkes. Unpriced* WMJ (B71-51102)

Enfance du Christ. Op.25: chorus and orchestra. (Berlioz, Hector). *Eulenburg. £4.75* EMDD (B71-50237)

Enfield, Patrick. Last voyage: part-song for S.A. and piano. *Elkin. £0.07* FDW (B71-50042)

Engelhart, Franz Xaver. Wenn ich ein Glocklein war. The Vesper bell. *Bosworth. Unpriced* DW (B71-50771)

English church music: a collection of essays

1971. *Royal School of Church Music. £0.76* AD/LD(D) (B71-16701) ISBN 0 85402 021 7

English country scenes: suite for brass band. (Ball, Eric). *Paxton. Unpriced* WMG (B71-50692)

English court odes, 1660-1820. (McGuinness, Rosamond). *Clarendon Press. £7.00* ADE/KM(YD/XEY161) (B71-27232) ISBN 0 19 816119 0

English Folk Dance and Song Society.

Folk directory

1971. *English Folk Dance and Song Society. £1.00(£0.75 to members)* A/G(BC) (B71-07864) ISBN 0 85418 029 x

A popular selection of English dance airs

Book 4: Sword and ceremony. (Fleming-Williams, Nan). *English Folk Dance and Song Society. £0.25* LH/G/AYD (B71-50896)

English lute songs, 1597-1632. *(Scolar Press)*

Coprario, John. Funeral teares, 1606; and, Songs of mourning, 1613, by John Coprario; and, Ayres to sing and play to the lute, 1610; and, The second book of ayres, 1612, by William Corkine; and, Songs for the lute, 1606 by John Danyel. *Scolar Press. £10.00* ADW(YD) (B71-04595) ISBN 0 85417 413 3

Dowland, John. The first booke of songes or ayres, 1597 and, The first booke of songs, 1613; and, The second booke of songs or ayres, 1600; and, The third and last booke of songs or ayres, 1603; and, A pilgrimes solace, 1612, by John Dowland; and, A musicall banquet, 1610 by Robert Dowland. *Scolar Press. £10.00* BDTWADW (B71-04594) ISBN 0 85417 414 1

English mass: two-part with organ accompaniment by Josef Henriksen. (Henriksen, Josef). *St Gregory Publishing Co. £0.40* FDG (B71-50825)

English sacred music

1: Anthems. (Tallis, Thomas). *Stainer and Bell. Unpriced* CB/LD (B71-50726)

2: Service music. (Tallis, Thomas). *Stainer and Bell. Unpriced* CB/LD (B71-50727)

Episodi: per pianoforte. (Sari, Jozsef). *Boosey and Hawkes. Unpriced* QPJ (B71-50499)

Epperson, Gordon.

Gallery: suite for unaccompanied cello. (Muczynski, Robert). *Schirmer; Chappell. Unpriced* SRPMG (B71-50599)

Sonata for cello & piano. Op.25. Sonata for cello and piano. Op.25. (Muczynski, Robert). *Schirmer; Chappell. Unpriced* SRPE (B71-50123)

Erdenklavier: pastorale for piano. (Berio, Luciano). *Universal. Unpriced* QPJ (B71-50473)

Eric Coates for brass: musical extracts from At the dance, The jester at the wedding, London Bridge, The three Elizabeths, The three bears; arranged for brass and reed band by Allan Street. (Coates, Eric). *Chappell. Unpriced* WMK (B71-50704)

Erickson, Frank. Tuesday in November. Excerpts. Fugue and chorale on Yankee Doodle. (Thomson, Virgil). *Schirmer; Chappell. Unpriced* UMK/Y/JR (B71-50622)

Erkin, Ulvi Cemal. Six Turkish songs. *Schott. £0.60* FEZDW/G/AYVB (B71-50849)

Ernest George White Society. Think afresh about the voice: a reappraisal of the teaching of Ernest George White. (Hewlett, Arthur Donald). *The Ernest George White Society. £0.45* AB/E (B71-19971) ISBN 0 9501610 0 4

Espana. Op. 165 - Excerpts. Malaguena. Op. 165, no.3 (Albeniz, Isaac). *Schott. Unpriced* SRPK/AHPP (B71-51038)

'Essay and General Literature Index' reprint series. *(Kennikat Press)* Hoover, Kathleen O'Donnell. Makers of opera. *Kennikat Press. £5.50* AC(XE311) (B71-21649) ISBN 0 8046 1412 1

Etudes: piano solo

Book 1. (Hopkins, Bill). *Schott. Unpriced* QPJ (B71-50093)

Eugene Onegin: lyric scenes in three acts and seven scenes. (Tchaikovsky, Peter). *Schauer and May. Unpriced* CC (B71-50730)

Europaische Volks-und Tanzweisen: fur Flote, Akkordeon I/II, Gitarre (banjo), Bass und Schlagzeug. (Buhe, Klaus). *Schott. £1.20* NYDRK/DW/AYB (B71-50432)

European songs for children: 15 traditional songs. (Offer, Charles Karel). *Paxton. Unpriced* JFDW/GJ/AYB (B71-50324)

Evaluation of music teaching and learning. (Colwell, Richard). *Prentice-Hall. Unpriced* A(VF/VCM) (B71-11816) ISBN 0 13 292151 0

Evans, Howard.

Bitter sweet: easy-to-play piano selection. (Coward, Noel). *Chappell. £0.25* QPK/CM (B71-50102)

Christmas songs for descant recorder. *Chappell. Unpriced* VSRPMK/DW/LF/AY (B71-51082)

The dancing years. (Novello, Ivor). *Chappell. £0.25* QPK/CM (B71-50103)

On a clear day you can see forever. (Lane, Burton). *Chappell. Unpriced* WMK/CM (B71-50153)

Evans, Ken. Creative singing: the story of an experiment in music and creativity in the Primary classroom. *Oxford University Press. £1.25* AB/E(VG) (B71-20921) ISBN 0 19 317411 1

Evans, Williams B. Come, O thou God of grace: for three-part chorus of mixed voices a cappella. (Ford, Virgil T). *Schirmer; Chappell. Unpriced* EZDH (B71-50790)

Evening draws in: for solo vocalist, chorus, piano and percussion. (Self, George). *Universal. Unpriced* FE/NYLDW (B71-50299)

Everyman's dictionary of music. (Blom, Eric). 5th ed. *Dent. £4.00* A(C) (B71-21647) ISBN 0 460 03022 1

Everyman's reference library. *(Dent)* Blom, Eric. Everyman's dictionary of music. 5th ed. *Dent. £4.00* A(C) (B71-21647) ISBN 0 460 03022 1

Evocacao: tema con variacoes for piano. (Viera Rios, Graziela). *Arthur Napoleao. Unpriced* QP/T (B71-50970)

Ewen, David. David Ewen introduces modern music: a history and appreciation - from Wagner to the avant-garde. Revised, enlarged ed. *Chilton Book Company. £2.75* A(XKC107) (B71-24687)

ISBN 0 8019 5487 8
Examinations in pianoforte playing and singing: sight reading tests, sight singing tests as set throughout 1970. Grades I-VIII & diplomas. (London College of Music). *Ashdown. £0.25* Q/EG (B71-50084)
Exodus. Excerpts. The Exodus song: S.A.B. (Gold, Ernest). *Chappell. Unpriced* DW/JR (B71-50236)
Exodus song. (Gold, Ernest). *Chappell. £0.09* DW/JR (B71-50235)
Exodus song: S.A.B. (Gold, Ernest). *Chappell. Unpriced* DW/JR (B71-50236)
Faber, Frederick W. Oh, come and mourn with us: SATB. (Matthews, Walter E). *Warner; Blossom. Unpriced* DH/LG (B71-50748)
Fabulas caracteristicas. Op.65. Excerpts. O Gato e o rato: piano. (Villa-Lobos, Heitor). *Arthur Napoleao; Essex Music. Unpriced* QPJ (B71-50501)
Fagg, William. The Raffles 'gamelan': a historical note. *British Museum. £0.40* BZGVJAL/B(WJ) (B71-04179) ISBN 0 7141 1514 2
Fair morning. (Binkerd, Gordon). *Boosey and Hawkes. £0.65* KDW (B71-50332)
Fair Organ Preservation Society. The Key Frame: the journal of the Fair Organ Preservation Society
No.1- ; Dec. 1964-. *The Fair Organ Preservation Society. £0.125(£1.00 yearly)* A/FM(B) (B71-18715)
Fairbanks, Terry. Noah and all that jazz: cantata for unison voices with piano accompaniment. *Leeds Music. Unpriced* JFDE (B71-50049)
Faith, Richard. Music I heard with you: for four-part chorus of mixed voices with piano accompaniment. *Schirmer; Chappell. Unpriced* DW (B71-50232)
Falla, Manuel de. El Amor brujo-Danza ritual del fuego. Ritual fire dance. *Chester. Unpriced* WMK/AH (B71-51106)
Fancy free: for piano. (Longmire, John). *Freeman. £0.30* QPJ (B71-50978)
Fanfare for heroes: for 3 trumpets, 3 trombones, timpani & cymbals. (Bliss, *Sir* Arthur). *Novello. Unpriced* NYHXPNNGN (B71-50438)
Fanfares and elegies: for brass and organ. (Dickinson, Peter). *Novello. £1.25* NWXPNP (B71-50426)
Fantasia for bassoon in D minor. V Fantasia ex D: fur Fagott und Basso continuo. (Selma y Salaverde, Bartolomeo de). *Schott. £1.10* VWPJ (B71-50685)
Fantasia no.7: per liuto. (Dowland, John). *Schott. £0.80* TWPMJ (B71-50618)
Fantasie pastorale hongroise: for flute and piano. (Doppler, Albrecht Franz). *Schirmer; Chappell. Unpriced* VRPJ (B71-50142)
Fantasy on Hungarian themes. Op.35. Hungarian phantasy: for two flutes and piano. (Doppler, Franz). *Musica rara. Unpriced* VRNTQK (B71-50519)
Fantel, Hans. Johann Strauss: father and son, and their era. *David and Charles. £2.75* BSQB(N) (B71-30149) ISBN 0 7153 5421 3
Fanu, Nicola Le. *See* Le Fanu, Nicola.
Fare you well, my friends: SATB a cappella. (Billings, William). *Peters; Hinrichsen. £0.75* EZDW/LC (B71-50286)
Farewell. (Ridout, Alan). *Stainer and Bell. Unpriced* DW (B71-50020)
Farinello, Orestes. Intermezzo, Impressoes do teatro: piano. *Arthur Napoleao; Essex Music. Unpriced* QPJ (B71-50484)
Farkas, Istvan. Bela Bartok - letters. (Bartok, Bela). *Faber and Faber Ltd. £5.50* BBG(N) (B71-18713) ISBN 0 571 09638 7
Farnon, Dennis. Clarinet caprice. *Boosey and Hawkes. £2.05* UMMJ (B71-51060)
Farnon, Robert J. Robert Farnon for brass: arranged for brass and reed band by Allan Street. *Chappell. Unpriced* WMK (B71-51104)
Favorite duet: for two bassoons or violoncellos. (Alcock, John, *b.1740*). *Piers Press. Unpriced* VWNU (B71-50148)
Featherstone, David. Words and music. (Lawrence, Ian). *Longman. £0.40* A(VG) (B71-08785) ISBN 0 582 18694 3
Fechner, Manfred.
Concerto for violin in B flat major, (The Posthorn). P.350. Konzert, B-dur (das Posthorn): fur Violine und Streichorchester Klavierauszug. (Vivaldi, Antonio). *Peters; Hinrichsen. £0.90* SPK/LF (B71-50576)
Concerto for violin in B flat major, (The Posthorn), P.350. Konzert, B-dur (das Posthorn): fur Violino und Streichorchester. (Vivaldi, Antonio). *Peters; Hinrichsen. £1.25* RXMPSF (B71-50536)
Romances for violin & orchestra. Op.40 & 50. Romanzen. Op.40 (G-dur), Op.50 (F-dur): fur Violine und Orchester. (Beethoven, Ludwig van). *Peters; Hinrichsen. £0.90* SPK (B71-50571)
Federation Internationale de Documentation. Publications. *(British Standards Institution)* Universal Decimal Classification
78: Music. English full ed. (4th international ed.). *British Standards Institution. £0.80* A(UJ) (B71-19565) ISBN 0 580 06563 4
Feld, Jindrich. Sonatina for bassoon & piano (1969). Sonatine: fur Fagott und Klavier. *Schott. £1.30* VWPEM (B71-50149)
Feldman, Morton.
Madame Press died last week at ninety: for small orchestra. *Universal. Unpriced* MRJ (B71-50411)
On time and the instrumental factor. *Universal. Unpriced* MMJ (B71-50390)
Fellowes, Edmund Horace.
The collected works of William Byrd
Vol.15: Consort songs for voice & viols. (Byrd, William). *Stainer and Bell. Unpriced* C/AZ (B71-50003)
Fifty songs for high voice
Book 1. (Dowland, John). Revised ed. *Stainer and Bell. Unpriced* KFTDW (B71-50063)
Book 2. (Dowland, John). Revised ed. *Stainer and Bell. Unpriced* KFTDW (B71-50064)
Fifty songs for low voice
Book 1. (Dowland, John). Revised ed. *Stainer and Bell. Unpriced* KFXDW (B71-50065)
Book 2. (Dowland, John). Revised ed. *Stainer and Bell. Unpriced* KFXDW (B71-50066)
Fellowes, Edmund horace. Mr Henry Noell, his funerall psalmes. Seven hymn tunes. Lamentio Henrici Noel: S.A.T.B.
Nos. 1-4. (Dowland, John). Revised ed. *Oxford University Press. Unpriced* EZDR/KDN (B71-50809) ISBN 0 19 352157 1
Fellowes, Edmund Horace.
Mr Henry Noell, his funerall psalmes. Seven hymn tunes. Lamentio Henrici Noel: S.A.T.B.
Nos. 5-7. (Dowland, John). Revised ed. *Oxford University Press. Unpriced* EZDR/KDN (B71-50810) ISBN 0 19 352160 1
Short service. Excerpts. Magnificat and Nunc dimittis: SAATTB and organ. (Byrd, William). Revised ed. *Oxford University Press. £0.25* DGPP (B71-50181) ISBN 0 19 352024 9
Fenby, Eric. Delius. *Faber and Faber Ltd. £1.50* BDL(N) (B71-19346) ISBN 0 571 09296 9
Ferguson, Howard.
Complete keyboard works of William Tisdall. (Tisdall, William). 2nd, revised ed. *Stainer and Bell. Unpriced* QSQ/AZ (B71-50515)
Early English keyboard music: an anthology
Vol.1. *Oxford University Press. £0.95* PWP/AYD (B71-50081) ISBN 0 19 372622 x
Vol.2. *Oxford University Press. £0.95* PWP/AYD (B71-50082) ISBN 0 19 372623 8
Style and interpretation: an anthology of keyboard music. *Oxford University Press. £1.25* PWNV/AY (B71-50938) ISBN 0 19 372628 9
Style and interpretation: an anthology of keyboard music. *Oxford University Press. £1.25* PWNV/AY (B71-50939) ISBN 0 19 372629 7
Fernandez, Oscar Lorenzo. *See* Lorenzo Fernandez, Oscar.
Ferneyhough, Brian.
Coloratura: for oboe and piano. *Hinrichsen. £1.10* VTPJ (B71-50665)
Three pieces: for piano. *Peters, Hinrichsen. £1.10* QPJ (B71-50485)
Ferris, William. Blues from the Delta. *Studio Vista. £1.35* AKDW/HHW(YTQ) (B71-06291) ISBN 0 289 70072 8
Fesch, Willem de. *See* Defesch, Willem.
Festival Benedicite in D: in shortened form. (Sumsion, Herbert). *Lengnick. Unpriced* DGNR (B71-50741)
Festival service book
5. (Royal School of Church Music). *Royal School of Church Music. Unpriced* DGM (B71-50178) ISBN 0 85402 018 7
Festival!: the book of American music celebrations... (Hopkins, Jerry). *Macmillan (N.Y.); Collier-Macmillan. £4.00* A/GB(YT/WE) (B71-11123) ISBN 0 02 580170 8
Fifty hymn melodies for school assembly. (Henriksen, Josef). *St Gregory Publishing Co. £0.825* SMK/DM/AY (B71-51012)
Fifty simple rounds: for singers, recorders and other instruments. (Lawrence, Ian). *Novello. £0.30* FE/VSDW/XC (B71-50301)
Figured bass accompaniments. (Williams, Peter, *b.1937*). *Edinburgh University Press. £5.00* A/RGD (B71-05794) ISBN 0 85224 054 6
Fill thou my life: anthem for SATB organ. (Aldridge, Richard). *Lengnick. £0.13* DH (B71-50184)
Fink, Siegfried.
Percussio antiqua: improvisations based on Sundgauer Marsch 1469 on historic percussion instruments, for percussion solo. *Simrock. £0.65* XNGM (B71-51122)
Ritmo (Latin-American music): for percussion ensemble (7 players). *Simrock. £1.10* XNP (B71-51123)
Serenade in percussione: for clarinet, double-bass and percussion (3 players). *Simrock. £0.85* NYEVNR (B71-50435)
Finney, Ross Lee. Summer in Valley City: for band. *Peters Hinrichsen. £3.50* UMJ (B71-50621)
Fioriture: for orchestra. (Durko, Zsolt). *Boosey and Hawkes. £0.75* MMJ (B71-50907)
First book of oboe solos. (Craxton, Janet). *Faber Music. £0.75* VTPK/AAY (B71-50147)
First booke of songes or ayres, 1597; and, The first booke of songs, 1613; and, The second booke of songs or ayres, 1600; and, The third and last booke of songs or ayres, 1603; and, A pilgrimes solace, 1612, by John Dowland and, A musicall banquet, 1610, by Robert Dowland. (Dowland, John). *Scolar Press. £10.00* BDTWADW (B71-04594) ISBN 0 85417 414 1
Fischer, Theo. Die goldene Zeit: vorweihnachtliche Musik in neun Satzen, fur gleiche Stimmen, Mannerchor und Kammerorchester (klavier oder Orgel) by Theo Fischer. *Bosworth. £0.50* DE/LEZ (B71-50739)
Fiske, Roger. L'Enfance du Christ. Op.25: chorus and orchestra. (Berlioz, Hector). *Eulenburg. £4.75* EMDD (B71-50237)
Five carol fantasies: for piano. (Beck, John Ness). *Schirmer Chappell. Unpriced* QP/LF (B71-50457)
Five fantasies for brass choir. Op. 70 Fantasy no.1: trumpets, horns, trombones. (Hovhaness, Alan). *Peters; Hinrichsen. £0.60* WMJ (B71-50698)
Fantasy no.2: trumpets, horns, trombones. (Hovhaness, Alan). *Peters; Hinrichsen. £0.625* WMJ (B71-50699)
Fantasy no.3: trumpets, horns, trombones. (Hovhaness, Alan). *Peters; Hinrichsen. £0.625* WMJ (B71-50700)
Fantasy no.4: 2 trumpets, horns, trombones (tubas). (Hovhaness, Alan). *Peters; Hinrichsen. £0.875* WMJ (B71-50701)
Fantasy no.5: 2 trumpets, horns, trombones (tubas). (Hovhaness, Alan). *Peters; Hinrichsen. £0.90* WMJ (B71-50702)
Five Hungarian folksongs: for voice and piano. (Bartok Bela). *Boosey and Hawkes. Unpriced* KDW/G/AYG (B71-50346)
Five inventions: for two or more treble-clef instruments of equal pitch. (Arnell, Richard). *Hinrichsen. Unpriced* LNU (B71-50375)
Five spiritual songs (Geistliche Lieder). (Bach, Johann Sebastian). *Faber Music. £1.00* KFTDH (B71-50062)
Fizdale, Robert. Four little duets for two pianos. Wq.155. (Bach, Carl Philipp Emanuel). *Schirmer; Chappell. Unpriced* QNU (B71-50962)
Flackton, William. Sonata for cello and keyboard in F major. Op.2, No.3 - Excerpts. Minuet and variation. *Schott. Unpriced* SRPHR/T (B71-51022)
Flanders, Michael. Captain Noah and his floating zoo: cantata in popular style for unison or two-part voices & piano, with optional bass & drums. *Novello. £0.40* FDE (B71-50035)
Fleming-Williams, Nan. A popular selection of English dance airs
Book 4: Sword and ceremony. *English Folk Dance and Song Society. £0.25* LH/G/AYD (B71-50896)
Flemish carol: tune old Flemish, SATB. (Rutter, John). *Oxford University Press. Unpriced* DP/LF (B71-50213) ISBN 0 19 343014 2
Fletcher, Stanley.
New tunes for strings. *Boosey and Hawkes. £4.90* RXN/AY (B71-51010)
Sonatina for violin duet. Sonatina for two violins. *Boosey and Hawkes. £1.10* SNUEM (B71-50557)
Fluck, Alan. Children's dances. Excerpts. Four dances nos 9, 5, 4 & 12. (Kodaly, Zoltan). *Boosey and Hawkes. £4.00* MK/AH (B71-50069)
Fluttuazioni: per violino e pianoforte. (Sary, Laszlo). *Boosey and Hawkes. Unpriced* SPJ (B71-50568)
Fly, Leslie. Forest themes: piano duets. *Forsyth. Unpriced* QNV (B71-50450)
Fold to thy heart thy brother: for four-part chorus of mixed voices a cappella. (Hovdesven, E A). *Schirmer; Chappell. Unpriced* EZDW (B71-50816)
Folk and vision: book of words and melody. (Rose, Margaret E). *Hart-Davis. Unpriced* JFE/TSDW/G/AY (B71-50879) ISBN 0 247 54443 4
Folk directory
1971. *English Folk Dance and Song Society. £1.00(£0.75 to members)* A/G(BC) (B71-07864) ISBN 0 85418 029 x
Folk songs for schools and camps: 81 favourite songs. (Silverman, Jerry). *Robbins Music; Francis, Day and Hunter. £0.75* JFEZDW/G/AY (B71-50328)
Folk songs from Newfoundland. (Karpeles, Maud). *Faber and Faber Ltd. £7.00* ADW/G(YSXD) (B71-07869) ISBN 0 571 09297 7
Folk-songs of the Upper Thames: with an essay on folk-song activity in the Upper Thames neighbourhood. (Williams, Alfred). 1st ed. reprinted. *S.R. Publishers. £3.15* ADW/G(YDEVU) (B71-10430) ISBN 0 85409 610 8
Folk tunes to accompany: a guide to simple accompaniment for beginners of all ages in schools, clubs, colleges or the home
Book 3: Modes and minors. (Noble, Robert). *Novello. £0.90* TSPMK/DW/G/AYB (B71-51056)
Folksongs sung in Ulster. (Morton, Robin). *The Mercier Press. £0.50* ADW/G(YDT) (B71-06293) ISBN 0 85342 221 4
Follow me: eight songs for young people. (Doherty, Christopher). *Weinberger. Unpriced* JFDW (B71-50868)
Fontaine, Jean de la. *See* La Fontaine, Jean de.
For children. Excerpts. For children: 25 selected pieces. (Bartok, Bela). *Boosey and Hawkes. £0.75* TSPMK (B71-50611)
For I went with the multitude: anthem for SATB and organ. (Aston, Peter). *Novello. Unpriced* DK (B71-50750)
Forbes, Sebastian. Quartet for strings, no.1. String quartet no.1. *Chester. Unpriced* RXNS (B71-50547)
Forbes, Watson. Easy classics for cello
Book 2. *Oxford University Press. £0.40* SRPK/AAY (B71-50594) ISBN 0 19 356578 1
Ford, Anthony. Arias from the Vienna operas. (Bononcini, Giovanni Battista). *Oxford University Press for the University of Hull. £2.50* KDW (B71-50337) ISBN 0 19 713412 2
Ford, Virgil T. Come, O thou God of grace: for three-part chorus of mixed voices a cappella. *Schirmer; Chappell. Unpriced* EZDH (B71-50790)
Forest themes: piano duets. (Fly, Leslie). *Forsyth. Unpriced* QNV (B71-50450)
Form IV: broken sequences: for piano. (Wolpe, Stefan). *Peters; Hinrichsen. Unpriced* QPJ (B71-50507)
Forman, Denis. Mozart's concerto form: the first movements of the piano concertos. *Hart-Davis. £6.95* BMSAMPQ/U (B71-30154) ISBN 0 246 64008 1
Formative films series. *(Primestyle Ltd)* Burrows, Michael. Mario Lanza; and, Max Steiner. *Primestyle Ltd. £0.75* AKGH/E(P) (B71-27972) ISBN 0 902421 14 x
Formazion. Op.16: per violoncello solo. (Bozay, Attila). *Boosey and Hawkes. Unpriced* SRPMJ (B71-50600)
Forrest, George.
Song of Norway. (Grieg, Edvard). *Chappell; Frank Music.*

£0.60 KDW/JR (B71-50058)

Song of Norway. (Grieg, Edvard). *Chappell. Unpriced* WMK/CM/JR (B71-51108)

Song of Norway: selection for all organs. (Grieg, Edvard). *Chappell. £0.40* RK/CM/JR (B71-50999)

The song of Norway: piano selection from the film. (Greig, Edvard). *Chappell; Frank Music. £0.25* QPK/CM/JR (B71-50104)

Forrester, Leon. St Christopher. Stupendous thought. *Banks. Unpriced* DH (B71-50011)

Fortig, Peter. Stationes fur Orgel. *Schott. £3.00* R/LH (B71-50992)

Fortner, Wolfgang. Zyklus (1964): Fassung fur Violoncello, Blaser, Harfen und Schlagzeug (1969). *Schott. £2.00* MRJ (B71-50412)

Fortune, Nigel. The Beethoven companion. (Arnold, Denis). *Faber and Faber Ltd. £7.00* BBJ(N) (B71-05266) ISBN 0 571 09003 6

Forty tunes: for the viola. (Widdicombe, Trevor). *Curwen. Unpriced* SQPK/DW/G/AYB (B71-50582)

Forza del destino: opera in three acts. (Verdi, Giuseppe). *Schirmer; Chappell. Unpriced* CC (B71-50162)

Foulsham-Sams technical books. *(Foulsham)* Middleton, Robert Gordon. Electronic organ servicing guide. *Foulsham. £2.25* ARPV/BT (B71-25917) ISBN 0 572 00785 x

Foundations of music education series. *(Prentice-Hall)* Hood, Marguerite Vivian. Teaching rhythm and using classroom instruments. *Prentice-Hall. £3.10* A(VG) (B71-08201) ISBN 0 13 894089 4

Four carols. Op.109: for mixed or S.A. voices

1: Chanticleer's carol. (Gardner, John). *Oxford University Press. Unpriced* DP/LF (B71-50759) ISBN 0 19 343017 7

2: Balulalow. (Gardner, John). *Oxford University Press. Unpriced* DP/LF (B71-50760) ISBN 0 19 343018 5

3: Remember. (Gardner, John). *Oxford University Press. Unpriced* DP/LF (B71-50761) ISBN 0 19 343019 3

4: A gallery carol. (Gardner, John). *Oxford University Press. Unpriced* DP/LF (B71-50762) ISBN 0 19 343020 7

Four easy scores: arranged for recorder, guitar and percussion. (Sadleir, Richard). *Feldman. £0.25* NYESK/AAY (B71-50937)

Four German songs: medium (high) voice and piano. (Griffes, Charles Tomlinson). *Peters; Hinrichsen. £1.10* KFVDW (B71-50365)

Four impressions: medium (high) voice and piano. (Griffes, Charles Tomlinson). *Peters; Hinrichsen. £1.10* KFVDW (B71-50366)

Four introits: for SATB and organ. (Webber, Lloyd). *Novello. £0.09* DH (B71-50013)

Four little duets for two pianos. Wq.155. (Bach, Carl Philipp Emanuel). *Schirmer; Chappell. Unpriced* QNU (B71-50962)

Four miniature songs from Ezra Pound: S.A.T.B. unaccompanied. (Dalby, Martin). *Lengnick. Unpriced* EZDW (B71-50031)

Four songs from the Japanese. Op.9:: voice and piano. (Goehr, Alexander). *Schott. Unpriced* KDW (B71-50339)

Four Stefan George songs: voice and piano. (Webern, Anton von). *Boosey and Hawkes. Unpriced* KDW (B71-50343)

Foursome for brass. (Spurgin, Anthony). *Feldman. Unpriced* WNS (B71-51114)

Francaix, Jean. Concerto for harpsichord. Concerto pour clavecin et ensemble instrumental. *Schott. £2.40* PWNUK/LF (B71-50444)

Francesco, *da Milano*. The lute music of Francesco Canova da Milano (1497-1543)

Vols I and II. *Harvard University Press. Unpriced* TW/AZ (B71-50617)

Franco, Fernando. Dios itlazu nantzine. *Schott. £0.40* VSNSK/DH (B71-51077)

Francoeur, Francois. Sonata for violin, cello and basso continuo in E major. Liv.2, no.12. Triosonate, E-Dur: fur Violine, Violoncello oder Viola da gamba und Basso continuo. *Schott. £1.20* NXNTE (B71-50430)

Frank Bridge. (Pirie, Peter John). *Triad Press. £0.80* BBTP (B71-24084) ISBN 0 902070 02 9

Franke, Erhard. Concerto for violin in B flat major, (The Posthorn). P.350. Konzert, B-dur (das Posthorn): fur Violine und Streichorchester Klavierauszug. (Vivaldi, Antonio). *Peters; Hinrichsen. £0.90* SPK/LF (B71-50576)

Franklin, Adele. We piano teachers. (Booth, Victor). 1st ed. 8th impression (revised). *Hutchinson. £1.25* AQ/E(VC) (B71-05270) ISBN 0 09 106190 3

Franz Schubert and his times. (Kobald, Karl). *Kennikat Press. £6.25* BSF(N) (B71-02479) ISBN 0 8046 0756 7

Fraser, Shena. Easy classics for cello

Book 2. (Forbes, Watson). *Oxford University Press. £0.40* SRPK/AAY (B71-50594) ISBN 0 19 356578 1

Freedom technique: exercises and studies for piano

Book 1: Beginners to grade 3 (USA2). (Last, Joan). *Oxford University Press. £0.40* Q/AF (B71-50941) ISBN 0 19 373117 7

Book 2: Grades 3-4 (USA 2-2 1/2). (Last, Joan). *Oxford University Press. £0.40* Q/AF (B71-50942) ISBN 0 19 373118 5

Book 3: Grade 5 (USA3) upwards. (Last, Joan). *Oxford University Press. £0.50* Q/AF (B71-50943) ISBN 0 19 373119 3

French, Percy. Best Irish songs of Percy French. *Wolfe. £0.25* BFURAKDW (B71-11819) ISBN 0 7234 0428 3

French song from Berlioz to Duparc: the origin and development of the melodie. (Noske, Frits). 2nd ed. *Dover; Constable. £3.00* ADW(YH/XHK51) (B71-05796) ISBN 0 486 22104 0

Frere, Walter Howard. A manual of plainsong for Divine Service. (Briggs, H B). *Novello. £1.25* DTD (B71-50019)

Fricker, Peter Racine. Praeludium. Opus. 60: for organ. *Oxford University Press. £0.80* RJ (B71-50522) ISBN 0 19 375390 1

Frickert, Walter. Walzer-Capricen, deutsche Tanze und andere Stucke: fur Klavier zu vier Handen. (Reger, Max). *Peters; Hinrichsen. £1.40* QNV (B71-50452)

Friend, Jerry R.

Hear my dream: S.A.B. and piano. *Warner; Blosso Music. Unpriced* DW (B71-50772)

On my way to the hill I saw my Lord: S.A.B. with piano and optional string bass. *Warner; Blossom Music. Unpriced* DH (B71-50745)

Friss, Antal. Violoncello tutor

Vol.3. *Boosey and Hawkes. Unpriced* SR/AC (B71-50587)

From the North Country: overture for band. (Hattori, Koh-Ichi). *Boosey and Hawkes. £2.00* UMMJ (B71-51061)

Froom, Jacqueline. A garden of weeds: 5 songs for soprano, clarinet and piano. (Greaves, Terence). *Thames. Unpriced* KFLE/VVPDW (B71-50892)

Fugal answer. (Nalden, Charles). *Auckland University Press; Oxford University Press. £5.75* AL/Y (B71-04593) ISBN 0 19 647552 x

Fugue. (Bullivant, Roger). *Hutchinson. £2.25* A/Y (B71-25915) ISBN 0 09 108440 7

Fugue and chorale on Yankee Doodle. (Thomson, Virgil). *Schirmer; Chappell. Unpriced* UMK/Y/JR (B71-50622)

Funeral teares, 1606; and, Songs of mourning, 1613, by John Coprario; and, Ayres to sing and play to the lute, 1610; and, The second book of ayres, 1612, by William Corkine; and, Songs for the lute, 1606, by John Danyel. (Coprario, John). *Scolar Press. £10.00* ADW(YD) (B71-04595) ISBN 0 85417 413 3

Funk, Heinrich. Contemporary organ music for liturgical use. *Eulenburg, Hinrichsen. £2.50* R/AY (B71-50516)

Fur Elise. (Beethoven, Ludwig van). *British and Continental. Unpriced* TSPMK (B71-50135)

Furnivall, Anthony. Si tu veux, nous nous aimerons: for soprano and piano. *Sycamore Press. Unpriced* KFLDW (B71-50356)

Furstenau, Anton Bernhard. L'Union: introduction and rondo brilliant. Op.115, on themes from Norma (Bellini), for two flutes and piano. *Musica rara. Unpriced* VRNTQ (B71-51068)

Gabrieli, Giovanni.

Beata es virgo: part chorus of mixed voices with organ accompaniment (optional). *Schirmer; Chappell. Unpriced* EZDGKJ (B71-50024)

Hodie Christus natus est: for double chorus of mixed voices with organ accompaniment. *Schirmer; Chappell. Unpriced* DGKJ/LF (B71-50740)

Jubilemus singuli: for eight-part chorus of mixed voices with organ accompaniment. *Schirmer; Chappell. Unpriced* DJ (B71-50016)

Gabschuss, Klaus Ulbrich. Kinderlieder und Volkslieder: fur den systematischen Unterricht am Klavier. *Schott. £1.30* QPK/DW/GJ/AY (B71-50513)

Gal, Hans.

Sonata for two violins & pianoforte. Op. 96. *Simrock. £1.75* SNTQE (B71-51013)

Trio for violin, clarinet and pianoforte. Op.97. *Simrock. Unpriced* NUVNT (B71-50924)

Galatopoulos, Stelios. Italian opera. *Dent. £2.00* AC/E(YJ/X) (B71-07324) ISBN 0 460 05798 7

Galgenlieder nach Gedichten von Christian Morgenstern: Aleatorische Komposition fur Kinder, Solosprecher, Sprech-und Sing-Chor, Blaser Streicher, Stabspiel Gerauschinstrumente und Schlagwerk. (Eckert, Alex). *Schott. £1.70* JFE/XMDW (B71-50326)

Gallery: suite for unaccompanied cello. (Muczynski, Robert). *Schirmer; Chappell. Unpriced* SRPMG (B71-50599)

Galliard, Johann Ernst. Sonata for bassoon and basso continuo in G major. Sonata, G-Dur: fur Fagott oder Violoncello und Basso continuo. *Schott. £0.90* VWPE (B71-50684)

Game for eight: choreographic suite for chamber orchestra. (Blomdahl, Karl-Birger). *Schott. £1.75* MRG (B71-50914)

Garden of weeds: 5 songs for soprano, clarinet and piano. (Greaves, Terence). *Thames. Unpriced* KFLE/VVPDW (B71-50892)

Gardiner, John Eliot. Meslanges. Liv. 2 - Excerpts. Helas! mon Dieu: SAATB unacc. (Le Jeune, Claude). *Oxford University Press. Unpriced* EZDH (B71-50791)

Gardner, John.

Four carols. Op.109: for mixed or S.A. voices

1: Chanticleer's carol. *Oxford University Press. Unpriced* DP/LF (B71-50759) ISBN 0 19 343017 7

2: Balulalow. *Oxford University Press. Unpriced* DP/LF (B71-50760) ISBN 0 19 343018 5

3: Remember. *Oxford University Press. Unpriced* DP/LF (B71-50761) ISBN 0 19 343019 3

4: A gallery carol. *Oxford University Press. Unpriced* DP/LF (B71-50762) ISBN 0 19 343020 7

Three amorous airs. Op.104: for female voices and piano

1: Waly waly: three-part. *Oxford University Press. Unpriced* FDW (B71-50293) ISBN 0 19 342587 4

2: The German flute: three-part. *Oxford University Press. Unpriced* FDW (B71-50294) ISBN 0 19 342588 2

3: The ballad of Nancy Dee: four-part. *Oxford University Press. Unpriced* FDW (B71-50295) ISBN 0 19 342589 0

Garlick, George T. A little tune for St Mark's Day. Op.71, no.1: organ solo. *George T. Garlick. Unpriced* RJ (B71-50995)

Garnett, Hugh. Practical music making with juniors. *Schoolmaster Publishing. £0.55* A(VJ) (B71-12945) ISBN 0 900642 10 6

Garon, Paul. The Devil's son-in-law: the story of Peetie Wheatstraw and his songs. *Studio Vista. £1.40* AKDW/HHW/(P) (B71-25346) ISBN 0 289 70212 7

Garrington, J L St C. The cherub carol: unison. (Coates, Douglas). *Bosworth. £0.05* JFDP/LF (B71-50867)

Gastoldi, Giovanni.

Balletti for five voices (1591). Fifteen balletti: SSATB a cappella (recorders and strings ad libitum) Introduttioni a i Balletti: O compagni allegrezza. (Companions, be happy). New ed. *Peters; Hinrichsen. £0.40* EZDU (B71-50263)

Balletti for five voices (1591). Fifteen balletti: SSATB a cappella (recorders and strings ad libitum)

Set 3. New ed. *Peters; Hinrichsen. £0.40* EZDU (B71-50264)

Balletti for five voices (1591). Fifteen balletti: SSATB a cappella (recorders and strings ad libitum)

Set 4. New ed. *Peters; Hinrichsen. £0.40* EZDU (B71-50265)

Gastoldi, Giovanni Giacomo.

A lieta vita. Such happy living: SSATB. *Warner; Blossom Music. Unpriced* EZDU (B71-50266)

Acht Duette: fur Gitarren. *Schott. £0.80* TSNU (B71-50607)

Gathered together: a service book for senior schools. *Oxford University Press. Unpriced* DM/AY (B71-50203)

Gato e o rato: piano. (Villa-Lobos, Heitor). *Arthu Napoleao; Essex Music. Unpriced* QPJ (B71-50501)

Gaudeamus igitur: traditional German melody arranged for chorus of mixed voices a cappella. (Bartholomew, Marshall). *Schirmer; Chappell. Unpriced* EZDW (B71-50268)

Gay, Bram. Sinfonietta: for brass band. (Horovitz, Joseph). *Novello. £3.00* WMEM (B71-51094)

Gay gnu galop. (Barsotti, Roger). *Bosworth. £1.25* UMMHLF (B71-51059)

Gay recorders: for descant or treble recorder with piano accompaniment. (Rudrum, Kenneth). *Paterson. Unpriced* VSPJ (B71-51078)

Geibel, Emanuel. Lied. Op. 29, no.2. In meinen Garten. In my garden. (Schumann, Robert). *Schirmer; Chappell. Unpriced* FDW (B71-50839)

Genesis: a cassation for audience and instruments. (Williamson, Malcolm). *Weinberger. Unpriced* DE (B71-50738)

Genzmer, Harald.

Concerto for trumpet & string orchestra. Konzert: fur Trompete und Streicher. *Litolff, Peters; Hinrichsen. £1.50* RXMPWSF (B71-50542)

Sextet for wind instruments. Sextett: 2 Klarinetten, 2 Fagotte, 2 Horner. *Litolff, Peters; Hinrichsen. £6.00* UNQ (B71-50629)

Sextet for wind instruments. Sextett: fur Klarinetten in B, 2 Fagotte, 2 Horner. *Litolff, Peters; Hinrichsen. £1.50* UNQ (B71-50628)

Die Tageszeiten: fur Orgel. *Litolff, Peters; Hinrichsen. £0.75* RJ (B71-50523)

Geordie song book. (Graham, Frank, *b.1913*). *Graham. £0.31* ADW/G(YDJJ) (B71-18090) ISBN 0 902833 81 2

George, Stefan. Four Stefan George songs: voice and piano. (Webern, Anton von). *Boosey and Hawkes. Unpriced* KDW (B71-50343)

George Beverley Shea solos: songs. *Marshall, Morgan and Scott. £0.40* KDH (B71-50881) ISBN 0 551 05069 1

Gerhard, Roberto. Symphony 4 'New York'. *Oxford University Press. £4.50* MME (B71-50379) ISBN 0 19 363614 x

Gershwin, George. George Gershwin: a symphonic portrait for concert band; arranged by Bruce Chase. *Chappell. Unpriced* UMMK/DW (B71-51062)

Gesti: for alto recorder. (Berio, Luciano). *Universal. Unpriced* VSSPMJ (B71-50661)

Get to know Mister Bach: an informal introduction with simple piano arrangements of his music. (Bach, Johann Sebastian). *Chappell. Unpriced* QPK (B71-50981)

Gibbons, Orlando. Almighty God, which hast given: verse anthem for Christmas Day. *Novello. £0.15* DK/LF (B71-50017)

Gibbs, Alan. Spell out the news: carol for unison voices with divisions, and organ or piano (or brass). *Novello. £0.06* FDP/LF (B71-50288)

Gibbs, Wolcott. Declaration of independence: arranged for three-part chorus of women's voices with piano accompaniment. (Dougherty, Celius). *Schirmer; Chappell. Unpriced* FDW (B71-50836)

Giesbert, Franz Julius.

Gitarrenbuch. (Visee, Robert de). *Schott. £1.20* TSPMJ (B71-50610)

Sonatas for two treble recorders, nos. 1-6. Sechs Sonaten fur zwei Altblockfloten. (Courtiville, Raphael). *Schott. £0.80* VSSNUE (B71-50656)

Gilbert, Anthony. The incredible flute music. Op.11: for flute and piano. *Schott. Unpriced* VRPJ (B71-50643)

Gilbert, Bryan Edward. Playing the guitar for the Lord's work. Revised ed. *Marshall, Morgan and Scott Ltd. £0.30* TS/AC (B71-50130) ISBN 0 551 05435 2

Gimpel, Herbert J. Beethoven: master composer. *Franklin Watts Ltd. £1.25* BBJ(N) (B71-12554) ISBN 0 85166 321 4

Girls and boys come out to play. (Poston, Elizabeth). *Bodley Head. £1.10* JFDW/GK/AY (B71-50872) ISBN 0 370 01527 4

Glarum, Leonard Stanley.

Canticle of Mary (Magnificat) for four-part chorus of mixed voices with organ accompaniment. *Schirmer; Chappell.*

Unpriced DGPQ (B71-50183)
Canticle of Mary (Magnificat) for unison voices with organ accompaniment. *Schirmer; Chappell. Unpriced* JDGPQ (B71-50315)
When one knows thee: for four-part chorus of mixed voices a cappella. *Schirmer; Chappell. Unpriced* EZDH (B71-50253)
Glennon, James. Making friends with music. *Foulsham. £0.60* A (B71-27970) ISBN 0 572 00774 4
'Gloria tibi trinitas': mass for six-part unaccompanied choir, S.A.T.T.B.B. (Taverner, John). *Stainer and Bell. £1.15* EZDG (B71-50302)
Glory to God in the highest: for mixed voices, organ (piano) and strings (ad lib). (Hammerschmidt, Andreas). *Peters Hinrichsen. £0.45* GDH/LF (B71-50313)
Gluck, Christoph Willibald von.
Alceste. Excerpts. Overture: arranged for school, amateur or professional orchestras or for strings with optional full orchestra. *Bosworth. £0.375* MJ (B71-50068)
Orfeo. Che faro. Air from 'Orpheus and Euridice': popularly known as 'What is life?'. *Studio Music. Unpriced* WMK/DW (B71-50707)
Go tell it on the mountain. He's got the whole world in His hands: a quodlibet based on two negro spirituals. (Hudson, Hazel). *Ashdown. £0.10* DW/LC (B71-50776)
God is our refuge, God is our strength: SATB chorus of choral and speaking voices with optional congregational declamation. (Hopson, Hal H). *Warner; Blossom Music. Unpriced* EZDR (B71-50807)
God rest you merry. (Robinson, Douglas). *Ashdown. £0.09* EZDP/LF (B71-50803)
Goehr, Alexander. Four songs from the Japanese. Op.9:: voice and piano. *Schott. Unpriced* KDW (B71-50339)
Goethe, Johann Wolfgang von. Warum. Wherefore should our singing soar. Op.91, no.4: for four-part chorus of mixed voices with piano accompaniment. (Brahms, Johannes). *Schirmer; Chappell. Unpriced* DW (B71-50230)
Going to see my long-haired babe. (Williams, Arnold). *Banks. Unpriced* GDW (B71-50046)
Gold, Arthur. Four little duets for two pianos. Wq.155. (Bach, Carl Philipp Emanuel). *Schirmer; Chappell. Unpriced* QNU (B71-50962)
Gold, Ernest.
Exodus. Excerpts. The Exodus song. *Chappell. £0.09* DW/JR (B71-50235)
Exodus. Excerpts. The Exodus song: S.A.B. *Chappell. Unpriced* DW/JR (B71-50236)
Goldsmith, Jerry. Two episodes from Lenau's Faust. No.2. First Mephisto waltz. The Mephisto waltz. (Liszt, Franz). *Twentieth Century Music. £0.20* QPK/JR (B71-50514)
Goliath jazz: for unison voices with piano accompaniment and guitar chords. (Chappell, Herbert). *Clarabella Music. Unpriced* CN/L (B71-50166)
Gomes, Antonio Carlos. Il Guarany - Excerpts. O Guarani: sinfonia. *Arthur Napoleao; Essex Music. Unpriced* QNVK (B71-50454)
Good cheer: a Christmas carol. (Hamilton, Alasdair). *Oxford University Press. Unpriced* FLDP/LF (B71-50851) ISBN 0 19 341505 4
Good King Wenceslas. (Robinson, Douglas). *Ashdown. £0.09* EZDP/LF (B71-50804)
Gordon, Edwin. The psychology of music teaching. *Prentice-Hall. £3.50* A/CS(VC) (B71-30146) ISBN 0 13 736215 3
Gordon, Philip. Within thy light: SATB with organ or piano. *Blossom Music. Unpriced* DH (B71-50186)
Goudimel, Claude. Psalm 42. Ainsi qu'on oit le cerf bruire. So my heart seeks ever after: for four-part chorus of mixed voices a cappella. *Schirmer; Chappell. Unpriced* EZDR (B71-50262)
Goymour, Michael. Last voyage: part-song for S.A. and piano. (Enfield, Patrick). *Elkin. £0.07* FDW (B71-50042)
Graded aural tests for all purposes: with suggested methods of working. (Warburton, Annie O). *Longman. Unpriced* C/EF (B71-50724) ISBN 0 582 32585 4
Graham, Frank, *b.1913*. The Geordie song book. *Graham. £0.31* ADW/G(YDJJ) (B71-18090) ISBN 0 902833 81 2
Grahame, Kenneth. The carol of the field mice. (Head, Michael). *Boosey and Hawkes. Unpriced* KDP/LF (B71-50331)
Graves, John. Cathedral city. *Schott. Unpriced* SRPJ (B71-51028)
Graves, Richard. Calypso praise. *Bosworth. £0.06* JFDH (B71-50050)
Great composers. *(Faber and Faber Ltd)*
Fenby, Eric. Delius. *Faber and Faber Ltd. £1.50* BDL(N) (B71-19346) ISBN 0 571 09296 9
Helm, Everett. Bartok. *Faber and Faber Ltd. £1.25* BBG(N) (B71-17373) ISBN 0 571 09105 9
Padmore, Elaine. Wagner. *Faber and Faber Ltd. £1.50* BWC(N) (B71-29387) ISBN 0 571 08785 x
Walker, Alan, *b.1930*. Liszt. *Faber and Faber Ltd. £1.50* BLJ(N) (B71-10425) ISBN 0 571 09120 2
Great is the Lord: for full chorus of mixed voices with organ or piano accompaniment. (Newbury, Kent A). *Schirmer Chappell. Unpriced* DK (B71-50196)
Great mover of all hearts: anthem. (Smith, Noel). *Lengnick. Unpriced* DH (B71-50747)
Great pianists of our time. (Kaiser, Joachim). *Allen and Unwin. £3.25* AQ/E(M) (B71-16015) ISBN 0 04 780019 4
Greaves, Terence. A garden of weeds: 5 songs for soprano, clarinet and piano. *Thames. Unpriced* KFLE/VVPDW (B71-50892)
Greek scenes. (Lambert, Cecily). *Forsyth. Unpriced* QPJ (B71-50094)
Green, Frederick Pratt. 26 hymns. *Epworth Press. £0.40* DM/AY (B71-50754) ISBN 0 7162 0181 x
Greening, Anthony.
Short service. Excerpts. Magnificat and Nunc dimittis: SAATTB and organ. (Byrd, William). Revised ed. *Oxford University Press. £0.25* DGPP (B71-50181) ISBN 0 19 352024 9
Turn thy face from my sins: verse anthem for A.T.B. and chorus, SSATB. (Locke, Matthew). *Oxford University Press. Unpriced* DK (B71-50195)
Variations on 'O Lord in Thee is all my trust': for organ. (Amner, John). *Schott. Unpriced* R/T (B71-50108)
Greig, Edvard.
Song of Norway. *Chappell; Frank Music. £0.60* KDW/JR (B71-50058)
The song of Norway: piano selection from the film. *Chappell; Frank Music. £0.25* QPK/CM/JR (B71-50104)
Grieg, Edvard.
Song of Norway. *Chappell. Unpriced* WMK/CM/JR (B71-51108)
Song of Norway: selection for all organs. *Chappell. £0.40* RK/CM/JR (B71-50999)
Grieve not the holy Spirit of God: anthem for SATB and organ. (Pasfield, W R). *Ashdown. Unpriced* DK (B71-50752)
Griffes, Charles T. Poem: for flute and band. *Schirmer; Chappell. Unpriced* UMPVR (B71-50626)
Griffes, Charles Tomlinson.
Four German songs: medium (high) voice and piano. *Peters; Hinrichsen. £1.10* KFVDW (B71-50365)
Four impressions: medium (high) voice and piano. *Peters Hinrichsen. £1.10* KFVDW (B71-50366)
Roman sketches. Op.7: for piano. *Schirmer; Chappell. Unpriced* QPJ (B71-50092)
Groom, Bob. The blues revival. *Studio Vista. £1.40* AKDW/HHW (B71-16011) ISBN 0 289 70149 x
Gruber, Franz. Stille Nacht, heilige Nacht. Silent night. *Oxford University Press. Unpriced* DP/LF (B71-50763) ISBN 0 19 343022 3
Grun, Bernard. Alban Berg: letters to his wife. (Berg, Alban). *Faber and Faber Ltd. £4.50* BBKR(N) (B71-05267) ISBN 0 571 08395 1
Grundman, Clare.
An Irish rhapsody: for military band. *Boosey and Hawkes. £8.75* UMMJ (B71-50623)
Puppets: for two B flat clarinets. *Boosey and Hawkes. £0.45* VVNU (B71-50672)
Grunfeld, Frederic V. The art and times of the guitar: an illustrated history of guitars and guitarists. *Macmillan (N.Y.); Collier-Macmillan. £2.50* ATS/B(X) (B71-19972) ISBN 0 02 546290 3
Guarani: sinfonia. (Gomes, Antonio Carlos). *Arthu Napoleao; Essex Music. Unpriced* QNVK (B71-50454)
Guide to Bartok's 'Mikrokosmos'. (Suchoff, Benjamin). Revised ed. *Boosey and Hawkes. £2.50* BBGAQ (B71-09061) ISBN 0 85162 002 7
Guildhall School of Music and Drama.
Pianoforte examinations
Grade 1. *Lengnick. £0.35* Q/AL (B71-50956)
Grade 2. *Lengnick. £0.35* Q/AL (B71-50957)
Grade 3. *Lengnick. £0.35* Q/AL (B71-50958)
Grade 4. *Lengnick. £0.35* Q/AL (B71-50959)
Junior. *Lengnick. £0.35* Q/AL (B71-50955)
Preliminary. *Lengnick. £0.35* Q/AL (B71-50954)
Pianoforte examinations, series 9
Introductory. *Lengnick. £0.35* Q/AL (B71-50960)
Guillaume de Machaut. (Reaney, Gilbert). *Oxford University Press. £0.90* BMBH (B71-30148) ISBN 0 19 315218 5
Gulda, Friedrich. Sonata for cello & piano. Cello sonata: for cello and piano. (Webern, Anton von). *Boosey and Hawkes. Unpriced* SRPE (B71-50593)
Guthrie, Arlo. This is the Arlo Guthrie book. *Amsco Music Publishing; Distributed by Collier-Macmillan. £0.90* KE/TSDW (B71-50888) ISBN 0 02 060680 x
Gutman, Robert William. Richard Wagner: the man, his mind and his music. *Penguin. £0.75* BWC(N) (B71-05793) ISBN 0 14 021168 3
Gweithdy cerddorol y plant. (Jones, E Olwen). *Christopher Davies. Unpriced* CB/NM (B71-50728)
Haddo House Choral Society. The music of the north. (Linklater, Eric). *Haddo House Choral Society. £0.30* AD/E(QB/YDLSH) (B71-09739) ISBN 0 9501767 0 2
Haggar, Reginald. Music and its story. (Young, Percy Marshall). Revised ed. *Dobson. £1.25* A(X) (B71-05265) ISBN 0 234 77346 4
Hail to the Lord's annointed: anthem for SATB and organ (or brass band). (Ball, Eric). *Novello. £0.15* DH (B71-50185)
Halevy, Ludovic. Ba-ta-clan: a masquerade in one act. (Offenbach, Jacques). *Schirmer; Chappell. Unpriced* CF (B71-50163)
Halffter, Cristobal. Anillos: for orchestra. Revised version. *Universal. Unpriced* MMJ (B71-50391)
Halfin, Bob. The power and the glory. (Leonard, Harry). *Novello. £1.75* EMDH (B71-50023)
Hall, Alan. The classical guitar: a method for beginners. *Scratchwood Music. £0.75* TS/AC (B71-50605)
Hall, Richard. Suite for piano. Suite. *Novello. £0.50* QPG (B71-50973)
Hallelujah. (Beethoven, Ludwig van). *Schirmer; Chappell. Unpriced* EUMDH (B71-50242)
Hallowell, John. Inside Creedence. *Bantam. £0.40* AKDW/HK/E(Y)M (B71-14240) ISBN 0 552 66901 6
Hamburger, Paul. Hamlet. Op. 48: opera in three acts. (Searle, Humphrey). *Faber. Unpriced* CC (B71-50160)
Hamilton, Alasdair. Good cheer: a Christmas carol. *Oxford University Press. Unpriced* FLDP/LF (B71-50851) ISBN 0 19 341505 4
Hamilton, Iain. Cantus: for orchestra (1964). *Schott. £0.60* MMJ (B71-50908)
Hamlet. Op. 48: opera in three acts. (Searle, Humphrey). *Faber. Unpriced* CC (B71-50160)
Hammerschmidt, Andreas.
Alleluja. Freuet euch ihr Christen alle. Alleluia! O rejoice ye Christians loudly: for mixed voices, organ (piano) and strings (ad lib). *Peters; Hinrichsen. £0.45* DH/LF (B71-50191)
Ehre sey Gott in der Hohe. Glory to God in the highest: for mixed voices, organ (piano) and strings (ad lib). *Peters Hinrichsen. £0.45* GDH/LF (B71-50313)
Wer walset uns den Stein. An Easter dialogue: for mixed voices, organ (piano), 2 trumpets, 4 trombones and double bass. *Peters; Hinrichsen. £0.45* ENUXPNQDH/LL (B71-50240)
Hammond, Tom. Hansel and Gretel: a fairy opera in three acts. (Humperdinck, Engelbert). *Schott. Unpriced* CC (B71-50157)
Hand, Colin.
Petite suite champetre. Op.67: for descant recorder (or flute or oboe) and piano. *Boosey and Hawkes. Unpriced* VSRPG (B71-51080)
Variations and fugue on a Cheshire souling song: for orchestra. *Novello. Unpriced* M/T (B71-50899)
Handel, George Frideric.
Coronation anthem no.2 (The King shall rejoice): for six-part chorus of mixed voices. *Schirmer; Chappell. Unpriced* DK (B71-50194)
Coronation anthem no.3 (My heart is inditing): for five-part chorus of mixed voices and solo quartet (ad lib.) with organ or piano accompaniment. *Schirmer; Chappell. Unpriced* DK (B71-50193)
A Handel solo album: for trumpet or trombone & piano (or bassoon & piano). *Oxford University Press. £0.60* WSPK/DH (B71-50717) ISBN 0 19 356971 x
Handel, George Frideric. My heart is inditing. *See* Handel, George Frideric. Coronation anthem no.3.
Handel, George Frideric.
Rinaldo - Sorge nel petto. Sarabande. *Schott. Unpriced* SRPK/AHVL (B71-51040)
Rodelinda. - Dove sei. Art thou troubled?: organ. *Paxton. Unpriced* RK/DW (B71-50532)
Sing unto God. (Wedding anthem for Frederick, Prince of Wales, 1736): for soloists, chorus and orchestra. *Oxford University Press. £0.80* DK/KDD (B71-50201) ISBN 0 19 336660 6
Sonata for two flutes in E minor. Triosonate e-Moll: fur 2 Querfloten und Basso continuo. *Schott. £1.10* VRNTPWE (B71-50637)
Handel, George Frideric. The King shall rejoice. *See* Handel, George Frideric. Coronation anthem.
Handel, George Frideric. Wedding anthem for Frederick, Prince of Wales. *See* Handel, George Frideric. Sing unto God.
Hanmer, Ronald.
Mexican fiesta: for brass band. *Studio Music. Unpriced* WMG (B71-50693)
Orfeo. Che faro. Air from 'Orpheus and Euridice': popularly known as 'What is life?'. (Gluck, Christoph Willibald von). *Studio Music. Unpriced* WMK/DW (B71-50707)
Viva Mexico!: a comedy musical in three acts. *Weinberger. Unpriced* CM (B71-50164)
Hansel and Gretel: a fairy opera in three acts. (Humperdinck, Engelbert). *Schott. Unpriced* CC (B71-50157)
Happy anniversary: a well-known tune. (Copland, Aaron). *Boosey and Hawkes. Unpriced* MMJ (B71-50911)
Hardy, Thomas. The oxen: a carol for women's voices and piano. (Britten, Benjamin). *Faber Music. Unpriced* FDP/LF (B71-50036)
Harewood, Marion.
The young pianist's repertoire
Book 1. (Waterman, Fanny). *Faber. Unpriced* QP/AY (B71-50455)
Book 2. (Waterman, Fanny). *Faber. Unpriced* QP/AY (B71-50456)
Harrap opera guide. (Morley, *Sir* Alexander Francis). *Harrap. £2.10* AC (B71-00713) ISBN 0 245 50509 1
Harris, A D. Symphony, no.99, in E flat major. B and H. 99. Adagio. Adagio. (Haydn, Joseph). *Feldman. Unpriced* VVNTK (B71-51088)
Harris, Will. The cold encounter: unison song. *Bosworth. £0.06* JFDW (B71-50052)
Harrison, Frank Ll. Resonemus laudibus: SATB. (Willcocks, David). *Oxford University Press. Unpriced* DP/LF (B71-50216) ISBN 0 19 343011 8
Hartmann, Karl Amadeus.
Jazz-Toccata und - Fuge: fur Klavier. *Schott. £1.20* QP/Y (B71-50085)
Sonatina for piano. Sonatine fur Klavier. *Schott. £0.90* QPEM (B71-50087)
Harutjunian, Alexander. Concerto for horn. Konzert: fur Horn und Orchester
Ausgabe fur Horn und Klavier vom Komponisten. *Peters; Hinrichsen. £1.20* WTPK/LF (B71-50718)
Harutjunjan, Alexander. *See* Harutjunian, Alexander.
Harvey, Jonathan. Laus Deo: for organ. *Novello. £0.30* RJ (B71-50524)
Has sorrow thy young days shaded?: for soprano and alto. (Parke, Dorothy). *Cramer. £0.09* FDW (B71-50837)
Hassall, Christopher. Twice in a blue moon: a fantasy operetta, the accompaniment for two pianos, percussion and double bass. (Tate, Phyllis). *Oxford University Press. £1.25* CQF (B71-50733) ISBN 0 19 338377 2
Hassler, Hans Leo. Variationen 'Ich ging einmal Spatieren': fur Cembalo (Orgel, Klavier). *Schott. £1.50* PWP/T (B71-50445)
Hattori, Koh-Ichi. From the North Country: overture for

band. Boosey and Hawkes. £2.00 UMMJ (B71-51061)

Hauser, Karlheinz Schultz-. See Schultz-Hauser, Karlheinz.

Hauser, Karlheinz Schultz-. See Schultz-Hauser, Karlheinz.

Haydn, Joseph.

Concerto for cello in D major. Hob. VII b/2. - Excerpts. Adagio. Schott. Unpriced SRPK (B71-51023)

A Haydn solo album: eleven short pieces. Oxford University Press. £0.60 WSPK (B71-50716) ISBN 0 19 357066 1

Mass, no.6 'Harmoniemesse'. - Dona nobis pacem. Dona nobis pacem. Schirmer; Chappell. Unpriced DH (B71-50746)

Mass no.16, 'Theresa mass'. Mass in B flat (Theresien messe): for four-part chorus of mixed voices and solo quartet. Schirmer; Chappell. Unpriced DG (B71-50176)

Symphony no.50 in C major. Eulenburg. Unpriced MME (B71-50380)

Symphony, no.99, in E flat major. B and H. 99. Adagio. Adagio. Feldman. Unpriced VVNTK (B71-51088)

Trios for strings. Hob.IV, 1-3. London trios. Schirmer Chappell. Unpriced TSNTK (B71-51049)

Haydn, Michael.

Divertimento for viola, cello and double bass in E fla major. Yorke Edition. Unpriced RXNT (B71-50551)

Divertimento for viola, cello & double bass in E flat major. Yorke. Unpriced RXNT (B71-50552)

Haydn. (Hughes, Rosemary). Revised ed. Dent. £1.50 BHE(N) (B71-07862) ISBN 0 460 03111 2

He is born. Il est ne: traditional French carol. (Higdon, George). Willis Music. Unpriced EZDP/LF (B71-50799)

Head, Michael. The carol of the field mice. Boosey and Hawkes. Unpriced KDP/LF (B71-50331)

Hear my dream: S.A.B. and piano. (Friend, Jerry R). Warner; Blossom Music. Unpriced DW (B71-50772)

Hearn, Lafcadio. Four songs from the Japanese. Op.9:: voice and piano. (Goehr, Alexander). Schott. Unpriced KDW (B71-50339)

Heart's adoration: two-part. (Marcello, Benedetto). Oxford University Press. Unpriced DH/LFL (B71-50014)

Hebbel, Friedrich. Abendlied. Evening song. Op.91, no.3: for four-part chorus of mixed voices with piano accompaniment. (Brahms, Johannes). Schirmer; Chappell. Unpriced DW (B71-50225)

Heber, Reginald. Psalm 45. Excerpts. Heart's adoration: two-part. (Marcello, Benedetto). Oxford University Press. Unpriced DH/LFL (B71-50014)

Hedges, Anthony. Quartet for strings (1970). Op. 41. String quartet (1970). Op. 41. British & Continental Music. Unpriced RXNS (B71-50548)

Heider, Werner.

Edition: multiple Musik fur Instrumental - oder Vokalgruppen. Litolff, Peters; Hinrichsen. £0.90 LN (B71-50374)

Landschaftspartitur: fur Klavier. Litolff; Hinrichsen. £3.25 QPJ (B71-50486)

Helas! mon Dieu: SAATB unacc. (Le Jeune, Claude). Oxford University Press. Unpriced EZDH (B71-50791)

Hellendaal, Pieter, b.1721. Sonata for cello and keyboard in B flat major. Op.5, no.3 - Excerpts. Rondo: for cello and piano. Schott. Unpriced SRP/W (B71-51018)

Hellmann, Diethard.

Alleluja. Freuet euch ihr Christen alle. Alleluia! O rejoice ye Christians loudly: for mixed voices, organ (piano) and strings (ad lib). (Hammerschmidt, Andreas). Peters Hinrichsen. £0.45 DH/LF (B71-50191)

Ehre sey Gott in der Hohe. Glory to God in the highest: for mixed voices, organ (piano) and strings (ad lib). (Hammerschmidt, Andreas). Peters; Hinrichsen. £0.45 GDH/LF (B71-50313)

Wer walset uns den Stein. An Easter dialogue: for mixed voices, organ (piano), 2 trumpets, 4 trombones and double bass. (Hammerschmidt, Andreas). Peters; Hinrichsen. £0.45 ENUXPNQDH/LL (B71-50240)

Hellyer, Roger.

Octet-partita. Op.79: for 2 oboes, 2 clarinets, 2 horns, 2 bassoons and contrabassoon ad lib. (Krommer, Franz). Musica rara. Unpriced UNNG (B71-50627)

Quartet for bassoon, 2 violas & cello in B flat major. Op.46, no.1. Quartet in B flat. Op,46, no.1: for bassoon, 2 violas & cello or bassoon, violin, viola and cello. (Krommer, Franz). Musica rara. Unpriced NVNS (B71-50422)

Sextet for wind instruments, no.1 in E flat major. Sextet no.1 in E flat for 2 clarinets, 2 horns and 2 bassoons. (Castil-Blaze, Francois Henri Joseph). Musica rara. Unpriced UNQ (B71-51065)

Suite for wind octet, no.4, in F major. Octet-partita: for 2 oboes, 2 clarinets, 2 horns, 2 bassoons and contrabassoon ad. lib. Op.57. (Krommer, Franz). Musica rara. £5.50 UNNG (B71-50138)

Suite for wind octet, no.5, in B flat major. Octet-partita: for 2 oboes, 2 clarinets, 2 horns, 2 bassoons and contrabassoon ad. lib. Op.67. (Krommer, Franz). Musica rara. £5.25 UNNG (B71-50139)

Helm, Everett. Bartok. Faber and Faber Ltd. £1.25 BBG(N) (B71-17373) ISBN 0 571 09105 9

Helps, Robert. Saccade: piano, four hands. Peters Hinrichsen. £0.90 QNV (B71-50451)

Hendrie, Gerald.

Introduction to music. Open University Press. £0.80 A (B71-08374) ISBN 0 335 00509 8

Mendelssohn's rediscovery of Bach. Open University Press. £1.20 A(VX/P) (B71-24686) ISBN 0 335 00516 0

Henriksen, Josef.

English mass: two-part with organ accompaniment by Josef Henriksen. St Gregory Publishing Co. £0.40 FDG (B71-50825)

Fifty hymn melodies for school assembly. St Gregory Publishing Co. £0.825 SMK/DM/AY (B71-51012)

Variations for organ on the Lourdes Hymn. St Gregory Publishing Co. £0.53 R/T (B71-50993)

Henze, Hans Werner.

Compases para preguntas ensimismadas: music for viola and 22 players. Schott. £3.20 MPSQ (B71-50913)

Versuch uber Schweine: fur Stimme und Orchester. Schott. £3.20 KE/MDX (B71-50059)

Hercules dux Ferrariae: Nomos no.1 for strings. (O Riada, Sean). Woodtown Music. Unpriced RXMG (B71-50114)

Hereford Cathedral. A portrait of John Bull, c.1563-1628. (Chappell, Paul). Hereford Cathedral. £0.10 BBV(N) (B71-03035) ISBN 0 9501011 2 5

Here's Jupiter: SATB a cappella (or improvised rock accompaniment ad lib). (Kent, Richard). Warner; Seven Arts; Blossom Music. Unpriced EZDW (B71-50032)

Herfurth, Clarence Paul. A tune a day: for classical guitar: a third instruction book. Chappell. £0.40 TS/AC (B71-50606)

Herlitschka, Herbert E. A ceremony of carols. Ein Kranz von Lobechorens. Op.28: for treble voices and harp. (Britten, Benjamin). New English-German ed. Boosey and Hawkes. Unpriced FLDEDP/LF (B71-50309)

Herman, Gary. The Who. Studio Vista. £1.40 AB/E(P) (B71-16698) ISBN 0 289 70135 x

Hernando's hideaway: T.T.B.B. (Adler, Richard). Frank Music. £0.90 GDW (B71-50314)

Herr segne euch. The Lord shall increase you: for SSAB chorus (or SATB). (Peter, Johann Friedrich). Boosey and Hawkes. £0.09 DH (B71-50189)

Herrick, Robert.

Charms and ceremonies: for unison voices, S(S)A and piano. (Hurd, Michael). Novello. £0.30 FDX (B71-50842)

Six songs. (Lawes, William). Schott. £0.65 KDW (B71-50883)

What sweeter musick: high voice. (Binkerd, Gordon). Boosey and Hawkes. £0.40 KFTDW (B71-50363)

What sweeter musick: low voice. (Binkerd, Gordon). Boosey and Hawkes. £0.40 KFXDW (B71-50367)

Herrmann, William.

Coronation anthem no.2 (The King shall rejoice): for six-part chorus of mixed voices. (Handel, George Frideric). Schirmer; Chappell. Unpriced DK (B71-50194)

Coronation anthem no.3 (My heart is inditing): for five-part chorus of mixed voices and solo quartet (ad lib.) with organ or piano accompaniment. (Handel, George Frideric). Schirmer; Chappell. Unpriced DK (B71-50193)

Mass, no.6 'Harmoniemesse'. - Dona nobis pacem. Dona nobis pacem. (Haydn, Joseph). Schirmer; Chappell. Unpriced DH (B71-50746)

Mass no.16, 'Theresa mass'. Mass in B flat (Theresien messe): for four-part chorus of mixed voices and solo quartet. (Haydn, Joseph). Schirmer; Chappell. Unpriced DG (B71-50176)

Tantum ergo in E flat (1828). D.962: for four-part chorus of mixed voices and solo quartet (ad lib.) with organ or piano accompaniment. (Schubert, Franz). Schirmer Chappell. Unpriced DGLBT (B71-50177)

Hess, Ernst.

Overture for strings in C minor. D.8. Ouverture, C-moll: fur Streicher (Zweite Fassung). (Schubert, Franz). Litolff, Peters; Hinrichsen. £1.60 RXN (B71-50543)

Overture for strings in C minor. D.8. Overture, C-moll: fur Streicher. (Schubert, Franz). Litolff, Peters; Hinrichsen. £1.60 RXN (B71-50544)

Hewlett, Arthur Donald. Think afresh about the voice: a reappraisal of the teaching of Ernest George White. The Ernest George White Society. £0.45 AB/E (B71-19971) ISBN 0 9501610 0 4

Higdon, George. He is born. Il est ne: traditional French carol. Willis Music. Unpriced EZDP/LF (B71-50799)

Higginson, Cornelia. I remember it well. (Chevalier, Maurice). W.H. Allen. £2.00 AKG/E(P) (B71-06910) ISBN 0 491 00436 2

Highlander march. (Turner, J Godfrey). Feldman. Unpriced UMMGM (B71-51057)

Hill, John D.

Sonata for two violins, trombone & basso continuo, no.1, in D minor. Sonata a 3, no.1 in D minor: for 2 violins, trombone & organ continuo. (Bertali, Antonio). Musica rara. Unpriced NUXUNSE (B71-50419)

Sonata for two violins, trombone & basso continuo, no.2, in D minor. Sonata a 3, no.2 in D minor: for 2 violins, trombone & organ continuo. (Bertali, Antonio). Musica rara. Unpriced NUXUNSE (B71-50420)

Hiller, Wilfried. Catalogue for percussion III: 3 players. Schott. £1.60 XNT (B71-51124)

Hilton, Lewis B. Learning to teach through playing: a woodwind method. Addison-Wesley. Unpriced V/AC (B71-50140)

Hindemith, Paul.

Kammermusik no.6. Op.46, no.1: Konzert fur Viola d'amore und Kammerorchester. Schott. £1.60 MPSQQF (B71-50403)

Kammermusik no.7: Konzert fur Orgel und Kammerorchester. Opus 46, no.2. Schott. £1.70 MPR (B71-50912)

Thema mit vier Variationen: die Vier Temperamente, fur Klavier und Streichorchester. Schott. £2.80 MPQ/T (B71-50402)

Hindley, Geoffrey. Larousse encyclopaedia of music. Hamlyn. £6.30 A(C) (B71-25341) ISBN 0 600 02396 6

Hines, Robert S. Christus factus est. Jesus who for our salvation: four-part chorus of mixed voices a cappella. (Anerio, Felice). Schirmer; Chappell. Unpriced EZDJ (B71-50794)

Hingeston, John.

Fantasia for 2 trumpets (cornetti), bass trombone (sackbutt) and organ continuo. Musica rara. Unpriced NWXPNS (B71-50936)

Fantasia for cornetto (trumpet), sackbutt (bass trombone) and organ continuo. Musica rara. Unpriced NWXPNT (B71-50934)

Hinojosa, Javier.

Sonatas for harpsichord in A minor. S.K.74, 80. Zwei Sonaten. (Seixas, Carlos de). Schott. £0.50 TSPMK/AE (B71-50614)

Varietie of lute-lessons. Excerpts. Fantasia no.7: per liuto. (Dowland, John). Schott. £0.80 TWPMJ (B71-50618)

Hirsch, Hans Ludwig. Omaggi a Rossini: fur Orchester. Litolff, Peters; Hinrichsen. £2.50 MMJ (B71-50392)

History of song. (Stevens, Denis). Hutchinson. £3.75 ADW(X) (B71-06292) ISBN 0 09 104680 7

History of the Royal Manchester College of Music, 1893-1972. (Kennedy, Michael, b.1926). Manchester University Press. £2.40 A(VP/YDJE/X) (B71-16699) ISBN 0 7190 0435 7

Hoag, Charles K.

May God have mercy upon us: for four-part chorus of mixed voices with organ accompaniment. Schirmer Chappell. Unpriced DR (B71-50768)

Sing softly: for two-part chorus of young voices with organ accompaniment (ad lib.). Schirmer; Chappell. Unpriced FEZDH/LF (B71-50845)

Hoddinott, Alun.

Concerto for harp. Opus 11. Oxford University Press. £3.00 MPTQF (B71-50406) ISBN 0 19 364487 8

Investiture dances: for orchestra. Opus 66. Oxford University Press. £2.00 MMH (B71-50386) ISBN 0 19 364505 x

Symphony no.3. Opus 61. Oxford University Press. £3.00 MME (B71-50381) ISBN 0 19 364551 3

Symphony no.4. Op.70. Oxford University Press. y3.50 MME (B71-50904) ISBN 0 19 364553 x

Hodgson, Martyn. Seven easy pieces by Elizabethan composers. Regina Music. Unpriced TSPMK (B71-50134)

Hodie apparuit. On this day the Christ appears: SSA or TTB. (Lasso, Orlando di). Schirmer; Chappell. Unpriced FEZDJ/LF (B71-50304)

Hodie Christus natus est: Christmas introit for women's or boys' voices. (Hunter, Ian T). Thames. Unpriced FEZDP/LF (B71-50846)

Hodie Christus natus est: for double chorus of mixed voices with organ accompaniment. (Gabrieli, Giovanni). Schirmer; Chappell. Unpriced DGKJ/LF (B71-50740)

Hodie Christus natus est. On this day Christ appears: motet for three-part chorus of women's voices a cappella. (Monteverdi, Claudio). Schirmer; Chappell. Unpriced EZDJ/LF (B71-50256)

Hoffmeister, Franz Anton. Duet for clarinet & piano in A major. Duo fur Klarinette und Klavier, A-Dur. Schott. £2.00 VVPJ (B71-50676)

Hoffstetter, Roman. Concerto for viola in C major. Konzert, C-Dur: fur Viola, Streicher, 2 Oboen und 2 Horner Klavierauszug von Helmut May. Schott. £1.80 SQPK/LF (B71-50583)

Hofmann, Wolfgang.

Concerto for double bass & string orchestra. Konzert: fur Kontrabass und Streicher. Litolff, Peters; Hinrichsen. £1.00 RXMPSSF (B71-50537)

Overture for strings in C minor. D.8. Ouverture, C-moll: fur Kammerorchester, nach der Ouverture C-moll fur Streicher. (Schubert, Franz). Litolff, Peters; Hinrichsen. Unpriced MRK (B71-50414)

Hogner, Friedrich. Zwei Trauungsgesange und Tanflied: fur Singstimme, Violine und Orgel. Litolff, Peters; Hinrichsen. £1.75 KE/SPLRDH (B71-50352)

Holborne, Antony.

Pavans, galiards, almains and other short airs. Complete music for brass: for 2 trumpets and 3 trombones (2 trumpets, horn and 2 trombones)

Vol.1. Musica rara. Unpriced WNR/AZ (B71-51112)

Pavans, galiards, almains and other short airs. Complete music for brass: for 2 trumpets and 3 trombones (2 trumpets, horn and 2 trombones)

Vol.2. Musica rara. Unpriced WNR/AZ (B71-51113)

Holderlin, Friedrich. Der Tod des Empedokles. Excerpts. Drei Monologue des Empedokles von Friedrich Holderlin: fur Bariton und Klavier oder Orchester. (Reutter, Hermann). Schott. £1.30 KGNDW (B71-50370)

Holiday tunes: 18 easy pieces for pianoforte. (Robinson, L Woodroffe). Freeman. Unpriced QPJ (B71-50098)

Holliger, Heinz. Trio for oboe, viola and harp. Trio fur Oboe, Viola und Harfe. Schott. Unpriced NVTNS (B71-50930)

Hollingworth, Paul. The power and the glory. (Leonard, Harry). Novello. £1.75 EMDH (B71-50023)

Hollowood, Bernard. Organo pleno. (Reynolds, Gordon). Novello. £0.35(non-net) AR/E (B71-04183) ISBN 0 85360 004 x

Holman, Derek. Versicles, Responses and the Lord's Prayer: for treble voices. Lengnick. Unpriced FLEZDGM (B71-50312)

Holst, Gustav. The tale of the wandering scholar. Op.50. The wandering scholar. Op.50: a chamber opera in one act. Faber. Unpriced CQC (B71-50172)

Holst, Imogen.

Quem pastores laudavere. Shepherds left their flocks a-straying: German carol SATB unacc. (Rutter, John). Oxford University Press. Unpriced EZDP/LF (B71-50260) ISBN 0 19 343012 6

The tale of the wandering scholar. Op.50. The wandering scholar. Op.50: a chamber opera in one act. (Holst, Gustav). Faber. Unpriced CQC (B71-50172)

Honeybrook: part-song for SSA and piano. (Thiman, Eric Harding). Novello. Unpriced FDW (B71-50043)

Hood, Marguerite Vivian. Teaching rhythm and using classroom instruments. Prentice-Hall. £3.10 A(VG)

(B71-08201) ISBN 0 13 894089 4

Hoover, Kathleen O'Donnell. Makers of opera. Kennikat Press. £5.50 AC(XE311) (B71-21649) ISBN 0 8046 1412 1

Hopkins, Antony.

Doctor Musicus: an opera designed especially for the young. Chester. Unpriced CN (B71-50732)

Music face to face. (Previn, Andre). Hamilton. £1.75 A (B71-26599) ISBN 0 241 02036 0

Talking about sonatas: a book of analytical studies, based on a personal view. Heinemann Educational. £2.50 AQPE (B71-26602) ISBN 0 435 81425 7

Hopkins, Bill. Etudes: piano solo

Book 1. Schott. Unpriced QPJ (B71-50093)

Hopkins, Bill, b.1943. Antonio Vivaldi: his life and works. (Kolneder, Walter). Faber and Faber Ltd. £6.00 BVJ (B71-07863) ISBN 0 571 09386 8

Hopkins, Douglas.

Postlude on 'Love divine' by John Stainer: for organ. Paxton. Unpriced RJ (B71-50525)

Rodelinda. - Dove sei. Art thou troubled?: organ. (Handel, George Frideric). Paxton. Unpriced RK/DW (B71-50532)

Hopkins, Jerry. Festival!: the book of American music celebrations... Macmillan (N.Y.); Collier-Macmillan. £4.00 A/GB(YT/WE) (B71-11123) ISBN 0 02 580170 8

Hopson, Hal H. God is our refuge, God is our strength: SATB chorus of choral and speaking voices with optional congregational declamation. Warner; Blossom Music. Unpriced EZDR (B71-50807)

Horovitz, Joseph.

Captain Noah and his floating zoo: cantata in popular style for unison or two-part voices & piano, with optional bass & drums. (Flanders, Michael). Novello. £0.40 FDE (B71-50035)

Sinfonietta: for brass band. Novello. £3.00 WMEM (B71-51094)

Horsch, Hans. Suite for brass, no.2. Blechblaser Suite No.2. Schott. £1.60 WNS (B71-50712)

Horscroft, Elizabeth. Space songs for infants. Ashdown. £0.25 JFDW/GJ (B71-50323)

House, L Marguerite. We three: two-part chorus with piano, optional guitars and claves. Warner; Blossom Music. Unpriced DW (B71-50233)

Hovdesven, E A. Fold to thy heart thy brother: for four-part chorus of mixed voices a cappella. Schirmer; Chappell. Unpriced EZDW (B71-50816)

Hovhaness, Alan.

Five fantasies for brass choir. Op. 70 Fantasy no.1: trumpets, horns, trombones. Peters; Hinrichsen. £0.60 WMJ (B71-50698)

Fantasy no.2: trumpets, horns, trombones. Peters Hinrichsen. £0.625 WMJ (B71-50699)

Fantasy no.3: trumpets, horns, trombones. Peters Hinrichsen. £0.625 WMJ (B71-50700)

Fantasy no.4: 2 trumpets, horns, trombones (tubas). Peters; Hinrichsen. £0.875 WMJ (B71-50701)

Fantasy no.5: 2 trumpets, horns, trombones (tubas). Peters; Hinrichsen. £0.90 WMJ (B71-50702)

I will lift up mine eyes. Op.93. Excerpts. My help cometh from the Lord: for mixed voices and organ. Peters Hinrichsen. £0.30 DH (B71-50187)

I will lift up mine eyes. Opus 93: mixed voices (boys choir and bass solo ad lib.) and organ. Peters; Hinrichsen. £0.75 DR (B71-50221)

Mountains and rivers without end. Op.225: chamber symphony for 10 players. Peters; Hinrichsen. £1.50 MRJ (B71-50413)

Sanahin: partita for organ. Peters; Hinrichsen. £0.90 RG (B71-50518)

How amiable are thy dwellings: anthem for SATB and organ. (Standford, Patric). Novello. Unpriced DK (B71-50199)

How far is it to Bethlehem?: English traditional melody, S.A.A. unacc. (Willcocks, David). Oxford University Press. Unpriced FEZDP/LF (B71-50305) ISBN 0 19 342592 0

How far is it to Bethlehem?: West country carol. (Lawson, Gordon). Royal School of Church Music. £0.05 EZDP/LF (B71-50800)

How sweet I roamed from field to field: two part song. (Williams, Patrick). Bosworth. £0.07 FDW (B71-50840)

Howells, Herbert. Thee will I love: motet for SATB and organ. Novello. £0.15 DH (B71-50012)

Huber, Klaus. Tenebrae: fur grosses Orchester. Ars Viva; Schott. £5.60 MMJ (B71-50393)

Hudson, Hazel.

Go tell it on the mountain. He's got the whole world in His hands: a quodlibet based on two negro spirituals. Ashdown. £0.10 DW/LC (B71-50776)

Oh Mary, and all that jazz!: a quodlibet. Ashdown. £0.10 DW/LC (B71-50777)

The old ark's a-moverin' (amongst other things): a quodlibet for two female, two male, or one female and one male voice parts. Ashdown. Unpriced DW/LC (B71-50778)

Hughes, Gervase. The music lover's companion. Eyre and Spottiswoode. £3.00 A(D) (B71-18712) ISBN 0 413 27920 0

Hughes, Rosemary. Haydn. Revised ed. Dent. £1.50 BHE(N) (B71-07862) ISBN 0 460 03111 2

Hughes, Ted. The demon Adachigahara. Op. 21. Excerpts. Night wind: S.A.T.B. (Crosse, Gordon). Oxford University Press. Unpriced EZDW (B71-50815) ISBN 0 19 342986 1

Humanities foundation course. (Open University Press)

Hendrie, Gerald. Introduction to music. Open University Press. £0.80 A (B71-08374) ISBN 0 335 00509 8

Hendrie, Gerald. Mendelssohn's rediscovery of Bach. Open University Press. £1.20 A(VX/P) (B71-24686) ISBN 0 335 00516 0

Hume, Arthur Wolfgang Julius Gerald Ord-. See Ord-Hume, Arthur Wolfgang Julius Gerald.

Humour in music. (Sharp, Mary, b.1907). Stockwell. £0.175 AQ/E(VC) (B71-04182) ISBN 0 7223 0133 2

Humperdinck, Engelbert. Hansel and Gretel: a fairy opera in three acts. Schott. Unpriced CC (B71-50157)

Humphrey, Pelham. Evening Service: SATB and organ with verses for SSAATB. Oxford University Press. £0.20 DGPP (B71-50182) ISBN 0 19 351634 9

Hungarian folksongs (1906). Excerpts. Five Hungarian folksongs: for voice and piano. (Bartok, Bela). Boosey and Hawkes. Unpriced KDW/G/AYG (B71-50346)

Hungarian phantasy: for two flutes and piano. (Doppler, Franz). Musica rara. Unpriced VRNTQK (B71-51069)

Hunt, Edgar. An introduction to playing the Spanish guitar. Schott. £0.25 TS/AC (B71-51047)

Hunt, Reginald. I had a hippopotamus. Ashdown. Unpriced JFDW (B71-50869)

Hunter, Ian T.

Ding dong! merrily on high: carol arranged for women's or boys' voices & organ/piano. Thames. Unpriced FDP/LF (B71-50828)

Hodie Christus natus est: Christmas introit for women's or boys' voices. Thames. Unpriced FEZDP/LF (B71-50846)

The shadows are falling: Tyrolean cradle song; words by T.A. Armstrong; with, Christmas day: Lancashire carol: carols for women's or boys' voices. Thames. Unpriced FEZDP/LF (B71-50847)

Huntley, John. The technique of film music. (Manvell, Roger). 1st ed. reprinted. Focal Press. £3.00 A/JR (B71-05268) ISBN 0 240 44943 6

Hupfeld player-piano: Solophonola, Duophonola, Triphonola catalogue, c.1910. 'Talking Machine Review'. £0.50 A/FP(WM) (B71-27974) ISBN 0 902338 11 0

Huray, Peter le. See Le Huray, Peter.

Hurd, Michael. Charms and ceremonies: for unison voices, S(S)A and piano. Novello. £0.30 FDX (B71-50842)

Hurford, Peter.

Bethlehem, of noblest cities: Australian folk melody and a melody from Psalmodia sacra, Gotha, 1715, for SATB. Oxford University Press. Unpriced DP/LFP (B71-50218)

Magdalen, cease from sobs and sighs: SATB unacc. Oxford University Press. Unpriced EZDP/LL (B71-50028)

Hutchinson, Godfrey. The Lambton worm: a folk tale from the North, for speakers, singers and tuned percussion. Leeds Music. Unpriced JFE/XMDX (B71-50327)

Hymn for children: a selection of hymns from the television series. High-Fye Music. £0.50 JFDM/AY (B71-50321)

Hymns for all seasons. (20th Century Church Light Music Group). Weinberger. Unpriced JDM/AY (B71-50047)

I arise from dreams of thee: two-part song, optional unison. (Dale, Mervyn). Ashdown. Unpriced FDW (B71-50831)

I don't know how to love him. (Webber, Andrew Lloyd). Leeds Music. £0.20 KFDW (B71-50890)

I had a hippopotamus. (Hunt, Reginald). Ashdown. Unpriced JFDW (B71-50869)

I had a little nut tree. (Poston, Elizabeth). Bodley Head. £1.10 JFDW/GK/AY (B71-50873) ISBN 0 370 01528 2

I hear a song: for full chorus of mixed voices a cappella. (Leaf, Robert). Schirmer; Chappell. Unpriced EZDW (B71-50276)

I heard a great voice: SAATBB a cappella. (Billings, William). Peters; Hinrichsen. £0.35 EZDK (B71-50257)

I remember it well. (Chevalier, Maurice). W.H. Allen. £2.00 AKG/E(P) (B71-06910) ISBN 0 491 00436 2

I will exalt thee: full anthem for four voices. (Tye, Christopher). Novello. £0.15 EZDK (B71-50027)

I will freely sacrifice to thee: for SSTB chorus (or SATB). (Peter, Johann Friedrich). Boosey and Hawkes. £0.15 DH (B71-50190)

I will lift up mine eyes. Op.93. Excerpts. My help cometh from the Lord: for mixed voices and organ. (Hovhaness, Alan). Peters; Hinrichsen. £0.30 DH (B71-50187)

I will lift up mine eyes. Opus 93: mixed voices (boys choir and bass solo ad lib.) and organ. (Hovhaness, Alan). Peters; Hinrichsen. £0.75 DR (B71-50221)

I will lift up mine eyes unto the hills. Op. 63: anthem for SSAA and piano. (Joubert, John). Novello. £0.15 DR (B71-50222)

Ich spiele vom Blatt: Schule des Prima-Vista-Spiels fur Klavier und andere Tasteninstrumente. (Keilmann, Wilhelm). Litolff, Peters; Hinrichsen. £3.00 PW/EG (B71-50443)

Ich will dir ein Frendenopfer. I will freely sacrifice to thee: for SSTB chorus (or SATB). (Peter, Johann Friedrich). Boosey and Hawkes. £0.15 DH (B71-50190)

If thou wilt ease thine heart. (Binkerd, Gordon). Boosey and Hawkes. £0.40 KDW (B71-50333)

Illustrated calderbooks. (Calder and Boyars) Samuel, Claude. Prokofiev. Calder and Boyars. £2.25 BPP(N) (B71-24085) ISBN 0 7145 0489 0

Immortals of mankind. (Franklin Watts Ltd) Gimpel, Herbert J. Beethoven: master composer. Franklin Watts Ltd. £1.25 BBJ(N) (B71-12554) ISBN 0 85166 321 4

Improvvisazione: per flauto e pianoforte. (Rozmann, Akos). Boosey and Hawkes. Unpriced VRPJ (B71-50644)

Improvvisazione: per pianoforte. (Papp, Lajos). Boosey and Hawkes. Unpriced QPJ (B71-50497)

Improvvisazioni: per quintetto a fiati. (Durko, Zsolt). Boosey and Hawkes. £0.50 UNR (B71-50631)

In Ireland. (Corker, Marjorie). Schott. Unpriced SRPJ (B71-51026)

In meinen Garten. In my garden. (Schumann, Robert). Schirmer; Chappell. Unpriced FDW (B71-50839)

In the forest: suite. (Johnson, Thomas Arnold). Freeman. £0.20 QPG (B71-50089)

In the present tense. Songs of Sydney Carter

4: Riding a tune. (Carter, Sydney). Galliard. Unpriced JDW (B71-50860)

Incorporated Society of Musicians. Careers with music. Incorporated Society of Musicians. £0.60 A(MN) (B71-09060) ISBN 0 902900 02 1

Incredible flute music. Op.11: for flute and piano. (Gilbert, Anthony). Schott. Unpriced VRPJ (B71-50643)

Inside Creedence. (Hallowell, John). Bantam. £0.40 AKDW/HK/E(Y)M (B71-14240) ISBN 0 552 66901 6

Instants: pour piano. (Lehmann, Hans Ulrich). Schott. £1.50 QPJ (B71-50488)

Institutional canons: for mixed chorus

1: The wealth of Illinois: S.A.T.B. (Binkerd, Gordon). Boosey and Hawkes. £0.15 EZ/X (B71-50243)

2: There is in souls: SATB. (Binkerd, Gordon). Boosey and Hawkes. £0.09 EZ/X (B71-50244)

3: To thy happy children: SSATBB. (Binkerd, Gordon). Boosey and Hawkes. £0.09 EZ/X (B71-50245)

Instruments of the orchestra. (Benn) Rendall, Francis Geoffrey. The clarinet: some notes upon its history and construction. 3rd ed. Benn. £2.75 AVV/B(X) (B71-20593) ISBN 0 510 36701 1

Intermezzo, Impressoes do teatro: piano. (Farinello, Orestes). Arthur Napoleao; Essex Music. Unpriced QPJ (B71-50484)

Introduction, allegro and finale: organ. (Barrett, Gavin). Boosey and Hawkes. £0.55 RJ (B71-50110)

Introduction to music. (Boyden, David Dodge). 2nd ed. Faber and Faber Ltd. £2.25 A (B71-16009) ISBN 0 571 04745 9

Introduction to music. (Hendrie, Gerald). Open University Press. £0.80 A (B71-08374) ISBN 0 335 00509 8

Introduction to playing the Spanish guitar. (Hunt, Edgar). Schott. £0.25 TS/AC (B71-51047)

Introduction to western music: Bach, Beethoven, Wagner, Stravinsky. (Kirby, F E). Free Press; Collier-Macmillan. £4.00 A(X) (B71-10428) ISBN 0 02 917360 4

Investiture dances: for orchestra. Opus 66. (Hoddinott, Alun). Oxford University Press. £2.00 MMH (B71-50386) ISBN 0 19 364505 x

Invitation to madrigals

5: for SATB. (Dart, Thurston). Stainerand Bell. £0.40 EZDU/AY (B71-50813)

Invocation of peace: Bekesser ohajtas: S.A.T.B. unaccompanied. (Kodaly, Zoltan). Boosey and Hawkes. Unpriced EZDW (B71-50274)

Ireland, John.

The overlanders. Two symphonic studies on themes from 'The overlanders'. Boosey and Hawkes. £0.65 MMJ (B71-50072)

The overlanders: suite for orchestra. Boosey and Hawkes. £2.50 MMG (B71-50070)

Scherzo & cortege, on themes from Julius Caesar. Boosey and Hawkes. £1.10 MMK/JM (B71-50075)

Irish and Highland harps. (Armstrong, Robert Bruce). Irish University Press. £10.00 ATQ/B (B71-30155) ISBN 0 7165 0073 6

Irish fiddler: unison. (Veal, Arthur). Oxford University Press. Unpriced JFDW (B71-50053)

Irish rhapsody: for military band. (Grundman, Clare). Boosey and Hawkes. £8.75 UMMJ (B71-50623)

Ist nicht Ephraim mein teurer Sohn? Is not Ephraim my precious Son?: Motete a 8 e 16 con due cappelle in fine, for mixed voices and instruments. (Schutz, Heinrich). Oxford University Press. £0.95 EWNNDH (B71-50788) ISBN 0 19 338084 6

Italian opera. (Galatopoulos, Stelios). Dent. £2.00 AC/E(YJ/X) (B71-07324) ISBN 0 460 05798 7

Ivey, Donald. Song: anatomy, imagery, and styles. Free Press; Collier-Macmillan. £3.00 ADW (B71-19968) ISBN 0 02 091580 2

Jacob, Gordon. Two chorale preludes: for brass band. Novello. £1.45 WMJ (B71-50703)

Jacob, Ruth Apprich. Miracles of Christmas: for four-part mixed chorus and organ (or piano). (Rorem, Ned). Boosey and Hawkes. £1.05 DE/LF (B71-50175)

Jacobs, Arthur. Opera: a modern guide. David and Charles. £3.00 AC (B71-08377) ISBN 0 7153 5013 7

Jacobs, Charles. El Maestro. (Milan, Luis). Pennsylvania University Press. Unpriced TVPMJ (B71-50616) ISBN 0 271 00091 0

Jacques, Reginald. Carols for choirs. Bk.1, nos. 33, 27, 13. Three carol orchestrations. Oxford University Press. Unpriced EMDP/LF (B71-50782)

Jagdmusik: 12 kleine Stucke, fur zwei Horner. (Sperger, Johann Matthias). Schott. £0.70 WTNU/GT (B71-50155)

Jairazbhoy, Nazir Ali. The rags of North Indian music: their structure and evolution. Faber and Faber Ltd. £10.00 BZFL (B71-11817) ISBN 0 571 08315 3

James, Peter. An anthology of English church music. (Wulstan, David). Chester. Unpriced EZDH/AYD (B71-50793)

Jamson, Bruce. Songs of America. Stainer and Bell. Unpriced JFE/NYESDW/G/AYT (B71-50875) ISBN 0 903000 01 6

Janitsch, Johann Gottlieb.

Sonata for flute, violin, oboe and basso continuo in C major. Op.4. Sonata da camera in C major: for flute, violin, oboe and basso continuo. Musica rara. £1.50 NWPNSE (B71-50424)

Sonata for flute, violin, oboe & basso continuo in C major. Op.4. Sonata da camera in C major. Op.4: for flute, violin, oboe & basso continuo. Musica rara. £1.50 NUPNSE (B71-50079)

Jasper, Tony. Pop. S.C.M. Press. £0.20 A/GB (B71-05264)

ISBN 0 334 01270 8

Jazz-Toccata und - Fuge: fur Klavier. (Hartmann, Karl Amadeus). *Schott.* £1.20 QP/Y (B71-50085)

Jeffery, Brian. Elizabethan duets. *Schott.* £0.40 TSNUK (B71-50131)

Jeffreys, John, *b.1927.* A book of songs. Private facsimile ed. *B. Hill. Unpriced* KDW (B71-50340)

Jenkins, John. Consort music in five parts. *Faber Music. Unpriced* STNQR (B71-50126)

Jeremiah, Dorothy Adams. Yes! I can play: songs and singing games. *Leeds Music. Unpriced* JFE/TQTDW/GS/AY (B71-50878)

Jergensen, Dale. Hodie Christus natus est: for double chorus of mixed voices with organ accompaniment. (Gabrieli, Giovanni). *Schirmer; Chappell. Unpriced* DGKJ/LF (B71-50740)

Jergenson, Dale.

Beata es virgo: part chorus of mixed voices with organ accompaniment (optional). (Gabrieli, Giovanni). *Schirmer; Chappell. Unpriced* EZDGKJ (B71-50024)

Jubilemus singuli: for eight-part chorus of mixed voices with organ accompaniment. (Gabrieli, Giovanni). *Schirmer; Chappell. Unpriced* DJ (B71-50016)

Jericho jazz: for unison voices with piano accompaniment and guitar chords. (Chappell, Herbert). *Clarabella Music. Unpriced* CN/L (B71-50167)

Jesus and the traders: for S.A.T.B. (Kodaly, Zoltan). Revised ed. *Universal Music. Unpriced* EZDH (B71-50254)

Jesus Christ Superstar- Excerpts. I don't know how to love him. (Webber, Andrew Lloyd). *Leeds Music.* £0.20 KFDW (B71-50890)

Jeune, Claude Le. *See* Le Jeune, Claude.

Johann Strauss: father and son, and their era. (Fantel, Hans). *David and Charles.* £2.75 BSQB(N) (B71-30149)

ISBN 0 7153 5421 3

John, Malcolm. Music drama in schools. *Cambridge University Press.* £3.80 ACN(VF) (B71-20590)

ISBN 0 521 08003 7

John, Miriam. Prokofiev. (Samuel, Claude). *Calder and Boyars.* £2.25 BPP(N) (B71-24085)

ISBN 0 7145 0489 0

John Barbirolli: a biography. (Reid, Charles, *b.1900*). *Hamilton.* £2.75 A/EC(P) (B71-18089)

ISBN 0 241 01819 6

John Cage. (Kostelanetz, Richard). *Allen Lane.* £3.15 BCBG (B71-14242) ISBN 0 7139 0210 8

John Damascene, *Saint.* Come, ye faithful, raise the strain: Easter anthem, for SATB and organ. (Thiman, Eric Harding). *Novello. Unpriced* DH/LL (B71-50015)

John of the Cross, *Saint.* Coplas: chorus (SATB-16 voices), soloists-SATB. (Tavener, John). *Chester. Unpriced* DE (B71-50174)

Johnny Appleseed: a cantata for all ages, for narrator, speaking chorus, singing chorus, dancers, mimers. (Verrall, Pamela). *Feldman.* £0.30 FE/NYFSDE (B71-50843)

Johnson, Edward. Robert Simpson: fiftieth birthday essays. *Triad Press.* £0.75 BSHM (B71-10427)

ISBN 0 902070 01 0

Johnson, Peter. Sing up: a guide and encouragement to sing in church. (Tamblyn, Bill). *G. Chapman.* £0.80 AD/LSB/E (B71-16702) ISBN 0 225 65904 2

Johnson, Thomas Arnold.

A day in the country: suite. *Freeman.* £0.20 QPG (B71-50088)

In the forest: suite. *Freeman.* £0.20 QPG (B71-50089)

Puppets on parade: suite. *Freeman.* £0.20 QPG (B71-50090)

Johnson preserved: opera in 3 acts. (Stoker, Richard). *Peters. Hinrichsen.* £5.00 CC (B71-50161)

Jones, David Lloyd-. *See* Lloyd-Jones, David.

Jones, E Olwen. Gweithdy cerddorol y plant. *Christopher Davies. Unpriced* CB/NM (B71-50728)

Jones, Edward Huws. Six songs. (Lawes, William). *Schott.* £0.65 KDW (B71-50883)

Jones, Max. Louis: the Louis Armstrong story, 1900-1971. *Studio Vista.* £3.20 AMT/E(P) (B71-25343)

ISBN 0 289 70215 1

Josquin des Pres.

Three six-part pieces. *Schott.* £0.30 VSNQK/DW (B71-51075)

Two five-part pieces. *Schott.* £0.40 VSNRK/DW (B71-51076)

Joubert, John.

I will lift up mine eyes unto the hills. Op. 63: anthem for SSAA and piano. *Novello.* £0.15 DR (B71-50222)

Six poems of Emily Bronte. Op.63: for high voice and piano. *Novello.* £1.75 KFTDW (B71-50895)

Journey to America. Excerpts. Pilgrims and pioneers: for orchestra. (Thomson, Virgil). *Schirmer; Chappell. Unpriced* MM/JR (B71-50376)

Joy. Excerpts. Brown baby: for chorus of treble voices (SSA) and piano. (Brown, Oscar). *Novello.* £0.09 FDW (B71-50041)

Joyce, James. Simples: a setting of James Joyce's poem. (Bliss, *Sir* Arthur). *Oxford University Press.* £0.80 KDW (B71-50336) ISBN 0 19 345165 4

Joyful song: SATB. (Rocherolle, Eugenie R). *Warner; Seven Arts; Blossom Music. Unpriced* DW (B71-50021)

Juan de la Cruz, *Saint. See* John of the Cross, *Saint.*

Jubilate: for organ and brass. (Weeks, John). *Hinrichsen.* £1.50 NWXPNM (B71-50425)

Jubilemus singuli: for eight-part chorus of mixed voices with organ accompaniment. (Gabrieli, Giovanni). *Schirmer; Chappell. Unpriced* DJ (B71-50016)

Jungk, Klaus.

Alterationen. Op.54: fur Violine, Violoncello und Klavier. *Litolff, Peters; Hinrichsen.* £3.00 NXNT (B71-50427)

Appunti: fur Flote. *Litolff, Peters; Hinrichsen. Unpriced*

VRPMJ (B71-50648)

Kadosa, Pal. Symphony no.8. Op.66. *Boosey and Hawkes. Unpriced* MME (B71-50382)

Kagel, Mauricio. Ludwig van: hommage von Beethoven. *Universal. Unpriced* PS (B71-50441)

Kaiser, Joachim. Great pianists of our time. *Allen and Unwin.* £3.25 AQ/E(M) (B71-16015)

ISBN 0 04 780019 4

Kalabis, Viktor. Variations for horn & piano. Opus 31. Variationen fur Horn und Klavier. Op.31. *Schott.* £1.10 WTP/T (B71-51119)

Kalevala. Op.95: fantasy on Finnish folksongs for concert band. (Creston, Paul). *Schirmer; Chappell. Unpriced* UMJ (B71-50620)

Kamenetz, U. Lenin in Siberia. (Muradeli, Vano). *Workers' Music Association.* £0.13 DW (B71-50773)

Kammermusik no.6. Op.46, no.1: Konzert fur Viola d'amore und Kammerorchester. (Hindemith, Paul). *Schott.* £1.60 MPSQQF (B71-50403)

Kammermusik no.7: Konzert fur Orgel und Kammerorchester. Opus 46, no.2. (Hindemith, Paul). *Schott.* £1.70 MPR (B71-50912)

Karpeles, Maud. Folk songs from Newfoundland. *Faber and Faber Ltd.* £7.00 ADW/G(YSXD) (B71-07869)

ISBN 0 571 09297 7

Kasschau, Howard. Country concerto for young pianists: for piano and orchestra. *Schirmer; Chappell. Unpriced* QNUK/LF (B71-50964)

Kastner, M S.

Canzon for two bassoons & basso continuo. XXIII Canzon a 2 Bassi: fur 2 Fagotte oder Posaune und Fagott und Basso continuo. (Selma y Salaverde, Bartolomeo de). *Schott.* £1.00 VWNTPW (B71-50682)

Fantasia for bassoon in D minor. V Fantasia ex D: fur Fagott und Basso continuo. (Selma y Salaverde, Bartolomeo de). *Schott.* £1.10 VWPJ (B71-50685)

Sonata for bassoon and basso continuo, no.1, in D minor. Sonata prima: fur Fagott und Basso continuo. (Bertoli, Giovanni Antonio). *Schott.* £1.10 VWPE (B71-50683)

Kathleen Ferrier: comprising: The life of Kathleen Ferrier by her sister Winifred Ferrier, and; Kathleen Ferrier: a memoir; edited by Neville Cardus. *Pan Books.* £0.50 AKFQ/E(P) (B71-27231) ISBN 0 330 02627 5

Kay, Norman. Shostakovich. *Oxford University Press.* £0.90 BSGR(N) (B71-29386) ISBN 0 19 315422 6

Kearney, Peter. Songs of brotherhood. *Feldman. Unpriced* JDM (B71-50317)

Keats, Donald. Sonata for piano. Piano sonata. *Boosey and Hawkes.* £1.10 QPE (B71-50463)

Kehr, Gunter. Symphony with fugue in G minor. Sinfonia con fuga, g-Moll. (Richter, Franz Xaver). *Schott.* £1.50 MRE (B71-50409)

Keilmann, Wilhelm. Ich spiele vom Blatt: Schule des Prima-Vista-Spiels fur Klavier und andere Tasteninstrumente. *Litolff, Peters; Hinrichsen.* £3.00 PW/EG (B71-50443)

Kelemen, Milko. Motion: fur Streichquartett. *Litolff, Peters Hinrichsen.* £0.90 RXNS (B71-50549)

Keller, Hans. Hamlet. Op. 48: opera in three acts. (Searle, Humphrey). *Faber. Unpriced* CC (B71-50160)

Kelly, Brian. Sonata for piano. *Novello. Unpriced* QPE (B71-50971)

Kelly, Bryan.

March: Washington D.C. *Novello. Unpriced* WMGM (B71-51097)

O be joyful in the Lord: a Caribbean Jubilate, for SATB and organ. *Novello.* £0.15 DGNT (B71-50008)

Out of the deep. De profundis: anthem for SATB and organ (or brass band). *Novello.* £0.15 DR (B71-50223)

Kelsey, B.

Symphony no.40 in G minor. K.550 - Molto allegro. Mozart 40. (Mozart, Wolfgang Amadeus). *Feldman. Unpriced* WMK (B71-51105)

Symphony no.40 in G minor. K.550. Molto allegro. Mozart 40. (Mozart, Wolfgang Amadeus). *Feldman. Unpriced* QPK (B71-50509)

Kemp's music and recording industry year book (international): a comprehensive reference source and marketing guide to the music and recording industry in Great Britain and overseas

1969/70. *Kemp's Printing and Publishing.* £3.25 A/GB(YC/BC) (B71-08164) ISBN 0 901268 28 3

1970/71. *Kemp's Printing and Publishing.* £3.50 A/GB(YC/BC) (B71-03857) ISBN 0 901268 24 0

Kendell, Iain. Sonata for strings. *Chester. Unpriced* RXME (B71-51007)

Kennan, Kent Wheeler. The technique of orchestration. 2nd ed. *Prentice-Hall.* £4.00 AM/DF (B71-01701)

ISBN 0 13 900316 9

Kennedy, Michael, *b.1926.*

Barbirolli: conductor laureate: the authorised biography. *MacGibbon and Kee.* £2.95 A/EC(P) (B71-27973)

ISBN 0 261 63336 8

The history of the Royal Manchester College of Music, 1893-1972. *Manchester University Press.* £2.40 A(VP/YDJE/X) (B71-16699) ISBN 0 7190 0435 7

The works of Ralph Vaughan Williams. *Oxford University Press.* £0.90 BVD(N) (B71-30151) ISBN 0 19 315423 4

Kennington, Donald. The literature of jazz: a critical guide. *Library Association.* £1.75(£1.40 to members) AMT(T) (B71-03232) ISBN 0 85365 074 8

Kent, Richard. Here's Jupiter: SATB a cappella (or improvised rock accompaniment ad lib). *Warner; Seven Arts; Blossom Music. Unpriced* EZDW (B71-50032)

Kern, Jerome. Show boat. *Chappell.* £0.30 RPVK/CM (B71-51003)

Kettlewell, Dave. The Yetties song book. (Wales, Tony). *English Folk Dance and Song Society. Unpriced* KE/TSDW/G/AYD (B71-50353)

Key Frame: the journal of the Fair Organ Preservation Society

No.1- ; Dec. 1964-. *The Fair Organ Preservation Society.* £0.125(£1.00 yearly) A/FM(B) (B71-18715)

Key to music. (Wishart, Peter). *British Broadcasting Corporation.* £0.90 A/S (B71-24688)

ISBN 0 563 10589 5

Keyboard musicianship. (Duckworth, Guy). *Free Press; Collier-Macmillan. Unpriced* Q/AC (B71-50446)

Khachaturian, Aram. Spartak - Excerpts. Spartacus: love theme. *Plantagenet Music.* £0.20 QPK/JS (B71-50987)

Kidson, Frank. Traditional tunes: a collection of ballad airs 1st ed. reprinted. *S.R. Publishers.* £2.10 AKDW/K/G(YC) (B71-03034) ISBN 0 85409 637 x

Kinderlieder und Volkslieder: fur den systematischen Unterricht am Klavier. (Gabschuss, Klaus Ulbrich). *Schott.* £1.30 QPK/DW/GJ/AY (B71-50513)

King, Nel. Beneath the underdog: his world as composed by Mingus. (Mingus, Charles). *Weidenfeld and Nicolson.* £2.10 AMT/E(P) (B71-19348) ISBN 0 297 00446 8

King Arthur. *See* Purcell, Henry.

King shall rejoice. *See* Handel, George Frideric.

Kipling, Rudyard. The wishing caps. (Binkerd, Gordon). *Boosey and Hawkes.* £0.65 KDW (B71-50335)

Kirby, F E. An introduction to western music: Bach, Beethoven, Wagner, Stravinsky. *Free Press; Collier-Macmillan.* £4.00 A(X) (B71-10428)

ISBN 0 02 917360 4

Kiss, Georges.

Sonatas for treble recorder in C minor & F major. Zwei Sonaten, c-Moll, f-Dur: fur Altenblockflote und Basso continuo. (Konink, Servaas van). *Schott.* £0.80 VSSPE (B71-51083)

Variationen 'Ich geing einmal Spatieren': fur Cembalo (Orgel, Klavier). (Hassler, Hans Leo). *Schott.* £1.50 PWP/T (B71-50445)

Klein, Maynard.

Abendlied. Evening song. Op.91, no.3: for four-part chorus of mixed voices with piano accompaniment. (Brahms, Johannes). *Schirmer; Chappell. Unpriced* DW (B71-50225)

Angelus ad pastores ait. The angel hosts declare: motet for three-part chorus of women's voices a cappella. (Monteverdi, Claudio). *Schirmer; Chappell. Unpriced* FEZDJ (B71-50303)

Hodie Christus natus est. On this day Christ appears: motet for three-part chorus of women's voices a cappella. (Monteverdi, Claudio). *Schirmer; Chappell. Unpriced* EZDJ/LF (B71-50256)

Lied. Op. 29, no.2. In meinen Garten. In my garden. (Schumann, Robert). *Schirmer; Chappell. Unpriced* FDW (B71-50839)

Nachtens. Nightly visions. Op.112, no.2: for four-part chorus of mixed voices with piano accompaniment. (Brahms, Johannes). *Schirmer; Chappell. Unpriced* DW (B71-50226)

Noel: Sus, debout gentilz pasteurs. Now arise ye shepherds mild: for four-part chorus of mixed voices a capella. (Costeley, Guillaume). *Schirmer; Chappell. Unpriced* EZDP/LF (B71-50798)

O schone Nacht. O lovely night. Op.92, no.1: for four-part chorus of mixed voices with piano accompaniment. (Brahms, Johannes). *Schirmer; Chappell. Unpriced* DW (B71-50227)

Psalm 112: for double chorus of mixed voices. (Bruckner, Anton). *Schirmer; Chappell. Unpriced* DR (B71-50220)

Resonet in laudibus. Excerpts. Hodie apparuit. On this day the Christ appears: SSA or TTB. (Lasso, Orlando di). *Schirmer; Chappell. Unpriced* FEZDJ/LF (B71-50304)

Sehnsucht. Longing. Op.112, no.1: for four-part chorus of mixed voices with piano accompaniment. (Brahms, Johannes). *Schirmer; Chappell. Unpriced* DW (B71-50228)

Spatherbst. Late autumn. Op.92, no.2: for four-part chorus of mixed voices with piano accompaniment. (Brahms, Johannes). *Schirmer; Chappell. Unpriced* DW (B71-50229)

Warum. Wherefore should our singing soar. Op.91, no.4: for four-part chorus of mixed voices with piano accompaniment. (Brahms, Johannes). *Schirmer; Chappell. Unpriced* DW (B71-50230)

Kleine Nachtmusik. K.525. Allegro. Mozart 13: serenade no.13 in G major. (Mozart, Wolfgang Amadeus). *Rondor Music; Hansen.* £0.20 QPK (B71-50982)

Kleinmichel, R. Hansel and Gretel: a fairy opera in three acts. (Humperdinck, Engelbert). *Schott. Unpriced* CC (B71-50157)

Klemm, Eberhardt.

Selected piano works of Claude Debussy Vol.3: Preludes, 2e livre. (Debussy, Claude). *Peters; Hinrichsen.* £1.75 QPJ (B71-50478)

Selected piano works ofClaude Debussy Vol.4: Images. (Debussy, Claude). *Peters; Hinrichsen.* £1.50 QPJ (B71-50479)

Klemperer, Otto. Symphony no.2. *Hinrichsen.* £5.00 MME (B71-50383)

Klerk, Albert de. Twelve images b for organ. *Novello.* £0.50 RJ (B71-50996)

Knight, Gerald Hocken.

Accompaniments for unison hymn-singing. *Royal School of Church Music. Unpriced* RK/DM/ED/AY (B71-50531)

A manual of plainsong for Divine Service. (Briggs, H B). *Novello.* £1.25 DTD (B71-50019)

Kobald, Karl. Franz Schubert and his times. *Kennikat Press.* £6.25 BSF(N) (B71-02479) ISBN 0 8046 0756 7

Koch, Edwin. Sonata for cello & basso continuo in G minor. Op.8, no.5. Sonata, g moll: fur Violoncello und Basso continuo. (Defesch, Willem). *Schott.* £0.80 SRPE (B71-50592)

Kodaly, Zoltan. Bicinia hungarica
Vol.4: 60 progressive two-part songs. Revised English ed. *Boosey and Hawkes. Unpriced* FEZDW (B71-50045)
Kodaly, Zoltan.
Children's dances. Excerpts. Four dances nos 9, 5, 4 & 12. *Boosey and Hawkes. £4.00* MK/AH (B71-50069)
Invocation of peace: Bekesser ohajtas: S.A.T.B. unaccompanied. *Boosey and Hawkes. Unpriced* EZDW (B71-50274)
Kodaly, Zoltan. Jesus and the traders: for S.A.T.B. Revised ed. *Universal Music. Unpriced* EZDH (B71-50254)
Kodaly, Zoltan.
Matra pictures: a set of Hungarian folksongs for S.A.T.B. Revised ed. *Universal. Unpriced* EZDW/G/AYG (B71-50285)
Prayer for honour: Szep Konyorges: S.A.T.B. unaccompanied. *Boosey and Hawkes. Unpriced* EZDW (B71-50275)
Kodaly choral method. *(Boosey and Hawkes)* Kodaly Zoltan. Bicinia hungarica
Vol.4: 60 progressive two-part songs. Revised English ed. *Boosey and Hawkes. Unpriced* FEZDW (B71-50045)
Kolneder, Walter.
Antonio Vivaldi: his life and works. *Faber and Faber Ltd. £6.00* BVJ (B71-07863) ISBN 0 571 09386 8
Concerto for bassoon in F major. P.318. Konzert, F-dur fur Fagott und Streichorchester. (Vivaldi, Antonio). *Peters; Hinrichsen. £1.75* RXMPVWF (B71-50541)
Concerto for bassoon in F major. P.318. Konzert, F-dur fur Fagott und Streichorchester
Ausgabe fur Fagott und Klavier. (Vivaldi, Antonio). *Peters; Hinrichsen. £1.20* VWPK/LF (B71-50686)
Sonatas for violin & harpsichord. Op.2. Sonate accademiche. Op.2: fur Violine und bezifferten Bass, Violine und Klavier (Cembalo, Orgel) mit Violoncello ad libitum
Sonata 1, D-dur. (Veracini, Francesco Maria). *Peters Hinrichsen. £0.525* SPE (B71-50560)
Sonatas for violin & harpsichord. Op.2. Sonate accademiche. Op.2: fur Violine und bezifferten Bass, Violine und Klavier (Cembalo, Orgel) mit Violoncello ad libitum
Sonata 2, B-dur. (Veracini, Francesco Maria). *Peters Hinrichsen. £0.525* SPE (B71-50561)
Sonatas for violin & harpsichord. Op.2. Sonate accademiche. Op.2: fur Violine und bezifferten Bass, Violine und Klavier (Cembalo, Orgel) mit Violoncello ad libitum
Sonata 3, C-dur. (Veracini, Francesco Maria). *Peters Hinrichsen. £0.525* SPE (B71-50562)
Sonatas for violin & harpsichord. Op.2. Sonate accademiche. Op.2: fur Violine und bezifferten Bass, Violine und Klavier (Cembalo, Orgel) mit Violoncello ad libitum
Sonata 4, F-dur. (Veracini, Francesco Maria). *Peters Hinrichsen. £0.725* SPE (B71-50563)
Sonatas for violin & harpsichord. Op.2. Sonate accademiche. Op.2: fur Violine und bezifferten Bass, Violine und Klavier (Cembalo, Orgel) mit Violoncello ad libitum
Sonata 7, d-moll. (Veracini, Francesco Maria). *Peters Hinrichsen. Unpriced* SPE (B71-50564)
Sonatas for violin & harpsichord. Op.2. Sonate accademiche. Op.2: fur Violine und bezifferten Bass, Violine und Klavier (Cembalo, Orgel) mit Violoncello ad libitum
Sonata 8, e-moll. (Veracini, Francesco Maria). *Peters Hinrichsen. £0.80* SPE (B71-50565)
Sonatas for violin & harpsichord. Op.2. Sonate accademiche. Op.2: fur Violine und bezifferten Bass, Violine und Klavier (Cembalo, Orgel) mit Violoncello ad libitum
Sonata 9, A-dur. (Veracini, Francesco Maria). *Peters Hinrichsen. £0.80* SPE (B71-50566)
Sonatas for violin & harpsichord. Op.2. Sonate accademiche. Op.2: fur Violine und bezifferten Bass, Violine und Klavier (Cembalo, Orgel) mit Violoncello ad libitum
Sonata 12, d-moll. (Veracini, Francesco Maria). *Peters Hinrichsen. £0.80* SPE (B71-50567)
Konink, Servaas van. Sonatas for treble recorder in C minor & F major. Zwei Sonaten, c Moll, f Dur fu Altenblockflote und Basso continuo. *Schott. £0.80* VSSPE (B71-51083)
Konzert, C-Dur: fur Viola und Orchestra. (Brixi, Franz Xaver). *Schott. £1.30* SQPK/LF (B71-50120)
Korn, Peter Jona. Rhapsody: for oboe and strings (1951). Piano score. *Simrock. £1.00* VTPK (B71-50666)
Kostelanetz, Richard. John Cage. *Allen Lane. £3.15* BCBG (B71-14242) ISBN 0 7139 0210 8
Kovats, Barna.
Malinconia: funf Gitarrenstucke. (Bresgen, Cesar). *Schott. £0.80* TSPMJ (B71-50608)
Minutenstucke: fur Gitarre. *Schott. £0.70* TSPMJ (B71-50132)
Kowal, Ada May. Music in school. *Bond Street Publishers. £1.00* A(VC) (B71-10424) ISBN 0 901373 08 7
Kraft, Walter. Toccata, 'Ite, missa est': fur Orgel. *London; Schott. £1.00* RJ (B71-50526)
Krivak, Margaret. Make your own musical instruments. (Mandell, Muriel). New ed. *Bailey Bros and Swinfen. £1.40* AL/BC (B71-01700) ISBN 0 561 00083 2
Krommer, Franz.
Octet-partita. Op.79: for 2 oboes, 2 clarinets, 2 horns, 2 bassoons and contrabassoon ad lib. *Musica rara. Unpriced* UNNG (B71-50627)
Quartet for bassoon, 2 violas & cello in B flat major. Op.46, no.1. Quartet in B flat. Op,46, no.1: for bassoon, 2 violas & cello or bassoon, violin, viola and cello. *Musica rara. Unpriced* NVNS (B71-50422)
Suite for wind octet, no.4, in F major. Octet-partita: for 2 oboes, 2 clarinets, 2 horns, 2 bassoons and contrabassoon ad. lib. Op.57. *Musica rara. £5.50* UNNG (B71-50138)
Suite for wind octet, no.5, in B flat major. Octet-partita: for 2 oboes, 2 clarinets, 2 horns, 2 bassoons and contrabassoon ad. lib. Op.67. *Musica rara. £5.25* UNNG (B71-50139)
Kubelik, Rafael. Sonatina for piano, 2 hands. Sonatina: fur Klavier zu zwei Handen. *Litolff, Peters; Hinrichsen. £1.50* QNVEM (B71-50453)
Kugler, Frans. Sehnsucht. Longing. Op.112, no.1: for four-part chorus of mixed voices with piano accompaniment. (Brahms, Johannes). *Schirmer; Chappell. Unpriced* DW (B71-50228)
Kuhnau, Johann. Clavier Ubung. Tl.2. Partie for keyboard, no.3 in E minor. Suite in A minor. *Novello. Unpriced* TSNUK/AG (B71-51050)
Kupkovic, Ladislav. Dio: Orchesterspiele mit Dirigieren. *Universal. Unpriced* MMJ (B71-50394)
Kurzbach, Paul. Trio for violin, cello & piano. Trio fur Violine, Violoncello und Klavier. *Litolff; Hinrichsen. £1.40* NXNT (B71-50428)
Kutsch, K J. A concise biographical dictionary of singers: from the beginning of recorded sound to the present. *Chilton Book Company. £7.50* AB/E(M/C) (B71-24692) ISBN 0 8019 5516 5
Kwmbayah: African tune. (Dinham, Kenneth J). *Oxford University Press. £0.04* GEZDW (B71-50857) ISBN 0 19 341019 2
La Fontaine, Jean de. Due voci: per soprano, martenot solo ed orchestra su un frammento di Jean de la Fontaine. (Bussotti, Sylvano). *Universal. Unpriced* KFLE/MPPSDW (B71-50357)
La lo and lullaby: berceuse de Noe: two part song. (Nelson, Havelock). *Lengnick. £0.05* FDP/LF (B71-50037)
La suite infantil: colecao de 5 pecas for piano No.2: Nene vai dormir. (Villa-Lobos, Heitor). *Arthur Napoleao; Essex Music. Unpriced* QPG (B71-50468)
Lachner, Franz. Octet for wind instruments in B flat major. Op.156. Octet for flute, oboe, 2 clarinets, 2 horns and 2 bassoons. Op.156. *Musica rara. £5.25* UNN (B71-50137)
Lai, Francis.
Love story: theme from the film. *Chappell. Unpriced* WMK/JR (B71-50710)
Love story: theme from the film. *Chappell. Unpriced* UMMK/JR (B71-51064)
Lalo, Edouard. Concerto for violin in G minor, 'Concerto russe'. Op. 29 - Excerpts. Chants russes. *Schott. Unpriced* SRPK (B71-51034)
Lamb: for full chorus of mixed voices a cappella. (Chorbajian, John). *Schirmer; Chappell. Unpriced* EZDH (B71-50252)
Lambert, Cecily. Greek scenes. *Forsyth. Unpriced* QPJ (B71-50094)
Lambton worm: a folk tale from the North, for speakers, singers and tuned percussion. (Hutchinson, Godfrey). *Leeds Music. Unpriced* JFE/XMDX (B71-50327)
Lanchbery, John.
Tales of Beatrix Potter: music from the film. *E.M.I. Film Music; Keith Prowse Music. £0.40* QPK/AHM/JR (B71-50512)
Tales of Beatrix Potter: selection from the ballet. *E.M.I. Film Music; Keith Prowse Music. y1.50* WMK/AHM/JR (B71-51107)
Landon, Howard Chandler Robbins. Symphony no.35 in D major. K.385, 'Haffner'. Symphony in D. K.385, 'Haffner' symphony. (Mozart, Wolfgang Amadeus). *Faber Music. £2.75* MME (B71-50905)
Landor, Walter Savage. Mother, I cannot mind my wheel. (Chagrin, Francis). *Ricordi. Unpriced* EZDW (B70-50030)
Landschaftspartitur: fur Klavier. (Heider, Werner). *Litolff Hinrichsen. £3.25* QPJ (B71-50486)
Lane, Burton.
On a clear day you can see forever. *Chappell. Unpriced* WMK/CM (B71-50153)
On a clear day you can see forever. *Chappell. £0.25* QPK/CM (B71-50984)
Langdon, John.
I will exalt thee: full anthem for four voices. (Tye, Christopher). *Novello. £0.15* EZDK (B71-50027)
O God be merciful unto us. (Deus misereatur): SATB (full). (Tye, Christopher). Revised ed. *Oxford University Press. Unpriced* EZDGPS (B71-50250) ISBN 0 19 352146 6
O God be merciful unto us. (Deus misereatur): SATB (full) with verse for SATB. (Tye, Christopher). Revised ed. *Oxford University Press. Unpriced* EZDGPS (B71-50251) ISBN 0 19 352147 4
Langley, Michael. The Lambton worm: a folk tale from the North, for speakers, singers and tuned percussion. (Hutchinson, Godfrey). *Leeds Music. Unpriced* JFE/XMDX (B71-50327)
Laporte, Andre. Reflections. Inner-space music: clarinet solo. *Chester. Unpriced* VVPMJ (B71-50680)
Largo and allegretto. (Bach, Johann Sebastian). *Schott. Unpriced* SRPK (B71-51032)
Larner, Gerald. The lion, the witch and the wardrobe: an opera. (McCabe, John). *Novello. £1.25* CC (B71-50158)
Larousse encyclopaedia of music. *Hamlyn. £6.30* A(C) (B71-25341) ISBN 0 600 02396 6
Lasocki, David.
Quintet for horn and strings in E major. Op.106. Quintet in E major. Op.106: for horn and string quartet (double bass ad lib). (Reicha, Anton Joseph). *Musica rara. Unpriced* NVNR (B71-50926)
Sonata for flute, violin, oboe and basso continuo in C major. Op.4. Sonata da camera in C major: for flute, violin, oboe and basso continuo. (Janitsch, Johann Gottlieb). *Musica rara. £1.50* NWPNSE (B71-50424)
Sonata for flute, violin, oboe & basso continuo in C major. Op.4. Sonata da camera in C major. Op.4: for flute, violin, oboe & basso continuo. (Janitsch, Johann Gottlieb). *Musica rara. £1.50* NUPNSE (B71-50079)
Lasso, Orlando di. Resonet in laudibus. Excerpts. Hodie apparuit. On this day the Christ appears: SSA or TTB. *Schirmer; Chappell. Unpriced* FEZDJ/LF (B71-50304)
Last, Joan.
Freedom technique: exercises and studies for piano
Book 1: Beginners to grade 3 (USA2). *Oxford University Press. £0.40* Q/AF (B71-50941) ISBN 0 19 373117 7
Book 2: Grades 3-4 (USA 2-2 1/2). *Oxford University Press. £0.40* Q/AF (B71-50942) ISBN 0 19 373118 5
Book 3: Grade 5 (USA3) upwards. *Oxford University Press. £0.50* Q/AF (B71-50943) ISBN 0 19 373119 3
Last voyage: part-song for S.A. and piano. (Enfield, Patrick). *Elkin. £0.07* FDW (B71-50042)
Laudate Dominum. K.339, no.5. (Mozart, Wolfgang Amadeus). *Oxford University Press. Unpriced* FDGKJ (B71-50826) ISBN 0 19 342590 4
Laurie, Margaret. The works of Henry Purcell
Vol.26: King Arthur; edited by Dennis Arundell, revised by Margaret Laurie. (Purcell, Henry). *Novello. £4.50* C/AZ (B71-50156)
Laus Deo: for organ. (Harvey, Jonathan). *Novello. £0.30* RJ (B71-50524)
Lawes, William. Six songs. *Schott. £0.65* KDW (B71-50883)
Lawrence, Ian.
Fifty simple rounds: for singers, recorders and other instruments. *Novello. £0.30* FE/VSDW/XC (B71-50301)
A Haydn solo album: eleven short pieces. (Haydn, Joseph). *Oxford University Press. £0.60* WSPK (B71-50716) ISBN 0 19 357066 1
Words and music. *Longman. £0.40* A(VG) (B71-08785) ISBN 0 582 18694 3
Words and music
Introduction. *Longman. £2.50* A(VG) (B71-22574) ISBN 0 582 18695 1
Stage 1. *Longman. £0.40* A(VG) (B71-06126) ISBN 0 582 18691 9
Stage 2. *Longman. £0.40* A(VG) (B71-06127) ISBN 0 582 18692 7
Stage 3. *Longman. £0.40* A(VG) (B71-06128) ISBN 0 582 18693 5
Lawson, Gordon. How far is it to Bethlehem?: West country carol. *Royal School of Church Music. £0.05* EZDP/LF (B71-50800)
Lawson, Peter. Momenta 94: for solo piano. *Peters, Hinrichsen. £1.25* QPJ (B71-50487)
Laycock, Geoffrey. New Catholic hymnal. (Petti, Anthony). *Faber Music. Unpriced* DM/LSB/AY (B71-50758) ISBN 0 571 10001 5
Le Fanu, Nicola. Variations for oboe quartet. *Novello. £1.75* NVTNS (B71-50931)
Le Huray, Peter. Mr Henry Noell, his funerall psalmes. Seven hymn tunes. Lamentio Henrici Noel: S.A.T.B. Nos. 1-4. (Dowland, John). Revised ed. *Oxford University Press. Unpriced* EZDR/KDN (B71-50809) ISBN 0 19 352157 1
Le Jeune, Claude. Meslanges. Liv. 2 - Excerpts. Helas! mon Dieu: SAATB unacc. *Oxford University Press. Unpriced* EZDH (B71-50791)
Leaf, Robert. I hear a song: for full chorus of mixed voices a cappella. *Schirmer; Chappell. Unpriced* EZDW (B71-50276)
Lear, Edward. Seven limericks: for two-part choir & small orchestra. (Bush, Geoffrey). *Novello. £0.50* FE/MDX (B71-50044)
Learning to teach through playing: a woodwind method. (Hilton, Lewis B). *Addison-Wesley. Unpriced* V/AC (B71-50140)
Lebermann, Walter.
Adagio and fugue for two flutes & string orchestra. Adagio und Fuge: fur 2 Querfloten und Streicher. Falck 65. (Bach, Wilhelm Friedemann). *Schott. £1.00* RXMPVRNU/Y (B71-50540)
Il Cimentia dell'armonia e dell'inventione. Op.8. Concerto for oboe & string orchestra in C major. Konzert, C-Dur fur Oboe, Streichorchester und General bass. (Vivaldi, Antonio). *Schott. £0.90* VTPK/LF (B71-50667)
Concerto for cello & string orchestra, no.3 in G major. WV480. Konzert no.3, G-Dur: fur Violoncello und Streichorchester. (Boccherini, Luigi). *Schott. £1.50* VRPK/LF (B71-50143)
Concerto for clarinet & string orchestra, no.1, in F major. Konzert no.1, F-Dur: fur Klarinette (B) und Streicher, zwei Oboen und zwei Horner ad lib. (Stamitz, Carl). Klavierauszug. *Schott. £2.00* VVPK/LF (B71-50678)
Concerto for two violas, strings & basso continuo in G major. Konzert, G-Dur: fur 2 Violen, Streicher und Basso continuo. (Telemann, Georg Philip). *Schott. Unpriced* SQNTPWK/LF (B71-50119)
Concerto for viola in C major. Konzert, C-Dur: fur Viola, Streicher, 2 Oboen und 2 Horner
Klavierauszug von Helmut May. (Hoffstetter, Roman). *Schott. £1.80* SQPK/LF (B71-50583)
Concerto fur viola in C major. Konzert, C-Dur: fur Viola und Orchestra. (Brixi, Franz Xaver). *Schott. £1.30* SQPK/LF (B71-50120)
Duets for cellos, nos.1-3. Op.51. Drei Duette: fur Violoncelli. Op.51. (Offenbach, Jacques). *Schott. £1.20* SRNU (B71-50590)
Sinfonia in D major. Sinfonia, D-Dur. (Dittersdorf, Carl Ditters von). *Schott. £1.50* MRE (B71-50408)
Symphony in D major. Falck 64. Sinfonie D-Dur. Falck 64. (Bach, Wilhelm Friedemann). *Schott. £1.20* MRE

(B71-50407)
Lee, S. Abendlied. Op.85, no.12. (Schumann, Robert). *Schott. Unpriced* SRPK (B71-51036)
Legendes. Two legends. (Liszt, Franz). *Peters; Hinrichsen. £0.40* QPJ (B71-50490)
Lehmann, Hans Ulrich. Instants: pour piano. *Schott. £1.50* QPJ (B71-50488)
Lehmann, Lotte. Eighteen song cycles: studies in their interpretations. *Cassell. £2.40* AB/E (B71-25345) ISBN 0 304 93842 4
Lehn, Franz. Vortragsbuchlein fur das Zusammenspiel: Sopran-und Altblockflote, Schlagwerk ad lib. (Rohr, Heinrich). *Schott. Unpriced* VSNUK/AAY (B71-50654)
Leigh, Eric. Two hymn preludes: for organ. *Feldman. £0.20* RJ (B71-50997)
Leighton, Kenneth.
Conflicts. Op. 51: fantasy on two themes for piano. *Novello. Unpriced* QPJ (B71-50977)
Sonata for cello solo. Op.52. *Novello. £0.50* SRPME (B71-50598)
Lekberg, Sven.
Come o'er the eastern hills: for four-part chorus of mixed voices a cappella. *Schirmer; Chappell. Unpriced* EZDW (B71-50278)
Little sorrows sit and weep: for four-part chorus of mixed voices a cappella. *Schirmer; Chappell. Unpriced* EZDW (B71-50279)
Three peavinations: for mixed chorus
1: Pavane. *Schirmer; Chappell. Unpriced* EZDW (B71-50280)
2: Moment musical. *Schirmer; Chappell. Unpriced* EZDW (B71-50281)
3: Counterpoint. *Schirmer; Chappell. Unpriced* EZDW (B71-50282)
Lendvai, Erno. Bela Bartok: an analysis of his music. *Kahn and Averill. £2.00* BBG (B71-30147) ISBN 0 900707 04 6
Lengyel, Endre. Violoncello music for beginners. *Boosey and Hawkes. £0.80* SRPK/AAY (B71-50595)
Lenin in Siberia. (Muradeli, Vano). *Workers' Music Association. £0.13* DW (B71-50773)
Lenin Lieder: fur Gesang und Klavier von Komponisten der Deutschen Demokratischen Republik. *Peters; Hinrichsen. £1.05* KDW/AYEE (B71-50345)
Lenkei, Gabriella. Violin music for beginners. *Boosey and Hawkes. £0.80* SPK/AAY (B71-50572)
Lennon, John.
50 great songs. *Northern Songs (Music Sales). £1.50* RK/DW (B71-51000)
50 great songs. *Northern Songs (Music Sales). £1.25* RPVK/DW (B71-51005)
Let it be: souvenir song album of 8 songs from the film. *Northern Songs. £0.75* JNCDW/JR (B71-50330)
Songs of John Lennon. *Wise Publications, Music Sales. £1.50* KDW (B71-50884)
Leonard, Harry. The power and the glory. *Novello. £1.75* EMDH (B71-50023)
Leonard Bernstein's young people's concerts. (Bernstein, Leonard). Revised and expanded ed.. *Cassell. £2.10* A (B71-25914) ISBN 0 304 93819 x
Lerchner, Juliane. New compendium of piano technique Book 2: Reiteration with and without changing fingers. *Peters; Hinrichsen. £1.25* Q/AF (B71-50448)
Lerner, Alan Jay. Paint your wagon: a musical play. (Loewe, Frederick). *Chappell. Unpriced* CM (B71-50731)
Leslie, John. Tyrolean carnival: accordion solo. *Bosworth. £0.15* RSPMJ (B71-50112)
Let it be: souvenir song album of 8 songs from the film. (Lennon, John). *Northern Songs. £0.75* JNCDW/JR (B71-50330)
Lethbridge, Lionel.
A Handel solo album: for trumpet or trombone & piano (or bassoon & piano). (Handel, George Frideric). *Oxford University Press. £0.60* WSPK/DH (B71-50717) ISBN 0 19 356971 x
Psalm 45. Excerpts. Heart's adoration: two-part. (Marcello, Benedetto). *Oxford University Press. Unpriced* DH/LFL (B71-50014)
Leufgen, Natalie. Die Sonne der Inkas: fur Sopran, 3 Sprecher und II Instrumentalisten. (Denisov, Edisson). *Universal. Unpriced* KFLE/MRDX (B71-50358)
Levey, Michael. The life & death of Mozart. *Weidenfeld and Nicolson. £3.00* BMS(N) (B71-28693) ISBN 0 297 00477 8
Lewis, Clive Staples. The lion, the witch and the wardrobe. *Adaptations.* The lion, the witch and the wardrobe: an opera. (McCabe, John). *Novello. £1.25* CC (B71-50158)
Lewis, Eiluned. Song of the refugee children; and, Chorus of the Holy Innocents. (Simpson, Lionel). *Feldman. Unpriced* EZDP/LF (B71-50802)
Lewkovitch, Bernhard. Twelve motets of the Spanish golden age. *Chester. Unpriced* EZDJ/AYK (B71-50795)
Liber organi. Altitalienische Orgelmeister
2. (Szigeti, Kilian). *Schott. £0.30* R/AYJ (B71-50991)
Library Association. The literature of jazz: a critical guide. (Kennington, Donald). *Library Association. £1.75(£1.40 to members)* AMT(T) (B71-03232) ISBN 0 85365 074 8
Library of communication techniques. *(Focal Press)* Manvell, Roger. The technique of film music. 1st ed. reprinted. *Focal Press. £3.00* A/JR (B71-05268) ISBN 0 240 44943 6
Lieder und Tanze der Vorklassik: Stuke aus dem 16. bis 18. Jahrhundert fur Gitarre sehr leicht gesetzt. (Brodszky, Ferenc). *Schott. Unpriced* TSPMK (B71-50612)
Life & death of Mozart. (Levey, Michael). *Weidenfeld and Nicolson. £3.00* BMS(N) (B71-28693) ISBN 0 297 00477 8
Lift up your heads. (The ascension). (Rorem, Ned). *Boosey and Hawkes. y4.50* DH/LM (B71-50749)
Lift up your heads. (The ascension). (Rorem, Ned). *Boosey and Hawkes. £1.10* ENYHXPNRDH/LM (B71-50784)
Ligeti, Gyorgy. Artikulation: electronic music: an aural score. *Schott. Unpriced* PS (B71-50080)
Ligeti, Gyorgy. Continuum: fur Cembalo. *Schott. £1.20* QRPJ (B71-50106)
Light of Christmas: unison with piano or 2-stave organ, the winner of the 1970 'Carol for a future' competition. (Thorpe, Frank). *Weinberger. £0.05* JFDP/LF (B71-50051)
Linde, Hans Martin. Music for a bird: for treble recorder solo. *Schott. £0.70* VSSPMJ (B71-50660)
Linklater, Eric. The music of the north. *Haddo House Choral Society. £0.30* AD/E(QB/YDLSH) (B71-09739) ISBN 0 9501767 0 2
Lion, the witch and the wardrobe: an opera. (McCabe, John). *Novello. £1.25* CC (B71-50158)
Lipkin, Malcolm. Mosaics: for chamber orchestra. *Chester. Unpriced* MRJ (B71-50921)
Lisken, Gerd. Vibration: model for a group improvisation with Orff instrumentation or other intstruments sic. *Schott. £1.20* XN (B71-51121)
Liszt, Franz.
Ballades for piano. Two ballades. *Peters, Hinrichsen. £0.50* QPJ (B71-50489)
Complete organ works of Franz Liszt
Vol.1. *Boosey and Hawkes. Unpriced* R/AZ (B71-50517)
Dante symphony. Symphonie zu Dantes Divina commedia: fur Frauenchor und Orchester. *Eulenburg. £2.10* FE/MDX (B71-50298)
Legendes. Two legends. *Peters; Hinrichsen. £0.40* QPJ (B71-50490)
Two episodes from Lenau's Faust. No.2. First Mephisto waltz. The Mephisto waltz. *Twentieth Century Music. £0.20* QPK/JR (B71-50514)
Liszt. (Walker, Alan, *b.1930*). *Faber and Faber Ltd. £1.50* BLJ(N) (B71-10425) ISBN 0 571 09120 2
Literature of jazz: a critical guide. (Kennington, Donald). *Library Association. £1.75(£1.40 to members)* AMT(T) (B71-03232) ISBN 0 85365 074 8
Little African suite: for piano. Opus 44. (Camilleri, Charles). *Novello. Unpriced* QPG (B71-50469)
Little cycle: for solo clarinet. (Waters, Charles Frederick). *Hinrichsen. £0.35* VVPMJ (B71-50681)
Little dance; and, Waltz: for cello and piano. (Maxwell, Michael). *Schott. Unpriced* SRPH (B71-51021)
Little hymn to Mary: carol for SATB and piano or organ. (Wilson-Dickson, Andrew). *Novello. Unpriced* DP/LF (B71-50766)
Little sorrows sit and weep: for four-part chorus of mixed voices a cappella. (Lekberg, Sven). *Schirmer; Chappell. Unpriced* EZDW (B71-50279)
Little tune for St Mark's Day. Op.71, no.1: organ solo. (Garlick, George T). *George T. Garlick. Unpriced* RJ (B71-50995)
Lives of the great composers. (Schonberg, Harold C). *Davis-Poynter Ltd. £5.00* A/D(YB/M) (B71-26600) ISBN 0 7067 0001 5
Lloyd, Tracey.
The Christmas jazz: for unison voices with piano accompaniment and guitar chords. (Chappell, Herbert). *Clarabella Music. Unpriced* CN/LF (B71-50171)
The Goliath jazz: for unison voices with piano accompaniment and guitar chords. (Chappell, Herbert). *Clarabella Music. Unpriced* CN/L (B71-50166)
The Jericho jazz: for unison voices with piano accompaniment and guitar chords. (Chappell, Herbert). *Clarabella Music. Unpriced* CN/L (B71-50167)
The Noah jazz: for unison voices with piano accompaniment and guitar chords. (Chappell, Herbert). *Clarabella Music. Unpriced* CN/L (B71-50168)
The prodigal son jazz: for unison voices with piano accompaniment and guitar chords. (Chappell, Herbert). *Clarabella Music. Unpriced* CN/L (B71-50169)
The Red Sea jazz: for unison voices with piano accompaniment and guitar chords. (Chappell, Herbert). *Clarabella Music. Unpriced* CN/L (B71-50170)
Lloyd-Jones, David. Eugene Onegin: lyric scenes in three acts and seven scenes. (Tchaikovsky, Peter). *Schauer and May. Unpriced* CC (B71-50730)
Lobos, Heitor Villa-. *See* Villa-Lobos, Heitor.
Locke, Matthew. Turn thy face from my sins: verse anthem for A.T.B. and chorus, SSATB. *Oxford University Press. Unpriced* DK (B71-50195)
Loewe, Frederick. Paint your wagon: a musical play. *Chappell. Unpriced* CM (B71-50731)
Logan's complete tutor: for the Highland bagpipe, and with a selection of marches, quicksteps, laments, strathspeys, reels & country dances followed by piobaireachd exercises & the famous piobaireachd, Cha till McCruimein (MacCrimmon will never return). Revised ed. *Paterson. Unpriced* VY/AC (B71-50687)
Logs: for 1 or more string basses. (Chihara, Paul). *Protone Music; Henmar Music; Hinrichsen. £1.00* SSN (B71-50601)
London College of Music. Examinations in pianoforte playing and singing: sight reading tests, sight singing tests as set throughout 1970. Grades I-VIII & diplomas. *Ashdown. £0.25* Q/EG (B71-50084)
London trios. (Haydn, Joseph). *Schirmer; Chappell. Unpriced* TSNTK (B71-51049)
Long, Maureen W. Music in British libraries: a directory of resources. *Library Association. £1.50(£1.20 to members of the Library Association)* A(U/YC/BC) (B71-26836) ISBN 0 85365 005 5
Longmire, John.
Fancy free: for piano. *Freeman. £0.30* QPJ (B71-50978)
Playing for pleasure: for piano
Book 3: Grade 1. *Bosworth. £0.225* QPJ (B71-50095)
Twelve floral sketches: for piano. *Bosworth. £0.20* QPJ (B71-50096)
Lookin' ahead (six feet under): S.A.B. (Rocherolle, Eugenie R). *Warner; Blossom Music. Unpriced* DW (B71-50774)
Lord, David. A prayer for peace: SATB unacc. *Oxford University Press. Unpriced* EZDH (B71-50025) ISBN 0 19 350320 4
Lord shall increase you: for SSAB chorus (or SATB). (Peter, Johann Friedrich). *Boosey and Hawkes. £0.09* DH (B71-50189)
Lorenzo Fernandez, Oscar.
Cancao do mar: canto e piano. *Arthur Napoleao; Essex Music. Unpriced* KDW (B71-50341)
Noturno: canto e piano. *Arthur Napoleao; Essex Music. Unpriced* KDW (B71-50342)
Suites for piano. Excerpts. Caminho da serra; and Cacando Borboletas; and, Madrugada; and, Na Beira do Rio. *Arthur Napoleao; Essex Music. Unpriced* SPMK (B71-50580)
Los Rios, Waldo de. *See* Rios, Waldo de los.
Louis: the Louis Armstrong story, 1900-1971. (Jones, Max). *Studio Vista. £3.20* AMT/E(P) (B71-25343) ISBN 0 289 70215 1
Love came down at Christmas: SATB. (Rutter, John). *Oxford University Press. Unpriced* DP/LF (B71-50764) ISBN 0 19 343025 8
Love story: theme from the film. (Lai, Francis). *Chappell. Unpriced* WMK/JR (B71-50710)
Love story: theme from the film. (Lai, Francis). *Chappell. Unpriced* UMMK/JR (B71-51064)
Lovelock, William. Elementary accompaniment writing. *Bell. £1.40* AQ/D/ED (B71-24689) ISBN 0 7135 1961 4
Lucie-Smith, Edward. Three surrealist songs: for mezzo-soprano, tape and piano doubling bongos by John Tavener; poems by Edward Lucie-Smith. (Tavener, John). *Chester. Unpriced* KFNE/NYLNUDW (B71-50893)
Ludwig van: hommage von Beethoven. (Kagel, Mauricio). *Universal. Unpriced* PS (B71-50441)
Lullaby: for four solo instruments, optional solo bassoon or solo cello, and string orchestra or piano. (Chagrin, Francis). *Novello. £1.55* MJ (B71-50902)
Lunn, John E. Ralph Vaughan Williams: a pictorial biography. *Oxford University Press. £3.30* BVD(N) (B71-30150) ISBN 0 19 315420 x
Lute music of Francesco Canova da Milano (1497-1543) Vols I and II. (Francesco, *da Milano*). *Harvard University Press. Unpriced* TW/AZ (B71-50617)
Lynn, George. Psalm 42. Ainsi qu'on oit le cerf bruire. So my heart seeks ever after: for four-part chorus of mixed voices a cappella. (Goudimel, Claude). *Schirmer; Chappell. Unpriced* EZDR (B71-50262)
Lynn, Lucile. Psalm 42. Ainsi qu'on oit le cerf bruire. So my heart seeks ever after: for four-part chorus of mixed voices a cappella. (Goudimel, Claude). *Schirmer; Chappell. Unpriced* EZDR (B71-50262)
McAuley, James. Six miniatures. (Wishart, Peter). *Stainer and Bell. £1.50* KDW (B71-50344)
McBradd, Leigh.
Three peavinations: for mixed chorus
1: Pavane. (Lekberg, Sven). *Schirmer; Chappell. Unpriced* EZDW (B71-50280)
2: Moment musical. (Lekberg, Sven). *Schirmer; Chappell. Unpriced* EZDW (B71-50281)
3: Counterpoint. (Lekberg, Sven). *Schirmer; Chappell. Unpriced* EZDW (B71-50282)
McCabe, John.
Capriccio (1969): for piano. *Novello. £0.50* QPJ (B71-50491)
Concertante music. *Novello. £2.50* MMJ (B71-50395)
Concertino for piano duet & orchestra (1968). *Novello. Unpriced* MPQNVFL (B71-50076)
The lion, the witch and the wardrobe: an opera. *Novello. £1.25* CC (B71-50158)
McCarthy, Albert John. The dance band era: the dancing decades from ragtime to swing, 1910-1950. *Studio Vista. £4.20* AMT/E(M/XMK41) (B71-30152) ISBN 0 289 70218 6
McCartney, Paul.
50 great songs. (Lennon, John). *Northern Songs (Music Sales). £1.50* RK/DW (B71-51000)
50 great songs. (Lennon, John). *Northern Songs (Music Sales). £1.25* RPVK/DW (B71-51005)
Let it be: souvenir song album of 8 songs from the film. (Lennon, John). *Northern Songs. £0.75* JNCDW/JR (B71-50330)
MacColl, Ewan. Sweet Thames flow softly: part-song, SATB. (Roe, Betty). *Thames. Unpriced* EZDW (B71-50817)
McDonald, Jacqueline. Songs for singing folk: Jackie and Bridies second song book. *Galliard. Unpriced* KFE/TSDW/G/AYC (B71-50355)
Macdonald starters. *(Macdonald and Co.)* Music. *Macdonald and Co. £0.25* A (B71-19965) ISBN 0 356 03759 2
Macero, Ted. One-three quarters: piccolo (flute), violin, violoncello, trombone, tuba and two pianos. *Peters Hinrichsen. £1.75* NUXPNP (B71-50418)
McFarland, Ollie. Joy. Excerpts. Brown baby: for chorus of treble voices (SSA) and piano. (Brown, Oscar). *Novello. £0.09* FDW (B71-50041)
McGuinness, Rosamond. English court odes, 1660-1820. *Clarendon Press. £7.00* ADE/KM(YD/XEY161) (B71-27232) ISBN 0 19 816119 0
Mackerras, Charles. The overlanders: suite for orchestra. (Ireland, John). *Boosey and Hawkes. £2.50* MMG (B71-50070)
McLean, Hugh. Two voluntaries: for organ. (Blow, John). *Novello. £0.35* RJ (B71-50521)
McLeish, Kenneth.

Three six-part pieces. (Josquin des Pres). *Schott. £0.30* VSNQK/DW (B71-51075)
Two five-part pieces. (Josquin des Pres). *Schott. £0.40* VSNRK/DW (B71-51076)
MacLellan, Gene.
Snowbird. *Ardmore and Beechwood. Unpriced* UMMK/DW (B71-51063)
Snowbird. *Ardmore and Beechwood. Unpriced* WMK/DW (B71-51109)
McLeod, Donald, *b.1921*. The classical guitar: design and construction. *Dryad Press. £2.50* ATS/BC (B71-14735) ISBN 0 85219 077 8
Macleod, Kenneth. Rune of hospitality. Op. 15: song with piano accompaniment. (Rubbra, Edmund). Revised ed.. *Lengnick. Unpriced* KDW (B71-50886)
McMullen, Elli. Twelve folk dances from many lands. *Schott. £0.70* VSRPK/DW/G/AYB (B71-51081)
McNeill, Mary. Songs of the seaside: three songs for unison voices, piano, tuned and rhythm percussion. *Keith Prowse Music. £0.90* JFE/NYLDW (B71-50325)
Maconchy, Elizabeth. Music for double bass and piano. *Yorke. Unpriced* SSPJ (B71-50125)
Macpherson, Charles. Thou, O God art praised in Sion: short anthem. *Novello. £0.06* FLDH (B71-50310)
Madame Press died last week at ninety: for small orchestra. (Feldman, Morton). *Universal. Unpriced* MRJ (B71-50411)
Madonna, per voi ardo. Ah love, my heart is burning: for SATB chorus. (Verdelot, Philippe). *Warner; Blossom Music. Unpriced* EZDU (B71-50267)
Maestro. (Milan, Luis). *Pennsylvania University Press. Unpriced* TVPMJ (B71-50616) ISBN 0 271 00091 0
Magdalen, cease from sobs and sighs: SATB unacc. (Hurford, Peter). *Oxford University Press. Unpriced* EZDP/LL (B71-50028)
Mahler, Gustav. Symphony no.5 in C minor. Excerpts. Adagietto. The timeless moment: song. *Chappell. £0.20* KDW (B71-50885)
Maine, Basil. Three plainsong preludes: for organ. *Boosey and Hawkes. Unpriced* RJ (B71-50527)
Mairants, Ivor.
Fur Elise. (Beethoven, Ludwig van). *British and Continental. Unpriced* TSPMK (B71-50135)
Six easy pieces: for classic guitar. *British and Continental. Unpriced* TSPMJ (B71-50133)
Make your own musical instruments. (Mandell, Muriel). New ed. *Bailey Bros and Swinfen. £1.40* AL/BC (B71-01700) ISBN 0 561 00083 2
Makers of opera. (Hoover, Kathleen O'Donnell). *Kennikat Press. £5.50* AC(XE311) (B71-21649) ISBN 0 8046 1412 1
Making friends with music. (Glennon, James). *Foulsham. £0.60* A (B71-27970) ISBN 0 572 00774 4
Making more music: a book of musical experiments for young people. (Addison, Richard). *Holmes-McDougall. £0.35(non-net* A(VK) (B71-17372) ISBN 0 7157 0749 3
Malinconia: funf Gitarrenstucke. (Bresgen, Cesar). *Schott. £0.80* TSPMJ (B71-50608)
Mallarme, Stephen. Si tu veux, nous nous aimerons: for soprano and piano. (Furnivall, Anthony). *Sycamore Press. Unpriced* KFLDW (B71-50356)
Man on the move: songs on the past, present and future of transport. (Rowe, Christopher). *Galliard. Unpriced* JE/TSDW (B71-50319)
Mandell, Muriel. Make your own musical instruments. New ed. *Bailey Bros and Swinfen. £1.40* AL/BC (B71-01700) ISBN 0 561 00083 2
Manicke, Dietrich. Aria: for violin and orchestra (1949/69). Piano score. *Simrock. £0.55* SPK (B71-50570)
Manson, M D. Melodies. (Mendelssohn, Felix). *Schott. £0.25* VSRPMK (B71-50146)
Manual of plainsong for Divine Service. (Briggs, H B). *Novello. £1.25* DTD (B71-50019)
Manvell, Roger. The technique of film music. 1st ed. reprinted. *Focal Press. £3.00* A/JR (B71-05268) ISBN 0 240 44943 6
Marcello, Benedetto. Psalm 45. Excerpts. Heart's adoration: two-part. *Oxford University Press. Unpriced* DH/LFL (B71-50014)
March: Washington D.C. (Kelly, Bryan). *Novello. Unpriced* WMGM (B71-51097)
Margittay, Sandor. Complete organ works of Franz Liszt Vol.1. (Liszt, Franz). *Boosey and Hawkes. Unpriced* R/AZ (B71-50517)
Mario Lanza; and, Max Steiner. (Burrows, Michael). *Primestyle Ltd. £0.75* AKGH/E(P) (B71-27972) ISBN 0 902421 14 x
Mariposa na luz: violino e piano. (Villa-Lobos, Heitor). *Arthur Napoleao; Essex Music. Unpriced* SPJ (B71-50569)
Marlowe, Sylvia. Pieces de clavecin. Excerpts. Selected harpischord music. (Couperin, Francois). *Schirmer; Chappell. Unpriced* QRPJ (B71-50105)
Marshall, Beatrice. Franz Schubert and his times. (Kobald, Karl). *Kennikat Press. £6.25* BSF(N) (B71-02479) ISBN 0 8046 0756 7
Marshall, Jim. Festival!: the book of American music celebrations... (Hopkins, Jerry). *Macmillan (N.Y.); Collier-Macmillan. £4.00* A/GB(YT/WE) (B71-11123) ISBN 0 02 580170 8
Marshall, Nicholas. Two minuets. *Schott. Unpriced* SRPK/AHR (B71-51039)
Martin, Ruth. La Forza del destino: opera in three acts. (Verdi, Giuseppe). *Schirmer; Chappell. Unpriced* CC (B71-50162)
Martin, Thomas. La Forza del destino: opera in three acts. (Verdi, Giuseppe). *Schirmer; Chappell. Unpriced* CC (B71-50162)
Martirios dos insetos - Excerpts. A Mariposa na luz: violino e piano. (Villa-Lobos, Heitor). *Arthur Napoleao; Essex Music. Unpriced* SPJ (B71-50569)
Mary Ann. (Down by the sea-shore siftin' sand): a popular Jamaican sic song in calypso style. (Dexter, Harry). *Ashdown. Unpriced* FDW (B71-50835)
Mason, Colin. Bela Bartok - letters. (Bartok, Bela). *Faber and Faber Ltd. £5.50* BBG(N) (B71-18713) ISBN 0 571 09638 7
Mass, no.6 'Harmoniemesse'. - Dona nobis pacem. Dona nobis pacem. (Haydn, Joseph). *Schirmer; Chappell. Unpriced* DH (B71-50746)
Master method for guitar: based on progressive arrangements of excerpts from the works of great masters. (Sadleir, Richard). *Feldman. £0.50* TS/AC (B71-51048)
Master musicians series. *(Dent)*
Hughes, Rosemary. Haydn. Revised ed. *Dent. £1.50* BHE(N) (B71-07862) ISBN 0 460 03111 2
Parrott, Ian. Elgar. *Dent. £1.75* BEP(N) (B71-14243) ISBN 0 460 03109 0
Masters in this hall: French traditional carol, SATB. (Willcocks, David). *Oxford University Press. Unpriced* DP/LF (B71-50214) ISBN 0 19 343009 6
Masters of music. *(Benn)*
Young, Percy Marshall. Dvorak. *Benn. £0.90* BDX(N) (B71-01698) ISBN 0 510 13717 2
Young, Percy Marshall. Schubert. *Benn. £0.90* BSF(N) (B71-01699) ISBN 0 510 13732 6
Mathias, William.
Ave rex. Excerpts. Sir Christemas: SATB. *Oxford University Press. Unpriced* DP/LF (B71-50212) ISBN 0 19 343008 8
Culhwch and Olwen. Op. 32: an entertainment. *University of Wales Press. Unpriced* ENYLNSDX (B71-50785)
Matra pictures: a set of Hungarian folksongs for S.A.T.B. (Kodaly, Zoltan). Revised ed. *Universal. Unpriced* EZDW/G/AYG (B71-50285)
Mattfeld, Julius. 'Variety' music cavalcade, 1620-1969: a chronology of vocal and instrumental music popular in the United States. 2nd ed. *Prentice-Hall. £7.50* A/GB(YT/XEW350/TC) (B71-23694) ISBN 0 13 940718 9
Matthews, David. The rising of the moon: an opera in three acts. (Maw, Nicholas). *Boosey and Hawkes. Unpriced* CC (B71-50159)
Matthews, Denis.
Sonata for piano in B flat major. K281. Sonata in B flat: pianoforte. K.281. (Mozart, Wolfgang Amadeus). *Associated Board of the Royal Schools of Music. £0.35* QPE (B71-50086)
Sonata for piano in D major. K.311. Sonata in D. K.311. (Mozart, Wolfgang Amadeus). *Associated Board of the Royal Schools of Music. £0.35* QPE (B71-50464)
Sonata for piano in E flat major. K.282. Sonata in E flat. K.282. (Mozart, Wolfgang Amadeus). *Associated Board of the Royal Schools of Music. £0.35* QPE (B71-50465)
Matthews, Thomas. The splendid art: a history of the opera. *Crowell-Collier; Collier-Macmillan. £1.75* AC(X) (B71-19967) ISBN 0 02 765290 4
Matthews, Walter E. Oh, come and mourn with us: SATB. *Warner; Blossom. Unpriced* DH/LG (B71-50748)
Maw, Nicholas.
The rising of the moon: an opera in three acts. *Boosey and Hawkes. Unpriced* CC (B71-50159)
Scenes and arias. *Boosey and Hawkes. £2.50* JNFDE/MDW (B71-50880)
Maxwell, Michael. A little dance; and, Waltz: for cello and piano. *Schott. Unpriced* SRPH (B71-51021)
May, Helmut. Concerto for viola in C major. Konzert, C-Dur: fur Viola, Streicher, 2 Oboen und 2 Horner Klavierauszug von Helmut May. (Hoffstetter, Roman). *Schott. £1.80* SQPK/LF (B71-50583)
May God have mercy upon us: for four-part chorus of mixed voices with organ accompaniment. (Hoag, Charles K). *Schirmer; Chappell. Unpriced* DR (B71-50768)
Meadows, Gail.
Balletti for five voices (1591). Fifteen balletti: SSATB a cappella (recorders and strings ad libitum) Introduttioni a i Balletti: O compagni allegrezza. (Companions, be happy). (Gastoldi, Giovanni). New ed. *Peters; Hinrichsen. £0.40* EZDU (B71-50263)
Balletti for five voices (1591). Fifteen balletti: SSATB a cappella (recorders and strings ad libitum) Set 3. (Gastoldi, Giovanni). New ed. *Peters; Hinrichsen. £0.40* EZDU (B71-50264)
Balletti for five voices (1591). Fifteen balletti: SSATB a cappella (recorders and strings ad libitum) Set 4. (Gastoldi, Giovanni). New ed. *Peters; Hinrichsen. £0.40* EZDU (B71-50265)
Meck, Barbara von-. *See* Von Meck, Barbara.
Medailles: for piano. (Bozay, Attila). *Boosey and Hawkes. £0.57* QPJ (B71-50476)
Medley of folk songs. (Stuart, Forbes). *Longman Young Books. £2.50* JDW/G/AY (B71-50861) ISBN 0 582 15331 x
Medley of melodies for descant recorder: arranged for classroom ensemble with chord symbol guide for piano, guitar, uke and chime bars, with chord diagrams for guitar and ukelele. *Feldman. Unpriced* NVSRNK/DW/AY (B71-50929)
Mellnas, Arne. Capricorn flakes: for keyboard & percussion. *Peters; Hinrichsen. £2.00* NYLNS (B71-50439)
Mendel, Arthur. Mozart: his character - his work. (Einstein, Alfred). *Panther. £0.75* BMS(N) (B71-06907) ISBN 0 586 03277 0
Mendelssohn, Felix.
Melodies. *Schott. £0.25* VSRPMK (B71-50146)
Preludes and fugues for piano. Op.35. Six preludes and fugues. Op.35: piano solo. *Peters, Hinrichsen. £0.60* QP/Y (B71-50462)
Mendelssohn's rediscovery of Bach. (Hendrie, Gerald). *Open University Press. £1.20* A(VX/P) (B71-24686) ISBN 0 335 00516 0
Mendl, Robert William Sigismund. Reflections of a music lover. *Spearman. £2.50* A (B71-05263) ISBN 0 85435 011 x
Mendoza, Anne. A children's Christmas festival: for voices, recorders and percussion. *Oxford University Press. £0.50* JFE/NYHSDE/LF (B71-50876) ISBN 0 19 330566 6
Mephisto waltz. (Liszt, Franz). *Twentieth Century Music. £0.20* QPK/JR (B71-50514)
Mersson, Boris. Sonatas for piano. Op.49, nos.1,2 - Excerpts. Divertimento in G major. (Beethoven, Ludwig van). *Bosworth. £2.25* UNRK (B71-51066)
Meslanges. Liv. 2 - Excerpts. Helas! mon Dieu: SAATB unacc. (Le Jeune, Claude). *Oxford University Press. Unpriced* EZDH (B71-50791)
Messenger, Thomas. Two-part counterpoint from the great Masters. *Faber. £0.55* QP/RM/AY (B71-50458)
Messina, Alfredo. Confidencia: mazurca no.3, piano. *Arthur Napoleao; Essex Music. Unpriced* QPHQ (B71-50974)
Mexican fiesta: for brass band. (Hanmer, Ronald). *Studio Music. Unpriced* WMG (B71-50693)
Mexican march. (Rosas, Juventino). *Bosworth. £0.875* WMK/AGM (B71-50152)
Meylan, Raymond.
Sonata for violin & harp in G major. Sonate: Violine (Flote) und Harfe. (Donizetti, Gaetano). *Litolff, Peters Hinrichsen. £0.80* SPLTQE (B71-50577)
Study for clarinet, no.1. Studie: fur Klarinette. (Donizetti, Gaetano). *Litolff, Peters; Hinrichsen. £0.50* VVPMJ (B71-50679)
Michaels, Jost. Duo for clarinet & piano in E flat major. Op.15. Duo. Op.15: for clarinet and piano. (Burgmuller, Norbert). *Simrock. Unpriced* VVPJ (B71-50675)
Middleton, Robert Gordon. Electronic organ servicing guide. *Foulsham. £2.25* ARPV/BT (B71-25917) ISBN 0 572 00785 x
Milan, Luis. El Maestro. *Pennsylvania University Press. Unpriced* TVPMJ (B71-50616) ISBN 0 271 00091 0
Millar, Bill. The Drifters: the rise and fall of the black vocal group. *Studio Vista. £1.40* AB/E(P) (B71-16703) ISBN 0 289 70133 3
Miller, Allan. Beginning piano for adults. *Collier Books; Collier-Macmillan. £1.00* Q/AC (B71-50083) ISBN 0 02 080890 9
Miller, Geoffrey. The Bournemouth Symphony Orchestra. *Dorset Publishing Company. £4.00* AMM/E(DCVB/X/QB) (B71-05269) ISBN 0 902129 06 6
Milton, John. Paradise lost. Op. 34: a dramatic cantata in two parts, for soprano, tenor and baritone soli, SATB and orchestra. (Steel, Christopher). *Novello. £0.90* DD (B71-50737)
Mingus, Charles. Beneath the underdog: his world as composed by Mingus. *Weidenfeld and Nicolson. £2.10* AMT/E(P) (B71-19348) ISBN 0 297 00446 8
Mini-blues suite: for descant, treble and tenor recorders. (Clover, David). *Feldman. Unpriced* VSNSG (B71-50651)
Miniature scores:.
Berkeley, Lennox. Symphony no.3 in one movement. *Chester. Unpriced* MME (B71-50378)
Blomdahl, Karl-Birger. Game for eight: choreographic suite for chamber orchestra. *Schott. £1.75* MRG (B71-50914)
Boyce, William. Concerto grosso in B minor: for two solo violins, solo violoncello and string orchestra. *Eulenburg. £0.60* RXMPSNTSRF (B71-51009)
Chavez, Carlos. Clio: symphonic ode. *Schirmer; Chappell. Unpriced* MMJ (B71-50071)
Durko, Zsolt. Fioriture: for orchestra. *Boosey and Hawkes. £0.75* MMJ (B71-50907)
Einem, Gottfried von. Concerto for violin. Op.33. Violin concerto. Op.33. *Boosey and Hawkes. Unpriced* MPSF (B71-50077)
Elgar, *Sir* Edward, *bart.* Quintet for piano and strings in A minor. Op. 84. Piano quintet in A minor. Op. 84. *Eulenburg. £0.35* NXNR (B71-50935)
Feldman, Morton. On time and the instrumental factor. *Universal. Unpriced* MMJ (B71-50390)
Gerhard, Roberto. Symphony 4 'New York'. *Oxford University Press. £4.50* MME (B71-50379) ISBN 0 19 363614 x
Hamilton, Iain. Cantus: for orchestra (1964). *Schott. £0.60* MMJ (B71-50908)
Haydn, Joseph. Symphony no.50 in C major. *Eulenburg. Unpriced* MME (B71-50380)
Hedges, Anthony. Quartet for strings (1970). Op. 41. String quartet (1970). Op. 41. *British & Continental Music. Unpriced* RXNS (B71-50548)
Hindemith, Paul. Thema mit vier Variationen: die Vier Temperamente, fur Klavier und Streichorchester. *Schott. £2.80* MPQ/T (B71-50402)
Hoddinott, Alun. Investiture dances: for orchestra. Opus 66. *Oxford University Press. £2.00* MMH (B71-50386) ISBN 0 19 364505 x
Hovhaness, Alan. Mountains and rivers without end. Op.225: chamber symphony for 10 players. *Peters; Hinrichsen. £1.50* MRJ (B71-50413)
Ireland, John. The overlanders: suite for orchestra. *Boosey and Hawkes. £2.50* MMG (B71-50070)
Ireland, John. Scherzo & cortege, on themes from Julius Caesar. *Boosey and Hawkes. £1.10* MMK/JM (B71-50075)
Liszt, Franz. Dante symphony. Symphonie zu Dantes Divina commedia: fur Frauenchor und Orchester. *Eulenburg. £2.10* FE/MDX (B71-50298)
McCabe, John. Concertino for piano duet & orchestra (1968). *Novello. Unpriced* MPQNVFL (B71-50076)

Maw, Nicholas. Scenes and arias. *Boosey and Hawkes. £2.50* JNFDE/MDW (B71-50880)
Panufnik, Andrzej. Autumn music. *Boosey and Hawkes. £0.50* MRJ (B71-50923)
Panufnik, Andrzej. Nocturne: for orchestra. *Boosey and Hawkes. Unpriced* MMJ (B71-50396)
Schubert, Franz. Overture in C major (in the Italian style) D. 591. *Eulenburg. £0.75* MMJ (B71-50909)
Schubert, Franz. Overture in D major (in the Italian style) D. 590. *Eulenberg. £0.75* MMJ (B71-50910)
Stravinsky, Igor. Four etudes for orchestra. Quatre etudes: pour orchestre. Revision 1952. *Boosey and Hawkes. £0.65* MMJ (B71-50073)
Zimmerman, Bernd Alois. Stille und Umkehr: Orchesterskizzen. *Schott. £1.90* MMJ (B71-50401)
Minutenstucke: fur Gitarre. (Kovats, Barna). *Schott. £0.70* TSPMJ (B71-50132)
Miracles of Christmas: for four-part mixed chorus and organ (or piano). (Rorem, Ned). *Boosey and Hawkes. £1.05* DE/LF (B71-50175)
Mistral, Gabriela. Die Sonne der Inkas: fur Sopran, 3 Sprecher und II Instrumentalisten. (Denisov, Edisson). *Universal. Unpriced* KFLE/MRDX (B71-50358)
Mitchell, Ronald Elwy. Opera dead or alive: production performance, and enjoyment of musical theatre. *University of Wisconsin Press. £6.00* AC/E (B71-19966) ISBN 0 299 05811 5
Mitchell, William John. The music forum
Vol.2. *Columbia University Press. £6.05* A(D) (B71-06290) ISBN 0 231 03153 x
Modern flute music. *Oxford University Press. £0.90* VRP/AY (B71-51070) ISBN 0 19 357821 2
Modern flute music. (Parry, William Howard). *Oxford University Press. £0.90* VRP/AY (B71-51071) ISBN 0 19 357820 4
Modern French music: its evolution and cultural background from 1900 to the present day. (Myers, Rollo Hugh). *Blackwell. £3.25* A(YH/XM71) (B71-26601) ISBN 0 631 13020 9
Moderne Orchester-Studien: fur Flote
Band 1. (Zoller, Karlheinz). *Schott. £3.00* VR/AF/AY (B71-50635)
Band 2. (Zoller, Karlheinz). *Schott. £2.75* VR/AF/AY (B71-50636)
Modinha Serestas no.5: 1 violao with Adeus, Bela Morena and, Cirandinhas no.2: 2 violaoes. (Villa-Lobos, Heitor). *Arthur Napoleao; Essex Music. Unpriced* SPMK (B71-50581)
Moffat, Alfred.
Air in D minor. (Purcell, Henry). *Schott. Unpriced* SRPK (B71-51035)
Rinaldo - Sorge nel petto. Sarabande. (Handel, George Frideric). *Schott. Unpriced* SRPK/AHVL (B71-51040)
Mohr, Joseph. Stille Nacht, heilige Nacht. Silent night. (Gruber, Franz). *Oxford University Press. Unpriced* DP/LF (B71-50763) ISBN 0 19 343022 3
Moll: fur das Pianoforte. (Castaldi, Paolo). *Universal. Unpriced* QPJ (B71-50477)
Momenta 94: for solo piano. (Lawson, Peter). *Peters, Hinrichsen. £1.25* QPJ (B71-50487)
Monteverdi, Claudio.
Angelus ad pastores ait. The angel hosts declare: motet for three-part chorus of women's voices a cappella. *Schirmer; Chappell. Unpriced* FEZDJ (B71-50303)
Hodie Christus natus est. On this day Christ appears: motet for three-part chorus of women's voices a cappella. *Schirmer; Chappell. Unpriced* EZDJ/LF (B71-50256)
Selve morale e spirituale. Excerpts. Deus tuorum militum: himnus unius martyris for T.T.B. with two violins and continuo. *Oxford University Press. Unpriced* GE/SNTPWDJ (B71-50900) ISBN 0 19 353272 7
Montgomery, James. Hail to the Lord's annointed: anthem for SATB and organ (or brass band). (Ball, Eric). *Novello. £0.15* DH (B71-50185)
Montgomery, Pamela.
Words and music. (Lawrence, Ian). *Longman. £0.40* A(VG) (B71-08785) ISBN 0 582 18694 3
Words and music
Introduction. (Lawrence, Ian). *Longman. £2.50* A(VG) (B71-22574) ISBN 0 582 18695 1
Stage 1. (Lawrence, Ian). *Longman. £0.40* A(VG) (B71-06126) ISBN 0 582 18691 9
Stage 2. (Lawrence, Ian). *Longman. £0.40* A(VG) (B71-06127) ISBN 0 582 18692 7
Stage 3. (Lawrence, Ian). *Longman. £0.40* A(VG) (B71-06128) ISBN 0 582 18693 5
Moravian duets. Op.32. Songs from Moravia
Book 1. (Dvorak, Antonin). *Chappell. Unpriced* FLDW (B71-50855)
Moravian duets. Op.32. Songs from Moravia
Book 1. (Dvorak, Antonin). *Chappell. Unpriced* FLDW (B71-50856)
Moravian duets. Op.32. Songs from Moravia
Book 2. (Dvorak, Antonin). *Chappell. Unpriced* FLDW (B71-50854)
More Biblical hymns and psalms. (Deiss, Lucien). *G. Chapman. £1.00* EZDR (B71-50806)
More carols for Christmas. (Brooks, Nigel). *Boosey and Hawkes. Unpriced* EZDP/LF/AY (B71-50261)
More folk songs from Lincolnshire: guitar chords added. (O'Shaughnessy, Patrick). *Oxford University Press in conjunction with the Lincolnshire Association. £0.75* KE/TSDW/G/AYDGH (B71-50354) ISBN 0 19 343687 6
Morgan, Haydn. They who considereth the poor shall be blest: SATB, ad. lib. *Warner; Blossom Music. Unpriced* EZDK (B71-50258)
Morley, *Sir* Alexander Francis. The Harrap opera guide. *Harrap. £2.10* AC (B71-00713) ISBN 0 245 50509 1
Morris, William. Masters in this hall: French traditional carol, SATB. (Willcocks, David). *Oxford University Press. Unpriced* DP/LF (B71-50214) ISBN 0 19 343009 6
Morton, Robin. Folksongs sung in Ulster. *The Mercier Press. £0.50* ADW/G(YDT) (B71-06293) ISBN 0 85342 221 4
Mosaics: for chamber orchestra. (Lipkin, Malcolm). *Chester. Unpriced* MRJ (B71-50921)
Mostras, Konstantin. Concerto for violin in D major. Op.35. Konzert, D-dur. Op.35: fur Violine und Orchester Ausgabe fur Violine und Klavier von Komponisten. (Tchaikovsky, Peter). *Peters; Hinrichsen. £1.40* SPK/LF (B71-50575)
Mother, I cannot mind my wheel. (Chagrin, Francis). *Ricordi. Unpriced* EZDW (B71-50030)
Mountain scenes: for cello and piano. (Alwyn, William). *Schott. Unpriced* SRPJ (B71-51025)
Mountains and rivers without end. Op.225: chamber symphony for 10 players. (Hovhaness, Alan). *Peters; Hinrichsen. £1.50* MRJ (B71-50413)
Mountney, Virginia Ruth. Class piano for adult beginners. (Squire, Russel Nelson). 2nd ed. *Prentice-Hall. £3.00* Q/AC (B71-50447) ISBN 0 13 135160 5
Moyse, Louis.
Fantasie pastorale hongroise: for flute and piano. (Doppler, Albrecht Franz). *Schirmer; Chappell. Unpriced* VRPJ (B71-50142)
Suite for flute & string orchestra in A minor. Suite in A minor: for flute and strings. (Telemann, Georg Philip). *Schirmer; Chappell. Unpriced* RXMPVRG (B71-50539)
Mozart, Wolfgang Amadeus.
Don Giovanni; libretto by Lorenzo da Ponte to the opera by W.A. Mozart; and, Idomeneo; libretto by Giambattista Varesco to the opera by W.A. Mozart. (Da Ponte, Lorenzo). *Cassell. £1.75* BMSAC (B71-24691) ISBN 0 304 93824 6
Eine kleine Nachtmusik. K.525. Allegro. Mozart 13: serenade no.13 in G major. *Rondor Music; Hansen. £0.20* QPK (B71-50982)
Le Nozze di Figaro; and, Cosi fan tutte; librettos by Lorenzo da Ponte to the operas by W.A. Mozart. (Da Ponte, Lorenzo). *Cassell. £1.75* BMSAC (B71-25344) ISBN 0 304 93826 2
O du eselhafter Peierl. K.559a. Peter, Peter: a round for four groups of singers. *Ashdown. £0.10* FDW/XC (B71-50841)
Six German dances for violins, bass and wind instruments. K.600, no.2. German dance. *Schott. Unpriced* SRPK/AH (B71-51037)
Sonata for piano in B flat major. K281. Sonata in B flat: pianoforte. K.281. *Associated Board of the Royal Schools of Music. £0.35* QPE (B71-50086)
Sonata for piano in D major. K.311. Sonata in D. K.311. *Associated Board of the Royal Schools of Music. £0.35* QPE (B71-50464)
Sonata for piano in E flat major. K.282. Sonata in E flat. K.282. *Associated Board of the Royal Schools of Music. £0.35* QPE (B71-50465)
Symphony no.35 in D major. K.385, 'Haffner'. Symphony in D. K.385, 'Haffner' symphony. *Faber Music. £2.75* MME (B71-50905)
Symphony no.40 in G minor. K.550 - Molto allegro. Mozart 40. *Feldman. Unpriced* WMK (B71-51105)
Symphony no.40 in G minor. K.550. Molto allegro. Mozart 40. *Feldman. Unpriced* QPK (B71-50509)
Symphony no.40 in G minor. K.550. Molto allegro. Mozart (Symphony no.40). *Rondor Music. £0.20* QPK (B71-50510)
Vesperae solennes de confessore. K.339 - Excerpts. Laudate Dominum. K.339, no.5. *Oxford University Press. Unpriced* FDGKJ (B71-50826) ISBN 0 19 342590 4
Die Zauberflote; libretto by Emanuel Schikaneder to the opera by W.A. Mozart; and, Die Entfuhrung aus dem Serail; libretto by Gottlieb Stephanie to the opera by W.A. Mozart. (Schikaneder, Emanuel). *Cassell. £1.75* BMSAC (B71-24690) ISBN 0 304 93825 4
Mozart 13: serenade no.13 in G major. (Mozart, Wolfgang Amadeus). *Rondor Music; Hansen. £0.20* QPK (B71-50982)
Mozart and his world. (Valentin, Erich). *Thames and Hudson. £1.75* BMS(N) (B71-08375) ISBN 0 500 13029 9
Mozart: his character - his work. (Einstein, Alfred). *Panther. £0.75* BMS(N) (B71-06907) ISBN 0 586 03277 0
Mozart's concerto form: the first movements of the piano concertos. (Forman, Denis). *Hart-Davis. £6.95* BMSAMPQ/U (B71-30154) ISBN 0 246 64008 1
Mr Henry Noell, his funerall psalmes. Seven hymn tunes. Lamentio Henrici Noel: S.A.T.B.
Nos. 1-4. (Dowland, John). Revised ed. *Oxford University Press. Unpriced* EZDR/KDN (B71-50809) ISBN 0 19 352157 1
Mr Henry Noell, his funerall psalmes. Seven hymn tunes. Lamentio Henrici Noel: S.A.T.B.
Nos. 5-7. (Dowland, John). Revised ed. *Oxford University Press. Unpriced* EZDR/KDN (B71-50810) ISBN 0 19 352160 1
Muczynski, Robert.
Gallery: suite for unaccompanied cello. *Schirmer; Chappell. Unpriced* SRPMG (B71-50599)
Sonata for cello & piano. Op.25. Sonata for cello and piano. Op.25. *Schirmer; Chappell. Unpriced* SRPE (B71-50123)
Toccata: for piano. *Schirmer; Chappell. Unpriced* QPJ (B71-50492)
Muffin man: for orchestra. (Bacon, Ernst). *Schirmer Chappell. Unpriced* MMJ (B71-50387)
Muir, Denise Narcisse-. *See* Narcisse-Muir, Denise.
Muradeli, Vano. Lenin in Siberia. *Workers' Music Association. £0.13* DW (B71-50773)
Murgier, Henri. Sonatas for treble recorder in C minor & F major. Zwei Sonaten, c-Moll, f-Dur: fur Altenblockflote und Basso continuo. (Konink, Servaas van). *Schott. £0.80* VSSPE (B71-51083)
Murray, Tom. Three Jamaican folk-songs. *Oxford University Press. £0.25* EZDW/G/AYULD (B71-50034)
Music. *Macdonald and Co. £0.25* A (B71-19965) ISBN 0 356 03759 2
Music and its story. (Young, Percy Marshall). Revised ed. *Dobson. £1.25* A(X) (B71-05265) ISBN 0 234 77346 4
Music and the young school leaver: problems and opportunities. (Schools Council). *Evans Bros; Methuen Educational. £0.23* A(MN/YD) (B71-18711) ISBN 0 423 46500 7
Music course for the Intermediate Certificate. (Cleary, Vincent). *Folens and Co. Ltd. £0.35* A (B71-06906) ISBN 0 902592 07 6
Music drama in schools. (John, Malcolm). *Cambridge University Press. £3.80* ACN(VF) (B71-20590) ISBN 0 521 08003 7
Music face to face. (Previn, Andre). *Hamilton. £1.75* A (B71-26599) ISBN 0 241 02036 0
Music for a bird: for treble recorder solo. (Linde, Hans Martin). *Schott. £0.70* VSSPMJ (B71-50660)
Music forum. Sonata for cello & piano, no.3 in A major. Op.69. Sonata for violoncello and pianoforte. Opus 69, first movement by Ludwig van Beethoven: facsimile of the autograph. (Beethoven, Ludwig van). *Columbia University Press. £1.75* BBJASRPE (B71-06294) ISBN 0 231 03417 2
Music forum
Vol.2. *Columbia University Press. £6.05* A(D) (B71-06290) ISBN 0 231 03153 x
Music I heard with you: for four-part chorus of mixed voices with piano accompaniment. (Faith, Richard). *Schirmer; Chappell. Unpriced* DW (B71-50232)
Music in British libraries: a directory of resources. (Long, Maureen W). *Library Association. £1.50(£1.20 to members of the Library Association)* A(U/YC/BC) (B71-26836) ISBN 0 85365 005 5
Music in Europe and the United States: a history. (Borroff, Edith). *Prentice-Hall. £6.00* A(X) (B71-21648) ISBN 0 13 608083 9
Music in opera: a historical anthology. (Brody, Elaine). *Prentice-Hall. £7.50* AC(X) (B71-12556) ISBN 0 13 608109 6
Music in school. (Kowal, Ada May). *Bond Street Publishers. £1.00* A(VC) (B71-10424) ISBN 0 901373 08 7
Music Library Association. Reprint series. *(Dover; Constable)* Noske, Frits. French song from Berlioz to Duparc: the origin and development of the melodie. 2nd ed. *Dover; Constable. £3.00* ADW(YH/XHK51) (B71-05796) ISBN 0 486 22104 0
Music lover's companion. (Hughes, Gervase). *Eyre and Spottiswoode. £3.00* A(D) (B71-18712) ISBN 0 413 27920 0
Music lovers: the story of Tchaikowsky and Nadejda von Meck. (Bowen, Catherine Drinker). 2nd ed. abridged. *Hodder Paperbacks. £0.35* BTD(N) (B71-04592) ISBN 0 340 15154 4
Music makers: in 5 stages Stage 4. (Berry, Marion). *Longman. £0.40* A(QU) (B71-06129) ISBN 0 582 18544 0
Stage 5. (Berry, Marion). *Longman. £0.40* A(QU) (B71-06130) ISBN 0 582 18545 9
Music of the north. (Linklater, Eric). *Haddo House Choral Society. £0.30* AD/E(QB/YDLSH) (B71-09739) ISBN 0 9501767 0 2
Musica Britanica: a national collection of music. 2nd revised ed. *Stainer and Bell. Unpriced* C/AYD (B71-50002)
Musica Britannica: a national collection of music
Vol.33: English songs, 1625-1660. *Stainer and Bell. Unpriced* C/AYD (B71-50001)
Musica Deo Sacra. Service no.1. Excerpts. Magnificat and Nunc dimittis: for SATB. (Tomkins, Thomas). *Novello. Unpriced* DGPP (B71-50743)
Musical boxes. (Tallis, David). *Muller. £3.00* A/FN (B71-17375) ISBN 0 584 10187 2
Musical excerpts of the masters. *Campbell Connelly. £0.60* QPK (B71-50100)
Musical instruments. The Irish and Highland harps. (Armstrong, Robert Bruce). *Irish University Press. £10.00* ATQ/B (B71-30155) ISBN 0 7165 0073 6
Musical instruments from the Renaissance to the 19th century. (Paganelli, Sergio). *Hamlyn. £0.90* AL/B(XDWC378) (B71-07323) ISBN 0 600 35920 4
Musical interpretation. (Westrup, *Sir* Jack Allan). *British Broadcasting Corporation. £0.90* A/E (B71-06909) ISBN 0 563 10352 3
Mussorgsky, Modeste. Boris Goudonov - Excerpts. Varlaam's song. *Ascherberg, Hopwood and Crew. £0.25* QPK/DW (B71-50985)
Mutanza: per pianoforte. (Szalonek, Witold). *Chester. Unpriced* QPJ (B71-50980)
My cats: for speaker, chorus and percussion. (Pehkonen, Elis). *Universal. £0.20* FHYE/NYLDX (B71-50308)
My heart is inditing. *See* Handel, George Frideric.
My help cometh from the Lord: for mixed voices and organ. (Hovhaness, Alan). *Peters; Hinrichsen. £0.30* DH (B71-50187)
Myers, Rollo Hugh.
Modern French music: its evolution and cultural background from 1900 to the present day. *Blackwell. £3.25* A(YH/XM71) (B71-26601) ISBN 0 631 13020 9
Ravel: life and works. *Duckworth. £1.00* BRE (B71-10426) ISBN 0 7156 0566 6
Myers, Stanley. Cavatina: arranged for guitar by John Williams. *Francis, Day and Hunter. £0.40* TSPMK

(B71-51052)
Na rede: piano. (Netto, Barrozo). Arthur Napoleao; Essex Music. Unpriced QPJ (B71-50495)
Nachtens. Nightly visions. Op.112, no.2: for four-part chorus of mixed voices with piano accompaniment. (Brahms, Johannes). Schirmer; Chappell. Unpriced DW (B71-50226)
Nagel, Frank.
Sonata for treble recorder & basso continuo in F major. Rinaldi op.67. Sonate F-Dur: fur Altblockflote und Basso continuo. (Vivaldi, Antonio). Schott. £0.80 VSSPE (B71-50657)
Sonata for two flutes in E minor. Triosonate e-Moll: fur 2 Querfloten und Basso continuo. (Handel, George Frideric). Schott. £1.10 VRNTPWE (B71-50637)
Nagy, Oliver. Concerto for flute & string orchestra in G major. Concerto in sol maggiore: per flauto, archi e continuo. (Quantz, Johann Joachim). Boosey and Hawkes. Unpriced RXMPVRF (B71-50117)
Nagy, Oliver. Concerto for flute & string orchestra in G major. Concerto in sol maggiore: per flauto, archi e continuo. (Quantz, Johann Joachim). Boosey and Hawkes. £1.45 VRPK/LF (B71-50144)
Nalden, Charles. Fugal answer. Auckland University Press; Oxford University Press. £5.75 AL/Y (B71-04593) ISBN 0 19 647552 x
Napoleao, Arthur.
Il Guarany - Excerpts. O Guarani: sinfonia. (Gomes, Antonio Carlos). Arthur Napoleao; Essex Music. Unpriced QNVK (B71-50454)
Romance and habanera: piano. Op.71. Arthur Napoleao; Essex Music. Unpriced QPJ (B71-50493)
Narcisse-Muir, Denise. Space songs for infants. (Horscroft, Elizabeth). Ashdown. £0.25 JFDW/GJ (B71-50323)
Nares, James. Try me, O God: short full anthem. Novello. £0.06 EZDK (B71-50026)
National Federation of Women's Institutes. Accent on music. N.F.W.I. £0.30 AF/E (B71-07868) ISBN 0 900556 12 9
National Operatic and Dramatic Association. Year book 1971. National Operatic and Dramatic Association. £0.75 AC/E(YC/Q) (B71-05795) ISBN 0 901318 02 7
Nativity carol: S.S.A. (Rutter, John). Oxford University Press. Unpriced FDP/LF (B71-50289) ISBN 0 19 342591 2
Naylor, F. Wenn ich ein Glocklein war. The Vesper bell. (Engelhart, Franz Xaver). Bosworth. Unpriced DW (B71-50771)
Neale, J M. Come, ye faithful, raise the strain: Easter anthem, for SATB and organ. (Thiman, Eric Harding). Novello. Unpriced DH/LL (B71-50015)
Neapolitan song. (Scandello, Antonio). Warner; Blossom Music. Unpriced EZDU (B71-50812)
Neary, Martin. Concerto for organ solo in E flat major. Concerto in E flat: for two manuals and pedals. (Bach, Monsieur). Oxford University Press. Unpriced RF (B71-50109)
Nelson, Havelock. La lo and lullaby: berceuse de Noe: two part song. Lengnick. £0.05 FDP/LF (B71-50037)
Nemessuri, Mihaly. The physiology of violin playing. (Szende, Otto). Collet's. £3.50 AS/EB (B71-16546) ISBN 0 569 06196 2
Nepomuceno, Alberto. Noturno: piano. Arthur Napoleao; Essex Music. Unpriced QPJ (B71-50494)
Ness, Arthur J. The lute music of Francesco Canova da Milano (1497-1543)
Vols I and II. (Francesco, da Milano). Harvard University Press. Unpriced TW/AZ (B71-50617)
Netto, Barrozo.
Carnaval das criancas: colecao de 8 pecas for piano No.7: A Gaita de um precoce fantasiado. (Villa-Lobos, Heitor). Arthur Napoleao; Essex Music. Unpriced QPG (B71-50470)
Na rede: piano. Arthur Napoleao; Essex Music. Unpriced QPJ (B71-50495)
Romance sem palavras: piano. Arthur Napoleao; Essex Music. Unpriced QPJ (B71-50496)
Nevens, David. 3 canticles of Thomas a Kempis: for unaccompanied mixed voices. Novello. Unpriced EZDH (B71-50792)
New catalogue of historical records, 1898-1908/09. (Bauer, Roberto). Sidgwick and Jackson. £6.50 A/FD(WT/XLT12) (B71-18315) ISBN 0 283 48420 9
New Catholic hymnal. (Petti, Anthony). Faber Music. Unpriced DM/LSB/AY (B71-50758) ISBN 0 571 10001 5
New compendium of piano technique
Book 2: Reiteration with and without changing fingers. (Lerchner, Juliane). Peters; Hinrichsen. £1.25 Q/AF (B71-50448)
New morning: complete vocal/piano folio with guitar diagrams & chord symbols. (Dylan, Bob). Feldman. Unpriced KDW (B71-50056)
New road to clarinet playing. (Dawe, Margery). Cramer. y0.45 VV/AC (B71-51086)
New tunes for strings. (Fletcher, Stanley). Boosey and Hawkes. £4.90 RXN/AY (B71-51010)
Newbury, Kent A.
Behold, I stand at the door: for four-part chorus of mixed voices a cappella. Schirmer; Chappell. Unpriced EZDK (B71-50259)
Great is the Lord: for full chorus of mixed voices with organ or piano accompaniment. Schirmer; Chappell. Unpriced DK (B71-50196)
Ring out, wild bells: for four-part chorus of mixed voices a cappella. Schirmer; Chappell. Unpriced EZDW (B71-50283)
Newell, N. Spartak - Excerpts. Spartacus: love theme. (Khachaturian, Aram). Plantagenet Music. £0.20 QPK/JS (B71-50987)
Newell, Norman. Symphony no.5 in C minor. Excerpts. Adagietto. The timeless moment: song. (Mahler, Gustav). Chappell. £0.20 KDW (B71-50885)
Newland, Paul.
Dvorak. (Young, Percy Marshall). Benn. £0.90 BDX(N) (B71-01698) ISBN 0 510 13717 2
Schubert. (Young, Percy Marshall). Benn. £0.90 BSF(N) (B71-01699) ISBN 0 510 13732 6
Nicholson, Richard. Consort music in five parts. (Jenkins, John). Faber Music. Unpriced STNQR (B71-50126)
Nicolai, P. Wachet auf. S.140. Excerpts. Zion hears the watchmen's voices: for unison & SATB chorale. (Bach, Johann Sebastian). Oxford University Press. Unpriced DM (B71-50202) ISBN 0 19 343013 4
Night people: reminiscences of a jazzman. (Wells, Dicky). Hale. £2.00 AMT/E(P) (B71-25916) ISBN 0 7091 2397 3
Night wind: S.A.T.B. (Crosse, Gordon). Oxford University Press. Unpriced EZDW (B71-50815) ISBN 0 19 342986 1
Noah and all that jazz: cantata for unison voices with piano accompaniment. (Fairbanks, Terry). Leeds Music. Unpriced JFDE (B71-50049)
Noah jazz: for unison voices with piano accompaniment and guitar chords. (Chappell, Herbert). Clarabella Music. Unpriced CN/L (B71-50168)
Noble, Robert. Folk tunes to accompany: a guide to simple accompaniment for beginners of all ages in schools, clubs, colleges or the home
Book 3: Modes and minors. Novello. £0.90 TSPMK/DW/G/AYB (B71-51056)
Nocturne: for orchestra. (Panufnik, Andrzej). Boosey and Hawkes. Unpriced MMJ (B71-50396)
Nocturne: for orchestra. (Panufnik, Andrzej). Boosey and Hawkes. Unpriced MMJ (B71-50397)
Noel: Sus, debout gentilz pasteurs. Now arise ye shepherds mild: for four-part chorus of mixed voices a capella. (Costeley, Guillaume). Schirmer; Chappell. Unpriced EZDP/LF (B71-50798)
Nolte, Ewald V. Der Herr segne euch. The Lord shall increase you: for SSAB chorus (or SATB). (Peter, Johann Friedrich). Boosey and Hawkes. £0.09 DH (B71-50189)
Nomos: for orchestra. (Birtwistle, Harrison). Universal. Unpriced MMJ (B71-50388)
Norfolk rhapsody: founded on folk-tunes collected orally in Norfolk and set as an orchestral piece. (Vaughan Williams, Ralph). Oxford University Press. £1.75 MMJ (B71-50400) ISBN 0 19 369227 9
Norman, Theodore. Trios for strings. Hob.IV, 1-3. London trios. (Haydn, Joseph). Schirmer; Chappell. Unpriced TSNTK (B71-51049)
Norrington, Roger. Selve morale e spirituale. Excerpts. Deus tuorum militum: himnus unius martyris for T.T.B. with two violins and continuo. (Monteverdi, Claudio). Oxford University Press. Unpriced GE/SNTPWDJ (B71-50900) ISBN 0 19 353272 7
Norris, John. A Bemerton cantata. Op.59: for mezzo-soprano solo, chorus, organ, string orchestra, harp, percussion. (Cruft, Adrian). Leeds Music. Unpriced DE (B71-50006)
Norriss, Eileen. Folk songs for guitar. Keith Prowse. £0.30 KE/TSDW/G/AY (B71-50060)
Noske, Frits. French song from Berlioz to Duparc: the origin and development of the melodie. 2nd ed. Dover; Constable. £3.00 ADW(YH/XHK51) (B71-05796) ISBN 0 486 22104 0
Notte, Ewald V. Ich will dir ein Frendenopfer. I will freely sacrifice to thee: for SSTB chorus (or SATB). (Peter, Johann Friedrich). Boosey and Hawkes. £0.15 DH (B71-50190)
Nott'num Town. (Street, Allan). Boosey and Hawkes. £2.90 WMG (B71-51096)
Noturno: canto e piano. (Lorenzo Fernandez, Oscar). Arthur Napoleao; Essex Music. Unpriced KDW (B71-50342)
Noturno: piano. (Nepomuceno, Alberto). Arthur Napoleao; Essex Music. Unpriced QPJ (B71-50494)
Novello, Ivor. The dancing years. Chappell. £0.25 QPK/CM (B71-50103)
Nozze di Figaro; and, Cosi fan tutte; librettos by Lorenzo da Ponte to the operas by W.A. Mozart. (Da Ponte, Lorenzo). Cassell. £1.75 BMSAC (B71-25344) ISBN 0 304 93826 2
Nursery ode. (Binkerd, Gordon). Boosey and Hawkes. £0.40 KDW (B71-50334)
Nyman, Michael. Down by the greenwood side: a dramatic pastoral. (Birtwistle, Harrison). Universal. Unpriced CQM (B71-50734)
Nys, Carl de. Mass for eight voices & eight violins & flutes. Mass: for soloists, double chorus & orchestra. (Charpentier, Marc Antoine). Oxford University Press. £3.50 EMDG (B71-50238) ISBN 0 19 335500 0
O be joyful in the Lord: a Caribbean Jubilate, for SATB and organ. (Kelly, Bryan). Novello. £0.15 DGNT (B71-50008)
O clap your hands together. Op.50: anthem for SATB and organ (or brass). (Steel, Christopher). Novello. £0.15 DK (B71-50200)
O du eselhafter Peierl. K.559a. Peter, Peter: a round for four groups of singers. (Mozart, Wolfgang Amadeus). Ashdown. £0.10 FDW/XC (B71-50841)
O God be merciful unto us. (Deus misereatur): SATB (full). (Tye, Christopher). Revised ed. Oxford University Press. Unpriced EZDGPS (B71-50250) ISBN 0 19 352146 6
O God be merciful unto us. (Deus misereatur): SATB (full) with verse for SATB. (Tye, Christopher). Revised ed. Oxford University Press. Unpriced EZDGPS (B71-50251) ISBN 0 19 352147 4
O Riada, Sean. Hercules dux Ferrariae: Nomos no.1 for strings. Woodtown Music. Unpriced RXMG (B71-50114)
O schone Nacht. O lovely night. Op.92, no.1: for four-part chorus of mixed voices with piano accompaniment. (Brahms, Johannes). Schirmer; Chappell. Unpriced DW (B71-50227)
O the morn, the merry merry morn. (Curtis, Frederick Vernon). Banks. Unpriced DP/LF (B71-50018)
Oboussier, Philippe. Workbook for woodwind: an elementary group method. Novello. £0.90 V/AC (B71-51067)
Octave variations: for recorder quartet. (Cook, Douglas). Schott. £0.50 VSNS/T (B71-50650)
Octet-partita: for 2 oboes, 2 clarinets, 2 horns, 2 bassoons and contrabassoon ad. lib. Op.67. (Krommer, Franz). Musica rara. £5.25 UNNG (B71-50139)
Odd man out: for double bass and piano. (Elliott, Vernon). Yorke. Unpriced SSPJ (B71-50124)
O'Donnell, Bridie. Songs for singing folk: Jackie and Bridies second song book. (McDonald, Jacqueline). Galliard. Unpriced KFE/TSDW/G/AYC (B71-50355)
Offenbach, Jacques.
Ba-ta-clan: a masquerade in one act. Schirmer; Chappell. Unpriced CF (B71-50163)
La belle Helene. United Music. Unpriced CF (B71-50004)
Duets for cellos, nos.1-3. Op.51. Drei Duette: fur Violoncelli. Op.51. Schott. £1.20 SRNU (B71-50590)
Offer, Charles Karel. European songs for children: 15 traditional songs. Paxton. Unpriced JFDW/GJ/AYB (B71-50324)
Ogdon, John. Boris Goudonov - Excerpts. Varlaam's song. (Mussorgsky, Modeste). Ascherberg, Hopwood and Crew. £0.25 QPK/DW (B71-50985)
Oh, come and mourn with us: SATB. (Matthews, Walter E). Warner; Blossom. Unpriced DH/LG (B71-50748)
Oh Mary, and all that jazz!: a quodlibet. (Hudson, Hazel). Ashdown. £0.10 DW/LC (B71-50777)
Oh! Noah. (Sansom, Clive A). Studio Music. Unpriced CN (B71-50165)
Oistrach, David.
Concerto for violin in D major. Op.35. Konzert, D-dur. Op.35: fur Violine und Orchester
Ausgabe fur Violine und Klavier von Komponisten. (Tchaikovsky, Peter). Peters; Hinrichsen. £1.40 SPK/LF (B71-50575)
Concerto for violin, no.2. Op.129. Konzert No.2 fur Violine und Orchester. Op.129
Ausgabe fur Violine und Klavier vom Komponisten. (Shostakovich, Dmitri). Peters; Hinrichsen. £2.00 SPK/LF (B71-50574)
Oistrach, Igor. Romances for violin & orchestra. Op.40 & 50. Romanzen. Op.40 (G-dur), Op.50 (F-dur): fur Violine und Orchester. (Beethoven, Ludwig van). Peters Hinrichsen. £0.90 SPK (B71-50571)
Okun, Milton. Something to sing about!: the personal choices of America's folk singers. Collier Books; Collier-Macmillan. £1.25 KDW/G/AYT (B71-50347)
Old, Margaret V. Sing to God: Christian songs for juniors. Scripture Union. £1.25 DM/AY (B71-50755) ISBN 0 85421 302 3
Old ark's a-movering' (amongst other things): a quodlibet for two female, two male, or one female and one male voice parts. (Hudson, Hazel). Ashdown. Unpriced DW/LC (B71-50778)
Oliver, Hazel. Born to be King. (Broad, D F). Banks. Unpriced FDP/LF (B71-50287)
Omaggi a Rossini: fur Orchester. (Hirsch, Hans Ludwig). Litolff, Peters; Hinrichsen. £2.50 MMJ (B71-50392)
On a clear day you can see forever. (Lane, Burton). Chappell. Unpriced WMK/CM (B71-50153)
On a clear day you can see forever. (Lane, Burton). Chappell. £0.25 QPK/CM (B71-50984)
On my way to the hill I saw my Lord: S.A.B. with piano and optional string bass. (Friend, Jerry R). Warner; Blossom Music. Unpriced DH (B71-50745)
On time and the instrumental factor. (Feldman, Morton). Universal. Unpriced MMJ (B71-50390)
Ondulando: estudo for piano. Op.31. (Villa-Lobos, Heitor). Arthur Napoleao; Essex Music. Unpriced QPJ (B71-50502)
One-three quarters: piccolo (flute), violin, violoncello, trombone, tuba and two pianos. (Macero, Ted). Peters Hinrichsen. £1.75 NUXPNP (B71-50418)
Open University. Humanities Foundation Course Team. Introduction to music. (Hendrie, Gerald). Open University Press. £0.80 A (B71-08374) ISBN 0 335 00509 8
Mendelssohn's rediscovery of Bach. (Hendrie, Gerald). Open University Press. £1.20 A(VX/P) (B71-24686) ISBN 0 335 00516 0
Opera: a modern guide. (Jacobs, Arthur). David and Charles. £3.00 AC (B71-08377) ISBN 0 7153 5013 7
Opera dead or alive: production performance, and enjoyment of musical theatre. (Mitchell, Ronald Elwy). University of Wisconsin Press. £6.00 AC/E (B71-19966) ISBN 0 299 05811 5
Operas of Leos Janacek. (Chisholm, Erik). Pergamon. £2.50 BJFAC (B71-07865) ISBN 0 08 012854 8
Ord-Hume, Arthur Wolfgang Julius Gerald. Player piano: the history of the mechanical piano and how to repair it. Allen and Unwin. £4.50 A/FP (B71-00206) ISBN 0 04 789003 7
O'Reilly, John. Three episodes: for percussion ensemble. Schirmer; Chappell. Unpriced XN (B71-50721)
Orfeo. Che faro. Air from 'Orpheus and Euridice': popularly known as 'What is life?'. (Gluck, Christoph Willibald von). Studio Music. Unpriced WMK/DW (B71-50707)
Orfeo: Kantate fur Sopran, Streicher und Basso continuo. (Pergolesi, Giovanni Battista). Litolff; Hinrichsen. £1.80 KFLE/RXNDX (B71-50360)

Organ blowing: its history and development. (Elvin, Laurence). *L. Elvin. £3.75* AR/BL (B71-16704) ISBN 0 9500049 1 x

Organ books
No.3. (Trevor, Caleb H). *Oxford University Press. £0.65* R/AY (B71-50990)

Organ, from its invention in the Hellenistic period to the end of the thirteenth century. (Perrot, Jean). *Oxford University Press. £8.50* AR/B(X) (B71-14734) ISBN 0 19 318418 4

Organo pleno. (Reynolds, Gordon). *Novello. £0.35(non-net)* AR/E (B71-04183) ISBN 0 85360 004 x

Orleans, Ilo. Within thy light: SATB with organ or piano. (Gordon, Philip). *Blossom Music. Unpriced* DH (B71-50186)

Orpheus with his lute: arranged by the composer for four-part chorus of mixed voices with piano accompaniment. (Schuman, William). *Schirmer; Chappell. £0.10* DW (B71-50022)

Orton, Richard. Cycle: for two or four players. *Ars Viva; Schott. £2.25* LNU (B71-50067)

Osborne, Charles. Letters of Giuseppe Verdi. (Verdi, Giuseppe). *Gollancz. £3.00* BVE(N) (B71-21046) ISBN 0 575 00759 1

O'Shaughnessy, Patrick. More folk songs from Lincolnshire: guitar chords added. *Oxford University Press in conjunction with the Lincolnshire Association. £0.75* KE/TSDW/G/AYDGH (B71-50354) ISBN 0 19 343687 6

Osterling, Eric. Sunburst: concert march. *Chappell. Unpriced* WMK/AGM (B71-50151)

Out of the deep. De profundis: anthem for SATB and organ (or brass band). (Kelly, Bryan). *Novello. £0.15* DR (B71-50223)

Out of your sleep arise and wake: carol for SATB and trumpet, horn, cello and percussion. (Roe, Betty). *Thames. Unpriced* ENYEXPNSDP/LF (B71-50783)

Over the stone: Welsh folk-song. (Arch, Gwyn). *Feldman. Unpriced* FDW (B71-50038)

Overlanders. Two symphonic studies on themes from 'The overlanders'. (Ireland, John). *Boosey and Hawkes. £0.65* MMJ (B71-50072)

Overlanders: suite for orchestra. (Ireland, John). *Boosey and Hawkes. £2.50* MMG (B71-50070)

Overture for a festival. (Stapleton, Eric). *Feldman. Unpriced* WMJ (B71-51099)

Overture in C major (in the Italian style) D. 591. (Schubert, Franz). *Eulenburg. £0.75* MMJ (B71-50909)

Overture in D major (in the Italian style) D. 590. (Schubert, Franz). *Eulenberg. £0.75* MMJ (B71-50910)

Owen, Wilfred. Shadwell Stair: part-song for SATB and flute. (Roe, Betty). *Thames. Unpriced* EVRDW (B71-50787)

Oxen: a carol for women's voices and piano. (Britten, Benjamin). *Faber Music. Unpriced* FDP/LF (B71-50036)

Oxford monographs on music. *(Clarendon Press)*
McGuinness, Rosamond. English court odes, 1660-1820. *Clarendon Press. £7.00* ADE/KM(YD/XEY161) (B71-27232) ISBN 0 19 816119 0

Oxford studies of composers. *(Oxford University Press)*
Kay, Norman. Shostakovich. *Oxford University Press. £0.90* BSGR(N) (B71-29386) ISBN 0 19 315422 6
Reaney, Gilbert. Guillaume de Machaut. *Oxford University Press. £0.90* BMBH (B71-30148) ISBN 0 19 315218 5
Roche, Jerome. Palestrina. *Oxford University Press. £0.90* BPC(N) (B71-29385) ISBN 0 19 314117 5

Padmore, Elaine. Wagner. *Faber and Faber Ltd. £1.50* BWC(N) (B71-29387) ISBN 0 571 08785 x

Paganelli, Sergio. Musical instruments from the Renaissance to the 19th century. *Hamlyn. £0.90* AL/B(XDWC378) (B71-07323) ISBN 0 600 35920 4

Paganini, Niccolo. Kleine Stucke: fur Gitarre. *Schott. £1.40* TSPMJ (B71-51051)

Paganini, Nicolo. Concerto for violin, no.3, in E major. Concerto no.3: per violino ed orchestra. *N.V. Philips' Photographische Industrie; Chappell. Unpriced* SPK/LF (B71-51015)

Paint your wagon: a musical play. (Loewe, Frederick). *Chappell. Unpriced* CM (B71-50731)

Pajama game - Excerpts. Hernando's hideaway: T.T.B.B. (Adler, Richard). *Frank Music. £0.90* GDW (B71-50314)

Palestrina, Giovanni Pierluigi da. Assumpta est Maria: motet for six voices. *Chester. Unpriced* EZDGKJ (B71-50249)

Palestrina. (Roche, Jerome). *Oxford University Press. £0.90* BPC(N) (B71-29385) ISBN 0 19 314117 5

Palmer, Roy. Room for company: folk songs and ballads selected and edited by. *Cambridge University Press. y1.38* JFDW/G/AYD (B71-50870) ISBN 0 521 08173 4

Pan book of opera. Opera: a modern guide. (Jacobs, Arthur). *David and Charles. £3.00* AC (B71-08377) ISBN 0 7153 5013 7

Panufnik, Andrzej.
Autumn music. *Boosey and Hawkes. £1.50* MRJ (B71-50922)
Autumn music. *Boosey and Hawkes. £0.50* MRJ (B71-50923)
Nocturne: for orchestra. *Boosey and Hawkes. Unpriced* MMJ (B71-50396)
Nocturne: for orchestra. *Boosey and Hawkes. Unpriced* MMJ (B71-50397)

Papp, Lajos. Improvvisazione: per pianoforte. *Boosey and Hawkes. Unpriced* QPJ (B71-50497)

Paradise lost. Op. 34: a dramatic cantata in two parts, for soprano, tenor and baritone soli, SATB and orchestra. (Steel, Christopher). *Novello. £0.90* DD (B71-50737)

Paradisi, Pietro Domenico.
Sonatas for harpsichord. Sonate di gravicembalo
Band 1: Sonate 1 -6. *Schott. £1.40* QRPE (B71-50989)
Sonatas for harpsichord. Sonate di gravicembalo
Band 2: Sonate 7-12. *Schott. £1.40* QRPE (B71-50988)

Park, Phil. Viva Mexico!: a comedy musical in three acts. (Hanmer, Ronald). *Weinberger. Unpriced* CM (B71-50164)

Parke, Dorothy. Has sorrow thy young days shaded?: for soprano and alto. *Cramer. £0.09* FDW (B71-50837)

Parkinson, John Alfred. Renaissance song book: seven songs for mixed voices. *Oxford University Press. £0.23* EZDW/AY (B71-50033) ISBN 0 19 330610 7

Parkinson, Patricia. Two little pieces: for recorders & strings. *Feldman. Unpriced* NVSK (B71-50928)

Parrott, Ian. Elgar. *Dent. £1.75* BEP(N) (B71-14243) ISBN 0 460 03109 0

Parry, William Howard.
Modern flute music. *Oxford University Press. £0.90* VRP/AY (B71-51071) ISBN 0 19 357820 4
Riding into Bethlehem: for unison or two-part voices with piano, optional recorders, and optional percussion by W.H. Parry; words by L. Bell. *Oxford University Press. Unpriced* FDP/LF (B71-50829) ISBN 0 19 342048 1

Pasfield, W R. Grieve not the holy Spirit of God: anthem for SATB and organ. *Ashdown. Unpriced* DK (B71-50752)

Path across the moor: for brass band. (Butterworth, Arthur). *Hinrichsen. £0.90* WMJ (B71-50697)

Paths to modern music: aspects of music from Wagner to the present day. (Davies, Laurence, *b.1926*). *Barrie and Jenkins. £4.00* A(D/XKR96) (B71-14731) ISBN 0 214 65249 1

Paul, Walter. On a clear day you can see forever. (Lane, Burton). *Chappell. £0.25* QPK/CM (B71-50984)

Paul of Tarsus: three episodes in the life of Paul the apostle, for four-part chorus of mixed voices with baritone solo, strings and organ. (Effinger, Cecil). *Schirmer; Chappell. Unpriced* ERXMDE (B71-50241)

Pax, C E . You! you!: a German folk tune. *Ashdown. £0.05* FDW (B71-50838)

Paxton, Stephen.
Allegro moderato. Op.3, no. 5. *Schott. Unpriced* SRPJ (B71-51029)
Sonata for cello and keyboard in D major. Op.3, No.2. Sonata. Op.3, No.2. *Schott. Unpriced* SRPE (B71-51020)

Paynter, John. There is no rose: a Christmas carol, mixed, or female or male voices unacc. *Oxford University Press. Unpriced* EZDP/LF (B71-50801) ISBN 0 19 353340 5

Peace to every neighbour: a carol. (Diplock, Cyril). *Royal School of Church Music. Unpriced* EZDP (B71-50796)

Pears, Peter. Five spiritual songs (Geistliche Lieder). (Bach, Johann Sebastian). *Faber Music. £1.00* KFTDH (B71-50062)

Pearse, John.
The classical guitar: a method for beginners. (Hall, Alan). *Scratchwood Music. £0.75* TS/AC (B71-50605)
The dulcimer book. *A.T.V. Kirshner Music; Distributed by Rosetti and Co. Ltd. £0.75* ATWTJ (B71-18091) ISBN 0 903052 00 8

Pedrette, Edward. Almighty God: for four-part chorus of mixed voices with organ or piano accompaniment. *Schirmer; Chappell. Unpriced* DH (B71-50188)

Pehkonen, Elis. My cats: for speaker, chorus and percussion. *Universal. £0.20* FHYE/NYLDX (B71-50308)

Pelican biographies. *(Penguin)* Gutman, Robert William. Richard Wagner: the man, his mind and his music. *Penguin. £0.75* BWC(N) (B71-05793) ISBN 0 14 021168 3

Pelikan, Maria.
Six folksongs from Yugoslavia: arranged for four-part chorus of mixed voices a cappella
1: The things my mother buys. (Srebotnjak, Alojz). *Schirmer; Chappell. Unpriced* EZDW/G/AYPK (B71-50818)
2: Katya and the Czar. (Srebotnjak, Alojz). *Schirmer Chappell. Unpriced* EZDW/G/AYPK (B71-50819)
3: The farmer's daughter. (Srebotnjak, Alojz). *Schirmer Chappell. Unpriced* EZDW/G/AYPK (B71-50820)
4: Love song from Ohrid. (Srebotnjak, Alojz). *Schirmer Chappell. Unpriced* EZDW/G/AYPK (B71-50821)
5: Wake up, Melinda. (Srebotnjak, Alojz). *Schirmer Chappell. Unpriced* EZDW/G/AYPK (B71-50822)
6: Oro (Yugoslav dance). (Srebotnjak, Alojz). *Schirmer Chappell. Unpriced* EZDW/G/AYPK (B71-50823)

Penna, Joseph. Beau soir. Beautiful evening. (Debussy, Claude). *Boosey and Hawkes. Unpriced* FDW (B71-50833)

Per pianoforte. (Boguslawski, Edward). *Ars viva; Schott. £1.80* QPJ (B71-50475)

Percussio antiqua: improvisations based on Sundgauer Marsch 1469 on historic percussion instruments, for percussion solo. (Fink, Siegfried). *Simrock. £0.65* XNGM (B71-51122)

Percussion instruments and their history. (Blades, James). *Faber and Faber Ltd. £10.00* AX(X) (B71-05797) ISBN 0 571 08858 9

Pergolesi, Giovanni Battista. Orfeo: Kantate fur Sopran, Streicher und Basso continuo. *Litolff; Hinrichsen. £1.80* KFLE/RXNDX (B71-50360)

Periodicals:, *New periodicals and those issued with changed titles.*
Chelys: the journal of the Viola da Gamba Society Vol.1-. *Viola da Gamba Society. £2.10(free to members)* ASTU(B) (B71-01190)
The Key Frame: the journal of the Fair Organ Preservation Society
No.1- ; Dec. 1964-. *The Fair Organ Preservation Society. £0.125(£1.00 yearly)* A/FM(B) (B71-18715)
Salvation Army. Salvation Army Brass Band Journal (General series). *Salvationist Publishing and Supplies. £0.50* WM/AY (B71-50689)

Perrot, Jean. The organ, from its invention in the Hellenistic period to the end of the thirteenth century. *Oxford University Press. £8.50* AR/B(X) (B71-14734) ISBN 0 19 318418 4

Pestel, Thomas. Behold the great Creator: carol for SATB unaccompanied. (Tomblings, Philip). *Ashdown. £0.05* EZDP/LF (B71-50805)

Peter, Johann Friedrich.
Der Herr segne euch. The Lord shall increase you: for SSAB chorus (or SATB). *Boosey and Hawkes. £0.09* DH (B71-50189)
Ich will dir ein Frendenopfer. I will freely sacrifice to thee: for SSTB chorus (or SATB). *Boosey and Hawkes. £0.15* DH (B71-50190)

Peter, Peter: a round for four groups of singers. (Mozart, Wolfgang Amadeus). *Ashdown. £0.10* FDW/XC (B71-50841)

Peterson, John W. George Beverley Shea solos: songs. *Marshall, Morgan and Scott. £0.40* KDH (B71-50881) ISBN 0 551 05069 1

Petite Musique de Chambre. Excerpts. Partita no.3 in C minor: for descant recorder and piano. (Telemann, Georg Philipp). *Faber Music. Unpriced* VRPG (B71-50642)

Petite suite champetre. Op.67: for descant recorder (or flute or oboe) and piano. (Hand, Colin). *Boosey and Hawkes. Unpriced* VSRPG (B71-51080)

Petite suite. Excerpts. Ballet. (Debussy, Claude). *Boosey and Hawkes. £1.05* MH (B71-50901)

Petjsik, Arpad. Violoncello music for beginners. (Lengyel, Endre). *Boosey and Hawkes. £0.80* SRPK/AAY (B71-50595)

Petti, Anthony. New Catholic hymnal. *Faber Music. Unpriced* DM/LSB/AY (B71-50758) ISBN 0 571 10001 5

Petti, Anthony G. Beata viscera, Hail Mary, full of grace: motet for five voices, S.A.A.T.B. for feasts of the Blessed Virgin. (Byrd, William). *Chester. Unpriced* EZDGKAH (B71-50248)

Pezel, Johann. Bicinia variorum instrumentum. Excerpts. Sonatinas nos. 61, 62, 65 and 66: for 2 trumpets in B flat (C) & continuo. *Musica rara. Unpriced* WSNTPWEM (B71-50715)

Pezzo concertato. Op.11: per viola solo e orchestra. (Bozay, Attila). *Boosey and Hawkes. £1.15* MPSQ (B71-50078)

Phelps.
Music makers: in 5 stages Stage 4. (Berry, Marion). *Longman. £0.40* A(QU) (B71-06129) ISBN 0 582 18544 0
Stage 5. (Berry, Marion). *Longman. £0.40* A(QU) (B71-06130) ISBN 0 582 18545 9

Philidor, Anne Danican. Suite for oboe and basso continuo no.1 in G minor (1er livre). Suite 1, g-Moll: fur Oboe (Querflote, Violine) und Basso continuo,. *Schott. £0.90* VTPG (B71-50664)

Philips, Ambrose. Nursery ode. (Binkerd, Gordon). *Boosey and Hawkes. £0.40* KDW (B71-50334)

Philips Group. Catalogue. *Philips Records Ltd. Unpriced* A/FD(WM) (B71-28930) ISBN 0 902225 01 4

Philips philicorda cassette album. *Chappell. Unpriced* RPVK/B/FL (B71-50533)

Phillips, John Charles.
Eight negro spirituals: arranged for SSA unaccompanied. *Novello. £0.35* FEZDW/LC/AY (B71-50850)
World rejoice!: a suite of traditional carols from five nations arranged for female and/or boys' voices, piano, strings and percussion, with alternative accompaniment for piano and optional percussion only. *Novello. £0.25* FDP/LF/AYB (B71-50292)

Phillips, Sally. Two pictures: for piano. *Oxford University Press. Unpriced* QPJ (B71-50097)

Photoptosis: Prelude fur grosser Orchester. (Zimmerman, Bernd Alois). *Schott. £3.20* MMJ (B71-50074)

Physiology of violin playing. (Szende, Otto). *Collet's. £3.50* AS/EB (B71-16546) ISBN 0 569 06196 2

Pianissimo... (Schnittke, Alfred). *Universal. Unpriced* MMJ (B71-50398)

Piano teachers' yearbook for the Associated Board Syllabus 1970. *H. Freeman. £0.50* AQ/E(VCL) (B71-02482) ISBN 0 900385 00 6
1971. *H. Freeman. £0.50* AQ/E(VCL) (B71-02481) ISBN 0 900385 01 4

Pianoforte. (Sumner, William Leslie). 3rd ed., with corrections and additions. *Macdonald and Co. £2.50* AQ(X) (B71-11124) ISBN 0 356 03516 6

Piave, Francesco Maria. La Forza del destino: opera in three acts. (Verdi, Giuseppe). *Schirmer; Chappell. Unpriced* CC (B71-50162)

Pieces de clavecin. Excerpts. Selected harpischord music. (Couperin, Francois). *Schirmer; Chappell. Unpriced* QRPJ (B71-50105)

Pied piper: a play with music. (Berger, Jean). *Schirmer Chappell. Unpriced* CQM (B71-50173)

Pilgrims and pioneers: for orchestra. (Thomson, Virgil). *Schirmer; Chappell. Unpriced* MM/JR (B71-50376)

Pinkham, Daniel.
Trio for trumpet, horn & trombone. Brass trio: trumpet, horn, trombone. *Peters; Hinrichsen. £1.25* WNT (B71-50714)
Variations: for oboe and organ by Daniel Pinkham. *Peters; Hinrichsen. £1.10* VTPLR/T (B71-50669)

Piper o'Dundee: for S.A.B. (Simpson, John). *Feldman. Unpriced* DW (B71-50234)

Pirie, Peter John. Frank Bridge. *Triad Press. £0.80* BBTP (B71-24084) ISBN 0 902070 02 9

Pitfield, Thomas.
Conversations: suite for B flat clarinet and piano (or string orchestra and harp). *Leeds Music. Unpriced* VVPG (B71-51089)
Sonatina for piano in C major. Sonatina in C: for piano.

Freeman. Unpriced QPEM (B71-50467)
Pitfield, Thomas Baron. Rhymes and rhythms: pieces for youth choir, piano, perc. and various optional instruments. *Hinrichsen. £1.60* FLE/NYLDW (B71-50311)
Platt, Richard.
Twelve overtures: in D major; for oboes, trumpets, horns, timpani, strings, and continuo. (Boyce, William). *Oxford University Press. £1.25* MRJ (B71-50918) ISBN 0 19 361834 6
Twelve overtures: in G major; for oboes, flutes, horns, strings, and continuo. (Boyce, William). *Oxford University Press. £1.25* MRJ (B71-50916) ISBN 0 19 361812 5
Twelve overtures
No.1: in D major; for oboes, strings and continuo. (Boyce, William). *Oxford University Press. £1.25* MRJ (B71-50915) ISBN 0 19 361802 8
No.3: in Bflat major; for oboes, strings and continuo. (Boyce, William). *Oxford University Press. Unpriced* MRJ (B71-50917) ISBN 0 19 361824 9
No.5: in F major; for oboes, strings and continuo. (Boyce, William). *Oxford University Press. £1.25* MRJ (B71-50919) ISBN 0 19 361849 4
No.6: in D minor; for oboes, flutes, horns, strings, and continuo. (Boyce, William). *Oxford University Press. £1.25* MRJ (B71-50920) ISBN 0 19 361859 1
Play guitar!: a comprehensive tutor for the complete beginner, of classical folk and creative techniques for the finger style Spanish guitar. (Crimlisk, Anthony). *Boosey and Hawkes. Unpriced* TS/AC (B71-51045)
Play guitar!: a comprehensive tutor, for the complete beginner, of classical, folk and creative techniques for the finger style Spanish guitar
Vol.1. (Crimlisk, Anthony). *Boosey and Hawkes. Unpriced* TS/AC (B71-50603)
Vol.2. (Crimlisk, Anthony). *Boosey and Hawkes. Unpriced* TS/AC (B71-50604)
Player piano: the history of the mechanical piano and how to repair it. (Ord-Hume, Arthur Wolfgang Julius Gerald). *Allen and Unwin. £4.50* A/FP (B71-00206) ISBN 0 04 789003 7
Playing for pleasure: for piano
Book 3: Grade 1. (Longmire, John). *Bosworth. £0.225* QPJ (B71-50095)
Playing the cello: an approach through live music making. (Cole, Hugo). *Novello. 1.50* SR/AC (B71-50586)
Playing the guitar for the Lord's work. (Gilbert, Bryan Edward). Revised ed. *Marshall, Morgan and Scott Ltd. £0.30* TS/AC (B71-50130) ISBN 0 551 05435 2
Playing the harpsichord. (Schott, Howard). *Faber and Faber Ltd. £2.75* AQR/E (B71-29388) ISBN 0 571 09203 9
Poem: for flute and band. (Griffes, Charles T). *Schirmer; Chappell. Unpriced* UMPVR (B71-50626)
Polnauer, Frederick F. Trattenimenti armonici per camera divisi in dodici sonate. Op.6, no. 2. Sonata for string orchestra. Op. 6, no. 2. (Albinoni, Tommaso). *Chester. Unpriced* RXME (B71-51008)
Ponder' songs of the seasons: for high voice and piano. (Roe, Betty). *Thames. Unpriced* KFTDW (B71-50894)
Ponte, Lorenzo da. *See* Da Ponte, Lorenzo.
Pooler, Marie. Simple gifts: American Shaker song. *Schirmer; Chappell. Unpriced* DW (B71-50769)
Poor Richard. Three contemporary madrigals: for four-part chorus of mixed voices a cappella
My love and I for kisses played. (Effinger, Cecil). *Schirmer; Chappell. Unpriced* EZDW (B71-50272)
Pop. (Jasper, Tony). *S.C.M. Press. £0.20* A/GB (B71-05264) ISBN 0 334 01270 8
Pope, Roger Hugh. Five short solos: for piano. *Bosworth. £0.18* QPJ (B71-50979)
Popper, David. 10 mittelschwere grosse Etuden. Op.76,II. Studies (preparatory to the high school of cello playing). Op. 76. *Schirmer; Chappell. Unpriced* SR/AF (B71-51016)
Popular selection of English dance airs
Book 4: Sword and ceremony. (Fleming-Williams, Nan). *English Folk Dance and Song Society. £0.25* LH/G/AYD (B71-50896)
Porter, Quincy. Quartet for strings, no.3. String quartet no.3. *Peters; Hinrichsen. £1.10* RXNS (B71-50550)
Portrait of John Bull, c.1563-1628. (Chappell, Paul). *Hereford Cathedral. £0.10* BBV(N) (B71-03035) ISBN 0 9501011 2 5
Postlude on 'Love divine' by John Stainer: for organ. (Hopkins, Douglas). *Paxton. Unpriced* RJ (B71-50525)
Poston, Elizabeth.
Bye, Baby Bunting. *Bodley Head. £1.10* JFDW/GK/AY (B71-50871) ISBN 0 370 01526 6
Girls and boys come out to play. *Bodley Head. £1.10* JFDW/GK/AY (B71-50872) ISBN 0 370 01527 4
I had a little nut tree. *Bodley Head. £1.10* JFDW/GK/AY (B71-50873) ISBN 0 370 01528 2
Poston, Elizabeth. The baby's song book. *(Bodley Head)*
Poston, Elizabeth. Bye, Baby Bunting. *Bodley Head. £1.10* JFDW/GK/AY (B71-50871) ISBN 0 370 01526 6
Poston, Elizabeth. Girls and boys come out to play. *Bodley Head. £1.10* JFDW/GK/AY (B71-50872) ISBN 0 370 01527 4
Poston, Elizabeth. I had a little nut tree. *Bodley Head. £1.10* JFDW/GK/AY (B71-50873) ISBN 0 370 01528 2
Poston, Elizabeth. Where are you going to, my pretty maid?. *Bodley Head. £1.10* JFDW/GK/AY (B71-50874) ISBN 0 370 01529 0
Poston, Elizabeth. Where are you going to, my pretty maid?. *Bodley Head. £1.10* JFDW/GK/AY (B71-50874) ISBN 0 370 01529 0
Pottenger, Harold. Christus am Olberger. Excerpts. Hallelujah. (Beethoven, Ludwig van). *Schirmer; Chappell. Unpriced* EUMDH (B71-50242)
Poulton, Diana. The first booke of songes or ayres, 1597 and, The first booke of songs, 1613; and, The second booke of songs or ayres, 1600; and, The third and last booke of songs or ayres, 1603; and, A pilgrimes solace, 1612, by John Dowland; and, A musicall banquet, 1610 by Robert Dowland. (Dowland, John). *Scolar Press. £10.00* BDTWADW (B71-04594) ISBN 0 85417 414 1
Pound, Ezra. Four miniature songs from Ezra Pound: S.A.T.B. unaccompanied. (Dalby, Martin). *Lengnick. Unpriced* EZDW (B71-50031)
Practical music making with juniors. (Garnett, Hugh). *Schoolmaster Publishing. £0.55* A(VJ) (B71-12945) ISBN 0 900642 10 6
Praeludium and gigue: for orchestra. (Rathaus, Karol). *Boosey and Hawkes. £2.10* MRHP (B71-50410)
Praeludium. Opus. 60: for organ. (Fricker, Peter Racine). *Oxford University Press. £0.80* RJ (B71-50522) ISBN 0 19 375390 1
Praise ye the Lord: anthem for SATB with divisions, and organ (or brass). (Aston, Peter). *Novello. £0.13* DR (B71-50219)
Prayer for honour: Szep Konyorges: S.A.T.B. unaccompanied. (Kodaly, Zoltan). *Boosey and Hawkes. Unpriced* EZDW (B71-50275)
Prayer for peace: SATB unacc. (Lord, David). *Oxford University Press. Unpriced* EZDH (B71-50025) ISBN 0 19 350320 4
Prelude and dance. Op.68: two light pieces, for double bass and pianoforte. (Cruft, Adrian). *Leeds Music. Unpriced* SSPH (B71-51043)
Prelude and march. Op.60: for double bass or other bass clef instrument and pianoforte. (Cruft, Adrian). *Leeds Music. Unpriced* SSPGM (B71-51042)
Prelude and scherzo. Op.65: for double bass or other bass clef instrument and pianoforte. (Cruft, Adrian). *Leeds Music. Unpriced* SSPJ (B71-51044)
Prentice-Hall contemporary perspectives in music education series. *(Prentice-Hall)*
Colwell, Richard. The evaluation of music teaching and learning. *Prentice-Hall. Unpriced* A(VF/VCM) (B71-11816) ISBN 0 13 292151 0
Gordon, Edwin. The psychology of music teaching. *Prentice-Hall. £3.50* A/CS(VC) (B71-30146) ISBN 0 13 736215 3
Previn, Andre. Music face to face. *Hamilton. £1.75* A (B71-26599) ISBN 0 241 02036 0
Price, Beryl. Emerald isle: five Irish airs arranged for cello (1st position) and piano. *Oxford University Press. £0.40* SRPK/DW/G/AYDM (B71-50596) ISBN 0 19 358302 x
Pride of lions: a story for singing and staging. (Tate, Phyllis). *Oxford University Press. Unpriced* CQN (B71-50735)
Probe. *(S.C.M. Press)* Jasper, Tony. Pop. *S.C.M. Press. £0.20* A/GB (B71-05264) ISBN 0 334 01270 8
Prodigal son jazz: for unison voices with piano accompaniment and guitar chords. (Chappell, Herbert). *Clarabella Music. Unpriced* CN/L (B71-50169)
Prokofiev, Sergei. Sonata for violin solo. Op.115. Sonate fur Violine solo. Opus 115. *Peters; Hinrichsen. £0.90* SPME (B71-50579)
Prokofiev. (Samuel, Claude). *Calder and Boyars. £2.25* BPP(N) (B71-24085) ISBN 0 7145 0489 0
Prokofjew, Sergej. *See* Prokofiev, Sergei.
Prudentius, Aurelius Clemens. Bethlehem, of noblest cities: Australian folk melody and a melody from Psalmodia sacra, Gotha, 1715, for SATB. (Hurford, Peter). *Oxford University Press. Unpriced* DP/LFP (B71-50218)
Psychology of music teaching. (Gordon, Edwin). *Prentice-Hall. £3.50* A/CS(VC) (B71-30146) ISBN 0 13 736215 3
Puppets: for two B flat clarinets. (Grundman, Clare). *Boosey and Hawkes. £0.45* VVNU (B71-50672)
Puppets on parade: suite. (Johnson, Thomas Arnold). *Freeman. £0.20* QPG (B71-50090)
Purcell, Daniel. Magnificat and Nunc dimittis in E minor: for SATB and organ. *Novello. £0.15* DGPP (B71-50742)
Purcell, Henry. Air in D minor. *Schott. Unpriced* SRPK (B71-51035)
Purcell, Henry. King Arthur. *See* Purcell, Henry. The works of Henry Purcell. Vol.26.
Purcell, Henry. The works of Henry Purcell
Vol.26: King Arthur; edited by Dennis Arundell, revised by Margaret Laurie. *Novello. £4.50* C/AZ (B71-50156)
Putterill, Jack. Thaxted Mass: three part unaccompanied. *St Gregory Publishing Co. £0.20* EZDG (B71-50789)
Quantz, Johann Joachim.
Concerto for flute & string orchestra in G major. Concerto in sol maggiore: per flauto, archi e continuo. *Boosey and Hawkes. Unpriced* RXMPVRF (B71-50117)
Concerto for flute & string orchestra in G major. Concerto in sol maggiore: per flauto, archi e continuo. *Boosey and Hawkes. £1.45* VRPK/LF (B71-50144)
Quartet for strings (1970). Op. 41. String quartet (1970). Op. 41. (Hedges, Anthony). *British & Continental Music. Unpriced* RXNS (B71-50548)
Quatre etudes: pour orchestre. (Stravinsky, Igor). Revision 1952. *Boosey and Hawkes. £0.65* MMJ (B71-50073)
Quatre etudes: pour orchestre. (Stravinsky, Igor). Revision 1952. *Boosey and Hawkes. Unpriced* MMJ (B71-50399)
Quelle est cette odeur agreable? Whence is that goodly fragrance flowing?: French traditional carol, S.A.T.B. (Willcocks, David). *Oxford University Press. Unpriced* DP/LF (B71-50215) ISBN 0 19 343010 x
Quem pastores laudavere. Shepherds left their flocks a-straying: German carol SATB unacc. (Rutter, John). *Oxford University Press. Unpriced* EZDP/LF (B71-50260) ISBN 0 19 343012 6
Rabindranath Tagore. *See* Tagore, *Sir* Rabindranath.
Radeke, Winfried.
Sonata for treble recorder & basso continuo in F major. Rinaldi op.67. Sonate F-Dur: fur Altblockflote und Basso continuo. (Vivaldi, Antonio). *Schott. £0.80* VSSPE (B71-50657)
Sonata for two flutes in E minor. Triosonate e-Moll: fur 2 Querfloten und Basso continuo. (Handel, George Frideric). *Schott. £1.10* VRNTPWE (B71-50637)
Raffles 'gamelan': a historical note. (Fagg, William). *British Museum. £0.40* BZGVJAL/B(WJ) (B71-04179) ISBN 0 7141 1514 2
Rags of North Indian music: their structure and evolution. (Jairazbhoy, Nazir Ali). *Faber and Faber Ltd. £10.00* BZFL (B71-11817) ISBN 0 571 08315 3
Ralph Vaughan Williams: a pictorial biography. (Lunn, John E). *Oxford University Press. £3.30* BVD(N) (B71-30150) ISBN 0 19 315420 x
Rameau, Jean Philippe. Arias: for tenor, flute, continuo
Vol.1. *Musica rara. £3.15* KGHE/VRPDW (B71-50368)
Ramsey, A B. Quelle est cette odeur agreable? Whence is that goodly fragrance flowing?: French traditional carol, S.A.T.B. (Willcocks, David). *Oxford University Press. Unpriced* DP/LF (B71-50215) ISBN 0 19 343010 x
Rands, Bernard.
Ballad 1: mezzo-soprano, flute/altoflute, tenor, trombone, contra-bass, piano, percussion. *Universal. Unpriced* KFNE/NYDDW (B71-50362)
Tableau: flute/alto flute, B flat clarinet/bass clarinet, viola, cello, piano/celesta, percussion. *Universal. Unpriced* NYDPNQ (B71-50431)
Rantin' pipe and tremblin' string: a history of Scottish dance music. (Emmerson, George Sinclair). *Dent. £5.00* A/H/G(YDL/XQP) (B71-16700) ISBN 0 460 03891 5
Rapley, Felton. Get to know Mister Bach: an informal introduction with simple piano arrangements of his music. (Bach, Johann Sebastian). *Chappell. Unpriced* QPK (B71-50981)
Rapp, E. Six German dances for violins, bass and wind instruments. K.600, no.2. German dance. (Mozart, Wolfgang Amadeus). *Schott. Unpriced* SRPK/AH (B71-51037)
Ratcliffe, Desmond. The power and the glory. (Leonard, Harry). *Novello. £1.75* EMDH (B71-50023)
Rathaus, Karol. Praeludium and gigue: for orchestra. *Boosey and Hawkes. £2.10* MRHP (B71-50410)
Ravel: life and works. (Myers, Rollo Hugh). *Duckworth. £1.00* BRE (B71-10426) ISBN 0 7156 0566 6
Ravenscroft, T. Four carols. Op.109: for mixed or S.A. voices
3: Remember. (Gardner, John). *Oxford University Press. Unpriced* DP/LF (B71-50761) ISBN 0 19 343019 3
Rayner, Josephine.
The music of Claude Debussy
Book 1: La Fille aux cheveux de lin; and, The little shepherd; and, Jimbo's lullaby. (Debussy, Claude). *Forsyth. Unpriced* QPJ (B71-50480)
Book 2: Clair de lune; and, Des Pas sur la neige; and, Snow is dancing. (Debussy, Claude). *Forsyth. Unpriced* QPJ (B71-50481)
Book 3: Serenade of the doll; and, La Puerta del vino; and Sarabande. (Debussy, Claude). *Forsyth. Unpriced* QPJ (B71-50482)
Reaney, Gilbert. Guillaume de Machaut. *Oxford University Press. £0.90* BMBH (B71-30148) ISBN 0 19 315218 5
Red Sea jazz: for unison voices with piano accompaniment and guitar chords. (Chappell, Herbert). *Clarabella Music. Unpriced* CN/L (B71-50170)
Reeves, Betty. The piano teachers' yearbook for the Associated Board Syllabus
1971. *H. Freeman. £0.50* AQ/E(VCL) (B71-02481) ISBN 0 900385 01 4
Reflections. Inner-space music: clarinet solo. (Laporte Andre). *Chester. Unpriced* VVPMJ (B71-50680)
Reflections of a music lover. (Mendl, Robert William Sigismund). *Spearman. £2.50* A (B71-05263) ISBN 0 85435 011 x
Reger, Max.
Ausgewahlte Klavierwerke
Band 3: Aus meinem Tagebuch. Op.82. *Peters; Hinrichsen. £1.25* QPJ (B71-50498)
Walzer-Capricen, deutsche Tanze und andere Stucke: fur Klavier zu vier Handen. *Peters; Hinrichsen. £1.40* QNV (B71 50452)
Reich, Willi. Schoenberg: a critical biography. *Longman. £3.50* BSET (B71-16010) ISBN 0 582 12753 x
Reicha, Anton. Two andantes and adagio 'pour le Cor Anglais': for flute, cor anglais, clarinet, horn and bassoon. *Universal Edition. Unpriced* UNR (B71-50632)
Reicha, Anton Joseph. Quintet for horn and strings in E major. Op.106. Quintet in E major. Op.106: for horn and string quartet (double bass ad lib). *Musica rara. Unpriced* NVNR (B71-50926)
Reid, Charles, *b.1900.* John Barbirolli: a biography. *Hamilton. £2.75* A/EC(P) (B71-18089) ISBN 0 241 01819 6
Reimann, Christian. Alleluja. Freuet euch ihr Christen alle. Alleluia! O rejoice ye Christians loudly: for mixed voices, organ (piano) and strings (ad lib). (Hammerschmidt, Andreas). *Peters; Hinrichsen. £0.45* DH/LF (B71-50191)
Renaissance song book: seven songs for mixed voices. (Parkinson, John Alfred). *Oxford University Press. £0.23* EZDW/AY (B71-50033) ISBN 0 19 330610 7
Rendall, Francis Geoffrey. The clarinet: some notes upon its history and construction. 3rd ed. *Benn. £2.75* AVV/B(X) (B71-20593) ISBN 0 510 36701 1
Resonemus laudibus: SATB. (Willcocks, David). *Oxford University Press. Unpriced* DP/LF (B71-50216) ISBN 0 19 343011 8
Resonet in laudibus. Excerpts. Hodie apparuit. On this day

the Christ appears: SSA or TTB. (Lasso, Orlando di). *Schirmer; Chappell. Unpriced* FEZDJ/LF (B71-50304)

Resources of music series. *(Cambridge University Press)*
John, Malcolm. Music drama in schools. *Cambridge University Press. £3.80* ACN(VF) (B71-20590) ISBN 0 521 08003 7

Response to music: principles of music education. (Brocklehurst, Brian). *Routledge and K. Paul. £1.40* A(VK/YC) (B71-03584) ISBN 0 7100 6949 9

Reutter, Hermann. Der Tod des Empedokles. Excerpts. Drei Monologue des Empedokles von Friedrich Holderlin: fur Bariton und Klavier oder Orchester. *Schott. £1.30* KGNDW (B71-50370)

Revelation and fall. Offenbarung und Untergang: for soprano and sixteen instrumentalists. (Davies, Peter Maxwell). *Boosey and Hawkes. Unpriced* KFLE/MRDX (B71-50359)

Reynolds, Gordon.
101 tunes to explore. (Chatterley, Albert). *Novello. £0.75* Q/R (B71-50961)
Organo pleno. *Novello. £0.35(non-net)* AR/E (B71-04183) ISBN 0 85360 004 x

Reynolds, Roger. Traces: piano, cello, signal generator, ring modulator; 6 channels of taped sound. *Peters; Hinrichsen. £2.50* PS (B71-50442)

Rhapsody: for oboe and strings (1951). (Korn, Peter Jona). Piano score. *Simrock. £1.00* VTPK (B71-50666)

Rhodes, Anthony. Musical instruments from the Renaissance to the 19th century. (Paganelli, Sergio). *Hamlyn. £0.90* AL/B(XDWC378) (B71-07323) ISBN 0 600 35920 4

Rhodes, Joseph W. They shall see the glory of the Lord: SATB. *Warner, Seven Arts; Blossom Music. Unpriced* DK (B71-50197)

Rhymes and rhythms: pieces for youth choir, piano, perc. and various optional instruments. (Pitfield, Thomas Baron). *Hinrichsen. £1.60* FLE/NYLDW (B71-50311)

Rhythm of the beating wings: a carol. (Ager, Lawrence). *Feldman. Unpriced* JFDP/LF (B71-50865)

Rhythmic dance: for four B flat clarinets. (Dillon, Robert). *Boosey and Hawkes. £0.65* VVNSH (B71-50670)

Ricci, Ruggiero. Sonata for violin solo. Op.115. Sonate fur Violine solo. Opus 115. (Prokofiev, Sergei). *Peters Hinrichsen. £0.90* SPME (B71-50579)

Rice, Tim. Jesus Christ Superstar- Excerpts. I don't know how to love him. (Webber, Andrew Lloyd). *Leeds Music. £0.20* KFDW (B71-50890)

Rich, Ellis.
Symphony no.40 in G minor. K.550 - Molto allegro. Mozart 40. (Mozart, Wolfgang Amadeus). *Feldman. Unpriced* WMK (B71-51105)
Symphony no.40 in G minor. K.550. Molto allegro. Mozart 40. (Mozart, Wolfgang Amadeus). *Feldman. Unpriced* QPK (B71-50509)

Richard Wagner: the man, his mind and his music. (Gutman, Robert William). *Penguin. £0.75* BWC(N) (B71-05793) ISBN 0 14 021168 3

Richardson, Alan.
First book of oboe solos. (Craxton, Janet). *Faber Music. £0.75* VTPK/AAY (B71-50147)
Sonatina for flute and piano. *Weinberger. Unpriced* VRPE (B71-50639)

Richardson, Norman.
Avalon: diversions on an original theme. *Boosey and Hawkes. Unpriced* WMJ (B71-51101)
Six more trumpet tunes. *Boosey and Hawkes. £0.65* WSPK/AAY (B71-51117)

Richter, Franz Xaver. Symphony with fugue in G minor. Sinfonia con fuga, g-Moll. *Schott. £1.50* MRE (B71-50409)

Ricketts, Michael. Music. *Macdonald and Co. £0.25* A (B71-19965) ISBN 0 356 03759 2

Riding into Bethlehem: for unison or two-part voices with piano, optional recorders, and optional percussion by W.H. Parry; words by L. Bell. (Parry, William Howard). *Oxford University Press. Unpriced* FDP/LF (B71-50829) ISBN 0 19 342048 1

Ridout, Alan.
Bagatelles. *Schott. Unpriced* SRPJ (B71-51030)
A farewell. *Stainer and Bell. Unpriced* DW (B71-50020)

Ries, Ferdinand. Sonate sentimentale: for flute or clarinet. Op.169. *Musica rara. £2.25* VRPE (B71-50141)

Rimbaud, Arthur. Think on dredful domesday: for s.S.A.T.B and chamber orchestra. (Burgon, Geoffrey). *Stainer and Bell. Unpriced* DX (B71-50779)

Rimmer, Joan. A children's Christmas festival: for voices, recorders and percussion. (Mendoza, Anne). *Oxford University Press. £0.50* JFE/NYHSDE/LF (B71-50876) ISBN 0 19 330566 6

Rinaldo - Sorge nel petto. Sarabande. (Handel, George Frideric). *Schott. Unpriced* SRPK/AHVL (B71-51040)

Ring out, wild bells: for four-part chorus of mixed voices a cappella. (Newbury, Kent A). *Schirmer; Chappell. Unpriced* EZDW (B71-50283)

Rios, Graziela Viera. *See* Viera Rios, Graziela.

Rios, Waldo de los.
Eine kleine Nachtmusik. K.525. Allegro. Mozart 13: serenade no.13 in G major. (Mozart, Wolfgang Amadeus). *Rondor Music; Hansen. £0.20* QPK (B71-50982)
Symphonies for the seventies. *Rondor Music. £1.25* QPK (B71-50983)
Symphony no.40 in G minor. K.550. Molto allegro. Mozart (Symphony no.40). (Mozart, Wolfgang Amadeus). *Rondor Music. £0.20* QPK (B71-50510)

Ripley, Graham. La Belle Helene. (Offenbach, Jacques). *United Music. Unpriced* CF (B71-50004)

Rising generation. (Siebert, Edrich). *Boosey and Hawkes. y2.64* WMG (B71-51095)

Rising of the moon: an opera in three acts. (Maw, Nicholas). *Boosey and Hawkes. Unpriced* CC (B71-50159)

Ritmo (Latin-American music): for percussion ensemble (7 players). (Fink, Siegfried). *Simrock. £1.10* XNP (B71-51123)

Ritual fire dance. (Falla, Manuel de). *Chester. Unpriced* WMK/AH (B71-51106)

Rivera y Rivera, Roberto. Dios itlazu nantzine. (Franco, Fernando). *Schott. £0.40* VSNSK/DH (B71-51077)

Rivers, Patrick. Ten canonic studies for recorders, nos. 1-7. Seven canonic studies. (Bergmann, Walter). *Schott. Unpriced* WNUK/AF (B71-51115)

Robert Farnon for brass: arranged for brass and reed band by Allan Street. (Farnon, Robert J). *Chappell. Unpriced* WMK (B71-51104)

Robert Simpson: fiftieth birthday essays. (Johnson, Edward). *Triad Press. £0.75* BSHM (B71-10427) ISBN 0 902070 01 0

Robinson, Douglas.
God rest you merry. *Ashdown. £0.09* EZDP/LF (B71-50803)
Good King Wenceslas. *Ashdown. £0.09* EZDP/LF (B71-50804)

Robinson, L Woodroffe. Holiday tunes: 18 easy pieces for pianoforte. *Freeman. Unpriced* QPJ (B71-50098)

Roche, Jerome. Palestrina. *Oxford University Press. £0.90* BPC(N) (B71-29385) ISBN 0 19 314117 5

Rocherolle, Eugenie R.
A joyful song: SATB. *Warner; Seven Arts; Blossom Music. Unpriced* DW (B71-50021)
Lookin' ahead (six feet under): S.A.B. *Warner; Blossom Music. Unpriced* DW (B71-50774)

Rockbooks. *(Studio Vista)*
Herman, Gary. The Who. *Studio Vista. £1.40* AB/E(P) (B71-16698) ISBN 0 289 70135 x
Millar, Bill. The Drifters: the rise and fall of the black vocal group. *Studio Vista. £1.40* AB/E(P) (B71-16703) ISBN 0 289 70133 3

Rodelinda. - Dove sei. Art thou troubled?: organ. (Handel, George Frideric). *Paxton. Unpriced* RK/DW (B71-50532)

Roe, Betty.
As I sat on a sunny bank: carol for treble voices and piano. *Thames. Unpriced* FLDP/LF (B71-50852)
Children's songs of the nativity: carol for woodwind (recorder, flute & clarinet or oboe), two-part women's or boy's voices, piano/organ and optional percussion. *Thames. Unpriced* FEZDP/LF (B71-50848)
Out of your sleep arise and wake: carol for SATB and trumpet, horn, cello and percussion. *Thames. Unpriced* ENYEXPNSDP/LF (B71-50783)
Ponder' songs of the seasons: for high voice and piano. *Thames. Unpriced* KFTDW (B71-50894)
Shadwell Stair: part-song for SATB and flute. *Thames. Unpriced* EVRDW (B71-50787)
Sweet Thames flow softly: part-song, SATB. *Thames. Unpriced* EZDW (B71-50817)
Unto us is born a son: carol for treble voices and piano. *Thames. Unpriced* FLDP/LF (B71-50853)

Roe, Paul F. Choral music education. *Prentice-Hall. £4.50* AD/E(VK) (B71-02480) ISBN 0 13 133348 8

Rohr, Heinrich. Vortragsbuchlein fur das Zusammenspiel: Sopran-und Altblockflote, Schlagwerk ad lib. *Schott. Unpriced* VSNUK/AAY (B71-50654)

Rokos, K W. Alceste. Excerpts. Overture: arranged for school, amateur or professional orchestras or for strings with optional full orchestra. (Gluck, Christoph Willibald von). *Bosworth. £0.375* MJ (B71-50068)

Roman sketches. Op.7: for piano. (Griffes, Charles Tomlinson). *Schirmer; Chappell. Unpriced* QPJ (B71-50092)

Romance and habanera: piano. Op.71. (Napoleao, Arthur). *Arthur Napoleao; Essex Music. Unpriced* QPJ (B71-50493)

Romance sans paroles. Op.23. (Davidov, Charles). *Schott. Unpriced* SRPJ (B71-51027)

Romance sem palavras: piano. (Netto, Barrozo). *Arthur Napoleao; Essex Music. Unpriced* QPJ (B71-50496)

Romances for violin & orchestra. Op.40 & 50. Romanzen. Op.40 (G-dur), Op.50 (F-dur): fur Violine und Orchester. (Beethoven, Ludwig van). *Peters; Hinrichsen. £0.90* SPK (B71-50571)

Romanzen. Op.40 (G-dur), Op.50 (F-dur): fur Violine und Orchester. (Beethoven, Ludwig van). *Peters; Hinrichsen. £0.90* SPK (B71-50571)

Rondino: solo for B flat trumpet (or cornet) with piano accompaniment. (Street, Allan). *Boosey and Hawkes. £0.35* WSP/W (B71-50154)

Room, Peter. Nursery rhymes. *Leeds Music. Unpriced* JFE/NYJDW/GK/AY (B71-50877)

Room for company: folk songs and ballads selected and edited by. (Palmer, Roy). *Cambridge University Press. y1.38* JFDW/G/AYD (B71-50870) ISBN 0 521 08173 4

Rorem, Ned.
Lift up your heads. (The ascension). *Boosey and Hawkes. y4.50* DH/LM (B71-50749)
Lift up your heads. (The ascension). *Boosey and Hawkes. £1.10* ENYHXPNRDH/LM (B71-50784)
Miracles of Christmas: for four-part mixed chorus and organ (or piano). *Boosey and Hawkes. £1.05* DE/LF (B71-50175)

Rosas, Juventino. Mexican march. *Bosworth. £0.875* WMK/AGM (B71-50152)

Rose, Arnold. The singer and the voice: vocal physiology and technique for singers. 2nd ed. *Faber and Faber Ltd. £3.00* AB/E (B71-10432) ISBN 0 571 04725 4

Rose, Bernard. Musica Deo Sacra. Service no.1. Excerpts. Magnificat and Nunc dimittis: for SATB. (Tomkins, Thomas). *Novello. Unpriced* DGPP (B71-50743)

Rose, Margaret E. Folk and vision: book of words and melody. *Hart-Davis. Unpriced* JFE/TSDW/G/AY (B71-50879) ISBN 0 247 54443 4

Rosen, Charles. The classical style: Haydn, Mozart, Beethoven. *Faber and Faber Ltd. £7.00* A(X) (B71-09738) ISBN 0 571 09118 0

Ross, Walter.
Concerto for brass quintet & orchestra. Piano reduction. *Boosey and Hawkes. £2.10* WNRK/LF (B71-50711)
Cryptical triptych: for trombone and piano. *Boosey and Hawkes. £1.05* WUPJ (B71-50720)

Rossetti, Christina.
A children's game: for women's voices with piano four-hand accompaniment. (Schoenfield, Paul). *Schirmer Chappell. Unpriced* FDX (B71-50297)
Love came down at Christmas: SATB. (Rutter, John). *Oxford University Press. Unpriced* DP/LF (B71-50764) ISBN 0 19 343025 8
Two doves: for full chorus of mixed voices a cappella by John Chorbajian; words by Christina Rossetti. (Chorbajian, John). *Schirmer; Chappell. Unpriced* EZDW (B71-50270)

Rostal, Max. Concerto for violin in D major. Op.61. Violin-Konzert, D-Dur: fur Violine und Orchester. Op.61. (Beethoven, Ludwig van). Klavierauszug. *Schott. £1.50* SPK/LF (B71-50573)

Rostropovich, Mstislav.
Concerto for cello & orchestra. (Bliss, *Sir* Arthur). *Novello. £2.50* MPSRF (B71-50404)
Concerto for cello & orchestra
Cello & piano score. (Bliss, *Sir* Arthur). *Novello. £1.50* SRPK/LF (B71-50597)

Rothenberg, Peter. Elektronische Orgel klassisch. *Schott. £1.20* RPVK (B71-51002)

Rowe, Christopher. Man on the move: songs on the past, present and future of transport. *Galliard. Unpriced* JE/TSDW (B71-50319)

Royal College of Organists. Year book 1970/1971. *Royal College of Organists. £0.525* AR(YC/VP/Q) (B71-04184) ISBN 0 902462 01 6

Royal School of Church Music.
Choral wedding service. Revised ed.. *Royal School of Church Music. Unpriced* DGM/KDD (B71-50179) ISBN 0 85402 019 5
English church music: a collection of essays 1971. *Royal School of Church Music. £0.76* AD/LD(D) (B71-16701) ISBN 0 85402 021 7
Festival service book
5. *Royal School of Church Music. Unpriced* DGM (B71-50178) ISBN 0 85402 018 7

Royston, N. Symphony no.40 in G minor. K.550 - Molto allegro. Mozart 40. (Mozart, Wolfgang Amadeus). *Feldman. Unpriced* WMK (B71-51105)

Rozmann, Akos. Improvvisazione: per flauto e pianoforte. *Boosey and Hawkes. Unpriced* VRPJ (B71-50644)

Rubbra, Edmund. Rune of hospitality. Op. 15: song with piano accompaniment. Revised ed.. *Lengnick. Unpriced* KDW (B71-50886)

Rudrum, Kenneth. Gay recorders: for descant or treble recorder with piano accompaniment. *Paterson. Unpriced* VSPJ (B71-51078)

Rudzinski, Zbigniew. Quartet for two pianos and percussion. Quartett fur zwei Klaviere und Schlagzeug. *Schott. £1.80* NYLNS (B71-50440)

Ruf, Hugo.
Einzelstucke und Suiten: fur Altblockflote solo. *Schott. £0.80* VSSPMG/AY (B71-50659)
Sonata for bassoon and basso continuo in G major. Sonata, G-Dur: fur Fagott oder Violoncello und Basso continuo. (Galliard, Johann Ernst). *Schott. £0.90* VWPE (B71-50684)
Sonata for oboe & basso continuo in E minor. Sonata e-Moll: fur Oboe (Querflote, Violine) und Basso continuo. (Chedeville, Nicolas). *Schott. £0.90* VTPE (B71-50663)
Sonata for violin, cello and basso continuo in E major. Liv.2, no.12. Triosonate, E-Dur: fur Violine, Violoncello oder Viola da gamba und Basso continuo. (Francoeur, Francois). *Schott. £1.20* NXNTE (B71-50430)
Sonatas for harpsichord. Sonate di gravicembalo
Band 1: Sonate 1 -6. (Paradisi, Pietro Domenico). *Schott. £1.40* QRPE (B71-50989)
Sonatas for harpsichord. Sonate di gravicembalo
Band 2: Sonate 7-12. (Paradisi, Pietro Domenico). *Schott. £1.40* QRPE (B71-50988)
Suite for flute & basso continuo in B minor. Op.35, no.5. Suite h-Moll: fur Querflote und Basso continuo. (Boismortier, Joseph Bodin de). *Schott. £1.10* VRPG (B71-50640)
Suite for flute & basso continuo in G major. Op.35, no.2. Suite, g-Dur: fur Querflote und Basso continuo. (Boismortier, Joseph Bodin de). *Schott. £1.00* VRPG (B71-50641)
Suite for oboe and basso continuo no.1 in G minor (1er livre). Suite 1, g-Moll: fur Oboe (Querflote, Violine) und Basso continuo,. (Philidor, Anne Danican). *Schott. £0.90* VTPG (B71-50664)
Suites for flute. Op.36 nos.1-6. Sechs Suiten: fur Querflote solo. (Boismortier, Joseph Bodin de). *Schott. £1.20* VRPMG (B71-50647)
Zwei Duos alter englischer Meister: fur Altblockfloten (Querfloten, Oboen). *Schott. £0.70* VSNUE/AYD (B71-50653)

Rund um die Welt: folkloristische Tanzmelodien fu Blockflotenquartett (Streicher) und Schlagwerke, Gitarre ad lib;. (Draths, Willi). *Schott. £1.00* NYESK/DW/G/AYB (B71-50434)

Rune of hospitality. Op. 15: song with piano accompaniment. (Rubbra, Edmund). Revised ed.. *Lengnick. Unpriced* KDW (B71-50886)

Runze, Klaus. Zwei Hande-zwolf Tasten
Band 1: Ein Buch mit Bildern fur kleine Klavierspieler. *Schott. £2.40* Q/AC (B71-50940)
Rushmore, Robert. The singing voice. *Hamilton. £3.00* AB/E (B71-12557) ISBN 0 241 01947 8
Russell, Leslie. Suite for flute & piano, no.1. Suite one: for flute (or violin) and piano. *Boosey and Hawkes. y0.50* VRPJ (B71-51072)
Russell-Smith, Geoffry.
Bicinia hungarica
Vol.4: 60 progressive two-part songs. (Kodaly, Zoltan). Revised English ed. *Boosey and Hawkes. Unpriced* FEZDW (B71-50045)
Invocation of peace: Bekesser ohajtas: S.A.T.B. unaccompanied. (Kodaly, Zoltan). *Boosey and Hawkes. Unpriced* EZDW (B71-50274)
Jesus and the traders: for S.A.T.B. (Kodaly, Zoltan). Revised ed. *Universal Music. Unpriced* EZDH (B71-50254)
Matra pictures: a set of Hungarian folksongs for S.A.T.B. (Kodaly, Zoltan). Revised ed. *Universal. Unpriced* EZDW/G/AYG (B71-50285)
Prayer for honour: Szep Konyorges: S.A.T.B. unaccompanied. (Kodaly, Zoltan). *Boosey and Hawkes. Unpriced* EZDW (B71-50275)
Ruthardt, A. Preludes and fugues for piano. Op.35. Six preludes and fugues. Op.35: piano solo. (Mendelssohn, Felix). *Peters, Hinrichsen. £0.60* QP/Y (B71-50462)
Rutter, John.
Christ the Lord is risen again: SATB. *Oxford University Press. £0.09* DM/LL (B71-50209) ISBN 0 19 351109 6
Flemish carol: tune old Flemish, SATB. *Oxford University Press. Unpriced* DP/LF (B71-50213) ISBN 0 19 343014 2
Love came down at Christmas: SATB. *Oxford University Press. Unpriced* DP/LF (B71-50764) ISBN 0 19 343025 8
Nativity carol: S.S.A. *Oxford University Press. Unpriced* FDP/LF (B71-50289) ISBN 0 19 342591 2
Quem pastores laudavere. Shepherds left their flocks a-straying: German carol SATB unacc. *Oxford University Press. Unpriced* EZDP/LF (B71-50260) ISBN 0 19 343012 6
Wachet auf. S.140. Excerpts. Zion hears the watchmen's voices: for unison & SATB chorale. (Bach, Johann Sebastian). *Oxford University Press. Unpriced* DM (B71-50202) ISBN 0 19 343013 4
Sabre las olas. Mexican march. (Rosas, Juventino). *Bosworth. £0.875* WMK/AGM (B71-50152)
Saccade: piano, four hands. (Helps, Robert). *Peters Hinrichsen. £0.90* QNV (B71-50451)
Sadie, Stanley.
A favorite duet: for two bassoons or violoncellos. (Alcock, John, *b.1740*). *Piers Press. Unpriced* VWNU (B71-50148)
Opera: a modern guide. (Jacobs, Arthur). *David and Charles. £3.00* AC (B71-08377) ISBN 0 7153 5013 7
Sonata for piano in B flat major. K281. Sonata in B flat: pianoforte. K.281. (Mozart, Wolfgang Amadeus). *Associated Board of the Royal Schools of Music. £0.35* QPE (B71-50086)
Sonata for piano in D major. K.311. Sonata in D. K.311. (Mozart, Wolfgang Amadeus). *Associated Board of the Royal Schools of Music. £0.35* QPE (B71-50464)
Sonata for piano in E flat major. K.282. Sonata in E flat. K.282. (Mozart, Wolfgang Amadeus). *Associated Board of the Royal Schools of Music. £0.35* QPE (B71-50465)
Sadleir, Dick. Album for guitar. *Feldman. £0.35* TSPMK/AAY (B71-50613)
Sadleir, Richard.
Four easy scores: arranged for recorder, guitar and percussion. *Feldman. £0.25* NYESK/AAY (B71-50937)
Master method for guitar: based on progressive arrangements of excerpts from the works of great masters. *Feldman. £0.50* TS/AC (B71-51048)
St Christopher. Stupendous thought. (Forrester, Leon). *Banks. Unpriced* DH (B71-50011)
Salaverde, Bartolomeo de Selma y. *See* Selma y Salaverde, Bartolomeo de.
Salter, Lionel.
Don Giovanni; libretto by Lorenzo da Ponte to the opera by W.A. Mozart; and, Idomeneo; libretto by Giambattista Varesco to the opera by W.A. Mozart. (Da Ponte, Lorenzo). *Cassell. £1.75* BMSAC (B71-24691) ISBN 0 304 93824 6
Le Nozze di Figaro; and, Cosi fan tutte; librettos by Lorenzo da Ponte to the operas by W.A. Mozart. (Da Ponte, Lorenzo). *Cassell. £1.75* BMSAC (B71-25344) ISBN 0 304 93826 2
Die Zauberflote; libretto by Emanuel Schikaneder to the opera by W.A. Mozart; and, Die Entfuhrung aus dem Serail; libretto by Gottlieb Stephanie to the opera by W.A. Mozart. (Schikaneder, Emanuel). *Cassell. £1.75* BMSAC (B71-24690) ISBN 0 304 93825 4
Salvation Army.
Salvation Army Brass Band Journal (Festival series). *Salvationist Publishing and Supplies. Unpriced* WM/AY (B71-51091)
Salvation Army Brass Band Journal (General series). *Salvationist Publishing. Unpriced* WM/AY (B71-50688)
Salvation Army Brass Band Journal (General series). *Salvationist Publishing and Supplies. £0.50* WM/AY (B71-50689)
Salvation Army Brass Band Journal (General series). *Salvationist Publishing and Supplies. Unpriced* WM/AY (B71-51092)
Salvation Army Brass Band Journal (Triumph series). *Salvationist Publishing. Unpriced* WM/AY (B71-50690)
Salvation Army Brass Band Journal (Triumph series). *Salvationist Publishing. Unpriced* WM/AY (B71-50691)
Salvation Army Brass Band Journal (Triumph series). *Salvationist Publishing and Supplies. Unpriced* WM/AY (B71-51093)
Salvation Army Brass Band Journal (General series). (Salvation Army). *Salvationist Publishing. Unpriced* WM/AY (B71-50688)
Salvatore, Gaston. Versuch uber Schweine: fur Stimme und Orchester. (Henze, Hans Werner). *Schott. £3.20* KE/MDX (B71-50059)
Salzer, Felix. The music forum
Vol.2. *Columbia University Press. £6.05* A(D) (B71-06290) ISBN 0 231 03153 x
Samuel, Claude. Prokofiev. *Calder and Boyars. £2.25* BPP(N) (B71-24085) ISBN 0 7145 0489 0
Sanahin: partita for organ. (Hovhaness, Alan). *Peters Hinrichsen. £0.90* RG (B71-50518)
Sandy, Stephen. Soaking: for four-part chorus of mixed voices a cappella. (Wilson, Richard). *Schirmer; Chappell. Unpriced* EZDW (B71-50284)
Sansom, Clive. The Irish fiddler: unison. (Veal, Arthur). *Oxford University Press. Unpriced* JFDW (B71-50053)
Sansom, Clive A. Oh! Noah. *Studio Music. Unpriced* CN (B71-50165)
Sari, Jozsef. Episodi: per pianoforte. *Boosey and Hawkes. Unpriced* QPJ (B71-50499)
Sary, Laszlo. Catacoustics: for two pianos. *Boosey and Hawkes. £0.86* QNU (B71-50449)
Sary, Laszlo. Fluttuazioni: per violino e pianoforte. *Boosey and Hawkes. Unpriced* SPJ (B71-50568)
Satz fur Klavier. (Webern, Anton von). *Boosey and Hawkes. Unpriced* QPJ (B71-50505)
Sauer, Emil von.
Ballades for piano. Two ballades. (Liszt, Franz). *Peters Hinrichsen. £0.50* QPJ (B71-50489)
Legendes. Two legends. (Liszt, Franz). *Peters; Hinrichsen. £0.40* QPJ (B71-50490)
Savio, Isaias.
Modinha Serestas no.5: 1 violao with Adeus, Bela Morena and, Cirandinhas no.2: 2 violaoes. (Villa-Lobos, Heitor). *Arthur Napoleao; Essex Music. Unpriced* SPMK (B71-50581)
Suites for piano. Excerpts. Caminho da serra; and Cacando Borboletas; and, Madrugada; and, Na Beira do Rio. (Lorenzo Fernandez, Oscar). *Arthur Napoleao; Essex Music. Unpriced* SPMK (B71-50580)
Sawitsch, Owady. Die Sonne der Inkas: fur Sopran, 3 Sprecher und II Instrumentalisten. (Denisov, Edisson). *Universal. Unpriced* KFLE/MRDX (B71-50358)
Scandello, Antonio. Canzoni napoletane. Lib 1, no.14. Voria che ta cantass'. Neapolitan song. *Warner; Blossom Music. Unpriced* EZDU (B71-50812)
Scenes and arias. (Maw, Nicholas). *Boosey and Hawkes. £2.50* JNFDE/MDW (B71-50880)
Scherzo & cortege, on themes from Julius Caesar. (Ireland, John). *Boosey and Hawkes. £1.10* MMK/JM (B71-50075)
Schikaneder, Emanuel. Die Zauberflote; libretto by Emanuel Schikaneder to the opera by W.A. Mozart; and, Di Entfuhrung aus dem Serail; libretto by Gottlieb Stephanie to the opera by W.A. Mozart. *Cassell. £1.75* BMSAC (B71-24690) ISBN 0 304 93825 4
Schiotz, Aksel. The singer and his art. *Hamilton. £3.00* AB/E (B71-06912) ISBN 0 241 01949 4
Schmidt, Harold.
Balletti for five voices (1591). Fifteen balletti: SSATB a cappella (recorders and strings ad libitum)
Introduttioni a i Balletti: O compagni allegrezza. (Companions, be happy). (Gastoldi, Giovanni). New ed. *Peters; Hinrichsen. £0.40* EZDU (B71-50263)
Balletti for five voices (1591). Fifteen balletti: SSATB a cappella (recorders and strings ad libitum)
Set 3. (Gastoldi, Giovanni). New ed. *Peters; Hinrichsen. £0.40* EZDU (B71-50264)
Schmidt, Harold C. Balletti for five voices (1591). Fifteen balletti: SSATB a cappella (recorders and strings ad libitum)
Set 4. (Gastoldi, Giovanni). New ed. *Peters; Hinrichsen. £0.40* EZDU (B71-50265)
Schneider, Max. Die Anfange des Basso continuo und seiner Bezifferung. *Gregg. £7.20* A/RGD (B71-17374) ISBN 0 576 28963 9
Schneider, Willy. Suite for brass, no.2. Blechblaser Suite No.2. (Horsch, Hans). *Schott. £1.60* WNS (B71-50712)
Schnittke, Alfred. Pianissimo... *Universal. Unpriced* MMJ (B71-50398)
Schoenberg: a critical biography. (Reich, Willi). *Longman. £3.50* BSET (B71-16010) ISBN 0 582 12753 x
Schoenfield, Paul. A children's game: for women's voices with piano four-hand accompaniment. *Schirme Chappell. Unpriced* FDX (B71-50297)
Scholey, Arthur. The song of Caedmon. (Swann, Donald). *Bodley Head. £1.50* FDD (B71-50824)
Schonberg, Harold C. The lives of the great composers. *Davis-Poynter Ltd. £5.00* A/D(YB/M) (B71-26600) ISBN 0 7067 0001 5
School of English Church Music. *See* Royal School of Church Music.
Schools Council. Music and the young school leaver: problems and opportunities. *Evans Bros; Methuen Educational. £0.23* A(MN/YD) (B71-18711) ISBN 0 423 46500 7
Schostakowitsch, Dmitri. *See* Shostakovich, Dmitri.
Schostakowitsch, Dmitri. *See* Shostakovich, Dmitri.
Schott, Howard. Playing the harpsichord. *Faber and Faber Ltd. £2.75* AQR/E (B71-29388) ISBN 0 571 09203 9
Schubert, Franz.
Overture for strings in C minor. D.8. Ouverture, C-moll: fur Kammerorchester, nach der Ouverture C-moll fur Streicher. *Litolff, Peters; Hinrichsen. Unpriced* MRK (B71-50414)
Overture for strings in C minor. D.8. Ouverture, C-moll: fur Streicher (Zweite Fassung). *Litolff, Peters; Hinrichsen. £1.60* RXN (B71-50543)
Overture for strings in C minor. D.8. Overture, C-moll: fur Streicher. *Litolff, Peters; Hinrichsen. £1.60* RXN (B71-50544)
Overture in C major (in the Italian style) D. 591. *Eulenburg. £0.75* MMJ (B71-50909)
Overture in D major (in the Italian style) D. 590. *Eulenberg. £0.75* MMJ (B71-50910)
Sonata for piano duet in B flat major. Grand sonata. Op.30: for pianoforte duet. *Associated Board of the Royal Schools of Music. Unpriced* QNVE (B71-50969)
Tantum ergo in E flat (1828). D.962: for four-part chorus of mixed voices and solo quartet (ad lib.) with organ or piano accompaniment. *Schirmer; Chappell. Unpriced* DGLBT (B71-50177)
Wiegenlied. Op.98, no.2. *Schott. Unpriced* SRPK/DW (B71-51041)
Schubert. (Einstein, Alfred). *Panther. £0.75* BSF (B71-14241) ISBN 0 586 03480 3
Schubert. (Young, Percy Marshall). *Benn. £0.90* BSF(N) (B71-01699) ISBN 0 510 13732 6
Schultz-Hauser, Karlheinz.
Jagdmusik: 12 kleine Stucke, fur zwei Horner. (Sperger, Johann Matthias). *Schott. £0.70* WTNU/GT (B71-50155)
Sonata for violin, viola da gamba & harpsichord in G minor. Sonate g-moll fur Violine, Viola da gamba (Viola) und Cembalo by Georg Philipp Telemann; herausgegeben von Karlheinz Schultz-Hauser. (Telemann, Georg Philipp). *Peters; Hinrichsen. £1.05* NXNTE (B71-50429)
Schuman, William. Orpheus with his lute: arranged by the composer for four-part chorus of mixed voices with piano accompaniment. *Schirmer; Chappell. £0.10* DW (B71-50022)
Schumann, Robert.
Abendlied. Op.85, no.12. *Schott. Unpriced* SRPK (B71-51036)
Lied. Op. 29, no.2. In meinen Garten. In my garden. *Schirmer; Chappell. Unpriced* FDW (B71-50839)
Schutz, Heinrich. Psalmen Davids sampt etlichen Moteten und Concerten, no.19. Ist nicht Ephraim mein teurer Sohn? Is not Ephraim my precious Son?: Motete a 8 e 16 con due cappelle in fine, for mixed voices and instruments. *Oxford University Press. £0.95* EWNNDH (B71-50788) ISBN 0 19 338084 6
Score of nursery rhymes. (Blackburn, Maria). *Feldman. y0.25* QPJ (B71-50975)
Scott, David.
Fifty songs for high voice
Book 1. (Dowland, John). Revised ed. *Stainer and Bell. Unpriced* KFTDW (B71-50063)
Book 2. (Dowland, John). Revised ed. *Stainer and Bell. Unpriced* KFTDW (B71-50064)
Fifty songs for low voice
Book 1. (Dowland, John). Revised ed. *Stainer and Bell. Unpriced* KFXDW (B71-50065)
Book 2. (Dowland, John). Revised ed. *Stainer and Bell. Unpriced* KFXDW (B71-50066)
Scottish cameo. (Siebert, Edrich). *Studio Music. Unpriced* WMK/DW/AYDL (B71-50709)
Scottish folk-song. (Angus-Butterworth, Lionel Milner). *L.M. Angus-Butterworth. Unpriced* ADW/G(YDL) (B71-19970) ISBN 0 9501956 0 x
Search: songs of the sun. (Campbell, David). *Galliard. Unpriced* JEZDW (B71-50862) ISBN 0 85249 160 3
Searle, Humphrey. Hamlet. Op. 48: opera in three acts. *Faber. Unpriced* CC (B71-50160)
Second Penguin book of English madrigals: for five voices. (Stevens, Denis). *Penguin. £0.50* EZDU/AYD (B71-50029) ISBN 0 14 070837 5
Seeley, Charles. To a young music lover. *Stockwell. £1.25* A (B71-14239) ISBN 0 7223 0050 6
Sehnsucht. Longing. Op.112, no.1: for four-part chorus of mixed voices with piano accompaniment. (Brahms, Johannes). *Schirmer; Chappell. Unpriced* DW (B71-50228)
Seixas, Carlos de. Sonatas for harpsichord in A minor. S.K.71, 80. Zwei Sonaten. *Schott. £0.50* TSPMK/AE (B71-50614)
Selections. Piano arrangements for all to play. (Tchaikovsky, Peter). *Francis, Day and Hunter. £0.90* QPK (B71-50511)
Self, George.
The evening draws in: for solo vocalist, chorus, piano and percussion. *Universal. Unpriced* FE/NYLDW (B71-50299)
Shriek: for 4, 8 or more descant recorders. *Universal. £0.15* VSRN (B71-50655)
Take a shape: for voices. *Universal. £0.20* FEZDX (B71-50307)
Selma y Salaverde, Bartolomeo de.
Canzon for two bassoons & basso continuo. XXIII Canzon a 2 Bassi: fur 2 Fagotte oder Posaune und Fagott und Basso continuo. *Schott. £1.00* VWNTPW (B71-50682)
Fantasia for bassoon in D minor. V Fantasia ex D: fur Fagott und Basso continuo. *Schott. £1.10* VWPJ (B71-50685)
Seltzer, Isadore. Leonard Bernstein's young people's concerts. (Bernstein, Leonard). Revised and expanded ed.. *Cassell. £2.10* A (B71-25914) ISBN 0 304 93819 x
Selve morale e spirituale. Excerpts. Deus tuorum militum: himnus unius martyris for T.T.B. with two violins and continuo. (Monteverdi, Claudio). *Oxford University Press. Unpriced* GE/SNTPWDJ (B71-50900) ISBN 0 19 353272 7

Senator, Ronald. A basket of eggs and other rhymes: for infants and juniors. *Boosey and Hawkes. £0.75* JFE/NYLDW (B71-50055)

Sequenza VI: per viola solo. (Berio, Luciano). *Universal. Unpriced* SQPMJ (B71-50585)

Serenade in percussione: for clarinet, double-bass and percussion (3 players). (Fink, Siegfried). *Simrock. £0.85* NYEVNR (B71-50435)

Serenade pour Montreux: pour 2 hautbois, 2 cors et orchestre a cordes. (Sutermeister, Heinrich). *Schott. £1.60* RXMPUNS (B71-50538)

Serestas. Excerpts. Cancao do Carreiro ou Cancao u crepusculo caricioso: canto e piano. (Villa-Lobos, Heitor). *Arthur Napoleao; Essex Music. Unpriced* KDW (B71-50057)

Serious I-VIII: piano accordion. (Surdin, Morris). *Boosey and Hawkes. Unpriced* RSPMJ (B71-50113)

Serraillier, Ian. A pride of lions: a story for singing and staging. (Tate, Phyllis). *Oxford University Press. Unpriced* CQN (B71-50735)

Seven canonic studies. (Bergmann, Walter). *Schott. Unpriced* WNUK/AF (B71-51115)

Seven easy pieces by Elizabethan composers. (Hodgson, Martyn). *Regina Music. Unpriced* TSPMK (B71-50134)

Seven limericks: for two-part choir & small orchestra. (Bush, Geoffrey). *Novello. £0.50* FE/MDX (B71-50044)

Seven polyphonic amens: for unaccompanied voices. (Blyton, Carey). *Leeds Music. Unpriced* EZDTM (B71-50811)

Shadwell Stair: part-song for SATB and flute. (Roe, Betty). *Thames. Unpriced* EVRDW (B71-50787)

Shakespeare, William.
 Come away, come away, Death: for full chorus of mixed voices a cappella. (Chorbajian, John). *Schirmer; Chappell. Unpriced* EZDW (B71-50814)
 Orpheus with his lute: arranged by the composer for four-part chorus of mixed voices with piano accompaniment. (Schuman, William). *Schirmer; Chappell. £0.10* DW (B71-50022)

Sharp, Mary, *b.1907*. Humour in music. *Stockwell. £0.175* AQ/E(VC) (B71-04182) ISBN 0 7223 0133 2

Sharpe, Frederick.
 The bells of the Isles of Scilly. *Sharpe. £0.10* AXSR/B(YDFS) (B71-07870) ISBN 0 9500835 2 6
 The church bells of Herefordshire: their inscriptions and founders
 Vol.3: Kington-Pudlestone. *F. Sharpe. £1.75* AXSR/B(YDHR) (B71-04597) ISBN 0 9500835 1 8

Shaw, Pat. A popular selection of English dance airs
 Book 4: Sword and ceremony. (Fleming-Williams, Nan). *English Folk Dance and Song Society. £0.25* LH/G/AYD (B71-50896)

Shaw, Watkins. Try me, O God: short full anthem. (Nares, James). *Novello. £0.06* EZDK (B71-50026)

Shelley, Percy Bysshe. I arise from dreams of thee: two-part song, optional unison. (Dale, Mervyn). *Ashdown. Unpriced* FDW (B71-50831)

Shenfield, Margaret. Mozart and his world. (Valentin, Erich). *Thames and Hudson. £1.75* BMS(N) (B71-08375) ISBN 0 500 13029 9

Shepherd, Burt. Here's Jupiter: SATB a cappella (or improvised rock accompaniment ad lib). (Kent, Richard). *Warner; Seven Arts; Blossom Music. Unpriced* EZDW (B71-50032)

Shepherd, Edwin T.
 Emmanuel songs. *Marshall, Morgan and Scott. £0.45* DM/AY (B71-50757) ISBN 0 551 05416 6
 Emmanuel songs
 Vol.3. *Marshall, Morgan and Scott. £0.45* DM/AY (B71-50756) ISBN 0 551 05049 7

Shilovsky, Konstantin. Eugene Onegin: lyric scenes in three acts and seven scenes. (Tchaikovsky, Peter). *Schauer and May. Unpriced* CC (B71-50730)

Shore's trumpet: eight pieces for B flat trumpet and piano. (Barsham, Eve). *Boosey and Hawkes. £0.55* WSPK (B71-51116)

Shostakovich, Dmitri.
 Concerto for violin, no.2. Op.129. Konzert No.2 fur Violine und Orchester. Op.129
 Ausgabe fur Violine und Klavier vom Komponisten. *Peters; Hinrichsen. £2.00* SPK/LF (B71-50574)
 Piano compositions. *Peters; Hinrichsen. £1.00* QPJ (B71-50500)
 Sonata for piano, no.1. Opus 12. Sonate fur Klavier, no.1. Opus 12. *Peters; Hinrichsen. £0.90* QPE (B71-50466)

Shostakovich. (Kay, Norman). *Oxford University Press. £0.90* BSGR(N) (B71-29386) ISBN 0 19 315422 6

Show boat. (Kern, Jerome). *Chappell. £0.30* RPVK/CM (B71-51003)

Shriek: for 4, 8 or more descant recorders. (Self, George). *Universal. £0.15* VSRN (B71-50655)

Shuldham-Shaw, Pat. *See* Shaw, Pat.

Shuttleworth, Anna. Playing the cello: an approach through live music making. (Cole, Hugo). *Novello. 1.50* SR/AC (B71-50586)

Si tu veux, nous nous aimerons: for soprano and piano. (Furnivall, Anthony). *Sycamore Press. Unpriced* KFLDW (B71-50356)

Siebert, Edrich.
 Amazing grace: traditional. *Studio Music. Unpriced* WMK (B71-50705)
 The big parade: quick march. *Studio Music. Unpriced* WMGM (B71-50694)
 Quartets for strings, nos.1, 6 and 2 - Excerpts. Quartet no.1 on themes from Beethoven. (Beethoven, Ludwig van). *Studio Music. Unpriced* WNSK (B71-50713)
 The rising generation. *Boosey and Hawkes. y2.64* WMG (B71-51095)
 A Scottish cameo. *Studio Music. Unpriced* WMK/DW/AYDL (B71-50709)

Snowbird. (MacLellan, Gene). *Ardmore and Beechwood. Unpriced* UMMK/DW (B71-51063)

Snowbird. (MacLellan, Gene). *Ardmore and Beechwood. Unpriced* WMK/DW (B71-51109)

Tales of Beatrix Potter: selection from the ballet. (Lanchbery, John). *E.M.I. Film Music; Keith Prowse Music. y1.50* WMK/AHM/JR (B71-51107)

Tango militaire: cornet solo. *Studio Music. Unpriced* WMHVR (B71-51098)

A Welsh cameo. *Studio Music. Unpriced* WMK/DW/AYDK (B71-50708)

Silent night. (Gruber, Franz). *Oxford University Press. Unpriced* DP/LF (B71-50763) ISBN 0 19 343022 3

Silk, Richard. Sing and rejoice: SATB. *Oxford University Press. Unpriced* DK (B71-50198) ISBN 0 19 350315 8

Silverman, Jerry. Folk songs for schools and camps: 81 favourite songs. *Robbins Music; Francis, Day and Hunter. £0.75* JFEZDW/G/AY (B71-50328)

Simple gifts: American Shaker song. (Pooler, Marie). *Schirmer; Chappell. Unpriced* DW (B71-50769)

Simples: a setting of James Joyce's poem. (Bliss, *Sir* Arthur). *Oxford University Press. £0.80* KDW (B71-50336) ISBN 0 19 345165 4

Simples coletanea: colecao de 3 pecas for piano
 No.1: Valsa mistica. (Villa-Lobos, Heitor). *Arthu Napoleao; Essex Music. Unpriced* QPJ (B71-50503)
 No.3: Rodante. (Villa-Lobos, Heitor). *Arthur Napoleao; Essex Music. Unpriced* QPJ (B71-50504)

Simpson, John.
 Divertimento: for 3 clarinets in B flat. *Feldman. Unpriced* VVNT (B71-51087)
 The piper o'Dundee: for S.A.B. *Feldman. Unpriced* DW (B71-50234)

Simpson, Lionel. Song of the refugee children; and, Chorus of the Holy Innocents. *Feldman. Unpriced* EZDP/LF (B71-50802)

Simpson, Robert. Energy: symphonic study for brass band. *Boosey and Hawkes. Unpriced* WMJ (B71-51102)

Sinfonia (1968): for eight voices and orchestra. (Berio, Luciano). *Universal. Unpriced* JNAYE/MDX (B71-50329)

Sing a lullabye for Jesus. (Verrall, Pamela Motley). *Freeman. Unpriced* FDP/LF (B71-50290)

Sing and rejoice: SATB. (Silk, Richard). *Oxford University Press. Unpriced* DK (B71-50198) ISBN 0 19 350315 8

Sing Emmanuel: the story of Edwin Shepherd and the London Emmanuel Choir. (Capon, John). *Word Books. £0.50* AD/E(QB/DB) (B71-27971) ISBN 0 85009 031 8

Sing softly: for two-part chorus of young voices with organ accompaniment (ad lib.). (Hoag, Charles K). *Schirmer Chappell. Unpriced* FEZDH/LF (B71-50845)

Sing to God: Christian songs for juniors. (Old, Margaret V). *Scripture Union. £1.25* DM/AY (B71-50755) ISBN 0 85421 302 3

Sing unto God. (Wedding anthem for Frederick, Prince of Wales, 1736): for soloists, chorus and orchestra. (Handel, George Frideric). *Oxford University Press. £0.80* DK/KDD (B71-50201) ISBN 0 19 336660 6

Sing up: a guide and encouragement to sing in church. (Tamblyn, Bill). *G. Chapman. £0.80* AD/LSB/E (B71-16702) ISBN 0 225 65904 2

Singer and his art. (Schiotz, Aksel). *Hamilton. £3.00* AB/E (B71-06912) ISBN 0 241 01949 4

Singer and the voice: vocal physiology and technique for singers. (Rose, Arnold). 2nd ed. *Faber and Faber Ltd. £3.00* AB/E (B71-10432) ISBN 0 571 04725 4

Singers all: ten songs arranged for four-part singing (unchanged and changing voices). (Cooper, Irvin). *Oxford University Press. £0.45* DW/G/AY (B71-50775) ISBN 0 19 330240 3

Singing voice. (Rushmore, Robert). *Hamilton. £3.00* AB/E (B71-12557) ISBN 0 241 01947 8

Sir Arthur Sullivan. (Young, Percy Marshall). *Dent. £4.00* BSW(N) (B71-28694) ISBN 0 460 03934 2

Sir Christemas: SATB. (Mathias, William). *Oxford University Press. Unpriced* DP/LF (B71-50212) ISBN 0 19 343008 8

Six Christmas hymns: for mixed voices and organ (or orchestra). (Willcocks, David). *Oxford University Press. £0.20* DP/LF/AY (B71-50217) ISBN 0 19 353568 8

Six conversations: for clarinet with piano accompaniment. (Verrall, Pamela). *Feldman. Unpriced* VVPJ (B71-50677)

Six easy pieces: for classic guitar. (Mairants, Ivor). *British and Continental. Unpriced* TSPMJ (B71-50133)

Six folksongs from Yugoslavia: arranged for four-part chorus of mixed voices a cappella
 1: The things my mother buys. (Srebotnjak, Alojz). *Schirmer; Chappell. Unpriced* EZDW/G/AYPK (B71-50818)
 2: Katya and the Czar. (Srebotnjak, Alojz). *Schirmer Chappell. Unpriced* EZDW/G/AYPK (B71-50819)
 3: The farmer's daughter. (Srebotnjak, Alojz). *Schirmer Chappell. Unpriced* EZDW/G/AYPK (B71-50820)
 4: Love song from Ohrid. (Srebotnjak, Alojz). *Schirmer Chappell. Unpriced* EZDW/G/AYPK (B71-50821)
 5: Wake up, Melinda. (Srebotnjak, Alojz). *Schirmer Chappell. Unpriced* EZDW/G/AYPK (B71-50822)
 6: Oro (Yugoslav dance). (Srebotnjak, Alojz). *Schirmer Chappell. Unpriced* EZDW/G/AYPK (B71-50823)

Six German dances for violins, bass and wind instruments. K.600, no.2. German dance. (Mozart, Wolfgang Amadeus). *Schott. Unpriced* SRPK/AH (B71-51037)

Six miniatures. (Wishart, Peter). *Stainer and Bell. £1.50* KDW (B71-50344)

Six miniatures: for oboe and piano. (Darke, Harold). *Schott. £0.60* VTPJ (B71-51085)

Six more trumpet tunes. (Richardson, Norman). *Boosey and Hawkes. £0.65* WSPK/AAY (B71-51117)

Six poems of Emily Bronte. Op.63: for high voice and piano. (Joubert, John). *Novello. £1.75* KFTDW (B71-50895)

Six string-crossing studies: for cello solo. (Bunting, Christopher). *Oxford University Press. Unpriced* SR/AF (B71-50588) ISBN 0 19 355751 7

Six velocity studies: for cello solo. (Bunting, Christopher). *Oxford University Press. £0.40* SR/AF (B71-50589) ISBN 0 19 355752 5

Skelton, Geoffrey. Wieland Wagner: the positive sceptic. *Gollancz. £2.80* AC/EP(P) (B71-16012) ISBN 0 575 00709 5

Slatford, Rodney.
 Divertimento for viola, cello and double bass in E fla major. (Haydn, Michael). *Yorke Edition. Unpriced* RXNT (B71-50551)
 Divertimento for viola, cello & double bass in E flat major. (Haydn, Michael). *Yorke. Unpriced* RXNT (B71-50552)
 Sonatas in canon for two bass instruments. Opus 5
 Vol.2: Sonata in C minor, no.3; and, Sonata in C major, no.4. (Telemann, Georg Philipp). *Yorke. Unpriced* LXNUE/X (B71-50898)

Smallman, Basil. The background of Passion music: J.S. Bach and his predecessors. 2nd revised and enlarged ed. *Dover; Constable. £0.75* ADD/LH (B71-13108) ISBN 0 486 22250 0

Smith, A G Warren-. *See* Warren-Smith, A.G.

Smith, Charles N.
 Exodus. Excerpts. The Exodus song. (Gold, Ernest). *Chappell. £0.09* DW/JR (B71-50235)
 Exodus. Excerpts. The Exodus song: S.A.B. (Gold, Ernest). *Chappell. Unpriced* DW/JR (B71-50236)

Smith, Edward Lucie-. *See* Lucie-Smith, Edward.

Smith, Geoffry Russell-. *See* Russell-Smith, Geoffry.

Smith, Gregg.
 Ave Maria: for chorus of treble voices and four-part chorus of mixed voices with celeste (or bells) and organ (or piano) accompaniment. *Schirmer; Chappell. Unpriced* EPWNUDJ (B71-50786)
 Babel: for four-part chorus of mixed voices (or solo quartet), five speaking groups and piano (2 players). *Schirmer; Chappell. £0.25* DE (B71-50007)

Smith, Isabel. Six carols for guitar. *Schott. £0.30* TSPMK/DP/LF/AYB (B71-51055)

Smith, Noel. Great mover of all hearts: anthem. *Lengnick. Unpriced* DH (B71-50747)

Smith, Patrick John. The tenth muse: a historical study of the opera libretto. *Gollancz. £4.00* ACBM(X) (B71-13107) ISBN 0 575 00669 2

Smith, Stevie. My cats: for speaker, chorus and percussion. (Pehkonen, Elis). *Universal. £0.20* FHYE/NYLDX (B71-50308)

Snowbird. (MacLellan, Gene). *Ardmore and Beechwood. Unpriced* UMMK/DW (B71-51063)

So we'll go no more a-roving: two-part song, optional unison. (Dale, Mervyn). *Ashdown. Unpriced* FDW (B71-50832)

Soaking: for four-part chorus of mixed voices a cappella. (Wilson, Richard). *Schirmer; Chappell. Unpriced* EZDW (B71-50284)

Softley, Barbara. Ponder' songs of the seasons: for high voice and piano. (Roe, Betty). *Thames. Unpriced* KFTDW (B71-50894)

Soler, Josep. Sonidas de la noche. Sounds in the night: for six percussionists. *Schott. Unpriced* XNN (B71-50722)

Something to play: an instrumental workbook for the classroom. (Brace, Geoffrey). *Cambridge University Press. Unpriced* LN (B71-50897)

Something to sing about!: the personal choices of America's folk singers. (Okun, Milton). *Collier Books; Collier-Macmillan. £1.25* KDW/G/AYT (B71-50347)

Something to sing at assembly. (Brace, Geoffrey). *Cambridge University Press. Unpriced* JFDM/AY (B71-50322) ISBN 0 521 07570 x

Sonata for cello & piano, no.3 in A major. Op.69. Sonata for violoncello and pianoforte. Opus 69, first movement by Ludwig van Beethoven: facsimile of the autograph. (Beethoven, Ludwig van). *Columbia University Press. £1.75* BBJASRPE (B71-06294) ISBN 0 231 03417 2

Sonata for violin, cello and basso continuo in E major. Liv.2, no.12. Triosonate, E-Dur: fur Violine, Violoncello oder Viola da gamba und Basso continuo. (Francoeur Francois). *Schott. £1.20* NXNTE (B71-50430)

Sonata for violoncello and pianoforte. Opus 69, first movement by Ludwig van Beethoven: facsimile of the autograph. (Beethoven, Ludwig van). *Columbia University Press. £1.75* BBJASRPE (B71-06294) ISBN 0 231 03417 2

Sonatas in canon for two bass instruments. Opus 5
 Vol.2: Sonata in C minor, no.3; and, Sonata in C major, no.4. (Telemann, Georg Philipp). *Yorke. Unpriced* LXNUE/X (B71-50898)

Sonate accademiche. Op.2: fur Violine und bezifferten Bass, Violine und Klavier (Cembalo, Orgel) mit Violoncello ad libitum
 Sonata 1, D-dur. (Veracini, Francesco Maria). *Peters Hinrichsen. £0.525* SPE (B71-50560)
 Sonata 2, B-dur. (Veracini, Francesco Maria). *Peters Hinrichsen. £0.525* SPE (B71-50561)
 Sonata 3, C-dur. (Veracini, Francesco Maria). *Peters Hinrichsen. £0.525* SPE (B71-50562)
 Sonata 4, F-dur. (Veracini, Francesco Maria). *Peters Hinrichsen. £0.725* SPE (B71-50563)
 Sonata 7, d-moll. (Veracini, Francesco Maria). *Peters Hinrichsen. Unpriced* SPE (B71-50564)
 Sonata 8, e-moll. (Veracini, Francesco Maria). *Peters Hinrichsen. £0.80* SPE (B71-50565)
 Sonata 9, A-dur. (Veracini, Francesco Maria). *Peters Hinrichsen. £0.80* SPE (B71-50566)
 Sonata 12, d-moll. (Veracini, Francesco Maria). *Peters Hinrichsen. £0.80* SPE (B71-50567)

Sonate sentimentale: for flute or clarinet. Op.169. (Ries, Ferdinand). *Musica rara. £2.25* VRPE (B71-50141)
Sonatensatz (Rondo) fur Klavier. (Webern, Anton von). *Boosey and Hawkes. Unpriced* QP/W (B71-50461)
Song: anatomy, imagery, and styles. (Ivey, Donald). *Free Press; Collier-Macmillan. £3.00* ADW (B71-19968) ISBN 0 02 091580 2
Song and dances: brassband. (Street, Allan). *Boosey and Hawkes. Unpriced* WMH (B71-50150)
Song for every season: a hundred years of a Sussex farming family. (Copper, Bob). *Heinemann. £2.75* ADW/G(YDCR) (B71-28161) ISBN 0 434 14455 x
Song of Caedmon. (Swann, Donald). *Bodley Head. £1.50* FDD (B71-50824)
Song of Norway. (Grieg, Edvard). *Chappell; Frank Music. £0.60* KDW/JR (B71-50058)
Song of Norway. (Grieg, Edvard). *Chappell. Unpriced* WMK/CM/JR (B71-51108)
Song of Norway: selection for all organs. (Grieg, Edvard). *Chappell. £0.40* RK/CM/JR (B71-50999)
Song of the refugee children; and, Chorus of the Holy Innocents. (Simpson, Lionel). *Feldman. Unpriced* EZDP/LF (B71-50802)
Songs and dances of many nations: for recorder. (Bayford, Dudley Escott). *Francis, Day and Hunter. £0.25* VSPMK/AAY (B71-51079)
Songs for Easter. (Brooks, Nigel). *Boosey and Hawkes. Unpriced* DM/LL/AY (B71-50210)
Songs for little children
Set 1. (Beaumont, Adrian). *Boosey and Hawkes. £0.50* JFDW/GJ (B71-50054)
Songs for singing folk: Jackie and Bridies second song book. (McDonald, Jacqueline). *Galliard. Unpriced* KFE/TSDW/G/AYC (B71-50355)
Songs from Moravia
Book 1. (Dvorak, Antonin). *Chappell. Unpriced* FLDW (B71-50855)
Book 1. (Dvorak, Antonin). *Chappell. Unpriced* FLDW (B71-50856)
Book 2. (Dvorak, Antonin). *Chappell. Unpriced* FLDW (B71-50854)
Songs of America. (Jamson, Bruce). *Stainer and Bell. Unpriced* JFE/NYESDW/G/AYT (B71-50875) ISBN 0 903000 01 6
Songs of brotherhood. (Kearney, Peter). *Feldman. Unpriced* JDM (B71-50317)
Songs of old age: a song cycle for voice and piano. (Warren, Raymond). *Novello. £0.75* KDW (B71-50887)
Songs of struggle. (Bush, Alan). *Workers' Music Association. Unpriced* JDW (B71-50048)
Songs of struggle. (Bush, Alan). *Workers' Music Association. £0.35* JDW (B71-50859)
Songs of Sydney Carter
4: Riding a tune. (Carter, Sydney). *Galliard. Unpriced* JDW (B71-50860)
Songs of the seaside: three songs for unison voices, piano, tuned and rhythm percussion. (McNeill, Mary). *Keith Prowse Music. £0.90* JFE/NYLDW (B71-50325)
Sonidas de la noche. Sounds in the night: for six percussionists. (Soler, Josep). *Schott. Unpriced* XNN (B71-50722)
Sonne der Inkas: fur Sopran, 3 Sprecher und II Instrumentalisten. (Denisov, Edisson). *Universal. Unpriced* KFLE/MRDX (B71-50358)
Sorrentino, Gilbert. Ballad 1: mezzo-soprano, flute/altoflute, tenor, trombone, contra-bass, piano, percussion. (Rands, Bernard). *Universal. Unpriced* KFNE/NYDDW (B71-50362)
Sound pictures: for piano. (Diemer, Emma Lou). *Boosey and Hawkes. £0.65* QPJ (B71-50483)
Southward bound. (Alexander, Arthur). *Schott. Unpriced* SRPJ (B71-51024)
Space songs for infants. (Horscroft, Elizabeth). *Ashdown. £0.25* JFDW/GJ (B71-50323)
Spartacus: love theme. (Khachaturian, Aram). *Plantagenet Music. £0.20* QPK/JS (B71-50987)
Spartak - Excerpts. Spartacus: love theme. (Khachaturian, Aram). *Plantagenet Music. £0.20* QPK/JS (B71-50987)
Spatherbst. Late autumn. Op.92, no.2: for four-part chorus of mixed voices with piano accompaniment. (Brahms, Johannes). *Schirmer; Chappell. Unpriced* DW (B71-50229)
Spell out the news: carol for unison voices with divisions, and organ or piano (or brass). (Gibbs, Alan). *Novello. £0.06* FDP/LF (B71-50288)
Spenser, Edmund. Think on dredful domesday: for s.S.A.T.B and chamber orchestra. (Burgon, Geoffrey). *Stainer and Bell. Unpriced* DX (B71-50779)
Sperger, Johann Matthias. Jagdmusik: 12 kleine Stucke, fur zwei Horner. *Schott. £0.70* WTNU/GT (B71-50155)
Spinelli, V. Cancao do mar: canto e piano. (Lorenz Fernandez, Oscar). *Arthur Napoleao; Essex Music. Unpriced* KDW (B71-50341)
Spink, Ian. Musica Britannica: a national collection of music Vol.33: English songs, 1625-1660. *Stainer and Bell. Unpriced* C/AYD (B71-50001)
Spinner, Leopold. Quintet for clarinet, horn, bassoon, guitar and double bass. Op.14. *Boosey and Hawkes. Unpriced* NVNR (B71-50421)
Spitfire fugue. (Walton, *Sir* William). *Boosey and Hawkes. Unpriced* UMMK/Y/JR (B71-50136)
Splendid art: a history of the opera. (Matthews, Thomas). *Crowell-Collier; Collier-Macmillan. £1.75* AC(X) (B71-19967) ISBN 0 02 765290 4
Spurgin, Anthony. Foursome for brass. *Feldman. Unpriced* WNS (B71-51114)
Squire, Russel Nelson. Class piano for adult beginners. 2nd ed. *Prentice-Hall. £3.00* Q/AC (B71-50447) ISBN 0 13 135160 5
Srebotnjak, Alojz.
Six folksongs from Yugoslavia: arranged for four-part chorus of mixed voices a cappella
1: The things my mother buys. *Schirmer; Chappell. Unpriced* EZDW/G/AYPK (B71-50818)
2: Katya and the Czar. *Schirmer; Chappell. Unpriced* EZDW/G/AYPK (B71-50819)
3: The farmer's daughter. *Schirmer; Chappell. Unpriced* EZDW/G/AYPK (B71-50820)
4: Love song from Ohrid. *Schirmer; Chappell. Unpriced* EZDW/G/AYPK (B71-50821)
5: Wake up, Melinda. *Schirmer; Chappell. Unpriced* EZDW/G/AYPK (B71-50822)
6: Oro (Yugoslav dance). *Schirmer; Chappell. Unpriced* EZDW/G/AYPK (B71-50823)
Stable bare. (Verrall, Pamela Motley). *Freeman. Unpriced* FDP/LF (B71-50291)
Stainer, *Sir* John. Magnificat and Nunc dimittis in E minor: for SATB and organ. (Purcell, Daniel). *Novello. £0.15* DGPP (B71-50742)
Stamitz, Carl. Concerto for clarinet & string orchestra, no.1, in F major. Konzert no.1, F-Dur: fur Klarinette (B) und Streicher, zwei Oboen und zwei Horner ad lib. Klavierauszug. *Schott. £2.00* VVPK/LF (B71-50678)
Standford, Patric. How amiable are thy dwellings: anthem for SATB and organ. *Novello. Unpriced* DK (B71-50199)
Standing in the need of prayer: spiritual. (Arch, Gwyn). *Feldman. Unpriced* FDW/LC (B71-50296)
Stapleton, Eric. Overture for a festival. *Feldman. Unpriced* WMJ (B71-51099)
Star bright, starlight. (Verrall, Pamela Motley). *Freeman. Unpriced* JDP/LF (B71-50318)
Stedman, Fabian. Tintinnalogia; or, The art of ringing. (Duckworth, Richard). 1st ed. reprinted. *Kingsmead Reprints. £2.10* AXSR/E (B71-04185) ISBN 0 901571 41 5
Steel, Christopher.
O clap your hands together. Op.50: anthem for SATB and organ (or brass). *Novello. £0.15* DK (B71-50200)
Paradise lost. Op. 34: a dramatic cantata in two parts, for soprano, tenor and baritone soli, SATB and orchestra. *Novello. £0.90* DD (B71-50737)
Steer, Michael. Easter song: for unison voices and organ. *Novello. Unpriced* JDH (B71-50316)
Steinitz, Paul. Sing unto God. (Wedding anthem for Frederick, Prince of Wales, 1736): for soloists, chorus and orchestra. (Handel, George Frideric). *Oxford University Press. £0.80* DK/KDD (B71-50201) ISBN 0 19 336660 6
Steinitz, Paul790000. Psalmen Davids sampt etlichen Moteten und Concerten, no.19. Ist nicht Ephraim mein teurer Sohn? Is not Ephraim my precious Son?: Motete a 8 e 16 con due cappelle in fine, for mixed voices and instruments. (Schutz, Heinrich). *Oxford University Press. £0.95* EWNNDH (B71-50788) ISBN 0 19 338084 6
Stephens, David. Avodath Hakodesh. Sacred service: a Sabbath morning service according to the Union Prayer Book, for baritone (cantor), mixed chorus and organ or full orchestra. (Bloch, Ernest). *Boosey and Hawkes. Unpriced* DGUB (B71-50010)
Stephenson, Elspeth M.
Come and sing: a selection of Christian songs for under-eights. (Dowman, Pamela). *Scripture Union. Unpriced* JFDM/GJ/AY (B71-50863) ISBN 0 85421 301 5
Sing to God: Christian songs for juniors. (Old, Margaret V). *Scripture Union. £1.25* DM/AY (B71-50755) ISBN 0 85421 302 3
Stert, Wolfgang. Duetto for viola & violone (or double bass in E flat major. (Dittersdorf, Carl Ditters von). *Yorke. Unpriced* SQPLSSVE (B71-50584)
Stevens, Bernard. Quartet for strings, no.2. String quartet no.2. *Galliard. Unpriced* RXNS (B71-51011)
Stevens, Denis.
A history of song. *Hutchinson. £3.75* ADW(X) (B71-06292) ISBN 0 09 104680 7
The second Penguin book of English madrigals: for five voices. *Penguin. £0.50* EZDU/AYD (B71-50029) ISBN 0 14 070837 5
Stickles, William. The pajama game - Excerpts. Hernando's hideaway: T.T.B.B. (Adler, Richard). *Frank Music. £0.90* GDW (B71 50314)
Stille Nacht, heilige Nacht. Silent night. (Gruber, Franz). *Oxford University Press. Unpriced* DP/LF (B71-50763) ISBN 0 19 343022 3
Stille und Umkehr: Orchesterskizzen. (Zimmerman, Bernd Alois). *Schott. £1.90* MMJ (B71-50401)
Stillwell, Roy E. Ich will dir ein Frendenopfer. I will freely sacrifice to thee: for SSTB chorus (or SATB). (Peter, Johann Friedrich). *Boosey and Hawkes. £0.15* DH (B71-50190)
Stilwell, Roy E. Der Herr segne euch. The Lord shall increase you: for SSAB chorus (or SATB). (Peter, Johann Friedrich). *Boosey and Hawkes. £0.09* DH (B71-50189)
Stofer, Doris.
Duet for clarinet & piano in A major. Duo fur Klarinette und Klavier, A-Dur. (Hoffmeister, Franz Anton). *Schott. £2.00* VVPJ (B71-50676)
Sonata for clarinet & piano in E flat major. Sonate, Es-Dur: fur Klarinette in B und Klavier. (Wanhal, Johann Baptist). *Schott. £2.00* VVPE (B71-50673)
Stoker, Richard.
Johnson preserved: opera in 3 acts. *Peters. Hinrichsen. £5.00* CC (B71-50161)
Quintet for wind instruments. Wind quintet: for flute, oboe, clarinet, bassoon, horn. *Hinrichsen. Unpriced* UNR (B71-50633)
Stone, David. Petite suite. Excerpts. Ballet. (Debussy, Claude). *Boosey and Hawkes. £1.05* MH (B71-50901)
Stone wall: a cassation for audience and orchestra. (Williamson, Malcolm). *Weinberger. Unpriced* DX (B71-50780)
Storey, David. Follow me: eight songs for young people. (Doherty, Christopher). *Weinberger. Unpriced* JFDW (B71-50868)
Stow, Randolph. Eight songs for a mad king: for voice, flute (doubling piccolo), clarinet, piano (doubling harpsichord and dulcimer), violin, violoncello and percussion. (Davies, Peter Maxwell). *Boosey and Hawkes. Unpriced* KE/NYDPNQDW (B71-50351)
Strasfogel, Ian. Ba-ta-clan: a masquerade in one act. (Offenbach, Jacques). *Schirmer; Chappell. Unpriced* CF (B71-50163)
Stravinsky, Igor.
Four etudes for orchestra. Quatre etudes: pour orchestre. Revision 1952. *Boosey and Hawkes. £0.65* MMJ (B71-50073)
Four etudes for orchestra. Quatre etudes: pour orchestre. Revision 1952. *Boosey and Hawkes. Unpriced* MMJ (B71-50399)
Stravinsky, Soulima.
Variations for piano. Piano variations
1st series. *Peters; Hinrichsen. £0.90* QP/T (B71-50459)
Variations for piano. Piano variations
2nd series. *Peters; Hinrichsen. £0.90* QP/T (B71-50460)
Street, Allan.
El Amor brujo-Danza ritual del fuego. Ritual fire dance. (Falla, Manuel de). *Chester. Unpriced* WMK/AH (B71-51106)
Eric Coates for brass: musical extracts from At the dance, The jester at the wedding, London Bridge, The three Elizabeths, The three bears; arranged for brass and reed band by Allan Street. (Coates, Eric). *Chappell. Unpriced* WMK (B71-50704)
Love story: theme from the film. (Lai, Francis). *Chappell. Unpriced* WMK/JR (B71-50710)
Nott'num Town. *Boosey and Hawkes. £2.90* WMG (B71-51096)
Robert Farnon for brass: arranged for brass and reed band by Allan Street. (Farnon, Robert J). *Chappell. Unpriced* WMK (B71-51104)
Rondino: solo for B flat trumpet (or cornet) with piano accompaniment. *Boosey and Hawkes. £0.35* WSP/W (B71-50154)
Song and dances: brassband. *Boosey and Hawkes. Unpriced* WMH (B71-50150)
Song of Norway. (Grieg, Edvard). *Chappell. Unpriced* WMK/CM/JR (B71-51108)
Strike sound: a collection of Padstow carols. (Worden, John). *Lodenek Press. Unpriced* DP/LF/AYDFRP (B71-50767)
Stuart, Forbes. A medley of folk songs. *Longman Young Books. £2.50* JDW/G/AY (B71-50861) ISBN 0 582 15331 x
Studie: fur Klarinette. (Donizetti, Gaetano). *Litolff, Peters; Hinrichsen. £0.50* VVPMJ (B71-50679)
Studies in Eastern Chant
Vol.2. (Wellesz, Egon). *Oxford University Press. £3.50* ADTDS (B71-16013) ISBN 0 19 316318 7
Study of the guitar simplified: a complete guitar course in 30 lessons
Vol.1. (Economides, George C). *Keith Prowse Music. Unpriced* TS/AC (B71-50129)
Stutschewsky, J. Espana. Op. 165 - Excerpts. Malaguena. Op. 165, no.3. (Albeniz, Isaac). *Schott. Unpriced* SRPK/AHPP (B71-51038)
Style and interpretation: an anthology of keyboard music. (Ferguson, Howard). *Oxford University Press. £1.25* PWNV/AY (B71-50938) ISBN 0 19 372628 9
Style and interpretation: an anthology of keyboard music. (Ferguson, Howard). *Oxford University Press. £1.25* PWNV/AY (B71-50939) ISBN 0 19 372629 7
Such, P. Air in D minor. (Purcell, Henry). *Schott. Unpriced* SRPK (B71-51035)
Suchoff, Benjamin. Guide to Bartok's 'Mikrokosmos'. Revised ed. *Boosey and Hawkes. £2.50* BBGAQ (B71-09061) ISBN 0 85162 002 7
Suite floral: colecao de 3 pecas for piano. Op.97
No.3: Alegria na Horta. (Villa-Lobos, Heitor). *Arthur Napoleao; Essex Music. Unpriced* QPG (B71-50471)
Suite for flute & string orchestra in A minor. Suite in A minor: for flute and strings. (Telemann, Georg Philip). *Schirmer; Chappell. Unpriced* RXMPVRG (B71-50539)
Suite in miniature: three movements in contrasting styles for two trombones or baritones or euphoniums. (Catelinet, Philip B). *Hinrichsen. £0.20* WUNUG (B71-50719)
Suite infantil no.2. Excerpts. Allegro. (Villa-Lobos, Heitor). *Arthur Napoleao; Essex Music. Unpriced* QPJ (B71-50099)
Sullivan, *Sir* Arthur. Gilbert and Sullivan songs. *Francis, Day and Hunter. £0.50* RPVK/CM/AY (B71-51004)
Sulyok, Imre. Dante symphony. Symphonie zu Dantes Divina commedia: fur Frauenchor und Orchester. (Liszt, Franz). *Eulenburg. £2.10* FE/MDX (B71-50298)
Summer in Valley City: for band. (Finney, Ross Lee). *Peters; Hinrichsen. £3.50* UMJ (B71-50621)
Summer water: a cantata for recorders and percussion, two-part singing chorus, soprano solo and speaking chorus. (Verrall, Pamela Motley). *Bosworth. £0.75* FE/NYHSDX (B71-50844)
Sumner, William Leslie. The pianoforte. 3rd ed., with corrections and additions. *Macdonald and Co. £2.50* AQ(X) (B71-11124) ISBN 0 356 03516 6
Sumsion, Herbert. Festival Benedicite in D: in shortened form. *Lengnick. Unpriced* DGNR (B71-50741)
Sunburst: concert march. (Osterling, Eric). *Chappell. Unpriced* WMK/AGM (B71-50151)
Surdin, Morris. Serious I-VIII: piano accordion. *Boosey and*

Hawkes. *Unpriced* RSPMJ (B71-50113)

Sussex bells and belfries. (Elphick, George Philip). *Phillimore. £5.50* AXSR(YDCR) (B71-11121) ISBN 0 900592 08 7

Sutermeister, Heinrich.
Serenade pour Montreux: pour 2 hautbois, 2 cors et orchestre a cordes. *Schott. £1.60* RXMPUNS (B71-50538)
Vier Lieder Bariton: Fassung mit Violine, Flote, Oboe, Faggott und Cembalo. *Schott. £2.40* KGNE/NUPNRDW (B71-50371)

Suzuki, Shinichi.
Suzuki violin school: Suzuki method
Vol.1. Revised ed. *Boosey and Hawkes. Unpriced* S/AC (B71-50553)
Vol.2. Revised ed. *Boosey and Hawkes. Unpriced* S/AC (B71-50554)
Vol.3. Revised ed. *Boosey and Hawkes. Unpriced* S/AC (B71-50555)
Vol.4. Revised ed. *Boosey and Hawkes. Unpriced* S/AC (B71-50556)

Swain, Freda. Walking; and, Dream tide. *Schott. Unpriced* SRPJ (B71-51031)

Swallow, Su. Music. *Macdonald and Co. £0.25* A (B71-19965) ISBN 0 356 03759 2

Swann, Donald. The song of Caedmon. *Bodley Head. £1.50* FDD (B71-50824)

Sweet Thames flow softly: part-song, SATB. (Roe, Betty). *Thames. Unpriced* EZDW (B71-50817)

Symphonic fanfare for brass choir. (Uber, David). *Schirmer; Chappell. Unpriced* WMGN (B71-50695)

Symphonie zu Dantes Divina commedia: fur Frauenchor und Orchester. (Liszt, Franz). *Eulenburg. £2.10* FE/MDX (B71-50298)

Symphonies for the seventies. (Rios, Waldo de los). *Rondor Music. £1.25* QPK (B71-50983)

Szalonek, Witold. Mutanza: per pianoforte. *Chester. Unpriced* QPJ (B71-50980)

Szende, Otto. The physiology of violin playing. *Collet's. £3.50* AS/EB (B71-16546) ISBN 0 569 06196 2

Szigeti, Kilian. Liber organi. Altitalienische Orgelmeister 2. *Schott. £0.30* R/AYJ (B71-50991)

Szmodis, Ivan. The physiology of violin playing. (Szende Otto). *Collet's. £3.50* AS/EB (B71-16546) ISBN 0 569 06196 2

Szonyi, Erzsebet. Allegro: per orchestra. *Boosey and Hawkes. y1.10* MJ (B71-50903)

Tableau: flute/alto flute, B flat clarinet/bass clarinet, viola, cello, piano/celesta, percussion. (Rands, Bernard). *Universal. Unpriced* NYDPNQ (B71-50431)

Taft, Loredo. Institutional canons: for mixed chorus
3: To thy happy children: SSATBB. (Binkerd, Gordon). *Boosey and Hawkes. £0.09* EZ/X (B71-50245)

Tageszeiten: fur Orgel. (Genzmer, Harald). *Litolff, Peters Hinrichsen. £0.75* RJ (B71-50523)

Tagore, *Sir* Rabindranath. When one knows thee: for four-part chorus of mixed voices a cappella. (Glarum, Leonard Stanley). *Schirmer; Chappell. Unpriced* EZDH (B71-50253)

Take a shape: for voices. (Self, George). *Universal. £0.20* FEZDX (B71-50307)

Tale of the wandering scholar. Op.50. The wandering scholar. Op.50: a chamber opera in one act. (Holst, Gustav). *Faber. Unpriced* CQC (B71-50172)

Tales of Beatrix Potter: music from the film. (Lanchbery, John). *E.M.I. Film Music; Keith Prowse Music. £0.40* QPK/AHM/JR (B71-50512)

Tales of Beatrix Potter: selection from the ballet. (Lanchbery, John). *E.M.I. Film Music; Keith Prowse Music. y1.50* WMK/AHM/JR (B71-51107)

Talking about sonatas: a book of analytical studies, based on a personal view. (Hopkins, Antony). *Heinemann Educational. £2.50* AQPE (B71-26602) ISBN 0 435 81425 7

Tallis, David. Musical boxes. *Muller. £3.00* A/FN (B71-17375) ISBN 0 584 10187 2

Tallis, Thomas.
English sacred music
1: Anthems. *Stainer and Bell. Unpriced* CB/LD (B71-50726)
2: Service music. *Stainer and Bell. Unpriced* CB/LD (B71-50727)

Tamblyn, Bill. Sing up: a guide and encouragement to sing in church. *G. Chapman. £0.80* AD/LSB/E (B71-16702) ISBN 0 225 65904 2

Tamblyn, William.
Antiphons and Psalm 150: for cantor, congregation, SATB choir and organ. *Boosey and Hawkes. Unpriced* DR (B71-50224)
You are Peter: anthem for SATB, organ and/or brass. *Boosey and Hawkes. Unpriced* DJ (B71-50192)

Tango militaire: cornet solo. (Siebert, Edrich). *Studio Music. Unpriced* WMHVR (B71-51098)

Tannau moliant. (Williams, W Matthews). *Llyfrfa'r Methodistiaid Calfinaidd. Unpriced* DM (B71-50753)

Tarantella: for B flat clarinet. (Dillon, Robert). *Boosey and Hawkes. £0.65* VVPHVS (B71-50674)

Tate, Phyllis.
Coastal ballads: Northumbrian sea songs
No.1: The water of Tyne. *Oxford University Press. £0.25* KDW/KC/AYDJJ (B71-50348) ISBN 0 19 345820 9
No.2: O the bonny fisher lad. *Oxford University Press. £0.25* KDW/KC/AYDJJ (B71-50349) ISBN 0 19 345819 5
No.3: Billy boy. *Oxford University Press. £0.25* KDW/KC/AYDJJ (B71-50350) ISBN 0 19 345821 7
A pride of lions: a story for singing and staging. *Oxford University Press. Unpriced* CQN (B71-50735)
Twice in a blue moon: a fantasy operetta, the accompaniment for two pianos, percussion and double bass. *Oxford University Press. £1.25* CQF (B71-50733) ISBN 0 19 338377 2

Tauber, Diana Napier. This was Richard Tauber. (Castle, Charles, *b.1939*). *W.H. Allen. £3.50* AKGH/E(P) (B71-11818) ISBN 0 491 00117 7

Tavener, John.
Coplas: chorus (SATB-16 voices), soloists-SATB. *Chester. Unpriced* DE (B71-50174)
Three surrealist songs: for mezzo-soprano, tape and piano doubling bongos by John Tavener; poems by Edward Lucie-Smith. *Chester. Unpriced* KFNE/NYLNUDW (B71-50893)

Taverner, John. 'Gloria tibi trinitas': mass for six-part unaccompanied choir, S.A.T.T.B.B. *Stainer and Bell. £1.15* EZDG (B71-50302)

Tchaikovsky, Peter.
1812 overture. Op.49: a festive overture. *Sunbury Music. £0.40* DADW (B71-50736)
Concerto for violin in D major. Op.35. Konzert, D-dur. Op.35: fur Violine und Orchester
Ausgabe fur Violine und Klavier von Komponisten. *Peters; Hinrichsen. £1.40* SPK/LF (B71-50575)
Eugene Onegin: lyric scenes in three acts and seven scenes. *Schauer and May. Unpriced* CC (B71-50730)
Piano arrangements for all to play. *Francis, Day and Hunter. £0.90* QPK (B71-50511)

Teaching rhythm and using classroom instruments. (Hood, Marguerite Vivian). *Prentice-Hall. £3.10* A(VG) (B71-08201) ISBN 0 13 894089 4

Technique of film music. (Manvell, Roger). 1st ed. reprinted. *Focal Press. £3.00* A/JR (B71-05268) ISBN 0 240 44943 6

Technique of orchestration. (Kennan, Kent Wheeler). 2nd ed. *Prentice-Hall. £4.00* AM/DF (B71-01701) ISBN 0 13 900316 9

Telemann, Georg Philip.
Concerto for two violas, strings & basso continuo in G major. Konzert, G-Dur: fur 2 Violen, Streicher und Basso continuo. *Schott. Unpriced* SQNTPWK/LF (B71-50119)
Suite for flute & string orchestra in A minor. Suite in A minor: for flute and strings. *Schirmer; Chappell. Unpriced* RXMPVRG (B71-50539)

Telemann, Georg Philipp.
Petite Musique de Chambre. Excerpts. Partita no.3 in C minor: for descant recorder and piano. *Faber Music. Unpriced* VRPG (B71-50642)
Sonata for violin, viola da gamba & harpsichord in G minor. Sonate g-moll fur Violine, Viola da gamba (Viola) und Cembalo by Georg Philipp Telemann; herausgegeben von Karlheinz Schultz-Hauser. *Peters; Hinrichsen. £1.05* NXNTE (B71-50429)
Sonatas in canon for two bass instruments. Opus 5
Vol.2: Sonata in C minor, no.3; and, Sonata in C major, no.4. *Yorke. Unpriced* LXNUE/X (B71-50898)
Twenty little fugues for organ. Excerpts. Four fugue nos.20, 7, 9, 13. *Faber Music. Unpriced* VSNSK/Y (B71-50652)

Ten canonic studies for recorders, nos. 1-7. Seven canonic studies. (Bergmann, Walter). *Schott. Unpriced* WNUK/AF (B71-51115)

Tenebrae: fur grosses Orchester. (Huber, Klaus). *Ars Viva; Schott. £5.60* MMJ (B71-50393)

Tennyson, Alfred, *Baron Tennyson.*
A farewell. (Ridout, Alan). *Stainer and Bell. Unpriced* DW (B71-50020)
Ring out, wild bells: for four-part chorus of mixed voices a cappella. (Newbury, Kent A). *Schirmer; Chappell. Unpriced* EZDW (B71-50283)

Tenth muse: a historical study of the opera libretto. (Smith, Patrick John). *Gollancz. £4.00* ACBM(X) (B71-13107) ISBN 0 575 00669 2

Tetelpar: two movements for oboe and piano. (Bozay, Attila). *Boosey and Hawkes. Unpriced* VTPJ (B71-51084)

Thal, Herbert Van. *See* Van Thal, Herbert.

Thaxted Mass: three part unaccompanied. (Putterill, Jack). *St Gregory Publishing Co. £0.20* EZDG (B71-50789)

The Oxford organ method. (Trevor, Caleb Henry). *Oxford University Press. Unpriced* R/AC (B71-50107)

The shadows are falling: Tyrolean cradle song; words by T.A. Armstrong; with, Christmas day: Lancashire carol: carols for women's or boys' voices. (Hunter, Ian T). *Thames. Unpriced* FEZDP/LF (B71-50847)

The song of Norway: piano selection from the file. (Greig, Edvard). *Chappell; Frank Music. £0.25* QPK/CM/JR (B71-50104)

Thee will I love: motet for SATB and organ. (Howells, Herbert). *Novello. £0.15* DH (B71-50012)

Thema mit vier Variationen: die Vier Temperamente, fur Klavier und Streichorchester. (Hindemith, Paul). *Schott. £2.80* MPQ/T (B71-50402)

There is no rose: a Christmas carol, mixed, or female or male voices unacc. (Paynter, John). *Oxford University Press. Unpriced* EZDP/LF (B71-50801) ISBN 0 19 353340 5

They shall see the glory of the Lord: SATB. (Rhodes, Joseph W). *Warner, Seven Arts; Blossom Music. Unpriced* DK (B71-50197)

They who considereth the poor shall be blest: SATB, ad. lib. (Morgan, Haydn). *Warner; Blossom Music. Unpriced* EZDK (B71-50258)

Thiman, Eric Harding.
Come, ye faithful, raise the strain: Easter anthem, for SATB and organ. *Novello. Unpriced* DH/LL (B71-50015)
Honeybrook: part-song for SSA and piano. *Novello. Unpriced* FDW (B71-50043)

Think afresh about the voice: a reappraisal of the teaching of Ernest George White. (Hewlett, Arthur Donald). *The Ernest George White Society. £0.45* AB/E (B71-19971) ISBN 0 9501610 0 4

Think on dredful domesday: for s.S.A.T.B and chamber orchestra. (Burgon, Geoffrey). *Stainer and Bell. Unpriced* DX (B71-50779)

This is the Arlo Guthrie book. (Guthrie, Arlo). *Amsco Music Publishing; Distributed by Collier-Macmillan. £0.90* KE/TSDW (B71-50888) ISBN 0 02 060680 x

This was Richard Tauber. (Castle, Charles, *b.1939*). *W.H. Allen. £3.50* AKGH/E(P) (B71-11818) ISBN 0 491 00117 7

Thomas a Kempis, *Saint.* 3 canticles of Thomas a Kempis: for unaccompanied mixed voices. (Nevens, David). *Novello. Unpriced* EZDH (B71-50792)

Thomas Aquinas, *Saint.* Tantum ergo in E flat (1828) D.962: for four-part chorus of mixed voices and solo quartet (ad lib.) with organ or piano accompaniment. (Schubert, Franz). *Schirmer; Chappell. Unpriced* DGLBT (B71-50177)

Thomas Gwyn. Culhwch and Olwen. Op. 32: an entertainment. (Mathias, William). *University of Wales Press. Unpriced* ENYLNSDX (B71-50785)

Thomson, Virgil.
Journey to America. Excerpts. Pilgrims and pioneers: for orchestra. *Schirmer; Chappell. Unpriced* MM/JR (B71-50376)
Tuesday in November. Excerpts. Fugue and chorale on Yankee Doodle. *Schirmer; Chappell. Unpriced* UMK/Y/JR (B71-50622)
Twentieth century composers
Vol.1: American music since 1910. *Weidenfeld and Nicolson. £3.50* A(XM) (B71-14732) ISBN 0 297 00264 3

Thornton, James. Poem: for flute and band. (Griffes, Charles T). *Schirmer; Chappell. Unpriced* UMPVR (B71-50626)

Thorpe, Frank. The light of Christmas: unison with piano or 2-stave organ, the winner of the 1970 'Carol for a future' competition. *Weinberger. £0.05* JFDP/LF (B71-50051)

Thou, O God art praised in Sion: short anthem. (Macpherson, Charles). *Novello. £0.06* FLDH (B71-50310)

Three amorous airs. Op.104: for female voices and piano
1: Waly waly: three-part. (Gardner, John). *Oxford University Press. Unpriced* FDW (B71-50293) ISBN 0 19 342587 4
2: The German flute: three-part. (Gardner, John). *Oxford University Press. Unpriced* FDW (B71-50294) ISBN 0 19 342588 2
3: The ballad of Nancy Dee: four-part. (Gardner, John). *Oxford University Press. Unpriced* FDW (B71-50295) ISBN 0 19 342589 0

Three carol orchestrations. (Jacques, Reginald). *Oxford University Press. Unpriced* EMDP/LF (B71-50782)

Three contemporary madrigals: for four-part chorus of mixed voices a cappella
If you your lips would keep from slips. (Effinger, Cecil). *Schirmer; Chappell. Unpriced* EZDW (B71-50271)
My love and I for kisses played. (Effinger, Cecil). *Schirmer; Chappell. Unpriced* EZDW (B71-50272)
Why was Cupid a boy?. (Effinger, Cecil). *Schirmer Chappell. Unpriced* EZDW (B71-50273)

Three episodes: for percussion ensemble. (O'Reilly, John). *Schirmer; Chappell. Unpriced* XN (B71-50721)

Three into five: for descant, treble (divisi) and tenor (divisi) recorders and piano. (Bonsor, Brian). *Schott. £0.50* VSNQQ (B71-50933)

Three lazy gents. (Barraclough, C). *Studio Music. Unpriced* WMJ (B71-50696)

Three peavinations: for mixed chorus
1: Pavane. (Lekberg, Sven). *Schirmer; Chappell. Unpriced* EZDW (B71-50280)
2: Moment musical. (Lekberg, Sven). *Schirmer; Chappell. Unpriced* EZDW (B71-50281)
3: Counterpoint. (Lekberg, Sven). *Schirmer; Chappell. Unpriced* EZDW (B71-50282)

Three plainsong preludes: for organ. (Maine, Basil). *Boosey and Hawkes. Unpriced* RJ (B71-50527)

Three surrealist songs: for mezzo-soprano, tape and piano doubling bongos by John Tavener; poems by Edward Lucie-Smith. (Tavener, John). *Chester. Unpriced* KFNE/NYLNUDW (B71-50893)

Tilmouth, Michael. Sonata for violin and basso continuo in G minor. Sonata in G minor: for violin and continuo (cello ad lib.). (Croft, William). *£0.60* SPE (B71-51014)

Timeless moment: song. (Mahler, Gustav). *Chappell. £0.20* KDW (B71-50885)

Tintinnalogia; or, The art of ringing. (Duckworth, Richard) 1st ed. reprinted. *Kingsmead Reprints. £2.10* AXSR/E (B71-04185) ISBN 0 901571 41 5

Tisdall, William. Complete keyboard works of William Tisdall. 2nd, revised ed. *Stainer and Bell. Unpriced* QSQ/AZ (B71-50515)

Tivanna, Kinsky 125: canzonetta for medium voice and piano. (Beethoven, Ludwig van). *Novello. £0.20* KFVDW (B71-50364)

To a young music lover. (Seeley, Charles). *Stockwell. £1.25* A (B71-14239) ISBN 0 7223 0050 6

To be sung on the water. Op. 42, no.2: transcribed for four-part chorus of women's voices a cappella. (Barber, Samuel). *Schirmer; Chappell. £0.35* FEZDW (B71-50306)

Toccata: for piano. (Muczynski, Robert). *Schirmer Chappell. Unpriced* QPJ (B71-50492)

Toccata, 'Ite, missa est': fur Orgel. (Kraft, Walter). *London; Schott. £1.00* RJ (B71-50526)

Tod des Empedokles. Excerpts. Drei Monologue des Empedokles von Friedrich Holderlin: fur Bariton und Klavier oder Orchester. (Reutter, Hermann). *Schott. £1.30* KGNDW (B71-50370)

Toda songs. (Emeneau, Murray Barnson). *Clarendon Press.*

£11.00 BZFMNT (B71-06911) ISBN 0 19 815129 2

Tomblings, Philip. Behold the great Creator: carol for SATB unaccompanied. *Ashdown. £0.05* EZDP/LF (B71-50805)

Tomkins, Thomas. Musica Deo Sacra. Service no.1. Excerpts. Magnificat and Nunc dimittis: for SATB. *Novello. Unpriced* DGPP (B71-50743)

Tomlinson, Geoffrey. Divertimento: for string orchestra. *Boosey and Hawkes. £4.10* RXMJ (B71-50116)

Tourinho, Eduardo. Noturno: canto e piano. (Lorenz Fernandez, Oscar). *Arthur Napoleao; Essex Music. Unpriced* KDW (B71-50342)

Traces: piano, cello, signal generator, ring modulator; 6 channels of taped sound. (Reynolds, Roger). *Peters; Hinrichsen. £2.50* PS (B71-50442)

Traditional tunes: a collection of ballad airs. (Kidson, Frank). 1st ed. reprinted. *S.R. Publishers. £2.10* AKDW/K/G(YC) (B71-03034) ISBN 0 85409 637 x

Trakl, Georg. Revelation and fall. Offenbarung und Untergang: for soprano and sixteen instrumentalists. (Davies, Peter Maxwell). *Boosey and Hawkes. Unpriced* KFLE/MRDX (B71-50359)

Trattenimenti armonici per camera divisi in dodici sonate. Op.6, no. 2. Sonata for string orchestra. Op. 6, no. 2. (Albinoni, Tommaso). *Chester. Unpriced* RXME (B71-51008)

Travis, Dave. 103 folk songs. *Campbell, Connelly. £0.95* JE/TSDW/G/AYT (B71-50320)

Treatise handbook including Bun no.2, Volo solo. (Cardew, Cornelius). *Peters, Hinrichsen. £3.50* LJ (B71-50372)

Trevelyan, R C. Flemish carol: tune old Flemish, SATB. (Rutter, John). *Oxford University Press. Unpriced* DP/LF (B71-50213) ISBN 0 19 343014 2

Trevor, C H. Thou, O God art praised in Sion: short anthem. (Macpherson, Charles). *Novello. £0.06* FLDH (B71-50310)

Trevor, Caleb H. Organ books
No.3. *Oxford University Press. £0.65* R/AY (B71-50990)

Trevor, Caleb Henry.
A Bach organ book for students. (Bach, Johann Sebastian). *Elkin. £1.50* RJ (B71-50519)
The Oxford organ method. *Oxford University Press. Unpriced* R/AC (B71-50107)

Trimble, Lester. Notturno: for strings. *Peters; Hinrichsen. £1.60* RXMJ (B71-50535)

Trombone technique. (Wick, Denis). *Oxford University Press. £1.15* AWU/E (B71-14736) ISBN 0 19 318704 3

Try me, O God: short full anthem. (Nares, James). *Novello. £0.06* EZDK (B71-50026)

Tschaikowski, Peter. *See* Tchaikovsky, Peter.

Tuesday in November. Excerpts. Fugue and chorale on Yankee Doodle. (Thomson, Virgil). *Schirmer; Chappell. Unpriced* UMK/Y/JR (B71-50622)

Tune a day: for classical guitar: a third instruction book. (Herfurth, Clarence Paul). *Chappell. £0.40* TS/AC (B71-50606)

Turn thy face from my sins: verse anthem for A.T.B. and chorus, SSATB. (Locke, Matthew). *Oxford University Press. Unpriced* DK (B71-50195)

Turner, J Godfrey.
The highlander march. *Feldman. Unpriced* UMMGM (B71-51057)
Youth on parade: for military band. *Feldman. Unpriced* UMMGM (B71-51058)

Turok, Paul. Elegy in memory of Karol Rathaus. Op.23: for 3 trumpets, 2 horns, 3 trombones and baritone and tuba. *Musica rara. Unpriced* WMJ (B71-51103)

Twelve floral sketches: for piano. (Longmire, John). *Bosworth. £0.20* QPJ (B71-50096)

Twelve images
b for organ. (Klerk, Albert de). *Novello. £0.50* RJ (B71-50996)

Twelve motets of the Spanish golden age. (Lewkovitch, Bernhard). *Chester. Unpriced* EZDJ/AYK (B71-50795)

Twelve overtures: in D major; for oboes, trumpets, horns, timpani, strings, and continuo. (Boyce, William). *Oxford University Press. £1.25* MRJ (B71-50918) ISBN 0 19 361834 6

Twelve overtures: in G major; for oboes, flutes, horns, strings, and continuo. (Boyce, William). *Oxford University Press. £1.25* MRJ (B71 50916) ISBN 0 19 361812 5

Twelve overtures
No.1: in D major; for oboes, strings and continuo. (Boyce, William). *Oxford University Press. £1.25* MRJ (B71-50915) ISBN 0 19 361802 8
No.3: in Bflat major; for oboes, strings and continuo. (Boyce, William). *Oxford University Press. Unpriced* MRJ (B71-50917) ISBN 0 19 361824 9
No.5: in F major; for oboes, strings and continuo. (Boyce, William). *Oxford University Press. £1.25* MRJ (B71-50919) ISBN 0 19 361849 4
No.6: in D minor; for oboes, flutes, horns, strings, and continuo. (Boyce, William). *Oxford University Press. £1.25* MRJ (B71-50920) ISBN 0 19 361859 1

Twentieth Century Church Light Music Group. *See* 20th Century Church Light Music Group.

Twentieth century composers
Vol.1: American music since 1910. *Weidenfeld and Nicolson. £3.50* A(XM) (B71-14732) ISBN 0 297 00264 3

Twenty-four etudes. *See* 24 etudes.

Twice in a blue moon: a fantasy operetta, the accompaniment for two pianos, percussion and double bass. (Tate, Phyllis). *Oxford University Press. £1.25* CQF (B71-50733) ISBN 0 19 338377 2

Two andantes and adagio 'pour le Cor Anglais': for flute, cor anglais, clarinet, horn and bassoon. (Reicha, Anton). *Universal Edition. Unpriced* UNR (B71-50632)

Two ballads: for S.A. and piano
1: The mountain-plover. Ushagreaisht. (Bliss, *Sir* Arthur). *Novello. £0.125* FDW (B71-50039)
2: Flowers in the valley. (Bliss, *Sir* Arthur). *Novello. £0.19* FDW (B71-50040)

Two doves: for full chorus of mixed voices a cappella by John Chorbajian; words by Christina Rossetti. (Chorbajian, John). *Schirmer; Chappell. Unpriced* EZDW (B71-50270)

Two-part counterpoint from the great Masters. (Messenger, Thomas). *Faber. £0.55* QP/RM/AY (B71-50458)

Two pictures: for piano. (Phillips, Sally). *Oxford University Press. Unpriced* QPJ (B71-50097)

Two symphonic studies on themes from 'The overlanders'. (Ireland, John). *Boosey and Hawkes. £0.65* MMJ (B71-50072)

Tye, Christopher.
I will exalt thee: full anthem for four voices. *Novello. £0.15* EZDK (B71-50027)
O God be merciful unto us. (Deus misereatur): SATB (full). Revised ed. *Oxford University Press. Unpriced* EZDGPS (B71-50250) ISBN 0 19 352146 6
O God be merciful unto us. (Deus misereatur): SATB (full) with verse for SATB. Revised ed. *Oxford University Press. Unpriced* EZDGPS (B71-50251) ISBN 0 19 352147 4

Tyrolean carnival: accordion solo. (Leslie, John). *Bosworth. £0.15* RSPMJ (B71-50112)

Tyson, Alan. La Tivanna, Kinsky 125: canzonetta for medium voice and piano. (Beethoven, Ludwig van). *Novello. £0.20* KFVDW (B71-50364)

Uber, David. Symphonic fanfare for brass choir. *Schirmer Chappell. Unpriced* WMGN (B71-50695)

Under the willow tree: country dance, for orchestra. (Barber, Samuel). *Schirmer; Chappell. Unpriced* MMH (B71-50385)

Unfinished symphonies: voices from the beyond. (Brown, Rosemary). *Souvenir Press. £1.75* A/D(ZF) (B71-15624) ISBN 0 285 62009 6

Union: introduction and rondo brilliant. Op.115, on themes from Norma (Bellini), for two flutes and piano. (Furstenau, Anton Bernhard). *Musica rara. Unpriced* VRNTQ (B71-51068)

Universal Decimal Classification
78: Music. English full ed. (4th international ed.). *British Standards Institution. £0.80* A(UJ) (B71-19565) ISBN 0 580 06563 4

Unto us is born a son: carol for treble voices and piano. (Roe, Betty). *Thames. Unpriced* FLDP/LF (B71-50853)

Unwin, George, *b.1920*. Great pianists of our time. (Kaiser, Joachim). *Allen and Unwin. £3.25* AQ/E(M) (B71-16015) ISBN 0 04 780019 4

Urwin, Stanley George. A tune a day: for classical guitar: a third instruction book. (Herfurth, Clarence Paul). *Chappell. £0.40* TS/AC (B71-50606)

Usborne, Peter. Music. *Macdonald and Co. £0.25* A (B71-19965) ISBN 0 356 03759 2

Uto traverso. *(Schott)* Doflein, Erich. 16 Stucke: fur Flote allein. *Schott. £0.80* VRPM/AY (B71-50145)

V Fantasia ex D: fur Fagott und Basso continuo. (Selma y Salaverde, Bartolomeo de). *Schott. £1.10* VWPJ (B71-50685)

Valentin, Erich. Mozart and his world. *Thames and Hudson. £1.75* BMS(N) (B71-08375) ISBN 0 500 13029 9

Van Beethoven, Ludwig. *See* Beethoven, Ludwig van.

Van Beethoven, Ludwig. *See* Beethoven, Ludwig van.

Van Beethoven, Ludwig van. *See* Beethoven, Ludwig van.

Vanessa. Excerpts. Under the willow tree: country dance, for orchestra. (Barber, Samuel). *Schirmer; Chappell. Unpriced* MMH (B71-50385)

Vanhal, Jan Krtitel. *See* Wanhal, Johann Baptist.

Vann, Stanley. Behold, how good and joyful: S.A.T.B. unacc.,. *Oxford University Press. Unpriced* EZDR (B71-50808) ISBN 0 19 350327 1

Variations for organ on the Lourdes Hymn. (Henriksen, Josef). *St Gregory Publishing Co. £0.53* R/T (B71-50993)

Variations on 'Good morrow, gossip Joan'. (Dinn, Freda). *Schott. Unpriced* SRP/T (B71-51017)

Variations on 'O Lord in Thee is all my trust': for organ. (Amner, John). *Schott. Unpriced* R/T (B71-50108)

Varietie of lute-lessons. Excerpts. Fantasia no.7: per liuto. (Dowland, John). *Schott. £0.80* TWPMJ (B71-50618)

'Variety' music cavalcade, 1620-1969: a chronology of vocal and instrumental music popular in the United States. (Mattfeld, Julius). 2nd ed. *Prentice-Hall. £7.50* A/GB(YT/XEW350/TC) (B71-23694) ISBN 0 13 940718 9

Varlaam's song. (Mussorgsky, Modeste). *Ascherberg, Hopwood and Crew. £0.25* QPK/DW (B71-50985)

Vaughan, Jennifer. Music. *Macdonald and Co. £0.25* A (B71-19965) ISBN 0 356 03759 2

Vaughan Williams, Ralph.
Dona nobis pacem: a cantata for soprano and baritone soli, chorus and orchestra. *Oxford University Press. £3.50* EMDE (B71-50781) ISBN 0 19 338860 x
Norfolk rhapsody: founded on folk-tunes collected orally in Norfolk and set as an orchestral piece. *Oxford University Press. £1.75* MMJ (B71-50400) ISBN 0 19 369227 9

Veal, Arthur. The Irish fiddler: unison. *Oxford University Press. Unpriced* JFDW (B71-50053)

Velimirovic, Milos Milorad. Studies in Eastern Chant
Vol.2. (Wellesz, Egon). *Oxford University Press. £3.50* ADTDS (B71-16013) ISBN 0 19 316318 7

Veracini, Francesco Maria.
Sonatas for violin & harpsichord. Op.2. Sonate accademiche. Op.2: fur Violine und bezifferten Bass, Violine und Klavier (Cembalo, Orgel) mit Violoncello ad libitum
Sonata 1, D-dur. *Peters; Hinrichsen. £0.525* SPE (B71-50560)
Sonatas for violin & harpsichord. Op.2. Sonate accademiche. Op.2: fur Violine und bezifferten Bass, Violine und Klavier (Cembalo, Orgel) mit Violoncello ad libitum
Sonata 2, B-dur. *Peters; Hinrichsen. £0.525* SPE (B71-50561)
Sonatas for violin & harpsichord. Op.2. Sonate accademiche. Op.2: fur Violine und bezifferten Bass, Violine und Klavier (Cembalo, Orgel) mit Violoncello ad libitum
Sonata 3, C-dur. *Peters; Hinrichsen. £0.525* SPE (B71-50562)
Sonatas for violin & harpsichord. Op.2. Sonate accademiche. Op.2: fur Violine und bezifferten Bass, Violine und Klavier (Cembalo, Orgel) mit Violoncello ad libitum
Sonata 4, F-dur. *Peters; Hinrichsen. £0.725* SPE (B71-50563)
Sonatas for violin & harpsichord. Op.2. Sonate accademiche. Op.2: fur Violine und bezifferten Bass, Violine und Klavier (Cembalo, Orgel) mit Violoncello ad libitum
Sonata 7, d-moll. *Peters; Hinrichsen. Unpriced* SPE (B71-50564)
Sonatas for violin & harpsichord. Op.2. Sonate accademiche. Op.2: fur Violine und bezifferten Bass, Violine und Klavier (Cembalo, Orgel) mit Violoncello ad libitum
Sonata 8, e-moll. *Peters; Hinrichsen. £0.80* SPE (B71-50565)
Sonatas for violin & harpsichord. Op.2. Sonate accademiche. Op.2: fur Violine und bezifferten Bass, Violine und Klavier (Cembalo, Orgel) mit Violoncello ad libitum
Sonata 9, A-dur. *Peters; Hinrichsen. £0.80* SPE (B71-50566)
Sonatas for violin & harpsichord. Op.2. Sonate accademiche. Op.2: fur Violine und bezifferten Bass, Violine und Klavier (Cembalo, Orgel) mit Violoncello ad libitum
Sonata 12, d-moll. *Peters; Hinrichsen. £0.80* SPE (B71-50567)

Verdelot, Philippe. Madonna, per voi ardo. Ah love, my heart is burning: for SATB chorus. *Warner; Blossom Music. Unpriced* EZDU (B71-50267)

Verdi, Giuseppe.
La Forza del destino: opera in three acts. *Schirmer; Chappell. Unpriced* CC (B71-50162)
Letters of Giuseppe Verdi. *Gollancz. £3.00* BVE(N) (B71-21046) ISBN 0 575 00759 1

Vereczkey, Laszlo. Kleine Stucke: fur Gitarre. (Paganini, Niccolo). *Schott. £1.40* TSPMJ (B71-51051)

Verrall, Pamela.
Johnny Appleseed: a cantata for all ages, for narrator, speaking chorus, singing chorus, dancers, mimers. *Feldman. £0.30* FE/NYFSDE (B71-50843)
Six conversations: for clarinet with piano accompaniment. *Feldman. Unpriced* VVPJ (B71-50677)

Verrall, Pamela Motley.
Sing a lullabye for Jesus. *Freeman. Unpriced* FDP/LF (B71-50290)
A stable bare. *Freeman. Unpriced* FDP/LF (B71-50291)
Star bright, starlight. *Freeman. Unpriced* JDP/LF (B71-50318)
Summer water: a cantata for recorders and percussion, two-part singing chorus, soprano solo and speaking chorus. *Bosworth. £0.75* FE/NYHSDX (B71-50844)

Versuch uber Schweine: fur Stimme und Orchester. (Henze, Hans Werner). *Schott. £3.20* KE/MDX (B71-50059)

Very, Jones. The fair morning. (Binkerd, Gordon). *Boosey and Hawkes. £0.65* KDW (B71-50332)

Vesper bell. (Engelhart, Franz Xaver). *Bosworth. Unpriced* DW (B71-50771)

Vesperae solennes de confessore. K.339 - Excerpts. Laudate Dominum. K.339, no.5. (Mozart, Wolfgang Amadeus). *Oxford University Press. Unpriced* FDGKJ (B71-50826) ISBN 0 19 342590 4

Vester, Frans.
Five pieces for the musical clock, nos.1,3. Adagio and allegro for the musical clock. (Beethoven, Ludwig van). *Universal. Unpriced* UNRK/A/FK (B71-50634)
Two andantes and adagio 'pour le Cor Anglais': for flute, cor anglais, clarinet, horn and bassoon. (Reicha, Anton). *Universal Edition. Unpriced* UNR (B71-50632)

Vibration: model for a group improvisation with Orff instrumentation or other intstruments sic. (Lisken, Gerd). *Schott. £1.20* XN (B71-51121)

Viera Rios, Graziela. Evocacao: tema con variacoes for piano. *Arthur Napoleao. Unpriced* QP/T (B71-50970)

Villa-Lobos, Heitor.
Carnaval das criancas: colecao de 8 pecas for piano
No.7: A Gaita de um precoce fantasiado. *Arthu Napoleao; Essex Music. Unpriced* QPG (B71-50470)
Fabulas caracteristicas. Op.65. Excerpts. O Gato e o rato: piano. *Arthur Napoleao; Essex Music. Unpriced* QPJ (B71-50501)
La suite infantil: colecao de 5 pecas for piano No.2: Nene vai dormir. *Arthur Napoleao; Essex Music. Unpriced* QPG (B71-50468)
Os martirios dos insetos - Excerpts. A Mariposa na luz: violino e piano. *Arthur Napoleao; Essex Music. Unpriced* SPJ (B71-50569)
Modinha Serestas no.5: 1 violao with Adeus, Bela Morena and, Cirandinhas no.2: 2 violaoes. *Arthur Napoleao Essex Music. Unpriced* SPMK (B71-50581)
Ondulando: estudo for piano. Op.31. *Arthur Napoleao; Essex Music. Unpriced* QPJ (B71-50502)
Serestas. Excerpts. Cancao do Carreiro ou Cancao u crepusculo caricioso: canto e piano. *Arthur Napoleao;*

Essex Music. Unpriced KDW (B71-50057)

Simples coletanea: colecao de 3 pecas for piano

No.1: Valsa mistica. *Arthur Napoleao; Essex Music. Unpriced* QPJ (B71-50503)

No.3: Rodante. *Arthur Napoleao; Essex Music. Unpriced* QPJ (B71-50504)

Suite floral: colecao de 3 pecas for piano. Op.97

No.3: Alegria na Horta. *Arthur Napoleao; Essex Music. Unpriced* QPG (B71-50471)

Suite infantil no.2. Excerpts. Allegro. *Arthur Napoleao; Essex Music. Unpriced* QPJ (B71-50099)

Vining, Paul. Almighty God, which hast given: verse anthem for Christmas Day. (Gibbons, Orlando). *Novello. £0.15* DK/LF (B71-50017)

Viola da Gamba Society. Chelys: the journal of the Viola da Gamba Society

Vol.1-. *Viola da Gamba Society. £2.10(free to members)* ASTU(B) (B71-01190)

Viollier, Renee. Arias: for tenor, flute, continuo

Vol.1. (Rameau, Jean Philippe). *Musica rara. £3.15* KGHE/VRPDW (B71-50368)

Virag, Benedek. Invocation of peace: Bekesser ohajtas: S.A.T.B. unaccompanied. (Kodaly, Zoltan). *Boosey and Hawkes. Unpriced* EZDW (B71-50274)

Visee, Robert de. Gitarrenbuch. *Schott. £1.20* TSPMJ (B71-50610)

Viva Mexico!: a comedy musical in three acts. (Hanmer, Ronald). *Weinberger. Unpriced* CM (B71-50164)

Vivaldi, Antonio.

Il Cimentia dell'armonia e dell'inventione. Op.8. Concerto for oboe & string orchestra in C major. Konzert, C-Dur fur Oboe, Streichorchester und General bass. *Schott. £0.90* VTPK/LF (B71-50667)

Concerto for bassoon in F major. P.318. Konzert, F-dur fur Fagott und Streichorchester. *Peters; Hinrichsen. £1.75* RXMPVWF (B71-50541)

Concerto for bassoon in F major. P.318. Konzert, F-dur fur Fagott und Streichorchester

Ausgabe fur Fagott und Klavier. *Peters; Hinrichsen. £1.20* VWPK/LF (B71-50686)

Concerto for violin in B flat major, (The Posthorn). P.350. Konzert, B-dur (das Posthorn): fur Violine und Streichorchester

Klavierauszug. *Peters; Hinrichsen. £0.90* SPK/LF (B71-50576)

Concerto for violin in B flat major, (The Posthorn), P.350. Konzert, B-dur (das Posthorn): fur Violino und Streichorchester. *Peters; Hinrichsen. £1.25* RXMPSF (B71-50536)

Sonata for treble recorder & basso continuo in F major. Rinaldi op.67. Sonate F-Dur: fur Altblockflote und Basso continuo. *Schott. £0.80* VSSPE (B71-50657)

Volger, Heinz. Ausgewahlte Klavierwerke

Band 3: Aus meinem Tagebuch. Op.82. (Reger, Max). *Peters; Hinrichsen. £1.25* QPJ (B71-50498)

Volks- und Tanzweisen aus Amerika: fur Flote, Akkordeon I/II (E-Gitarre), Gitarre (Banjo), Bass und Schlagzeug. (Buhe, Klaus). *Schott. £1.20* NYDRK/DW/AYT (B71-50433)

Volo solo: for a virtuoso performer on any instrument. (Cardew, Cornelius). *Peters, Hinrichsen. £0.90* LJ (B71-50373)

Von Dittersdorf, Carl Ditters. *See* Dittersdorf, Carl Ditters von.

Von Dittersdorf, Carl Ditters. *See* Dittersdorf, Carl Ditters von.

Von Einem, Gottfried. *See* Einem, Gottfried von.

Von Einem, Gottfried. *See* Einem, Gottfried von.

Von Gluck, Christoph Willibald. *See* Gluck, Christoph Willibald von.

Von Goethe, Johann Wolfgang. *See* Goethe, Johann Wolfgang von.

Von Meck, Barbara. The music lovers: the story of Tchaikowsky and Nadejda von Meck. (Bowen, Catherine Drinker). 2nd ed. abridged. *Hodder Paperbacks. £0.35* BTD(N) (B71-04592) ISBN 0 340 15154 4

Von Sauer, Emil. *See* Sauer, Emil von.

Von Webern, Anton. *See* Webern, Anton von.

Von Webern, Anton. *See* Webern, Anton von.

Vortragsbuchlein fur das Zusammenspiel: Sopran-und Altblockflote, Schlagwerk ad lib. (Rohr, Heinrich). *Schott. Unpriced* VSNUK/AAY (B71-50654)

Wachet auf. S.140. Excerpts. Zion hears the watchmen's voices: for unison & SATB chorale. (Bach, Johann Sebastian). *Oxford University Press. Unpriced* DM (B71-50202) ISBN 0 19 343013 4

Wagner. (Padmore, Elaine). *Faber and Faber Ltd. £1.50* BWC(N) (B71-29387) ISBN 0 571 08785 x

Wales, Tony.

Songs for singing folk: Jackie and Bridies second song book. (McDonald, Jacqueline). *Galliard. Unpriced* KFE/TSDW/G/AYC (B71-50355)

The Yetties song book. *English Folk Dance and Song Society. Unpriced* KE/TSDW/G/AYD (B71-50353)

Walker, Alan, *b.1930*. Liszt. *Faber and Faber Ltd. £1.50* BLJ(N) (B71-10425) ISBN 0 571 09120 2

Walker, George. The Anthony Gell suite (in olden style): for strings and woodwind (optional). *Bosworth. Unpriced* RXMG (B71-50115)

Walker, Malcolm. Barbirolli: conductor laureate: the authorised biography. (Kennedy, Michael, *b.1926*). *MacGibbon and Kee. £2.95* A/EC(P) (B71-27973) ISBN 0 261 63336 8

Walking; and, Dream tide. (Swain, Freda). *Schott. Unpriced* SRPJ (B71-51031)

Wallace, J L. Prelude & fugue, 'The Spitfire'. Excerpts. Spitfire fugue. (Walton, *Sir* William). *Boosey and Hawkes. Unpriced* UMMK/Y/JR (B71-50136)

Walton, *Sir* William. Prelude & fugue, 'The Spitfire'. Excerpts. Spitfire fugue. *Boosey and Hawkes. Unpriced* UMMK/Y/JR (B71-50136)

Walzer-Capricen, deutsche Tanze und andere Stucke: fur Klavier zu vier Handen. (Reger, Max). *Peters; Hinrichsen. £1.40* QNV (B71-50452)

Wandering scholar. Op.50: a chamber opera in one act. (Holst, Gustav). *Faber. Unpriced* CQC (B71-50172)

Wanhal, Johann Baptist. Sonata for clarinet & piano in E flat major. Sonate, Es-Dur: fur Klarinette in B und Klavier. *Schott. £2.00* VVPE (B71-50673)

Warburton, Annie O. Graded aural tests for all purposes: with suggested methods of working. *Longman. Unpriced* C/EF (B71-50724) ISBN 0 582 32585 4

Warburton, Annie Osborne. Analyses of musical classics Book 3. *Longman. £1.40* A/S (B71-27230) ISBN 0 582 32487 4

Warburton, K M. Honeybrook: part-song for SSA and piano. (Thiman, Eric Harding). *Novello. Unpriced* FDW (B71-50043)

Warlock, Peter. Capriol suite. *Curwen, R. Smith. Unpriced* WMK/AHG (B71-50706)

Warren, Raymond. Songs of old age: a song cycle for voice and piano. *Novello. £0.75* KDW (B71-50887)

Warren-Smith, A G. Born to be King. (Broad, D F). *Banks. Unpriced* FDP/LF (B71-50287)

Warum. Wherefore should our singing soar. Op.91, no.4: for four-part chorus of mixed voices with piano accompaniment. (Brahms, Johannes). *Schirmer; Chappell. Unpriced* DW (B71-50230)

Wasserklavier: for piano. (Berio, Luciano). *Universal. Unpriced* QPJ (B71-50474)

Waterman, Fanny.

The young pianist's repertoire

Book 1. *Faber. Unpriced* QP/AY (B71-50455)

Book 2. *Faber. Unpriced* QP/AY (B71-50456)

Waters, Charles Frederick.

Cornet fantasy: for the organ. *Leonard, Gould and Bolttler. £0.18* RJ (B71-50998)

Little cycle: for solo clarinet. *Hinrichsen. £0.35* VVPMJ (B71-50681)

Watson, Walter. Music for organ and horns. *Schirmer Chappell. Unpriced* WTNRR (B71-51118)

Watt, Jill. Johnson preserved: opera in 3 acts. (Stoker, Richard). *Peters. Hinrichsen. £5.00* CC (B71-50161)

We piano teachers. (Booth, Victor). 1st ed. 8th impression (revised). *Hutchinson. £1.25* AQ/E(VC) (B71-05270) ISBN 0 09 106190 3

We three: two-part chorus with piano, optional guitars and claves. (House, L Marguerite). *Warner; Blossom Music. Unpriced* DW (B71-50233)

Webb, Graham. The disc musical box handbook. *Faber and Faber Ltd. £3.50* A/FND (B71-18092) ISBN 0 571 09378 7

Webb, Roger. Symphony no.5 in C minor. Excerpts. Adagietto. The timeless moment: song. (Mahler, Gustav). *Chappell. £0.20* KDW (B71-50885)

Webber, Andrew Lloyd. Jesus Christ Superstar- Excerpts. I don't know how to love him. *Leeds Music. £0.20* KFDW (B71-50890)

Webber, Lloyd. Four introits: for SATB and organ. *Novello. £0.09* DH (B71-50013)

Webern, Anton von.

Four Stefan George songs: voice and piano. *Boosey and Hawkes. Unpriced* KDW (B71-50343)

Satz fur Klavier. *Boosey and Hawkes. Unpriced* QPJ (B71-50505)

Sonata for cello & piano. Cello sonata: for cello and piano. *Boosey and Hawkes. Unpriced* SRPE (B71-50593)

Sonatensatz (Rondo) fur Klavier. *Boosey and Hawkes. Unpriced* QP/W (B71-50461)

Wedding anthem for Frederick, Prince of Wales. *See* Handel, George Frideric.

Weeks, John. Jubilate: for organ and brass. *Hinrichsen. £1.50* NWXPNM (B71-50425)

Wehinger, Rainer. Artikulation: electronic music: an aural score. (Ligeti, Gyorgy). *Schott. Unpriced* PS (B71-50080)

Wehrle, Heinz. Vier Orgelstucke. *Eulenburg, Hinrichsen. £1.10* RJ (B71-50528)

Weigart, Bernhard.

Duets for cellos. Opus 15. Duos: fur zwei Violoncelli. Opus 15. (Dotzauer, Justus Johann Friedrich). *Schott. £0.90* SRNU (B71-50121)

Sonata for cello & basso continuo in G minor. Op.8, no.5. Sonata, g moll: fur Violoncello und Basso continuo. (Defesch, Willem). *Schott. £0.80* SRPE (B71-50592)

Weisse, Michael. Christ the Lord is risen again: SATB. (Rutter, John). *Oxford University Press. £0.09* DM/LL (B71-50209) ISBN 0 19 351109 6

Welford, Robert. The classical guitar: design and construction. (McLeod, Donald, *b.1921*). *Dryad Press. £2.50* ATS/BC (B71-14735) ISBN 0 85219 077 8

Well, what do you know!: SATB, with piano accompaniment and optional violins, strings bass and guitar. (Artman, Ruth). *Warner; Blossom Music. Unpriced* DW (B71-50770)

Wellesz, Egon. Studies in Eastern Chant

Vol.2. *Oxford University Press. £3.50* ADTDS (B71-16013) ISBN 0 19 316318 7

Wells, Dicky. The night people: reminiscences of a jazzman. *Hale. £2.00* AMT/E(P) (B71-25916) ISBN 0 7091 2397 3

Welsh cameo. (Siebert, Edrich). *Studio Music. Unpriced* WMK/DW/AYDK (B71-50708)

Welsh flavour: a selection of Welsh hymn tunes set to English words

Vol.1. (Battye, Ken). *K. Battye. Unpriced* DM/AYDK (B71-50204)

Vol.2. (Battye, Ken). *K. Battye. Unpriced* DM/AYDK (B71-50205)

Vol.3. (Battye, Ken). *K. Battye. Unpriced* DM/AYDK (B71-50206)

Vol.4. (Battye, Ken). *K. Battye. Unpriced* DM/AYDK (B71-50207)

Vol.5. (Battye, Ken). *K. Battye. Unpriced* DM/AYDK (B71-50208)

Wenn ich ein Glocklein war. The Vesper bell. (Engelhart, Franz Xaver). *Bosworth. Unpriced* DW (B71-50771)

Wennington, William. La Tivanna, Kinsky 125: canzonetta for medium voice and piano. (Beethoven, Ludwig van). *Novello. £0.20* KFVDW (B71-50364)

Wer walset uns den Stein. An Easter dialogue: for mixed voices, organ (piano), 2 trumpets, 4 trombones and double bass. (Hammerschmidt, Andreas). *Peters; Hinrichsen. £0.45* ENUXPNQDH/LL (B71-50240)

Wesley, Charles. 6 Wesley songs for the young. (Williamson, Malcolm). *Weinberger. £0.30* JFDM (B71-50864)

West, Elisabeth. Bela Bartok - letters. (Bartok, Bela). *Faber and Faber Ltd. £5.50* BBG(N) (B71-18713) ISBN 0 571 09638 7

Westergaard, Peter. Four Stefan George songs: voice and piano. (Webern, Anton von). *Boosey and Hawkes. Unpriced* KDW (B71-50343)

Westmore, Peter.

Come to Bethlehem: twelve original carols. *Vanguard Music. Unpriced* KDP/LF/AY (B71-50882)

Come to Bethlehem: twelve original carols. (Westmore, Peter). *Vanguard Music. Unpriced* KDP/LF/AY (B71-50882)

Weston, Pamela.

Clarinet virtuosi of the past. *Hale. £5.00* AVV/E(M/XA1950) (B71-30156) ISBN 0 7091 2442 2

Classical album: for 2 clarinets in B flat and piano. *Boosey and Hawkes. Unpriced* VVPK/AAY (B71-51090)

Eight clarinet trios of the 18th century. *Schott. £0.40* VVNT/AY (B71-50671)

Weston, Philip. The disc musical box handbook. (Webb, Graham). *Faber and Faber Ltd. £3.50* A/FND (B71-18092) ISBN 0 571 09378 7

Westrup, *Sir* Jack Allan.

Everyman's dictionary of music. (Blom, Eric). 5th ed. *Dent. £4.00* A(C) (B71-21647) ISBN 0 460 03022 1

Musical interpretation. *British Broadcasting Corporation. £0.90* A/E (B71-06909) ISBN 0 563 10352 3

What sweeter musick: high voice. (Binkerd, Gordon). *Boosey and Hawkes. £0.40* KFTDW (B71-50363)

When one knows thee: for four-part chorus of mixed voices a cappella. (Glarum, Leonard Stanley). *Schirmer; Chappell. Unpriced* EZDH (B71-50253)

Where are you going to, my pretty maid?. (Poston, Elizabeth). *Bodley Head. £1.10* JFDW/GK/AY (B71-50874) ISBN 0 370 01529 0

Where sleeps the infant Jesus: Mexican carol, SATB. (Ehret, Walter). *Warner; Blossom Music. Unpriced* DP/LF (B71-50211)

White (Ernest George) Society. *See* Ernest George White Society.

White, Ian.

Divertimento for viola, cello and double bass in E fla major. (Haydn, Michael). *Yorke Edition. Unpriced* RXNT (B71-50551)

Divertimento for viola, cello & double bass in E flat major. (Haydn, Michael). *Yorke. Unpriced* RXNT (B71-50552)

Whittier, John Greenleaf. Fold to thy heart thy brother: for four-part chorus of mixed voices a cappella. (Hovdesven, E A). *Schirmer; Chappell. Unpriced* EZDW (B71-50816)

Who. (Herman, Gary). *Studio Vista. £1.40* AB/E(P) (B71-16698) ISBN 0 289 70135 x

Wick, Denis. Trombone technique. *Oxford University Press. £1.15* AWU/E (B71-14736) ISBN 0 19 318704 3

Widdicombe, Trevor. Forty tunes: for the viola. *Curwen. Unpriced* SQPK/DW/G/AYB (B71-50582)

Wiegenlied. Op.98, no.2. (Schubert, Franz). *Schott. Unpriced* SRPK/DW (B71-51041)

Wieland Wagner: the positive sceptic. (Skelton, Geoffrey). *Gollancz. £2.80* AC/EP(P) (B71-16012) ISBN 0 575 00709 5

Wienandt, Elwyn Arthur. The anthem in England and America. *Free Press; Collier-Macmillan. £6.00* ADH(YT/X) (B71-20591) ISBN 0 02 093523 4

Wilde, Oscar. Four impressions: medium (high) voice and piano. (Griffes, Charles Tomlinson). *Peters; Hinrichsen. £1.10* KFVDW (B71-50366)

Willan, Healey. Elegie heroique. *Boosey and Hawkes. Unpriced* UMMJ (B71-50624)

Willcocks, David.

Carols for choirs. Bk.1, nos. 33, 27, 13. Three carol orchestrations. (Jacques, Reginald). *Oxford University Press. Unpriced* EMDP/LF (B71-50782)

Carols for choirs. Excerpts. Six Christmas hymns: for mixed voices and organ (or orchestra). *Oxford University Press. £0.20* DP/LF/AY (B71-50217) ISBN 0 19 353568 8

How far is it to Bethlehem?: English traditional melody, S.A.A. unacc. *Oxford University Press. Unpriced* FEZDP/LF (B71-50305) ISBN 0 19 342592 0

Masters in this hall: French traditional carol, SATB. *Oxford University Press. Unpriced* DP/LF (B71-50214) ISBN 0 19 343009 6

Mr Henry Noell, his funerall psalmes. Seven hymn tunes. Lamentio Henrici Noel: S.A.T.B.

Nos. 1-4. (Dowland, John). Revised ed. *Oxford University Press. Unpriced* EZDR/KDN (B71-50809) ISBN 0 19 352157 1

Quelle est cette odeur agreable? Whence is that goodly fragrance flowing?: French traditional carol, S.A.T.B. *Oxford University Press. Unpriced* DP/LF (B71-50215) ISBN 0 19 343010 x

Resonemus laudibus: SATB. *Oxford University Press.*
Unpriced DP/LF (B71-50216)   ISBN 0 19 343011 8
Stille Nacht, heilige Nacht. Silent night. (Gruber, Franz).
Oxford University Press. Unpriced DP/LF (B71-50763)
                                     ISBN 0 19 343022 3
Williams, Alfred. Folk-songs of the Upper Thames: with an
essay on folk-song activity in the Upper Thames
neighbourhood. 1st ed. reprinted. *S.R. Publishers. £3.15*
ADW/G(YDEVU) (B71-10430)   ISBN 0 85409 610 8
Williams, Arnold. Going to see my long-haired babe. *Banks.*
Unpriced GDW (B71-50046)
Williams, I. Great mover of all hearts: anthem. (Smith,
Noel). *Lengnick. Unpriced* DH (B71-50747)
Williams, John. Cavatina: arranged for guitar by John
Williams. (Myers, Stanley). *Francis, Day and Hunter.*
£0.40 TSPMK (B71-51052)
Williams, Nan Fleming-. *See* Fleming- Williams, Nan.
Williams, Patrick.
First easy album for the organ. *Bosworth. £0.30* RK/AAY
(B71-50529)
How sweet I roamed from field to field: two part song.
Bosworth. £0.07 FDW (B71-50840)
Second easy album for the organ. *Bosworth. Unpriced*
RK/AAY (B71-50530)
Williams, Peter, *b.1937.* Figured bass accompaniments.
Edinburgh University Press. £5.00 A/RGD (B71-05794)
                                     ISBN 0 85224 054 6
Williams, Ralph Vaughan. *See* Vaughan Williams, Ralph.
Williams, Ursula Vaughan. *See* Vaughan Williams, Ursula.
Williams, W Matthews. Tannau moliant. *Llyfrfa'r*
Methodistiaid Calfinaidd. Unpriced DM (B71-50753)
Williamson, Malcolm.
6 Wesley songs for the young. *Weinberger. £0.30* JFDM
(B71-50864)
Genesis: a cassation for audience and instruments.
Weinberger. Unpriced DE (B71-50738)
Williamson, Malcolm. Six Wesley songs for the young. *See*
Williamson, Malcolm. 6 Wesley songs for the young.
Williamson, Malcolm.
The stone wall: a cassation for audience and orchestra.
Weinberger. Unpriced DX (B71-50780)
Symphony: for organ. *Novello. £1.50* RE (B71-50994)
Te Deum: for S.A.T.B. choir, organ and optional brass
ensemble. *Weinberger. £0.25* DGNQ (B71-50180)
Willow, willow: for flute, tuba, and three percussionists.
(Chihara, Paul). *Protone Music; Henmer Music;*
Hinrichsen. £1.75 NYHNR (B71-50436)
Wills, Arthur. Communion service in C: for congregation,
SATB and organ. *Royal School of Church Music.*
Unpriced DGS (B71-50009)
Wilson, Richard. Soaking: for four-part chorus of mixed
voices a cappella. *Schirmer; Chappell. Unpriced* EZDW
(B71-50284)
Wilson, Robert Barclay.
All poor men and humble. O deued pob Christio: a Welsh
carol. *Cramer. £0.06* DP/LF (B71-50765)
Two short pieces: piano. *Cramer. Unpriced* QPJ
(B71-50506)
Wilson, Thomas. Sonata for piano (1959, rev. 1964). Piano
sonata (1959: revised 1964). *Stainer & Bell. Unpriced*
QPE (B71-50972)
Wilson-Dickson, Andrew. A little hymn to Mary: carol for
SATB and piano or organ. *Novello. Unpriced* DP/LF
(B71-50766)
Winkworth, Catherine.
Alleluja. Freuet euch ihr Christen alle. Alleluia! O rejoice ye
Christians loudly: for mixed voices, organ (piano) and
strings (ad lib). (Hammerschmidt, Andreas). *Peters*
Hinrichsen. £0.45 DH/LF (B71-50191)
Christ the Lord is risen again: SATB. (Rutter, John).
Oxford University Press. £0.09 DM/LL (B71-50209)
                                     ISBN 0 19 351109 6
Winters, Geoffrey. A medley of folk songs. (Stuart, Forbes).
Longman Young Books. £2.50 JDW/G/AY (B71-50861)
                                     ISBN 0 582 15331 x
Wise, Herbert H. This is the Arlo Guthrie book. (Guthrie,
Arlo). *Amsco Music Publishing; Distributed by*
Collier-Macmillan. £0.90 KE/TSDW (B71-50888)
                                     ISBN 0 02 060680 x
Wishart, Peter.
Key to music. *British Broadcasting Corporation. £0.90*
A/S (B71-24688)   ISBN 0 563 10589 5
Six miniatures. *Stainer and Bell. £1.50* KDW (B71-50344)

Wishing caps. (Binkerd, Gordon). *Boosey and Hawkes.*
£0.65 KDW (B71-50335)
Withers, Herbert.
Concerto for cello in D major. Hob. VII b/2. - Excerpts.
Adagio. (Haydn, Joseph). *Schott. Unpriced* SRPK
(B71-51023)
Concerto for clavier in F minor. S1056 - Excerpts. Largo
and allegretto. (Bach, Johann Sebastian). *Schott. Unpriced*
SRPK (B71-51032)
Concerto for violin in G minor, 'Concerto russe'. Op. 29 -
Excerpts. Chants russes. (Lalo, Edouard). *Schott.*
Unpriced SRPK (B71-51034)
Dream children. Op.43,no.2. (Elgar, *Sir* Edward, *bart*).
Schott. Unpriced SRPK (B71-51033)
Southward bound. (Alexander, Arthur). *Schott. Unpriced*
SRPJ (B71-51024)
Within thy light: SATB with organ or piano. (Gordon,
Philip). *Blossom Music. Unpriced* DH (B71-50186)
Wolfe, Daniel.
Beata es virgo: part chorus of mixed voices with organ
accompaniment (optional). (Gabrieli, Giovanni).
Schirmer; Chappell. Unpriced EZDGKJ (B71-50024)
Hodie Christus natus est: for double chorus of mixed voices
with organ accompaniment. (Gabrieli, Giovanni).
Schirmer; Chappell. Unpriced DGKJ/LF (B71-50740)

Jubilemus singuli: for eight-part chorus of mixed voices with
organ accompaniment. (Gabrieli, Giovanni). *Schirmer;*
Chappell. Unpriced DJ (B71-50016)
Wolman, Baron. Festival!: the book of American music
celebrations... (Hopkins, Jerry). *Macmillan (N.Y.);*
Collier-Macmillan. £4.00 A/GB(YT/WE) (B71-11123)
                                     ISBN 0 02 580170 8
Wolpe, Stefan. Form IV: broken sequences: for piano.
Peters; Hinrichsen. Unpriced QPJ (B71-50507)
Women's Institutes. *See* National Federation of Women's
Institutes.
Wood, Graham. An A-Z of rock and roll. *Studio Vista.*
£2.50 AKDW/HK(C) (B71-12553)
                                     ISBN 0 289 70006 x
Wood, Robert B. Make your own musical instruments.
(Mandell, Muriel). New ed. *Bailey Bros and Swinfen.*
£1.40 AL/BC (B71-01700)   ISBN 0 561 00083 2
Woodward, G R.
Ding dong! merrily on high: carol arranged for women's or
boys' voices & organ/piano. (Hunter, Ian T). *Thames.*
Unpriced FDP/LF (B71-50828)
O the morn, the merry merry morn. (Curtis, Frederick
Vernon). *Banks. Unpriced* DP/LF (B71-50018)
Unto us is born a son: carol for treble voices and piano.
(Roe, Betty). *Thames. Unpriced* FLDP/LF (B71-50853)
Wooldridge, David. Great pianists of our time. (Kaiser,
Joachim). *Allen and Unwin. £3.25* AQ/E(M) (B71-16015)
                                     ISBN 0 04 780019 4
Worden, John. Strike sound: a collection of Padstow carols.
Lodenek Press. Unpriced DP/LF/AYDFRP (B71-50767)

Words and music. (Lawrence, Ian). *Longman. £0.40* A(VG)
(B71-08785)   ISBN 0 582 18694 3
Words and music
Introduction. (Lawrence, Ian). *Longman. £2.50* A(VG)
(B71-22574)   ISBN 0 582 18695 1
Stage 1. (Lawrence, Ian). *Longman. £0.40* A(VG)
(B71-06126)   ISBN 0 582 18691 9
Stage 2. (Lawrence, Ian). *Longman. £0.40* A(VG)
(B71-06127)   ISBN 0 582 18692 7
Stage 3. (Lawrence, Ian). *Longman. £0.40* A(VG)
(B71-06128)   ISBN 0 582 18693 5
Workbook for woodwind: an elementary group method.
(Oboussier, Philippe). *Novello. £0.90* V/AC (B71-51067)
Works of Ralph Vaughan Williams. (Kennedy, Michael,
b.1926). Oxford University Press. £0.90 BVD(N)
(B71-30151)   ISBN 0 19 315423 4
World of Duke Ellington. (Dance, Stanley). *Macmillan.*
£3.50 AMT/E(P) (B71-30153)   ISBN 0 333 13019 7
World rejoice!: a suite of traditional carols from five nations
arranged for female and/or boys' voices, piano, strings and
percussion, with alternative accompaniment for piano and
optional percussion only. (Phillips, John Charles). *Novello.*
£0.25 FDP/LF/AYB (B71-50292)
Worshipful Company of Musicians: a short history.
(Crewdson, Henry Alastair Ferguson). New ed. *C. Knight.*
£4.00 A(Q/YDBCJ/XD471) (B71-30640)
                                     ISBN 0 85314 086 3
Wright, Robert.
Song of Norway. (Greig, Edvard). *Chappell; Frank Music.*
£0.60 KDW/JR (B71-50058)
Song of Norway. (Grieg, Edvard). *Chappell. Unpriced*
WMK/CM/JR (B71-51108)
Song of Norway: selection for all organs. (Grieg, Edvard).
Chappell. £0.40 RK/CM/JR (B71-50999)
The song of Norway: piano selection from the film. (Greig,
Edvard). *Chappell; Frank Music. £0.25* QPK/CM/JR
(B71-50104)
Wulstan, David. An anthology of English church music.
Chester. Unpriced EZDH/AYD (B71-50793)
Wyttenbach, Jurg. Drei Klavierstucke (1969). *Schott. £1.20*
QPJ (B71-50508)
XXIII Canzon a 2 Bassi: fur 2 Fagotte oder Posaune und
Fagott und Basso continuo. (Selma y Salaverde,
Bartolomeo de). *Schott. £1.00* VWNTPW (B71-50682)
Yeats, William Butler. Songs of old age: a song cycle for
voice and piano. (Warren, Raymond). *Novello. £0.75*
KDW (B71-50887)
Yepes y Alvarez, Juan de. *See* John of the Cross, *Saint.*
Yes! I can play: songs and singing games. (Jeremiah,
Dorothy Adams). *Leeds Music. Unpriced*
JFE/TQTDW/GS/AY (B71-50878)
Yetties song book. (Wales, Tony). *English Folk Dance and*
Song Society. Unpriced KE/TSDW/G/AYD
(B71-50353)
You are Peter: anthem for SATB, organ and/or brass.
(Tamblyn, William). *Boosey and Hawkes. Unpriced* DJ
(B71-50192)
You! you!: a German folk tune. (Pax, C E). *Ashdown. £0.05*
FDW (B71-50838)
Young, Percy Marshall.
Bicinia hungarica
Vol.4: 60 progressive two-part songs. (Kodaly, Zoltan).
Revised English ed. *Boosey and Hawkes. Unpriced*
FEZDW (B71-50045)
Dvorak. *Benn. £0.90* BDX(N) (B71-01698)
                                     ISBN 0 510 13717 2
Music and its story. Revised ed. *Dobson. £1.25* A(X)
(B71-05265)   ISBN 0 234 77346 4
Schubert. *Benn. £0.90* BSF(N) (B71-01699)
                                     ISBN 0 510 13732 6
Sir Arthur Sullivan. *Dent. £4.00* BSW(N) (B71-28694)
                                     ISBN 0 460 03934 2
Young, Robert Hexter. The anthem in England and America.
(Wienandt, Elwyn Arthur). *Free Press; Collier-Macmillan.*
£6.00 ADH(YT/X) (B71-20591)   ISBN 0 02 093523 4
Young people's concerts. *See* Bernstein, Leonard.
Young pianist's repertoire
Book 1. (Waterman, Fanny). *Faber. Unpriced* QP/AY

(B71-50455)
Book 2. (Waterman, Fanny). *Faber. Unpriced* QP/AY
(B71-50456)
Youth on parade: for military band. (Turner, J Godfrey).
Feldman. Unpriced UMMGM (B71-51058)
Zauberflote; libretto by Emanuel Schikaneder to the opera
by W.A. Mozart; and, Die Entfuhrung aus dem Serail
libretto by Gottlieb Stephanie to the opera by W.A.
Mozart. (Schikaneder, Emanuel). *Cassell. £1.75* BMSAC
(B71-24690)   ISBN 0 304 93825 4
Zehm, Friedrich. Concerto da camera: fur Oboe und
Streichorchester. Klavierauszug. *Schott. £2.00* VTPK/LF
(B71-50668)
Zimmerman, Bernd Alois.
Photoptosis: Prelude fur grosser Orchester. *Schott. £3.20*
MMJ (B71-50074)
Stille und Umkehr: Orchesterskizzen. *Schott. £1.90* MMJ
(B71-50401)
Zion hears the watchmen's voices: for unison & SATB
chorale. (Bach, Johann Sebastian). *Oxford University*
Press. Unpriced DM (B71-50202)   ISBN 0 19 343013 4
Zoller, Karlheinz.
Moderne Orchester-Studien: fur Flote
Band 1. *Schott. £3.00* VR/AF/AY (B71-50635)
Band 2. *Schott. £2.75* VR/AF/AY (B71-50636)
Zschiesche, Alf. Acht Duette: fur Gitarren. (Gastoldi,
Giovanni Giacomo). *Schott. £0.80* TSNU (B71-50607)
Zwei Duos alter englischer Meister: fur Altblockfloten
(Querfloten, Oboen). (Ruf, Hugo). *Schott. £0.70*
VSNUE/AYD (B71-50653)
Zwei Hande-zwolf Tasten
Band 1: Ein Buch mit Bildern fur kleine Klavierspieler.
(Runze, Klaus). *Schott. £2.40* Q/AC (B71-50940)
Zwei Trauungsgesange und Tanflied: fur Singstimme, Violine
und Orgel. (Hogner, Friedrich). *Litolff, Peter*
Hinrichsen. £1.75 KE/SPLRDH (B71-50352)
Zyklus (1964): Fassung fur Violoncello, Blaser, Harfen und
Schlagzeug (1969). (Fortner, Wolfgang). *Schott. £2.00*
MRJ (B71-50412)

SUBJECT INDEX

Choral societies AD/E(QB)
Chord organ RPVC
Christmas: Anthems DK/LF
Christmas: Anthems, Hymns, Carols, etc.
  DH/LF
Christmas: Arrangements for chord organ
  RPVCK/DP/LP
Christmas: Cantatas DE/LF
Christmas: Carol cantatas: Soprano voices
  FLDPDE/LF
Christmas: Carols DP/LF
Christmas: Carols: Accompanied by brass, strings
  & percussion quartet
  ENYEXPNSDP/LF
Christmas: Carols: Arrangements for guitar solo
  TSPMK/DP/LF
Christmas: Carols: Female voices, Children's
  voices FDP/LF
Christmas: Carols: Female voices, Children's
  voices: Accompanied by flute
  FE/VRDP/LF
Christmas: Carols: Full scores EMDP/LF
Christmas: Carols: Solo voice KDP/LF
Christmas: Carols: Soprano voices
  FLDP/LF
Christmas: Carols: Unaccompanied female voices,
  children's voices FEZDP/LF
Christmas: Carols: Unaccompanied works
  EZDP/LF
Christmas: Carols: Unison JDP/LF
Christmas: Motets, Anthems, Hymns, etc.: Male
  voices GDH/LF
Christmas: Motets, Anthems, Hymns, etc.:
  Unaccompanied female voices, children's
  voices FEZDH/LF
Christmas: Motets: Unaccompanied female voices,
  children's voices FEZDJ/LF
Christmas: Motets: Unaccompanied works
  EZDJ/LF
Christmas: Piano solos QP/LF
Christmas: Religious cantatas: Female voices,
  children's voices: Unison: Accompanied by
  recorder & percussion
  JFE/NYHSDE/LF
Christmas: Songs: Arrangements for
  unaccompanied descant recorder
  VSRPMK/DW/LF
Christmas: Vespers: Roman liturgy
  DGKJ/LF
Church bells: Books AXSR
Church choral music: Books AD/LD
Church music: Vocal music CB/LD
Cinema: Arrangements for military band
  UMMK/JR
Cinema: Ballet: Arrangements for brass band
  WMK/AHM/JR
Cinema: Ballet: Arrangements for piano solo
  QPK/AHM/JR
Cinema: Music: Arrangements for brass band
  WMK/JR
Cinema: Music: Books A/JR
Cinema: Music: Fugues: Arrangements for military
  band UMMK/Y/JR
Cinema: Music: Fugues: Arrangements for wind
  band UMK/Y/JR
Cinema: Musical plays: Arrangements for brass
  band WMK/CM/JR
Cinema: Musical plays: Arrangements for organ
  RK/CM/JR
Cinema: Musical plays: Arrangements for piano
  solo QPK/CM/JR
Cinema: Orchestral works: Arrangements for piano
  solo QPK/JR
Cinema: Songs DW/JR
Cinema: Songs: Solo voice KDW/JR
Cinema: Symphony orchestra MM/JR
Cinema: Vocal quartets: Songs
  JNCDW/JR
City of London: Organisations: Books
  A(Q/YDBCJ)
Clarinet (B flat) VV
Clarinet (B flat): Accompanying soprano voice
  KFLE/VV
Clarinet: Books AVV
Clarinet, strings & percussion HYEV
Clarinet, strings & piano: Chamber music
  NUV
Classification: Libraries: Music A(UJ)
Collected works of individual composers
  C/AZ
Collected works of individual composers: Brass
  quintet WNR/AZ
Collected works of individual composers: Lute
  TW/AZ
Collected works of individual composers: Organ
  R/AZ
Collected works of individual composers: Virginals
  QSQ/AZ
Communion: Anglican liturgy: Choral music
  DGS
Communion: Proper of the Mass: Roman liturgy:
  Unaccompanied works EZDGKAH
Composers: European music: Books
  A/D(YB/M)
Composers, Individual: Books B
Composition: Accompaniment: Books
  AQ/ED/D
Composition: Books A/D

Composition influenced by spiritualism
  A/D(ZF)
Composition: Orchestral music AM/D
Composition: Piano music AQ/D
Concertinos: Piano, 4 hands & orchestra
  MPQNVFL
Concertos: Arrangements for brass quintet
  WNRK/LF
Concertos: Arrangements for keyboard instruments
  (2) PWNUK/LF
Concertos: Arrangements for oboe, string &
  keyboard trio NUTNTK/LF
Concertos: Arrangements for viola & piano
  SQPK/LF
Concertos: Arrangements for violas (2) & keyboard
  SQNTPWK/LF
Concertos: Bassoon & orchestra: Arrangements for
  bassoon & piano VWPK/LF
Concertos: Bassoon & string orchestra
  RXMPVWF
Concertos: Cello & orchestra MPSRF
Concertos: Cello & orchestra: Arrangements for
  cello & piano SRPK/LF
Concertos: Clarinet & orchestra: Arrangements for
  clarinet (B flat) & piano VVPK/LF
Concertos: Double bass & string orchestra
  RXMPSSF
Concertos: Flute & orchestra: Arrangements for
  flute & piano VRPK/LF
Concertos: Flute & string orchestra
  RXMPVRF
Concertos: Flute & wind band UMPVRF
Concertos: Harp & orchestra MPTQF
Concertos: Horn & orchestra: Arrangements for
  horn & piano WTPK/LF
Concertos: Oboe & orchestra: Arrangements for
  oboe & piano VTPK/LF
Concertos: Organ RF
Concertos: Piano & orchestra: Arrangements for
  pianos (2), 4 hands QNUK/LF
Concertos: Toy instruments: Orchestral works
  MVF
Concertos: Trumpet & string orchestra
  RXMPWSF
Concertos: Viola & orchestra: Arrangements for
  viola & piano SQPK/LF
Concertos: Viola d'amore & orchestra
  MPSQQF
Concertos: Violin & orchestra MPSF
Concertos: Violin & orchestra: Arrangements for
  violin & piano SPK/LF
Concertos: Violin & string orchestra
  RXMPSF
Concertos: Violins (2), cello & string orchestra
  RXMPSNTSRF
Concrete music PS
Conducting: Books A/EC
Conductors A/EC(M)
Contralto voice: Books AKFQ
Cor anglais & two oboes VTNTVTT
Cornwall: Christmas carols: Collections
  DP/LF/AYDFR
Counterpoint: Piano solos QP/RM
Court odes: Secular cantatas: Books
  ADX/KM

Dance music: Books A/H
Dance suites: Arrangements for brass band
  WMK/AHG
Dances LH
Dances: Arrangements for brass band
  WMK/AH
Dances: Arrangements for cello & piano
  SRPK/AH
Dances: Arrangements for guitar solo, unaccom-
  panied TSPMK/AH
Dances: Arrangements for orchestra
  MK/AH
Dances: Brass band WMH
Dances: Cello & piano SRPH
Dances: Chamber orchestra MRH
Dances: Clarinet & piano VVPH
Dances: Clarinet quartets VVNSH
Dances: Double bass & piano SSPH
Dances: Light orchestral works MSH
Dances: Military band UMMH
Dances: Orchestral music MH
Dances: Piano solo QPH
Dances: Symphony orchestra MMH
Delius, Frederick: Books BDL
Descant recorder VSR
Descant recorder & strings: Chamber music
  NVSR
Deus misereatur: Evening Prayer: Anglican liturgy
  EZDGPS
Directories: Great Britain: Books
  A(U/YC/BC)
Disc musical boxes: Books A/FND
Divine Office: Roman liturgy DGKB
Double bass SS
Double bass & string orchestra RXMPSS
Dowland, John: Books BDT
Drifters, The: Books AB/E(P)
Duets: Baritones WTZNU
Duets: Bassoon VWNU
Duets: Brass instruments WNU
Duets: Cello SRNU
Duets: Clarinet VVNU

Duets: Guitar TSNU
Duets: Horn WTNU
Duets: Keyboard instrument, 4 hands
  PWNV
Duets: Keyboard instruments PWNUK
Duets: Keyboard instruments (2) PWNU
Duets: Instrumental music LNU
Duets: Keyboard & percussion: Accompanying
  mezzo-soprano voice KFNE/NYLNU
Duets: Piano, 4 hands QNV
Duets: Pianos (2), 4 hands QNU
Duets: Recorder VSNU
Duets: Treble recorder VSSNU
Duets: Trombone WUNU
Dulcimer, Appalachian: Books ATWTT
Durham, County: Folksongs: Books
  ADW/G(YDJJ)
Dvořák, Antonín: Books BDX

East Germany: Song collections: Vocal solos
  KDW/AYEE
Easter: Carols: Unaccompanied works
  EZDP/LL
Easter: Hymns DM/LL
Easter: Motets, Anthems, Hymns, etc.
  DH/LL
Easter: Motets, Anthems, Hymns, etc.:
  Accompanied by keyboard, brass & string
  sextet ENUXPNQDH/LL
Easter: Motets, Anthems, Hymns, etc.: Arrange-
  ments for recorder VSK/DH/LL
Education: Books A(V)
Education: Organ: Great Britain
  AR(YC/V)
Einem, Gottfried von: Books BEN
Electric organ RPV
Electric organ: Books ARPV
Electronic instrument & orchestra: Accompanying
  soprano voice KFLE/MPPS
Electronic organ RPV
Electronic organ: Books ARPV
Elgar, Sir Edward, bart.: Books BEP
Ellington, Duke: Books AMT(P)
Encyclopaedias: Music A(C)
Encyclopaedias: Rock 'n' roll
  AKDW/HK(C)
Encyclopaedias: Singers: Books
  AB/E(M/C)
England: Anthems, Hymns, etc.: Collections:
  Unaccompanied works EZDH/AYD
England: Court odes: Secular cantatas: Books
  ADX/KM(YD)
England: Dance collections: Arrangement for
  guitar solo, unaccompanied
  TSPMK/AH/AYD
England: Folk dance collections
  LH/G/AYD
England: Folk song collections: Arrangements for
  guitar solo TSPMK/DW/G/AYD
England: Folk-song collections: Solos: Accom-
  panied by guitar KE/TSDW/G/AYD
England: Folk songs: Books ADW/G(YD)
England: Keyboard solos PWP/AYD
England: Madrigal collections: Unaccompanied
  works EZDU/AYD
England: Music: Collections C/AYD
England: Sonata collections: Recorder duets
  VSNUE/AYD
England: Songs: Books ADW(YD)
Ensemble: Bassoons VWN
Ensemble: Brass WN
Ensemble: Cellos SRN
Ensemble: Chamber music N
Ensemble: Chamber music: Double bass
  SSN
Ensemble: Clarinets VVN
Ensemble: Descant recorders VSRN
Ensemble: Horns WTN
Ensemble: Percussion XN
Ensemble: Recorders VSN
Ensemble: Strings RXN
Ensemble: Treble recorders VSSN
Ensemble: Trombones WUN
Ensemble: Trumpets WSN
Ensemble: Voices JN
Ensemble: Wind UN
Ensembles: Baritones WTZN
Ensembles: Chamber music: Accompanying choral
  works EWN
Ensembles: Chamber music: Accompanying soprano
  voice KFLE/RXN
Ensembles: Instrumental music LN
Epiphany: Carols DP/LFP
Epiphany: Motets, Anthems, Hymns, etc.
  DH/LFL
Europe: Children's song collections: Female voices,
  Children's voices: Unison
  JFDW/GJ/AYB
Europe: Christmas carol collections: Arrangements
  for chord organ
  RPVCK/DP/LF/AYB
Europe: Christmas carol collections: Female
  voices, Children's voices
  FDP/LF/AYB
Europe: Collections: Christmas carols: Arrange-
  ments for guitar solo, unaccompanied
  TSPMK/DP/LF/AYB
Europe: Composition: Books A/D(YB)

LIST OF MUSIC PUBLISHERS

While every effort has been made to check the information given in this list with the publishers concerned, the Council of the British National Bibliography cannot hold itself responsible for any errors or omissions.

ALEXANDER Broude Inc., New York.
British Agent: Boosey & Hawkes, Music Publishers Ltd.

ALLAN & Co. (Pty.), Ltd., Australia.
British Agent: Freeman, H., & Co.

ALLEN, George, & Unwin, Ltd. 40 Museum St., London, W.C.2: *Tel:* 01-405 8577. *Grams:* Deucalion.
Trade: Park Lane, Hemel Hempstead, Herts.
Tel: 0442 3244

AMERICAN Institute of Musicology, U.S.A.
British Agent: Hinrichsen Edition, Ltd.

AMICI della Musica da Camera, Rome.
British Agent: Hinrichsen Edition, Ltd.

ARNOLD, Edward, (Publishers), Ltd. (Music Scores). *See* Novello & Co., Ltd.

ARTIA, Prague.
British Agent: **Boosey & Hawkes, Music Publishers Ltd.**

ASCHERBURG, Hopwood & Crewe, 50 New Bond St., W.1.

ASHDOWN, Edwin, Ltd. 275-281 Cricklewood Broadway, London, NW2 6QR. *Tel:* 01-450 5237.

ASSOCIATED Board of the Royal Schools of Music (Publications Dept.). 14 Bedford Sq., London, WC1B 3JG. *Tel:* 01-636 6919. *Grams:* Musexam London WC1.

AVENUE Music Publishing Co., Ltd. 50 New Bond St., London, W.1. *Tel:* 01-629 7600. *Grams:* Symphony Wesdo London.

BANK, Annie, Editions, Amsterdam.
British Agent: J. & W. Chester, Ltd.

BARENREITER, Ltd. 32 Gt. Titchfield St., London, W.1. *Tel:* 01-580 9008

BARON, H. 136 Chatsworth Rd., London, NW2 5QU. *Tel:* 01-459 2035. *Grams:* Musicbaron, London.

BARRY & Co., Buenos Aires.
British Agent: **Boosey & Hawkes, Music Publishers Ltd.**

BAYLEY & Ferguson, Ltd. 65 Berkeley St., Glasgow C3. *Tel:* CENtral 7240. *Grams:* Bayley Glasgow.

BELWIN-MILLS Music, Ltd. 230 Purley Way, Croydon, CR9 4QD. *Tel:* 01-681 0855.

BERLIN, Irving, Ltd. 14 St. George St., London, W.1. *Tel:* 01-629 7600.

BESSEL, W. & Co. Paris.
British Agent: Boosey & Hawkes, Music Publishers Ltd.

BIELER, Edmund, Musikverlag, Cologne.
British Agent: J. & W. Chester, Ltd.

BLOSSOM Music, Ltd. 139 Piccadilly, London, W.1. *Tel:* 01-629 7211. *Grams:* Leedsmusik London, W.1.

BOOSEY & Hawkes Music Publishers, Ltd. 295 Regent St., London, W1A 1BR. *Tel:* 01-580 2060. *Grams:* Sonorous London W.1.

BOSTON Music Co., Boston (Mass.).
British Agent: Chappell & Co., Ltd.

BOSWORTH & Co., Ltd. 14-18 Heddon St., London, W.1. *Tel:* 01-734 4961/2. *Grams:* Bosedition Piccy London.

BOTE & Bock, Berlin.
British Agent: Schott & Co., Ltd.

BOURNE MUSIC Ltd. 34/36 Maddox St., London, W1R 9PD. *Tel:* 01-493 6412/6583. *Grams:* Bournemusic London, W.1.

BRADBURY Wood, Ltd. 16 St. George St., London, W.1.

BREGMAN, Vocco & Conn, Ltd. 50 New Bond St., London, W.1. *Tel:* 01-629 7600.

BREITKOPF & Härtel, Leipzig.
British Agent: Breitkopf & Härtel (London), Ltd.

BREITKOPF & Härtel (London), Ltd. 8 Horse and Dolphin Yard, London, W1V 7LG.

BREITKOPF & Härtel, Wiesbaden, W. Germany.
British Agent: Breitkopf & Härtel (London), Ltd.

BRITISH & Continental Music Agencies, Ltd. 64 Dean St., London, W.1. *Tel:* GERrard 9336. *Grams:* Humfriv Wesdo London.

BROCKHAUS, Max, Germany.
British Agent (Orchestral music only): Novello & Co., Ltd.

BROUDE Bros., New York.
British Agent: Schott & Co., Ltd.

BRUZZICHELLI, Aldo, Florence.
British Agent: Hinrichsen Edition. Ltd.

CAMPBELL, Connelly, & Co., Ltd. *See* CONNELLY, Campbell, & Co., Ltd.

CARY, L. J., & Co., Ltd. 16 Mortimer St., London, W.1. *Tel:* 01-636 3562. *Grams:* Ascherberg London W.1.

CEBEDEM Foundation, Brussels.
British Agent: Lengnick & Co., Ltd.

CHAPPELL & Co., Ltd. 50 New Bond St., London, W.1. *Tel:* 01-629 7600. *Grams:* Symphony Wesdo London.

CHESTER, J. & W., Ltd. Eagle Court, London, E.C.1. *Tel:* 01-253-6947. *Grams:* Guarnerius, London E.C.1.

CHURCH, John, Co., Pennsylvania
British Agent: Alfred A. Kalmus, Ltd.

CLIFFORD Essex Music Co., Ltd. *See* ESSEX, Clifford, Music Co., Ltd.

COLLIER/DEXTER Music Ltd. 21-25 Earl St., London, E.C.2. *Tel:* 01-247 0237/8.

COMPASS Music Ltd. 50 New Bond St., London, W.1. *Tel:* 01-629 7600

CONNELLY, Campbell & Co., Ltd. 10 Denmark St., London, W.C.2. *Tel:* TEMple Bar 1653. *Grams:* Dansmelodi Westcent London.

CONSTABLE & Co., Ltd. 10 Orange St., London, W.C.2. *Tel:* 01-930 0801. *Grams:* Dhagoba London WC2.
Trade: Tiptree Book Services Ltd., Tiptree, Colchester, Essex. *Tel:* Tiptree 6362/7

CONTINUO Music Press Inc., New York.
British Agent: Boosey & Hawkes, Music Publishers Ltd.

CRAMER, J. B., & Co., Ltd. 99 St. Martin's Lane, London, WC2N 4AZ. *Tel:* 01-240 1612.

CURWEN, J., & Sons, Ltd.
Agents: Faber Music, & Roberton Publications.

DELHI Publications, Inc., Cincinnati.
British Agent: Chappell & Co., Ltd.

DELRIEU, Georges, & Cie, Nice.
British Agent: Galliard, Ltd.

DE SANTIS, Rome.
British Agent: Hinrichsen Edition, Ltd.

DEUTSCH, André, Ltd. 105 Gt. Russell St., London, W.C.1. *Tel:* 01-580 2746. *Grams:* Adlib London.
Trade: Amabel House, 14-24 Baches St., London, N.1. *Tel:* 01-253 8589.

DE WOLFE, Ltd. 80-82 Wardour St., London, W.1. *Tel:* 01-437 4933. *Grams:* Musicall London.

DISNEY, Walt, Music Co., Ltd. 52 Maddox St., London, W.1. *Tel:* 01-629 7600.

DITSON, Oliver, Co., Pennsylvania.
British Agent: Alfred A. Kalmus, Ltd.

DOBLINGER Edition, Vienna.
British Agent: Alfred A. Kalmus, Ltd.

DONEMUS Foundation, Amsterdam.
British Agent: Alfred Lengnick, & Co., Ltd.

EDITIO Musica, Budapest.
British Agent: Boosey & Hawkes, Music Publishers Ltd.

EDITION Tonos, Darmstadt.
British Agent: Breitkopf & Härtel (London), Ltd.

EDIZIONI Suvini Zerboni, Milan.
British Agent: Schott & Co., Ltd.

EDWARD B. Marks Music Corporation, New York.
British Agent: Boosey & Hawkes, Music Publishers Ltd.

ELKIN & Co., Ltd. Borough Green, Sevenoaks, Kent. *Tel:* Borough Green 3261. *Grams:* Novellos Sevenoaks

ENGLISH Folk Dance and Song Society. Cecil Sharp House, 2 Regent's Park Road, London, NW1 7AY. *Tel:* 01-485 2206.

ENGSTROM & Soedring, Copenhagen.
British Agent: Hinrichsen Edition, Ltd.

ESCHIG, Max, Paris.
British Agent: Schott & Co., Ltd.

ESSEX, Clifford, Music Co., Ltd. 20 Earlham St., London, W.C.2. *Tel:* 01-836 2810. *Grams:* Triomphe London, W.C.2.

ESSEX Music Group. Dumbarton House, 68 Oxford St., London, WIN 9LA. *Tel:* 01-636 7906. *Grams:* Sexmus, London.
Trade: Music Sales Ltd. 78 Newman St., London, W.1.

EULENBURG, Ernst, Ltd. 48 Great Marlborough St., London, W.1. *Tel:* GERrard 1246/8.

FABER Music, Ltd. 38 Russell Sq., London, W.C.1. *Tel:* 01-636 1344. *Grams:* Fabbaf London WC1.

FAITH Press, Ltd. 7 Tufton St., London, SW1P 3QD. *Tel:* 01-222 3940

FAMOUS Chappell, Ltd. 50 New Bond St., London, W.1. *Tel:* 01-629 7600. *Grams:* Symphony Wesdo London.

FELDMAN, B., & Co., Ltd. 64 Dean St., London, W.1. *Tel:* GERrard 9336. *Grams:* Humfriv Wesdo London.

FISCHER, Carl, New York.
British Agent: Hinrichsen Edition, Ltd.

FOETISCH Freres, Editions, Lausanne.
British Agent: J. & W. Chester, Ltd.

FORBERG, Robert, Bad Godesberg.
British Agent: Hinrichsen Edition, Ltd.

FORSYTH Brothers, Ltd. 190 Grays Inn Rd., London, WC1X 8EW. *Tel:* 01-837 4768.

FORTISSIMO-Verlag, Vienna.
British Agent: Clifford Essex Music Co., Ltd.

FOX, Sam, Publishing Co. *See* SAM Fox Publishing Co.

FRANCIS, Day & Hunter, Ltd. 138 Charing Cross Rd., London, W.C.2. *Tel:* 01-836 9351. *Grams:* Arpeggio Westcent London.

FRANK Music Co., Ltd. 50 New Bond St., London W.1. *Tel:* 01-629 7600.

FREEMAN, H., Ltd. 64 Dean St., London, W.1. *Tel:* 01-437 9336/9.

FRENCH, Samuel, Ltd. 26 Southampton St., Strand, London, W.C.2. *Tel:* 01-836 7513. *Grams:* Dramalogue London W.C.2.

G. & C. Music Corporation, New York.
British Agent: Chappell & Co., Ltd.

GALAXY Music Corporation, New York.
British Agent: Galliard, Ltd.

GALLIARD Ltd. Queen Anne's Rd., Great Yarmouth, Norfolk. *Tel:* 0493 4281.

GLOCKEN Verlag, Ltd. 10-16 Rathbone St., London, W1P 2BJ. *Tel:* 01-580 2827. *Grams:* Operetta London W1.

GRAPHIC, Graz, Austria.
British Agent: Alfred A. Kalmus, Ltd.

GREGG International Publishers, Ltd. Westmead, Farnborough, Hants.

GWASG Prifysgol Cymru, Merthyr House, James St., Cardiff, CF1 6EU. *Tel:* Cardiff 31919.

HANSEN, Wilhelm, Edition, Copenhagen.
British Agent: J. & W. Chester, Ltd.

HÄNSSLER, Verlag, Germany.
British Agent: Novello & Co., Ltd.

HARGAIL Music Press, New York.
British Agent: Alfred A. Kalmus, Ltd.

HARMONIA Uitgave, Hilversum.
British Agent: Alfred A. Kalmus, Ltd.

HART, F. Pitman, & Co., Ltd. 99 St. Martin's Lane, London, WC2N 4AZ. *Tel:* 01-240 1612.

HEINRICHSHOFEN, Wilhelmshaven.
British Agent: Hinrichsen Edition, Ltd.

HENLE, G., Verlag, Germany.
British Agent: Novello & Co., Ltd.

HENMAR Press, New York.
British Agent: Hinrichsen Edition, Ltd.

HEUWEKEMEIJER, Holland.
British Agent: Hinrichsen Edition, Ltd.

HINRICHSEN Edition, Ltd. Bach House, 10-12 Baches St., London, N1 6DN. *Tel:* 01-253 1638. *Grams:* Musipeters London.

HLADKY, Musikverlag V., Vienna.
British Agent: Clifford Essex Music Co., Ltd.

HOFMEISTER Figaro Verlag, Vienna.
British Agent: Alfred A. Kalmus, Ltd.

HUG & Co., Zurich.
British Agent: Hinrichsen Edition, Ltd.

HUGHES a'i Fab (Hughes & Son) Publishers, Ltd. 29 Rivulet Rd., Wrexham, Denbighshire, North Wales. *Tel:* Wrexham 4340.

HUNTZINGER, R. L., Inc., Cincinnati.
British Agent: Chappell & Co., Ltd.

IMPERIAL Society of Teachers of Dancing. 70 Gloucester Place, London, W1H 4AJ. *Tel:* 01-935 0825/6. *Grams:* Istod, London W1.

INTER-ART Music Publishers. 10-16 Rathbone St., London, W1P 2BJ. *Tel:* 01-580 2827. *Grams:* Operetta London W1.

INTERNATIONAL Music Co., New York.
British Agent: Alfred A. Kalmus, Ltd.

INTERNATIONALEN Musikbisliothek, Berlin.
British Agent: Breitkopf & Härtel (London), Ltd.

ISTITUTO Italiano per la Storia della Musica.
British Agent: Alfred A. Kalmus, Ltd.

JAMESON (St. Brides), Ltd. *No longer publishing.*

JUSKO, Ralph, Publications, Inc., Cincinnati.
British Agent: Chappell & Co., Ltd.

KAHNT, C. F., Germany.
British Agent: Novello & Co., Ltd.

KALMUS, Alfred A., Ltd. 2-3 Fareham St., London, W1V 4DU. *Tel:* 01-437 5203. *Grams:* Alkamus London W.1.

KALMUS, Edwin, New York.
British Agent: Alfred A. Kalmus, Ltd.

KEITH Prowse Music Publishing Co., Ltd. 21 Denmark St., London, WC2H 8NE. *Tel:* 01-836 5501.

KISTNER & Siegel & Co., Germany.
British Agent: Novello & Co., Ltd.

KNEUSSLIN, Switzerland.
British Agent: Hinrichsen Edition, Ltd.

LAUDY & Co. c/o Bosworth & Co., Ltd. 14-18 Heddon St., London, W.1. *Tel:* 01-734 4961/2. *Grams:* Bosedition Piccy London.

LEA Pocket Scores, New York.
British Agent: Alfred A. Kalmus, Ltd.

LEEDS Music, Ltd. 139 Piccadilly, London, W.1. *Tel:* MAYfair 7211. *Grams:* Leedsmusik London.

LENGNICK, Alfred, & Co., Ltd. Purley Oaks Studios, 421a Brighton Rd., South Croydon, Sy. *Tel:* 01-660-7646.

LEONARD, Gould & Bolttler. 99 St. Martin's Lane, London, WC2N 4AZ. *Tel:* 01-240 1612.

LEUCKART, F. E. C., Germany.
British Agent: Novello & Co., Ltd.

LIENAU, Robert (Schlesinger), Germany.
British Agent: Hinrichsen Edition, Ltd.

LITOLFF Verlag. Bach House, 10-12 Baches St., London, N1 6DN. *Tel:* 01-253 1638.

LUVERNE Inc., New York.
British Agent: Boosey & Hawkes, Music Publishers Ltd.

LYCHE, Oslo.
British Agent: Hinrichsen Edition, Ltd.

McGINNIS & Marx, New York.
British Agent: Hinrichsen Edition, Ltd.

MADDOX Music Co., Ltd. 52 Maddox St., London, W.1. *Tel:* MAYfair 7600.

MAURICE, Peter. *See* PETER Maurice.

MERION Music Co., Pennsylvania.
British Agent: Alfred A. Kalmus, Ltd.

MERSEBURGER Verlag, Berlin.
British Agent: Hinrichsen Edition, Ltd. ; Musica Rara.

METROPOLIS, Antwerp.
British Agent: Hinrichsen Edition, Ltd.

MEZHDUNARODNAJA Kniga, Moscow.
British Agent: Boosey & Hawkes, Music Publishers Ltd.

MIDLAND Music Ltd. 50 Ladbroke Grove, London, W.11. *Tel:* 01-229 1129

MILLS Music, Ltd. 20 Denmark St., London, W.C.2. *Tel:* 01-240 1745. *Grams:* Millsmusic London.

MOECK, Hermann, Germany.
British Agent: Schott & Co., Ltd.

MORRIS, Edwin H., & Co., Ltd. 15 St. George St., London, W.1. *Tel:* 01-499 8548.

MÖSELER Verlag, Germany.
British Agent: Novello & Co., Ltd.

MÜLLER, Willy, Germany.
British Agent: Novello & Co., Ltd.

MUSIA International (Export and Import), Frankfurt.
British Agent: Hinrichsen Edition, Ltd.

MUSIC Index, U.S.A.
British Agent: Hinrichsen Edition, Ltd.

MUSICA Rara. 2 Great Marlborough St., London, W.1. *Tel:* GERrard 1576.

NEW American Music Awards Series (Sigma Alpha Iota), New York.
British Agent: Hinrichsen Edition, Ltd.

NEW Music Edition, Pennsylvania.
British Agent: Alfred A. Kalmus, Ltd.

NEW Wind Music Co. 23 Ivor Pl., London, N.W.1. *Tel:* 01-262 3797.

NEW World Publishers, Ltd. 50 New Bond St., London, W.1. *Tel:* 01-629 7600. *Grams:* Symphony Wesdo London.

NOETZEL, Wilhelmshaven, Germany.
British Agent: Hinrichsen Edition, Ltd.

NORDISKA Musikforlaget, Stockholm.
British Agent: J. & W. Chester, Ltd.

NORMAN Richardson Band Arrangements. 8 King Edward Grove, Teddington, Middx.

NORSK Musikforlag, Oslo.
British Agent: J. & W. Chester, Ltd.

NORTHERN Songs, Ltd. James House, 71/75 New Oxford St., London, W.C.1. *Tel:* 01-836 4864. *Grams:* Dejamus London WC1.

NOVELLO & Co., Ltd. Borough Green, Sevenoaks, Kent. *Tel:* Borough Green 3261. *Grams:* Novello Sevenoaks

OCTAVA Music Co., Ltd.
British Agent: Josef Weinberger, Ltd.

OXFORD University Press (Music Department). 44 Conduit St., London, W1R ODE. *Tel:* 01-734 5364. *Grams and Cables:* Fulscore London W1.

PARAGON, New York.
British Agent: Hinrichsen Edition, Ltd.

PATERSON'S Publications, Ltd. 38 Wigmore St., London, W1H 0EX. *Tel:* 01-935 3551. *Grams:* Paterwia London W1.

PAXTON, W., & Co., Ltd. *No longer publishing.*

PENNSYLVANIA State University Press. 27 Whitfield St., London, W.1. *Tel;* 01-636 4940. *Grams:* Amunpress, London.

PETER Maurice Music Co., Ltd. 21 Denmark St., London, WC2H 8NE. *Tel:* 01-836 5501. *Grams:* Mauritunes London WC2.

PETERS Edition, Bach House, 10-12 Baches St., London, N1 6DN. *Tel:* 01-253 1638. *Grams:* Musipeters London.

PITMAN, Hart, & Co., Ltd. *See* HART, F. Pitman, & Co., Ltd.

PLAINSONG & Mediaeval Music Society. *Secretary:* Charles K. Colhoun, c/o Lloyds Bank Ltd., 112/114 Kensington High St., London, W.8.

POLISH Music Publications, Poland.
British Agent: Alfred A. Kalmus, Ltd.

POLYPHONIC Reproductions Ltd. 89-91 Vicarage Rd, London, N.W.10. *Tel:* 01-459 6194.

PRESSER, Theodore, Co., Pennsylvania.
British Agent: Alfred A. Kalmus, Ltd.

PRO ART Publications, Inc. New York.
British Agent: Alfred A. Kalmus, Ltd.

PROWSE, Keith, Music Publishing Co., Ltd. *See* KEITH
Prowse Music Publishing Co., Ltd.

RAHTER, D. 239/241 Shaftesbury Ave., London, W.C.2.
Tel: 01-836 3349.

REGINA Music Publishing Co., Ltd. Old Run Rd., Leeds,
LS10 2AA. *Tel:* Leeds 700527.

RICHARDSON, Norman, Ltd. *See* Norman Richardson Band
Arrangements.

RIES & Erler, Berlin.
British Agent: Hinrichsen Edition, Ltd.

ROBBINS Music Corporation, Ltd. 35 Soho Sq., London,
W.1. *Tel:* 01-437-0068.

ROBERTON Publications. The Windmill, Wendover,
Aylesbury, Bucks. *Tel:* Wendover 3107.

ROYAL Academy of Dancing. 251 Knightsbridge, London,
S.W.7. *Tel:* 01-584 9335. *Grams:* Radancing London
SW7.

ROYAL School of Church Music. Addington Palace, Croydon,
CR9 5AD. *Tel:* 01-654 7676. *Grams:* Cantoris,
Croydon.

ROYAL Scottish Country Dance Society. 12 Coates Crescent,
Edinburgh 3. *Tel:* 031-225 3854.

RUBANK Inc. U.S.A.
British agent: Novello & Co., Ltd.

ST. MARTINS Publications, Ltd. Addington Palace, Croydon
CR9 5AD. *Tel:* 01-654 7676

SAM Fox Publishing Co., New York.
British Agent: Keith Prowse Music Publishing Co., Ltd.

SCHIRMER, G., Inc., New York.
British Agents: Chappell & Co., Ltd.
    Curwen, J.C. & Sons. Ltd.

SCHMIDT, C. F., Heilbronn, Germany.
British Agent: Hinrichsen Edition, Ltd.

SCHOFIELD & Sims, Ltd. 35 St. John's Rd., Huddersfield,
Yorkshire HD1 5DT. *Tel:* Huddersfield 30684. *Grams:*
Schosims, Huddersfield.

SCHOTT & Co., Ltd. 48 Great Marlborough St., London, W.1.
Tel: 01-437-1246. *Grams:* Shotanco.

SCHULTHEISS, Tübingen.
British Agent: Hinrichsen Edition, Ltd.

SCRIPTURE Union. 5 Wigmore St., London, W.1.
Tel: 01-486 2561.
Trade: 79 Hackney Rd., London, E.2. *Tel:* 01-739 2941.

SIMROCK, N. Lyra House, 67 Belsize Lane, London,
NW3 5AX. *Tel:* 01-794 8038.

SIRIUS-Verlag, Berlin.
British Agent: Hinrichsen Edition, Ltd.

SOCIETAS Universalis Santae Ceciliae.
British Agent: Alfred A. Kalmus, Ltd.

SOUTHERN Music Company, San Antonio, Texas.
British Agent: Boosey & Hawkes, Music Publishers Ltd.

STAINER & Bell, Ltd. 82 High Road, London, N2 9PW.
Tel: 01-444 9135.

STEINGRABER Verlag, Germany.
British Agent: Bosworth & Co., Ltd.

STUDIO Music Co. 89-91 Vicarage Rd., London, N.W.10.
Tel: 01-459 6194/5

SUPRAPHON Czechoslovakia.
British Agent: Alfred A. Kalmus, Ltd.

TALZEHN Music Corporation, New York.
British Agent: Hinrichsen Edition, Ltd.

TAUNUS Verlag, Frankfurt.
British Agent: Hinrichsen Edition, Ltd.

TETRA Music Corporation, New York.
British Agent: Boosey & Hawkes, Music Publishers Ltd.

TURRET Books. 1B, 1C, 1D, Kensington Church Walk,
London, W8 4NB.
Tel: 01-937 7583.

UNIVERSAL Edition (London), Ltd. 2-3 Fareham St., London,
W1V 4DU.

UNIVERSAL Edition Vienna-London-Zurich
British Agent: Alfred A. Kalmus, Ltd.

UNIVERSITY of Wales Press. Merthyr House, James St.,
Cardiff, CF1 6EU. *Tel:* Cardiff 31919.

V.E.B. Deutscher Verlag für Musik, Leipzig.
British Agent: Breitkopf & Härtel (London), Ltd.

V.E.B. Friedrich Hofmeister, Leipzig.
British Agent: Breitkopf & Härtel (London), Ltd.

VALANDO Music Co., Ltd. 50 New Bond St., London, W.1.
Tel: 01-629 7600. *Grams:* Symphony Wesdo London.

VERLAG Neue Musik, Berlin.
British Agent: Breitkopf & Härtel (London), Ltd.

VICTORIA Music Publishing Co., Ltd. 52 Maddox St., London, W.1. *Tel:* MAYfair 7600.

WALTON Music Corporation, California.
British Agent: Walton Music, Ltd.

WALTON Music, Ltd. 50 New Bond St., London, W.1. *Tel:*
01-629 7600. *Grams:* Symphony Wesdo London.

WARNE, Frederick, & Co., Ltd. 40 Bedford Sq., London,
WC1B 3HE. *Tel:* 01-580 9622. *Grams:* Warne
London WC1

WEINBERGER, Josef, Ltd. 10-16 Rathbone St., London,
W1P 2BJ. *Tel;* 01-580 2827. *Grams;* Operetta London
W.1.

WILHELMIANA Musikverlag, Frankfurt am Main.
British Agent: J. & W. Chester, Ltd.

WILLIAMSON Music, Ltd. 14 St. George St., London, W.1.
Tel: 01-629 7600.

WILLIS Music Co., Cincinnat¹ (Ohio).
British Agent: Chappell & Co., Ltd.

WOOD, B.F., Music Co., Ltd. *See* BELWIN-Mills Music Ltd.

WOOD, Bradbury, Ltd. *See* BRADBURY Wood Ltd.

ZANIBON Edition, Padua.
British Agent: Hinrichsen Edition, Ltd.

ZIMMERMANN, Musikverlag, Germany.
British Agent: Novello & Co., Ltd.